Advanced Structured COBOL

Advanced Structured COBOL

JOHN A. J. WALSTROM
Eastern Illinois University

MARGUERITE K. SUMMERS
University of North Carolina, Charlotte

TATE F. LINDAHL
Western Illinois University

MACMILLAN PUBLISHING COMPANY NEW YORK
Collier Macmillan Publishers LONDON

Macmillan Publishing Company
866 Third Avenue, New York, New York 10022

Collier Macmillan Canada, Inc.

Library of Congress Cataloging in Publication Data
Walstrom, John A. J.
    Advanced structured COBOL.
    1. COBOL (Computer program language) 2. Structured
programming. I. Summers, Marguerite K. II. Lindahl,
Tate F.   III. Title.   IV. Title: Advanced structured
C.O.B.O.L.
QA76.73.C25W35 1985   001.64′24   84-12259
ISBN 0-02-424250-0

Printing: 3 4 5 6 7 8   Year: 6 7 8 9 0 1 2

ISBN 0-02-424250-0

Preface

Advanced Structured COBOL contains material appropriate for an advanced-level COBOL course. It is written with the assumption that students will have previously taken an introductory COBOL programming course.

Teaching advanced-level COBOL classes for several years has made us aware of the need for a strong advanced-level textbook designed to provide a greater depth of coverage of a number of topics we consider to be essential. COBOL supports several file structures and has excellent external file processing capabilities. Its table processing features are perhaps the most powerful and versatile of any found in today's widely used programming languages. The COBOL SORT feature provides options to allow flexibility in processing files where sorting is required. COBOL *is* a powerful language, and students need to clearly understand its most powerful features. The depth of detailed coverage these topics are given in *Advanced Structured COBOL* is, we believe, one of its major strengths.

Another strong feature of the text is the extensive use of illustrative programs. Over forty complete programs have been coded, compiled, and executed and are included at appropriate points throughout the textbook. Each program is a solution developed in response to a realistic problem stated in a realistic context. Each one is strategically placed to clearly illustrate the use of the specific COBOL statements, features, and concepts being considered at that point in the text.

End-of-chapter programming exercises are an important feature of the text. These exercises have been designed to provide students with the opportunity to develop and code programs that build on the material presented in the chapter and, at the same time, to allow them to experience the feeling of working with realistic problems.

A draft of the manuscript was class-tested for two semesters in multiple sections of an advanced COBOL class by several faculty members, including the authors. The response to the manuscript, from both students and faculty, has been excellent.

The arrangement of chapters will introduce topics to students in a reasonable sequence that we have found to work well. However, we have designed each chapter to be essentially self-contained, in order to allow maximum flexibility in using the text. With certain exceptions, the sequence in which chapters are covered can be a matter of preference.

Topics in Chapter 1 include structured program design, walkthroughs, and program testing. We believe it is an important chapter, one that should be covered to emphasize the importance of the program development process. Even though students will undoubtedly have been previously exposed to this process, time spent in reviewing (or for some, perhaps studying for the first time) the design of good programs is time well spent. Good programs are designed; they don't just happen by chance.

Chapter 2 provides extensive coverage of techniques for processing tables using indexes; subscripts; and the SET, SEARCH, and SEARCH ALL statements. In addition, programmer-written routines for table sorting and searching are illustrated. If students have already done a significant amount of work with techniques for processing tables, you may choose to skip over this material. However, knowledge of table processing techniques is required to fully comprehend several of the program examples presented in later chapters.

Students enrolled in an advanced COBOL class frequently have had only a cursory introduction to magnetic tape and disk devices. A clear understanding of the characteristics of these devices and of fundamental concepts such as physical and logical records is important. For this reason, Chapter 3, "Tape and Disk concepts," has been included in the text material and will be encountered prior to any chapters in which this knowledge is required. However, Chapter 3 contains no discussion of COBOL language elements; therefore, its coverage is optional and can easily be omitted if students already have sufficient understanding of the material.

Chapter 4 describes the process of creating and processing sequential disk and tape files. Fundamental concepts such as matching on key fields and control break processing are discussed and illustrated in program examples.

Chapter 5 focuses on the COBOL SORT feature and its options, including USING, GIVING, INPUT PROCEDUREs, and OUTPUT PROCEDUREs. This chapter can be introduced into the class at any time; however, it will be somewhat difficult for students to comprehend this material without previous exposure to sequential disk and/or tape files.

Three additional file structures are presented in Chapters 6, 7, and 8. Creating and processing indexed files (both ISAM and VSAM) are examined in Chapter 6. Relative file organization and concepts fundamental to the creation and processing of relative files are Chapter 7 topics. Chapter 8 focuses on creating and processing direct files. Division/remainder addressing and overflow record processing are included in programming examples. Because of time limitations, or perhaps for other reasons, some instructors may prefer to cover either relative files (Chapter 7) or direct files (Chapter 8) but not both. This can easily be done, since neither chapter is dependent upon knowledge of the content contained in the other.

Subprograms are considered in Chapter 9. The CALL statement, LINKAGE SECTION, and the relationship of the calling program to the called subprogram are described in detail.

Chapter 10 presents an overview of the COBOL Report Writer feature. Chapter 11 covers several important topics, including source program libraries and the COPY statement, string manipulation statements such as STRING and UNSTRING, and COBOL source language debugging.

The text conforms to 1974 American National Standards COBOL with the exception of the material presented on direct file organization, ISAM, and the IBM/ debugging language, which exists now as an IBM extension to the standard.

ACKNOWLEDGMENTS

We are indebted to many people for their contributions as we prepared the manuscript. Robert J. Macek, computer science editor for Macmillan Publishing Company, was always helpful and patient, giving his wholehearted support to the project from its very beginning.

We must acknowledge our sincere appreciation to Dr. Patrick J. Lamont, Ted Stenerson, Evelyn Thompson, and Geetha Rao for their willingness to classroom-test the manuscript. Without question, the finished product is stronger because of their constructive suggestions. Our thanks also to Pattie Riden and Phyllis Walstrom, who shared in typing the original manuscript draft and suffered through its revisions.

We are indebted to the IBM Corporation for allowing the use of materials in Appendixes A, B, and D and for supplying numerous illustrations used in the text.

COBOL ACKNOWLEDGMENT

The following information is reprinted from *COBOL Edition 1965*, published by the Conference on Data Systems Languages (CODASYL), and printed by the U.S. Government Printing Office.

"Any organization interested in reproducing the COBOL report and specification in whole or in part, using ideas taken from this report as the basis for an instruction manual or for any other purpose is free to do so. However, all such organizations are requested to reproduce this section as part of the introduction to the document. Those using a short passage, as in a book review, are requested to mention "COBOL" in acknowledgment of the source, but need not quote this entire section.

"COBOL is an industry language and is not the property of any company or group of companies, or of any organization or group of organizations.

"No warranty, expressed or implied, is made by any contributor or by the COBOL Committee as to the accuracy and functioning of the programming system and language. Moreover, no responsibility is assumed by any contributor, or by the committee, in connection therewith.

"Procedures have been established for the maintenance of COBOL. Inquiries concerning the procedures for proposing changes should be directed to the Executive Committee of the Conference on Data Systems Languages.

"The authors and copyright holders of the copyrighted material used herein

FLOW-MATIC (Trademark of Sperry Rand Corporation), Programming for the Univac (R) I and II, Data Automation Systems copyrighted 1958, 1959, by Sperry Rand Corporation; IBM Commercial Translator Form No. F28-8013, copyrighted 1959 by IBM; FACT, DSI 27A5260-2760, copyrighted 1960 by Minneapolis-Honeywell

have specifically authorized the use of this material in whole or in part, in the COBOL specifications. Such authorization extends to the reproduction and use of COBOL specifications in programming manuals of similar publications."

J. A. J. W.
M. K. S.
T. F. L.

Contents

3 TAPE AND DISK CONCEPTS   60

4 CREATING AND PROCESSING SEQUENTIAL FILES   77

5 SORTING   122

6 CREATING AND PROCESSING INDEXED SEQUENTIAL FILES   154

10 *REPORT WRITER OVERVIEW* **264**

11 *MISCELLANEOUS TOPICS* **296**

APPENDIXES **319**

INDEX **357**

Advanced Structured COBOL

1 The Program Development Process

It is more than possible for a student in a beginning programming course to conclude that

1. Programmers spend most of their time writing new programs.
2. As soon as the programs are working properly, they are thrown away.
3. All data values for which a program must perform properly are known prior to writing the program (i.e., the program must process only the test data supplied).

These conclusions seem reasonable, since this is the way the course frequently is taught.

Granted, there are throwaway programs in a data processing production environment; they are designed to be used once and then discarded. These programs are written in response to unusual one-time situations. It is much more likely, however, that a program you write will be a part of your life for a long time. In addition, changes will be required from time to time in the program. Making these changes, called *program maintenance,* will occupy a large part of a programmer's time. One authority states, "It is probably true that most programmer/analysts with ten years' experience have spent at least 60% of their time in maintenance."[1] A large segment of a programmer's time is also spent in testing and debugging. In a programming class, answering the question, "Did it work?" is usually done by checking answers with the instructor, comparing results with fellow students, or checking the results with those in the textbook. None of these approaches is feasible in a "real-world" data processing center. The length of programs (3000–4000-line COBOL programs are common) usually makes it difficult to verify that programs do what they are supposed to do.

Since much of a professional programmer's time is devoted to maintenance, testing, and debugging, new programs should be written to make the accomplishment of these tasks easier and faster. There have been a number of program development techniques designed to reduce the amount of time required to be spent on these activities. This chapter will provide a brief discussion of some widely used techniques for program development.

Theoretical foundations of *structured programming* evolved from a paper presented in 1964 by Bohm and Jacopini[2] and from Dijkstra's 1965 and 1968 publications.[3,4]

The fundamental concept is that all programming logic can be expressed using three basic control structures: (1) *sequence,* (2) *selection* (IF-THEN-ELSE), and (3) *repetition* (DO WHILE).

Actual production COBOL programs are frequently thousands of lines long. There may be hundreds of decision points and transfers of control made in a single program of that length. For a program to be easily understood, you must be able to determine which statements will actually be executed for a given set of input data. In the mid-1960s, there was a significant amount of interest in program transfer-of-control statements. Studies indicated that there were fewer errors in programs that contained very few GO TO* statements. Furthermore, programs without GO TO statements were much simpler to maintain. In 1965, Dijkstra published his now-famous work showing that the GO TO statement could be eliminated from a programming language.[3] There are many who think it should be. "GO TO less" programming has become closely identified with structured programming. COBOL was developed several years before Dijkstra's paper appeared; there are a few instances where COBOL syntax requires that a GO TO statement be used.

A different approach to program design is necessary for writing structured programs. In 1974, an article appeared in the *IBM Systems Journal* describing the basis for the design and evaluation of structured programs.[5] Fundamental to *structured design* is the idea of repeatedly subdividing a problem into smaller problems until the small problems can be translated easily into understandable program segments. The program segments are then assembled to form a program solution to the original problem. This is called *top–down* or *modular design.* The program segment corresponding to a subproblem is called a *module.* Modules in structured COBOL correspond to single paragraphs and single sections.

Program complexity, how difficult the program is to read and understand, is related to the complexity within each module and to the complexity in the way communication takes place between modules. Program complexity is also related to how data are communicated and changed by the modules.[6]

Structured design requires that a program be evaluated in terms of the following:

1. Cohesion.
2. Coupling.
3. Module complexity.
   a. Size of module.
   b. Span of control.
   c. Control variables.

Cohesion

Cohesion is a measurement of the strength of relationships between statements in a module.[5] The strongest relationship, *functional cohesion,* occurs when all statements in a module are used to accomplish a single task in the program (for example, a module to compute an employee's net pay). The weakest relationship, *coincidental cohesion,* occurs when a module contains statements that, by coincidence, need to be executed multiple times and a module is created to contain these statements to avoid repetition in the code. Several intermediate levels of cohesion have been

---

* A GO TO statement is a transfer-of-control statement found in virtually all of the older high-level computer languages, in one form or another.

defined. One commonly encountered is *temporal cohesion*. Temporal cohesion occurs when statements that are executed at the same time are grouped in a module (for example, writing final totals and closing of files).

Coupling

Coupling is a measure of the strength of relationships between modules.[5] Modules are independent if a change in a given module has no effect on other modules. This is the lowest form of coupling. It is not possible for all modules to be independent, but loose coupling is to be preferred over tight coupling.

Coupling occurs in two ways:

1. Transfers of control.
2. Shared data.

Coupling resulting from transfers of control is loosest if modules are entered at the beginning (top) and exited at the end (bottom) and if control is passed directly down the paths depicted in the *hierarchy chart.*

A hierarchy chart, often referred to simply as a *structure chart,* is a diagram that shows the relationship among program modules. It provides us with a visual presentation of module levels, that is, higher-level modules and the lower-level modules they control.

Data sharing occurs when two or more modules can reference and modify the same data items. A very simple rule of thumb for data sharing is this: If it isn't necessary, don't do it. In particular, don't share subscripts, counters, and named constants. These should be dedicated data items and should never have multiple uses.

Module Complexity

There have been several attempts at measuring the internal complexity of a module. Certainly the size of a module is related to its complexity. General guidelines indicate that the size of a module should not exceed the amount of code that can appear on one page of output. This will be approximately 50 COBOL statements. Another measure of internal complexity of a given module is the number of modules that it controls. This is referred to as the *span of control.* As a general rule, it should not exceed seven modules; otherwise, the process of determining which ones will be executed, given various sets of conditions, is more complicated than is desirable.

The complexity measures of size and span of control were part of the original structured design concepts. Later authorities have attempted other measures related to the execution sequence.

A *control variable* is any data item used to control the execution sequence of the program. A module accesses a control variable if it modifies or tests it. McClure has developed a module complexity measure based on the number and types of accesses to control variables in a module.[6] Although the actual numeric value assigned is based on a rather complicated formula, the basic premise is that modules that test and modify control variables are more complex than those that do not. A rough estimate of complexity is obtained by counting the number of comparisons and modifications of control variables. The higher the number, the greater the internal complexity.

Modules with high internal complexity should be examined to see if they can reasonably be subdivided or broken down into less complex modules. The design goal is to have modules with approximately equal internal complexity. Failing in this, testing efforts need to be concentrated on modules with high complexity.

STRUCTURED WALKTHROUGHS

Most of us have probably noticed that proofreading our own work is difficult. After our repeated checking, a friend will often discover an error that we missed. Programmers have the same kind of problem in detecting errors in their programs. A *structured walkthrough,* designed to provide a similar kind of editorial assistance, is a group review at some stage in the program development process for the purpose of detecting errors. The goal is to discover errors early in the development process.

The review is initiated by the programmer. The specific format will depend on the data processing department, but the emphasis is on *error detection,* not on programmer evaluation or error correction.

Walkthroughs may be conducted any time the programmer feels public review will be beneficial. However, they should normally be done upon completion of

1. Program specifications.
2. Design.
3. Coding.

Additional walkthroughs may be conducted, but there are generally fewer benefits realized at other stages.

The *design walkthrough* should review the design from the standpoint of

1. Does the design meet the program specifications?
2. Does the design meet structured design requirements?
3. Is the logic correct for each module?

The *coding walkthrough* should review the program code for

1. Correct implementation of the design logic.
2. Adherence to the departmental coding standards.

There is some question as to whether the coding walkthrough should be conducted before or after the code is compiled. We feel that a walkthrough after the code is compiled is likely to be more effective.

PROGRAM TESTING

The purpose of testing a program is to verify that the program is correct. To test a program, input data must be developed and the output results verified. By a correct program, we mean one that (1) generates correct results for correct input data and (2) generates a reasonable response to data that is not valid.

There are several ways to approach program testing. For structured programs, *top–down testing* is often chosen. Modules are coded and tested starting at the top of the hierarchy chart. For testing purposes, *stub modules* are used in place of those lower-level modules not yet coded. The content of a stub module (in reality a dummy module) will depend upon the function of the actual module that will eventually replace it. For example, a processing module stub might simply contain a statement to DISPLAY a message indicating that the stub had been entered.

For each program module, you verify that when input is supplied, the module produces correct output and calls the appropriate modules under its control.

To provide a specific example of top–down testing, your attention is directed to the structure chart shown in Fig. 1.1. All of the modules for a complete program are represented in this chart.

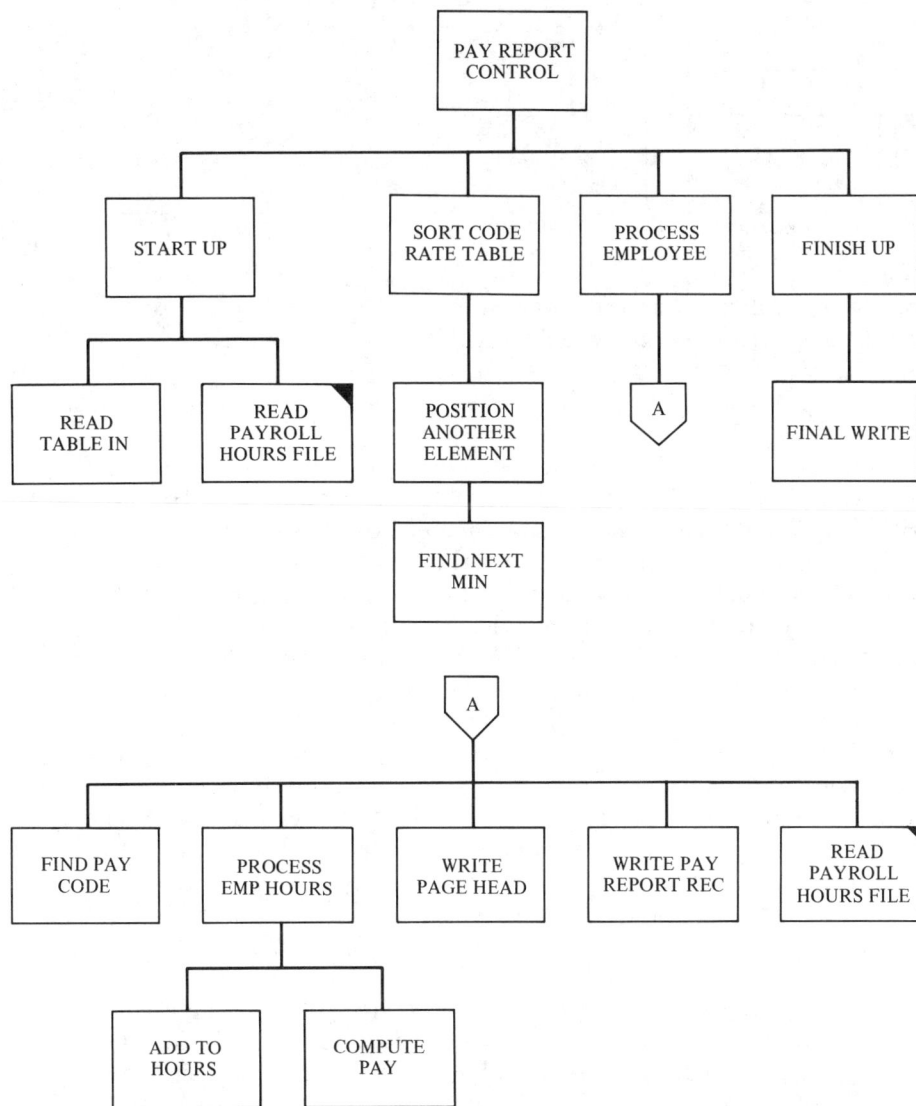

Figure 1.1
Complete structure (hierarchy) chart to be used in illustrating the concept of top–down program testing.

Modules selected for the initial stage of coding and testing are shown in Fig. 1.2. As can be seen, not all original program modules are depicted—just those modules actually needed at this stage. The shaded modules represent stub modules.

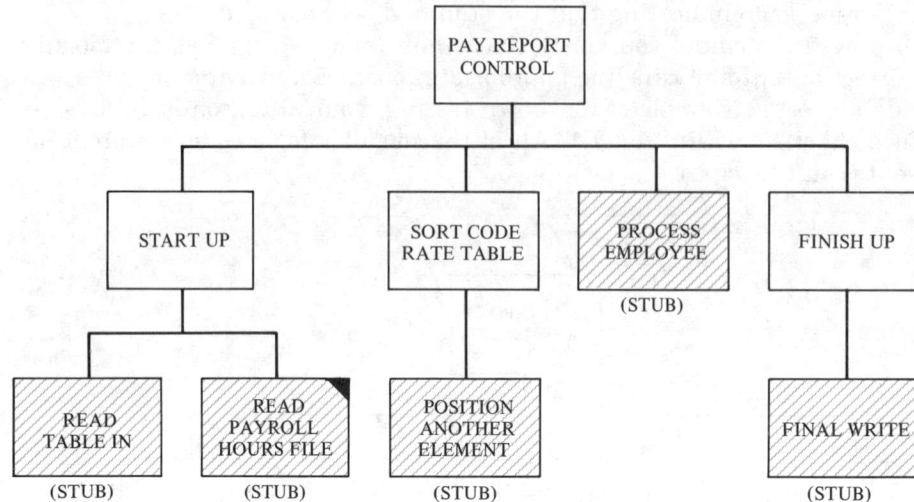

Figure 1.2

Initial stage for top–down testing the program represented in the structure chart in Figure 1.1. (Stub modules are shaded.)

In the initial stage, the modules to be coded for testing would be PAY REPORT CONTROL, START UP, SORT CODE RATE TABLE, and FINISH UP, with PROCESS EMPLOYEE and the remaining modules coded as stubs.

Modules that might logically be included in the second stage of testing are shown in Figure 1.3. Some modules, coded as stubs for initial testing purposes, are now completely coded and additional stub modules have been added.

The process of coding and testing in stages continues as we work our way down from higher-level modules through progressively lower levels, until every module in the program has been coded and fully tested.

An alternative to top–down testing is *bottom–up testing*. Using this approach, modules are coded and tested starting at the bottom of the hierarchy chart and then working up. Routines, called *drivers*, are written that call a module and pass data to it. As modules higher up in the chart are developed, the driver routines are replaced by the actual modules.

It is also possible to code the program completely before testing begins. This approach is usually limited to small programming projects that involve only one programmer.

In any case, data must be developed for use in testing. A good approach to use in designing test data is to develop the data to test a specific module when that module is written rather than waiting until later. At a minimum, test data should include data to test the following types of situations:

1. Each branch of a decision point.
2. Maximum and minimum values for data items.
3. Cases with too much (too little) data or no data.
4. Unusual values (blank or negative, for example).

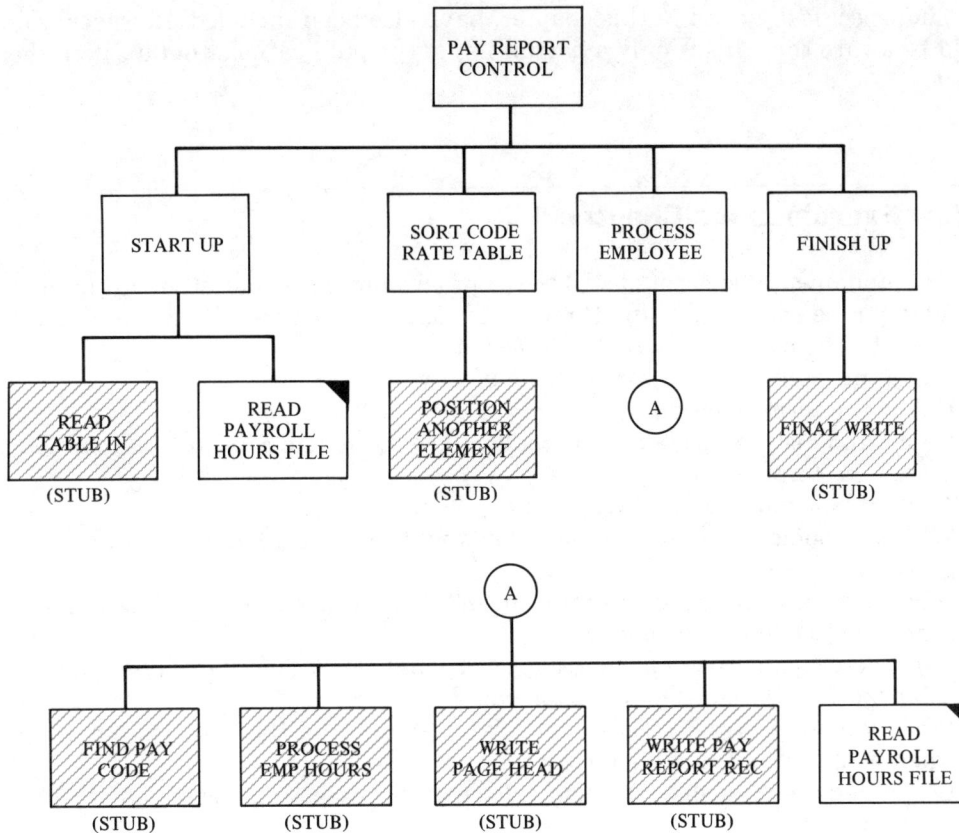

Figure 1.3
Second stage for top–down testing the program represented in the structure chart in Figure 1.1.

When you finish testing, every line of code in your program should have been executed.

CONCLUDING COMMENTS

The real objective of structured programming is *not* simply the elimination of GO TO statements, as some people with little understanding of the concept seem to think. Although this is one of the most visible characteristics of structured programs, it should be obvious that a program may contain no GO TO statements and still be of very poor quality.

The major objectives of structured program development should be to design programs that are easy to test, code, and maintain. This means writing programs that use straightforward logic and are easily understood, with internal complexity reduced to a low level. In accomplishing these objectives, modular top–down design emerges, which virtually eliminates the need to use GO TO statements.

You are encouraged to use the references provided at the end of this chapter to expand your knowledge of the program development process. Several major references, not specifically cited in this chapter, have also been included. However, you should be aware that this is only a partial list of the publications that exist on the subject.

Review Exercises for Chapter 1

1. The fundamental concept of structured programming is that all programming logic can be expressed using three basic control structures. What are they?
2. Describe the concept of *structured design*.
3. Explain the meaning of *program complexity*.
4. Define the term *cohesion*.
5. Define and distinguish between *functional cohesion* and *coincidental cohesion*.
6. Define the term *coupling*.
7. Explain how module coupling occurs.
8. What are some of the techniques that might be used to gauge module complexity?
9. What does module *span of control* mean? Should any limit be placed on the number of modules? If so, why?
10. If it is determined that a module has a very high degree of internal complexity, what course of action should be followed?
11. What is a *structured walkthrough*? What should be the primary emphasis when walkthroughs are conducted?
12. Define and distinguish between *top–down* program testing and *bottom–up* program testing.
13. What is the purpose of *stub modules*? What might be the initial content of such modules?
14. Certain types of situations (conditions) should be tested during the program testing phase. Thinking in terms of data values and processing conditions to be tested as a minimum, what should test data include?
15. The program development process is receiving an increasingly greater amount of attention. Based on the material presented in this chapter, in addition to any other pertinent information of which you may be aware, state the causes that you think are bringing about this increased attention.

Chapter References

1. Liu, C. "A Look at Software Maintenance," *Datamation*, Vol. 22, No. 11, November 1976, pp. 51–55.
2. Bohm, C., and G. Jacopini, "Flow Diagrams, Tuning Machines and Languages with Only Two Formation Rules," *Communications of the ACM*, Vol. 9, No. 3, May 1966, pp. 366–371.
3. Dijkstra, E. W. "GO TO Statement Considered Harmful," Letter to the Editor, *Communications of the ACM*, Vol. 11, No. 3, March 1968, pp. 147–148.
4. Dijkstra, E. W. "Programming Considered as a Human Activity," *Proceeding of IFIP Congress 65*. Washington, D.C.: Spartan Books, 1965.
5. Stevens, W., G. Myers, and L. Constantine. "Structured Design," *IBM Systems Journal*, Vol. 13, No. 2, 1974, pp. 115–139.

6. McClure, C. *Formalization and Application of Structured Programming and Program Complexity,* Ph.D. Thesis, Illinois Institute of Technology, May 1976, pp. 57–100.

Additional References

Baker, F. T. "Chief Programmer Team Management of Production Programming," *IBM Systems Journal,* Vol. 11, No. 1, January, 1972, pp. 56–73.

Martin, J., and C. McClure. *Software Maintenance: The Problem and Its Solutions.* Englewood Cliffs, N.J.: Prentice-Hall, 1983.

McCracken, Daniel D. "Revolution in Programming, an Overview," *Datamation,* Vol. 19, No. 12, December 1973, pp. 50–52.

Myers, Glenford J. *Reliable Software Through Composite Design.* Princeton, N.J.: Petrocelli/Charter, 1975.

Parnas, D. L. "On the Criteria to be Used in Decomposing Systems into Modules," *Communications of the ACM,* Vol. 15, No. 12, December 1972, pp. 1053–1058.

Yourdon, E. "Making the Move to Structured Programming," *Datamation,* June 1975, pp. 52–56.

Yourdon, E. *Techniques of Program Structure and Design.* Englewood Cliffs, N.J.: Prentice-Hall, 1975.

Yourdon, E., and L. Constantine. *Structured Design: Fundamentals of a Discipline of Computer Program and Systems Design.* Englewood Cliffs, N.J.: Prentice-Hall, 1979.

Indexing and the SEARCH Statement

INTRODUCTION

Programmers frequently encounter the need to work with data stored in tables. In your first course in COBOL, you probably studied tables and how to access data in tables using subscripts. However, you may not have worked with indexing or the SEARCH statement, which are the primary topics of discussion in this chapter. If you did not, a study of these topics should be rewarding. If you are already familiar with indexing and the use of SEARCH statements, you may wish to give only a light reading to this material or perhaps simply to move on to other topics.

Before we examine indexing (described a bit later), a brief look at table handling using subscripts seems appropriate.

For subscripting, a list of names might be described as follows.

```
01  NAME-LIST.
    02  NAME OCCURS 50 TIMES
        PIC X(25).
```

The individual names are then referenced as NAME (1) ... NAME (50) or, perhaps, NAME (NAME-COUNT), where NAME-COUNT, a user-defined data name used as a subscript, is described in the DATA DIVISION:

```
01  COUNTERS.
    02  NAME-COUNT          PIC 9(2).
            .
            .
            .
```

Recall that the PERFORM statement is frequently used to control accessing of data in tables. We might write out the list of names in the table with the following program segment:

```
WORKING-STORAGE SECTION.
01  COUNTERS.
    02  NUM-NAMES-IN-LIST   PIC 9(2).
    02  NAME-COUNT          PIC 9(2).
            .
            .
            .
```

```
      PROCEDURE DIVISION.
                         .
                         .
                         .
          PERFORM LIST-ALL-NAMES VARYING
              NAME-COUNT FROM 1 BY 1
              UNTIL NAME-COUNT IS GREATER
              THAN NUM-NAMES-IN-LIST.
                         .
                         .
                         .
      LIST-ALL-NAMES.
          DISPLAY NAME (NAME-COUNT).
                         .
                         .
                         .
```

The program segment just illustrated uses subscripts; however, COBOL provides an alternative technique, called *indexing,* for referencing elements in a table. In general, indexing provides more efficient access to table elements than subscripting, and, for some problems, allows the programmer to code a solution that is both simpler and more efficient.

In order to provide a basis for comparing the two methods, we will consider a simple subscripted table example.

Example 2.1

Input data consists of an employee's social security number, name, pay rate, and the number of hours worked on each of seven days. His gross pay is to be computed using a table containing the hours worked per day.

A structure chart is given in Figure 2.1 and, in order to give more complete documentation, the module descriptions are given in Figure 2.2. The programming logic should be familiar to you. (If not, perhaps a quick review of the table-handling chapter of your introductory COBOL textbook would be helpful.) In any event, the logic used is very simple. The program solution is given in Figure 2.3.

Special points about the program are:

1. On line 94, a table for PAY-IN-HOURS-WORKED is established. All seven of these table entries will be filled with data contained in seven consecutive fields in a single input record.
2. The value computed on line 147 for LINE-COUNT is 56. This means the condition tested on line 169 will be true for the first execution and hence, writing of the heading on the first page will be done.

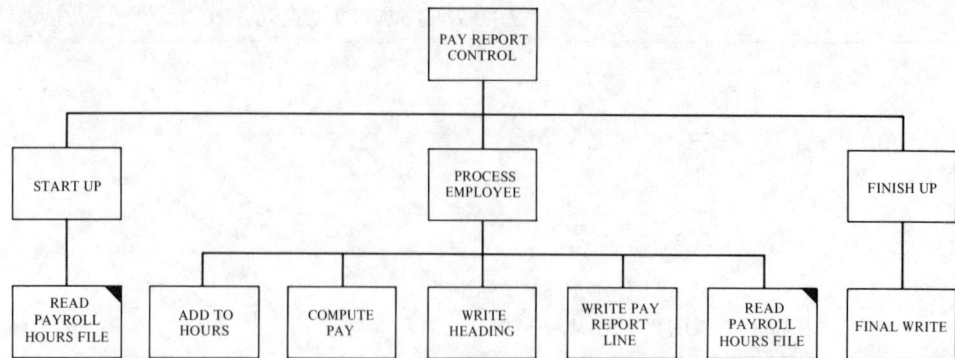

Figure 2.1
Structure chart for the program in Figure 2.3.

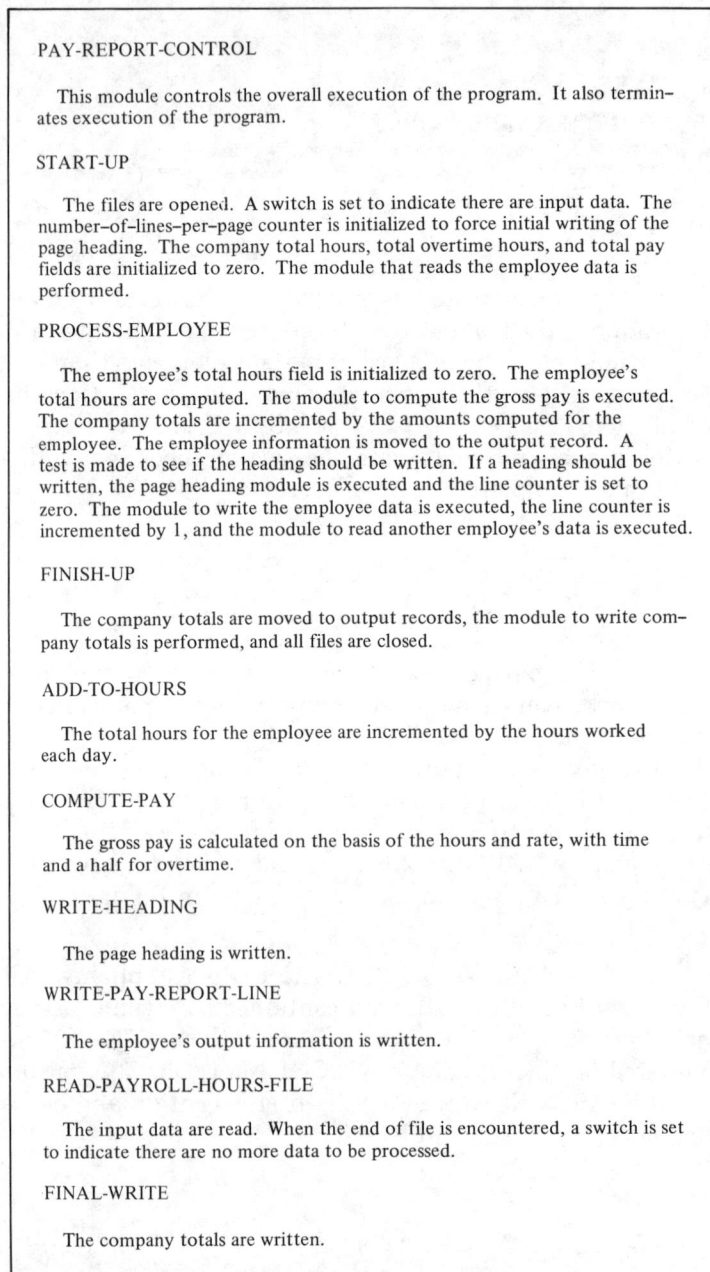

PAY-REPORT-CONTROL

This module controls the overall execution of the program. It also terminates execution of the program.

START-UP

The files are opened. A switch is set to indicate there are input data. The number–of–lines–per–page counter is initialized to force initial writing of the page heading. The company total hours, total overtime hours, and total pay fields are initialized to zero. The module that reads the employee data is performed.

PROCESS-EMPLOYEE

The employee's total hours field is initialized to zero. The employee's total hours are computed. The module to compute the gross pay is executed. The company totals are incremented by the amounts computed for the employee. The employee information is moved to the output record. A test is made to see if the heading should be written. If a heading should be written, the page heading module is executed and the line counter is set to zero. The module to write the employee data is executed, the line counter is incremented by 1, and the module to read another employee's data is executed.

FINISH-UP

The company totals are moved to output records, the module to write company totals is performed, and all files are closed.

ADD-TO-HOURS

The total hours for the employee are incremented by the hours worked each day.

COMPUTE-PAY

The gross pay is calculated on the basis of the hours and rate, with time and a half for overtime.

WRITE-HEADING

The page heading is written.

WRITE-PAY-REPORT-LINE

The employee's output information is written.

READ-PAYROLL-HOURS-FILE

The input data are read. When the end of file is encountered, a switch is set to indicate there are no more data to be processed.

FINAL-WRITE

The company totals are written.

Figure 2.2
Module description for the program in Figure 2.3.

```
00001                 IDENTIFICATION DIVISION.
00002           *
00003             PROGRAM-ID.
00004                 EX-2-1.
00005             ********************************************************************
00006           *                                                                  *
00007           *     PROGRAMMER TEAM           SUMMERS/WALSTROM/LINDAHL            *
00008           *     PROGRAM COMPLETION DATE OCTOBER 15, 1984                      *
00009           *                                                                  *
00010           *                    PROGRAM SUMMARY                               *
00011           *     INPUT                                                        *
00012           *         EACH EMPLOYEE INPUT RECORD CONTAINS                      *
00013           *             - SOCIAL SECURITY NUMBER                             *
00014           *             - NAME                                              *
00015           *             - HOURLY PAY RATE                                    *
00016           *             - NUMBER OF HOURS WORKED FOR EACH DAY OF THE WEEK    *
00017           *                                                                  *
00018           *     PROCESSING                                                   *
00019           *             - THE TOTAL NUMBER OF HOURS WORKED FOR AN EMPLOYEE   *
00020           *               IS COMPUTED USING A SUBSCRIPTED TABLE FOR          *
00021           *               THE DAILY HOURS WORKED                            *
00022           *             - THE GROSS PAY FOR AN EMPLOYEE IS COMPUTED          *
00023           *             - THE NUMBER OF REGULAR AND OVERTIME HOURS IS        *
00024           *               COMPUTED                                          *
00025           *             - TOTALS FOR REGULAR AND OVERTIME HOURS FOR ALL      *
00026           *               EMPLOYEES IS COMPUTED                             *
00027           *             - TOTAL GROSS PAY FOR ALL EMPLOYEES IS COMPUTED      *
00028           *                                                                  *
00029           *     OUTPUT                                                       *
00030           *         A PRINTED REPORT IS PRODUCED. OUTPUT FOR AN EMPLOYEE     *
00031           *         CONSISTS OF                                             *
00032           *             - SOCIAL SECURITY NUMBER                             *
00033           *             - NAME                                              *
00034           *             - NUMBER OF HOURS WORKED AT REGULAR RATE            *
00035           *             - NUMBER OF HOURS WORKED AT OVERTIME RATE           *
00036           *             - PAY RATE                                          *
00037           *             - GROSS PAY                                         *
00038           *         OUTPUT FOR THE COMPANY CONSISTS OF                      *
00039           *             - TOTAL OF ALL EMPLOYEE HOURS WORKED                *
00040           *             - TOTAL OF ALL EMPLOYEE OVERTIME HOURS WORKED       *
00041           *             - TOTAL AMOUNT OF THE PAYROLL                       *
00042             ********************************************************************
00043           *
00044             ENVIRONMENT DIVISION.
00045           *
00046             CONFIGURATION SECTION.
00047             SOURCE-COMPUTER.
00048                 IBM-370.
00049             OBJECT-COMPUTER.
00050                 IBM-370.
00051             SPECIAL-NAMES.
00052                 C01 IS TO-TOP-OF-PAGE.
00053             INPUT-OUTPUT SECTION.
00054             FILE-CONTROL.
00055                 SELECT PAYROLL-HOURS-FILE-IN
00056                     ASSIGN TO SYS007-UR-2501-S.
00057                 SELECT PAYROLL-REPORT-PRINT-FILE
00058                     ASSIGN TO SYS009-UR-1403-S.
00059           *
00060             DATA DIVISION.
00061           *
00062             FILE SECTION.
00063             FD  PAYROLL-HOURS-FILE-IN
00064                     LABEL RECORDS ARE OMITTED.
00065             01  PAYROLL-HOURS-IN-AREA          PIC X(80).
00066             FD  PAYROLL-REPORT-PRINT-FILE
00067                     LABEL RECORDS ARE OMITTED.
00068             01  PAYROLL-REPORT-PRINT-AREA      PIC X(133).
00069           *
00070             WORKING-STORAGE SECTION.
00071             01  SWITCHES.
00072                 02  END-OF-PAY-DATA-SW         PIC X.
00073                     88  NO-MORE-PAY-DATA   VALUE 'Y'.
```

Figure 2.3

Compute employee pay with subscripting for Example 2.1.

Figure 2.3 (cont.)

```
00074           01    COUNTERS.
00075                 02   HOURS-WORKED-COUNTER         PIC 9.
00076                 02   LINE-COUNT                   PIC 9(2).
00077           01    CONSTANTS.
00078                 02   NUM-DAYS-IN-WEEK             PIC 9 VALUE 7.
00079                 02   LINES-PER-PAGE              PIC 9(2) VALUE 55.
00080                 02   REG-PAY-PERIOD              PIC 9(2) VALUE 40.
00081                 02   OVERTIME-RATE               PIC V9(2) VALUE .50.
00082           01    EMP-TOTALS.
00083                 02   EMP-TOTAL-HOURS             PIC 9(2)V9(2).
00084                 02   EMP-TOTAL-OVERTIME          PIC 9(2)V9(2).
00085                 02   EMP-TOTAL-PAY               PIC 9(3)V9(2).
00086           01    COMPANY-TOTALS.
00087                 02   COM-TOTAL-HOURS             PIC 9(6)V9(2).
00088                 02   COM-TOTAL-OVERTIME          PIC 9(5)V9(2).
00089                 02   COM-TOTAL-PAY               PIC 9(8)V9(2).
00090           01    PAYROLL-HOURS-IN-REC.
00091                 02   PAY-IN-SS-NUM               PIC 9(9).
00092                 02   PAY-IN-NAME                 PIC X(20).
00093                 02   PAY-IN-RATE                 PIC 9(2)V9(3).
00094                 02   PAY-IN-HOURS-WORKED
00095                        OCCURS 7 TIMES            PIC 9(2)V9(2).
00096                 02   FILLER                      PIC X(18).
00097           01    PAY-REPORT-LINE.
00098                 02   FILLER                      PIC X(5) VALUE SPACE.
00099                 02   PAY-OUT-SS-NUM              PIC 9(9).
00100                 02   FILLER                      PIC X(5) VALUE SPACE.
00101                 02   PAY-OUT-NAME                PIC X(25).
00102                 02   PAY-OUT-REG-HOURS           PIC Z9.9(2).
00103                 02   FILLER                      PIC X(5) VALUE SPACE.
00104                 02   PAY-OUT-OVER-HOURS          PIC Z9.9(2).
00105                 02   FILLER                      PIC X(5) VALUE SPACE.
00106                 02   PAY-OUT-RATE                PIC Z9.9(3).
00107                 02   FILLER                      PIC X(5) VALUE SPACE.
00108                 02   PAY-OUT-TOTAL-PAY           PIC Z(2)9.9(2).
00109           01    HEADING-LINE.
00110                 02   FILLER                      PIC X(25)
00111                        VALUE '      SS NUM'.
00112                 02   FILLER                      PIC X(16)
00113                        VALUE 'NAME'.
00114                 02   FILLER                      PIC X(35)
00115                        VALUE 'REG HOURS   OVERTIME      RATE'.
00116                 02   FILLER                      PIC X(3) VALUE 'PAY'.
00117           01    STARLINE.
00118                 02   FILLER                      PIC X(133) VALUE ALL '*'.
00119           01    COMPANY-HOURS-LINE.
00120                 02   FILLER                      PIC X VALUE SPACE.
00121                 02   FILLER                      PIC X(30)
00122                        VALUE 'COMPANY TOTAL HOURS'.
00123                 02   COM-HOURS-OUT               PIC Z(5)9.9(2).
00124           01    COMPANY-OVERTIME-LINE.
00125                 02   FILLER                      PIC X VALUE SPACE.
00126                 02   FILLER                      PIC X(30)
00127                        VALUE 'COMPANY TOTAL OVERTIME'.
00128                 02   COM-OVERTIME-OUT            PIC Z(5)9.9(2).
00129           01    COMPANY-PAY-LINE.
00130                 02   FILLER                      PIC X VALUE SPACE.
00131                 02   FILLER                      PIC X(27)
00132                        VALUE 'COMPANY TOTAL PAYROLL'.
00133                 02   COM-PAY-OUT                 PIC $(8)9.9(2).
00134     *
00135     PROCEDURE DIVISION.
00136     *
00137     PAY-REPORT-CONTROL.
00138           PERFORM START-UP.
00139           PERFORM PROCESS-EMPLOYEE UNTIL NO-MORE-PAY-DATA.
00140           PERFORM FINISH-UP.
00141           STOP RUN.
00142     *
00143     START-UP.
00144           OPEN INPUT PAYROLL-HOURS-FILE-IN
00145                OUTPUT PAYROLL-REPORT-PRINT-FILE.
00146           MOVE 'N' TO END-OF-PAY-DATA-SW.
00147           COMPUTE LINE-COUNT = LINES-PER-PAGE + 1.
00148           MOVE ZERO TO COM-TOTAL-HOURS,
00149                        COM-TOTAL-OVERTIME,
00150                        COM-TOTAL-PAY.
00151           PERFORM READ-PAYROLL-HOURS-FILE.
```

Figure 2.3 (cont.)

```
00152              *
00153                  PROCESS-EMPLOYEE.
00154                      MOVE ZERO TO EMP-TOTAL-HOURS.
00155                      PERFORM ADD-TO-HOURS VARYING HOURS-WORKED-COUNTER
00156                          FROM 1 BY 1 UNTIL HOURS-WORKED-COUNTER IS
00157                          GREATER THAN NUM-DAYS-IN-WEEK.
00158                      PERFORM COMPUTE-PAY.
00159                      ADD EMP-TOTAL-HOURS TO COM-TOTAL-HOURS.
00160                      ADD EMP-TOTAL-OVERTIME TO COM-TOTAL-OVERTIME.
00161                      ADD EMP-TOTAL-PAY TO COM-TOTAL-PAY.
00162                      COMPUTE PAY-OUT-REG-HOURS = EMP-TOTAL-HOURS -
00163                                                  EMP-TOTAL-OVERTIME.
00164                      MOVE PAY-IN-SS-NUM TO PAY-OUT-SS-NUM.
00165                      MOVE PAY-IN-NAME TO PAY-OUT-NAME.
00166                      MOVE EMP-TOTAL-OVERTIME TO PAY-OUT-OVER-HOURS.
00167                      MOVE EMP-TOTAL-PAY TO PAY-OUT-TOTAL-PAY.
00168                      MOVE PAY-IN-RATE TO PAY-OUT-RATE.
00169                      IF LINE-COUNT IS GREATER THAN LINES-PER-PAGE
00170                          PERFORM WRITE-HEADING
00171                          MOVE ZERO TO LINE-COUNT.
00172                      PERFORM WRITE-PAY-REPORT-LINE.
00173                      ADD 1 TO LINE-COUNT.
00174                      PERFORM READ-PAYROLL-HOURS-FILE.
00175              *
00176                  FINISH-UP.
00177                      MOVE COM-TOTAL-HOURS TO COM-HOURS-OUT.
00178                      MOVE COM-TOTAL-OVERTIME TO COM-OVERTIME-OUT.
00179                      MOVE COM-TOTAL-PAY TO COM-PAY-OUT.
00180                      PERFORM FINAL-WRITE.
00181                      CLOSE PAYROLL-HOURS-FILE-IN
00182                          PAYROLL-REPORT-PRINT-FILE.
00183              *
00184                  ADD-TO-HOURS.
00185                      ADD PAY-IN-HOURS-WORKED (HOURS-WORKED-COUNTER)
00186                          TO EMP-TOTAL-HOURS.
00187              *
00188                  COMPUTE-PAY.
00189                      COMPUTE EMP-TOTAL-PAY = EMP-TOTAL-HOURS * PAY-IN-RATE.
00190                      IF EMP-TOTAL-HOURS IS GREATER THAN REG-PAY-PERIOD
00191                          COMPUTE EMP-TOTAL-OVERTIME = EMP-TOTAL-HOURS -
00192                                                       REG-PAY-PERIOD
00193                      ELSE
00194                          MOVE ZERO TO EMP-TOTAL-OVERTIME.
00195                      COMPUTE EMP-TOTAL-PAY = EMP-TOTAL-PAY + EMP-TOTAL-OVERTIME *
00196                                              PAY-IN-RATE * OVERTIME-RATE.
00197              *
00198                  WRITE-HEADING.
00199                      WRITE PAYROLL-REPORT-PRINT-AREA FROM HEADING-LINE
00200                          AFTER ADVANCING TO-TOP-OF-PAGE.
00201              *
00202                  WRITE-PAY-REPORT-LINE.
00203                      WRITE PAYROLL-REPORT-PRINT-AREA FROM PAY-REPORT-LINE
00204                          AFTER ADVANCING 1 LINES.
00205              *
00206                  READ-PAYROLL-HOURS-FILE.
00207                      READ PAYROLL-HOURS-FILE-IN INTO PAYROLL-HOURS-IN-REC
00208                          AT END MOVE 'Y' TO END-OF-PAY-DATA-SW.
00209              *
00210                  FINAL-WRITE.
00211                      WRITE PAYROLL-REPORT-PRINT-AREA FROM STARLINE
00212                          AFTER ADVANCING 3 LINES.
00213                      WRITE PAYROLL-REPORT-PRINT-AREA FROM COMPANY-HOURS-LINE
00214                          AFTER ADVANCING 2 LINES.
00215                      WRITE PAYROLL-REPORT-PRINT-AREA FROM COMPANY-OVERTIME-LINE
00216                          AFTER ADVANCING 1 LINES.
00217                      WRITE PAYROLL-REPORT-PRINT-AREA FROM COMPANY-PAY-LINE
00218                          AFTER ADVANCING 1 LINES.
```

DATA DIVISION ENTRIES

The use of an index requires a slightly modified version of the OCCURS clause.

```
┌─────────────────────────────────────────────────┐
│                      FORMAT                       │
├─────────────────────────────────────────────────┤
│  OCCURS  integer-2 TIMES                          │
│      ⎡⎧ASCENDING ⎫              ⎤                 │
│      ⎢⎨DESCENDING⎬ KEY IS data-name-1 . . .⎥     │
│      ⎣⎩          ⎭              ⎦                 │
│  INDEXED BY index-name-1, . . .                   │
└─────────────────────────────────────────────────┘
```

In order to use an index, the INDEXED BY clause must appear. The KEY clause may be specified if the table defined is in order by one or more fields.

An indexed version of our table of names now looks like this:

```
01  NAME-LIST.
    02  NAME OCCURS 50 TIMES
            INDEXED BY NAME-COUNT
            PIC X(25).
```

Unlike a data-name, an index (NAME-COUNT in this example) must *not* be further defined with a PICTURE clause in the DATA DIVISION. The internal form of an index is determined automatically by the compiler.

If our list of names is in alphabetical order, we would use the KEY clause and the description would be

```
01  NAME-LIST.
    02  NAME OCCURS 50 TIMES
            ASCENDING KEY IS NAME
            INDEXED BY NAME-COUNT
            PIC X(25).
```

Indexing may be either direct or relative. *Direct indexing,* as is true with subscripts, must directly reference a specific entry in the table. To illustrate:

```
NAME (NAME-COUNT).
```

Relative indexing is specified by following the index-name by one of the operators, + or −, followed by an integer numeric literal. There must be a space before and after the operator. Two examples are

```
NAME (NAME-COUNT + 2)
```
(For example, if NAME-COUNT has the value 4, NAME (NAME-COUNT + 2) references NAME (6),
```
NAME (NAME-COUNT − 1)
```
and NAME (NAME-COUNT − 1) references NAME (3).)

Of course, with both direct and relative forms of indexing, you should exercise care to make certain that references are made only to valid entries within the limits of the table. The relative form of referencing table entries is not allowed under the ANSI standard if you are using *subscripts*.

Sometimes we will need to save the value in an index for later use. The value in an index must be saved under a data-name associated with an elementary data item that has been defined as an *index data item*. For this purpose, we use a special form of the USAGE clause, USAGE IS INDEX, to define an index data item and associate it with a data-name.

```
┌─────────────────────────────────────────┐
│                  FORMAT                   │
├─────────────────────────────────────────┤
│  level-number   data-name   USAGE IS INDEX │
└─────────────────────────────────────────┘
```

```
01  SAVE-INDEX.
    02  SAVE-NAME-LOCATION
            USAGE IS INDEX.
                .
                .
                .
```

Before moving on, the distinction between an index data item and an index name should be clearly pointed out. An index data item is defined through the USAGE IS INDEX clause, whereas an index name is specified by the INDEXED BY index-name clause when the table is established, and it is associated with the table.

Formal restrictions on the use of index names and index data items are

1. An index name may be referenced only in a SET, SEARCH, or PERFORM with the VARYING option.
2. An index data item may be referenced in a SET statement or a relation condition.
3. An index data item may be part of a group that is referred to in a MOVE or I/O statement, but no conversion will be done.
4. An index data item cannot be a conditional variable.
5. The SYNCHRONIZED, JUSTIFIED, PICTURE, BLANK, or VALUE clauses may not be used jointly with the USAGE IS INDEX clause.
6. The comparison of two index-names is a comparison of the corresponding occurrence numbers.
7. In the comparison of an index name to a numeric integer data item or literal, the occurrence number is compared to the data item or literal.
8. If an index data item is compared to an index name or another index data item, the actual storage contents are compared with no conversion. Any other comparison involving an index data item is illegal.

Let's consider the payroll problem once again.

Example 2.2

For the same input and output data as Example 2.1, the program will be rewritten
to do the processing using an indexed table of hours.

Since an index may be referenced using a PERFORM statement with the VARY-
ING option in the same way a subscript is referenced, only DATA DIVISION entries
need to be changed. The solution is given in Figure 2.4. Since no changes were
made in the coding logic from Example 2.1, the structure chart is omitted. Note
the INDEXED BY clause on line 94 and the required absence of any PICTURE
clause for the index HOURS-WORKED-COUNTER.

```
00069          WORKING-STORAGE SECTION.
00070          01   SWITCHES.
00071               02   END-OF-PAY-DATA-SW              PIC X.
00072                    88   NO-MORE-PAY-DATA    VALUE 'Y'.
00073          01   COUNTERS.
00074               02   LINE-COUNT                      PIC 9(2).
00075          01   CONSTANTS.
00076               02   NUM-DAYS-IN-WEEK                PIC 9 VALUE 7.
00077               02   LINES-PER-PAGE                  PIC 9(2) VALUE 55.
00078               02   REG-PAY-PERIOD                  PIC 9(2) VALUE 40.
00079               02   OVERTIME-RATE                   PIC V9(2) VALUE .50.
00080          01   EMP-TOTALS.
00081               02   EMP-TOTAL-HOURS                 PIC 9(2)V9(2).
00082               02   EMP-TOTAL-OVERTIME              PIC 9(2)V9(2).
00083               02   EMP-TOTAL-PAY                   PIC 9(3)V9(2).
00084          01   COMPANY-TOTALS.
00085               02   COM-TOTAL-HOURS                 PIC 9(6)V9(2).
00086               02   COM-TOTAL-OVERTIME              PIC 9(5)V9(2).
00087               02   COM-TOTAL-PAY                   PIC 9(8)V9(2).
00088          01   PAYROLL-HOURS-IN-REC.
00089               02   PAY-IN-SS-NUM                   PIC 9(9).
00090               02   PAY-IN-NAME                     PIC X(20).
00091               02   PAY-IN-RATE                     PIC 9(2)V9(3).
00092               02   PAY-IN-HOURS-WORKED
00093                    OCCURS 7 TIMES
00094                    INDEXED BY HOURS-WORKED-COUNTER
00095                                                    PIC 9(2)V9(2).
00096               02   FILLER                          PIC X(18).
00097          01   PAY-REPORT-LINE.
00098               02   FILLER                          PIC X(5) VALUE SPACE.
00099               02   PAY-OUT-SS-NUM                  PIC 9(9).
00100               02   FILLER                          PIC X(5) VALUE SPACE.
00101               02   PAY-OUT-NAME                    PIC X(25).
00102               02   PAY-OUT-REG-HOURS               PIC Z9.9(2).
00103               02   FILLER                          PIC X(5) VALUE SPACE.
00104               02   PAY-OUT-OVER-HOURS              PIC Z9.9(2).
00105               02   FILLER                          PIC X(5) VALUE SPACE.
00106               02   PAY-OUT-RATE                    PIC Z9.9(3).
00107               02   FILLER                          PIC X(5) VALUE SPACE.
00108               02   PAY-OUT-TOTAL-PAY               PIC Z(2)9.9(2).
00109          01   HEADING-LINE.
00110               02   FILLER                          PIC X(25)
00111                    VALUE '        SS NUM'.
00112               02   FILLER                          PIC X(16)
00113                    VALUE 'NAME'.
00114               02   FILLER                          PIC X(35)
00115                    VALUE 'REG HOURS    OVERTIME    RATE'.
00116               02   FILLER                          PIC X(3) VALUE 'PAY'.
00117          01   STARLINE.
00118               02   FILLER                          PIC X(133) VALUE ALL '*'.
00119          01   COMPANY-HOURS-LINE.
00120               02   FILLER                          PIC X VALUE SPACE.
00121               02   FILLER                          PIC X(30)
00122                    VALUE 'COMPANY TOTAL HOURS'.
00123               02   COM-HOURS-OUT                   PIC Z(5)9.9(2).
```

Figure 2.4
Compute employee pay with indexing for Example 2.2.

Figure 2.4 (cont.)

```
00124            01    COMPANY-OVERTIME-LINE.
00125                  02    FILLER                          PIC X VALUE SPACE.
00126                  02    FILLER                          PIC X(30)
00127                        VALUE  'COMPANY TOTAL OVERTIME'.
00128                  02    COM-OVERTIME-OUT                PIC Z(5)9.9(2).
00129            01    COMPANY-PAY-LINE.
00130                  02    FILLER                          PIC X VALUE SPACE.
00131                  02    FILLER                          PIC X(27)
00132                        VALUE  'COMPANY TOTAL PAYROLL'.
00133                  02    COM-PAY-OUT                     PIC $(8)9.9(2).
00134         *
00135         PROCEDURE DIVISION.
00136         *
00137          PAY-REPORT-CONTROL.
00138               PERFORM START-UP.
00139               PERFORM PROCESS-EMPLOYEE UNTIL NO-MORE-PAY-DATA.
00140               PERFORM FINISH-UP.
00141               STOP RUN.
00142         *
00143          START-UP.
00144               OPEN INPUT PAYROLL-HOURS-FILE-IN
00145                    OUTPUT PAYROLL-REPORT-PRINT-FILE.
00146               MOVE 'N' TO END-OF-PAY-DATA-SW.
00147               COMPUTE LINE-COUNT = LINES-PER-PAGE + 1.
00148               MOVE ZERO TO COM-TOTAL-HOURS,
00149                            COM-TOTAL-OVERTIME,
00150                            COM-TOTAL-PAY.
00151               PERFORM READ-PAYROLL-HOURS-FILE.
00152         *
00153          PROCESS-EMPLOYEE.
00154               MOVE ZERO TO EMP-TOTAL-HOURS.
00155               PERFORM ADD-TO-HOURS VARYING HOURS-WORKED-COUNTER
00156                    FROM 1 BY 1 UNTIL HOURS-WORKED-COUNTER IS
00157                    GREATER THAN NUM-DAYS-IN-WEEK.
00158               PERFORM COMPUTE-PAY.
00159               ADD EMP-TOTAL-HOURS TO COM-TOTAL-HOURS.
00160               ADD EMP-TOTAL-OVERTIME TO COM-TOTAL-OVERTIME.
00161               ADD EMP-TOTAL-PAY TO COM-TOTAL-PAY.
00162               COMPUTE PAY-OUT-REG-HOURS = EMP-TOTAL-HOURS -
00163                                           EMP-TOTAL-OVERTIME.
00164               MOVE PAY-IN-SS-NUM TO PAY-OUT-SS-NUM.
00165               MOVE PAY-IN-NAME TO PAY-OUT-NAME.
00166               MOVE EMP-TOTAL-OVERTIME TO PAY-OUT-OVER-HOURS.
00167               MOVE EMP-TOTAL-PAY TO PAY-OUT-TOTAL-PAY.
00168               MOVE PAY-IN-RATE TO PAY-OUT-RATE.
00169               IF LINE-COUNT IS GREATER THAN LINES-PER-PAGE
00170                    PERFORM WRITE-HEADING
00171                    MOVE ZERO TO LINE-COUNT.
00172               PERFORM WRITE-PAY-REPORT-LINE.
00173               ADD 1 TO LINE-COUNT.
00174               PERFORM READ-PAYROLL-HOURS-FILE.
00175         *
00176          FINISH-UP.
00177               MOVE COM-TOTAL-HOURS TO COM-HOURS-OUT.
00178               MOVE COM-TOTAL-OVERTIME TO COM-OVERTIME-OUT.
00179               MOVE COM-TOTAL-PAY TO COM-PAY-OUT.
00180               PERFORM FINAL-WRITE.
00181               CLOSE PAYROLL-HOURS-FILE-IN
00182                     PAYROLL-REPORT-PRINT-FILE.
00183         *
00184          ADD-TO-HOURS.
00185               ADD PAY-IN-HOURS-WORKED (HOURS-WORKED-COUNTER)
00186                    TO EMP-TOTAL-HOURS.
00187         *
00188          COMPUTE-PAY.
00189               COMPUTE EMP-TOTAL-PAY = EMP-TOTAL-HOURS * PAY-IN-RATE.
00190               IF EMP-TOTAL-HOURS IS GREATER THAN REG-PAY-PERIOD
00191                    COMPUTE EMP-TOTAL-OVERTIME = EMP-TOTAL-HOURS -
00192                                                 REG-PAY-PERIOD
00193               ELSE
00194                    MOVE ZERO TO EMP-TOTAL-OVERTIME.
00195               COMPUTE EMP-TOTAL-PAY = EMP-TOTAL-PAY + EMP-TOTAL-OVERTIME *
00196                                       PAY-IN-RATE * OVERTIME-RATE.
00197         *
00198          WRITE-HEADING.
00199               WRITE PAYROLL-REPORT-PRINT-AREA FROM HEADING-LINE
00200                    AFTER ADVANCING TO-TOP-OF-PAGE.
```

Figure 2.4 (*cont.*)

```
00201        *
00202            WRITE-PAY-REPORT-LINE.
00203                WRITE PAYROLL-REPORT-PRINT-AREA FROM PAY-REPORT-LINE
00204                    AFTER ADVANCING 1 LINES.
00205        *
00206            READ-PAYROLL-HOURS-FILE.
00207                READ PAYROLL-HOURS-FILE-IN INTO PAYROLL-HOURS-IN-REC
00208                    AT END MOVE 'Y' TO END-OF-PAY-DATA-SW.
00209        *
00210            FINAL-WRITE.
00211                WRITE PAYROLL-REPORT-PRINT-AREA FROM STARLINE
00212                    AFTER ADVANCING 3 LINES.
00213                WRITE PAYROLL-REPORT-PRINT-AREA FROM COMPANY-HOURS-LINE
00214                    AFTER ADVANCING 2 LINES.
00215                WRITE PAYROLL-REPORT-PRINT-AREA FROM COMPANY-OVERTIME-LINE
00216                    AFTER ADVANCING 1 LINES.
00217                WRITE PAYROLL-REPORT-PRINT-AREA FROM COMPANY-PAY-LINE
00218                    AFTER ADVANCING 1 LINES.
```

THE SET STATEMENT

Since an index and an index data item have different internal representation from that of other numeric data items, they require a special verb to manipulate them. That is the function of the SET verb. It is used to initialize and increment an index.

$$\text{SET} \left\{ \begin{array}{l} \text{index-name-1} \\ \text{identifier-1} \end{array} \right\} \underline{\text{TO}} \left\{ \begin{array}{l} \text{index-name-2} \\ \text{identifier-2} \\ \text{literal-1} \end{array} \right\}$$

FORMAT 1

Format-1 of the SET statement is used to initialize an index.
This form may also be used to assign values to an index data item.

```
SET SAVE-NAME-LOCATION TO 1.
SET SAVE-NAME-LOCATION TO NAME-COUNT.
```

A second form to the SET statement:

FORMAT 2

$$\underline{\text{SET}} \text{ index-name-3} \left\{ \begin{array}{l} \underline{\text{UP}} \text{ BY} \\ \underline{\text{DOWN}} \text{ BY} \end{array} \right\} \left\{ \begin{array}{l} \text{identifier-3} \\ \text{literal-2} \end{array} \right\}$$

Format-2 of the SET statement is used to construct loops. For example, the following program segment gives the same loop control as that presented in Example 2.2.

```
              .
              .
              .

      SET HOURS-WORKED-COUNTER TO 1.
      PERFORM ADD-TO-HOURS UNTIL HOURS-WORKED-COUNTER
            IS GREATER THAN 7.
              .
              .
              .
   ADD-TO-HOURS.
      ADD PAY-IN-HOURS-WORKED (HOURS-WORKED-COUNTER)
            TO EMP-TOTAL-HOURS.
      SET HOURS-WORKED-COUNTER UP BY 1.
              .
              .
              .
```

Format-2 of the SET statement *may not* be used to manipulate index data items. The formal rules for the SET statements are given here.

**FORMAL RULES AND CONSIDERATIONS
PERTAINING TO THE SET STATEMENT**

All identifiers must name either index data items or fixed-point numeric elementary items described as integers; however, identifier-3 must not name an index data item. When a literal is used, it must be a positive nonzero integer. Index-names are related to a given table through the INDEXED BY option of the OCCURS clause, which automatically defines the index name.

Format-1 considerations—when the SET statement is executed, one of the following actions occurs:

1. Index-name-1 is converted to a value that corresponds to the same table element to which either index-name-2, identifier-2, or literal-1 corresponds. If identifier-2 is an index data item, or if index-name-2 is related to the same table as index-name-1, no conversion takes place.
2. If identifier-1 is an index data item, it is set equal to either the contents of index-name-2 or identifier-2, where identifier-2 is also an index data item. Literal-1 cannot be used in this case.
3. If identifier-1 is not an index data item, it is set to an occurrence number that corresponds to the value of index-name-3. Neither identifier-2 nor literal-1 can be used in this case.

Format-2 considerations—When the SET statement is executed, the contents of the index-name-3 are incremented (UP BY) or decremented (DOWN BY) by a value that corresponds to the number of occurrences represented by the value of literal-2 or identifier-3.

INTERNAL REPRESENTATION

The elements of the array NAME-LIST are stored consecutively.

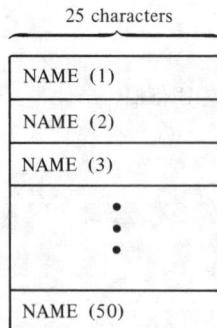

25 characters

NAME (1)
NAME (2)
NAME (3)
$\vdots$
NAME (50)

The numerical position of the entry in the table is called the *occurrence number*. For each entry, the value in the corresponding index is

$$(\text{occurrence-number} - 1) * \text{element length}.$$

In our example, for the array NAME-LIST, the element length is 25 characters. Thus, if the character representation is in bytes, SET NAME-COUNT TO 5 stores $((5 - 1) * 25) = 100$ in NAME-COUNT. Then, SET SAVE-NAME-LOCATION TO NAME-COUNT will also place 100 in SAVE-NAME-LOCATION.

Most of the time, the programmer will not be concerned with the internal form of the index. However, for indexes associated with tables with different entry lengths, and for index data-items, this internal form can give surprising results, as the following illustration using relation tests will show.

RELATION TESTS FOR INDEX NAMES AND INDEX DATA ITEMS

Suppose we have the following statements in a program.

```
          .
          .
          .
     01   SAVE-INDEX.
          02   SAVE-SHORT          USAGE IS INDEX.
     01   SHORT-NUM-TABLE.
          02   SHORT-NUM
               OCCURS 10 TIMES
               INDEXED BY SHORT        PIC 9(4).
     01   LONG-NUM-TABLE.
          02   LONG-NUM
```

```
            OCCURS 10 TIMES
            INDEXED BY LONG        PIC 9(6).
                    .
                    .
                    .

     PROCEDURE DIVISION.
                    .
                    .
                    .

         SET SHORT TO 5.
         SET LONG TO 5.
         SET SAVE-SHORT TO SHORT.
         IF SHORT = LONG
              PERFORM EQUAL-ENTRY.
         IF SAVE-SHORT = LONG
              PERFORM EQUAL-ENTRY.
                    .
                    .
                    .
```

For the first IF, the two occurrence numbers (both 5) would be compared and EQUAL-ENTRY would be executed. For the second IF, the actual contents are compared (16 in SAVE-SHORT and 24 in LONG) and EQUAL-ENTRY would not be executed.

A summary of the permissible comparisons is given in Table 2.1.

TABLE 2.1.   Permissible Comparison for Index Names and Index Data Items

Second Operand First Operand	*Index-name*	*Index Data Item*	*Data-name (numeric integer only)*	*Numeric Literal (integer only)*
Index-name	Compare occurrence number	Compare without conversion	Compare occurrence number with data-name	Compare occurrence number with literal
Index data item	Compare without conversion	Compare without conversion	Illegal	Illegal
Data-name (numeric integer only)	Compare occurrence number with data-name	Illegal	Legal	Legal
Numeric literal (integer only)	Compare occurrence number with literal	Illegal	Legal	Legal

TABLE LOOK-UP

You were probably introduced to the concept of a table look-up in your first course in COBOL. The idea, in a nonprogramming sense, is familiar. For example, shortly before April 15, millions of people are looking up the amount of their federal income tax in the tax tables that accompany the federal income tax forms.

Since the technique is encountered in everyday life, you might expect that it occurs frequently in programming, too. Consider a list of standard abbreviations for states:

Occurrence Number	Abbreviation	Full State Name
1	AK	ALASKA
2	AL	ALABAMA
3	AR	ARKANSAS
4	CA	CALIFORNIA
.		
.		
.		
14	IL	ILLINOIS
.		
.		
.		

Although the input data could contain the full name of the state, this involves unnecessary data entry time and wasted storage. We see that if the state abbreviation is AR, it has occurrence number 3, and the full state name (ARKANSAS) can be retrieved from the table using this occurrence number.

One frequently used table look-up technique is the *serial search,* also referred to as the *linear* search and the *sequential* search. This technique involves beginning at some point in the table (usually the first element) and testing each successive element until the desired element is found or until the end of the table is reached. If the end of the table is reached, we may assume that the element we are searching for is not in the table.

We will now present a programming example that illustrates the serial search table look-up technique.

Example 2.3

The employee data of Example 2.1 contained the employee's pay rate as part of the input data. Inspection of payroll data has revealed that there are only 10 distinct rates, based on an employee's job classification. It is decided to enter a pay code for the job classification, instead of the actual pay rate. The pay codes chosen, and the corresponding pay rates, are as follows:

Pay Codes	Pay Rates
A	5.350
B	4.400
R	10.100
S	2.000
T	3.505
X	7.750
0	6.105
1	3.625
4	4.800
5	9.500

Salary computations are the same once the appropriate pay rate is located in the rate table.

In Figure 2.5, a structure chart is given for a solution to this problem. A program solution using subscripted tables is given in Figure 2.6.

Note the following:

1. Remember that values may not be initialized for data items that have an OCCURS clause. Thus, we use REDEFINES (lines 159 and 165) to assign the tables to storage areas that were previously initialized to rate and code values.
2. Separate pay rate and pay code tables are defined, since they will allow for simpler initialization than is possible with a single combined table.
3. The IF statement on line 219 locates the correct pay code. Then the occurrence number of the pay rate is set to that for the pay code (line 220). At this point, we have the pay rate to be used, and the program proceeds as before.

The data entry clerks are pleased with the new data format. The accounting department is also pleased since (1) fewer errors are being made, and (2) illegal pay codes are detected by the program, which means more accuracy in the amounts being paid to employees. There is one problem with the new system—its execution time exceeds that of the old one.

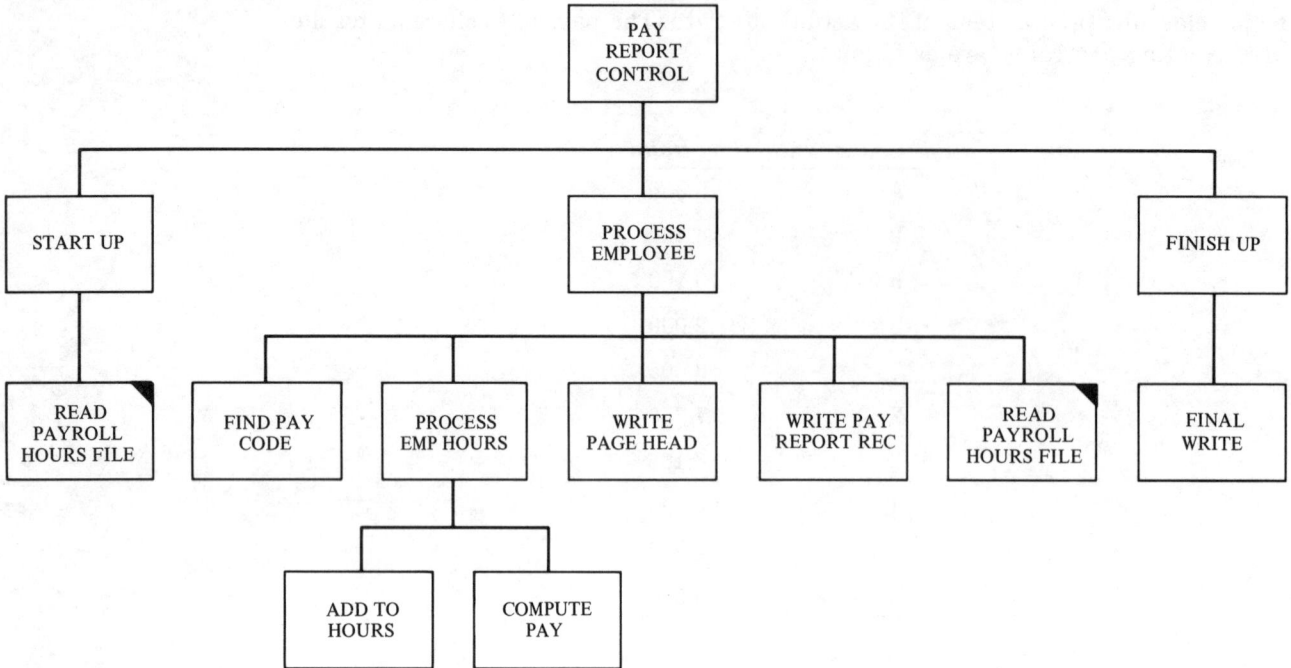

Figure 2.5
Structure chart for the program in Figure 2.6.

```
00001          IDENTIFICATION DIVISION.
00002        *
00003          PROGRAM-ID.
00004             EX-2-3.
00005        ***************************************************************
00006        *                                                             *
00007        *    PROGRAMMER TEAM          SUMMERS/WALSTROM/LINDAHL        *
00008        *    PROGRAM COMPLETION DATE NOVEMBER 7, 1984.               *
00009        *                                                             *
00010        *                   PROGRAM SUMMARY                          *
00011        *    INPUT                                                    *
00012        *        EACH EMPLOYEE INPUT RECORD CONTAINS                  *
00013        *              - SOCIAL SECURITY NUMBER                       *
00014        *              - NAME                                         *
00015        *              - PAY CODE                                     *
00016        *              - NUMBER OF HOURS WORKED FOR EACH DAY OF THE WEEK *
00017        *                                                             *
00018        *    PROCESSING                                               *
00019        *        FOR A VALID EMPLOYEE RECORD                          *
00020        *              - THE PAY RATE IS LOCATED IN THE RATE TABLE    *
00021        *              - THE TOTAL NUMBER OF HOURS WORKED FOR AN EMPLOYEE *
00022        *                IS COMPUTED                                  *
00023        *              - ALL TABLES ARE SUBSCRIPTED                   *
00024        *              - THE GROSS PAY FOR AN EMPLOYEE IS COMPUTED    *
00025        *              - THE NUMBER OF REGULAR AND OVERTIME HOURS     *
00026        *                IS COMPUTED                                  *
00027        *              - TOTALS FOR REGULAR AND OVERTIME HOURS FOR ALL *
00028        *                EMPLOYEES ARE ACCUMULATED                    *
00029        *              - TOTAL GROSS PAY FOR ALL EMPLOYEES IS COMPUTED *
00030        *                                                             *
```

Figure 2.6
Compute employee pay with programmer-written serial table look-up via subscripting for Example 2.3.

Figure 2.6 (cont.)

```
00031        *       OUTPUT                                              *
00032        *          A PRINTED REPORT IS PRODUCED.                    *
00033        *          VALID EMPLOYEE OUTPUT CONSISTS OF                *
00034        *             - SOCIAL SECURITY NUMBER                      *
00035        *             - NAME                                        *
00036        *             - NUMBER OF HOURS WORKED AT REGULAR RATE      *
00037        *             - NUMBER OF HOURS WORKED AT OVERTIME RATE     *
00038        *             - PAY RATE                                    *
00039        *             - GROSS PAY                                   *
00040        *          INVALID EMPLOYEE OUTPUT CONSISTS OF              *
00041        *             - SOCIAL SECURITY NUMBER                      *
00042        *             - NAME                                        *
00043        *             - ZERO FOR HOURS AT REGULAR RATE, HOURS AT    *
00044        *               OVERTIME RATE AND GROSS PAY                 *
00045        *             - THE INVALID PAY CODE                        *
00046        *             - AN ERROR MESSAGE                            *
00047        *          OUTPUT FOR THE COMPANY CONSISTS OF               *
00048        *             - TOTAL OF ALL EMPLOYEE HOURS WORKED          *
00049        *             - TOTAL OF ALL EMPLOYEE OVERTIME HOURS WORKED *
00050        *             - TOTAL AMOUNT OF THE PAYROLL                 *
00051        ************************************************************
00052        *
00053        ENVIRONMENT DIVISION.
00054        *
00055        CONFIGURATION SECTION.
00056        SOURCE-COMPUTER.
00057            IBM-370.
00058        OBJECT-COMPUTER.
00059            IBM-370.
00060        SPECIAL-NAMES.
00061            C01 IS TO-TOP-OF-PAGE.
00062        INPUT-OUTPUT SECTION.
00063        FILE-CONTROL.
00064            SELECT PAYROLL-HOURS-FILE-IN
00065                ASSIGN TO SYS007-UR-2501-S.
00066            SELECT PAYROLL-REPORT-PRINT-FILE
00067                ASSIGN TO SYS009-UR-1403-S.
00068        *
00069        DATA DIVISION.
00070        *
00071        FILE SECTION.
00072        FD  PAYROLL-HOURS-FILE-IN
00073                LABEL RECORDS ARE OMITTED.
00074        01  PAYROLL-HOURS-IN-AREA            PIC X(80).
00075        FD  PAYROLL-REPORT-PRINT-FILE
00076                LABEL RECORDS ARE OMITTED.
00077        01  PAYROLL-REPORT-PRINT-AREA        PIC X(133).
00078        *
00079        WORKING-STORAGE SECTION.
00080        01  SWITCHES.
00081            02  END-OF-PAY-DATA-SW           PIC X.
00082                88  NO-MORE-PAY-DATA VALUE 'Y'.
00083            02  PAY-CODE-FOUND-SW            PIC X.
00084                88  PAY-CODE-FOUND    VALUE 'Y'.
00085        01  COUNTERS.
00086            02  RATE-TABLE-COUNTER           PIC 9(2).
00087            02  PAY-CODE-TABLE-COUNTER       PIC 9(2).
00088            02  HOURS-WORKED-TABLE-COUNTER   PIC 9.
00089            02  LINE-COUNT                   PIC 9(2).
00090        01  CONSTANTS.
00091            02  NUM-DAYS-IN-WEEK             PIC 9 VALUE 7.
00092            02  NUM-OF-CODES                 PIC 9(2) VALUE 10.
00093            02  LINES-PER-PAGE               PIC 9(2) VALUE 55.
00094            02  REG-PAY-PERIOD               PIC 9(2) VALUE 40.
00095            02  OVERTIME-RATE                PIC V9(2) VALUE .50.
00096        01  EMPLOYEE-TOTALS.
00097            02  EMP-TOTAL-HOURS              PIC 9(2)V9(2).
00098            02  EMP-TOTAL-OVERTIME           PIC 9(2)V9(2).
00099            02  EMP-TOTAL-PAY                PIC 9(3)V9(2).
00100        01  COMPANY-TOTALS.
00101            02  COM-TOTAL-HOURS              PIC 9(6)V9(2).
00102            02  COM-TOTAL-OVERTIME           PIC 9(5)V9(2).
00103            02  COM-TOTAL-PAY                PIC 9(8)V9(2).
00104        01  PAYROLL-HOURS-IN-REC.
00105            02  PAY-IN-SS-NUM                PIC 9(9).
00106            02  PAY-IN-NAME                  PIC X(20).
00107            02  PAY-IN-CODE                  PIC X.
00108            02  PAY-IN-HOURS-WORKED
00109                OCCURS 7 TIMES               PIC 9(2)V9(2).
00110            02  FILLER                       PIC X(22).
```

Figure 2.6 (cont.)

```
00111              01   PAY-REPORT-LINE.
00112                   02   FILLER                        PIC X(5) VALUE SPACE.
00113                   02   PAY-OUT-SS-NUM                PIC 9(9).
00114                   02   FILLER                        PIC X(5) VALUE SPACE.
00115                   02   PAY-OUT-NAME                  PIC X(25).
00116                   02   PAY-OUT-REG-HOURS             PIC Z9.9(2).
00117                   02   FILLER                        PIC X(5) VALUE SPACE.
00118                   02   PAY-OUT-OVER-HOURS            PIC Z9.9(2).
00119                   02   FILLER                        PIC X(5) VALUE SPACE.
00120                   02   PAY-OUT-RATE                  PIC Z9.9(3).
00121                   02   FILLER                        PIC X(5) VALUE SPACE.
00122                   02   PAY-OUT-TOTAL-PAY             PIC Z(2)9.9(2).
00123                   02   PAY-OUT-MESSAGE-INFO.
00124                        03  PAY-OUT-MESSAGE           PIC X(30).
00125                        03  PAY-OUT-CODE              PIC X.
00126              01   HEADING-LINE.
00127                   02   FILLER                        PIC X(44)
00128                        VALUE '       SS NUM       EMPLOYEE NAME'.
00129                   02   FILLER                        PIC X(35)
00130                        VALUE ' REG HOURS  OVERTIME   RATE       PAY'.
00131              01   STARLINE.
00132                   02   FILLER                        PIC X(133) VALUE ALL '*'.
00133              01   COMPANY-HOURS-LINE.
00134                   02   FILLER                        PIC X VALUE SPACE.
00135                   02   FILLER                        PIC X(30)
00136                        VALUE 'COMPANY TOTAL HOURS'.
00137                   02   COM-HOURS-OUT                 PIC Z(5)9.9(2).
00138              01   COMPANY-OVERTIME-LINE.
00139                   02   FILLER                        PIC X VALUE SPACE.
00140                   02   FILLER                        PIC X(30)
00141                        VALUE 'COMPANY TOTAL OVERTIME'.
00142                   02   COM-OVERTIME-OUT              PIC Z(5)9.9(2).
00143              01   COMPANY-PAY-LINE.
00144                   02   FILLER                        PIC X VALUE SPACE.
00145                   02   FILLER                        PIC X(27)
00146                        VALUE 'COMPANY TOTAL PAYROLL'.
00147                   02   COM-PAY-OUT                   PIC $(8)9.9(2).
00148              01   RATES.
00149                   02   FILLER                        PIC 9(2)V9(3) VALUE 5.350.
00150                   02   FILLER                        PIC 9(2)V9(3) VALUE 4.400.
00151                   02   FILLER                        PIC 9(2)V9(3) VALUE 10.100.
00152                   02   FILLER                        PIC 9(2)V9(3) VALUE 2.000.
00153                   02   FILLER                        PIC 9(2)V9(3) VALUE 3.505.
00154                   02   FILLER                        PIC 9(2)V9(3) VALUE 7.750.
00155                   02   FILLER                        PIC 9(2)V9(3) VALUE 6.105.
00156                   02   FILLER                        PIC 9(2)V9(3) VALUE 3.625.
00157                   02   FILLER                        PIC 9(2)V9(3) VALUE 4.800.
00158                   02   FILLER                        PIC 9(2)V9(3) VALUE 9.500.
00159              01   RATE-TABLE REDEFINES RATES.
00160                   02   PAY-RATE
00161                        OCCURS 10 TIMES               PIC 9(2)V9(3).
00162              01   PAY-CODES.
00163                   02   FILLER                        PIC X(10)
00164                        VALUE 'ABRSTX0145'.
00165              01   PAY-CODE-TABLE REDEFINES PAY-CODES.
00166                   02   PAY-CODE
00167                        OCCURS 10 TIMES               PIC X.
00168       *
00169        PROCEDURE DIVISION.
00170       *
00171        PAY-REPORT-CONTROL.
00172              PERFORM START-UP.
00173              PERFORM PROCESS-EMPLOYEE UNTIL NO-MORE-PAY-DATA.
00174              PERFORM FINISH-UP.
00175              STOP RUN.
00176       *
00177        START-UP.
00178              OPEN INPUT PAYROLL-HOURS-FILE-IN
00179                   OUTPUT PAYROLL-REPORT-PRINT-FILE.
00180              MOVE 'N' TO END-OF-PAY-DATA-SW.
00181              COMPUTE LINE-COUNT = LINES-PER-PAGE + 1.
00182              MOVE ZERO TO COM-TOTAL-HOURS,
00183                           COM-TOTAL-OVERTIME,
00184                           COM-TOTAL-PAY.
00185              PERFORM READ-PAYROLL-HOURS-FILE.
```

Figure 2.6 (cont.)

```
00186          *
00187          PROCESS-EMPLOYEE.
00188              MOVE 'N' TO PAY-CODE-FOUND-SW.
00189              PERFORM FIND-PAY-CODE VARYING PAY-CODE-TABLE-COUNTER
00190                  FROM 1 BY 1 UNTIL PAY-CODE-FOUND
00191                              OR
00192                  PAY-CODE-TABLE-COUNTER IS GREATER THAN NUM-OF-CODES.
00193              MOVE PAY-IN-NAME TO PAY-OUT-NAME.
00194              MOVE PAY-IN-SS-NUM TO PAY-OUT-SS-NUM.
00195              IF PAY-CODE-FOUND
00196                  MOVE SPACE TO PAY-OUT-MESSAGE-INFO
00197                  PERFORM PROCESS-EMP-HOURS
00198              ELSE
00199                  MOVE 'INVALID PAY-CODE' TO PAY-OUT-MESSAGE
00200                  MOVE ZERO TO PAY-OUT-REG-HOURS, PAY-OUT-OVER-HOURS,
00201                      PAY-OUT-RATE, PAY-OUT-TOTAL-PAY
00202                  MOVE PAY-IN-CODE TO PAY-OUT-CODE.
00203              IF LINE-COUNT   IS GREATER THAN LINES-PER-PAGE
00204                  PERFORM WRITE-PAGE-HEAD
00205                  MOVE ZERO TO LINE-COUNT.
00206              PERFORM WRITE-PAY-REPORT-REC.
00207              ADD 1 TO LINE-COUNT.
00208              PERFORM READ-PAYROLL-HOURS-FILE.
00209          *
00210          FINISH-UP.
00211              MOVE COM-TOTAL-HOURS TO COM-HOURS-OUT.
00212              MOVE COM-TOTAL-OVERTIME TO COM-OVERTIME-OUT.
00213              MOVE COM-TOTAL-PAY TO COM-PAY-OUT.
00214              PERFORM FINAL-WRITE.
00215              CLOSE PAYROLL-HOURS-FILE-IN,
00216                  PAYROLL-REPORT-PRINT-FILE.
00217          *
00218          FIND-PAY-CODE.
00219              IF PAY-CODE (PAY-CODE-TABLE-COUNTER) = PAY-IN-CODE
00220                  MOVE PAY-CODE-TABLE-COUNTER TO  RATE-TABLE-COUNTER
00221                  MOVE 'Y' TO PAY-CODE-FOUND-SW.
00222          *
00223          PROCESS-EMP-HOURS.
00224              MOVE ZERO TO EMP-TOTAL-HOURS.
00225              PERFORM ADD-TO-HOURS VARYING HOURS-WORKED-TABLE-COUNTER
00226                  FROM 1 BY 1 UNTIL HOURS-WORKED-TABLE-COUNTER
00227                  GREATER THAN NUM-DAYS-IN-WEEK.
00228              PERFORM COMPUTE-PAY.
00229              ADD EMP-TOTAL-HOURS TO COM-TOTAL-HOURS.
00230              ADD EMP-TOTAL-OVERTIME TO COM-TOTAL-OVERTIME.
00231              ADD EMP-TOTAL-PAY TO COM-TOTAL-PAY.
00232              COMPUTE PAY-OUT-REG-HOURS = EMP-TOTAL-HOURS -
00233                              EMP-TOTAL-OVERTIME.
00234              MOVE EMP-TOTAL-OVERTIME  TO PAY-OUT-OVER-HOURS.
00235              MOVE PAY-RATE (RATE-TABLE-COUNTER) TO PAY-OUT-RATE.
00236              MOVE EMP-TOTAL-PAY TO PAY-OUT-TOTAL-PAY.
00237          *
00238          ADD-TO-HOURS.
00239              COMPUTE EMP-TOTAL-HOURS = EMP-TOTAL-HOURS +
00240                      PAY-IN-HOURS-WORKED (HOURS-WORKED-TABLE-COUNTER).
00241          *
00242          COMPUTE-PAY.
00243              COMPUTE EMP-TOTAL-PAY =   EMP-TOTAL-HOURS *
00244                              PAY-RATE (RATE-TABLE-COUNTER).
00245              IF EMP-TOTAL-HOURS IS GREATER THAN REG-PAY-PERIOD
00246                  COMPUTE EMP-TOTAL-OVERTIME = EMP-TOTAL-HOURS -
00247                              REG-PAY-PERIOD
00248              ELSE
00249                  MOVE ZERO TO EMP-TOTAL-OVERTIME.
00250              COMPUTE EMP-TOTAL-PAY =   EMP-TOTAL-PAY + EMP-TOTAL-OVERTIME
00251                          * PAY-RATE (RATE-TABLE-COUNTER)
00252                          * OVERTIME-RATE.
00253          *
00254          WRITE-PAGE-HEAD.
00255              WRITE PAYROLL-REPORT-PRINT-AREA FROM HEADING-LINE
00256                  AFTER ADVANCING TO-TOP-OF-PAGE.
00257          *
00258          WRITE-PAY-REPORT-REC.
00259              WRITE PAYROLL-REPORT-PRINT-AREA FROM PAY-REPORT-LINE
00260                  AFTER ADVANCING 1 LINES.
```

Figure 2.6 (*cont.*)

```
00261          *
00262              READ-PAYROLL-HOURS-FILE.
00263                  READ PAYROLL-HOURS-FILE-IN INTO PAYROLL-HOURS-IN-REC
00264                      AT END MOVE 'Y' TO END-OF-PAY-DATA-SW.
00265          *
00266              FINAL-WRITE.
00267                  WRITE PAYROLL-REPORT-PRINT-AREA FROM STARLINE
00268                      AFTER ADVANCING 3 LINES.
00269                  WRITE PAYROLL-REPORT-PRINT-AREA FROM COMPANY-HOURS-LINE
00270                      AFTER ADVANCING 2 LINES.
00271                  WRITE PAYROLL-REPORT-PRINT-AREA FROM COMPANY-OVERTIME-LINE
00272                      AFTER ADVANCING 1 LINES.
00273                  WRITE PAYROLL-REPORT-PRINT-AREA FROM COMPANY-PAY-LINE
00274                      AFTER ADVANCING 1 LINES.
```

Example 2.4

In an attempt to reduce the execution time needed to process the payroll, the program in Figure 2.6 is to be revised so that all tables are indexed.

The program modification is given in Figure 2.7. Since there is no change in the control structure, the structure chart is omitted. In fact, little change is required for the program. All tables now have an INDEXED BY clause (lines 107, 161, 169). On line 223, the occurrence number for the desired pay code is converted and placed in the index RATE-TABLE-COUNTER with a SET statement.

```
00078          *
00079              WORKING-STORAGE SECTION.
00080              01  SWITCHES.
00081                  02  END-OF-PAY-DATA-SW            PIC X.
00082                      88  NO-MORE-PAY-DATA VALUE 'Y'.
00083                  02  PAY-CODE-FOUND-SW             PIC X.
00084                      88  PAY-CODE-FOUND      VALUE 'Y'.
00085              01  COUNTERS.
00086                  02  LINE-COUNT                   PIC 9(2).
00087              01  CONSTANTS.
00088                  02  NUM-DAYS-IN-WEEK             PIC 9 VALUE 7.
00089                  02  NUM-OF-CODES                 PIC 9(2) VALUE 10.
00090                  02  LINES-PER-PAGE               PIC 9(2) VALUE 55.
00091                  02  REG-PAY-PERIOD               PIC 9(2) VALUE 40.
00092                  02  OVERTIME-RATE                PIC V9(2) VALUE .50.
00093              01  EMPLOYEE-TOTALS.
00094                  02  EMP-TOTAL-HOURS              PIC 9(2)V9(2).
00095                  02  EMP-TOTAL-OVERTIME           PIC 9(2)V9(2).
00096                  02  EMP-TOTAL-PAY                PIC 9(3)V9(2).
00097              01  COMPANY-TOTALS.
00098                  02  COM-TOTAL-HOURS              PIC 9(6)V9(2).
00099                  02  COM-TOTAL-OVERTIME           PIC 9(5)V9(2).
00100                  02  COM-TOTAL-PAY                PIC 9(8)V9(2).
00101              01  PAYROLL-HOURS-IN-REC.
00102                  02  PAY-IN-SS-NUM                PIC 9(9).
00103                  02  PAY-IN-NAME                  PIC X(20).
00104                  02  PAY-IN-CODE                  PIC X.
00105                  02  PAY-IN-HOURS-WORKED
00106                          OCCURS 7 TIMES
00107                          INDEXED BY HOURS-WORKED-TABLE-COUNTER
00108                                                   PIC 9(2)V9(2).
00109                  02  FILLER                       PIC X(22).
```

Figure 2.7
Compute employee pay with programmer-written serial table look-up via indexing for Example 2.4.

Figure 2.7 (cont.)

```
00110          01   PAY-REPORT-LINE.
00111               02   FILLER                         PIC X(5) VALUE SPACE.
00112               02   PAY-OUT-SS-NUM                 PIC 9(9).
00113               02   FILLER                         PIC X(5) VALUE SPACE.
00114               02   PAY-OUT-NAME                   PIC X(25).
00115               02   PAY-OUT-REG-HOURS              PIC Z9.9(2).
00116               02   FILLER                         PIC X(5) VALUE SPACE.
00117               02   PAY-OUT-OVER-HOURS             PIC Z9.9(2).
00118               02   FILLER                         PIC X(5) VALUE SPACE.
00119               02   PAY-OUT-RATE                   PIC Z9.9(3).
00120               02   FILLER                         PIC X(5) VALUE SPACE.
00121               02   PAY-OUT-TOTAL-PAY              PIC Z(2)9.9(2).
00122               02   PAY-OUT-MESSAGE-INFO.
00123                    03   PAY-OUT-MESSAGE           PIC X(30).
00124                    03   PAY-OUT-CODE              PIC X.
00125          01   HEADING-LINE.
00126               02   FILLER                         PIC X(44)
00127                    VALUE '       SS NUM       EMPLOYEE NAME'.
00128               02   FILLER                         PIC X(35)
00129                    VALUE ' REG HOURS   OVERTIME   RATE      PAY'.
00130          01   STARLINE.
00131               02   FILLER                         PIC X(133) VALUE ALL '*'.
00132          01   COMPANY-HOURS-LINE.
00133               02   FILLER                         PIC X VALUE SPACE.
00134               02   FILLER                         PIC X(30)
00135                    VALUE 'COMPANY TOTAL HOURS'.
00136               02   COM-HOURS-OUT                  PIC Z(5)9.9(2).
00137          01   COMPANY-OVERTIME-LINE.
00138               02   FILLER                         PIC X VALUE SPACE.
00139               02   FILLER                         PIC X(30)
00140                    VALUE 'COMPANY TOTAL OVERTIME'.
00141               02   COM-OVERTIME-OUT               PIC Z(5)9.9(2).
00142          01   COMPANY-PAY-LINE.
00143               02   FILLER                         PIC X VALUE SPACE.
00144               02   FILLER                         PIC X(27)
00145                    VALUE 'COMPANY TOTAL PAYROLL'.
00146               02   COM-PAY-OUT                    PIC $(8)9.9(2).
00147          01   RATES.
00148               02   FILLER                         PIC 9(2)V9(3) VALUE 5.350.
00149               02   FILLER                         PIC 9(2)V9(3) VALUE 4.400.
00150               02   FILLER                         PIC 9(2)V9(3) VALUE 10.100.
00151               02   FILLER                         PIC 9(2)V9(3) VALUE 2.000.
00152               02   FILLER                         PIC 9(2)V9(3) VALUE 3.505.
00153               02   FILLER                         PIC 9(2)V9(3) VALUE 7.750.
00154               02   FILLER                         PIC 9(2)V9(3) VALUE 6.105.
00155               02   FILLER                         PIC 9(2)V9(3) VALUE 3.625.
00156               02   FILLER                         PIC 9(2)V9(3) VALUE 4.800.
00157               02   FILLER                         PIC 9(2)V9(3) VALUE 9.500.
00158          01   RATE-TABLE REDEFINES RATES.
00159               02   PAY-RATE
00160                         OCCURS 10 TIMES
00161                         INDEXED BY RATE-TABLE-COUNTER
00162                                                   PIC 9(2)V9(3).
00163          01   PAY-CODES.
00164               02   FILLER                         PIC X(10)
00165                    VALUE 'ABRSTX0145'.
00166          01   PAY-CODE-TABLE REDEFINES PAY-CODES.
00167               02   PAY-CODE
00168                         OCCURS 10 TIMES
00169                         INDEXED BY PAY-CODE-TABLE-COUNTER
00170                                                   PIC X.
00171     *
00172      PROCEDURE DIVISION.
00173     *
00174      PAY-REPORT-CONTROL.
00175          PERFORM START-UP.
00176          PERFORM PROCESS-EMPLOYEE UNTIL NO-MORE-PAY-DATA.
00177          PERFORM FINISH-UP.
00178          STOP RUN.
00179     *
00180      START-UP.
00181          OPEN INPUT PAYROLL-HOURS-FILE-IN
00182               OUTPUT PAYROLL-REPORT-PRINT-FILE.
00183          MOVE 'N' TO END-OF-PAY-DATA-SW.
00184          COMPUTE LINE-COUNT = LINES-PER-PAGE + 1.
00185          MOVE ZERO TO COM-TOTAL-HOURS,
00186                       COM-TOTAL-OVERTIME,
00187                       COM-TOTAL-PAY.
00188          PERFORM READ-PAYROLL-HOURS-FILE.
```

Figure 2.7 (*cont.*)

```
00189          *
00190                PROCESS-EMPLOYEE.
00191                    MOVE 'N' TO PAY-CODE-FOUND-SW.
00192                    PERFORM FIND-PAY-CODE VARYING PAY-CODE-TABLE-COUNTER
00193                         FROM 1 BY 1 UNTIL PAY-CODE-FOUND
00194                                 OR
00195                         PAY-CODE-TABLE-COUNTER IS GREATER THAN NUM-OF-CODES.
00196                    MOVE PAY-IN-NAME TO PAY-OUT-NAME.
00197                    MOVE PAY-IN-SS-NUM TO PAY-OUT-SS-NUM.
00198                    IF PAY-CODE-FOUND
00199                         MOVE SPACE TO PAY-OUT-MESSAGE-INFO
00200                         PERFORM PROCESS-EMP-HOURS
00201                    ELSE
00202                         MOVE 'INVALID PAY-CODE' TO PAY-OUT-MESSAGE
00203                         MOVE ZERO TO PAY-OUT-REG-HOURS, PAY-OUT-OVER-HOURS,
00204                              PAY-OUT-RATE, PAY-OUT-TOTAL-PAY
00205                         MOVE PAY-IN-CODE TO PAY-OUT-CODE.
00206                    IF LINE-COUNT    IS GREATER THAN LINES-PER-PAGE
00207                         PERFORM WRITE-PAGE-HEAD
00208                         MOVE ZERO TO LINE-COUNT.
00209                    PERFORM WRITE-PAY-REPORT-REC.
00210                    ADD 1 TO LINE-COUNT.
00211                    PERFORM READ-PAYROLL-HOURS-FILE.
00212          *
00213               FINISH-UP.
00214                    MOVE COM-TOTAL-HOURS TO COM-HOURS-OUT.
00215                    MOVE COM-TOTAL-OVERTIME TO COM-OVERTIME-OUT.
00216                    MOVE COM-TOTAL-PAY TO COM-PAY-OUT.
00217                    PERFORM FINAL-WRITE.
00218                    CLOSE PAYROLL-HOURS-FILE-IN,
00219                         PAYROLL-REPORT-PRINT-FILE.
00220          *
00221               FIND-PAY-CODE.
00222                    IF PAY-CODE (PAY-CODE-TABLE-COUNTER) = PAY-IN-CODE
00223                         SET RATE-TABLE-COUNTER TO PAY-CODE-TABLE-COUNTER
00224                         MOVE 'Y' TO PAY-CODE-FOUND-SW.
00225          *
00226               PROCESS-EMP-HOURS.
00227                    MOVE ZERO TO EMP-TOTAL-HOURS.
00228                    PERFORM ADD-TO-HOURS VARYING HOURS-WORKED-TABLE-COUNTER
00229                         FROM 1 BY 1 UNTIL HOURS-WORKED-TABLE-COUNTER
00230                         GREATER THAN NUM-DAYS-IN-WEEK.
00231                    PERFORM COMPUTE-PAY.
00232                    ADD EMP-TOTAL-HOURS TO COM-TOTAL-HOURS.
00233                    ADD EMP-TOTAL-OVERTIME TO COM-TOTAL-OVERTIME.
00234                    ADD EMP-TOTAL-PAY TO COM-TOTAL-PAY.
00235                    COMPUTE PAY-OUT-REG-HOURS = EMP-TOTAL-HOURS -
00236                                               EMP-TOTAL-OVERTIME.
00237                    MOVE EMP-TOTAL-OVERTIME  TO PAY-OUT-OVER-HOURS.
00238                    MOVE PAY-RATE (RATE-TABLE-COUNTER) TO PAY-OUT-RATE.
00239                    MOVE EMP-TOTAL-PAY TO PAY-OUT-TOTAL-PAY.
00240          *
00241               ADD-TO-HOURS.
00242                    COMPUTE EMP-TOTAL-HOURS = EMP-TOTAL-HOURS +
00243                         PAY-IN-HOURS-WORKED (HOURS-WORKED-TABLE-COUNTER).
00244          *
00245               COMPUTE-PAY.
00246                    COMPUTE EMP-TOTAL-PAY =   EMP-TOTAL-HOURS *
00247                                          PAY-RATE (RATE-TABLE-COUNTER).
00248                    IF EMP-TOTAL-HOURS IS GREATER THAN REG-PAY-PERIOD
00249                         COMPUTE EMP-TOTAL-OVERTIME = EMP-TOTAL-HOURS -    '
00250                                               REG-PAY-PERIOD
00251                    ELSE
00252                         MOVE ZERO TO EMP-TOTAL-OVERTIME.
00253                    COMPUTE EMP-TOTAL-PAY =   EMP-TOTAL-PAY + EMP-TOTAL-OVERTIME
00254                                          * PAY-RATE (RATE-TABLE-COUNTER)
00255                                          * OVERTIME-RATE.
00256          *
00257               WRITE-PAGE-HEAD.
00258                    WRITE PAYROLL-REPORT-PRINT-AREA FROM HEADING-LINE
00259                         AFTER ADVANCING TO-TOP-OF-PAGE.
00260          *
00261               WRITE-PAY-REPORT-REC.
00262                    WRITE PAYROLL-REPORT-PRINT-AREA FROM PAY-REPORT-LINE
00263                         AFTER ADVANCING 1 LINES.
00264          *
00265               READ-PAYROLL-HOURS-FILE.
00266                    READ PAYROLL-HOURS-FILE-IN INTO PAYROLL-HOURS-IN-REC
00267                         AT END MOVE 'Y' TO END-OF-PAY-DATA-SW.
```

Figure 2.7 (cont.)

```
00268        *
00269         FINAL-WRITE.
00270             WRITE PAYROLL-REPORT-PRINT-AREA FROM STARLINE
00271                 AFTER ADVANCING 3 LINES.
00272             WRITE PAYROLL-REPORT-PRINT-AREA FROM COMPANY-HOURS-LINE
00273                 AFTER ADVANCING 2 LINES.
00274             WRITE PAYROLL-REPORT-PRINT-AREA FROM COMPANY-OVERTIME-LINE
00275                 AFTER ADVANCING 1 LINES.
00276             WRITE PAYROLL-REPORT-PRINT-AREA FROM COMPANY-PAY-LINE
00277                 AFTER ADVANCING 1 LINES.
```

THE SEARCH STATEMENT

In the previous examples, the table look-up was explicitly written by the programmer. However, COBOL has built-in facilities to search a table for an element that satisfies a given condition. There are two versions of the SEARCH statement, one for serial table searching and one for binary searching. The serial search concept was defined earlier in our discussion of table look-up prior to its use in Examples 2.3 and 2.4. Binary searching will be defined later.

The format of the SEARCH statement that does serial (sequential) table look-up is given here.

```
┌─────────────────────────────────────────────────────────────┐
│                        FORMAT 1                              │
│                                                              │
│                              ⎡          ⎧index-name-1⎫⎤      │
│  SEARCH identifier-1   ⎢VARYING ⎨identifier-2 ⎬⎥      │
│                              ⎣          ⎩            ⎭⎦      │
│                                                              │
│     [AT END imperative-statement-1]                          │
│                                                              │
│                         ⎧imperative-statement-2⎫             │
│     WHEN condition-1 ⎨NEXT SENTENCE          ⎬             │
│                         ⎩                     ⎭             │
│                                                              │
│     ⎡               ⎧imperative-statement-3⎫⎤               │
│     ⎢WHEN condition-2 ⎨NEXT SENTENCE          ⎬⎥               │
│     ⎣               ⎩                     ⎭⎦               │
└─────────────────────────────────────────────────────────────┘
```

The data entry specified as identifier-1 must have both an OCCURS clause and an INDEXED BY clause. No subscript or index may be specified for identifier-1. We will present the formal rules for a Format-1 SEARCH, but first let's consider an example:

```
WORKING-STORAGE SECTION.
01  SWITCHES.
    02  PART-NUM-FOUND-SW              PIC X.
        88  PART-FOUND      VALUE 'Y'.
            .
            .
            .
```

```
01   PART-REC-IN.
         .

         .

         .

     02   PART-NUM-IN                          PIC 9(6).
         .

         .

01   PARTS-TABLE.
     02   PARTS-INFO
              OCCURS 500 TIMES
              INDEXED BY PART-LOC.
          03   PART-NUM                         PIC 9(6).
          03   PART-DESCRIPTION                 PIC X(20).
         .

         .

         .

PROCEDURE DIVISION.
         .

         .

         .

     SET PART-LOC TO 1.
     SEARCH PART-INFO
         AT END MOVE 'N' TO PART-NUM-FOUND-SW
         WHEN PART-NUM (PART-LOC) = PART-NUM-IN
             MOVE 'Y' TO PART-NUM-FOUND-SW.
         .

         .

         .

     IF PART-FOUND
         PERFORM PROCESS-PART-IN
     ELSE
         PERFORM PROCESS-ERROR-IN-PART.
         .

         .

         .
```

In the preceding example, the SEARCH statement invokes a serial search of the PARTS-TABLE. The value in PART-LOC must be initialized to 1 before the search begins. If a match is found for PART-NUM-IN, the index PART-LOC will point to that entry in the table. This value then can be used to reference the desired information from PARTS-TABLE.

If the WHEN condition is not satisfied before the end-of-table is encountered (the desired element is not found), the imperative statement following the AT END option will be executed.

Now let's take another look at Example 2.4; however, this time the SEARCH statement will be used to locate the pay code in our program solution. No DATA DIVISION changes will be necessary, and only minor changes are needed in the two modules PROCESS-EMPLOYEE and FIND-PAY-CODE. In Figure 2.8, we present the alternative PROCEDURE DIVISION. Note the following points about the program:

1. The statement on line 192, SET PAY-CODE-TABLE-COUNTER TO 1, will cause the SEARCH to start with the first element of the table each time the SEARCH statement on line 220 is executed.
2. The SEARCH statement beginning on line 220 sets the switch PAY-CODE-FOUND-SW in the AT END clause if the matching pay code is not found. If the code is located in the table, the index for the corresponding rate is set in the WHEN clause (line 222).

```
00171          *
00172           PROCEDURE DIVISION.
00173          *
00174           PAY-REPORT-CONTROL.
00175               PERFORM START-UP.
00176               PERFORM PROCESS-EMPLOYEE UNTIL NO-MORE-PAY-DATA.
00177               PERFORM FINISH-UP.
00178               STOP RUN.
00179          *
00180           START-UP.
00181               OPEN INPUT PAYROLL-HOURS-FILE-IN
00182                    OUTPUT PAYROLL-REPORT-PRINT-FILE.
00183               MOVE 'N' TO END-OF-PAY-DATA-SW.
00184               COMPUTE LINE-COUNT = LINES-PER-PAGE + 1.
00185               MOVE ZERO TO COM-TOTAL-HOURS,
00186                            COM-TOTAL-OVERTIME,
00187                            COM-TOTAL-PAY.
00188               PERFORM READ-PAYROLL-HOURS-FILE.
00189          *
00190           PROCESS-EMPLOYEE.
00191               MOVE 'Y' TO PAY-CODE-FOUND-SW.
00192               SET PAY-CODE-TABLE-COUNTER TO 1.
00193               PERFORM FIND-PAY-CODE.
00194               MOVE PAY-IN-NAME TO PAY-OUT-NAME.
00195               MOVE PAY-IN-SS-NUM TO PAY-OUT-SS-NUM.
00196               IF PAY-CODE-FOUND
00197                   MOVE SPACE TO PAY-OUT-MESSAGE-INFO
00198                   PERFORM PROCESS-EMP-HOURS
00199               ELSE
00200                   MOVE 'INVALID PAY-CODE' TO PAY-OUT-MESSAGE
00201                   MOVE ZERO TO PAY-OUT-REG-HOURS, PAY-OUT-OVER-HOURS,
00202                        PAY-OUT-RATE, PAY-OUT-TOTAL-PAY
00203                   MOVE PAY-IN-CODE TO PAY-OUT-CODE.
00204               IF LINE-COUNT   IS GREATER THAN LINES-PER-PAGE
00205                   PERFORM WRITE-PAGE-HEAD
00206                   MOVE ZERO TO LINE-COUNT.
00207               PERFORM WRITE-PAY-REPORT-REC.
00208               ADD 1 TO LINE-COUNT.
00209               PERFORM READ-PAYROLL-HOURS-FILE.
00210          *
00211           FINISH-UP.
00212               MOVE COM-TOTAL-HOURS TO COM-HOURS-OUT.
00213               MOVE COM-TOTAL-OVERTIME TO COM-OVERTIME-OUT.
00214               MOVE COM-TOTAL-PAY TO COM-PAY-OUT.
00215               PERFORM FINAL-WRITE.
00216               CLOSE PAYROLL-HOURS-FILE-IN,
00217                     PAYROLL-REPORT-PRINT-FILE.
00218          *
00219           FIND-PAY-CODE.
00220               SEARCH PAY-CODE
00221                   AT END MOVE 'N' TO PAY-CODE-FOUND-SW
00222                   WHEN  PAY-CODE (PAY-CODE-TABLE-COUNTER) = PAY-IN-CODE
00223                       SET RATE-TABLE-COUNTER TO PAY-CODE-TABLE-COUNTER.
```

Figure 2.8
Compute employee pay with serial table look-up via the SEARCH statement for Example 2.4.

Figure 2.8 (*cont.*)

```
00224        *
00225            PROCESS-EMP-HOURS.
00226                MOVE ZERO TO EMP-TOTAL-HOURS.
00227                PERFORM ADD-TO-HOURS VARYING HOURS-WORKED-TABLE-COUNTER
00228                    FROM 1 BY 1 UNTIL HOURS-WORKED-TABLE-COUNTER
00229                    GREATER THAN NUM-DAYS-IN-WEEK.
00230                PERFORM COMPUTE-PAY.
00231                ADD EMP-TOTAL-HOURS TO COM-TOTAL-HOURS.
00232                ADD EMP-TOTAL-OVERTIME TO COM-TOTAL-OVERTIME.
00233                ADD EMP-TOTAL-PAY TO COM-TOTAL-PAY.
00234                COMPUTE PAY-OUT-REG-HOURS = EMP-TOTAL-HOURS -
00235                                            EMP-TOTAL-OVERTIME.
00236                MOVE EMP-TOTAL-OVERTIME  TO PAY-OUT-OVER-HOURS.
00237                MOVE PAY-RATE (RATE-TABLE-COUNTER) TO PAY-OUT-RATE.
00238                MOVE EMP-TOTAL-PAY TO PAY-OUT-TOTAL-PAY.
00239        *
00240            ADD-TO-HOURS.
00241                COMPUTE EMP-TOTAL-HOURS = EMP-TOTAL-HOURS +
00242                    PAY-IN-HOURS-WORKED (HOURS-WORKED-TABLE-COUNTER).
00243        *
00244            COMPUTE-PAY.
00245                COMPUTE EMP-TOTAL-PAY =   EMP-TOTAL-HOURS *
00246                    PAY-RATE (RATE-TABLE-COUNTER).
00247                IF EMP-TOTAL-HOURS IS GREATER THAN REG-PAY-PERIOD
00248                    COMPUTE EMP-TOTAL-OVERTIME = EMP-TOTAL-HOURS -
00249                                                 REG-PAY-PERIOD
00250                ELSE
00251                    MOVE ZERO TO EMP-TOTAL-OVERTIME.
00252                COMPUTE EMP-TOTAL-PAY =   EMP-TOTAL-PAY + EMP-TOTAL-OVERTIME
00253                    * PAY-RATE (RATE-TABLE-COUNTER)
00254                    * OVERTIME-RATE.
00255        *
00256            WRITE-PAGE-HEAD.
00257                WRITE PAYROLL-REPORT-PRINT-AREA FROM HEADING-LINE
00258                    AFTER ADVANCING TO-TOP-OF-PAGE.
00259        *
00260            WRITE-PAY-REPORT-REC.
00261                WRITE PAYROLL-REPORT-PRINT-AREA FROM PAY-REPORT-LINE
00262                    AFTER ADVANCING 1 LINES.
00263        *
00264            READ-PAYROLL-HOURS-FILE.
00265                READ PAYROLL-HOURS-FILE-IN INTO PAYROLL-HOURS-IN-REC
00266                    AT END MOVE 'Y' TO END-OF-PAY-DATA-SW.
00267        *
00268            FINAL-WRITE.
00269                WRITE PAYROLL-REPORT-PRINT-AREA FROM STARLINE
00270                    AFTER ADVANCING 3 LINES.
00271                WRITE PAYROLL-REPORT-PRINT-AREA FROM COMPANY-HOURS-LINE
00272                    AFTER ADVANCING 2 LINES.
00273                WRITE PAYROLL-REPORT-PRINT-AREA FROM COMPANY-OVERTIME-LINE
00274                    AFTER ADVANCING 1 LINES.
00275                WRITE PAYROLL-REPORT-PRINT-AREA FROM COMPANY-PAY-LINE
00276                    AFTER ADVANCING 1 LINES.
```

As an option, we might have chosen to let the SEARCH increment the index for the rate table, in addition to the index for the pay code table, as illustrated in the program segment that follows.

```
PROCEDURE DIVISION
            .
            .
            .

PROCESS EMPLOYEE.
    SET PAY-CODE-TABLE-COUNTER TO 1.
    PERFORM FIND-PAY-CODE.
            .
            .
            .
```

```
FIND-PAY-CODE.
    SEARCH PAY-CODE VARYING RATE-TABLE-COUNTER
        AT END MOVE 'N' TO PAY-CODE-FOUND-SW
        WHEN PAY-CODE (PAY-CODE-TABLE-COUNTER) =
            PAY-IN-CODE
            MOVE 'Y' TO PAY-CODE-FOUND-SW.
            .
            .
            .
```

Since both indexes must be incremented, it would be somewhat less efficient to write this version of the SEARCH for our specific problem.

BINARY SEARCHING

For a table that is in order on a key field, there is an alternative search technique, called a *binary search,* that can reduce the time spent searching a table. If the table is large, the savings can be substantial.

To perform a binary search, we first look at the *middle* element in the table. If that element is the desired one, we are finished; otherwise, we will be able to determine in which half of the table the desired element lies. Turning our attention to that half of the table, we again select the middle element, and so on.

In each step, we locate the middle element. If it is the desired element, we are finished. If it is smaller than the desired element, we will try the middle element in the upper half of the remaining portion of the table. If it is larger than the desired element, then we look in the lower half of the remaining portion of the table. With each step, we continue to eliminate from consideration one half of the remaining portion of the table until the desired element has been found or is ultimately deemed missing.

For the table of state abbreviations and names, suppose the desired abbreviation is IL.

Step	Lower Limit	Upper Limit	Midpoint	Value	
1	1	50	25	MS	
2	1	24	12	IA	
3	13	24	18	LA	
4	13	17	15	IN	
5	13	14	13	ID	
6	14	14	14	IL	Found

Comparing the binary technique to the sequential search technique, the maximum number of steps for the sequential search is 50, with the average being 25. The maximum number of steps for the binary search is the smallest value of k, such that $2^k \geq 50$. Since $2^5 < 50 < 2^6$, no more than 6 steps will ever be required for a 50-element table.

Because we are not able to do arithmetic with indexes for program comparison purposes, we will illustrate the technique using subscripted tables.

Example 2.5

To compare the binary search technique to the serial search technique for execution time, the program of Figure 2.6 is redone using the binary search.

The program solution to Example 2.5 is presented in Figure 2.9. Little savings would be expected in this case, since the difference is about two executions of the module FIND-PAY-CODE. Also note that the FIND-PAY-CODE module is more complex than the corresponding one in Figure 2.6. For large tables, the execution time savings can be considerable. (How much for a table with 500 elements?)

```
00079      *
00080         WORKING-STORAGE SECTION.
00081         01   SWITCHES.
00082              02   END-OF-PAY-DATA-SW              PIC X.
00083                   88   NO-MORE-PAY-DATA VALUE 'Y'.
00084              02   PAY-CODE-FOUND-SW              PIC X.
00085                   88   PAY-CODE-FOUND      VALUE 'Y'.
00086              02   ALL-LOCATIONS-TESTED-SW       PIC X.
00087                   88   ALL-LOCATIONS-TESTED VALUE 'Y'.
00088         01   COUNTERS.
00089              02   RATE-TABLE-COUNTER            PIC 9(2).
00090              02   PAY-CODE-TABLE-COUNTER        PIC 9(2).
00091              02   HOURS-WORKED-TABLE-COUNTER    PIC 9.
00092              02   LINE-COUNT                    PIC 9(2).
00093         01   CONSTANTS.
00094              02   NUM-DAYS-IN-WEEK              PIC 9 VALUE 7.
00095              02   NUM-OF-CODES                  PIC 9(2) VALUE 10.
00096              02   LINES-PER-PAGE                PIC 9(2) VALUE 55.
00097              02   REG-PAY-PERIOD                PIC 9(2) VALUE 40.
00098              02   OVERTIME-RATE                 PIC V9(2) VALUE .50.
00099         01   BINARY-SEARCH-LIMITS.
00100              02   MAX-LOCATION                  PIC 9(2).
00101              02   MIN-LOCATION                  PIC 9(2).
00102         01   EMPLOYEE-TOTALS.
00103              02   EMP-TOTAL-HOURS               PIC 9(2)V9(2).
00104              02   EMP-TOTAL-OVERTIME            PIC 9(2)V9(2).
00105              02   EMP-TOTAL-PAY                 PIC 9(3)V9(2).
00106         01   COMPANY-TOTALS.
00107              02   COM-TOTAL-HOURS               PIC 9(6)V9(2).
00108              02   COM-TOTAL-OVERTIME            PIC 9(5)V9(2).
00109              02   COM-TOTAL-PAY                 PIC 9(8)V9(2).
00110         01   PAYROLL-HOURS-IN-REC.
00111              02   PAY-IN-SS-NUM                 PIC 9(9).
00112              02   PAY-IN-NAME                   PIC X(20).
00113              02   PAY-IN-CODE                   PIC X.
00114              02   PAY-IN-HOURS-WORKED
00115                     OCCURS 7 TIMES              PIC 9(2)V9(2).
00116              02   FILLER                        PIC X(22).
00117         01   PAY-REPORT-LINE.
00118              02   FILLER                        PIC X(5) VALUE SPACE.
00119              02   PAY-OUT-SS-NUM                PIC 9(9).
00120              02   FILLER                        PIC X(5) VALUE SPACE.
00121              02   PAY-OUT-NAME                  PIC X(25).
00122              02   PAY-OUT-REG-HOURS             PIC Z9.9(2).
00123              02   FILLER                        PIC X(5) VALUE SPACE.
00124              02   PAY-OUT-OVER-HOURS            PIC Z9.9(2).
00125              02   FILLER                        PIC X(5) VALUE SPACE.
00126              02   PAY-OUT-RATE                  PIC Z9.9(3).
00127              02   FILLER                        PIC X(5) VALUE SPACE.
00128              02   PAY-OUT-TOTAL-PAY             PIC Z(2)9.9(2).
00129              02   PAY-OUT-MESSAGE-INFO.
00130                   03   PAY-OUT-MESSAGE          PIC X(30).
00131                   03   PAY-OUT-CODE             PIC X.
```

Figure 2.9

Compute employee pay with programmer-written binary table look-up via subscripting for Example 2.5.

Figure 2.9 (*cont.*)

```
00132             01  HEADING-LINE.
00133                 02  FILLER                       PIC X(44)
00134                     VALUE '         SS NUM       EMPLOYEE NAME'.
00135                 02  FILLER                       PIC X(35)
00136                     VALUE ' REG HOURS  OVERTIME   RATE      PAY'.
00137             01  STARLINE.
00138                 02  FILLER                       PIC X(133) VALUE ALL '*'.
00139             01  COMPANY-HOURS-LINE.
00140                 02  FILLER                       PIC X VALUE SPACE.
00141                 02  FILLER                       PIC X(30)
00142                     VALUE 'COMPANY TOTAL HOURS'.
00143                 02  COM-HOURS-OUT                PIC Z(5)9.9(2).
00144             01  COMPANY-OVERTIME-LINE.
00145                 02  FILLER                       PIC X VALUE SPACE.
00146                 02  FILLER                       PIC X(30)
00147                     VALUE 'COMPANY TOTAL OVERTIME'.
00148                 02  COM-OVERTIME-OUT             PIC Z(5)9.9(2).
00149             01  COMPANY-PAY-LINE.
00150                 02  FILLER                       PIC X VALUE SPACE.
00151                 02  FILLER                       PIC X(27)
00152                     VALUE 'COMPANY TOTAL PAYROLL'.
00153                 02  COM-PAY-OUT                  PIC $(8)9.9(2).
00154             01  RATES.
00155                 02  FILLER                       PIC 9(2)V9(3) VALUE 5.350.
00156                 02  FILLER                       PIC 9(2)V9(3) VALUE 4.400.
00157                 02  FILLER                       PIC 9(2)V9(3) VALUE 10.100.
00158                 02  FILLER                       PIC 9(2)V9(3) VALUE 2.000.
00159                 02  FILLER                       PIC 9(2)V9(3) VALUE 3.505.
00160                 02  FILLER                       PIC 9(2)V9(3) VALUE 7.750.
00161                 02  FILLER                       PIC 9(2)V9(3) VALUE 6.105.
00162                 02  FILLER                       PIC 9(2)V9(3) VALUE 3.625.
00163                 02  FILLER                       PIC 9(2)V9(3) VALUE 4.800.
00164                 02  FILLER                       PIC 9(2)V9(3) VALUE 9.500.
00165             01  RATE-TABLE REDEFINES RATES.
00166                 02  PAY-RATE
00167                     OCCURS 10 TIMES              PIC 9(2)V9(3).
00168             01  PAY-CODES.
00169                 02  FILLER                       PIC X(10)
00170                     VALUE 'ABRSTX0145'.
00171             01  PAY-CODE-TABLE REDEFINES PAY-CODES.
00172                 02  PAY-CODE
00173                     OCCURS 10 TIMES              PIC X.
00174         *
00175          PROCEDURE DIVISION.
00176         *
00177          PAY-REPORT-CONTROL.
00178              PERFORM START-UP.
00179              PERFORM PROCESS-EMPLOYEE UNTIL NO-MORE-PAY-DATA.
00180              PERFORM FINISH-UP.
00181              STOP RUN.
00182         *
00183          START-UP.
00184              OPEN INPUT PAYROLL-HOURS-FILE-IN
00185                   OUTPUT PAYROLL-REPORT-PRINT-FILE.
00186              MOVE 'N' TO END-OF-PAY-DATA-SW.
00187              COMPUTE LINE-COUNT = LINES-PER-PAGE + 1.
00188              MOVE ZERO TO COM-TOTAL-HOURS,
00189                           COM-TOTAL-OVERTIME,
00190                           COM-TOTAL-PAY.
00191              PERFORM READ-PAYROLL-HOURS-FILE.
```

Figure 2.9 (cont.)

```
00192        *
00193         PROCESS-EMPLOYEE.
00194              MOVE 'N' TO PAY-CODE-FOUND-SW,
00195                         ALL-LOCATIONS-TESTED-SW.
00196              MOVE 1 TO MIN-LOCATION
00197              MOVE NUM-OF-CODES TO MAX-LOCATION
00198              PERFORM FIND-PAY-CODE UNTIL ALL-LOCATIONS-TESTED
00199                                                          OR
00200                                          PAY-CODE-FOUND.
00201              MOVE PAY-IN-NAME TO PAY-OUT-NAME.
00202              MOVE PAY-IN-SS-NUM TO PAY-OUT-SS-NUM.
00203              IF PAY-CODE-FOUND
00204                  MOVE SPACE TO PAY-OUT-MESSAGE-INFO
00205                  PERFORM PROCESS-EMP-HOURS
00206              ELSE
00207                  MOVE 'INVALID PAY-CODE' TO PAY-OUT-MESSAGE
00208                  MOVE ZERO TO PAY-OUT-REG-HOURS, PAY-OUT-OVER-HOURS,
00209                               PAY-OUT-RATE, PAY-OUT-TOTAL-PAY
00210                  MOVE PAY-IN-CODE TO PAY-OUT-CODE.
00211              IF LINE-COUNT   IS GREATER THAN LINES-PER-PAGE
00212                  PERFORM WRITE-PAGE-HEAD
00213                  MOVE ZERO TO LINE-COUNT.
00214              PERFORM WRITE-PAY-REPORT-REC.
00215              ADD 1 TO LINE-COUNT.
00216              PERFORM READ-PAYROLL-HOURS-FILE.
00217        *
00218         FINISH-UP.
00219              MOVE COM-TOTAL-HOURS TO COM-HOURS-OUT.
00220              MOVE COM-TOTAL-OVERTIME TO COM-OVERTIME-OUT.
00221              MOVE COM-TOTAL-PAY TO COM-PAY-OUT.
00222              PERFORM FINAL-WRITE.
00223              CLOSE PAYROLL-HOURS-FILE-IN,
00224                         PAYROLL-REPORT-PRINT-FILE.
00225        *
00226         FIND-PAY-CODE.
00227              COMPUTE PAY-CODE-TABLE-COUNTER = (MAX-LOCATION +
00228                                          MIN-LOCATION) / 2.
00229              IF MAX-LOCATION = MIN-LOCATION
00230                  MOVE 'Y' TO ALL-LOCATIONS-TESTED-SW.
00231              IF PAY-CODE (PAY-CODE-TABLE-COUNTER) = PAY-IN-CODE
00232                  MOVE PAY-CODE-TABLE-COUNTER TO RATE-TABLE-COUNTER
00233                  MOVE 'Y' TO PAY-CODE-FOUND-SW
00234              ELSE
00235                  IF PAY-IN-CODE IS GREATER THAN
00236                     PAY-CODE (PAY-CODE-TABLE-COUNTER)
00237                  COMPUTE MIN-LOCATION = PAY-CODE-TABLE-COUNTER + 1
00238                  ELSE
00239                     COMPUTE MAX-LOCATION = PAY-CODE-TABLE-COUNTER   - 1.
00240        *
00241         PROCESS-EMP-HOURS.
00242              MOVE ZERO TO EMP-TOTAL-HOURS.
00243              PERFORM ADD-TO-HOURS VARYING HOURS-WORKED-TABLE-COUNTER
00244                  FROM 1 BY 1 UNTIL HOURS-WORKED-TABLE-COUNTER
00245                  GREATER THAN NUM-DAYS-IN-WEEK.
00246              PERFORM COMPUTE-PAY.
00247              ADD EMP-TOTAL-HOURS TO COM-TOTAL-HOURS.
00248              ADD EMP-TOTAL-OVERTIME TO COM-TOTAL-OVERTIME.
00249              ADD EMP-TOTAL-PAY TO COM-TOTAL-PAY.
00250              COMPUTE PAY-OUT-REG-HOURS = EMP-TOTAL-HOURS -
00251                                          EMP-TOTAL-OVERTIME.
00252              MOVE EMP-TOTAL-OVERTIME  TO PAY-OUT-OVER-HOURS.
00253              MOVE PAY-RATE (RATE-TABLE-COUNTER) TO PAY-OUT-RATE.
00254              MOVE EMP-TOTAL-PAY TO PAY-OUT-TOTAL-PAY.
00255        *
00256         ADD-TO-HOURS.
00257              COMPUTE EMP-TOTAL-HOURS = EMP-TOTAL-HOURS +
00258                     PAY-IN-HOURS-WORKED (HOURS-WORKED-TABLE-COUNTER).
00259        *
00260         COMPUTE-PAY.
00261              COMPUTE EMP-TOTAL-PAY =   EMP-TOTAL-HOURS *
00262                                    PAY-RATE (RATE-TABLE-COUNTER).
00263              IF EMP-TOTAL-HOURS IS GREATER THAN REG-PAY-PERIOD
00264                  COMPUTE EMP-TOTAL-OVERTIME = EMP-TOTAL-HOURS -
00265                                          REG-PAY-PERIOD
00266              ELSE
00267                  MOVE ZERO TO EMP-TOTAL-OVERTIME.
00268              COMPUTE EMP-TOTAL-PAY =   EMP-TOTAL-PAY + EMP-TOTAL-OVERTIME
00269                                    * PAY-RATE (RATE-TABLE-COUNTER)
00270                                    * OVERTIME-RATE.
```

Figure 2.9 (cont.)

```
00271        *
00272           WRITE-PAGE-HEAD.
00273              WRITE PAYROLL-REPORT-PRINT-AREA FROM HEADING-LINE
00274                 AFTER ADVANCING TO-TOP-OF-PAGE.
00275        *
00276           WRITE-PAY-REPORT-REC.
00277              WRITE PAYROLL-REPORT-PRINT-AREA FROM PAY-REPORT-LINE
00278                 AFTER ADVANCING 1 LINES.
00279        *
00280           READ-PAYROLL-HOURS-FILE.
00281              READ PAYROLL-HOURS-FILE-IN INTO PAYROLL-HOURS-IN-REC
00282                 AT END MOVE 'Y' TO END-OF-PAY-DATA-SW.
00283        *
00284           FINAL-WRITE.
00285              WRITE PAYROLL-REPORT-PRINT-AREA FROM STARLINE
00286                 AFTER ADVANCING 3 LINES.
00287              WRITE PAYROLL-REPORT-PRINT-AREA FROM COMPANY-HOURS-LINE
00288                 AFTER ADVANCING 2 LINES.
00289              WRITE PAYROLL-REPORT-PRINT-AREA FROM COMPANY-OVERTIME-LINE
00290                 AFTER ADVANCING 1 LINES.
00291              WRITE PAYROLL-REPORT-PRINT-AREA FROM COMPANY-PAY-LINE
00292                 AFTER ADVANCING 1 LINES.
```

THE SEARCH ALL STATEMENT

The preceding section was included to discuss how binary searching is done. The SEARCH ALL statement provides a convenient way of performing a binary search without the necessity of the programmer explicitly providing all of the code, as was the case in Example 2.5.

FORMAT 2
SEARCH ALL identifier-1
[AT END imperative-statement-1]
WHEN condition-1 $\begin{cases} \text{imperative-statement-2} \\ \text{NEXT SENTENCE} \end{cases}$

After we consider some examples of Format 2 of the SEARCH statement, we will look at the formal rules for both formats of the SEARCH statement.

Returning to the parts-table example of the previous section, to use SEARCH ALL, the parts table *must* be in order by part number. The revised program segment follows:

```
WORKING-STORAGE SECTION.
01  SWITCHES.
    02  PART-NUM-FOUND-SW           PIC X.
        88  PART-FOUND     VALUE 'Y'.
            .
            .
            .
```

```
01   PART-REC-IN.
          .
          .
          .
     02   PART-NUM-IN                          PIC 9(6).
          .
          .
          .
01   PARTS-TABLE.
     02   PART-INFO
               OCCURS 500 TIMES
         .     ASCENDING KEY IS PART-NUM
               INDEXED BY PART-LOC.
          03   PART-NUM                   PIC 9(6).
          03   PART-DESCRIPTION           PIC X(20).
          .
          .
          .
PROCEDURE DIVISION.
          .
          .
          .
     SEARCH ALL PART-INFO
          AT END MOVE 'N' TO PART-NUM-FOUND-SW
          WHEN PART-NUM (PART-LOC) = PART-NUM-IN
               MOVE 'Y' TO PART-NUM-FOUND-SW.
          .
          .
          .
     IF PART-FOUND
          PERFORM PROCESS-PART-IN
     ELSE
          PERFORM PROCESS-ERROR-IN-PART.
          .
          .
          .
```

Example 2.6

As another example, we will once again revise our payroll program of Example 2.4.
The table of pay codes is in ascending order. The program is to be modified to use
the SEARCH ALL statement.

The control structure is the same as in Figure 2.5. The program listing is in
Figure 2.10. Note the addition of a KEY clause to the description of PAY-CODE-

TABLE on line 170. Also, there is a change in the module FIND-PAY-CODE. The statement on line 221 is now SEARCH ALL. The SEARCH ALL statement automatically initializes the index prior to beginning a binary search of the table. Consequently, there is now no need for the programmer to initialize the index-name PAY-CODE-TABLE-COUNTER. One additional change should be noted: In module PROCESS-EMPLOYEE, the setting of switches has been modified since only one switch, PAY-CODE-FOUND-SW, on line 193, is now needed.

```
00079              *
00080              WORKING-STORAGE SECTION.
00081              01  SWITCHES.
00082                  02  END-OF-PAY-DATA-SW              PIC X.
00083                      88  NO-MORE-PAY-DATA VALUE 'Y'.
00084                  02  PAY-CODE-FOUND-SW              PIC X.
00085                      88  PAY-CODE-FOUND    VALUE 'Y'.
00086              01  COUNTERS.
00087                  02  LINE-COUNT                     PIC 9(2).
00088              01  CONSTANTS.
00089                  02  NUM-DAYS-IN-WEEK               PIC 9 VALUE 7.
00090                  02  NUM-OF-CODES                   PIC 9(2) VALUE 10.
00091                  02  LINES-PER-PAGE                 PIC 9(2) VALUE 55.
00092                  02  REG-PAY-PERIOD                 PIC 9(2) VALUE 40.
00093                  02  OVERTIME-RATE                  PIC V9(2) VALUE .50.
00094              01  EMPLOYEE-TOTALS.
00095                  02  EMP-TOTAL-HOURS                PIC 9(2)V9(2).
00096                  02  EMP-TOTAL-OVERTIME             PIC 9(2)V9(2).
00097                  02  EMP-TOTAL-PAY                  PIC 9(3)V9(2).
00098              01  COMPANY-TOTALS.
00099                  02  COM-TOTAL-HOURS                PIC 9(6)V9(2).
00100                  02  COM-TOTAL-OVERTIME             PIC 9(5)V9(2).
00101                  02  COM-TOTAL-PAY                  PIC 9(8)V9(2).
00102              01  PAYROLL-HOURS-IN-REC.
00103                  02  PAY-IN-SS-NUM                  PIC 9(9).
00104                  02  PAY-IN-NAME                    PIC X(20).
00105                  02  PAY-IN-CODE                    PIC X.
00106                  02  PAY-IN-HOURS-WORKED
00107                      OCCURS 7 TIMES
00108                      INDEXED BY HOURS-WORKED-TABLE-COUNTER
00109                                                     PIC 9(2)V9(2).
00110                  02  FILLER                         PIC X(22).
00111              01  PAY-REPORT-LINE.
00112                  02  FILLER                         PIC X(5) VALUE SPACE.
00113                  02  PAY-OUT-SS-NUM                 PIC 9(9).
00114                  02  FILLER                         PIC X(5) VALUE SPACE.
00115                  02  PAY-OUT-NAME                   PIC X(25).
00116                  02  PAY-OUT-REG-HOURS              PIC Z9.9(2).
00117                  02  FILLER                         PIC X(5) VALUE SPACE.
00118                  02  PAY-OUT-OVER-HOURS             PIC Z9.9(2).
00119                  02  FILLER                         PIC X(5) VALUE SPACE.
00120                  02  PAY-OUT-RATE                   PIC Z9.9(3).
00121                  02  FILLER                         PIC X(5) VALUE SPACE.
00122                  02  PAY-OUT-TOTAL-PAY              PIC Z(2)9.9(2).
00123                  02  PAY-OUT-MESSAGE-INFO.
00124                      03  PAY-OUT-MESSAGE            PIC X(30).
00125                      03  PAY-OUT-CODE               PIC X.
00126              01  HEADING-LINE.
00127                  02  FILLER                         PIC X(44)
00128                      VALUE '     SS NUM      EMPLOYEE NAME'.
00129                  02  FILLER                         PIC X(35)
00130                      VALUE ' REG HOURS   OVERTIME    RATE        PAY'.
00131              01  STARLINE.
00132                  02  FILLER                         PIC X(133) VALUE ALL '*'.
00133              01  COMPANY-HOURS-LINE.
00134                  02  FILLER                         PIC X VALUE SPACE.
00135                  02  FILLER                         PIC X(30)
00136                      VALUE 'COMPANY TOTAL HOURS'.
00137                  02  COM-HOURS-OUT                  PIC Z(5)9.9(2).
00138              01  COMPANY-OVERTIME-LINE.
00139                  02  FILLER                         PIC X VALUE SPACE.
00140                  02  FILLER                         PIC X(30)
00141                      VALUE 'COMPANY TOTAL OVERTIME'.
00142                  02  COM-OVERTIME-OUT               PIC Z(5)9.9(2).
```

Figure 2.10
Compute employee pay with binary table look-up via the SEARCH ALL statement for Example 2.6.

Figure 2.10 (cont.)

```
00143              01   COMPANY-PAY-LINE.
00144                   02   FILLER                              PIC X VALUE SPACE.
00145                   02   FILLER                              PIC X(27)
00146                        VALUE 'COMPANY TOTAL PAYROLL'.
00147                   02   COM-PAY-OUT                         PIC $(8)9.9(2).
00148              01   RATES.
00149                   02   FILLER                              PIC 9(2)V9(3) VALUE 5.350.
00150                   02   FILLER                              PIC 9(2)V9(3) VALUE 4.400.
00151                   02   FILLER                              PIC 9(2)V9(3) VALUE 10.100.
00152                   02   FILLER                              PIC 9(2)V9(3) VALUE 2.000.
00153                   02   FILLER                              PIC 9(2)V9(3) VALUE 3.505.
00154                   02   FILLER                              PIC 9(2)V9(3) VALUE 7.750.
00155                   02   FILLER                              PIC 9(2)V9(3) VALUE 6.105.
00156                   02   FILLER                              PIC 9(2)V9(3) VALUE 3.625.
00157                   02   FILLER                              PIC 9(2)V9(3) VALUE 4.800.
00158                   02   FILLER                              PIC 9(2)V9(3) VALUE 9.500.
00159              01   RATE-TABLE REDEFINES RATES.
00160                   02   PAY-RATE
00161                             OCCURS 10 TIMES
00162                             INDEXED BY RATE-TABLE-COUNTER
00163                                                            PIC 9(2)V9(3).
00164              01   PAY-CODES.
00165                   02   FILLER                              PIC X(10)
00166                        VALUE 'ABRSTX0145'.
00167              01   PAY-CODE-TABLE REDEFINES PAY-CODES.
00168                   02   PAY-CODE
00169                             OCCURS 10 TIMES
00170                             ASCENDING KEY IS PAY-CODE
00171                             INDEXED BY PAY-CODE-TABLE-COUNTER
00172                                                            PIC X.
00173              *
00174              PROCEDURE DIVISION.
00175              *
00176              PAY-REPORT-CONTROL.
00177                   PERFORM START-UP.
00178                   PERFORM PROCESS-EMPLOYEE UNTIL NO-MORE-PAY-DATA.
00179                   PERFORM FINISH-UP.
00180                   STOP RUN.
00181              *
00182              START-UP.
00183                   OPEN INPUT PAYROLL-HOURS-FILE-IN
00184                        OUTPUT PAYROLL-REPORT-PRINT-FILE.
00185                   MOVE 'N' TO END-OF-PAY-DATA-SW.
00186                   COMPUTE LINE-COUNT = LINES-PER-PAGE + 1.
00187                   MOVE ZERO TO COM-TOTAL-HOURS,
00188                                COM-TOTAL-OVERTIME,
00189                                COM-TOTAL-PAY.
00190                   PERFORM READ-PAYROLL-HOURS-FILE.
00191              *
00192              PROCESS-EMPLOYEE.
00193                   MOVE 'N' TO PAY-CODE-FOUND-SW.
00194                   PERFORM FIND-PAY-CODE.
00195                   MOVE PAY-IN-NAME TO PAY-OUT-NAME.
00196                   MOVE PAY-IN-SS-NUM TO PAY-OUT-SS-NUM.
00197                   IF PAY-CODE-FOUND
00198                        MOVE SPACE TO PAY-OUT-MESSAGE-INFO
00199                        PERFORM PROCESS-EMP-HOURS
00200                   ELSE
00201                        MOVE 'INVALID PAY-CODE' TO PAY-OUT-MESSAGE
00202                        MOVE ZERO TO PAY-OUT-REG-HOURS, PAY-OUT-OVER-HOURS,
00203                                PAY-OUT-RATE, PAY-OUT-TOTAL-PAY
00204                        MOVE PAY-IN-CODE TO PAY-OUT-CODE.
00205                   IF LINE-COUNT   IS GREATER THAN LINES-PER-PAGE
00206                        PERFORM WRITE-PAGE-HEAD
00207                        MOVE ZERO TO LINE-COUNT.
00208                   PERFORM WRITE-PAY-REPORT-REC.
00209                   ADD 1 TO LINE-COUNT.
00210                   PERFORM READ-PAYROLL-HOURS-FILE.
```

Figure 2.10 (*cont.*)

```
00211       *
00212                  FINISH-UP.
00213                      MOVE COM-TOTAL-HOURS TO COM-HOURS-OUT.
00214                      MOVE COM-TOTAL-OVERTIME TO COM-OVERTIME-OUT.
00215                      MOVE COM-TOTAL-PAY TO COM-PAY-OUT.
00216                      PERFORM FINAL-WRITE.
00217                      CLOSE PAYROLL-HOURS-FILE-IN,
00218                            PAYROLL-REPORT-PRINT-FILE.
00219       *
00220                  FIND-PAY-CODE.
00221                      SEARCH ALL PAY-CODE
00222                          WHEN PAY-CODE (PAY-CODE-TABLE-COUNTER) = PAY-IN-CODE
00223                              MOVE 'Y' TO PAY-CODE-FOUND-SW.
00224       *
00225                  PROCESS-EMP-HOURS.
00226                      MOVE ZERO TO EMP-TOTAL-HOURS.
00227                      PERFORM ADD-TO-HOURS VARYING HOURS-WORKED-TABLE-COUNTER
00228                          FROM 1 BY 1 UNTIL HOURS-WORKED-TABLE-COUNTER
00229                          GREATER THAN NUM-DAYS-IN-WEEK.
00230                      SET RATE-TABLE-COUNTER TO PAY-CODE-TABLE-COUNTER.
00231                      PERFORM COMPUTE-PAY.
00232                      ADD EMP-TOTAL-HOURS TO COM-TOTAL-HOURS.
00233                      ADD EMP-TOTAL-OVERTIME TO COM-TOTAL-OVERTIME.
00234                      ADD EMP-TOTAL-PAY TO COM-TOTAL-PAY.
00235                      COMPUTE PAY-OUT-REG-HOURS = EMP-TOTAL-HOURS -
00236                              EMP-TOTAL-OVERTIME.
00237                      MOVE EMP-TOTAL-OVERTIME  TO PAY-OUT-OVER-HOURS.
00238                      MOVE PAY-RATE (RATE-TABLE-COUNTER) TO PAY-OUT-RATE.
00239                      MOVE EMP-TOTAL-PAY TO PAY-OUT-TOTAL-PAY.
00240       *
00241                  ADD-TO-HOURS.
00242                      COMPUTE EMP-TOTAL-HOURS = EMP-TOTAL-HOURS +
00243                          PAY-IN-HOURS-WORKED (HOURS-WORKED-TABLE-COUNTER).
00244       *
00245                  COMPUTE-PAY.
00246                      COMPUTE EMP-TOTAL-PAY =   EMP-TOTAL-HOURS *
00247                              PAY-RATE (RATE-TABLE-COUNTER).
00248                      IF EMP-TOTAL-HOURS IS GREATER THAN REG-PAY-PERIOD
00249                          COMPUTE EMP-TOTAL-OVERTIME = EMP-TOTAL-HOURS -
00250                                  REG-PAY-PERIOD
00251                      ELSE
00252                          MOVE ZERO TO EMP-TOTAL-OVERTIME.
00253                      COMPUTE EMP-TOTAL-PAY =   EMP-TOTAL-PAY + EMP-TOTAL-OVERTIME
00254                              * PAY-RATE (RATE-TABLE-COUNTER)
00255                              * OVERTIME-RATE.
00256       *
00257                  WRITE-PAGE-HEAD.
00258                      WRITE PAYROLL-REPORT-PRINT-AREA FROM HEADING-LINE
00259                          AFTER ADVANCING TO-TOP-OF-PAGE.
00260       *
00261                  WRITE-PAY-REPORT-REC.
00262                      WRITE PAYROLL-REPORT-PRINT-AREA FROM PAY-REPORT-LINE
00263                          AFTER ADVANCING 1 LINES.
00264       *
00265                  READ-PAYROLL-HOURS-FILE.
00266                      READ PAYROLL-HOURS-FILE-IN INTO PAYROLL-HOURS-IN-REC
00267                          AT END MOVE 'Y' TO END-OF-PAY-DATA-SW.
00268       *
00269                  FINAL-WRITE.
00270                      WRITE PAYROLL-REPORT-PRINT-AREA FROM STARLINE
00271                          AFTER ADVANCING 3 LINES.
00272                      WRITE PAYROLL-REPORT-PRINT-AREA FROM COMPANY-HOURS-LINE
00273                          AFTER ADVANCING 2 LINES.
00274                      WRITE PAYROLL-REPORT-PRINT-AREA FROM COMPANY-OVERTIME-LINE
00275                          AFTER ADVANCING 1 LINES.
00276                      WRITE PAYROLL-REPORT-PRINT-AREA FROM COMPANY-PAY-LINE
00277                          AFTER ADVANCING 1 LINES.
```

Now that we have seen several examples using the SEARCH verb, let's look at the formal rules.

FORMAL RULES AND CONSIDERATIONS GOVERNING THE SEARCH STATEMENT

A. The following rules pertain to identifier-1 in both formats.

1. It must not be subscripted or indexed.
2. It must be the subject of an OCCURS clause with the INDEXED BY option.
3. It may be a data item subordinate to the data item containing an OCCURS clause, thus providing for a two- or three-dimensional table.

B. In the AT END and WHEN options, if any of the imperative statement(s) does not terminate with a GO TO statement, control passes automatically to the next sentence after execution of the imperative statement(s).

C. Format 1 considerations—Identifier-2, when specified, must be described as an index data item or it must be a fixed-point numeric elementary item described as an integer. When an occurrence number is incremented, identifier-2 is simultaneously incremented by the same amount.

Condition-1, condition-2, and so on may be any condition as follows:

Relation condition.
Class condition.
Condition-name condition.
Sign condition.
Switch-status condition.
Logical combinations of these conditions using AND, OR, and NOT.

Upon the execution of a SEARCH statement, a serial search takes place, starting with the current index setting.

If, at the start of the SEARCH, the value of the index-name associated with identifier-1 is not greater than the highest possible occurrence number for identifier-1, the following actions take place.

1. The condition(s) in the WHEN option is evaluated in the order written.
2. If none of the conditions is satisfied, the index-name for identifier-1 is incremented to reference the next table element, and step 1 is repeated.
3. If, upon evaluation, one of the WHEN conditions is satisfied, the search terminates immediately, and the imperative-statement associated with that condition is executed. The index-name points to the table element that satisfied the condition.
4. If the end of the table is reached without the WHEN condition being satisfied, the search terminates, as described in the next paragraph.

If at the start of the SEARCH, the value of the index-name associated with identifier-1 is greater than the highest permissible occurrence number for identifier-1, the search is terminated immediately; and if the AT END option is specified, imperative-statement-1 is executed. If this option is omitted, control passes to the next sentence.

When the VARYING index-name-1 option is specified, one of the following applies:

If index-name-1 is one of the indexes for identifier-1, index-name-1 is used for the search. Otherwise the first (or only) index-name for identifier-1 is used.
If index-name-1 is an index for another table entry, then when the index-name for identifier-1 is incremented to represent the next occurrence of the table, index-name-1 is simultaneously incremented to represent the next occurrence of the table it indexes.

D. Format 2 considerations—The first index-name assigned to identifier-1 will be used for the search.

The description of identifier-1 must contain the KEY option in its OCCURS clause.

Condition-1 must consist of one of the following:

1. A relation condition incorporating the EQUALS, EQUAL TO, or equal sign (=) relation. Either the subject or the object (but not both) of the relation condition must consist solely of one of the data-names that appear in the KEY clause of identifier-1.
2. A condition-name condition in which the VALUE clause describing the condition-name consists of a single literal only. The conditional variable associated with the condition-name must be one of the data-names that appear in the KEY clause of identifier-1.
3. A compound condition formed from simple conditions of the types just described, with AND as the only connective.

Any data-name that appears in the KEY clause of identifier-1 may be tested in condition-1. However, all data-names in the KEY clause preceding the one to be tested must also be so tested in condition-1. No other tests may be made in condition-1.

During execution of a Format 2 SEARCH statement, the setting of index-name is varied during the search so that at no time is it less than the value that corresponds to the first element of the table, nor is it ever greater than the value that corresponds to the last element of the table. If condition-1 cannot be satisfied for any setting of the index within this permitted range, control is passed to imperative-statement-1 when the AT END option appears or to the next sentence when this clause does not appear. In either case, the final setting of the index is not predictable. If the index indicates an occurrence that allows condition-1 to be satisfied, control passes to imperative-statement-2.

We have by no means used all of the options made available to us by the SEARCH statement. However, we have looked at examples of the most significant ones.

It is our firm belief that better programs result if the imperative statement of the SEARCH is restricted to either or both of the following:

1. Setting a switch to be tested later.
2. Saving the value in an index for use later.

MULTILEVEL INDEXED TABLES

An INDEXED BY clause may appear each time an OCCURS clause appears. Thus, indexing may be used in place of subscripting for two- and three-dimensional tables.

Suppose we have an attendance table for committee meetings. For each meeting in the past two years, it contains the meeting date and the list of names of members present.

```
01   MEETING-ATTENDANCE-TABLE.
     02   MEETING-DATA
             OCCURS 24 TIMES
             INDEXED BY MEETING-COUNTER.
```

```
03   MEETING-DATE                    PIC 9(6).
03   MEMBERS-PRESENT
     OCCURS 10 TIMES
     ASCENDING KEY IS MEMBER-NAME
     INDEXED BY MEMBER-COUNTER.
04   MEMBER-NAME                      PIC X(30).
```

Suppose you need to know if JONES, JOHN P. attended the meeting on January 28, 1983. The following program segment could be used.

```
ACCEPT DATE-IN.
SET MEETING-COUNTER TO 1.
SEARCH MEETING-DATA
    AT END MOVE 'N' TO DATE-FOUND-SW
    WHEN MEETING-DATE (MEETING-COUNTER) = DATE-IN
       MOVE 'Y' TO DATE-FOUND-SW.
IF DATE-FOUND
    ACCEPT NAME-IN
    SEARCH ALL MEMBERS-PRESENT
    AT END MOVE 'N' TO MEETING-ATTENDED-SW
    WHEN NAME-IN =
          MEMBER-NAME (MEETING-COUNTER, MEMBER-COUNTER)
       MOVE 'Y' TO MEETING-ATTENDED-SW.
```

The switches are self-descriptive. The location of the desired entry is referenced by the indexes (MEETING-COUNTER, MEMBER-COUNTER) after the execution of the SEARCH ALL statement (that is, if the member name being searched for in the preceding program segments is found, the following statements will move the entry referenced by the indexes from the table to a field in a print line).

```
IF MEMBER-FOUND
    MOVE MEMBER-NAME (MEETING-COUNTER, MEMBER-COUNTER)
       TO MEMBER-NAME-PRINT.
```

SORTING AN INDEXED TABLE

Use of the SEARCH ALL statement required that the table be in order by a key field. The table will not always be in order initially. A simple technique, called *selection sorting,* can be used to arrange the table elements in order.

To explain the technique, let's consider the table to be subdivided into two parts: a sorted part and an unsorted part. At first, everything is considered to be in the unsorted part. We find the smallest key in the unsorted part and place it at the beginning of the unsorted part (which will now become the end of the sorted part of the table). This transfers one element from the unsorted part to the sorted part.

This process is repeated until all elements are in the sorted part; then we are finished. To illustrate:

17	81	10	14

Unsorted part

Locate the smallest value, which is 10 in location 3; then interchange it with the value in the beginning element of the unsorted part.

10	81	17	14

Sorted part · Unsorted part

Locate the smallest value in the unsorted part, which is 14 in location 4; then interchange it with the value in the beginning element of the unsorted part.

10	14	17	81

Sorted part · Unsorted part

At this point, continuing to repeat the steps will not change the sequence of entries in the table, since the unsorted part is, in fact, in order. However, the specific sorting technique we have used has no way to recognize this fact. Therefore, it will continue to repeat the sorting steps until the last entry in the unsorted part has been transferred to the sorted part.

We will now apply this sorting technique to the payroll problem.

Example 2.7

Since the values for rates and codes change often, it was decided to read them into a single table. The table is then sorted, with the use of multiple indexing being illustrated. The computations are unchanged.

The structure chart for a solution to Example 2.7 is given in Figure 2.11. The program listing is in Figure 2.12.

Note that multiple index names are needed (lines 162-165) for use in the sorting routine.

The module SORT-CODE-RATE-TABLE controls a counter that determines where the beginning of the unsorted part of the table starts. START-UNSORTED will contain the new beginning location of the unsorted part of the table upon exit from the module POSITION-ANOTHER-ELEMENT.

Using a single table that contains both rates and codes, rather than the two tables used in our earlier example, has resulted in minor changes to various modules. The index-name PAY-CODE-TABLE-COUNTER is no longer needed. Other changes are self-explanatory.

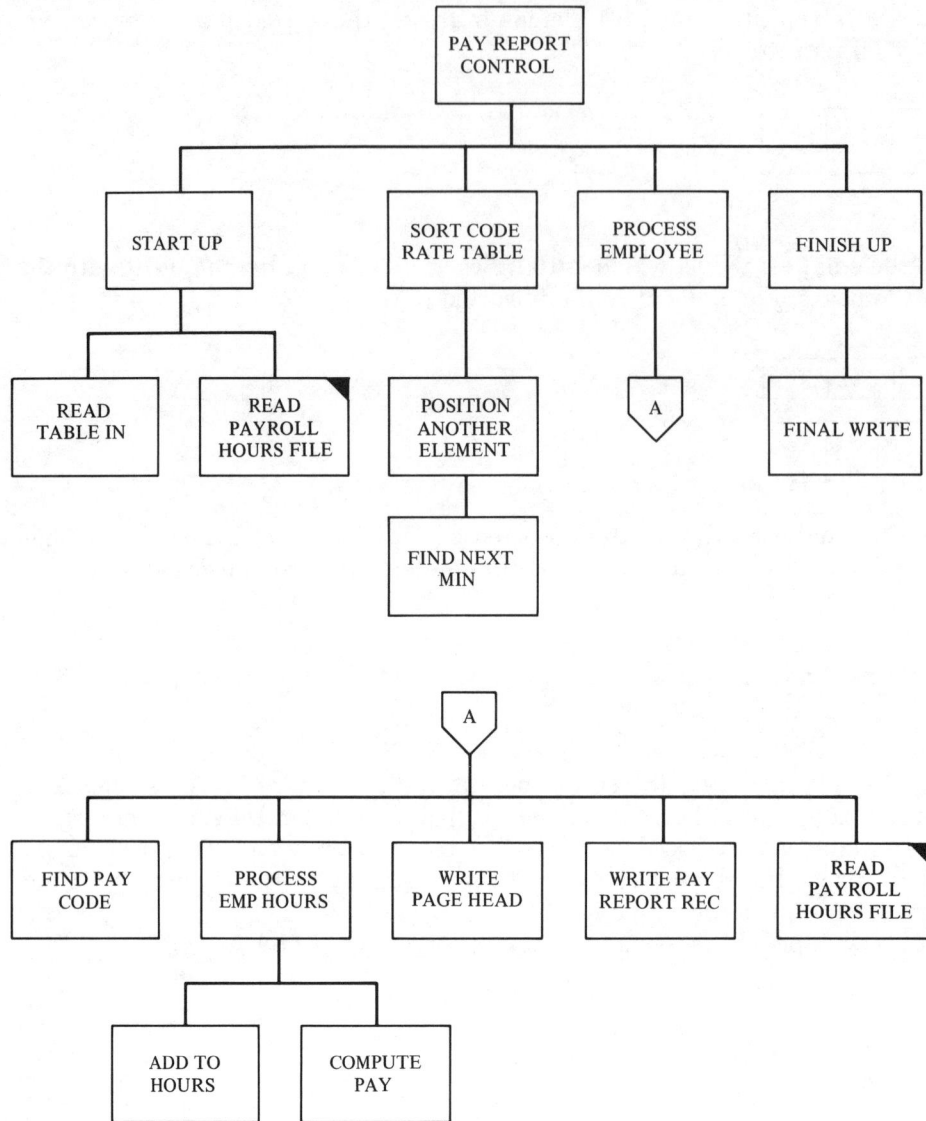

Figure 2.11
Structure chart for the program in Figure 2.12.

```
00001              IDENTIFICATION DIVISION.
00002          *
00003           PROGRAM-ID.
00004              EX-2-7.
00005          **********************************************************************
00006          *                                                                    *
00007          *    PROGRAMMER TEAM         SUMMERS/WALSTROM/LINDAHL                 *
00008          *    PROGRAM COMPLETION DATE DECEMBER 5, 1984.                        *
00009          *                                                                    *
00010          *                   PROGRAM SUMMARY                                   *
00011          *    INPUT                                                            *
00012          *        THE FIRST INPUT RECORD CONSISTS OF CODE RATE PAIRS           *
00013          *        FOR THE CODE RATE TABLE                                      *
00014          *             - PAY CODE                                             *
00015          *             - PAY RATE                                             *
00016          *        EACH EMPLOYEE INPUT RECORD CONTAINS                          *
00017          *             - SOCIAL SECURITY NUMBER                               *
00018          *             - NAME                                                 *
00019          *             - PAY CODE                                            *
00020          *             - NUMBER OF HOURS WORKED FOR EACH DAY OF THE WEEK       *
00021          *                                                                    *
00022          *    PROCESSING                                                       *
00023          *             - THE CODE RATE TABLE IS SORTED IN ASCENDING           *
00024          *               ORDER BY PAY CODE                                     *
00025          *        FOR A VALID EMPLOYEE RECORD                                  *
00026          *             - THE PAY RATE IS LOCATED IN THE CODE RATE TABLE        *
00027          *               USING A BINARY SEARCH TECHNIQUE                       *
00028          *             - THE TOAL NUMBER OF HOURS WORKED FOR AN EMPLOYEE       *
00029          *               IS COMPUTED                                          *
00030          *             - ALL TABLES ARE INDEXED                              *
00031          *             - THE GROSS PAY FOR AN EMPLOYEE IS COMPUTED            *
00032          *             - THE NUMBER OF REGULAR AND OVERTIME HOURS             *
00033          *               IS COMPUTED                                          *
00034          *             - TOTALS FOR REGULAR AND OVERTIME HOURS FOR ALL        *
00035          *               EMPLOYEES ARE ACCUMULATED                           *
00036          *             - TOTAL GROSS PAY FOR ALL EMPLOYEES IS COMPUTED        *
00037          *                                                                    *
00038          *    OUTPUT                                                           *
00039          *        A PRINTED REPORT IS PRODUCED                                 *
00040          *        VALID EMPLOYEE OUTPUT CONSISTS OF                            *
00041          *             - SOCIAL SECURITY NUMBER                               *
00042          *             - NAME                                                 *
00043          *             - NUMBER OF HOURS WORKED AT REGULAR RATE               *
00044          *             - NUMBER OF HOURS WORKED AT OVERTIME RATE              *
00045          *             - PAY RATE                                             *
00046          *             - GROSS PAY                                           *
00047          *        INVALID EMPLOYEE OUTPUT CONSISTS OF                          *
00048          *             - SOCIAL SECURITY NUMBER                               *
00049          *             - NAME                                                 *
00050          *             - ZERO FOR HOURS AT REGULAR RATE, HOURS AT             *
00051          *               OVERTIME RATE, AND GROSS PAY                          *
00052          *             - THE INVALID PAY CODE                                  *
00053          *             - AN ERROR MESSAGE                                     *
00054          *        COMPANY OUTPUT CONSISTS OF                                   *
00055          *             - TOTAL OF ALL EMPLOYEE HOURS WORKED                   *
00056          *             - TOTAL OF ALL EMPLOYEE OVERTIME HOURS WORKED          *
00057          *             - TOTAL AMOUNT OF THE PAYROLL                          *
00058          **********************************************************************
00059          *
00060           ENVIRONMENT DIVISION.
00061          *
00062           CONFIGURATION SECTION.
00063           SOURCE-COMPUTER.
00064              IBM-370.
00065           OBJECT-COMPUTER.
00066              IBM-370.
00067           SPECIAL-NAMES.
00068              C01 IS TO-TOP-OF-PAGE.
00069           INPUT-OUTPUT SECTION.
00070           FILE-CONTROL.
00071              SELECT PAYROLL-HOURS-FILE-IN
00072                  ASSIGN TO SYS007-UR-2501-S.
00073              SELECT PAYROLL-REPORT-PRINT-FILE
00074                  ASSIGN TO SYS009-UR-1403-S.
```

Figure 2.12
Compute employee pay with programmer-written sort of an indexed table for Example 2.7.

Figure 2.12 (cont.)

```
00075       *
00076       DATA DIVISION.
00077       *
00078       FILE SECTION.
00079       FD  PAYROLL-HOURS-FILE-IN
00080           LABEL RECORDS ARE OMITTED.
00081       01  PAYROLL-HOURS-IN-AREA            PIC X(80).
00082       FD  PAYROLL-REPORT-PRINT-FILE
00083           LABEL RECORDS ARE OMITTED.
00084       01  PAYROLL-REPORT-PRINT-AREA        PIC X(133).
00085       *
00086       WORKING-STORAGE SECTION.
00087       01  SWITCHES.
00088           02  END-OF-PAY-DATA-SW           PIC X.
00089               88  NO-MORE-PAY-DATA VALUE 'Y'.
00090           02  PAY-CODE-FOUND-SW            PIC X.
00091               88  PAY-CODE-FOUND    VALUE 'Y'.
00092       01  COUNTERS.
00093           02  LINE-COUNT                   PIC 9(2).
00094       01  CONSTANTS.
00095           02  NUM-DAYS-IN-WEEK             PIC 9 VALUE 7.
00096           02  NUM-OF-CODES                 PIC 9(2) VALUE 10.
00097           02  LINES-PER-PAGE               PIC 9(2) VALUE 55.
00098           02  REG-PAY-PERIOD               PIC 9(2) VALUE 40.
00099           02  OVERTIME-RATE                PIC V9(2) VALUE .50.
00100       01  EMPLOYEE-TOTALS.
00101           02  EMP-TOTAL-HOURS              PIC 9(2)V9(2).
00102           02  EMP-TOTAL-OVERTIME           PIC 9(2)V9(2).
00103           02  EMP-TOTAL-PAY                PIC 9(3)V9(2).
00104       01  COMPANY-TOTALS.
00105           02  COM-TOTAL-HOURS              PIC 9(6)V9(2).
00106           02  COM-TOTAL-OVERTIME           PIC 9(5)V9(2).
00107           02  COM-TOTAL-PAY                PIC 9(8)V9(2).
00108       01  SORT-SAVE-AREA.
00109           02  SAVE-RATE-BY-CODE.
00110               03  SAVE-PAY-CODE            PIC X.
00111               03  SAVE-PAY-RATE            PIC 9(2)V9(3).
00112       01  PAYROLL-HOURS-IN-REC.
00113           02  PAY-IN-SS-NUM                PIC 9(9).
00114           02  PAY-IN-NAME                  PIC X(20).
00115           02  PAY-IN-CODE                  PIC X.
00116           02  PAY-IN-HOURS-WORKED
00117               OCCURS 7 TIMES
00118               INDEXED BY HOURS-WORKED-TABLE-COUNTER
00119                                            PIC 9(2)V9(2).
00120           02  FILLER                       PIC X(22).
00121       01  PAY-REPORT-LINE.
00122           02  FILLER                       PIC X(5) VALUE SPACE.
00123           02  PAY-OUT-SS-NUM               PIC 9(9).
00124           02  FILLER                       PIC X(5) VALUE SPACE.
00125           02  PAY-OUT-NAME                 PIC X(25).
00126           02  PAY-OUT-REG-HOURS            PIC Z9.9(2).
00127           02  FILLER                       PIC X(5) VALUE SPACE.
00128           02  PAY-OUT-OVER-HOURS           PIC Z9.9(2).
00129           02  FILLER                       PIC X(5) VALUE SPACE.
00130           02  PAY-OUT-RATE                 PIC Z9.9(3).
00131           02  FILLER                       PIC X(5) VALUE SPACE.
00132           02  PAY-OUT-TOTAL-PAY            PIC Z(2)9.9(2).
00133           02  PAY-OUT-MESSAGE-INFO.
00134               03  PAY-OUT-MESSAGE          PIC X(30).
00135               03  PAY-OUT-CODE             PIC X.
00136       01  HEADING-LINE.
00137           02  FILLER                       PIC X(44)
00138               VALUE '       SS NUM     EMPLOYEE NAME'.
00139           02  FILLER                       PIC X(35)
00140               VALUE ' REG HOURS  OVERTIME  RATE      PAY'.
00141       01  STARLINE.
00142           02  FILLER                       PIC X(133) VALUE ALL '*'.
00143       01  COMPANY-HOURS-LINE.
00144           02  FILLER                       PIC X VALUE SPACE.
00145           02  FILLER                       PIC X(30)
00146               VALUE 'COMPANY TOTAL HOURS'.
00147           02  COM-HOURS-OUT                PIC Z(5)9.9(2).
00148       01  COMPANY-OVERTIME-LINE.
00149           02  FILLER                       PIC X VALUE SPACE.
00150           02  FILLER                       PIC X(30)
00151               VALUE 'COMPANY TOTAL OVERTIME'.
00152           02  COM-OVERTIME-OUT             PIC Z(5)9.9(2).
```

Figure 2.12 (cont.)

```
00153              01   COMPANY-PAY-LINE.
00154                   02   FILLER                         PIC X VALUE SPACE.
00155                   02   FILLER                         PIC X(27)
00156                        VALUE  'COMPANY TOTAL PAYROLL'.
00157                   02   COM-PAY-OUT                     PIC $(8)9.9(2).
00158              01   CODE-RATE-TABLE.
00159                   02   RATE-BY-CODE
00160                        OCCURS 10 TIMES
00161                        ASCENDING KEY IS PAY-CODE
00162                        INDEXED BY RATE-TABLE-COUNTER,
00163                                   SAVE-MIN-LOC,
00164                                   START-UNSORTED,
00165                                   UNSORTED-COUNTER.
00166                        03   PAY-CODE                   PIC X.
00167                        03   PAY-RATE                   PIC 9(2)V9(3).
00168         *
00169         PROCEDURE DIVISION.
00170         *
00171         PAY-REPORT-CONTROL.
00172              PERFORM START-UP.
00173              PERFORM SORT-CODE-RATE-TABLE.
00174              PERFORM PROCESS-EMPLOYEE UNTIL NO-MORE-PAY-DATA.
00175              PERFORM FINISH-UP.
00176              STOP RUN.
00177         *
00178         START-UP.
00179              OPEN INPUT PAYROLL-HOURS-FILE-IN
00180                   OUTPUT PAYROLL-REPORT-PRINT-FILE.
00181              MOVE 'N' TO END-OF-PAY-DATA-SW.
00182              COMPUTE LINE-COUNT = LINES-PER-PAGE + 1.
00183              MOVE ZERO TO COM-TOTAL-HOURS,
00184                           COM-TOTAL-OVERTIME,
00185                           COM-TOTAL-PAY.
00186              PERFORM READ-TABLE-IN.
00187              PERFORM READ-PAYROLL-HOURS-FILE.
00188         *
00189         SORT-CODE-RATE-TABLE.
00190              PERFORM POSITION-ANOTHER-ELEMENT VARYING
00191                   RATE-TABLE-COUNTER FROM 1 BY 1
00192                   UNTIL RATE-TABLE-COUNTER = NUM-OF-CODES.
00193         *
00194         POSITION-ANOTHER-ELEMENT.
00195              MOVE RATE-BY-CODE (RATE-TABLE-COUNTER) TO SAVE-RATE-BY-CODE.
00196              SET SAVE-MIN-LOC TO RATE-TABLE-COUNTER.
00197              SET START-UNSORTED TO RATE-TABLE-COUNTER.
00198              SET START-UNSORTED UP BY 1.
00199              PERFORM FIND-NEXT-MIN VARYING UNSORTED-COUNTER
00200                   FROM START-UNSORTED BY 1 UNTIL UNSORTED-COUNTER
00201                   IS GREATER THAN NUM-OF-CODES.
00202              MOVE RATE-BY-CODE (RATE-TABLE-COUNTER) TO
00203                   RATE-BY-CODE (SAVE-MIN-LOC).
00204              MOVE SAVE-RATE-BY-CODE TO
00205                   RATE-BY-CODE (RATE-TABLE-COUNTER).
00206         *
00207         FIND-NEXT-MIN.
00208              IF PAY-CODE (UNSORTED-COUNTER) IS LESS THAN SAVE-PAY-CODE
00209                   MOVE RATE-BY-CODE (UNSORTED-COUNTER) TO
00210                        SAVE-RATE-BY-CODE
00211                   SET SAVE-MIN-LOC TO UNSORTED-COUNTER.
00212         *
00213         PROCESS-EMPLOYEE.
00214              MOVE 'N' TO PAY-CODE-FOUND-SW.
00215              PERFORM FIND-PAY-CODE.
00216              MOVE PAY-IN-NAME TO PAY-OUT-NAME.
00217              MOVE PAY-IN-SS-NUM TO PAY-OUT-SS-NUM.
00218              IF PAY-CODE-FOUND
00219                   MOVE SPACE TO PAY-OUT-MESSAGE-INFO
00220                   PERFORM PROCESS-EMP-HOURS
00221              ELSE
00222                   MOVE 'INVALID PAY-CODE' TO PAY-OUT-MESSAGE
00223                   MOVE ZERO TO PAY-OUT-REG-HOURS, PAY-OUT-OVER-HOURS,
00224                        PAY-OUT-RATE, PAY-OUT-TOTAL-PAY
00225                   MOVE PAY-IN-CODE TO PAY-OUT-CODE.
00226              PERFORM WRITE-PAY-REPORT-REC.
00227              ADD 1 TO LINE-COUNT.
00228              PERFORM READ-PAYROLL-HOURS-FILE.
```

Figure 2.12 (cont.)

```
00229          *
00230            FINISH-UP.
00231                MOVE COM-TOTAL-HOURS TO COM-HOURS-OUT.
00232                MOVE COM-TOTAL-OVERTIME TO COM-OVERTIME-OUT.
00233                MOVE COM-TOTAL-PAY TO COM-PAY-OUT.
00234                PERFORM FINAL-WRITE.
00235                CLOSE PAYROLL-HOURS-FILE-IN,
00236                    PAYROLL-REPORT-PRINT-FILE.
00237          *
00238            FIND-PAY-CODE.
00239                SEARCH ALL RATE-BY-CODE
00240                    WHEN PAY-CODE (RATE-TABLE-COUNTER) = PAY-IN-CODE
00241                    MOVE 'Y' TO PAY-CODE-FOUND-SW.
00242          *
00243            PROCESS-EMP-HOURS.
00244                MOVE ZERO TO EMP-TOTAL-HOURS.
00245                PERFORM ADD-TO-HOURS VARYING HOURS-WORKED-TABLE-COUNTER
00246                    FROM 1 BY 1 UNTIL HOURS-WORKED-TABLE-COUNTER
00247                    GREATER THAN NUM-DAYS-IN-WEEK.
00248                PERFORM COMPUTE-PAY.
00249                ADD EMP-TOTAL-HOURS TO COM-TOTAL-HOURS.
00250                ADD EMP-TOTAL-OVERTIME TO COM-TOTAL-OVERTIME.
00251                ADD EMP-TOTAL-PAY TO COM-TOTAL-PAY.
00252                COMPUTE PAY-OUT-REG-HOURS = EMP-TOTAL-HOURS -
00253                    EMP-TOTAL-OVERTIME.
00254                MOVE EMP-TOTAL-OVERTIME  TO PAY-OUT-OVER-HOURS.
00255                MOVE PAY-RATE (RATE-TABLE-COUNTER) TO PAY-OUT-RATE.
00256                MOVE EMP-TOTAL-PAY TO PAY-OUT-TOTAL-PAY.
00257                IF LINE-COUNT   IS GREATER THAN LINES-PER-PAGE
00258                    PERFORM WRITE-PAGE-HEAD
00259                    MOVE ZERO TO LINE-COUNT.
00260          *
00261            ADD-TO-HOURS.
00262                COMPUTE EMP-TOTAL-HOURS = EMP-TOTAL-HOURS +
00263                    PAY-IN-HOURS-WORKED (HOURS-WORKED-TABLE-COUNTER).
00264          *
00265            COMPUTE-PAY.
00266                COMPUTE EMP-TOTAL-PAY =  EMP-TOTAL-HOURS *
00267                    PAY-RATE (RATE-TABLE-COUNTER).
00268                IF EMP-TOTAL-HOURS IS GREATER THAN REG-PAY-PERIOD
00269                    COMPUTE EMP-TOTAL-OVERTIME = EMP-TOTAL-HOURS -
00270                        REG-PAY-PERIOD
00271                ELSE
00272                    MOVE ZERO TO EMP-TOTAL-OVERTIME.
00273                COMPUTE EMP-TOTAL-PAY =  EMP-TOTAL-PAY + EMP-TOTAL-OVERTIME
00274                    * PAY-RATE (RATE-TABLE-COUNTER)
00275                    * OVERTIME-RATE.
00276          *
00277            READ-TABLE-IN.
00278                READ PAYROLL-HOURS-FILE-IN INTO CODE-RATE-TABLE
00279                    AT END MOVE 'Y' TO END-OF-PAY-DATA-SW.
00280          *
00281            WRITE-PAGE-HEAD.
00282                WRITE PAYROLL-REPORT-PRINT-AREA FROM HEADING-LINE
00283                    AFTER ADVANCING TO-TOP-OF-PAGE.
00284          *
00285            WRITE-PAY-REPORT-REC.
00286                WRITE PAYROLL-REPORT-PRINT-AREA FROM PAY-REPORT-LINE
00287                    AFTER ADVANCING 1 LINES.
00288          *
00289            READ-PAYROLL-HOURS-FILE.
00290                READ PAYROLL-HOURS-FILE-IN INTO PAYROLL-HOURS-IN-REC
00291                    AT END MOVE 'Y' TO END-OF-PAY-DATA-SW.
00292          *
00293            FINAL-WRITE.
00294                WRITE PAYROLL-REPORT-PRINT-AREA FROM STARLINE
00295                    AFTER ADVANCING 3 LINES.
00296                WRITE PAYROLL-REPORT-PRINT-AREA FROM COMPANY-HOURS-LINE
00297                    AFTER ADVANCING 2 LINES.
00298                WRITE PAYROLL-REPORT-PRINT-AREA FROM COMPANY-OVERTIME-LINE
00299                    AFTER ADVANCING 1 LINES.
00300                WRITE PAYROLL-REPORT-PRINT-AREA FROM COMPANY-PAY-LINE
00301                    AFTER ADVANCING 1 LINES.
```

COMMENTS ON INDEXING AND TABLE ORGANIZATION

Using an INDEX instead of a subscript nearly always results in more efficient processing. However, if arithmetic must be done to create the occurrence number of the item in the table, it cannot be done directly with an index. In this case, subscripting may be a better choice.

Some general guidelines on table organization are

1. The greater the number of levels of indexing or subscripting (COBOL allows a maximum of three levels), the longer the access time.
2. Using the most efficient numeric representation of the subscript will reduce the time required for locating a table element. Normally, this will be COMPUTATIONAL.
3. If a table element will be referenced several times, move the element to a work area. By doing so, this means that the address of the table element needs only to be calculated one time instead of every time the element is referenced.

For larger tables, a binary search will be more efficient than a linear search *if all elements* are accessed with approximately the same relative frequency. There are situations where this is not true. If you know which elements are accessed most frequently and they are placed first in the table, a linear search can be more effective.

When possible, organize tables so that input codes translate directly to corresponding table entries. For example, a table of month entries should be organized JAN, FEB, . . . DEC to correspond exactly with months of the year coded 1, 2, . . . 12 on input data.

Programming Exercises for Chapter 2

For the following exercises, all the tables are to be indexed. Your instructor may wish to provide instructions for the specific search technique to be used. If desired, all exercises may be done by writing your own search routine. Exercises 2.1 and 2.3 may be approached with either Format 1 or Format 2 of the SEARCH statement. What approach do you think is appropriate for Exercise 2.2? Why?

EXERCISE 2.1

S. W. Camera Supply store markets cameras and related supplies. A report is desired that will summarize total sales for the month. For each sale, a record containing the following data is kept:

Record Positions	Contents	Format
1–5	Product identifier	X(5)
6–8	Quantity sold	9(3)

Use the following sample test data in your sales records.

Product Identifier	Quantity Sold
3329T	1
3274T	1
3298·	4
3515	1
3298	1
3245T	1
3357	2
3328	1
3298	3
3230	2
3274T	1
3521	2
3328T	1

The following entries should be entered in an inventory table that will be searched as sales records are read.

Product Identifier	Description	Unit Price
3251	Camera bag	19.95
3356	SLR accessory kit	29.95
3665T	7-component SLR system	489.00
3391T	SLR body f/1.8 5 mm lens	299.50
3328T	f/2.8 telephoto lens	75.00
3404T	f/2.8 wide-angle lens	75.00
3329T	Tele-extender	35.00
3245T	Auto dedicated flash	39.95
3302T	Power winder	79.00
3357	SLR accessory kit	29.95
3274T	35mm system	259.00
3256T	35mm camera	199.00
3273T	Tele/wide-angle kit	79.95
3298	24-exp color film	2.95
3413T	Print-maker kit	199.00
3515	Nylon camera bag	39.95
3230	Polarizer	14.95

Use an appropriate search technique to search the inventory table and produce a monthly sales report similar to the one illustrated. For each item for which there were sales during the month, a detail line is to be printed. This line should contain the product number, quantity sold, unit price, and total sales for each item. Also, at the end of the report, print the combined total sales for all items.

```
                    S. W. CAMERA SUPPLY
                   MONTHLY SALES REPORT
  PRODUCT
 IDENTIFIER    PRODUCT DESCRIPTION        UNIT PRICE   QUANTITY SOLD   TOTAL SALES
  XXXXX    XXXXXXXXXXXXXXXXXXXXXXXXXX      XXX.XX           XXX         XXXXX.XX
    .               .                        .              .             .
    .               .                        .              .             .
    .               .                        .              .             .
    .               .                        .              .             .
                                             .
                       GRAND TOTAL SALES                               XXXXXX.XX
```

EXERCISE 2.2

Professor D. D. Heard would like to have a program written that will assign grades based on a numeric scale. This numeric scale might vary in the different courses he teaches. It may also vary from one semester to another.

Sample Grading Scale

Score	Grade
93–100	A
80–92	B
65–79	C
58–64	D
0–57	F

Since frequent changes are to be made, the numeric scale to be used should be read as input data. The values that indicate the minimum score required for each of the grade ranges (to be equated with A–F), are entered as five consecutive values on the first input record, each value in 9(3) format. This record also contains the class identifier in positions 16–21 in X(6) format.

Test Data

For loading the table and identifying the class:

```
093080065058000CS 204
```

For each student, the input record contains:

Record Position	Contents	Format
1–9	Student ID	X(9)
10–29	Student Name	X(20)
30–32	Student Score	9(3)

Test Data

For student input records:

Student ID	Name	Score
247355189	Connie Beach	80
238277002	Irwin Fulton	96
498808130	Anaya Keh	68
245252562	Ralph Rupert	64
246115133	Fred Smith	56
145976760	Jill Wilson	76

For each student, print student ID, name, score, and grade assigned:

```
                    REPORT FOR CLASS XXXXXX
 ID NUMBER                  NAME                    SCORE     GRADE
 XXXXXXXXX    XXXXXXXXXXXXXXXXXXXXXXXXXXXXXX          XXX       X
     .                       .                        .         .
     .                       .                        .         .
     .                       .                        .         .
```

EXERCISE 2.3

The Golden Age Retirement Plan markets lifetime retirement annuities. For each prospective customer, an illustration is prepared showing the amount that will be paid annually upon retirement. This amount is based on the customer's age, yearly premium payment, age at retirement, and sex.

A form is to be printed that provides the report to the prospective purchaser.

Sample Table Data

Amount of Yearly Life Annuity with 10-Year Guarantee Purchasable by a Single Premium of $100 One–twelfth of the amount shown is payable each month.													
Age Attained When Premium is Due	Male Annuitant, Annuity Beginning at			Female Annuitant, Annuity Beginning at			Age Attained When Premium is Due	Male Annuitant, Annuity Beginning at			Female Annuitant, Annuity Beginning at		
	Age 60	Age 65	Age 70	Age 60	Age 65	Age 70		Age 60	Age 65	Age 70	Age 60	Age 65	Age 70
20	$17.13	$22.21	$29.17	$15.02	$19.34	$25.32	45	$ 8.18	$10.61	$13.93	$ 7.17	$ 9.24	$12.09
21	16.63	21.56	28.32	14.58	18.78	24.58	46	7.94	10.30	13.52	6.96	8.97	11.74
22	16.15	20.94	27.49	14.16	18.23	23.86	47	7.71	10.00	13.13	6.76	8.70	11.39
23	15.68	20.33	26.69	13.75	17.70	23.17	48	7.49	9.71	12.74	6.56	8.45	11.06
24	15.22	19.73	25.91	13.35	17.18	22.49	49	7.27	9.42	12.37	6.37	8.21	10.74
25	14.78	19.16	25.16	12.96	16.68	21.84	50	7.06	9.15	12.01	6.19	7.97	10.43
26	14.35	18.60	24.42	12.58	16.20	21.20	51	6.85	8.88	11.66	6.01	7.73	10.12
27	13.93	18.06	23.71	12.21	15.73	20.58	52	6.65	8.62	11.32	5.83	7.51	9.83
28	13.52	17.53	23.02	11.86	15.27	19.98	53	6.46	8.37	10.99	5.66	7.29	9.54
29	13.13	17.02	22.35	11.51	14.82	19.40	54	6.27	8.13	10.67	5.50	7.08	9.26
30	12.75	16.53	21.70	11.18	14.39	18.84	55	6.09	7.89	10.36	5.33	6.87	8.99
31	12.38	16.04	21.07	10.85	13.97	18.29	56	5.91	7.66	10.06	5.18	6.67	8.73
32	12.01	15.58	20.45	10.53	13.56	17.75	57	5.74	7.44	9.77	5.03	6.48	8.48
33	11.66	15.12	19.86	10.23	13.17	17.74	58	5.57	7.22	9.48	4.88	6.29	8.23
34	11.32	14.68	19.28	9.93	12.79	16.73	59	5.41	7.01	9.21	4.74	6.10	7.99
35	10.99	14.25	18.72	9.64	12.41	16.25	60	5.25	6.81	8.94	4.60	5.93	7.76
36	10.67	13.84	18.17	9.36	12.05	15.77	61		6.61	8.68		5.75	7.53
37	10.36	13.44	17.64	9.09	11.70	15.31	62		6.41	8.42		5.59	7.31
38	10.06	13.04	17.13	8.82	11.36	14.87	63		6.23	8.18		5.42	7.10
39	9.77	12.66	16.63	8.56	11.03	14.43	64		6.05	7.94		5.26	6.89
40	9.48	12.30	16.15	8.31	10.71	14.01	65		5.87	7.71		5.11	6.69
41	9.21	11.94	15.68	8.07	10.40	13.61	66			7.48			6.50
42	8.94	11.59	15.22	7.84	10.09	13.21	67			7.27			6.31
43	8.68	11.25	14.78	7.61	9.80	12.82	68			7.05			6.12
44	8.43	10.92	14.34	7.39	9.51	12.45	69			6.85			5.94
							70			6.65			5.77

The table entries in your program should be organized as follows:

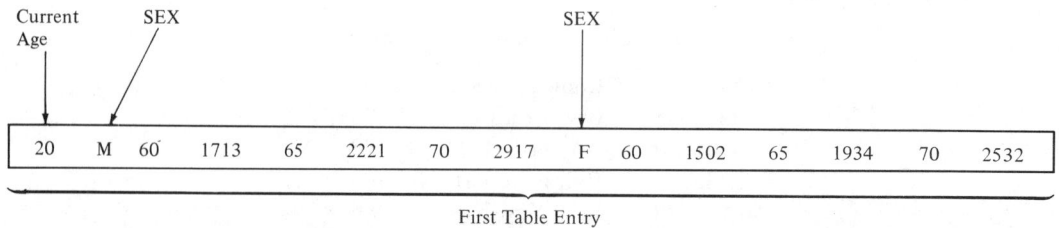

First Table Entry

For a given year, the amount available for purchase of annuity is the amount paid during the year plus 3 percent of the total invested in the plan.

Sample calculations for a 35-year-old female who plans annual payments of $1,000 and wants to retire at age 60 are given here.

Year 1

annuity purchased = (1000 ÷ 100) * 9.64

Year 2

  annuity purchased = (1030 ÷ 100) * 9.36

Year 3

  annuity purchased = (1123.6 ÷ 100) * 9.09

The input record contains:

Record Position	Contents	Format
1–25	Name	X(25)
26–27	Age	9(2)
28–29	Retirement age	9(2)
30–36	Yearly	9(5)V9(2)
37	Sex	X

Sample Input Data

Name	Age	Retirement Age	Yearly	Sex
James Lewis	20	60	400	M
Tom Brown	35	70	800	M
Suzie King	44	65	1,500	F
Lynn Anderson	50	70	1,000	F
Bob Short	26	60	120	M
Margaret Jones	60	65	5,000	F
James Squires	45	60	1,000	M
Liz Floyd	20	60	500	F

For each prospective purchaser, generate a benefits projection report similar to the one illustrated.

```
            GOLDEN AGE RETIREMENT PLAN
               BENEFITS PROJECTION

    THIS BENEFITS PROJECTION WAS PREPARED FOR
XXXXXXXXXXXXXX, WHO IS CURRENTLY XX YEARS OLD AND
PLANS PAYMENTS OF $XX,XXX.XX TO THE PLAN.
    THE ANNUAL INCOME BEGINNING AT AGE XX IS PROJECTED
TO BE $XXX,XXX.XX.
```

3 Tape and Disk Concepts

INTRODUCTION

You were probably introduced to the concept of secondary storage in your first computer course. Disk and tape are very commonly used secondary storage media. Let's discuss several important ideas concerning the way data are recorded on tape and disk.

TAPE RECORDS

Data records are recorded on tape magnetically and, once recorded, are permanent in the sense that they may be repeatedly accessed without being destroyed. In this respect, the process is very similar to recording and playing back on a home tape recorder. Magnetic tape comes in various widths, with 1/2 inch the most common. A typical reel of tape contains approximately 2400 feet of tape (Figure 3.1). A tape may be thought of as containing *tracks* (or channels) running along its length. Nine-track tape is most commonly used at the present time, but seven-track tape is also in use. For this discussion, we will assume nine-track tape, noting that from a programmer's point of view, the number of tracks is generally unimportant.

As a general rule, the way data are recorded on the tape will reflect the internal representation of the data for the specific computer system being used. Many computers, especially IBM, use the Extended Binary Coded Decimal Interchange Code (EBCDIC) to represent character data. Each character requires a group of 8 bits, called a *byte,* for its representation. For example, using a box to represent a byte, and 0 and 1 to denote the "off" and "on" status of a bit, respectively, the letter *A* would appear as follows:

```
11000001
```

Similarly, the character representation of the digit 4 would look like this:

```
11110100
```

Actually, each byte has 9 bits, but the ninth bit is never used to represent data; rather it is used to provide *parity checking*. Parity checking is one of several techniques used to help insure that data are correctly transferred from one internal

Figure 3.1
Magnetic tape reel. (Photo courtesy of Scott Walstrom.)

storage location to another, as well as from certain external storage media (such as magnetic tape) to internal storage. For example, if a computer uses odd parity, the number of 1-bits in a byte must always be odd. Therefore, if the data part of the byte contains an odd number of 1-bits, the parity bit is set to 0; otherwise, it is set to 1.

The revised version of the letter *A* is

0	11000001

Parity Data
 bit   portion

The letter *C* will have the parity bit set to 1:

1	11000011

Parity Data
 bit   portion

Actually, the setting and testing of the parity bit's value is strictly a hardware function. The idea of parity checking was introduced to explain why nine tracks (rather than eight) are needed on the tape.

The way EBCDIC characters are represented on magnetic tape is illustrated in Figure 3.2 for selected characters. You will notice that the relative position of corresponding bits is different in a byte from its representation on tape. This transformation is done automatically and is of no concern to the programmer.

Although not a feature of ANS COBOL, some computers, including IBM's, support another representation of numeric data known as *packed (internal) decimal*. In this representation, each byte, except the rightmost, contains two digits. The rightmost byte of the field contains a digit and a sign code. Several examples are given here.

Decimal Number	Internal Form
94863	94 86 3F
+3975	03 97 5C
−462138	04 62 13 8D

Boxes are again used to represent bytes.

This is a popular form of representation for numeric data being stored on tape, since one tape position can now represent two decimal digits rather than one. Thus, a considerable amount of space on tape will be saved.

Numbers may also be represented in binary format. Such numbers will generally occupy fewer bytes, and hence less tape, than the same numbers in either the EBCDIC or external decimal formats.

Magnetic tape is often characterized by the number of bytes per inch (bpi) recorded along its length. On older computer systems, representative tape densities were 200 and 556 bpi. Contemporary tape units typically record at densities of 800, 1600,

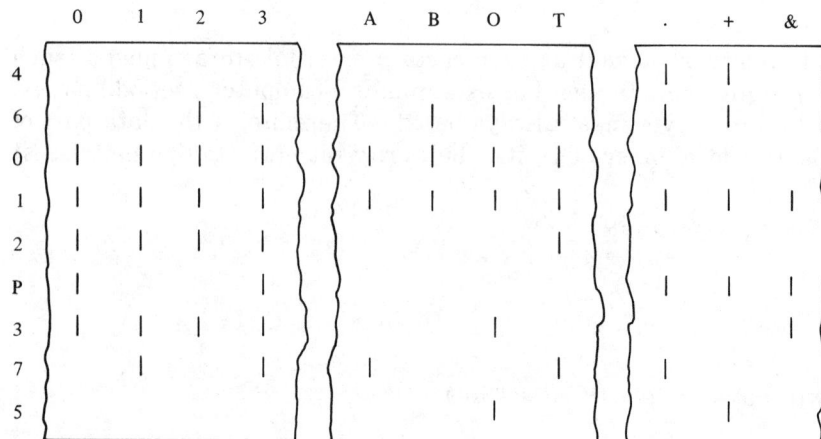

Figure 3.2
Data format for 9-track tapes. Vertical lines indicate 1-bits.

and 6250 bpi. Some tape units support tapes recorded at only one density, whereas others have a switch that allows the density to be changed to any of several values.

Organizations will commonly have hundreds, or even thousands, of reels of tape. Figure 3.3 shows a tape reel being pulled from a tape library.

An important feature of a tape unit is the speed, in inches per second, that the tape physically moves past the recording mechanism (read/write head). A reel of tape, the take-up reel, and the recording mechanism can be seen in Figure 3.4. Typical speeds are 75 and 125 inches per second.

The product of the tape unit's speed and its recording density is called the *data transfer rate*. This is the rate at which data will be read or recorded. Thus, if a tape unit's speed is 125 inches/second, and if the recording density is 800 bpi, its data transfer rate is (125 * 800), or 100,000 characters per second. Figure 3.5 shows an

Figure 3.3
Magnetic tape library. (Photo courtesy of International Business Machines Corporation.)

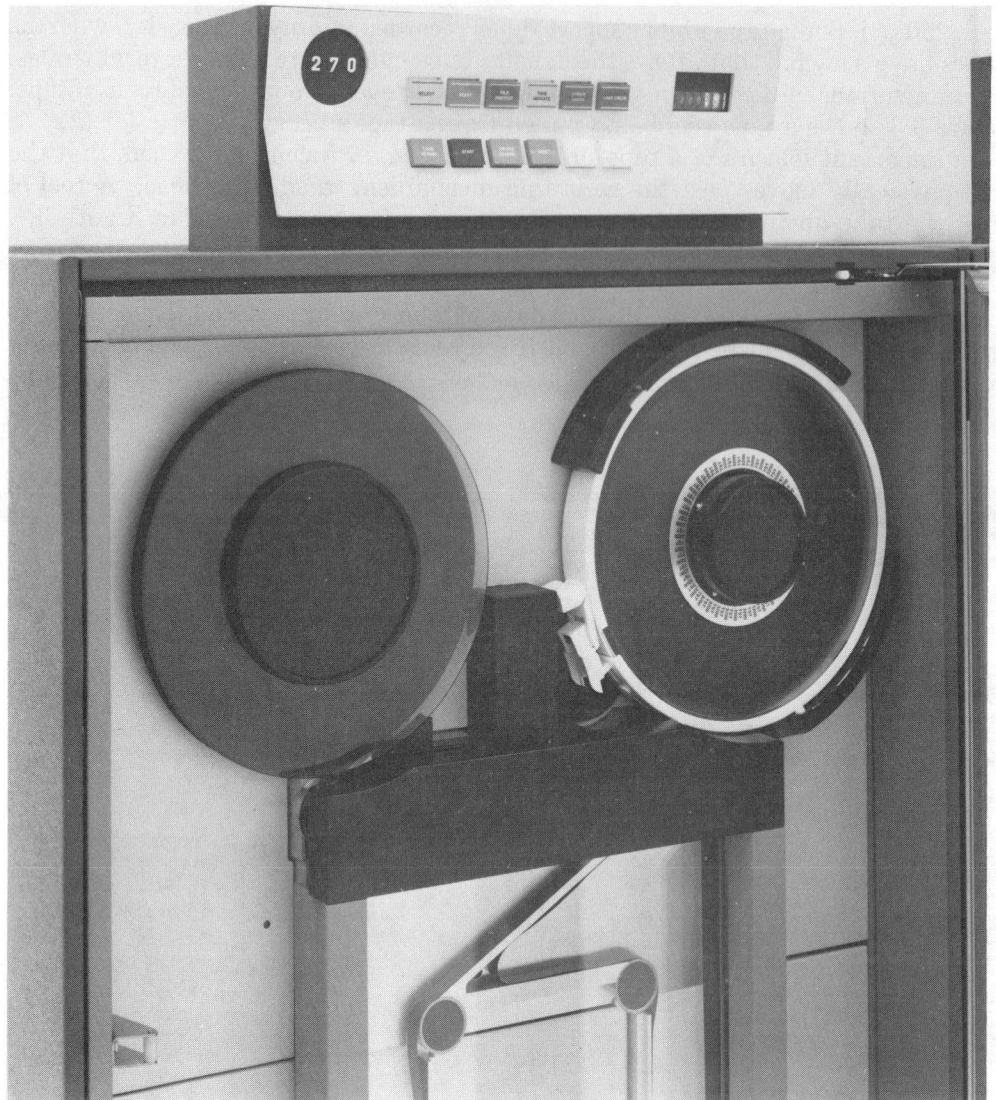

Figure 3.4
Recording mechanism (read/write head) for magnetic tape unit. (Photo courtesy of International Business Machines Corporation.)

IBM 3420 magnetic tape unit. This unit is available in six different models, and depending on the model, allows recording densities of 556, 800, 1600, or 6250 bpi and tape speeds of 75, 125, or 200 inches per second. Thus, the data transfer rate varies from a low of 41,700 bytes per second to a high of 1,250,000 bytes per second.

An organization will nearly always have more than one tape unit. Figure 3.6 pictures four IBM 3420 tape units grouped together. Another type of tape unit is shown in Figure 3.7.

Now that we know how to record individual characters on tape, let's consider how the characters are combined to form fields and records. As an example, suppose an inventory record were maintained on tape for each of 1000 parts. We assume the following record layout:

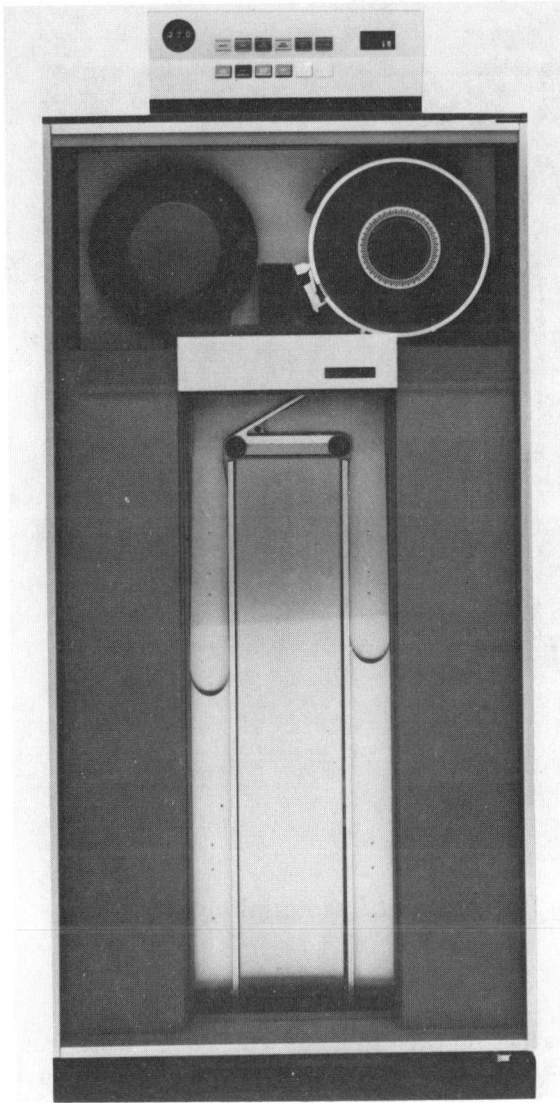

Figure 3.5
IBM 3420 magnetic tape unit. (Photo courtesy of International Business Machines Corporation.)

Record Position	Description	Sample Data Value
1–5	Part number	10346
6–25	Part description	LOCK NUT
26–32	Quantity on hand	0009860

Part number, part description, and quantity on hand are *fields*. These three fields constitute a *record*. The entire 1,000 records constitute a *file*.

Figure 3.6
Four IBM 3420 tape units grouped together. (Photo courtesy of International Business Machines Corporation.)

An *interrecord gap* (IRG) is a blank space on tape that separates one record from another. Older tape units typically created IRGs of .75 inch, whereas newer tape units typically create IRGs of .6 inch. The primary purpose of an IRG is to provide space where the tape unit may halt after reading one record and accelerate to full speed before reading the next. From the standpoint of recording data, IRGs are wasted space. If records are small, the IRGs can occupy most of the space on the tape.

Halting the tape unit between each record wastes computer time as well. The situation can be significantly improved by transferring several records to or from main memory each time the tape is read or written.

The term *record* is used in two different senses, and a programmer *must* be aware of which one is meant. A *logical record* refers to the related fields comprising some entity, whereas a *physical record* refers to the data transferred to (or from) memory in one input (or output) operation. When a physical record contains two or more logical records, the records are referred to as *blocked*. Records are said to be *unblocked* if a physical record contains only a single logical record. On tape, physical records are separated by IRGs. Figure 3.8 illustrates the tape structure for unblocked records and for records blocked five to a block.

Since by blocking both computer time and tape space are saved, records on tape should usually be blocked. Logical records may have the following formats:

Figure 3.7
IBM 3410 magnetic tape units. (Photo courtesy of International Business Machines Corporation.)

1. Fixed length.
2. Variable length.
3. Spanned.
4. Undefined.

Fixed length means that all records contain the same number of bytes. *Variable-length records* allow the record to occupy only the number of bytes necessary to

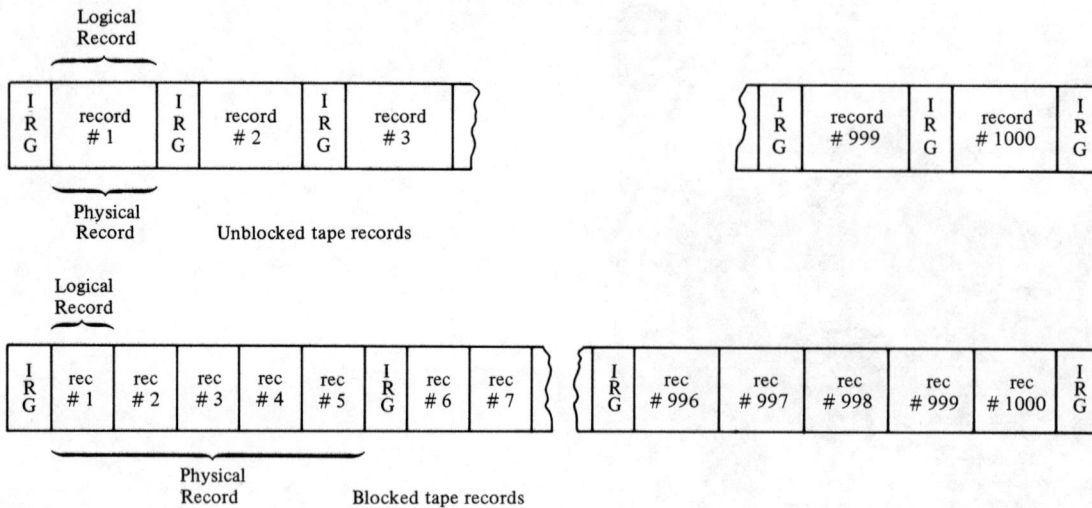

Figure 3.8
Blocked and unblocked records on magnetic tape.

contain the data. A record that contains course data for a student who is a senior requires more space than would a record for a sophomore. If logical records are longer than physical records, the records are *spanned.* The fourth type of record format, one with undefined length, is rarely encountered—consequently, it will not be discussed. In this text, we will only consider fixed-length logical records that are completely contained within a single block. This type was illustrated in Figure 3.8.

TAPE LABELS

Most tape files contain labels to protect against misuse or destruction. A label is a special record written at the beginning and/or the end of the file. Labels written at the beginning of the file are called *header labels,* whereas those written at the end of the file are called *trailer labels.*

There are a number of fields in a header label; some of the most important of them are

1. The file name.
2. The file creation date.
3. The file expiration date.

The file name is used to uniquely identify the file to the operating system file-access modules. The creation date is the date on which the file was initially created. The expiration date is the date after which the file may be overwritten and replaced by a new file.

Tape files that have a header label will normally have a trailer label. The most important field contained in the trailer label is the block count field. When the file is created, the number of physical records (blocks) in the file will be placed in this field automatically. Then, when the file is used for an input file, an automatic check is made to make sure the correct number of blocks was processed. If not, a message is issued to the console operator.

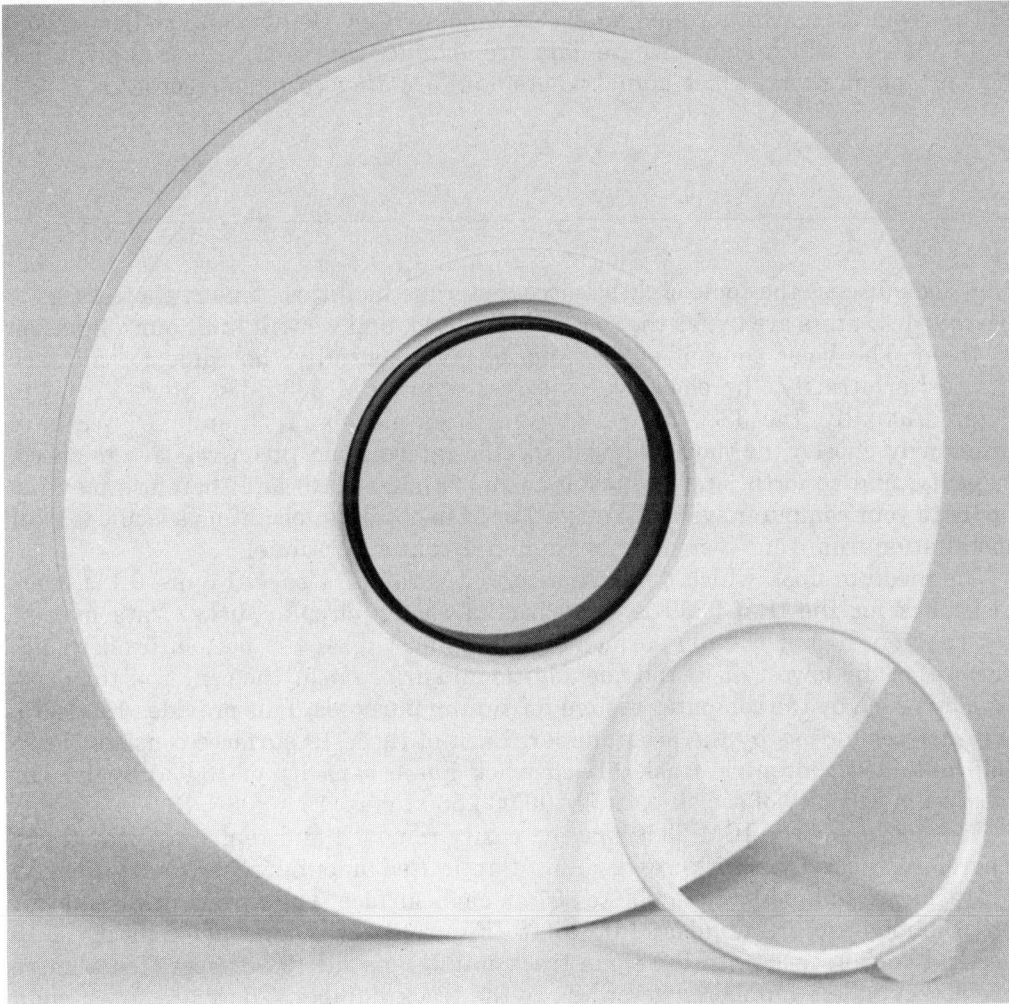

Figure 3.9
Magnetic tape reel with file protection ring pulled out. (Photo courtesy of Scott Walstrom.)

Another device used to protect tape files is the *file protection ring*. This is a small plastic ring (Figure 3.9) that may be inserted into a groove on the outside of the reel of tape. Writing on the tape is permitted *only* when the file protection ring is in place.

DELIMITING A TAPE FILE

The entire length of the reel of tape cannot be used for the recording of data. There is a short, reflective, metallic strip placed about ten feet from the physical beginning of the reel. This marks the beginning of the usable portion of the tape. This strip, called a *load point marker,* can be detected by the tape unit. A similar strip, approximately 15 feet from the end of the reel, marks the end of the usable portion of the reel. This strip is called an *end-of-tape marker*. Do not confuse header and trailer labels, which signal where data are *actually* recorded, with load point and end-of-tape markers, which signal where data are *allowed* to be recorded.

DISK CONCEPTS

Now let's discuss the topic of direct-access storage facilities. Among these types of devices disk units are by far the most widely used, and we will limit our discussion to them. The basic concept of disk storage is essentially the same for all such devices; arbitrarily, therefore, we will discuss an IBM 3330 disk storage unit in detail. Actually, the 3330 is available in three models (1, 2, and 11). We have arbitrarily chosen the model 11. All specific information given relative to speed, capacity, and so forth, applies to this model (Figure 3.10) and therefore may not apply to your computer system. You will need to obtain information specific to your installation from your instructor or computer center personnel.

The medium upon which data are recorded is the *disk pack* (Figure 3.11). Each disk pack for the IBM 3330 is comprised of eleven circular disks. Data may be recorded on all but the top surface of the topmost disk, the bottom (underneath surface) of the lowest disk, and one additional surface near the center of the pack, which is used by the computer system for timing purposes. This provides 19 recording surfaces for use by the programmer. Each of these 19 surfaces consists of 808 self-contained concentric tracks. Each track has a capacity of 13,030 bytes. The maximum capacity of a disk pack is 200,036,560 bytes (19 * 808 * 13,030).

Disk packs for the IBM 3330 may be easily removed and replaced with others. Therefore, these disk units provide almost unlimited amounts of secondary storage.

Tracks are numbered from 000 to 807 on each surface. The surfaces available for programmer use are numbered 00 to 18 (Figure 3.12). A *cylinder* consists of 19 vertical tracks, each with the same track number on all 19 surfaces. Thus, there are 808 cylinders numbered according to the track number. There are seven additional cylinders (808–814) that are used by the system as alternate tracks if any of the tracks available to the programmer become defective.

Figure 3.10
IBM 3330 disk storage unit. (Photo courtesy of International Business Machines Corporation.)

TAPE AND DISK CONCEPTS

Figure 3.11
*IBM 3336 disk pack. (Photo courtesy of International
Business Machines Corporation.)*

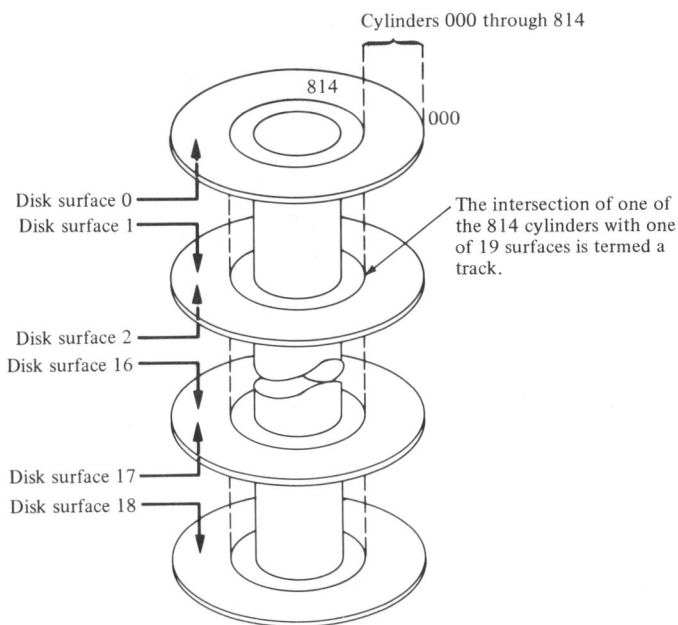

Cylinders 000 through 814

814

000

Disk surface 0
Disk surface 1

The intersection of one of
the 814 cylinders with one
of 19 surfaces is termed a
track.

Disk surface 2
Disk surface 16

Disk surface 17
Disk surface 18

Figure 3.12
Disk recording surface and track schematic.

Associated with each of the 19 recording surfaces is a movable *read/write head*. A read/write head is the mechanism whereby information is read from or recorded on the track. These heads do not actually touch the recording surface; instead, they float on an air cushion a few millionths of an inch from the surface. As with tape, the information is recorded magnetically in bit form. Although a parity check bit is not used with character representation on disk, other types of validity checking are done by the hardware.

The 19 read/write heads (numbered 0–18) are connected to form a single access mechanism, and all heads move in and out over the surfaces as a unit (Figure 3.13). At any given time, the heads are positioned to access the 19 tracks of a given cylinder. Only one head is used at any given time, so that only one track can be accessed at a time for reading or writing data.

The time required to position the read/write heads over the proper cylinder is called *seek time*. For the IBM 3330, the maximum seek time is 55 milliseconds, the minimum is 10 milliseconds, and the average is 30 milliseconds.

Once the access mechanism is positioned over the correct cylinder, the appropriate read/write head is turned on (called *head switching* or *head selection*); however, the desired record may or may not be under the read/write head. The time spent waiting for the record to rotate under the head is called *rotational delay*. For the IBM 3330, the maximum rotational delay is 16.7 milliseconds, and the average rotational delay is 8.4 milliseconds.

For the IBM 3330, the *data transfer rate* (the rate at which data may be read or recorded) is 806,000 bytes per second. Of the actions involved in disk drive access to records (seeking, head switching, rotational delay, and data transfer), seeking and rotational delay are the most time-consuming.

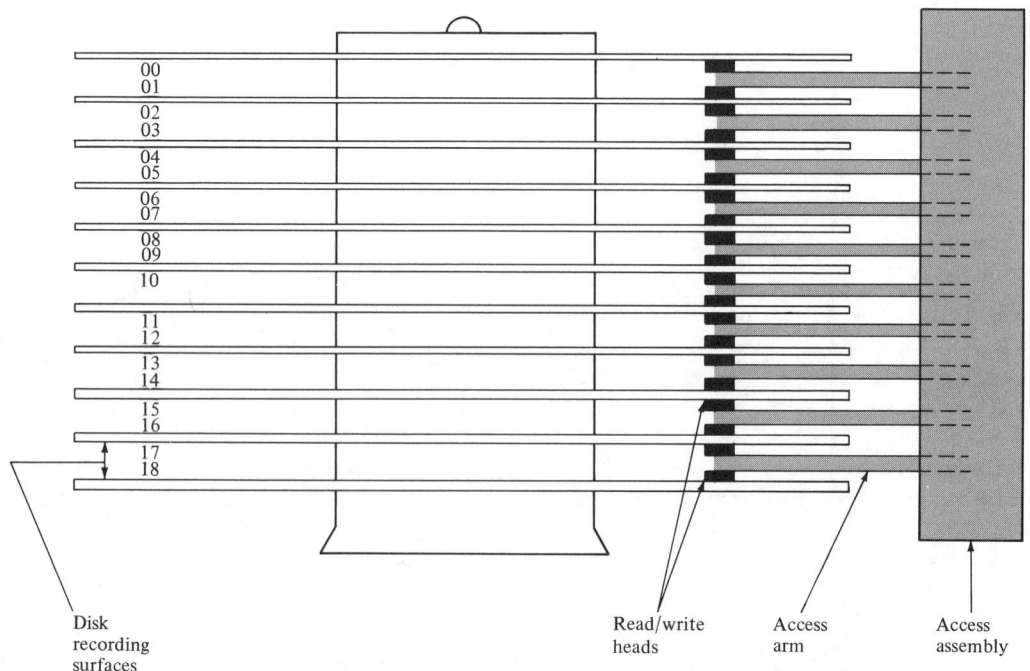

Figure 3.13
Schematic of disk access mechanism.

DELIMITING DISK FILES

To specify the portion of the disk to be used for a given file, information must be provided to indicate which cylinders and tracks are to be used for the file. This is done with a pair of *extents,* the first to specify the beginning of the file and the second to indicate the end of the disk space made available for the file. An extent is simply a track and cylinder designation. For example, a file might be between track 00 of cylinder 023 and track 14 of cylinder 117, inclusive. Files may also use noncontiguous cylinders, track 00 of cylinder 023 to track 14 of cylinder 043, and track 00 of cylinder 084 to track 10 of cylinder 090.

Disk extents for files may be supplied by job-control statements, program statements, or operating system routines. The specific data that you are required to provide and the manner in which it is to be supplied may vary greatly, depending on the computer hardware and operating system involved. In some systems, you must be very precise in providing detailed file-extent information. In contrast, other systems may operate on "space" only, meaning that file space is simply requested (without providing extent specifications), and the operating system locates and allocates space automatically. In fact, some systems do not even require a request for space; it is made available by the system as records are written. For further information, consult the manual specific to your installation.

DISK LABELS/FILE DIRECTORIES

The following information is the minimum necessary for accessing disk files:

1. File name.
2. Creation date.
3. Expiration date.
4. File organization.
5. Extents.
6. Space actually in use.

The operating system maintains this information through disk labels and/or file directories.

Typically, a *disk label* (information used to identify, locate, and so on, a disk file) is entered in a special table called the *Volume Table of Contents* (VTOC), which resides on the disk pack. The VTOC contains label information for all files on the pack.

We are using the term *file directory* here to mean a table, or index, used by the system to store file information, keep track of available (and allocated) file space, and the like. File directories are typically used in conjunction with powerful system software that manages file space and supplies its own file information with minimal, or no, user requirements for providing file specifications.

RECORD FORMATS ON DISK

Record formats on disk are essentially the same as record formats on tape. Physical records are separated by interrecord gaps. Not all file organization methods available on disk permit blocking of logical records, and there are situations where a particular use of a file may result in blocking being more of a disadvantage than an advantage. Blocking will, however, always result in a saving of disk space for file organizations that permit it.

A NOTE ON OTHER DISK UNITS

There are two types of disk units in wide use today that differ in their physical construction from the IBM 3330.

As an example of the first type, the IBM 3340 direct access storage facility (Figure 3.14), uses an IBM 3348 data module as the storage medium (Figure 3.15). The access arms and read/write heads are part of the data module itself. This is a sealed, self-contained unit containing the recording surfaces, access arms, and read/write heads. Since the entire unit is sealed, there is greater reliability. Data modules can be removed and replaced by others, again giving almost unlimited storage capacity.

In contrast, the IBM 3350 direct access storage facility (Figure 3.16) uses a sealed, *nonremovable* unit for the recording of data. The sealed unit contains disk, access arms, and read/write heads.

The track and cylinder concept described for the 3330 applies to the 3340 and 3350. The track and cylinder capacities, the data transfer rate, and the access time will vary widely.

For both the 3340 and the 3350, there are two read/write heads per surface and

Figure 3.14
IBM 3340 direct access storage facility. (Photo courtesy of International Business Machines Corporation.)

Figure 3.15
IBM 3348 data module. (Photo courtesy of International Business Machines Corporation.)

both have the option (at extra cost) of having some cylinders with fixed read/write heads. These features reduce access time.

The type of technology (sealed, self-contained data modules) used in the IBM 3340 and 3350 is commonly referred to as Winchester technology. When Winchester disk drives were originally introduced by IBM, they had two data modules, each of which could store 30 megabytes (a megabyte is a million bytes) of data. This 30-30 configuration led to the term *Winchester,* named after the famous 30-30 Winchester rifle. The recording density of data modules has since been increased; however, the term *Winchester* is still used to describe the technology.

Figure 3.16
IBM 3350 direct access storage facility. (Photo courtesy of International Business Machines Corporation.)

Although the 3340 and 3350 were specifically mentioned, IBM has other Winchester-type disk drives. Several other hardware vendors also have disk drives available that employ the so-called Winchester technology.

Review Exercises for Chapter 3

1. Explain in some detail the way in which data are recorded on magnetic tape.
2. How many channels (tracks) are used for recording purposes on most contemporary tape units?
3. What is the purpose of *parity checking?* Describe how it works.
4. What are some of the most commonly used recording densities on magnetic tape?
5. Define the term *data transfer rate.*
6. What are *interrecord gaps?* What purpose do they serve? What is a disadvantage of interrecord gaps, particularly when records are small?
7. Define and clearly distinguish between the terms *physical record* and *logical record.*
8. What are two advantages of having blocked records?
9. What are tape file header labels and what is their purpose?
10. Name at least three fields contained in a tape header label and state the purpose of each.
11. Describe the nature and purpose of the file protection ring on a reel of magnetic tape.
12. Explain the function of the *load point marker* and the *end-of-tape marker* as they pertain to a reel of magnetic tape.
13. Describe the physical makeup of a disk pack for the IBM 3330. Discuss such concepts as tracks, cylinders, number of tracks per cylinder, number of cylinders, track capacity, and so on.
14. What is meant by the term *seek time?*
15. Define the term *rotational delay.*
16. Of the actions involved in disk drive access to records, which are the most time-consuming?

4

Creating and Processing Sequential Files

Mega-Tronics, Inc. is a small but growing electronics company. The growth has overwhelmed the manual accounting procedures currently in use. The problem is most acute in the payroll process; it seems to be error-prone. Consequently, Mega's president, after considering computerization of accounting procedures, has made the decision to convert to a computer system and has decided the changeover should begin with payroll procedures. Of course, there are limited funds for this, which limits the amount of equipment and software that can be purchased, as well as the number of personnel available to be used for the changeover.

The constraints on Mega's funds and personnel cause the president to decide on a batch system using sequential files. Consequently, this chapter is devoted to the study of this type of system.

A *sequential file* is one in which the logical records are stored sequentially in the order in which they are created and must be retrieved in the order in which they are stored. A tape file is always sequential, whereas a file on disk may, but does not have to be, created as a sequential file.

A sequential file is generally created in either ascending or descending order on one or more key fields (control fields). For example, it may be in order by student identification number; in alphabetical order by name; or in alphabetical order by department name and ordered within each department by student identification number. The logic of most programs that process sequential files is based on the assumption that files are in order on some key field(s), and there are enough key fields specified to distinguish or identify records uniquely. If records contained in a sequential file are not ordered on a key field, some authorities prefer to call them *serial files*.

Sequential files are generally appropriate if processing of the file normally will involve a large percentage of the records in the file. They are very storage-efficient. If Mega-Tronics has a stable work force, then sequential files will be a satisfactory solution to the payroll problem.

There are three types of processing to be done:

1. Add a record to the file in the appropriate key sequence location.
2. Delete a record from the file that is no longer needed.
3. Update/change one or more nonkey fields in the file.

Since the records are physically sequential, processing types 1 and 2 involve re-creating the file by omitting existing records or adding new records to the file as necessary.

For disk files, processing type 3 may be done in the *existing* file by retrieving the record and updating and replacing it. Tape files do not allow this, since the tape is positioned past the end of the record just retrieved, hence, for all three types of transactions, a tape file must be re-created. All three types of processing activity are illustrated in Figure 4.1.

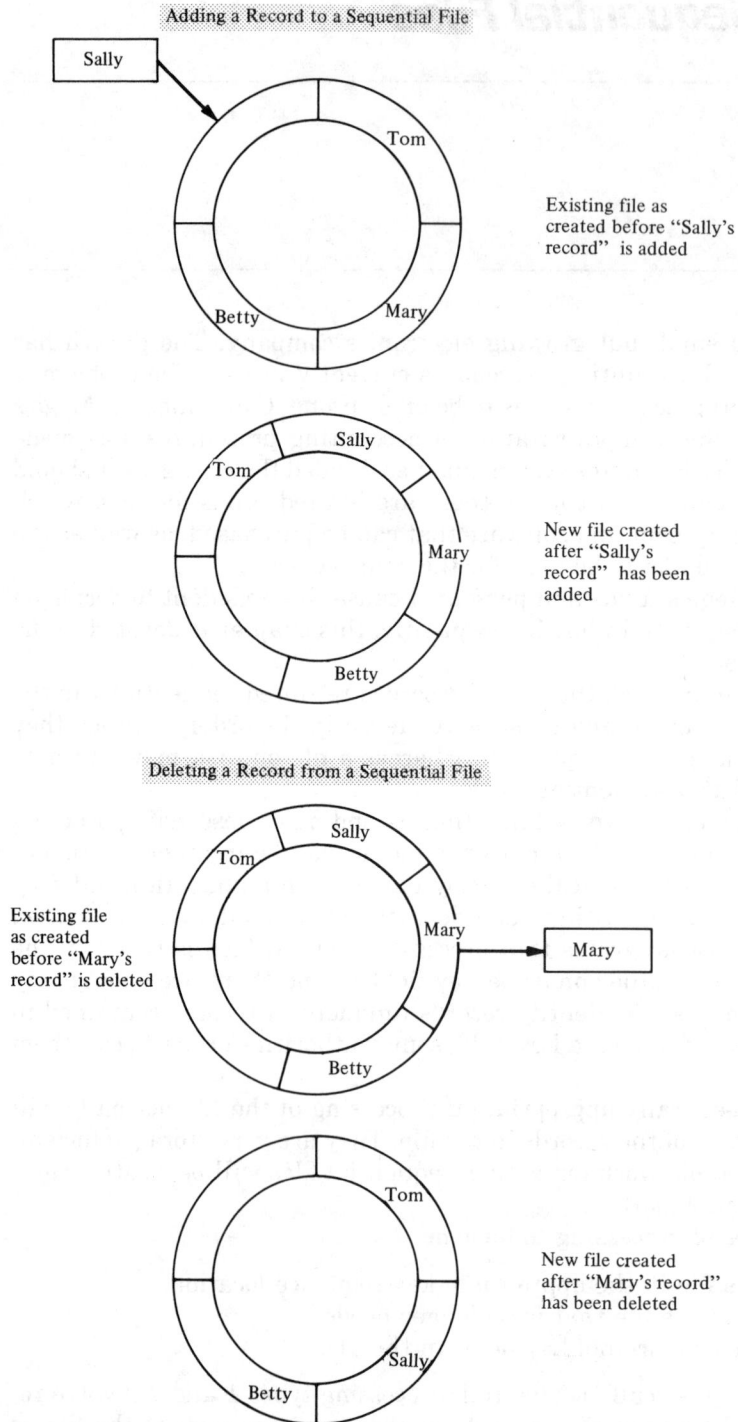

Figure 4.1
File-processing concepts for sequential files.

Figure 4.1 (*cont.*)

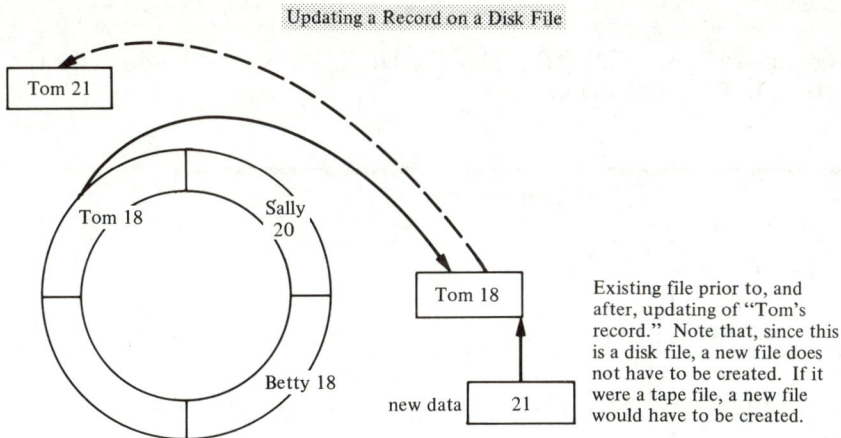

Updating a Record on a Disk File

Tom 21

Tom 18

Sally
20

Betty 18

Tom 18

new data   21

Existing file prior to, and
after, updating of "Tom's
record." Note that, since this
is a disk file, a new file does
not have to be created. If it
were a tape file, a new file
would have to be created.

ENVIRONMENT DIVISION ENTRIES

Every file in COBOL must have a SELECT sentence, which names the file and describes how the file is to be organized.

FORMAT

SELECT filename

ASSIGN TO system-name

$$\left[\text{ACCESS IS} \left\{ \begin{array}{l} \text{RANDOM} \\ \text{SEQUENTIAL} \end{array} \right\} \right].$$

For a sequential file, the ACCESS clause may be omitted, since ACCESS IS SEQUENTIAL will be assumed.

If a voter registration list is to be kept on a tape file, the following SELECT sentence could be used:

```
SELECT REG-VOTER-FILE-IN
     ASSIGN TO SYS035-UT-2400-S.
```

If the voter registration list is to be kept on a sequential disk file, the following SELECT sentence could be used:

```
SELECT REG-VOTER-FILE-IN
     ASSIGN TO SYS027-DA-3330-S-REGFILE.
```

The choice of system-name is highly installation-dependent. Your local computer center consultant can provide information specific to your installation.

DATA DIVISION ENTRIES

The file that was named in the ENVIRONMENT DIVISION must be described in an FD entry in the DATA DIVISION.

```
                              FORMAT

    FD file-name
         LABEL {RECORD IS  } {STANDARD}
               {RECORDS ARE} {OMITTED }
         [BLOCK CONTAINS integer {RECORDS   }].
                                 {CHARACTERS}
```

The file-name must match that given in the SELECT sentence.

The LABEL RECORDS clause is used for all files. For disk files, STANDARD labels will be specified. Tape labels may be specified as either STANDARD or OMITTED.

If REG-VOTER-FILE-IN has been assigned to an unlabeled tape:

```
    FD   REG-VOTER-FILE-IN
         LABEL RECORDS ARE OMITTED
         BLOCK CONTAINS 50 RECORDS.
    01   REG-VOTER-IN-AREA                PIC X(100).
```

If REG-VOTER-FILE-IN has been assigned to a disk or labeled tape:

```
    FD   REG-VOTER-FILE-IN
         LABEL RECORDS ARE STANDARD
         BLOCK CONTAINS 50 RECORDS.
    01   REG-VOTER-IN-AREA                PIC X(100).
```

PROCEDURE DIVISION ENTRIES

Statements to process files, like other processing statements, are coded in the PROCEDURE DIVISION.

All files must be OPENed before they can be accessed.

```
                              FORMAT

              {INPUT }
    OPEN      {OUTPUT} file-name, ...
              {I-O   }
```

As a result of an OPEN statement, labels are checked (if present), the access mechanism is positioned to the beginning of the file, and buffers may be filled. Whether a given file should be opened as INPUT, OUTPUT, or I-O depends on the type of processing to be done. When all processing is complete, the file must be CLOSEd.

FORMAT

CLOSE file-name-1, file-name-2, . . . [WITH LOCK]

The CLOSE statement causes the last block of records and the end-of-file indicator to be written to the file. The WITH LOCK option is used only for tape and causes the tape to be completely rewound and unloaded (that is, the file cannot be reopened during this execution of the program).

A program obtains the next logical record from the file with a READ statement.

FORMAT

READ file-name [INTO identifier]

AT END imperative-statement

After execution of the READ statement, the next logical record is made available for processing in the data area described by the 01-entry under the FD for file-name. If the INTO option is chosen, the next logical record is also moved to *identifier,* following the usual rules for a group-move. When the end-of-file indicator for the file is encountered, the imperative-statement following AT END will be executed.

To request that a record be transferred to the file, a WRITE statement is used.

FORMAT

WRITE record-name [FROM identifier]

The execution of the WRITE statement causes the current logical record to be added to the current block of records for transfer to the file. The block will then be copied (written) to the file when it is full (and also when the file is closed, regardless of whether the block is full).

If the FROM clause is specified, the contents of *identifier* are copied to the area specified under the 01-entry for the file (according to usual group-move rules), prior to transferring any records to the file.

To alter the contents of fields in an existing disk record, the REWRITE statement is used. It has the following format:

```
                  ┌─────────────────────────────────────┐
                  │              FORMAT                  │
                  ├─────────────────────────────────────┤
                  │  REWRITE record-name [FROM identifier]│
                  │  [INVALID KEY imperative-statement]  │
                  └─────────────────────────────────────┘
```

To use REWRITE, the file must be OPENed as *I-O*. The I-O option allows an existing file (which must reside on a direct-access storage facility) to be opened for both input and output operations. The procedure for updating a record involves READing the existing record, making the desired changes to appropriate data fields, and then using REWRITE to place the contents of the updated record back in the original location in the file. If the original record location cannot be found when attempting to REWRITE the record, then an INVALID KEY condition will result and the imperative-statement following the INVALID KEY clause will be executed.

PROBLEMS WITH PROCESSING IN THE BUFFER

During program testing and debugging, it is not uncommon to encounter unique problems when processing is done in the *buffer areas*. It is quite possible for the logic of a COBOL program to appear correct and yet not generate the results expected. To illustrate, let's assume that COMPARE-KEY and RECORD-COUNT are fields in WORKING-STORAGE and that ID-NUM is a field in the record called REG-VOTER-REC, which is in the buffer area. Further, assume that no two records will have the same ID-NUM value. Now consider the following statements, which, although coded in an inefficient manner, are nevertheless valid as written.

```
    MOVE ID-NUM TO COMPARE-KEY.
    IF ID-NUM = COMPARE KEY
        WRITE REG-VOTER-REC.
    IF ID-NUM = COMPARE-KEY
        ADD 1 TO RECORD-COUNT.
```

When this sequence of statements is executed, the results may surprise you. The first IF statement will test the condition ID-NUM = COMPARE-KEY and find it to be true; therefore, the record will be written. However, the second IF statement will test the same condition and will find it to be false; consequently, RECORD-COUNT will not be incremented by 1. How can this be?

The problem is caused by the fact that most operating systems normally allocate at least two input/output memory buffer areas for each sequential file in the program. Therefore, the data name described in the 01-level for an FD entry does not always refer to the *same* physical location in memory. The operating system keeps track of which storage area is currently being used. Therefore, the answer to the question posed in the preceding paragraph is that *after* the WRITE statement was executed, as a result of the first IF statement being true, the operating system moved its buffer pointer to indicate the next physical location in the buffer. This resulted in ID-NUM in REG-VOTER-REC no longer referring to the same storage location that it did prior to the WRITE. Therefore, the second IF statement is actually testing the contents of whatever happens to be at that location. It should be clearly pointed out, however, that different operating systems may move buffer pointers at different times. Although what we have described is very common, it is possible that your system might give different results.

The question of which specific storage locations are being used is more complicated with blocked records. Figure 4.2 illustrates the buffer areas normally allocated to the 01-record description entry associated with the FD-entry for a file containing blocked records (in this case, two logical records per block). The buffers represented in Figure 4.2 are for input, with READs used to show movement in the buffer areas (this same technique applies to WRITEs and output buffers). As can be seen, a single record might be placed in any one of four different physical locations. (How many possibilities exist if there are 20 logical records per block?)

Processing records while in the buffer areas frequently requires that the programmer know when the change from one physical location to another is made by the operating system. Since this is a difficult thing to do, we recommend that the INTO and FROM clauses always be used and that all processing be done in WORKING-STORAGE, except where COBOL syntax requirements specify otherwise.

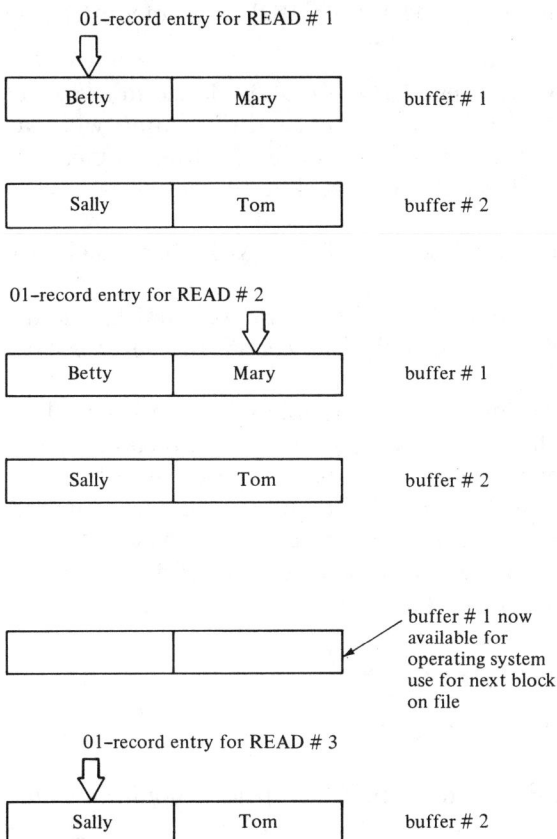

01–record entry for READ # 1

| Betty | Mary | buffer # 1 |

| Sally | Tom | buffer # 2 |

01–record entry for READ # 2

| Betty | Mary | buffer # 1 |

| Sally | Tom | buffer # 2 |

| | | buffer # 1 now available for operating system use for next block on file |

01–record entry for READ # 3

| Sally | Tom | buffer # 2 |

Figure 4.2
Information transfer to the buffers for an input file.

SEQUENTIAL FILE CREATION

Consideration will now be given to several examples that illustrate important types of processing for a sequential processing-based system.

| Example 4.1 |

Mega-Tronic's DP department has decided to make the changeover to the computerized system effective January 1. The initial program will create the employee master file. This file will contain employee personal data; certain company data about the employee; and the year-to-date totals for the employee's tax, total pay, and FICA. For fields that have restrictions on the numeric size or type of data, error checking will be done. For data to be valid, plant site codes must be either 1 or 2, department numbers must fall in the range of 1 through 15, pay rates must fall in the range of 3.35 through 18.75, and tax class and social security number must be numeric.

The overall program organization is given in Figure 4.3. Since the logic involved in the individual modules is somewhat complex, module descriptions are given in Figure 4.4. The program listing is given in Figure 4.5.

Following are some comments concerning specific COBOL statements in the program:

1. Lines 94, 96, and 102 involve special uses of the VALUE clause for 88-level items. On line 94, multiple values are attached to the condition name, whereas on lines 96 and 102, a range of values is attached to the condition name.
2. The BLOCK CONTAINS clause on line 78 specifies that each physical record will contain 10 logical records.
3. All disk files must have labels and, on line 77, STANDARD disk labels are specified.
4. On line 66, the ASSIGN clause is given. PAYFILE is the external file name, the name by which PAYROLL-MAST-FILE-OUT is known to the operating system.
5. Lines 130–147 set up a table to contain a list of possible error messages. This will allow easy printing of multiple error messages for a given record.
6. Line 168 checks to see if any error has been made on the input record.
7. On lines 195–197, all files are closed. The physical transfer of the last block of PAYROLL-MAST-FILE-OUT to the disk is done automatically at this time.
8. The test for a valid plant site on line 203 has been simplified by using the condition name POSSIBLE-PLANT-SITE. This test is equivalent to

```
IF PAY-IN-PLANT-SITE IS NOT EQUAL TO 1
              AND
    PAY-IN-PLANT-SITE IS NOT EQUAL TO 2
```

9. On line 210, the test for a valid department code using the condition name POSSIBLE-DEPT-CODE is equivalent to

```
IF PAY-IN-DEPT-CODE IS LESS THAN 1
              OR
    PAY-IN-DEPT-CODE IS GREATER THAN 15
```

10. The condition name test, VALID-PAY-RATE, on line 225, is used to simplify testing for a range of valid pay rates. This test is equivalent to

```
IF PAY-IN-PAY-RATE IS LESS THAN 3.35
                OR
   PAY-IN-PAY-RATE IS GREATER THAN 18.75
```

11. The statement that causes logical records to be transferred to PAYROLL-MAST-FILE-OUT is the WRITE statement on line 248.

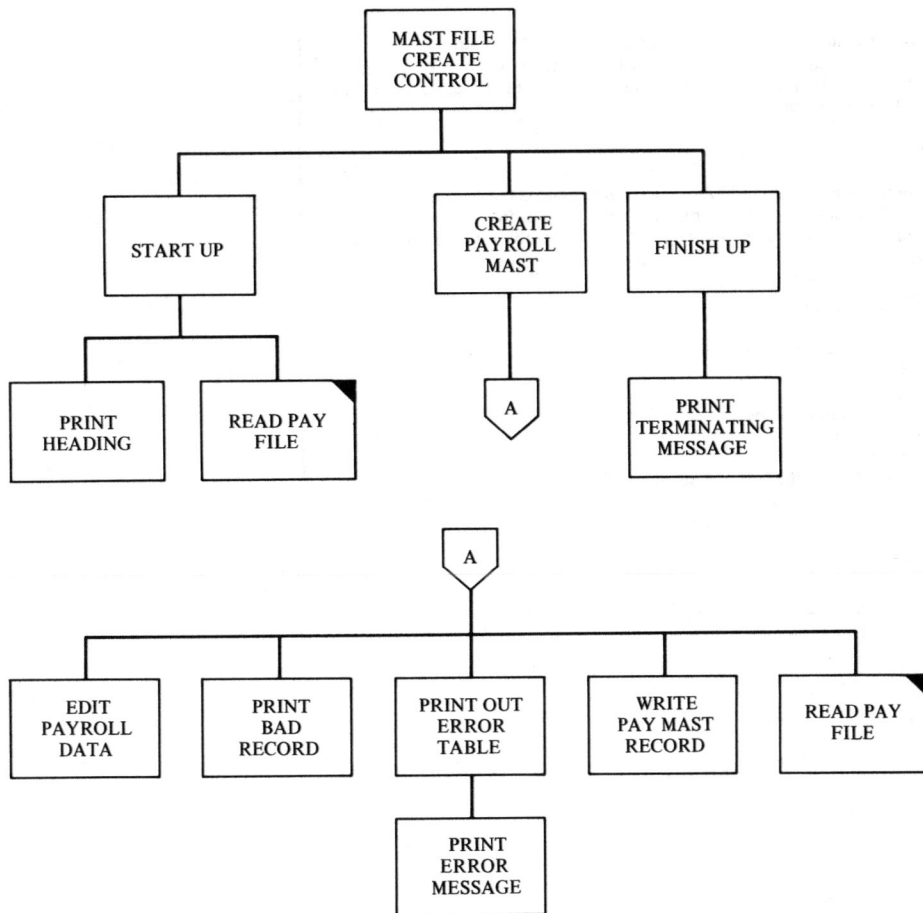

Figure 4.3
Structure chart for the program in Figure 4.5

MAST-FILE-CREATE-CONTROL

This module controls the execution sequence of the program. It also term-inates execution of the program.

START-UP

In this module:

- all files are opened
- a switch is set to indicate there are input data
- the read module is called
- the print heading module is called

CREATE-PAYROLL-MAST

This module calls a data validation routine to check the input data for errors. If errors have been found, the input data with the appropriate error messages are to be printed. If no errors are found, the fields for output are set up and routines are called to write the output records.

FINISH-UP

If the output file was successfully created, a message indicating this is moved to a terminating message line; otherwise, a message indicating that a problem was encountered is moved. A module is called to print the message. All files are closed.

EDIT-PAYROLL-DATA

This module checks for errors in:
- Plant site.
- Department code.
- Social security number.
- Tax classification.
- Pay rate.
If an error is found, the corresponding switch is set to 'Y'; otherwise, the switch is set to 'N'. The non–nesting of the test is intentional, since this allows detection of multiple errors for an input record.

PRINT-OUT-ERROR-TABLE

The error switches are checked and for all switches set to 'Y', the module to write error messages is executed.

PRINT-HEADING

The page heading is written.

PRINT-TERMINATING-MESSAGE

The terminating message line is printed.

PRINT-BAD-RECORD

A record that contains errors is printed.

WRITE-PAY-MAST-REC

A record is written to the payroll master file.

READ-PAY-FILE

The next logical record from the input file is obtained. If there are no more records on the file, a switch is set to indicate the file is exhausted.

PRINT-ERROR-MESSAGE

An error message is written.

Figure 4.4
Module descriptions for the program in Figure 4.5.

```
00001              IDENTIFICATION DIVISION.
00002          *
00003           PROGRAM-ID.
00004               EX-4-1.
00005          *****************************************************************
00006          *                                                               *
00007          *    PROGRAMMER TEAM          WALSTROM/SUMMERS/LINDAHL           *
00008          *    PROGRAM COMPLETION DATE NOVEMBER 28,1983                    *
00009          *                                                               *
00010          *                  PROGRAM SUMMARY                              *
00011          *    INPUT                                                      *
00012          *        THE INPUT FILE IS IN ASCENDING ORDER                   *
00013          *        BY SOCIAL SECURITY NUMBER. EACH INPUT RECORD CONSISTS OF*
00014          *             - CODE FOR THE PLANT LOCATION                     *
00015          *             - CODE FOR THE DEPARTMENT TO WHICH THE EMPLOYEE    *
00016          *               IS ASSIGNED                                     *
00017          *             - SOCIAL SECURITY NUMBER                          *
00018          *             - NAME                                            *
00019          *             - OTHER PERSONAL DATA                             *
00020          *             - TAX CLASSIFICATION                              *
00021          *             - PAY RATE                                        *
00022          *                                                               *
00023          *    PROCESSING                                                 *
00024          *             - THE EMPLOYEE DATA IS CHECKED FOR ERRORS IN       *
00025          *               THE PLANT LOCATION CODE, DEPARTMENT CODE,        *
00026          *               SOCIAL SECURITY NUMBER, TAX CLASSIFICATION, AND  *
00027          *               PAY RATE                                        *
00028          *             - FOR A VALID INPUT RECORD, ZERO IS MOVED TO THE   *
00029          *               YEAR-TO-DATE TOTALS FOR GROSS PAY, TAX WITHHELD  *
00030          *               AND FICA WITHHELD                               *
00031          *                                                               *
00032          *    OUTPUT                                                     *
00033          *        FOR VALID EMPLOYEE INPUT DATA A RECORD IS OUTPUT TO     *
00034          *        A SEQUENTIAL DISK FILE. THIS FILE IS ORDERED BY         *
00035          *        SOCIAL SECURITY NUMBER. EACH RECORD CONSISTS OF         *
00036          *             - CODE FOR THE PLANT LOCATION                     *
00037          *             - CODE FOR THE DEPARTMENT TO WHICH THE EMPLOYEE    *
00038          *               IS ASSIGNED                                     *
00039          *             - NAME                                            *
00040          *             - OTHER PERSONAL DATA                             *
00041          *             - TAX CLASSIFICATION                              *
00042          *             - PAY RATE                                        *
00043          *             - YEAR-TO-DATE TOTALS FOR GROSS PAY, TAX WITHHELD, *
00044          *               AND FICA WITHHELD                               *
00045          *        FOR EMPLOYEE DATA WITH ERRORS A PRINTED REPORT IS       *
00046          *        PRODUCED. THE OUTPUT CONSISTS OF                        *
00047          *             - THE INPUT RECORD                                *
00048          *             - A LIST OF ERROR MESSAGES DESCRIBING THE FIELDS   *
00049          *               WHICH WERE ERRONEOUS                            *
00050          *****************************************************************
00051          *
00052           ENVIRONMENT DIVISION.
00053          *
00054            CONFIGURATION SECTION.
00055            SOURCE-COMPUTER.
00056                IBM-370.
00057            OBJECT-COMPUTER.
00058                IBM-370.
00059            SPECIAL-NAMES.
00060                C01 IS TOP-OF-PAGE.
00061            INPUT-OUTPUT SECTION.
00062            FILE-CONTROL.
00063                SELECT PAYROLL-FILE-IN
00064                    ASSIGN TO SYS007-UR-2501-S.
00065                SELECT PAYROLL-MAST-FILE-OUT
00066                    ASSIGN TO SYS023-DA-3330-S-PAYFILE.
00067                SELECT ERROR-REPORT-PRINT-FILE
00068                    ASSIGN TO SYS009-UR-1403-S.
00069          *
00070           DATA DIVISION.
00071          *
00072            FILE SECTION.
00073            FD  PAYROLL-FILE-IN
00074                    LABEL RECORDS ARE OMITTED.
```

Figure 4.5
Data validation and creation of a sequential master file for Example 4.1.

Figure 4.5 (cont.)

```
00075          01    PAYROLL-IN-AREA                    PIC X(80).
00076          FD    PAYROLL-MAST-FILE-OUT
00077                      LABEL RECORDS ARE STANDARD
00078                      BLOCK CONTAINS 10 RECORDS.
00079          01    PAYROLL-MAST-OUT-AREA              PIC X(100).
00080          FD    ERROR-REPORT-PRINT-FILE
00081                      LABEL RECORDS ARE OMITTED.
00082          01    ERROR-LINE-OUT-AREA                PIC X(133).
00083          *
00084          WORKING-STORAGE SECTION.
00085          01    SWITCHES.
00086                02   END-OF-FILE-SW                PIC X.
00087                     88   END-OF-FILE   VALUE 'Y'.
00088          01    COUNTERS.
00089                02   ERR-SUB                       PIC 9.
00090          01    CONSTANTS.
00091                02   NUMB-OF-ERROR-MESSAGES        PIC 9 VALUE 5.
00092          01    PAYROLL-IN-REC.
00093                02   PAY-IN-PLANT-SITE             PIC 9.
00094                     88   POSSIBLE-PLANT-SITE   VALUES 1 2.
00095                02   PAY-IN-DEPT-CODE              PIC 9(2).
00096                     88   POSSIBLE-DEPT-CODE   VALUES 1 THRU 15.
00097                02   PAY-IN-SS-NUM                 PIC X(9).
00098                02   PAY-IN-EMP-NAME               PIC X(20).
00099                02   PAY-IN-PERSONAL-DATA          PIC X(42).
00100                02   PAY-IN-TAX-CLASS              PIC 9(2).
00101                02   PAY-IN-PAY-RATE               PIC 9(2)V9(2).
00102                     88   VALID-PAY-RATE   VALUES 3.35 THRU 18.75.
00103          01    PAYROLL-MAST-OUT-REC.
00104                02   PAY-OUT-PLANT-SITE            PIC S9.
00105                02   PAY-OUT-DEPT-CODE             PIC S9(2).
00106                02   PAY-OUT-SS-NUM                PIC X(9).
00107                02   PAY-OUT-EMP-NAME              PIC X(20).
00108                02   PAY-OUT-PERSONAL-DATA         PIC X(42).
00109                02   PAY-OUT-TAX-CLASS             PIC S9(2).
00110                02   PAY-OUT-PAY-RATE              PIC S9(2)V9(2).
00111                02   PAY-OUT-YTD-GROSS             PIC S9(5)V9(2).
00112                02   PAY-OUT-YTD-TAX               PIC S9(5)V9(2).
00113                02   PAY-OUT-YTD-FICA              PIC S9(4)V9(2).
00114          01    ERR-HDG-PRINT-LINE.
00115                02   FILLER                        PIC X(47) VALUE SPACES.
00116                02   FILLER                        PIC X(38)
00117                     VALUE 'LIST OF ERRORS IN PAYROLL DATA RECORDS'.
00118                02   FILLER                        PIC X(47) VALUE SPACES.
00119          01    ERR-DETAIL-PRINT-LINE-1.
00120                02   FILER                         PIC X(26) VALUE SPACES.
00121                02   BAD-REC-OUT                   PIC X(80).
00122                02   FILLER                        PIC X(26) VALUE SPACES.
00123          01    ERR-DETAIL-PRINT-LINE-2.
00124                02   FILLER                        PIC X(58) VALUE SPACES.
00125                02   ERR-MESSAGE-OUT               PIC X(17)
00126                02   FILLER                        PIC X(57) VALUE SPACES.
00127          01    TERMINATING-MSG-PRINT-LINE.
00128                02   FILLER                        PIC X(5) VALUE SPACE.
00129                02   TERMINATING-MESSAGE           PIC X(127).
00130          01    ERROR-PROCESSING-TABLES.
00131                02   ERROR-MESSAGE-SWITCH-TABLE.
00132                     03   ERROR-MESSAGE-SW
00133                          OCCURS 5 TIMES           PIC X.
00134                02   ERROR-MESSAGE-CONTENT.
00135                     03   FILLER                   PIC X(17)
00136                          VALUE 'PLANT SITE ERROR  '.
00137                     03   FILLER                   PIC X(17)
00138                          VALUE 'DEPT CODE ERROR   '.
00139                     03   FILLER                   PIC X(17)
00140                          VALUE 'SOC SEC NUM ERROR'.
00141                     03   FILLER                   PIC X(17)
00142                          VALUE 'TAX CLASS ERROR   '.
00143                     03   FILLER                   PIC X(17)
00144                          VALUE 'PAY RATE ERROR    '.
00145                02   ERROR-MESSAGE-TABLE REDEFINES ERROR-MESSAGE-CONTENT.
00146                     03   ERROR-MESSAGE
00147                          OCCURS 5 TIMES           PIC X(17).
00148          *
00149          PROCEDURE DIVISION.
00150          *
00151          MAST-FILE-CREATE-CONTROL.
00152                PERFORM START-UP.
00153                PERFORM CREATE-PAYROLL-MAST
00154                     UNTIL END-OF-FILE.
00155                PERFORM FINISH-UP.
00156                STOP RUN.
```

Figure 4.5 (*cont.*)

```
00157          *
00158              START-UP.
00159                  OPEN INPUT PAYROLL-FILE-IN
00160                       OUTPUT PAYROLL-MAST-FILE-OUT
00161                              ERROR-REPORT-PRINT-FILE.
00162                  MOVE 'N' TO END-OF-FILE-SW.
00163                  PERFORM PRINT-HEADING.
00164                  PERFORM READ-PAY-FILE.
00165          *
00166              CREATE-PAYROLL-MAST.
00167                  PERFORM EDIT-PAYROLL-DATA.
00168                  IF (ERROR-MESSAGE-SWITCH-TABLE IS NOT EQUAL TO ALL 'N')
00169                      MOVE PAYROLL-IN-REC TO BAD-REC-OUT
00170                      PERFORM PRINT-BAD-RECORD
00171                      PERFORM PRINT-OUT-ERROR-TABLE VARYING ERR-SUB FROM 1 BY 1
00172                          UNTIL ERR-SUB IS GREATER THAN NUMB-OF-ERROR-MESSAGES
00173                  ELSE
00174                      MOVE PAY-IN-PLANT-SITE TO PAY-OUT-PLANT-SITE
00175                      MOVE PAY-IN-DEPT-CODE TO PAY-OUT-DEPT-CODE
00176                      MOVE PAY-IN-SS-NUM TO PAY-OUT-SS-NUM
00177                      MOVE PAY-IN-EMP-NAME TO PAY-OUT-EMP-NAME
00178                      MOVE PAY-IN-PERSONAL-DATA TO PAY-OUT-PERSONAL-DATA
00179                      MOVE PAY-IN-TAX-CLASS TO PAY-OUT-TAX-CLASS
00180                      MOVE PAY-IN-PAY-RATE TO PAY-OUT-PAY-RATE
00181                      MOVE ZEROS TO PAY-OUT-YTD-GROSS
00182                                   PAY-OUT-YTD-TAX
00183                                   PAY-OUT-YTD-FICA
00184                      PERFORM WRITE-PAY-MAST-REC.
00185                  PERFORM READ-PAY-FILE.
00186          *
00187              FINISH-UP.
00188                  IF END-OF-FILE
00189                      MOVE 'PAYROLL MASTER FILE CREATED'
00190                          TO TERMINATING-MESSAGE
00191                  ELSE
00192                      MOVE 'PROBLEM ENCOUNTERED CREATING PAYROLL MASTER FILE'
00193                          TO TERMINATING-MESSAGE.
00194                  PERFORM PRINT-TERMINATING-MESSAGE.
00195                  CLOSE PAYROLL-FILE-IN
00196                        PAYROLL-MAST-FILE-OUT
00197                        ERROR-REPORT-PRINT-FILE.
00198          *
00199              EDIT-PAYROLL-DATA.
00200                  IF (PAY-IN-PLANT-SITE IS NOT NUMERIC)
00201                      MOVE 'Y' TO  ERROR-MESSAGE-SW (1)
00202                  ELSE
00203                      IF NOT POSSIBLE-PLANT-SITE
00204                          MOVE 'Y' TO ERROR-MESSAGE-SW (1)
00205                      ELSE
00206                          MOVE 'N' TO ERROR-MESSAGE-SW (1).
00207                  IF (PAY-IN-DEPT-CODE IS NOT NUMERIC)
00208                      MOVE 'Y' TO ERROR-MESSAGE-SW (2)
00209                  ELSE
00210                      IF NOT POSSIBLE-DEPT-CODE
00211                          MOVE 'Y' TO ERROR-MESSAGE-SW (2)
00212                      ELSE
00213                          MOVE 'N' TO ERROR-MESSAGE-SW (2).
00214                  IF (PAY-IN-SS-NUM IS NOT NUMERIC)
00215                      MOVE 'Y' TO ERROR-MESSAGE-SW (3)
00216                  ELSE
00217                      MOVE 'N' TO ERROR-MESSAGE-SW (3).
00218                  IF (PAY-IN-TAX-CLASS IS NOT NUMERIC)
00219                      MOVE 'Y' TO ERROR-MESSAGE-SW (4)
00220                  ELSE
00221                      MOVE 'N' TO ERROR-MESSAGE-SW (4).
00222                  IF (PAY-IN-PAY-RATE IS NOT NUMERIC)
00223                      MOVE 'Y' TO ERROR-MESSAGE-SW (5)
00224                  ELSE
00225                      IF NOT VALID-PAY-RATE
00226                          MOVE 'Y' TO ERROR-MESSAGE-SW (5)
00227                      ELSE
00228                          MOVE 'N' TO ERROR-MESSAGE-SW (5).
00229          *
00230              PRINT-OUT-ERROR-TABLE.
00231                  IF (ERROR-MESSAGE-SW (ERR-SUB) IS EQUAL TO 'Y')
00232                      MOVE ERROR-MESSAGE (ERR-SUB) TO ERR-MESSAGE-OUT
00233                      PERFORM PRINT-ERROR-MESSAGE.
00234          *
00235              PRINT-HEADING.
00236                  WRITE ERROR-LINE-OUT-AREA FROM ERR-HDG-PRINT-LINE
00237                      AFTER ADVANCING TOP-OF-PAGE.
```

Figure 4.5 (*cont.*)

```
00238          *                              .
00239           PRINT-TERMINATING-MESSAGE.
00240               WRITE ERROR-LINE-OUT-AREA FROM TERMINATING-MSG-PRINT-LINE
00241                    AFTER ADVANCING TOP-OF-PAGE.
00242          *
00243           PRINT-BAD-RECORD.
00244               WRITE ERROR-LINE-OUT-AREA FROM ERR-DETAIL-PRINT-LINE-1
00245                    AFTER ADVANCING 3 LINES.
00246          *
00247           WRITE-PAY-MAST-REC.
00248               WRITE PAYROLL-MAST-OUT-AREA FROM PAYROLL-MAST-OUT-REC.
00249          *
00250           READ-PAY-FILE.
00251               READ PAYROLL-FILE-IN INTO PAYROLL-IN-REC
00252                    AT END MOVE 'Y' TO END-OF-FILE-SW.
00253          *
00254           PRINT-ERROR-MESSAGE.
00255               WRITE ERROR-LINE-OUT-AREA FROM ERR-DETAIL-PRINT-LINE-2
00256                    AFTER ADVANCING 1 LINES.
```

CONTROL-BREAK PROCESSING

In our next example, we will be looking at a sequential processing technique known as *control-break processing*. Records with the same key value must be grouped together. Control-break processing involves testing each key value in turn until a change in key values is detected. The change in key values, called a *control break*, signals the end of one group and the beginning of the next. Records in the file must be ordered in key value sequence. For example, assuming name is used as the key value, a file might contain the following records:

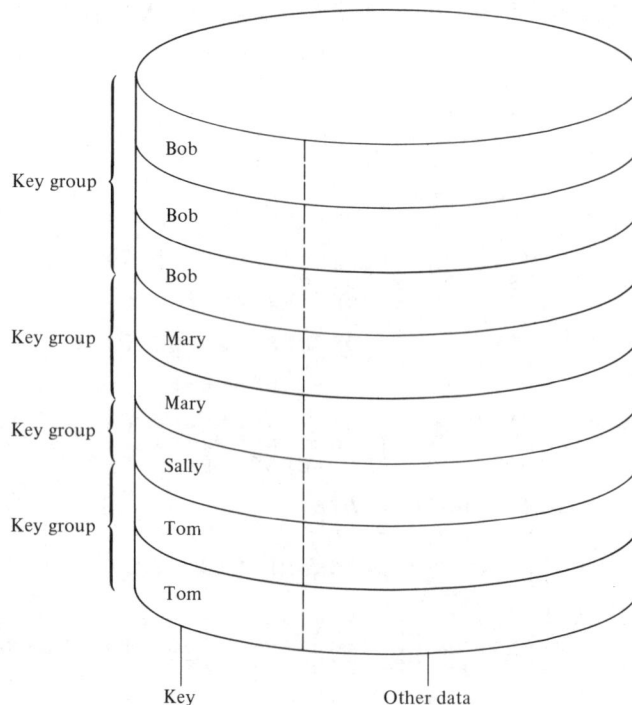

The individual records will require processing of a certain type. In addition, special processing will be required when all records in a key group have been processed. Special processing may also be needed at the start of the key group. Suppose the record contains the credit hours and quality points earned by a student in each of several courses. Special processing at the start of a group might involve setting total hours and total quality points to zero. The processing of a record would add hours and quality points to the totals. Special processing at the end of a group then could compute the grade point average for the semester.

Example 4.2

Employees of Mega-Tronics may work on several different projects during a pay period. Each employee has a time card, which contains the total time worked for a particular project. These data must be combined and used to create a file that will contain the total hours worked by each employee for the week.

The employee time-card file will be ordered on social security number; consequently, this is the key value field that will be tested for control breaks.

The program organization for processing employee time cards is given in Figure 4.6. Figure 4.7 contains the individual module logic, and the actual program listing is given in Figure 4.8.

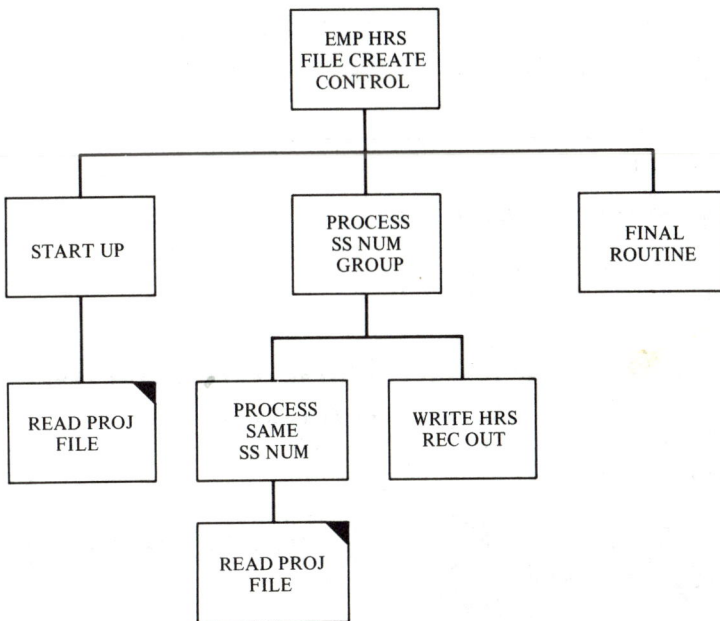

Figure 4.6
Structure chart for the program in Figure 4.8.

EMP-HRS-FILE-CREATE-CONTROL

This module causes the execution of START–UP, PROCESS–SS–NUM–GROUP, and FINAL–ROUTINE. It also terminates execution of the program.

START-UP

All files are opened. A switch is set to indicate that there are input data. The overall company total hours worked is set to zero. The input file is read.

PROCESS-SS-NUM-GROUP

Employee personal data are copied to the output record. The employee hours are initialized to zero. A switch is set to indicate that the group is not processed. Then the module PROCESS–SAME–SS–NUM is executed until a new SS number is found on the input file. The record constructed is written and the company total is incremented by the number of hours for this employee.

FINAL-ROUTINE

If the output file has been successfully created, the company total is written; otherwise, an error message is written. All files are closed.

PROCESS-SAME-SS-NUM

The total hours worked for the current employee are incremented by the hours for the current project. A new input record is read. If it is a different SS number from that currently in the output record, a switch is set to indicate that the group of records for an employee in output record is ended.

WRITE-HRS-REC-OUT

A record is written to the output file.

READ-PROJ-FILE

Obtains the next input record and sets a switch to terminate processing when all records have been read.

Figure 4.7
Module descriptions for the program in Figure 4.8.

```
00001          IDENTIFICATION DIVISION.
00002     *
00003          PROGRAM-ID.
00004             EX-4-2.
00005     ****************************************************************
00006     *                                                              *
00007     *   PROGRAMMER TEAM           WALSTROM/SUMMERS/LINDAHL          *
00008     *   PROGRAM COMPLETION DATE NOVEMBER 28,1983                   *
00009     *                                                              *
00010     *              PROGRAM SUMMARY                                 *
00011     *   INPUT                                                      *
00012     *       THE INPUT FILE IS A SEQUENTIAL FILE, ORDERED BY        *
00013     *       SOCIAL SECURITY NUMBER. THERE MAY BE MULTIPLE RECORDS  *
00014     *       FOR AN EMPLOYEE. EACH RECORD CONSISTS OF               *
00015     *          - SOCIAL SECURITY NUMBER                            *
00016     *          - TASK PERFORMED BY EMPLOYEE                        *
00017     *          - PROJECT BUDGET NUMBER                             *
00018     *          - HOURS WORKED BY EMPLOYEE FOR THE TASK             *
00019     *            AND PROJECT                                       *
00020     *                                                              *
00021     *   PROCESSING                                                 *
00022     *          - FOR EACH EMPLOYEE THE TOTAL NUMBER OF HOURS       *
00023     *            WORKED IS ACCUMULATED                             *
00024     *          - THE TOTAL NUMBER OF HOURS WORKED BY ALL           *
00025     *            EMPLOYEES IS ACCUMULATED                          *
00026     *                                                              *
```

Figure 4.8
Control-break processing and creation of a sequential transaction file for Example 4.2.

Figure 4.8 (cont.)

```
00027      *      OUTPUT                                                    *
00028      *          THE OUTPUT FILE IS A SEQUENTIAL FILE ORDERED BY       *
00029      *          SOCIAL SECURITY NUMBER. EACH RECORD CONSISTS OF       *
00030      *              - SOCIAL SECURITY NUMBER                          *
00031      *              - TOTAL HOURS WORKED                              *
00032      *          A PRINTED REPORT IS GENERATED. IT CONTAINS           *
00033      *              - THE TOTAL NUMBER OF HOURS WORKED BY ALL         *
00034      *                EMPLOYEES                                       *
00035      ****************************************************************
00036      *
00037       ENVIRONMENT DIVISION.
00038      *
00039       CONFIGURATION SECTION.
00040       SOURCE-COMPUTER.
00041           IBM-370.
00042       OBJECT-COMPUTER.
00043           IBM-370.
00044       INPUT-OUTPUT SECTION.
00045       FILE-CONTROL.
00046           SELECT HRS-WORKED-PAY-PERIOD-FILE-OUT
00047               ASSIGN TO SYS023-DA-3330-S-THRSFIL.
00048           SELECT HRS-WORKED-PROJ-FILE-IN
00049               ASSIGN TO SYS023-DA-3330-S-PHRSFIL.
00050      *
00051       DATA DIVISION.
00052      *
00053       FILE SECTION.
00054       FD  HRS-WORKED-PAY-PERIOD-FILE-OUT
00055               LABEL RECORDS ARE STANDARD
00056               BLOCK CONTAINS 10 RECORDS.
00057       01  HRS-WORKED-OUT-AREA            PIC X(13).
00058       FD  HRS-WORKED-PROJ-FILE-IN
00059               LABEL RECORDS ARE STANDARD
00060               BLOCK CONTAINS 20 RECORDS.
00061       01  HRS-WORKED-PROJ-IN-AREA        PIC X(20).
00062      *
00063       WORKING-STORAGE SECTION.
00064       01  SWITCHES.
00065           02  END-OF-FILE-SW                 PIC X.
00066               88  NO-MORE-RECORDS VALUE 'Y'.
00067           02  END-OF-SS-NUM-GROUP-SW     PIC X.
00068               88  NEW-SS-NUM         VALUE 'Y'.
00069       01  COMPANY-TOTALS.
00070           02  COMPANY-HRS-WORKED-TOTAL   PIC S9(6)V9(2).
00071           02  COMPANY-HRS-DISPLAY-TOTAL  PIC -Z(6).9(2).
00072       01  HRS-WORKED-IN-REC.
00073           02  HRS-IN-SS-NUM              PIC X(9).
00074           02  HRS-IN-TASK-CODE           PIC S9(2).
00075           02  HRS-IN-PROJ-NUM            PIC 9(5).
00076           02  HRS-IN-HRS-WORKED          PIC S9(2)V9(2).
00077       01  HRS-WORKED-OUT-REC.
00078           02  HRS-OUT-SS-NUM             PIC X(9).
00079           02  HRS-OUT-HRS-WORKED         PIC S9(2)V9(2).
00080      *
00081       PROCEDURE DIVISION.
00082      *
00083       EMP-HRS-FILE-CREATE-CONTROL.
00084           PERFORM START-UP.
00085           PERFORM PROCESS-SS-NUM-GROUP UNTIL NO-MORE-RECORDS.
00086           PERFORM FINAL-ROUTINE.
00087           STOP RUN.
00088      *
00089       START-UP.
00090           OPEN INPUT HRS-WORKED-PROJ-FILE-IN
00091                OUTPUT HRS-WORKED-PAY-PERIOD-FILE-OUT.
00092           MOVE 'N' TO END-OF-FILE-SW.
00093           PERFORM READ-PROJ-FILE.
00094           MOVE 0 TO COMPANY-HRS-WORKED-TOTAL.
00095      *
00096       PROCESS-SS-NUM-GROUP.
00097           MOVE HRS-IN-SS-NUM TO HRS-OUT-SS-NUM.
00098           MOVE 0 TO HRS-OUT-HRS-WORKED.
00099           MOVE 'N' TO END-OF-SS-NUM-GROUP-SW.
00100           PERFORM PROCESS-SAME-SS-NUM UNTIL NEW-SS-NUM.
00101           PERFORM WRITE-HRS-REC-OUT.
00102           ADD HRS-OUT-HRS-WORKED TO COMPANY-HRS-WORKED-TOTAL.
```

Figure 4.8 (*cont.*)

```
00103          *
00104              FINAL-ROUTINE.
00105                  IF NO-MORE-RECORDS
00106                      MOVE COMPANY-HRS-WORKED-TOTAL TO
00107                          COMPANY-HRS-DISPLAY-TOTAL
00108                  DISPLAY 'HOURS FOR ALL WORKERS '
00109                          COMPANY-HRS-DISPLAY-TOTAL
00110                  DISPLAY 'HOURS WORKED FILE PROCESSING COMPLETE'.
00111              CLOSE HRS-WORKED-PROJ-FILE-IN
00112                      HRS-WORKED-PAY-PERIOD-FILE-OUT.
00113          *
00114              PROCESS-SAME-SS-NUM.
00115                  ADD HRS-IN-HRS-WORKED TO HRS-OUT-HRS-WORKED.
00116                  PERFORM READ-PROJ-FILE.
00117                  IF HRS-IN-SS-NUM IS NOT EQUAL TO HRS-OUT-SS-NUM
00118                      MOVE 'Y' TO END-OF-SS-NUM-GROUP-SW.
00119          *
00120              WRITE-HRS-REC-OUT.
00121                  WRITE HRS-WORKED-OUT-AREA FROM HRS-WORKED-OUT-REC.
00122          *
00123              READ-PROJ-FILE.
00124                  READ HRS-WORKED-PROJ-FILE-IN INTO HRS-WORKED-IN-REC
00125                      AT END MOVE 'Y' TO END-OF-FILE-SW,
00126                          END-OF-SS-NUM-GROUP-SW.
```

MATCHING ON KEY FIELDS

Let us now turn our attention to a situation that requires that a file, usually referred to as a *transaction file*, be matched on the key field that is contained in its records to the key field that is contained in the records of the *master file*. To illustrate the concept of matching on key fields, assume the following files and keys:

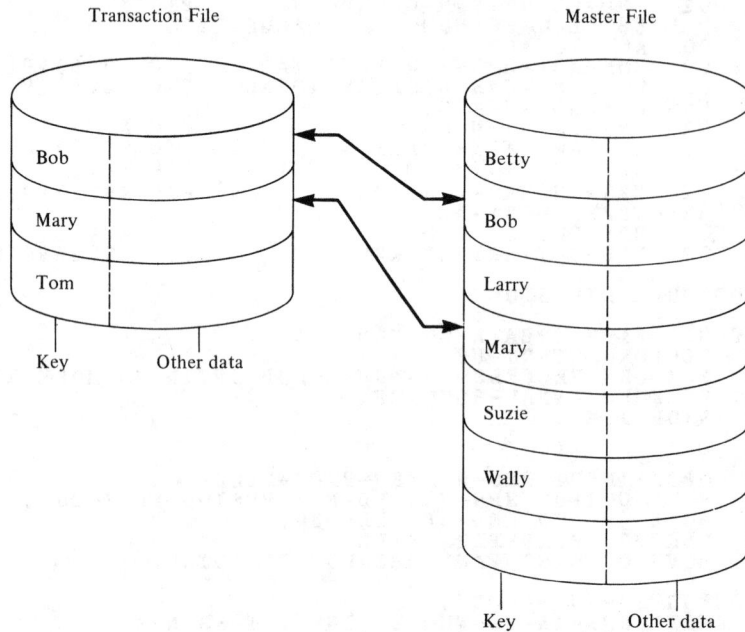

Since there is a record in both files for BOB and MARY, the required processing of those records can take place. However, TOM's transaction record cannot be processed, since he has no master record, whereas BETTY, LARRY, and SUZIE's master records will not be changed because they have no transaction record. Any updating of a master file will require this type of processing. In Example 4.3, we will look at a specific instance of updating a sequential master file using the key field matching technique.

Example 4.3

As part of the maintenance of the payroll master file, Mega's DP department will need to update the year-to-date totals on the master file at the end of each pay period. In addition, the accounting department wants a payroll register listing of all employees and their current payroll information. As an internal audit measure, check printing is done in another program and will not be of concern in this example.

The overall program organization is given in the structure chart of Figure 4.10. The logic of the program is given in the module descriptions of Figure 4.11, and the program listing appears in Figure 4.12.

The output format is given in Figure 4.9. We would like to point out the following specific features in the program:

1. The master file PAYROLL-MAST-FILE-IO must be OPENed as I-O (line 263), which allows records to be READ and to REWRITE them back to the file.
2. ALL 'N' in line 265 generates a string of N's the same length as SWITCHES. This single statement initializes each character position of SWITCHES to 'N'.
3. The statements on line 436 and 441 insure that whichever of the two files is completely read first will always have the highest key value and therefore will not be accessed again.
4. When the execution of the READ statement on line 435 is followed by the execution of the REWRITE statement on line 445 without a key change, the effect is to replace (update) a record on PAYROLL-MAST-FILE-IO.

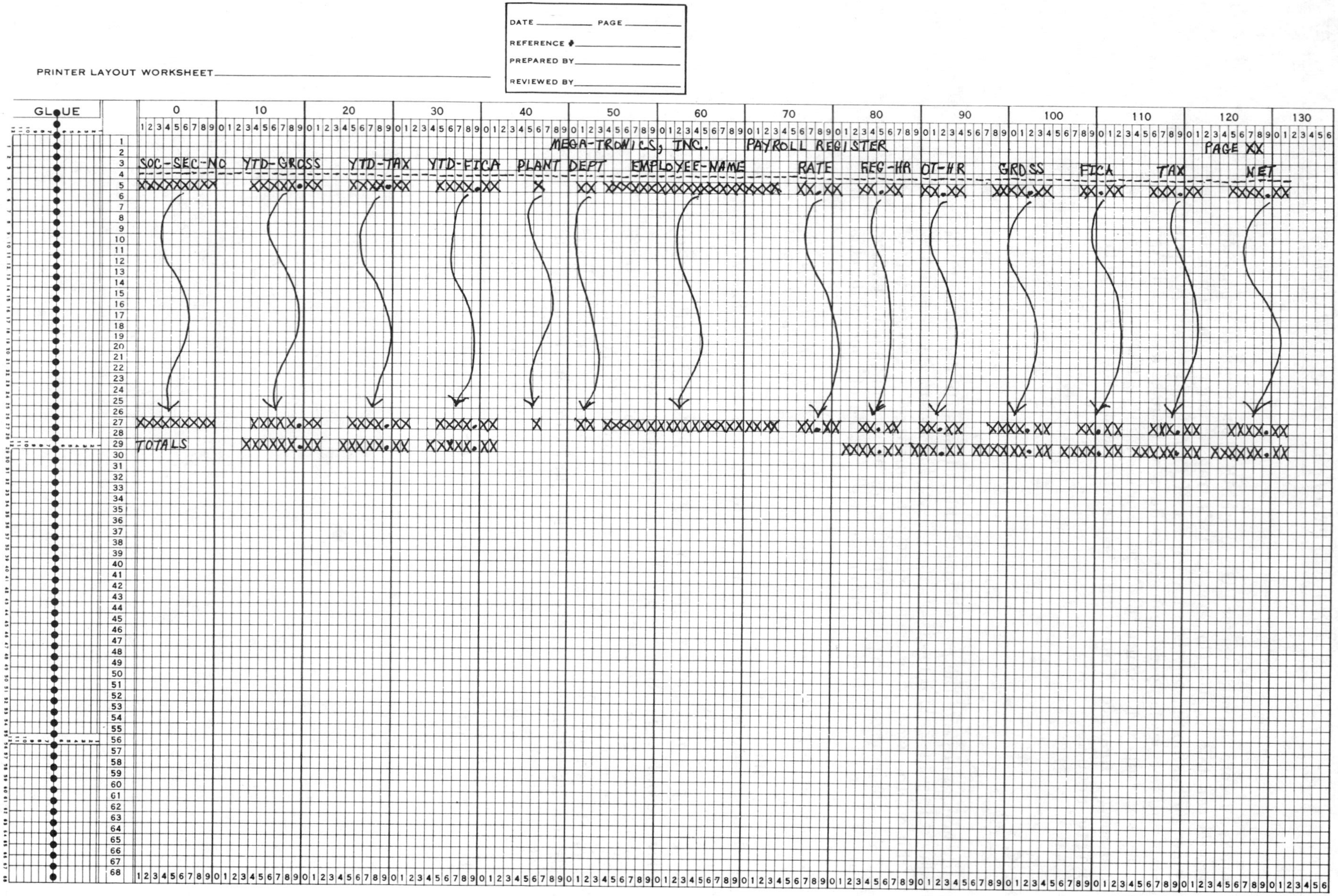

Figure 4.9
Printer layout for the program in Figure 4.12.

96

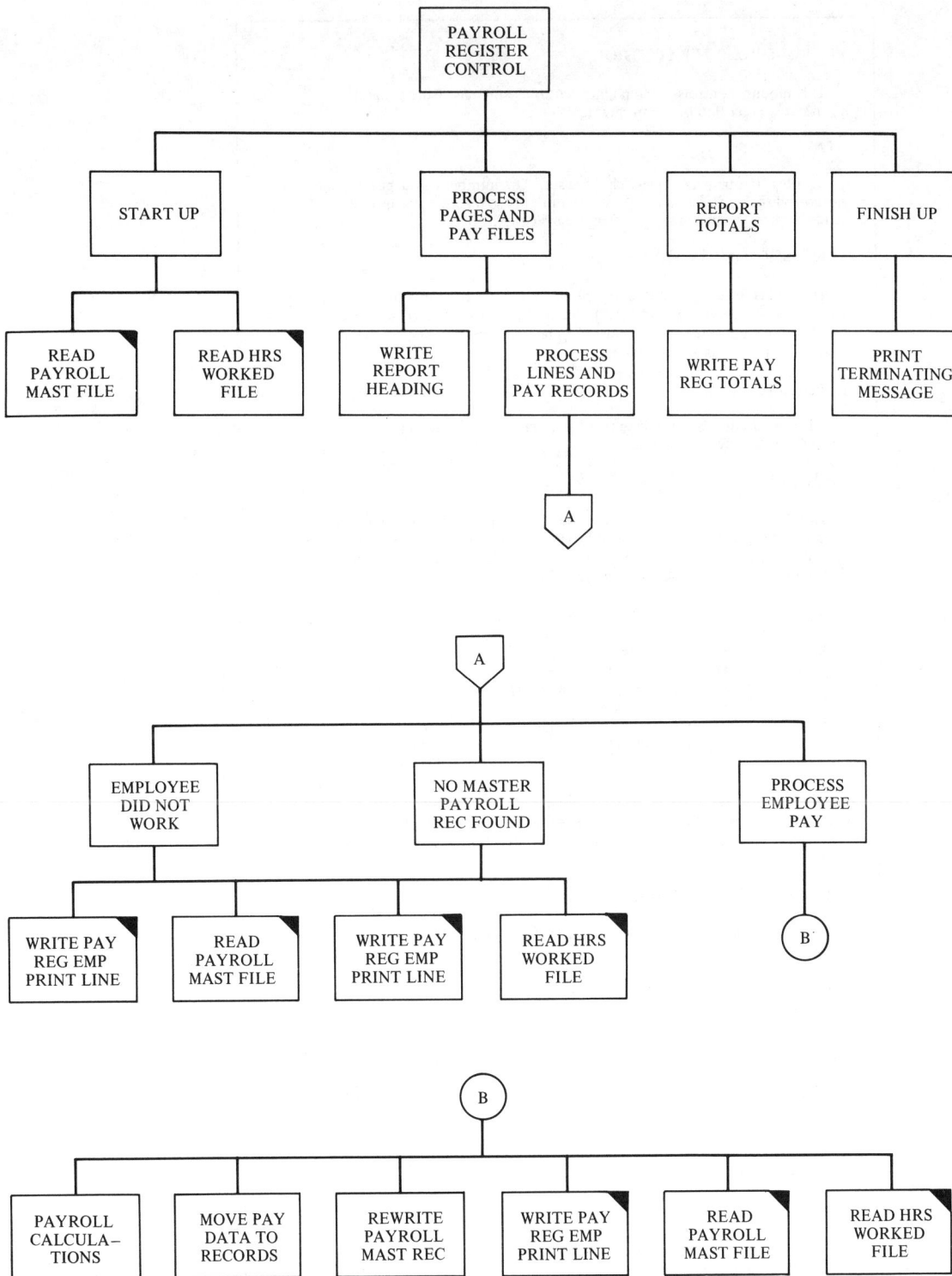

Figure 4.10
Structure chart for the program in Figure 4.12.

PAYROLL-REGISTER-CONTROL

This module controls the overall execution sequence of the program. It terminates execution of the program.

START–UP

All files are opened. All switches are set. The number of output pages is initialized to 1. All company totals are initialized to zero. The modules to read the master and transaction files are executed.

PROCESS-PAGES-AND-PAY-FILES

The report heading module is executed. The line counter is set to 1; the page counter is incremented by 1. Lines are then processed until a page is filled or both input files are exhausted. The page counter is moved to the output area. The page–full switch is reset.

REPORT-TOTALS

All company totals are moved to edited fields for output. The module to write the total line is executed.

FINISH-UP

Switches are tested to determine if the files are processed to completion. If so, a message indicating a successful file update is moved to a terminating message line; otherwise, a message indicating that problems were encountered is moved. A module is called to print the message. All files are closed.

PROCESS-LINES-AND-PAY-RECORDS

An employee is in one of three categories.
1. Not in pay status this period.
2. In pay status but not yet on the master file.
3. In pay status and on the master file.
This module tests to determine which category an employee is in. If an employee is in category 1, a module is called to process employees who did not work. If an employee is in category 2, a module is called to process employees who have no master record. For employees in category 3, a module is called to process employee pay. The line count is incremented by 1. If the page is full, the page–full switch is set to indicate this condition. Switches are tested to determine if all records in the master and transactions files have been read.

EMPLOYEE-DID-NOT-WORK

Data fields and a message indicating that the employee did not work are moved to the output record to be printed. YTD totals from the employee's master record are added to the company totals. The modules to write a line to the payroll register and to read the master file are executed.

NO-MASTER-PAYROLL-REC-FOUND

Social security number and a message indicating that no payroll master record was found are moved to an output line to be printed. Appropriate data fields in the output line are set to zero and spaces are moved to the name field. The modules to write a line to the payroll register and to read the transaction file are called.

PROCESS-EMPLOYEE-PAY

Modules are called to do the following:
- Compute payroll calculations.
- Move payroll data to output records.
- Rewrite the payroll master record.
- Write a line to the payroll register.
- Read the payroll master file.
- Read the hours worked transaction file.

Figure 4.11
Module descriptions for the program in Figure 4.12.

Figure 4.11 (cont.)

PAYROLL-CALCULATIONS

The employee's pay is computed, along with the tax and FICA. The employee YTD totals are updated, as are the company totals.

MOVE-PAY-DATA-TO-RECORDS

The data fields are moved to the output record for printing.

WRITE-REPORT-HEADING

The report title, and the page and column headings are printed.

WRITE-PAY-REG-TOTALS

The company totals are printed.

PRINT-TERMINATING-MESSAGE

The terminating message line is printed.

WRITE-PAY-REG-EMP-PRINT-LINE

A line is printed on the payroll register.

READ-PAYROLL-MAST-FILE

The master file is read. If there are no more records, the key field is set to HIGH-VALUES so that its key value will always be high.

READ–HRS–WORKED–FILE

The transaction file is read. If there are no more transactions, the key field is set to HIGH-VALUES so that its key value will always be high.

REWRITE-PAYROLL-MAST-REC

The updated employee record is written back to the master file.

```
00001          IDENTIFICATION DIVISION.
00002     *
00003          PROGRAM-ID.
00004             EX-4-3.
00005     ****************************************************************
00006     *                                                              *
00007     *    PROGRAMMER TEAM           WALSTROM/SUMMERS/LINDAHL         *
00008     *    PROGRAM COMPLETION DATE DECEMBER 8, 1983.                 *
00009     *                                                              *
00010     *                   PROGRAM SUMMARY                            *
00011     *    INPUT                                                     *
00012     *        INPUT FILES USED ARE THE PAYROLL MASTER FILE AND      *
00013     *        THE HOURS WORKED FILE. BOTH ARE ORDERED ON THE        *
00014     *        SOCIAL SECURITY NUMBER.                               *
00015     *        PAYROLL MASTER RECORDS CONSIST OF                     *
00016     *            - CODE FOR THE PLANT LOCATION                     *
00017     *            - CODE FOR THE DEPARTMENT TO WHICH THE EMPLOYEE   *
00018     *              IS ASSIGNED                                     *
00019     *            - SOCIAL SECURITY NUMBER                          *
00020     *            - NAME                                           *
00021     *            - OTHER PERSONAL DATA                             *
00022     *            - TAX CLASSIFICATION                             *
00023     *            - PAY RATE                                       *
00024     *            - YEAR-TO-DATE TOTALS FOR GROSS PAY,TAX WITHHELD, *
00025     *              AND FICA WITHHELD                               *
00026     *        HOURS WORKED RECORDS CONSIST OF                       *
00027     *            - SOCIAL SECURITY NUMBER                          *
00028     *            - TOTAL HOURS WORKED                             *
00029     *                                                              *
00030     *    PROCESSING                                                *
00031     *        THE STATUS OF EACH SOCIAL SECURITY NUMBER IS DETERMINED*
00032     *            - ONLY ON PAYROLL MASTER FILE                     *
00033     *            - ONLY ON HOURS WORKED FILE                       *
00034     *            - ON BOTH                                         *
00035     *        FOR EMPLOYEES APPEARING ON A SINGLE FILE A STATUS     *
00036     *        MESSAGE IS DETERMINED. FOR AN EMPLOYEE ON BOTH FILES  *
00037     *            - THE GROSS PAY FOR PAY PERIOD IS COMPUTED        *
00038     *            - THE TAX FOR PAY PERIOD IS COMPUTED             *
00039     *            - THE FICA FOR PAY PERIOD IS COMPUTED            *
00040     *            - THE NET PAY FOR PAY PERIOD IS COMPUTED         *
00041     *            - YEAR-TO-DATE TOTALS FOR GROSS PAY, TAX WITHHELD *
00042     *              AND FICA WITHHELD ARE UPDATED                   *
00043     *        COMPANY TOTALS ARE ACCUMULATED FOR                    *
00044     *            - YEAR-TO-DATE GROSS PAY, TAX WITHHELD,           *
00045     *              FICA WITHHELD                                   *
00046     *            - PAY PERIOD GROSS PAY, TAX WITHHELD,            *
00047     *              FICA WITHHELD, NET PAY, REGULAR HOURS WORKED,   *
00048     *              OVERTIME HOURS WORKED                          *
00049     *                                                              *
00050     *    OUTPUT                                                    *
00051     *        AN UPDATED PAYROLL MASTER FILE IS PRODUCED.           *
00052     *        A PRINTED REPORT IS PRODUCED. FOR AN EMPLOYEE ON      *
00053     *        BOTH FILES OUTPUT CONSISTS OF                         *
00054     *            - SOCIAL SECURITY NUMBER                          *
00055     *            - YEAR-TO-DATE GROSS TAX FICA                     *
00056     *            - PLANT LOCATION CODE                             *
00057     *            - DEPARTMENT CODE                                *
00058     *            - NAME                                           *
00059     *            - PAY RATE                                       *
00060     *            - REGULAR AND OVERTIME HOURS                      *
00061     *            - PAY PERIOD GROSS TAX FICA NET                  *
00062     *        OTHER EMPLOYEE OUTPUT CONSISTS OF                     *
00063     *            - SOCIAL SECURITY NUMBER                          *
00064     *            - STATUS MESSAGE                                 *
00065     *        COMPANY OUTPUT CONSISTS OF                            *
00066     *            - YEAR-TO-DATE GROSS TAX FICA                     *
00067     *            - REGULAR AND OVERTIME HOURS                      *
00068     *            - PAY PERIOD GROSS FICA TAX NET                  *
00069     ****************************************************************
00070     *
00071          ENVIRONMENT DIVISION.
```

Figure 4.12
Updating a sequential master file and generating a payroll register for Example 4.3.

Figure 4.12 (*cont.*)

```
00072             *
00073               CONFIGURATION SECTION.
00074               SOURCE-COMPUTER.
00075                  IBM-370.
00076               OBJECT-COMPUTER.
00077                  IBM-370.
00078               SPECIAL-NAMES.
00079                  C01 IS TO-TOP-OF-PAGE.
00080               INPUT-OUTPUT SECTION.
00081               FILE-CONTROL.
00082                  SELECT HRS-WORKED-PAY-PERIOD-FILE-IN
00083                      ASSIGN TO SYS023-DA-3330-S-THRSFIL.
00084                  SELECT PAYROLL-MAST-FILE-IO
00085                      ASSIGN TO SYS023-DA-3330-S-PAYFILE.
00086                  SELECT PAYROLL-REGISTER-REPORT-FILE
00087                      ASSIGN TO SYS009-UR-1403-S.
00088             *
00089               DATA DIVISION.
00090             *
00091               FILE SECTION.
00092               FD  HRS-WORKED-PAY-PERIOD-FILE-IN
00093                      LABEL RECORDS ARE STANDARD
00094                      BLOCK CONTAINS 10 RECORDS.
00095               01  HRS-WORKED-IN-AREA           PIC X(13).
00096               FD  PAYROLL-MAST-FILE-IO
00097                      LABEL RECORDS ARE STANDARD
00098                      BLOCK CONTAINS 10 RECORDS.
00099               01  PAY-MAST-IO-AREA             PIC X(100).
00100               FD  PAYROLL-REGISTER-REPORT-FILE
00101                      LABEL RECORDS ARE OMITTED.
00102               01  PAY-REG-REPORT-AREA          PIC X(133).
00103             *
00104               WORKING-STORAGE SECTION.
00105               01  SWITCHES.
00106                   02  END-OF-HRS-WORKED-FILE-SW    PIC X.
00107                       88  END-OF-HRS-WORKED-FILE   VALUE 'Y'.
00108                   02  END-OF-PAYROLL-MAST-FILE-SW PIC X.
00109                       88  END-OF-PAYROLL-MAST-FILE  VALUE 'Y'.
00110                   02  STOP-PROCESSING-SW          PIC X.
00111                       88  PROCESSING-SHOULD-STOP   VALUE 'Y'.
00112                   02  PAGE-IS-FULL-SW             PIC X.
00113                       88  PAGE-IS-FULL            VALUE 'Y'.
00114                   02  INVALID-REWRITE-PAY-MAST-SW PIC X.
00115                       88  INVALID-REWRITE-PAY-MAST VALUE 'Y'.
00116               01  COUNTERS.
00117                   02  PAGE-COUNT                  PIC S9(2).
00118                   02  LINE-COUNT                  PIC S9(2).
00119               01  CONSTANTS.
00120                   02  MAX-REG-HRS                 PIC S9(2)    VALUE +40.
00121                   02  OVERTIME-ADJUSTMENT         PIC S9V9     VALUE +1.5.
00122                   02  MAX-SS-WITHHOLD             PIC S9(5)    VALUE +29700.
00123                   02  SS-WITHHOLD-RATE            PIC SV9(3)   VALUE +.067.
00124                   02  TAXABLE-INCOME-ADJUSTMENT   PIC S9(2)    VALUE +13.
00125                   02  EST-FED-TAX-RATE            PIC SV9(2)   VALUE +.18.
00126                   02  PAGE-SIZE                   PIC S9(2)    VALUE +55.
00127               01  CALCULATION-WORK-AREAS.
00128                   02  EMPLOYEE-PAY-CALCULATION-AREA.
00129                       03  EMP-YTD-GROSS           PIC S9(5)V9(2).
00130                       03  EMP-YTD-TAX             PIC S9(4)V9(2).
00131                       03  EMP-YTD-FICA            PIC S9(4)V9(2).
00132                       03  EMP-REG-HR              PIC S9(2)V9(2).
00133                       03  EMP-OT-HR               PIC S9(2)V9(2).
00134                       03  EMP-GROSS               PIC S9(4)V9(2).
00135                       03  EMP-FICA                PIC S9(2)V9(2).
00136                       03  EMP-TAX                 PIC S9(3)V9(2).
00137                       03  EMP-NET                 PIC S9(4)V9(2).
00138                   02  CUMMULATIVE-TOTALS.
00139                       03  TOTAL-YTD-GROSS         PIC S9(7)V9(2).
00140                       03  TOTAL-YTD-TAX           PIC S9(5)V9(2).
00141                       03  TOTAL-YTD-FICA          PIC S9(5)V9(2).
00142                       03  TOTAL-REG-HR            PIC S9(4)V9(2).
00143                       03  TOTAL-OT-HR             PIC S9(4)V9(2).
00144                       03  TOTAL-GROSS             PIC S9(6)V9(2).
00145                       03  TOTAL-FICA              PIC S9(4)V9(2).
00146                       03  TOTAL-TAX               PIC S9(5)V9(2).
00147                       03  TOTAL-NET               PIC S9(6)V9(2).
```

Figure 4.12 (*cont.*)

```
00148                 01   HRS-WORKED-IN-REC.
00149                      02   HRS-IN-SS-NUM                  PIC X(9).
00150                      02   HRS-IN-HRS-WORKED              PIC S9(2)V9(2).
00151                 01   PAY-MAST-IO-REC.
00152                      02   PAY-IO-PLANT-SITE              PIC S9.
00153                      02   PAY-IO-DEPT-CODE               PIC S9(2).
00154                      02   PAY-IO-SS-NUM                  PIC X(9).
00155                      02   PAY-IO-EMP-NAME                PIC X(20).
00156                      02   PAY-IO-PERSONAL-DATA           PIC X(42).
00157                      02   PAY-IO-TAX-CLASS               PIC S9(2).
00158                      02   PAY-IO-PAY-RATE                PIC S9(2)V9(2).
00159                      02   PAY-IO-YTD-GROSS               PIC S9(5)V9(2).
00160                      02   PAY-IO-YTD-TAX                 PIC S9(5)V9(2).
00161                      02   PAY-IO-YTD-FICA                PIC S9(4)V9(2).
00162                 01   PAY-REG-HDG-LINE-1.
00163                      02   FILLER                         PIC X(47) VALUE SPACE.
00164                      02   FILLER                         PIC X(39)
00165                           VALUE 'MEGA-TRONICS, INC.    PAYROLL REGISTER'.
00166                      02   FILLER                         PIC X(35) VALUE SPACE.
00167                      02   FILLER                         PIC X(4)  VALUE 'PAGE'.
00168                      02   PAY-REG-PAGE-NUMBER            PIC Z9.
00169                      02   FILLER                         PIC X(4)  VALUE SPACE.
00170                 01   PAY-REG-HDG-LINE-2.
00171                      02   FILLER                         PIC X(11)
00172                           VALUE ' SOC-SEC-NO'.
00173                      02   FILLER                         PIC X(11)
00174                           VALUE '  YTD-GROSS'.
00175                      02   FILLER                         PIC X(10) VALUE '   YTD-TAX'.
00176                      02   FILLER                         PIC X(10) VALUE '  YTD-FICA'.
00177                      02   FILLER                         PIC X(6)  VALUE ' PLANT'.
00178                      02   FILLER                         PIC X(5)  VALUE ' DEPT'.
00179                      02   FILLER                         PIC X(17)
00180                           VALUE '      EMPLOYEE-NAME'.
00181                      02   FILLER                         PIC X(10) VALUE '      RATE'.
00182                      02   FILLER                         PIC X(9)  VALUE '   REG-HR'.
00183                      02   FILLER                         PIC X(6)  VALUE ' OT-HR'.
00184                      02   FILLER                         PIC X(9)  VALUE '    GROSS'.
00185                      02   FILLER                         PIC X(8)  VALUE '    FICA'.
00186                      02   FILLER                         PIC X(8)  VALUE '     TAX'.
00187                      02   FILLER                         PIC X(10) VALUE '       NET'.
00188                 01   PAY-REG-EMP-PRINT-LINE.
00189                      02   FILLER                         PIC X(1)  VALUE SPACE.
00190                      02   EMP-PRINT-SS-NUM               PIC X(9).
00191                      02   FILLER                         PIC X(4)  VALUE SPACE.
00192                      02   EMP-PRINT-YTD-GROSS            PIC Z(5).9(2).
00193                      02   FILLER                         PIC X(3)  VALUE SPACE.
00194                      02   EMP-PRINT-YTD-TAX              PIC Z(4).9(2).
00195                      02   FILLER                         PIC X(3)  VALUE SPACE.
00196                      02   EMP-PRINT-YTD-FICA             PIC Z(4).9(2).
00197                      02   FILLER                         PIC X(3)  VALUE SPACE.
00198                      02   EMP-PRINT-PLANT                PIC 9.
00199                      02   FILLER                         PIC X(4)  VALUE SPACE.
00200                      02   EMP-PRINT-DEPT                 PIC Z9.
00201                      02   FILLER                         PIC X(2)  VALUE SPACE.
00202                      02   EMP-PRINT-EMP-NAME             PIC X(20).
00203                      02   FILLER                         PIC X(2)  VALUE SPACE.
00204                      02   EMP-PRINT-RATE                 PIC Z9.9(2).
00205                      02   FILLER                         PIC X(2)  VALUE SPACE.
00206                      02   EMP-PRINT-PAY-PERIOD-RESULTS.
00207                           03   EMP-PRINT-REG-HR          PIC Z(2).9(2).
00208                           03   FILLER                    PIC X(2).
00209                           03   EMP-PRINT-OT-HR           PIC Z(2).9(2).
00210                           03   FILLER                    PIC X(3).
00211                           03   EMP-PRINT-GROSS           PIC Z(4).9(2).
00212                           03   FILLER                    PIC X(3).
00213                           03   EMP-PRINT-FICA            PIC Z(2).9(2).
00214                           03   FILLER                    PIC X(3).
00215                           03   EMP-PRINT-TAX             PIC Z(3).9(2).
00216                           03   FILLER                    PIC X(3).
00217                           03   EMP-PRINT-NET             PIC Z(4).9(2).
00218                           03   FILLER                    PIC X.
00219                      02   EXCEPTION-PRINT-MESSAGE REDEFINES
00220                           EMP-PRINT-PAY-PERIOD-RESULTS.
00221                           03   FILLER                    PIC X(50).
```

Figure 4.12 (cont.)

```
00222          01   PAY-REG-TOTALS-PRINT-LINE.
00223               02   FILLER                      PIC X(7) VALUE ' TOTALS'.
00224               02   FILLER                      PIC X(5) VALUE SPACE.
00225               02   TOT-PRINT-YTD-GROSS         PIC Z(7).9(2).
00226               02   FILLER                      PIC X(2) VALUE SPACE.
00227               02   TOT-PRINT-YTD-TAX           PIC Z(5).9(2).
00228               02   FILLER                      PIC X(2) VALUE SPACE.
00229               02   TOT-PRINT-YTD-FICA          PIC Z(5).9(2).
00230               02   FILLER                      PIC X(39) VALUE SPACE.
00231               02   TOT-PRINT-REG-HR            PIC Z(4).9(2).
00232               02   FILLER                      PIC X    VALUE SPACE.
00233               02   TOT-PRINT-OT-HR             PIC Z(4).9(2).
00234               02   FILLER                      PIC X    VALUE SPACE.
00235               02   TOT-PRINT-GROSS             PIC Z(6).9(2).
00236               02   FILLER                      PIC X    VALUE SPACE.
00237               02   TOT-PRINT-FICA              PIC Z(4).9(2).
00238               02   FILLER                      PIC X    VALUE SPACE.
00239               02   TOT-PRINT-TAX               PIC Z(5).9(2).
00240               02   FILLER                      PIC X    VALUE SPACE.
00241               02   TOT-PRINT-NET               PIC Z(6).9(2).
00242               02   FILLER                      PIC X    VALUE SPACE.
00243          01   TERMINATING-MSG-PRINT-LINE.
00244               02   FILLER                      PIC X(5) VALUE SPACE.
00245               02   TERMINATING-MESSAGE         PIC X(31).
00246               02   FILLER                      PIC X VALUE SPACE.
00247               02   TERMINATING-REC-CONTENTS    PIC X(100).
00248          01   PAY-REG-UNDERLINER-LINE.
00249               02   FILLER                      PIC X(133) VALUE ALL '-'.
00250     *
00251     PROCEDURE DIVISION.
00252     *
00253     PAYROLL-REGISTER-CONTROL.
00254          PERFORM START-UP.
00255          PERFORM PROCESS-PAGES-AND-PAY-FILES
00256               UNTIL PROCESSING-SHOULD-STOP.
00257          PERFORM REPORT-TOTALS.
00258          PERFORM FINISH-UP.
00259          STOP RUN.
00260     *
00261     START-UP.
00262          OPEN INPUT   HRS-WORKED-PAY-PERIOD-FILE-IN
00263               I-O     PAYROLL-MAST-FILE-IO
00264               OUTPUT  PAYROLL-REGISTER-REPORT-FILE.
00265          MOVE ALL 'N' TO SWITCHES.
00266          MOVE 1 TO PAGE-COUNT   PAY-REG-PAGE-NUMBER.
00267          MOVE ZEROES TO TOTAL-YTD-GROSS TOTAL-YTD-TAX   TOTAL-YTD-FICA
00268                         TOTAL-REG-HR   TOTAL-OT-HR   TOTAL-GROSS
00269                         TOTAL-FICA   TOTAL-TAX   TOTAL-NET.
00270          PERFORM READ-PAYROLL-MAST-FILE.
00271          PERFORM READ-HRS-WORKED-FILE.
00272     *
00273     PROCESS-PAGES-AND-PAY-FILES.
00274          PERFORM WRITE-REPORT-HEADING.
00275          MOVE 1 TO LINE-COUNT.
00276          ADD 1 TO PAGE-COUNT.
00277          PERFORM PROCESS-LINES-AND-PAY-RECORDS
00278               UNTIL (PAGE-IS-FULL) OR (PROCESSING-SHOULD-STOP).
00279          MOVE PAGE-COUNT TO PAY-REG-PAGE-NUMBER.
00280          MOVE 'N' TO PAGE-IS-FULL-SW.
00281     *
00282     REPORT-TOTALS.
00283          MOVE TOTAL-YTD-GROSS TO TOT-PRINT-YTD-GROSS.
00284          MOVE TOTAL-YTD-TAX TO TOT-PRINT-YTD-TAX.
00285          MOVE TOTAL-YTD-FICA TO TOT-PRINT-YTD-FICA.
00286          MOVE TOTAL-REG-HR TO TOT-PRINT-REG-HR.
00287          MOVE TOTAL-OT-HR TO TOT-PRINT-OT-HR.
00288          MOVE TOTAL-GROSS TO TOT-PRINT-GROSS.
00289          MOVE TOTAL-FICA TO TOT-PRINT-FICA.
00290          MOVE TOTAL-TAX TO TOT-PRINT-TAX.
00291          MOVE TOTAL-NET TO TOT-PRINT-NET.
00292          PERFORM WRITE-PAY-REG-TOTALS.
```

Figure 4.12 (cont.)

```
00293             *
00294                 FINISH-UP.
00295                     IF (END-OF-PAYROLL-MAST-FILE) AND (END-OF-HRS-WORKED-FILE)
00296                         MOVE 'PAYROLL MASTER FILE UPDATED'
00297                             TO TERMINATING-MESSAGE
00298                         MOVE SPACES TO TERMINATING-REC-CONTENTS
00299                     ELSE
00300                         IF INVALID-REWRITE-PAY-MAST
00301                             MOVE 'INVALID REWRITE--PAYROLL MASTER'
00302                                 TO TERMINATING-MESSAGE
00303                             MOVE PAY-MAST-IO-REC TO TERMINATING-REC-CONTENTS
00304                         ELSE
00305                             MOVE 'PROBLEM IN PROCESSING PAYROLL'
00306                                 TO TERMINATING-MESSAGE
00307                             MOVE PAY-MAST-IO-REC TO TERMINATING-REC-CONTENTS.
00308                     PERFORM PRINT-TERMINATING-MESSAGE.
00309                     CLOSE HRS-WORKED-PAY-PERIOD-FILE-IN      PAYROLL-MAST-FILE-IO
00310                         PAYROLL-REGISTER-REPORT-FILE.
00311             *
00312                 PROCESS-LINES-AND-PAY-RECORDS.
00313                     IF (PAY-IO-SS-NUM IS LESS THAN HRS-IN-SS-NUM)
00314                         PERFORM EMPLOYEE-DID-NOT-WORK
00315                     ELSE
00316                         IF (PAY-IO-SS-NUM IS GREATER THAN HRS-IN-SS-NUM)
00317                             PERFORM NO-MASTER-PAYROLL-REC-FOUND
00318                         ELSE
00319                             PERFORM PROCESS-EMPLOYEE-PAY.
00320                     ADD 1 TO LINE-COUNT.
00321                     IF LINE-COUNT = PAGE-SIZE
00322                         MOVE 'Y' TO PAGE-IS-FULL-SW.
00323                     IF (END-OF-PAYROLL-MAST-FILE) AND (END-OF-HRS-WORKED-FILE)
00324                         MOVE 'Y' TO STOP-PROCESSING-SW.
00325             *
00326                 EMPLOYEE-DID-NOT-WORK.
00327                     MOVE PAY-IO-SS-NUM TO EMP-PRINT-SS-NUM.
00328                     MOVE PAY-IO-PLANT-SITE TO EMP-PRINT-PLANT.
00329                     MOVE PAY-IO-DEPT-CODE TO EMP-PRINT-DEPT.
00330                     MOVE PAY-IO-EMP-NAME TO EMP-PRINT-EMP-NAME.
00331                     MOVE PAY-IO-PAY-RATE TO EMP-PRINT-RATE.
00332                     MOVE PAY-IO-YTD-GROSS TO EMP-PRINT-YTD-GROSS.
00333                     MOVE PAY-IO-YTD-TAX TO EMP-PRINT-YTD-TAX.
00334                     MOVE PAY-IO-YTD-FICA TO EMP-PRINT-YTD-FICA.
00335                     MOVE '   EMPLOYEE DID NOT WORK THIS PAY PERIOD'
00336                         TO EXCEPTION-PRINT-MESSAGE.
00337                     ADD PAY-IO-YTD-GROSS TO TOTAL-YTD-GROSS.
00338                     ADD PAY-IO-YTD-TAX TO TOTAL-YTD-TAX.
00339                     ADD PAY-IO-YTD-FICA TO TOTAL-YTD-FICA.
00340                     PERFORM WRITE-PAY-REG-EMP-PRINT-LINE.
00341                     PERFORM READ-PAYROLL-MAST-FILE.
00342             *
00343                 NO-MASTER-PAYROLL-REC-FOUND.
00344                     MOVE HRS-IN-SS-NUM TO EMP-PRINT-SS-NUM.
00345                     MOVE ZERO TO EMP-PRINT-YTD-GROSS EMP-PRINT-YTD-TAX
00346                         EMP-PRINT-YTD-FICA EMP-PRINT-PLANT EMP-PRINT-DEPT
00347                         EMP-PRINT-RATE.
00348                     MOVE SPACE TO EMP-PRINT-EMP-NAME.
00349                     MOVE '   NO PAYROLL MASTER RECORD IN FILE FOR EMPLOYEE'
00350                         TO EXCEPTION-PRINT-MESSAGE.
00351                     PERFORM WRITE-PAY-REG-EMP-PRINT-LINE.
00352                     PERFORM READ-HRS-WORKED-FILE.
00353             *
00354                 PROCESS-EMPLOYEE-PAY.
00355                     PERFORM PAYROLL-CALCULATIONS.
00356                     PERFORM MOVE-PAY-DATA-TO-RECORDS.
00357                     PERFORM REWRITE-PAYROLL-MAST-REC.
00358                     PERFORM WRITE-PAY-REG-EMP-PRINT-LINE.
00359                     PERFORM READ-PAYROLL-MAST-FILE.
00360                     PERFORM READ-HRS-WORKED-FILE.
```

Figure 4.12 (cont.)

```
00361          *
00362              PAYROLL-CALCULATIONS.
00363                  IF (HRS-IN-HRS-WORKED IS GREATER THAN MAX-REG-HRS)
00364                      MOVE MAX-REG-HRS TO EMP-REG-HR
00365                      COMPUTE EMP-OT-HR = (HRS-IN-HRS-WORKED) - (MAX-REG-HRS)
00366                      COMPUTE EMP-GROSS = (EMP-REG-HR * PAY-IO-PAY-RATE) +
00367                          (EMP-OT-HR * OVERTIME-ADJUSTMENT * PAY-IO-PAY-RATE)
00368                  ELSE
00369                      MOVE HRS-IN-HRS-WORKED TO EMP-REG-HR
00370                      MOVE ZEROES TO EMP-OT-HR
00371                      COMPUTE EMP-GROSS = (EMP-REG-HR * PAY-IO-PAY-RATE).
00372                  COMPUTE EMP-TAX = ((EMP-GROSS) - (PAY-IO-TAX-CLASS) *
00373                      (TAXABLE-INCOME-ADJUSTMENT)) * (EST-FED-TAX-RATE).
00374                  IF (PAY-IO-YTD-GROSS IS GREATER THAN MAX-SS-WITHHOLD)
00375                      MOVE ZEROS TO EMP-FICA
00376                  ELSE
00377                      IF ((PAY-IO-YTD-GROSS + EMP-GROSS)
00378                          IS LESS THAN MAX-SS-WITHHOLD)
00379                          COMPUTE EMP-FICA = EMP-GROSS * SS-WITHHOLD-RATE
00380                      ELSE
00381                          COMPUTE EMP-FICA = ((MAX-SS-WITHHOLD) -
00382                              (PAY-IO-YTD-GROSS)) * SS-WITHHOLD-RATE.
00383                  COMPUTE EMP-NET = EMP-GROSS - (EMP-FICA + EMP-TAX).
00384                  COMPUTE EMP-YTD-GROSS = PAY-IO-YTD-GROSS + EMP-GROSS.
00385                  COMPUTE EMP-YTD-TAX = PAY-IO-YTD-TAX + EMP-TAX.
00386                  COMPUTE EMP-YTD-FICA = PAY-IO-YTD-FICA + EMP-FICA.
00387                  COMPUTE TOTAL-YTD-GROSS = TOTAL-YTD-GROSS + EMP-YTD-GROSS.
00388                  COMPUTE TOTAL-YTD-TAX = TOTAL-YTD-TAX + EMP-YTD-TAX.
00389                  COMPUTE TOTAL-YTD-FICA = TOTAL-YTD-FICA + EMP-YTD-FICA.
00390                  COMPUTE TOTAL-REG-HR = TOTAL-REG-HR + EMP-REG-HR.
00391                  COMPUTE TOTAL-OT-HR = TOTAL-OT-HR + EMP-OT-HR.
00392                  COMPUTE TOTAL-GROSS = TOTAL-GROSS + EMP-GROSS.
00393                  COMPUTE TOTAL-FICA = TOTAL-FICA + EMP-FICA.
00394                  COMPUTE TOTAL-TAX = TOTAL-TAX + EMP-TAX.
00395                  COMPUTE TOTAL-NET = TOTAL-NET + EMP-NET.
00396          *
00397              MOVE-PAY-DATA-TO-RECORDS.
00398                  MOVE SPACES TO EXCEPTION-PRINT-MESSAGE.
00399                  MOVE PAY-IO-SS-NUM TO EMP-PRINT-SS-NUM.
00400                  MOVE EMP-YTD-GROSS TO EMP-PRINT-YTD-GROSS  PAY-IO-YTD-GROSS.
00401                  MOVE EMP-YTD-TAX TO EMP-PRINT-YTD-TAX   PAY-IO-YTD-TAX.
00402                  MOVE EMP-YTD-FICA TO EMP-PRINT-YTD-FICA  PAY-IO-YTD-FICA.
00403                  MOVE PAY-IO-PLANT-SITE TO EMP-PRINT-PLANT.
00404                  MOVE PAY-IO-DEPT-CODE TO EMP-PRINT-DEPT.
00405                  MOVE PAY-IO-EMP-NAME TO EMP-PRINT-EMP-NAME.
00406                  MOVE PAY-IO-PAY-RATE TO EMP-PRINT-RATE.
00407                  MOVE EMP-REG-HR TO EMP-PRINT-REG-HR.
00408                  MOVE EMP-OT-HR TO EMP-PRINT-OT-HR.
00409                  MOVE EMP-GROSS TO EMP-PRINT-GROSS.
00410                  MOVE EMP-FICA TO EMP-PRINT-FICA.
00411                  MOVE EMP-TAX TO EMP-PRINT-TAX.
00412                  MOVE EMP-NET TO EMP-PRINT-NET.
00413          *
00414              WRITE-REPORT-HEADING.
00415                  WRITE PAY-REG-REPORT-AREA FROM PAY-REG-HDG-LINE-1
00416                      AFTER ADVANCING TO-TOP-OF-PAGE.
00417                  WRITE PAY-REG-REPORT-AREA FROM PAY-REG-HDG-LINE-2
00418                      AFTER ADVANCING 2 LINES.
00419                  WRITE PAY-REG-REPORT-AREA FROM PAY-REG-UNDERLINER-LINE
00420                      AFTER ADVANCING 1 LINES.
00421          *
00422              WRITE-PAY-REG-TOTALS.
00423                  WRITE PAY-REG-REPORT-AREA FROM PAY-REG-TOTALS-PRINT-LINE
00424                      AFTER ADVANCING 2 LINES.
00425          *
00426              PRINT-TERMINATING-MESSAGE.
00427                  WRITE PAY-REG-REPORT-AREA FROM TERMINATING-MSG-PRINT-LINE
00428                      AFTER ADVANCING TO-TOP-OF-PAGE.
00429          *
00430              WRITE-PAY-REG-EMP-PRINT-LINE.
00431                  WRITE PAY-REG-REPORT-AREA FROM PAY-REG-EMP-PRINT-LINE
00432                      AFTER ADVANCING 1 LINES.
00433          *  READ-PAYROLL-MAST-FILE.
00434              READ-PAYROLL-MAST-FILE.
00435                  READ PAYROLL-MAST-FILE-IO INTO PAY-MAST-IO-REC
00436                      AT END MOVE HIGH-VALUES TO PAY-IO-SS-NUM
00437                          MOVE 'Y' TO END-OF-PAYROLL-MAST-FILE-SW.
```

Figure 4.12 (*cont.*)

```
00438          *
00439              READ-HRS-WORKED-FILE.
00440                  READ HRS-WORKED-PAY-PERIOD-FILE-IN INTO HRS-WORKED-IN-REC
00441                      AT END MOVE HIGH-VALUES TO HRS-IN-SS-NUM
00442                          MOVE 'Y' TO END-OF-HRS-WORKED-FILE-SW.
00443          *
00444              REWRITE-PAYROLL-MAST-REC.
00445                  REWRITE PAY-MAST-IO-AREA FROM PAY-MAST-IO-REC
00446                      INVALID KEY MOVE 'Y' TO INVALID-REWRITE-PAY-MAST-SW
00447                                            STOP-PROCESSING-SW.
```

MERGING TWO FILES

To add new records to a sequential file requires that the file be re-created if the key sequence is to be maintained.

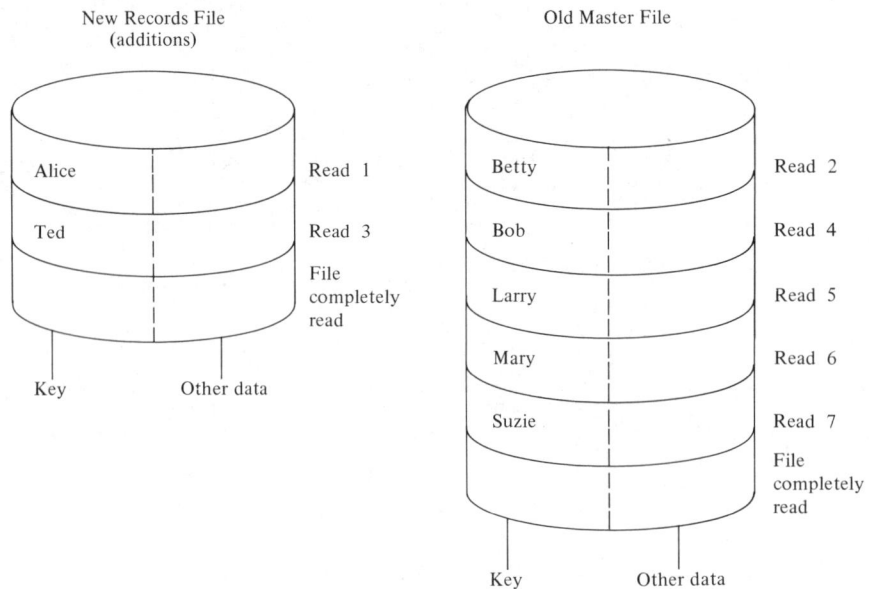

The technique used is a *file merge*. Both files are read; the record with the lowest key is written to the new file, and the file that contained that record is read again. This process is continued until one of the files is completely read. The rest of the other file is then copied to the new file.

New Records File
(additions)

Alice

Ted

Key   Other data

Old Master File
(existing file)

Betty

Bob

Larry

Mary

Suzie

Key   Other Data

New Master File

Alice

Betty

Bob

Larry

Mary

Suzie

Ted

Key   Other data

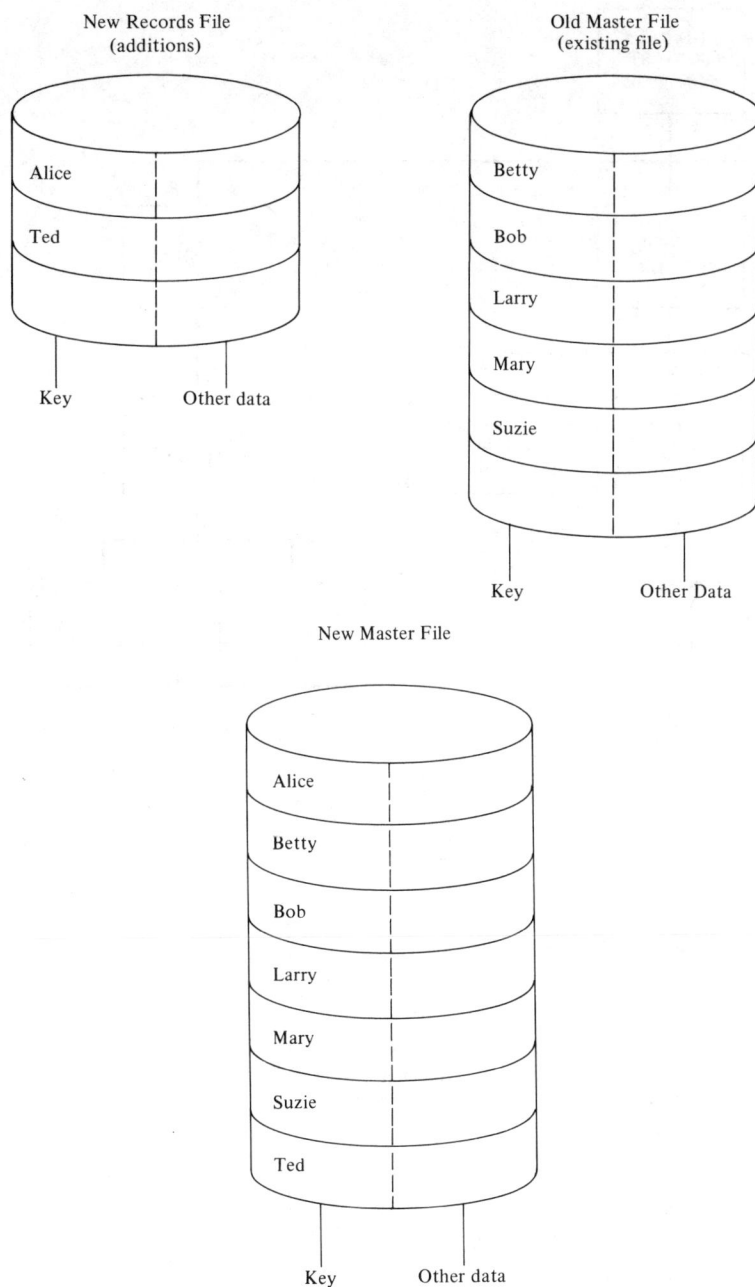

Our next example illustrates the technique.

Example 4.4

Several new employees have been hired by Mega-Tronics. Their records must be added to the payroll master file. A file exists containing the personal and company data for the new employees. This file is in order by social security number.

The control structure is illustrated in Figure 4.13. Details of the logic of the program are in Figure 4.14. The program listing is in Figure 4.15. All specifics of the COBOL statements have previously been covered.

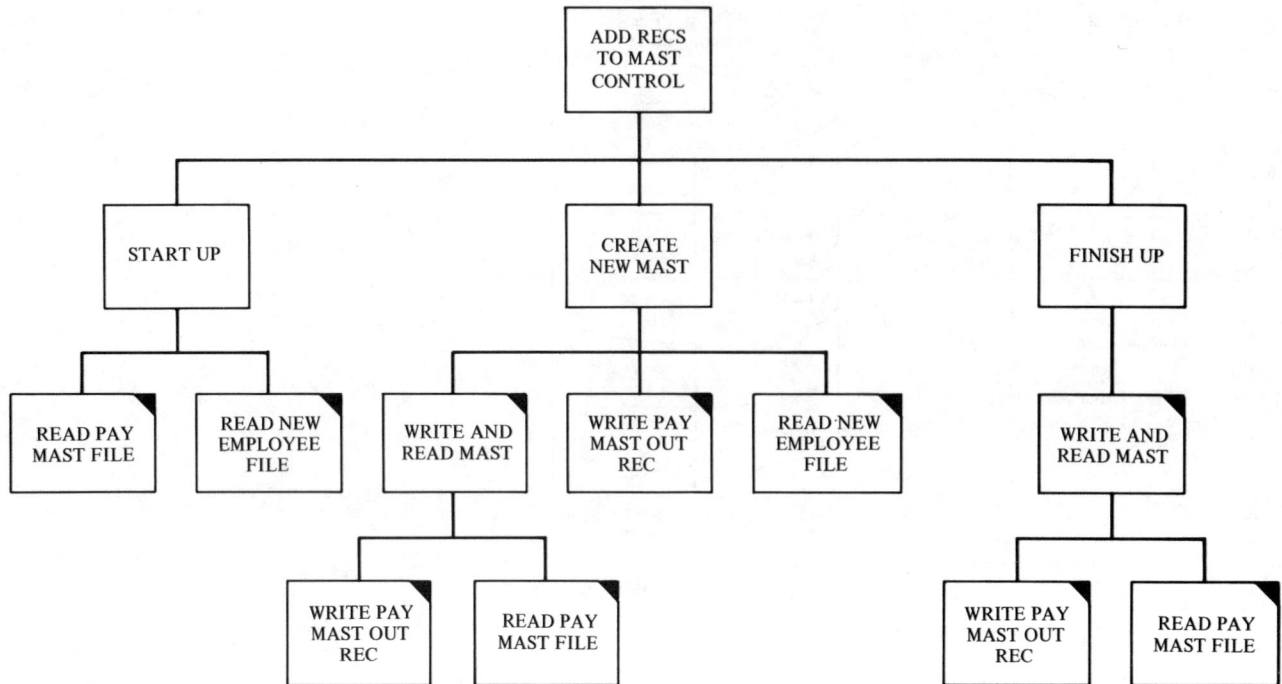

Figure 4.13
Structure chart for the program in Figure 4.15.

ADD-RECS-TO-MAST-CONTROL

    This module controls the execution sequence of the program. It also terminates execution of the program.

START-UP

    All files are opened. A switch is set to indicate that there are input data. The modules to read both input files are called. The counters for the number of new employees, and all employees, are initialized to zero. The year-to-date fields in a new employee's record are set to zero.

CREATE-NEW-MAST

    The module that controls reading and writing of master records is called repeatedly until the key value for a new employee's record is equal to, or greater than, the key value for the record read from the master file. If the key values are equal, a message indicating duplicate social security numbers is displayed along with the contents of the new employee's record, and the master input record is moved to the master output record. Otherwise, the new employee's record is moved to the master output record, the module to write the master output record is called, and the counts of total employees and of new employees are incremented. The module to read the new employee file is called.

FINISH-UP

    This module writes the counts for new employees and total employees. All files are closed.

Figure 4.14
Module description for the program in Figure 4.15.

Figure 4.14 (*cont.*)

WRITE-AND-READ-MAST

    The master input record is moved to the master output record. The module to write the master output record is called. The count of employees is incremented. The input master file is read.

READ-NEW-EMPLOYEE-FILE

    The additions file is read. When the end of file is encountered, switches are set to indicate that all processing of the input files is complete.

WRITE-PAY-MAST-OUT-REC

    A record is written to the new master file.

READ-PAY-MAST-FILE

    The old master file is read. When the end of file is encountered, the key is changed to HIGH-VALUES to prevent the file from being accessed again.

```
00001        IDENTIFICATION DIVISION.
00002      *
00003        PROGRAM-ID.
00004          EX-4-4.
00005      ***************************************************************
00006      *                                                             *
00007      *     PROGRAMMER TEAM          WALSTROM/SUMMERS/LINDAHL       *
00008      *     PROGRAM COMPLETION DATE DECEMBER 12, 1983              *
00009      *                                                             *
00010      *                    PROGRAM SUMMARY                          *
00011      *     INPUT                                                   *
00012      *         INPUT FILES ARE CURRENT PAYROLL MASTER FILE AND NEW *
00013      *         EMPLOYEE FILE. BOTH ARE ORDERED BY SOCIAL SECURITY  *
00014      *         NUMBER AND CONTAIN THE INFORMATION BELOW IN THE     *
00015      *         SAME RECORD POSITIONS                               *
00016      *             - CODE FOR THE PLANT LOCATION                   *
00017      *             - CODE FOR THE DEPARTMENT TO WHICH THE EMPLOYEE *
00018      *               IS ASSIGNED                                   *
00019      *             - SOCIAL SECURITY NUMBER                        *
00020      *             - NAME                                          *
00021      *             - OTHER PERSONAL INFORMATION                    *
00022      *             - TAX CLASSIFICATION                            *
00023      *             - PAY RATE                                      *
00024      *         IN ADDITION, RECORDS ON THE CURRENT PAYROLL MASTER  *
00025      *         FILE CONTAIN                                        *
00026      *             - YEAR-TO-DATE TOTALS FOR GROSS PAY, TAX WITHHELD*
00027      *               AND FICA WITHHELD                             *
00028      *                                                             *
00029      *     PROCESSING                                              *
00030      *             - THE YEAR-TO-DATE TOTALS ARE SET TO ZERO       *
00031      *             - THE TWO INPUT FILES ARE MERGED                *
00032      *             - COUNT OF THE NEW EMPLOYEES IS COMPUTED        *
00033      *             - COUNT OF ALL EMPLOYEES IS COMPUTED            *
00034      *                                                             *
00035      *     OUTPUT                                                  *
00036      *         AN UPDATED PAYROLL MASTER FILE IS PRODUCED. THIS FILE*
00037      *         IS IN THE SAME FORM AS THE ORIGINAL. IT CONTAINS    *
00038      *             - ALL EMPLOYEE DATA FROM BOTH INPUT FILES       *
00039      *         A PRINTED REPORT IS PRODUCED. IT CONTAINS           *
00040      *             - A LIST OF EMPLOYEES WITH RECORDS IN BOTH INPUT *
00041      *               FILES                                         *
00042      *             - COUNT OF ALL EMPLOYEES                        *
00043      *             - COUNT OF NEW EMPLOYEES                        *
00044      ***************************************************************
```

Figure 4.15
Adding new records to a sequential master file by merging for Example 4.4.

Figure 4.15 (*cont.*)

```
00045            *
00046              ENVIRONMENT DIVISION.
00047            *
00048               CONFIGURATION SECTION.
00049               SOURCE-COMPUTER.
00050                   IBM-370.
00051               OBJECT-COMPUTER.
00052                   IBM-370.
00053            *
00054               INPUT-OUTPUT SECTION.
00055               FILE-CONTROL.
00056                   SELECT PAYROLL-MAST-FILE-IN
00057                       ASSIGN TO SYS023-DA-3330-S-PAYFILE.
00058                   SELECT PAYROLL-MAST-FILE-OUT
00059                       ASSIGN TO SYS023-DA-3330-S-PAYOUT.
00060                   SELECT PAYROLL-NEW-EMPLOYEE-FILE-IN
00061                       ASSIGN TO SYS023-DA-3330-S-ADDFILE.
00062            *
00063              DATA DIVISION.
00064            *
00065              FILE SECTION.
00066              FD  PAYROLL-MAST-FILE-IN
00067                   LABEL RECORDS ARE STANDARD
00068                   BLOCK CONTAINS 10 RECORDS.
00069              01  PAYROLL-MAST-IN-AREA             PIC X(100).
00070              FD  PAYROLL-MAST-FILE-OUT
00071                   LABEL RECORDS ARE STANDARD
00072                   BLOCK CONTAINS 10 RECORDS.
00073              01  PAYROLL-MAST-OUT-AREA            PIC X(100).
00074              FD  PAYROLL-NEW-EMPLOYEE-FILE-IN
00075                   LABEL RECORDS ARE STANDARD
00076                   BLOCK CONTAINS 10 RECORDS.
00077              01  PAY-NEW-EMP-IN-AREA              PIC X(80).
00078            *
00079              WORKING-STORAGE SECTION.
00080              01  SWITCHES.
00081                  02  END-OF-NEW-EMP-SW            PIC X.
00082                      88  END-OF-NEW-EMP    VALUE 'Y'.
00083              01  COUNTERS.
00084                  02  EMP-RECORDS-COUNT           PIC 9(5).
00085                  02  NEW-EMP-RECORDS-COUNT       PIC 9(4).
00086              01  COUNTERS-OUT.
00087                  02  EMP-COUNT-OUT               PIC Z(4)9.
00088                  02  NEW-EMP-COUNT-OUT           PIC Z(3)9.
00089              01  NEW-EMP-IN-REC.
00090                  02  NEW-EMP-IN-INFO.
00091                      03  FILLER                  PIC X(3).
00092                      03  NEW-EMP-SS-NUM          PIC X(9).
00093                      03  FILLER                  PIC X(68).
00094                  02  NEW-EMP-YTD-GROSS           PIC S9(5)V9(2).
00095                  02  NEW-EMP-YTD-TAX             PIC S9(5)V9(2).
00096                  02  NEW-EMP-YTD-FICA            PIC S9(4)V9(2).
00097              01  PAYROLL-MAST-IN-REC.
00098                  02  FILLER                      PIC X(3).
00099                  02  PAY-IN-SS-NUM               PIC X(9).
00100                  02  FILLER                      PIC X(88).
00101              01  PAYROLL-MAST-OUT-REC            PIC X(100).
00102            *
00103              PROCEDURE DIVISION.
00104            *
00105              ADD-RECS-TO-MAST-CONTROL.
00106                  PERFORM START-UP.
00107                  PERFORM CREATE-NEW-MAST UNTIL END-OF-NEW-EMP.
00108                  IF END-OF-NEW-EMP
00109                      PERFORM FINISH-UP
00110                  ELSE
00111                      DISPLAY ' PROBLEM IN CREATING THE FILE.'.
00112                  STOP RUN.
```

Figure 4.15 (*cont.*)

```
00113         *
00114           START-UP.
00115             OPEN INPUT PAYROLL-MAST-FILE-IN,
00116                        PAYROLL-NEW-EMPLOYEE-FILE-IN
00117                  OUTPUT PAYROLL-MAST-FILE-OUT.
00118             MOVE 'N' TO END-OF-NEW-EMP-SW.
00119             PERFORM READ-PAY-MAST-FILE.
00120             PERFORM READ-NEW-EMPLOYEE-FILE.
00121             MOVE 0 TO EMP-RECORDS-COUNT,
00122                       NEW-EMP-RECORDS-COUNT.
00123             MOVE 0 TO NEW-EMP-YTD-GROSS,
00124                       NEW-EMP-YTD-TAX,
00125                       NEW-EMP-YTD-FICA.
00126         *
00127           CREATE-NEW-MAST.
00128             PERFORM WRITE-AND-READ-MAST
00129                UNTIL PAY-IN-SS-NUM IS NOT LESS THAN NEW-EMP-SS-NUM.
00130             IF PAY-IN-SS-NUM = NEW-EMP-SS-NUM
00131                DISPLAY ' DUPLICATE SS NUM', NEW-EMP-IN-REC
00132                MOVE PAYROLL-MAST-IN-REC TO PAYROLL-MAST-OUT-REC
00133             ELSE
00134                MOVE NEW-EMP-IN-REC TO PAYROLL-MAST-OUT-REC
00135                PERFORM WRITE-PAY-MAST-OUT-REC
00136                ADD 1 TO EMP-RECORDS-COUNT
00137                          NEW-EMP-RECORDS-COUNT.
00138             PERFORM READ-NEW-EMPLOYEE-FILE.
00139         *
00140           FINISH-UP.
00141             PERFORM WRITE-AND-READ-MAST
00142                UNTIL PAY-IN-SS-NUM = HIGH-VALUES.
00143             MOVE EMP-RECORDS-COUNT TO EMP-COUNT-OUT.
00144             MOVE NEW-EMP-RECORDS-COUNT TO NEW-EMP-COUNT-OUT.
00145             DISPLAY ' THERE ARE ', EMP-COUNT-OUT, ' EMPLOYEES.'.
00146             DISPLAY ' THERE ARE ', NEW-EMP-COUNT-OUT,
00147                     ' NEW EMPLOYEE RECORDS'.
00148             CLOSE PAYROLL-MAST-FILE-IN,
00149                   PAYROLL-MAST-FILE-OUT,
00150                   PAYROLL-NEW-EMPLOYEE-FILE-IN.
00151         *
00152           WRITE-AND-READ-MAST.
00153             MOVE PAYROLL-MAST-IN-REC TO PAYROLL-MAST-OUT-REC.
00154             PERFORM WRITE-PAY-MAST-OUT-REC.
00155             ADD 1 TO EMP-RECORDS-COUNT.
00156             PERFORM READ-PAY-MAST-FILE.
00157         *
00158           READ-NEW-EMPLOYEE-FILE.
00159             READ PAYROLL-NEW-EMPLOYEE-FILE-IN INTO NEW-EMP-IN-INFO
00160                AT END MOVE 'Y' TO END-OF-NEW-EMP-SW.
00161         *
00162           WRITE-PAY-MAST-OUT-REC.
00163             WRITE PAYROLL-MAST-OUT-AREA FROM PAYROLL-MAST-OUT-REC.
00164         *
00165           READ-PAY-MAST-FILE.
00166             READ PAYROLL-MAST-FILE-IN INTO PAYROLL-MAST-IN-REC
00167                AT END MOVE HIGH-VALUES TO PAY-IN-SS-NUM.
```

REPORT GENERATION AND CREATION OF AN ARCHIVAL FILE

As a last example, we will look at the creation of a tape file. Tape processing is quite similar to processing sequential disk files. If our complete system were on tape, Example 4.3 would require that the new master file with the updates be created on another tape. Other processing changes would be minor.

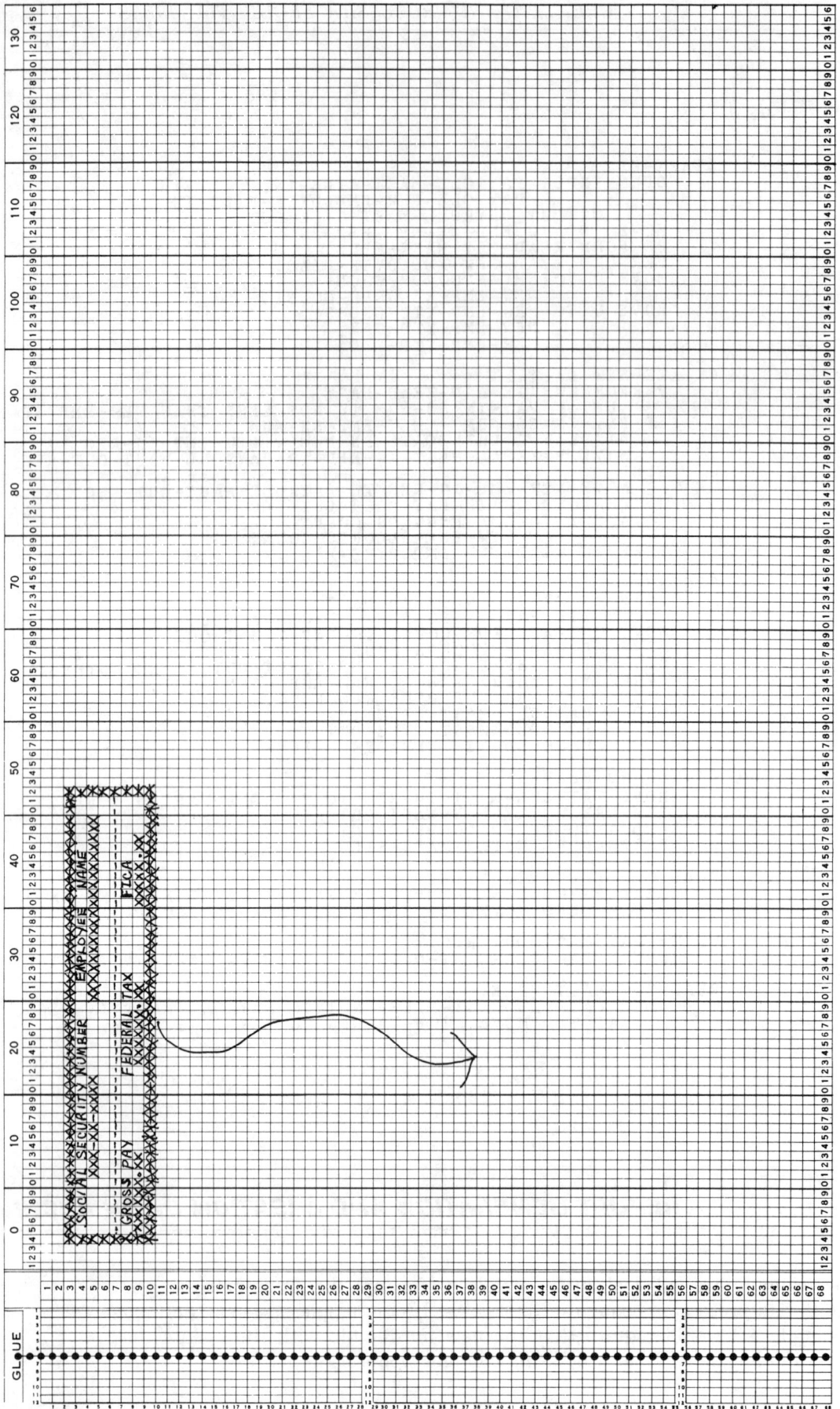

Figure 4.16
Printer layout for output from the program in Figure 4.19.

Example 4.5

At the end of each year, a copy of the payroll master file must be saved for possible IRS auditing. Since IRS is unlikely to question information on the file, Mega's DP department has decided to retain the permanent historical (archival) copy on a tape file. To reduce the number of runs against the file, they have decided that W-2 forms can efficiently be printed at the same time.

Printing of W-2 forms is complex; therefore, we will present a simplified version of the W-2 form. Its format is illustrated in Figure 4.16. The control structure of the program is presented in Figure 4.17. Logic for individual modules appears in Figure 4.18.

We would like to make several comments concerning the program of Figure 4.19.

1. TAPMAS is the external name by which the file is known (line 50).
2. A tape file with standard labels is being created (line 64).
3. Note that the entire W-2 form is described as a table in the DATA DIVISION (lines 101–151). Moving all output data to the table (lines 187–193) and then writing the table out (line 195) permits very simple coding logic for printing a form.
4. VALUE ALL '*' generates a string of the length specified in the Picture clause. For line 104, a string of 49 '*'s is generated.
5. A tape file should always be closed WITH LOCK when all processing of the tape is complete (line 184).

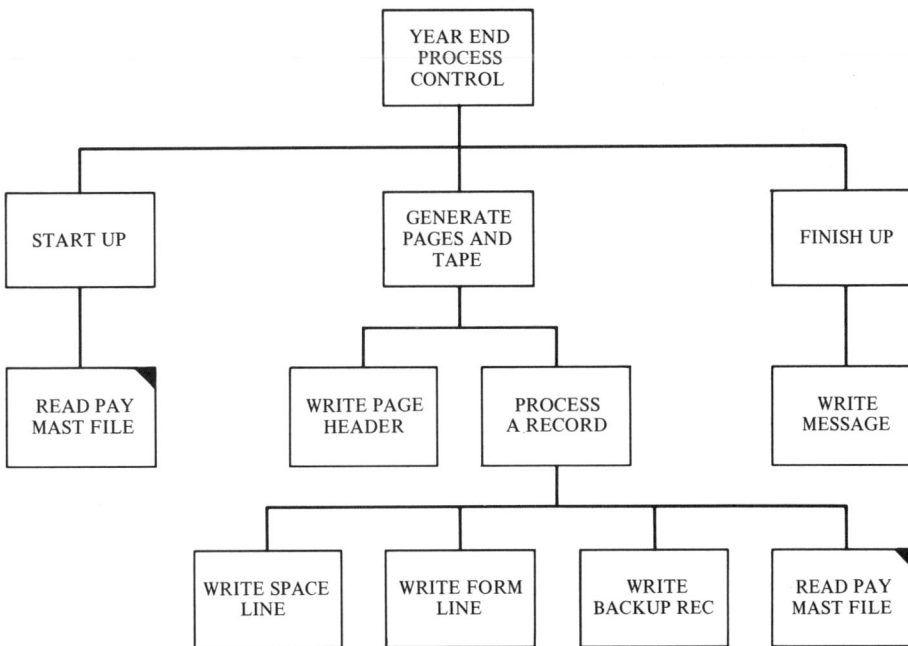

Figure 4.17
Structure chart for the program in Figure 4.19.

YEAR-END-PROCESS-CONTROL

The overall execution sequence of the program is controlled by this module. Execution of the program is terminated here.

START-UP

All files are opened. The count for the number of pages is set to 1 and a switch is set to indicate that there are input data. The module that reads the input file is executed.

GENERATE-PAGES-AND-TAPE

This module executes the page header routine. It increments the page counter. It also sets the counter controlling the number of forms on the page to zero. It then executes a module to process the input records until the page is filled.

FINISH-UP

A module is called to write a final message line. All files are closed.

PROCESS-A-RECORD

Data from the input record are edited and moved to the W–2 form lines.
A form is generated and the form count is incremented. If no more forms can be written on this page, the end–of–page switch is set. The module to write the master record to the tape is executed. The module is called to read the input file.

WRITE-PAGE-HEADER

This module writes a heading at the top of a new page.

WRITE-MESSAGE

A final message line is written

WRITE-SPACE-LINE

A blank line is written

WRITE-FORM-LINE

A line of the W–2 form is written.

WRITE-BACK-UP-REC

A record is written to the tape file.

READ-PAY-MAST-FILE

The next logical record is read. When the file has been completely read, all switches are set to 'Y'.

Figure 4.18
Module descriptions for the program in Figure 4.19.

```
00001          IDENTIFICATION DIVISION.
00002     *
00003        PROGRAM-ID.
00004          EX-4-5.
00005     *********************************************************************
00006     *                                                                   *
00007     *    PROGRAMMER TEAM         WALSTROM/SUMMERS/LINDAHL               *
00008     *    PROGRAM COMPLETION DATE FEBRUARY 9,1984.                       *
00009     *                                                                   *
00010     *                        PROGRAM SUMMARY                            *
00011     *    INPUT                                                          *
00012     *        THE PAYROLL MASTER FILE IS THE ONLY INPUT DATA. EACH       *
00013     *        RECORD CONTAINS                                            *
00014     *            - CODE FOR PLANT LOCATION                              *
00015     *            - CODE FOR DEPARTMENT                                  *
00016     *            - SOCIAL SECURITY NUMBER                               *
00017     *            - NAME                                                 *
00018     *            - OTHER PERSONAL DATA                                  *
00019     *            - TAX CLASSIFICATION                                   *
00020     *            - PAY RATE                                             *
00021     *            - YEAR-TO-DATE TOTALS FOR GROSS PAY TAX FICA           *
00022     *                                                                   *
00023     *    PROCESSING                                                     *
00024     *        FOR EACH EMPLOYEE, DATA IS ARRANGED AND EDITED             *
00025     *        FOR A SIMPLIFIED W-2 FORM.                                 *
00026     *                                                                   *
00027     *    OUTPUT                                                         *
00028     *        A COPY OF THE PAYROLL MASTER FILE IS GENERATED ON TAPE.    *
00029     *        A PRINTED W-2 FORM IS PRODUCED FOR EACH EMPLOYEE.          *
00030     *        EACH FORM CONTAINS                                         *
00031     *            - SOCIAL SECURITY NUMBER                               *
00032     *            - NAME                                                 *
00033     *            - GROSS PAY FOR THE YEAR                               *
00034     *            - TAX WITHHELD DURING THE YEAR                         *
00035     *            - FICA WITHHELD DURING THE YEAR                        *
00036     *********************************************************************
00037     *
00038        ENVIRONMENT DIVISION.
00039     *
00040        CONFIGURATION SECTION.
00041        SOURCE-COMPUTER.
00042            IBM-370.
00043        OBJECT-COMPUTER.
00044            IBM-370.
00045        SPECIAL-NAMES.
00046            C01 IS TO-TOP-OF-PAGE.
00047        INPUT-OUTPUT SECTION.
00048        FILE-CONTROL.
00049            SELECT PAYROLL-MAST-BACKUP-FILE-OUT
00050                ASSIGN TO SYS020-UT-3420-S-TAPEMAS.
00051            SELECT W-2-REPORT-PRINT-FILE
00052                ASSIGN TO SYS009-UR-1403-S.
00053            SELECT PAYROLL-MAST-FILE-IN
00054                ASSIGN TO SYS023-DA-3330-S-PAYFILE.
00055     *
00056        DATA DIVISION.
00057     *
00058        FILE SECTION.
00059        FD  PAYROLL-MAST-FILE-IN
00060                LABEL RECORDS ARE STANDARD
00061                BLOCK CONTAINS 10 RECORDS.
00062        01  PAYROLL-MAST-IN-AREA             PIC X(100).
00063        FD  PAYROLL-MAST-BACKUP-FILE-OUT
00064                LABEL RECORDS ARE STANDARD
00065                BLOCK CONTAINS 10 RECORDS.
00066        01  PAYROLL-BACKUP-MAST-OUT-AREA     PIC X(100).
00067        FD  W-2-REPORT-PRINT-FILE
00068                LABEL RECORDS ARE OMITTED.
00069        01  W-2-REPORT-LINE-OUT-AREA         PIC X(133).
00070     *
00071        WORKING-STORAGE SECTION.
00072        01  SWITCHES.
00073            02  END-OF-PAY-FILE-SW               PIC X.
00074                88  NO-MORE-RECORDS     VALUE 'Y'.
00075            02  END-OF-PAGE-SW                   PIC X.
00076                88  END-PAGE            VALUE 'Y'.
```

Figure 4.19

Printing a report from a sequential master file and creating an archival tape file for Example 4.5.

Figure 4.19 (cont.)

```
00077              01   COUNTERS.
00078                   02   PAGE-COUNT                   PIC 9(2).
00079                   02   FORM-COUNT                   PIC 9.
00080                   02   LINE-COUNT                   PIC 9.
00081              01   CONSTANTS.
00082                   02   FORMS-PER-PAGE               PIC 9 VALUE 5.
00083                   02   LINES-PER-FORM               PIC 9 VALUE 8.
00084              01   PAY-MAST-IN-REC.
00085                   02   FILLER                       PIC X(3).
00086                   02   PAY-IN-SS-NUM.
00087                        03   FIRST-3-IN              PIC X(3).
00088                        03   MIDDLE-2-IN             PIC X(2).
00089                        03   LAST-4-IN               PIC X(4).
00090                   02   PAY-IN-EMP-NAME              PIC X(20).
00091                   02   FILLER                       PIC X(48).
00092                   02   PAY-IN-YTD-GROSS             PIC S9(5)V9(2).
00093                   02   PAY-IN-YTD-TAX               PIC S9(5)V9(2).
00094                   02   PAY-IN-YTD-FICA              PIC S9(4)V9(2).
00095              01   FORM-SPACER.
00096                   02   FILLER                       PIC X(133) VALUE SPACE.
00097              01   PAGE-HEAD-LINE.
00098                   02   FILLER                       PIC X(120) VALUE SPACE.
00099                   02   FILLER                       PIC X(4)   VALUE 'PAGE'.
00100                   02   PAGE-COUNT-OUT               PIC Z(3).
00101              01   W-2-FORM-LINES-REGION.
00102                   02   ASTERISK-LINE-1.
00103                        03   FILLER                  PIC X(4) VALUE SPACE.
00104                        03   FILLER                  PIC X(49) VALUE ALL '*'.
00105                   02   HEAD-LINE-1.
00106                        03   FILLER                  PIC X(4) VALUE SPACE.
00107                        03   FILLER                  PIC X(28)
00108                        VALUE '* SOCIAL SECURITY NUMBER'.
00109                        03   FILLER                  PIC X(21)
00110                        VALUE 'EMPLOYEE NAME        *'.
00111                   02   OUT-LINE-1.
00112                        03   FILLER                  PIC X(5) VALUE '    *'.
00113                        03   FILLER                  PIC X(6) VALUE SPACE.
00114                        03   OUT-SS-NUM.
00115                             04   OUT-FIRST-3-DIGITS PIC X(3).
00116                             04   FILLER             PIC X VALUE '-'.
00117                             04   OUT-MIDDLE-2-DIGITS PIC X(2).
00118                             04   FILLER             PIC X VALUE '-'.
00119                             04   OUT-LAST-4-DIGITS  PIC X(4).
00120                        03   FILLER                  PIC X(8) VALUE SPACE.
00121                        03   OUT-EMP-NAME            PIC X(22).
00122                        03   FILLER                  PIC X VALUE '*'.
00123                   02   SEPARATOR-LINE.
00124                        03   FILLER                  PIC X(4) VALUE SPACE.
00125                        03   FILLER                  PIC X(48) VALUE '*'.
00126                        03   FILLER                  PIC X    VALUE '*'.
00127                   02   DASH-LINE.
00128                        03   FILLER                  PIC X(5) VALUE '    *'.
00129                        03   FILLER                  PIC X(47) VALUE ALL '-'.
00130                        03   FILLER                  PIC X    VALUE '*'.
00131                   02   HEAD-LINE-2.
00132                        03   FILLER                  PIC X(4) VALUE SPACE.
00133                        03   FILLER                  PIC X(18)
00134                        VALUE '* GROSS PAY'.
00135                        03   FILLER                  PIC X(19)
00136                        VALUE 'FEDERAL TAX'.
00137                        03   FILLER                  PIC X(12)
00138                        VALUE 'FICA       *'.
00139                   02   OUT-LINE-2.
00140                        03   FILLER                  PIC X(5) VALUE '    *'.
00141                        03   OUT-EMP-PAY             PIC $(5)9.99.
00142                        03   FILLER                  PIC X(9) VALUE SPACE.
00143                        03   OUT-EMP-TAX             PIC $(5)9.99.
00144                        03   FILLER                  PIC X(8) VALUE SPACE.
00145                        03   OUT-FICA                PIC $(4)9.99.
00146                        03   FILLER                  PIC X(5) VALUE '    *'.
00147                   02   ASTERISK-LINE-2.
00148                        03   FILLER                  PIC X(4) VALUE SPACE.
00149                        03   FILLER                  PIC X(49) VALUE ALL '*'.
00150              01   W2-FORM-LINES-TABLE REDEFINES W-2-FORM-LINES-REGION.
00151                   02   PAY-OUT-PRINT-REC            PIC X(53) OCCURS 8 TIMES.
00152              01   FINAL-MESSAGE-LINE.
00153                   02   FILLER                       PIC X(37)
00154                        VALUE ' W-2 FORMS AND BACKUP TAPE GENERATED'.
```

Figure 4.19 (cont.)

```
00155        *
00156         PROCEDURE DIVISION.
00157        *
00158         YEAR-END-PROCESS-CONTROL.
00159             PERFORM START-UP.
00160             PERFORM GENERATE-PAGES-AND-TAPE UNTIL NO-MORE-RECORDS.
00161             PERFORM FINISH-UP.
00162             STOP RUN.
00163        *
00164         START-UP.
00165             OPEN INPUT PAYROLL-MAST-FILE-IN
00166                  OUTPUT PAYROLL-MAST-BACKUP-FILE-OUT
00167                         W-2-REPORT-PRINT-FILE.
00168             MOVE 1 TO PAGE-COUNT.
00169             MOVE 'N' TO END-OF-PAY-FILE-SW.
00170             PERFORM READ-PAY-MAST-FILE.
00171        *
00172         GENERATE-PAGES-AND-TAPE.
00173             MOVE 'N' TO END-OF-PAGE-SW.
00174             MOVE PAGE-COUNT TO PAGE-COUNT-OUT.
00175             PERFORM WRITE-PAGE-HEADER.
00176             ADD 1 TO PAGE-COUNT.
00177             MOVE 0 TO FORM-COUNT.
00178             PERFORM PROCESS-A-RECORD UNTIL END-PAGE.
00179        *
00180         FINISH-UP.
00181             PERFORM WRITE-MESSAGE.
00182             CLOSE PAYROLL-MAST-FILE-IN
00183                   W-2-REPORT-PRINT-FILE.
00184             CLOSE PAYROLL-MAST-BACKUP-FILE-OUT WITH LOCK.
00185        *
00186         PROCESS-A-RECORD.
00187             MOVE FIRST-3-IN TO OUT-FIRST-3-DIGITS.
00188             MOVE MIDDLE-2-IN TO OUT-MIDDLE-2-DIGITS.
00189             MOVE LAST-4-IN TO OUT-LAST-4-DIGITS.
00190             MOVE PAY-IN-EMP-NAME TO OUT-EMP-NAME.
00191             MOVE PAY-IN-YTD-GROSS TO OUT-EMP-PAY.
00192             MOVE PAY-IN-YTD-TAX TO OUT-EMP-TAX.
00193             MOVE PAY-IN-YTD-FICA TO OUT-FICA.
00194             PERFORM WRITE-SPACE-LINE.
00195             PERFORM WRITE-FORM-LINE
00196                 VARYING LINE-COUNT FROM 1 BY 1
00197                     UNTIL LINE-COUNT IS GREATER THAN LINES-PER-FORM.
00198             ADD 1 TO FORM-COUNT.
00199             IF FORM-COUNT IS EQUAL TO FORMS-PER-PAGE
00200                 MOVE 'Y' TO END-OF-PAGE-SW.
00201             PERFORM WRITE-BACKUP-REC.
00202             PERFORM READ-PAY-MAST-FILE.
00203        *
00204         WRITE-PAGE-HEADER.
00205             WRITE W-2-REPORT-LINE-OUT-AREA FROM PAGE-HEAD-LINE
00206                 AFTER ADVANCING TO-TOP-OF-PAGE.
00207        *
00208         WRITE-MESSAGE.
00209             WRITE W-2-REPORT-LINE-OUT-AREA FROM FINAL-MESSAGE-LINE
00210                 AFTER ADVANCING TO-TOP-OF-PAGE.
00211        *
00212         WRITE-SPACE-LINE.
00213             WRITE W-2-REPORT-LINE-OUT-AREA FROM FORM-SPACER
00214                 AFTER ADVANCING 2 LINES.
00215        *
00216         WRITE-FORM-LINE.
00217             WRITE W-2-REPORT-LINE-OUT-AREA
00218                 FROM PAY-OUT-PRINT-REC (LINE-COUNT)
00219                 AFTER ADVANCING 1 LINES.
00220        *
00221         WRITE-BACKUP-REC.
00222             WRITE PAYROLL-BACKUP-MAST-OUT-AREA
00223                 FROM PAY-MAST-IN-REC.
00224        *
00225         READ-PAY-MAST-FILE.
00226             READ PAYROLL-MAST-FILE-IN INTO PAY-MAST-IN-REC
00227                 AT END MOVE ALL 'Y' TO SWITCHES.
```

ADVANTAGES AND DISADVANTAGES OF SEQUENTIAL FILES

The following are some of the advantages of sequential file organization:

1. It provides for very efficient processing if activity against the records in the file is high, that is, if most (a large percentage) of the records will be affected during a processing run.
2. It is the *most* efficient type of file organization in terms of space utilization of the storage medium.

Disadvantages of sequential files include:

1. A new file must be created whenever new records are inserted in the file or old records are deleted.
2. Processing of unsequenced transactions is very inefficient. Transactions must normally be held until a sufficient number have been accumulated to justify a file update run. Then, prior to the update run, the transaction records must be sorted into the same sequence as the records contained in the master file.
3. Processing of single transactions at the time they actually occur (real-time processing) is not feasible since a specific master record can not be accessed quickly for updating without first accessing all records in the file that precede it.

Programming Exercises for Chapter 4

The following exercises will involve writing programs that process sequential files.

EXERCISE 4.1

Mega-Tronics mails a quarterly report to its stockholders. The stockholder master address file contains the following information:

Record Positions	Contents	Format
1–15	Stockholder identification code	X(15)
16–45	Name	X(30)
46–75	Street address	X(30)
76–90	City	X(15)
91–92	State	X(2)
93–97	Zip Code	X(5)

A program is needed to update the information on the stockholder master file. Files are in order by stockholder identification code. Records used to update the file will be formated the same as the master file records except that an additional position, record position 98, will contain a code indicating what type of updating is needed. Records may be added, deleted, or changed. When data in a master record are to be changed, only the data necessary to process the change will actually be entered. The code in position 98 and its meaning is

Code	Meaning
A	Add a stockholder to file
D	Delete a stockholder from file
M	Change stockholder's record to new values contained in nonblank data fields

Your output should consist of an updated master file in the same form as the original one.

You should also edit the data in the records used to update the file and print a list of the records that you were unable to process because of errors in the data. Your data edit should check for invalid transaction codes and to determine that none of the fields in the records to be added to the file are blank.

EXERCISE 4.2

A program is needed to print mailing labels for the Mega-Tronics quarterly report to its stockholders.

The stockholders' master address file is to be used as input to your program. Format of the information contained in the stockholder records is given in Exercise 4.1.

The address mailing labels are arranged four across on the printer form, separated vertically by one print line. Each label is 30 columns wide, with four columns between each label.

See the following for an illustration of the label forms. To print on these labels, input records must be processed in groups of four.

Sample Output Form

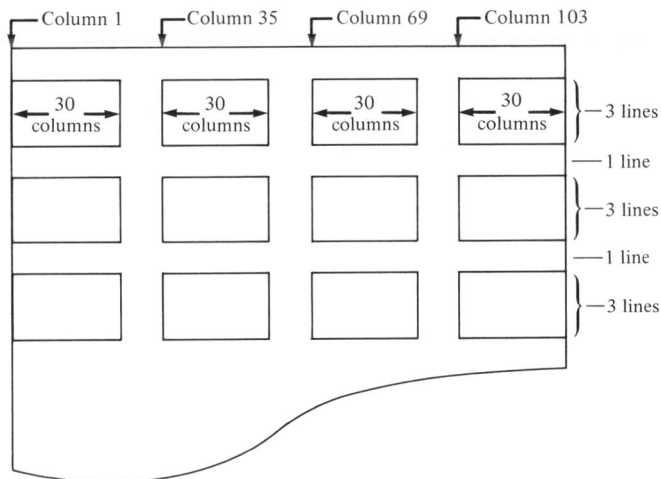

EXERCISE 4.3

The employees' credit union at Mega-Tronics has requested a program to compute and credit interest to accounts on a monthly basis. No interest is earned on deposits during the month in which the deposit is made. Interest for the month is forfeited on any withdrawals made during that month. The current interest rate is $5\frac{1}{2}$ percent annually.

The input file (the old master account file) is in order by account number. Each record contains the following information:

Record Position	Contents	Format
1–5	Account number	X(5)
6–7	Department code	9(2)
8–16	Social security number	X(9)
17–36	Name	X(20)
37–66	Address	X(30)
67–73	Current balance	S9(5)V9(2)
74–80	Total deposits (month)	S9(5)V9(2)
81–87	Total withdrawals (month)	S9(5)V9(2)
88	Account status (I if account is closed, blank otherwise)	X

Your program should create a new master account file in the same form as the old one, with

1. The interest earned added to the current balance.
2. The monthly totals for deposits and withdrawals set to zero.

EXERCISE 4.4

The Mega-Tronics Employee Credit Union needs a program for its daily updating of the master account file. See Exercise 4.3 for format of master file records.

The input data are in order by account number. A transaction code appears, which has the following meaning:

Transaction Code	Meaning
D	Deposit
W	Withdrawal
N	New account
C	Close account

If the transaction code is a D or W, the record contains:

Record Positions	Contents	Format
1–5	Account number	X(5)
6	Transaction code	X
7–13	Amount	9(5)V9(2)

If the transaction code is a C, the record contains:

Record Positions	Contents	Format
1–5	Account number	X(5)
6	Transaction code	X

If the transaction code is an N, the record contains:

Record Positions	Contents	Format
1–5	Account number	X(5)
6	Transaction code	X
7–8	Department code	9(2)
9–17	Social security number	X(9)
18–37	Name	X(20)
38–67	Address	X(30)
68–74	Initial deposit	9(5)V9(2)

Output should consist of an updated master file and a printed report. If an account is closed, its account status should be changed to I and its current balance set to zero.

There may be multiple transactions for an account, so do not write a new or updated master record until all transactions for an account have been processed.

The printed report (see following report layout) should indicate the kind of processing requested and the outcome of that request. Use descriptive messages. (For example: action requested, NEW ACCOUNT; action taken, ACCOUNT OPENED; or if an error message is needed, NO MASTER ACCOUNT FOUND.)

```
                    MEGA-TRONICS EMPLOYEE CREDIT UNION
              DAILY TRANSACTION REPORT FOR XX/XX/XX      PAGE XX

ACCOUNT        ACTION
NUMBER        REQUESTED         ACTION TAKEN                ERROR MESSAGE
XXXXX       XXXXXXXXXXX    XXXXXXXXXXXXXXXXXXX    XXXXXXXXXXXXXXXXXXXXXXXXXXXXX
   .             .                  .                          .
   .             .                  .                          .
   .             .                  .                          .
   .             .                  .                          .
   .             .                  .                          .
```

5 Sorting

You will recall from the previous chapter that the files had to be in order by social security number. The need for order is frequently encountered in the processing methods used in many other data processing applications. Typical of these are

1. Control-break processing (for example, expense reports by year, month, and day; census bureau reports by state, county, and city; student credit-hour production by college, department, and faculty member).
2. Matching records on a common control field (such as matching interest reports from banks and savings institutions with income tax returns for individual tax returns; eliminating the duplicates from files for mailing lists).
3. Use of the SEARCH ALL verb for internal table handling (not for files).

Previously, we have simply assumed that the files were in the correct order. In this chapter, we will be discussing COBOL techniques to arrange the records in the desired order. This process is referred to as *sorting a file*. Although the concept of sorting is the same for both tables and files, different techniques are used to do the sorting. We have already discussed some of the techniques for sorting tables in Chapter 2.

Since sorting of files is frequently done by many different users of a computer system, a sort routine is generally supplied as part of the software provided with the computer system. This routine is one of a set of programs called *utility programs* (or simply *utilities*). They provide a wide range of user services.

File sorting is a very complex process, so we will look at a greatly simplified version of the technique for a very small example. Let's assume a file with records containing, as a key field, the standard two-character state abbreviations developed by the U.S. Post Office. Each record also contains additional data. For our example, the original file to be sorted contains:

Key	Other data
IL	
AR	
AL	
SC	
AR	
IL	
AR	
LA	

First, this file is copied to a work file:

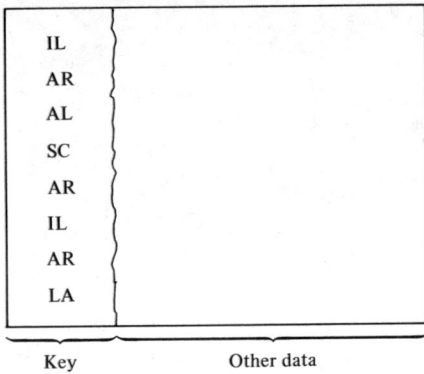

IL	
AR	
AL	
SC	
AR	
IL	
AR	
LA	
Key	Other data

The sorting process on the work file is illustrated in Figure 5.1.

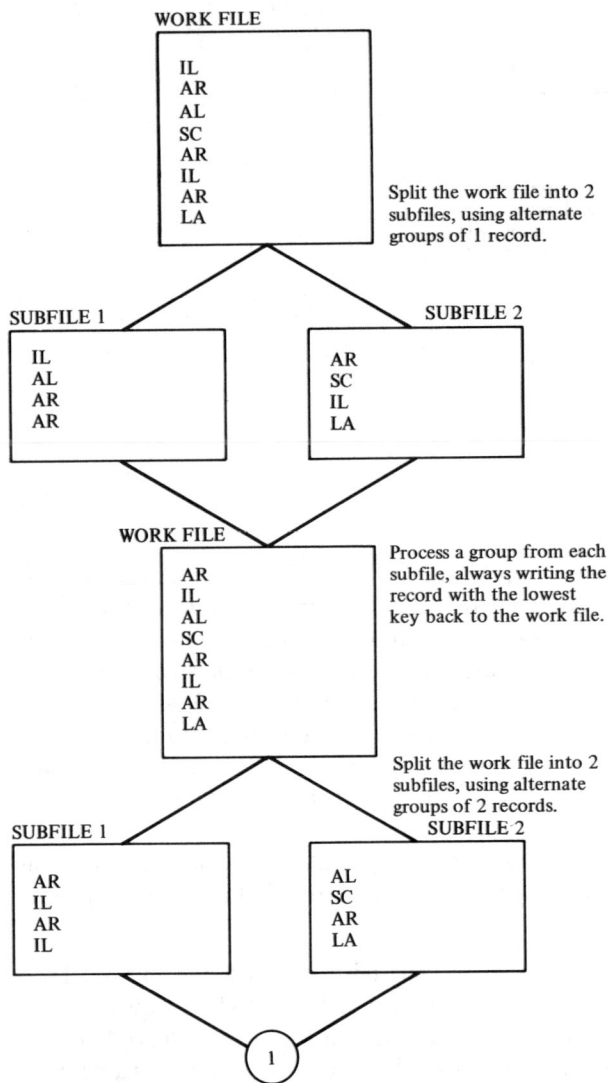

WORK FILE

IL
AR
AL
SC
AR
IL
AR
LA

Split the work file into 2 subfiles, using alternate groups of 1 record.

SUBFILE 1

IL
AL
AR
AR

SUBFILE 2

AR
SC
IL
LA

WORK FILE

AR
IL
AL
SC
AR
IL
AR
LA

Process a group from each subfile, always writing the record with the lowest key back to the work file.

Split the work file into 2 subfiles, using alternate groups of 2 records.

SUBFILE 1

AR
IL
AR
IL

SUBFILE 2

AL
SC
AR
LA

(1)

Figure 5.1
Illustration of sorting by merging.

Figure 5.1 (*cont.*)

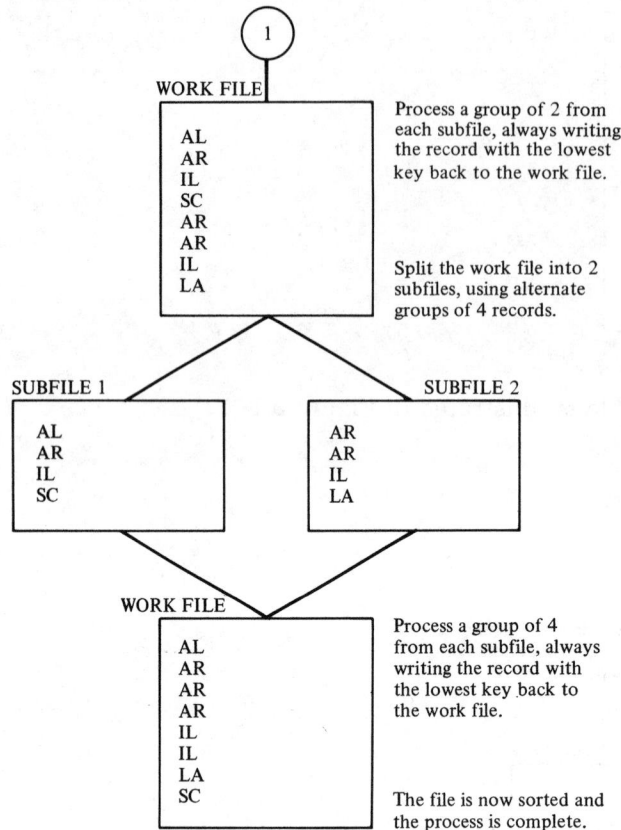

THE COBOL SORT FEATURE

The SORT feature of COBOL allows a programmer access to the sort utility within a COBOL program. The file to be sorted can be read, sorted, and processed by invoking a single COBOL statement. There are three distinct phases involved in the use of the SORT feature. These are (1) an input phase, in which the input file is transferred to the sort work file; (2) a sorting phase, in which the sort work file is actually sorted; and (3) an output phase, in which the sorted file is made available for processing. The point should be emphasized that it is *not* the input file itself that is sorted, but rather it is the sort work file that contains a copy, perhaps even a modified copy, of the input file that is actually sorted.

When the sort feature is used, either the input or output phase, or both, may be done automatically; or they may be under programmer control. Thus the programmer has the following options:

1. The input file can be sorted and a copy of the sorted file kept for later use. This situation, where we assume all files are on disk, is illustrated in Figure 5.2.
2. The input file can be processed to create the records to be transferred to the sort work file and a copy of the sorted file saved for later use. This situation is illustrated in Figure 5.3, where we assume all files are on disk.
3. The input file can be copied to the sort work file and the sorted sort work file processed to create records for the output file. This situation is illustrated in

INPUT phase

1. Opens input, sort work files.
2. Copies input file to sort work file.
3. Closes input file.

SORT phase

Sorts the sort work file.

OUTPUT phase

1. Opens output file.
2. Copies sort work file to output file.
3. Closes output, sort work files.

Input file

Sort work file

Output file

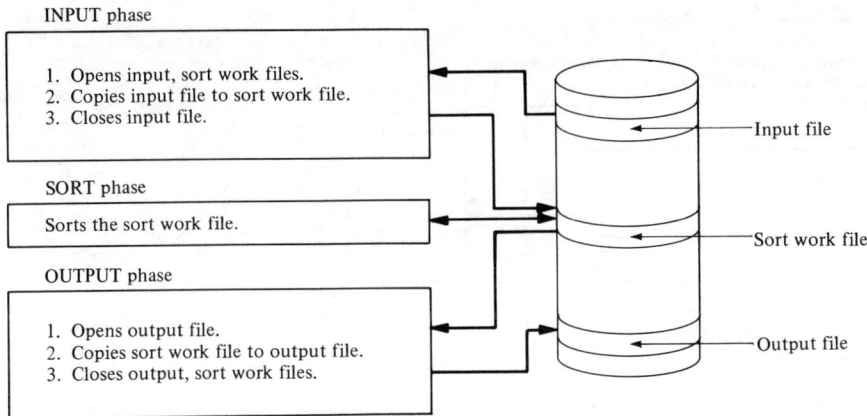

Figure 5.2
The SORT feature with all operations done automatically.

Figure 5.4, where the input and sort work files are on disk and the output file is a print file.

4. The input file can be processed to create the records to be transferred to the sort work file. Processing can also be performed on the sorted file. This situation is illustrated in Figure 5.5, where we assume the input and sort work files are on disk and that two copies of the output file are needed; one is a disk file and the second, a print file.

Since records must be transferred to the sort work file, it is possible for the input and output files to be one and the same; that is, the file is sorted and then the records for the output file overwrite the input file. However, you should be aware that, should a problem develop during the process and you need to rerun the job, the original input file will no longer exist.

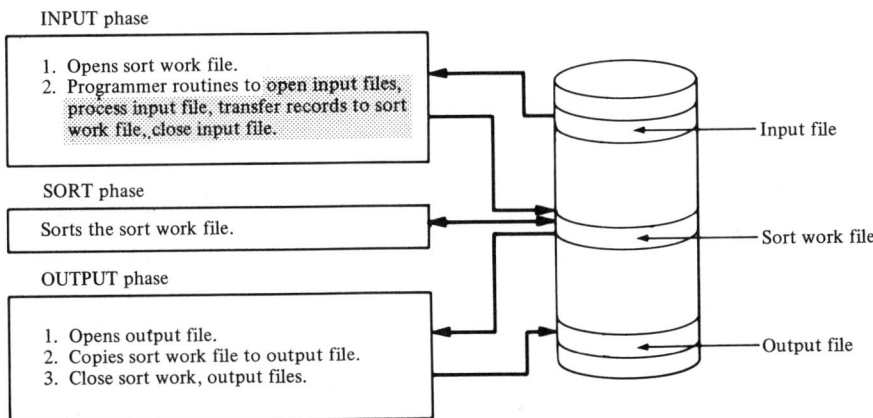

INPUT phase

1. Opens sort work file.
2. Programmer routines to open input files, process input file, transfer records to sort work file, close input file.

SORT phase

Sorts the sort work file.

OUTPUT phase

1. Opens output file.
2. Copies sort work file to output file.
3. Close sort work, output files.

Input file

Sort work file

Output file

Figure 5.3
The SORT feature with the INPUT phase under programmer control. Programmer-written routines are highlighted.

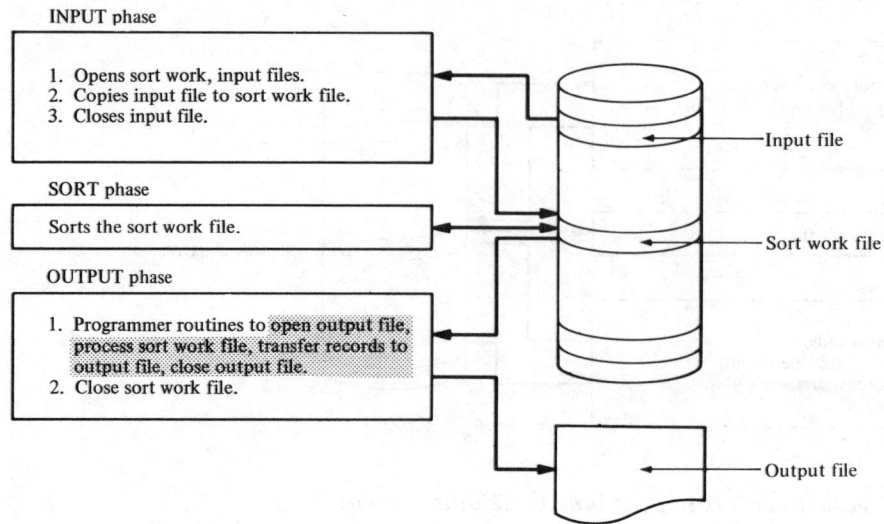

INPUT phase

1. Opens sort work, input files.
2. Copies input file to sort work file.
3. Closes input file.

SORT phase

Sorts the sort work file.

OUTPUT phase

1. Programmer routines to open output file, process sort work file, transfer records to output file, close output file.
2. Close sort work file.

Input file

Sort work file

Output file

Figure 5.4
The SORT feature with the OUTPUT phase under programmer control. Programmer-written routines are highlighted.

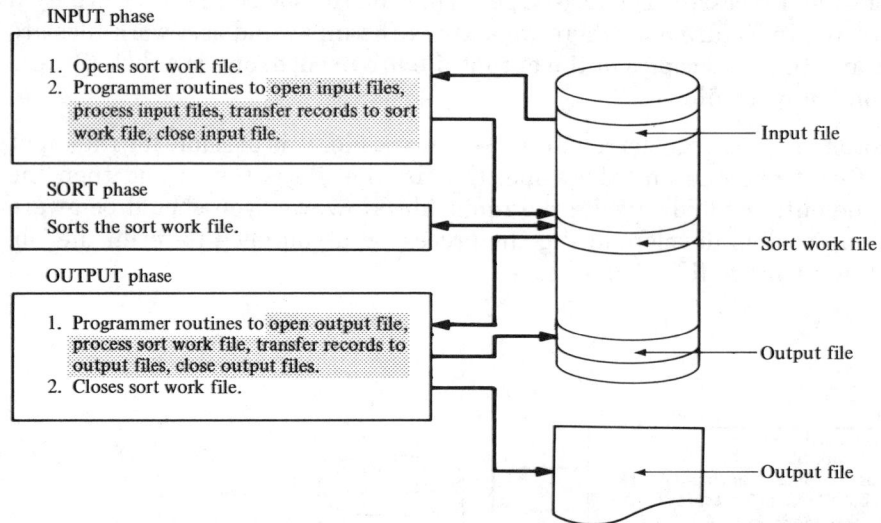

INPUT phase

1. Opens sort work file.
2. Programmer routines to open input files, process input files, transfer records to sort work file, close input file.

SORT phase

Sorts the sort work file.

OUTPUT phase

1. Programmer routines to open output file, process sort work file, transfer records to output files, close output files.
2. Closes sort work file.

Input file

Sort work file

Output file

Output file

Figure 5.5
The SORT feature with INPUT and OUTPUT phases under programmer control. Programmer-written routines are highlighted.

COBOL CONSIDERATIONS

Use of the SORT feature will require new entries in the ENVIRONMENT, DATA, and PROCEDURE DIVISIONs. The sort work file must have a SELECT entry in the ENVIRONMENT DIVISION. There must be a description of the sort work file in the DATA DIVISION. A new verb, SORT, is necessary in the PROCEDURE DIVISION, and the use of the SORT verb may require the use of SECTIONs (described later in this chapter) in the PROCEDURE DIVISION.

ENVIRONMENT DIVISION ENTRIES

Sort work files, like other files, must be named in a SELECT entry in the FILE-CONTROL paragraph in the ENVIRONMENT DIVISION.

```
                    FORMAT

        SELECT sort-work-file-name
        ASSIGN TO system-name
```

Sort-work-file-name: This is the programmer-supplied name assigned to the sort work file. It is this file that will actually be used by the sort utility program. This name must also appear in an SD entry in the DATA DIVISION.

System-name: This name will have the same form as the system names for other files. Although *system-name* may refer to either disk or tape, it will most often refer to disk, since disk sorts are generally faster. This name is highly installation-dependent. For example, for an IBM computer, we might use the following statement to assign the sort work file to a tape drive:

```
    SELECT SORTER-FILE
        ASSIGN TO SYSO01-UT-2400-S-SORTWK1.
```

Alternatively, the sort work file may be assigned to a disk drive:

```
    SELECT SORTER-FILE
        ASSIGN TO SYSO01-DA-3330-S-SORTWK1.
```

You are encouraged to contact your instructor or a computer center consultant for information specific to your installation.

DATA DIVISION ENTRIES

The same type of physical characteristics that are specified for input or output files must also be described for a sort work file. An SD entry is used for this purpose. Its form is similar to the FD entry for other files.

FORMAT
SD sort-work-file-name $\left[\text{DATA} \begin{Bmatrix} \underline{\text{RECORD}} \text{ IS} \\ \underline{\text{RECORDS}} \text{ ARE} \end{Bmatrix} \text{data-name-1, data-name-2, } \dots \right]$ [<u>RECORD CONTAINS</u> [integer-1 *TO*] integer-2 CHARACTERS]

Sort-work-file-name: This name must match that given in a SELECT entry in the ENVIRONMENT DIVISION.

The DATA RECORD and RECORD CONTAINS clauses have the same use as in an FD entry. For some systems—IBM, for example—the DATA RECORD and RECORD CONTAINS clauses are treated as comments.

Record description entries, similar to those associated with an FD entry, appear at the 01-level for each SD. In the SD record description entries, the names of the keys required for sorting *must* be specified; other record fields may require description, if needed for processing.

For an example of an SD description, assume that SORTER-FILE is to be sorted on two keys, first on state code and then on city name. Suppose the state code will appear in bytes 16 and 17 of the record and the city name will appear in bytes 26–40 of the record. Then the description

```
SD      SORTER-FILE.
01      SORT-AREA.
        02  FILLER              PIC X(15).
        02  SORT-STATE-CODE     PIC X(2).
        02  FILLER              PIC X(8).
        02  SORT-CITY-NAME      PIC X(15).
        02  FILLER              PIC X(20).
```

will provide all the information needed for sorting.

Although a file described in an SD is similar in many ways to a file described in an FD, the programmer's access to a file described in an SD is severely restricted. We will look at these restrictions in succeeding sections.

PROCEDURE DIVISION ENTRIES

The SORT verb, which actually causes the sorting process to take place, must be coded in the PROCEDURE DIVISION. In addition, any routines needed to process the input/output files will be coded here. Multiple SORT statements are permitted in a program; however, only one can be active at a time.

A simple version of the SORT statement is as follows:

FORMAT 1

SORT sort-work-file-name

ON $\left\{ \begin{array}{l} \text{ASCENDING} \\ \text{DESCENDING} \end{array} \right\}$ KEY data-name-1, . . .

$\left[\text{ON} \left\{ \begin{array}{l} \text{ASCENDING} \\ \text{DESCENDING} \end{array} \right\} \text{KEY data-name-2, . . .} \right]$

USING input-file-name
GIVING output-file-name

Sort-work-file-name is the name given in an SD entry and indicates the name of the sort work file. The ASCENDING/DESCENDING KEY clause will list the sort keys and indicates whether the records are to be in increasing or decreasing key sequence. Data-name-1, data-name-2, . . . are the names of the sort keys. Each *must* appear in a record description under the SD for sort-work-file-name.

The data fields may be any of the following types:

1. Alphabetic.
2. Alphanumeric.
3. Numeric.
4. Numeric edited.
5. Zoned (external) decimal.
6. Binary (COMPUTATIONAL).
7. Packed (internal) decimal (COMPUTATIONAL-3).[1]

At least one ASCENDING/DESCENDING clause must be specified. Keys are listed in order of decreasing importance. The first (or only) key is called the *major key*. If there are two or more keys, the last one is called the *minor key*. Any other keys are called *intermediate keys*.

ASCENDING KEY SORT-STATE-CODE specifies that the sort work file is to be sorted in alphabetical order by state code.

```
ASCENDING KEY SORT-STATE-CODE,
            SORT-CITY-NAME
```

would specify that the sort work file is to be in alphabetical order by state code and, within a state, to be in alphabetical order by city name. SORT-STATE-CODE is the major key and SORT-CITY-NAME is the minor key.

Rules for sort keys:

1. Keys must be physically located in the same position and have the same data description in every record in the sort work file. If there are multiple record

---

[1] Not in COBOL 74 Standard, but it is a commonly used type with some computer systems, such as IBM.

descriptions in an SD, it is sufficient to describe the sort keys in only one of the record descriptions.

2. Data items used for sort keys may not contain an OCCURS clause or be subordinate to items that contain an OCCURS clause.
3. Keys may not be located following a variable-length table in a record.
4. The data names that describe the keys may be qualified.

In addition to these rules, specific computer systems often have other rules concerning the number of keys one may specify, the length of the keys, and so on. Contact your instructor or computer center personnel at your installation for additional details, if needed.

The USING clause specifies the automatic transfer of all records in input-file-name to sort-work-file-name. The GIVING clause specifies that after sorting is complete, all records in sort-work-file-name are to be transferred automatically to output-file-name.

To help us understand how the different parts fit together, let's look at a program segment (Figure 5.6) to sort on the two keys, state code and city name.

```
      IDENTIFICATION DIVISION.
*
                           .
                           .
                           .
*
      ENVIRONMENT DIVISION.
*
                     .
                     .
                     .

      FILE-CONTROL.
          SELECT CENSUS-DATA-FILE-IN
              ASSIGN TO SYS023-DA-3330-S-CENFILE.
          SELECT CENSUS-DATA-FILE-OUT
              ASSIGN TO SYS023-DA-3330-S-STAFILE.
          SELECT SORTER-FILE
              ASSIGN TO SYS001-DA-3330-S-SORTWK1.
                     .
                     .
                     .
*
      DATA DIVISION.
*
      FILE SECTION.
      FD   CENSUS-DATA-FILE-IN
               LABEL RECORDS STANDARD.
      01   CEN-DATA-IN-AREA                   PIC X(60).
      FD   CENSUS-DATA-FILE-OUT
               LABEL RECORDS STANDARD
               BLOCK CONTAINS 50 RECORDS.
      01   CENSUS-DATA-OUT-AREA               PIC X(60).
      SD   SORTER-FILE.
      01   SORT-AREA.
           02   FILLER                        PIC X(15).
           02   SORT-STATE-CODE               PIC X(2).
           02   FILLER                        PIC X(8).
           02   SORT-CITY-NAME                PIC X(15).
           02   FILLER                        PIC X(20).
                     .
                     .
                     .
```

Figure 5.6

Program segment illustrating USING and GIVING options of the SORT statement.

Figure 5.6 (*cont.*)

```
*
 WORKING-STORAGE SECTION.

                 .
                 .
                 .
*
 PROCEDURE DIVISION.
*
                 .
                 .
                 .

      SORT SORTER-FILE
           ASCENDING KEY SORT-STATE-CODE,
                         SORT-CITY-NAME
           USING CENSUS-DATA-FILE-IN
           GIVING CENSUS-DATA-FILE-OUT.

                 .
                 .
                 .

      STOP RUN.
```

We will now consider a complete program.

> ## Example 5.1

It is sometimes necessary for Mega-Tronics, Inc. to provide information to government agencies concerning the employment status of individuals. Since the request for information may not include a social security number, a copy of the payroll master file (created for Example 4.1, Chapter 4) is to be created in alphabetical order so that employee payroll records can be located by employee name. This will allow processing several such requests in one search through the file.

A program solution to Example 5.1 is given in Figure 5.7. The following important points should be noted:

1. Only the sort key field PAY-WORK-EMP-NAME needs to be described in SORT-WORK-AREA. The records in PAYROLL-MAST-FILE-IN will be copied without change to SORT-WORK-FILE. No item in PAYROLL-MAST-IN-AREA need be named. Note, however, that PAY-IN-EMP-NAME (line 49) is in exactly the same location in the record as PAY-WORK-EMP-NAME (line 59).
2. There are no OPEN, CLOSE, READ, or WRITE statements for the files PAYROLL-MAST-FILE-IN and PAYROLL-MAST-ORD-FILE-OUT, since these functions are done *automatically* by the SORT.
3. The records in PAYROLL-MAST-FILE-IN and PAYROLL-MAST-ORD-FILE-OUT have the same format.
4. Assigning PAYROLL-MAST-FILE-IN and PAYROLL-MAST-ORD-OUT to the same disk assignment would cause the output file to overwrite the input file. This is a risky practice. At the end of this program there are two copies of the payroll file, the original in order by social security number and the new one in alphabetical order.

```
00001              IDENTIFICATION DIVISION.
00002         *
00003            PROGRAM-ID.
00004              EX-5-1.
00005         ********************************************************************
00006         *                                                                  *
00007         *    PROGRAMMER TEAM              SUMMERS/WALSTROM/LINDAHL          *
00008         *    PROGRAM COMPLETION DATE JANUARY 9 1984.                       *
00009         *                                                                  *
00010         *                    PROGRAM SUMMARY                               *
00011         *    INPUT                                                         *
00012         *        THE INPUT FILE IS THE PAYROLL MASTER FILE. THE ONLY       *
00013         *        DATA USED IS THE EMPLOYEE NAME IN RECORD POSITIONS        *
00014         *        21-40.                                                    *
00015         *                                                                  *
00016         *    PROCESSING                                                    *
00017         *        SORTING OF THE PAYROLL MASTER FILE IS DONE USING          *
00018         *        THE SORT VERB.                                            *
00019         *                                                                  *
00020         *    OUTPUT                                                        *
00021         *        A COPY OF THE PAYROLL MASTER FILE IN ALPHABETICAL         *
00022         *        ORDER BY EMPLOYEE NAME                                    *
00023         ********************************************************************
00024         *
00025            ENVIRONMENT DIVISION.
00026         *
00027            CONFIGURATION SECTION.
00028            SOURCE-COMPUTER.
00029              IBM-370-155.
00030            OBJECT-COMPUTER.
00031              IBM-370-155.
00032            INPUT-OUTPUT SECTION.
00033            FILE-CONTROL.
00034              SELECT PAYROLL-MAST-FILE-IN
00035                ASSIGN TO SYS023-DA-3330-S-PAYFILE.
00036              SELECT PAYROLL-MAST-ORD-FILE-OUT
00037                ASSIGN TO SYS023-DA-3330-S-SRTFILE.
00038              SELECT SORT-WORK-FILE
00039                ASSIGN TO SYS001-UT-3330-S-SORTWK1.
00040         *
00041            DATA DIVISION.
00042         *
00043            FILE SECTION.
00044            FD  PAYROLL-MAST-FILE-IN
00045                LABEL RECORDS STANDARD
00046                BLOCK CONTAINS 10 RECORDS.
00047            01  PAYROLL-MAST-IN-AREA.
00048                02  FILLER                        PIC X(12).
00049                02  PAY-IN-EMP-NAME               PIC X(20).
00050                02  FILLER                        PIC X(68).
00051            FD  PAYROLL-MAST-ORD-FILE-OUT
00052                LABEL RECORDS STANDARD
00053                BLOCK CONTAINS 10 RECORDS.
00054            01  PAYROLL-MAST-ORD-OUT-AREA         PIC X(100).
00055            SD  SORT-WORK-FILE.
00056
00057            01  SORT-WORK-AREA.
00058                02  FILLER                        PIC X(12).
00059                02  PAY-WORK-EMP-NAME             PIC X(20).
00060                02  FILLER                        PIC X(68).
00061         *
00062            PROCEDURE DIVISION.
00063         *
00064            SORTER-CONTROL.
00065                SORT SORT-WORK-FILE
00066                    ON ASCENDING KEY PAY-WORK-EMP-NAME
00067                    USING PAYROLL-MAST-FILE-IN
00068                    GIVING PAYROLL-MAST-ORD-FILE-OUT.
00069                STOP RUN.
```

Figure 5.7
Sorting a file using the USING/GIVING options for Example 5.1.

To use the more complex version of the SORT statement requires that the PRO-CEDURE DIVISION be written in SECTION(s).

A SECTION consists of one or more consecutive paragraphs and has the following format:

```
PROCEDURE DIVISION.
section-name-1 SECTION.
paragraph-name-1-1.
        .
        .
        .
[paragraph-name-1-2.
        .
        .
        .
                                ]
[section-name-2 SECTION.
                                ]
```

A SECTION header consists of a section-name followed by the COBOL reserved word SECTION. The usual rules for forming a procedure name also apply to SECTION names. A SECTION header begins in the A margin and must be on a line by itself.

The end of a SECTION is indicated by the appearance of a new SECTION header or the end of the program. Execution of a SECTION begins with the first statement in the first paragraph of the SECTION and ends with the last statement in the last paragraph of the SECTION. Statements will be executed in sequential order unless the programmer alters the execution sequence.

The reserved word EXIT is essentially a "do-nothing," yet useful, verb. It allows us to assign a procedure-name to a given point in a program. When used, EXIT must be the only statement in the paragraph.

FORMAT
paragraph name.   <u>EXIT</u>.

The EXIT paragraph typically follows a series of paragraphs for the purpose of providing a given end point that can be referenced.

Frequently, the EXIT statement is used as the last statement in a SECTION. We highly recommend this practice, because it is consistent with the design of structured programs.

The GO TO statement can be used to alter the normal execution sequence.

```
+-----------------------------+
|           FORMAT            |
+-----------------------------+
|     GO TO procedure-name    |
+-----------------------------+
```

The GO TO statement causes the first statement in procedure-name (paragraph) to be the next statement executed. Since the last paragraph of a SECTION must be executed, the GO TO statement can be used in conjunction with an EXIT statement to terminate the execution of a SECTION.

An example of SECTION organization is given in Figure 5.8. Note in this figure that the statement GO TO EXAMPLE-SECT-EXIT will transfer program control to a paragraph that contains an EXIT statement. This action will indicate that execution of statements in EXAMPLE-SECT SECTION is complete, since a new section-name will be encountered following execution of the EXIT statement.

```
            .
            .
            .
*
EXAMPLE-SECT SECTION.
*
 EXAMPLE-SECT-CONTROL.
     PERFORM START-SECT.
     PERFORM ADD-UP UNTIL A IS POSITIVE.
     DISPLAY 'A=', A, 'B=', B.
     GO TO EXAMPLE-SECT-EXIT.
*
 START-SECT.
     MOVE -2 TO A.
     MOVE 0 TO B.
*
 ADD-UP.
     ADD A TO B.
     ADD 1 TO A.
*
EXAMPLE-SECT-EXIT.
     EXIT.
*
 EXAMPLE-SECT-NEXT SECTION.
            .
            .
            .
```

Figure 5.8
Illustration of SECTION organization.

A general version of the SORT statement is as follows:

FORMAT

SORT   sort-work-file-name

      ON $\left\{ \begin{array}{l} \underline{\text{ASCENDING}} \\ \underline{\text{DESCENDING}} \end{array} \right\}$ KEY data-name-1 . . .

      $\left[\text{ON} \left\{ \begin{array}{l} \underline{\text{ASCENDING}} \\ \underline{\text{DESCENDING}} \end{array} \right\} \text{KEY data-name-2 . . .} \right]$

      $\left\{ \begin{array}{l} \underline{\text{INPUT PROCEDURE}} \text{ IS section-name-1 } [\underline{\text{THRU}} \text{ section-name-2}] \\ \underline{\text{USING}} \text{ input-file-name} \end{array} \right\}$

      $\left\{ \begin{array}{l} \underline{\text{OUTPUT PROCEDURE}} \text{ IS section-name-3 } [\underline{\text{THRU}} \text{ section-name-4}] \\ \underline{\text{GIVING}} \text{ output-file-name} \end{array} \right\}$

The features remaining to be discussed are INPUT/OUTPUT PROCEDURE(s).

INPUT PROCEDURE

An INPUT PROCEDURE contains statements to read input data and perform any preprocessing necessary to create and transfer the records to the sort work file. For most applications, the INPUT PROCEDURE will consist of a single SECTION; however, by specifying the THRU option, two or more SECTION(s) may be used.

    For example, if CENSUS-DATA-FILE-IN (Figure 5.6) requires preprocessing to generate the records to be sorted for CENSUS-DATA-FILE-OUT, then we may write

```
SORT SORTER-FILE
     ON ASCENDING KEY   SORT-STATE-CODE,
                        SORT-CITY-NAME
     INPUT PROCEDURE PROCESS-DATA-FILE-IN
     GIVING CENSUS-DATA-FILE-OUT.
```

PROCESS-DATA-FILE-IN is the name of a SECTION that will contain the preprocessing and transfer statements necessary to generate SORTER-FILE.

    Within the SECTION(s) named in the INPUT PROCEDURE clause, the records are transferred to the sort work file one at a time via the RELEASE statement.

FORMAT

<u>RELEASE</u> sort-record-name

    [<u>FROM</u> identifier]

The following rules apply:

1. A RELEASE statement may be used only within the SECTION(s) named in the INPUT PROCEDURE clause.
2. If the INPUT PROCEDURE option is specified, at least one RELEASE statement must be included.
3. Sort-record-name is the name of a logical record associated with sort-work-file-name.
4. When the FROM identifier is used, it makes the RELEASE statement equivalent to

```
MOVE identifier TO sort-record-name.
RELEASE sort-record-name.
```

The usual MOVE rules apply.
5. Sort-record-name and identifier must not refer to the same storage area.

To MOVE the data item NEW-CENSUS-DATA to SORT-AREA and add this new record to SORTER-FILE, we write

```
RELEASE SORT-AREA
      FROM NEW-CENSUS-DATA.
```

The effect is identical to a WRITE/FROM for a file opened as OUTPUT.

Example 5.2

This month, departments 1, 7, and 10 at the Mega-Tronics Corporation will be on vacation. The file kept in alphabetical order by the payroll/accounting department (Example 5.1) must have employees in these departments deleted. That is, employees in these departments will not be included in the *new* payroll file.

We will not discuss the program solution to Example 5.2 shown in Figure 5.10 in detail (structure charts are in Figure 5.9); however, the following points are important:

1. Since PAY-IN-DEPT-CODE (line 67) is the only data item of PAY-MAST-IN-REC that is referenced in the PROCEDURE DIVISION, it is the only one explicitly named. Other fields can be named if needed by the programming logic.
2. Only PAYROLL-MAST-FILE-IN was opened and closed in the program. The sort work file is always opened and closed automatically and, since the GIVING option was used, the output file is also opened and closed automatically.
3. The choice of the INPUT PROCEDURE option (line 83) causes one complete execution of the SECTION named READ-IN. Control passes to the SECTION named READ-IN (line 86), where the records are read, processed, and transferred to SORT-WORK-FILE. After completion of the execution of the SECTION named READ-IN, control returns to the SORT statement for the actual sorting of SORT-WORK-FILE.
4. The RELEASE (line 110) is similar to the WRITE in the sense that both are used to output records. Since RELEASE/FROM is used, data in SORT-WORK-AREA and PAYROLL-MAST-IN-REC will be identical, even though the fields are not all specified.
5. Where a choice is possible, statements related to the creation of SORT-WORK-FILE are placed in the INPUT PROCEDURE section. As an example of this,

PAYROLL-MAST-FILE-IN could have been OPENed and CLOSEd in the SORT-CONTROL section, but instead it was OPENed and CLOSEd in READ-IN, the INPUT PROCEDURE section. We believe that this organization is more consistent with structured design objectives.

Section organization

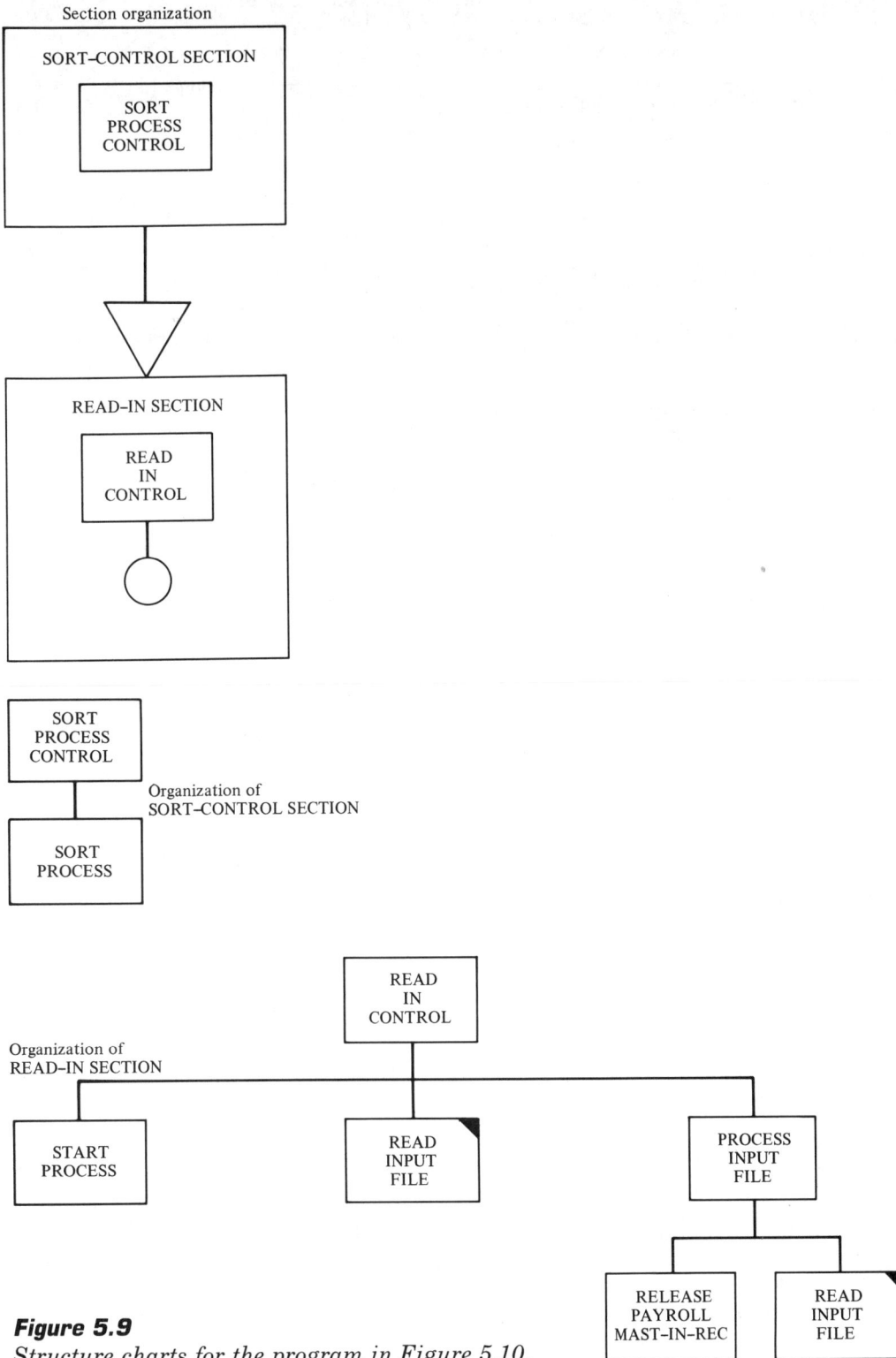

Organization of
SORT–CONTROL SECTION

Organization of
READ–IN SECTION

Figure 5.9
Structure charts for the program in Figure 5.10.

```
00001                IDENTIFICATION DIVISION.
00002           *
00003                PROGRAM-ID.
00004                    EX-5-2.
00005           ***********************************************************
00006           *                                                         *
00007           *    PROGRAMMER TEAM          SUMMERS/WALSTROM/LINDAHL     *
00008           *    PROGRAM COMPLETION DATE JANUARY 20, 1984.            *
00009           *                                                         *
00010           *                   PROGRAM SUMMARY                       *
00011           *    INPUT                                                *
00012           *        THE INPUT FILE IS THE PAYROLL MASTER FILE. THE DATA *
00013           *        NECESSARY FOR THIS APPLICATION                   *
00014           *            - NAME RECORD POSITIONS 21-40                *
00015           *            - DEPARTMENT CODE RECORD POSITIONS 2-3       *
00016           *                                                         *
00017           *    PROCESSING                                           *
00018           *            - RECORDS FOR VACATIONING DEPARTMENTS ARE DELETED *
00019           *            - SORTING OF THE FILE IS DONE USING THE SORT VERB *
00020           *                                                         *
00021           *    OUTPUT                                               *
00022           *        A COPY OF THE PAYROLL MASTER FILE WHICH          *
00023           *            - IS IN ALPHABETICAL ORDER BY EMPLOYEE NAME  *
00024           *            - DOES NOT CONTAIN RECORDS FOR EMPLOYEES ASSIGNED *
00025           *              TO VACATIONING DEPARTMENTS                 *
00026           ***********************************************************
00027           *
00028                ENVIRONMENT DIVISION.
00029           *
00030                CONFIGURATION SECTION.
00031                SOURCE-COMPUTER.
00032                    IBM-370-155.
00033                OBJECT-COMPUTER.
00034                    IBM-370-155.
00035                INPUT-OUTPUT SECTION.
00036                FILE-CONTROL.
00037                    SELECT PAYROLL-MAST-FILE-IN
00038                        ASSIGN TO SYS023-DA-3330-S-PAYFILE.
00039                    SELECT PAYROLL-MAST-ORD-FILE-OUT
00040                        ASSIGN TO SYS023-DA-3330-S-SRTFILE.
00041                    SELECT SORT-WORK-FILE
00042                        ASSIGN TO SYS001-DA-3330-S-SORTWK1.
00043           *
00044                DATA DIVISION.
00045           *
00046                FILE SECTION.
00047                FD  PAYROLL-MAST-FILE-IN
00048                        LABEL RECORDS STANDARD
00049                        BLOCK CONTAINS 10 RECORDS.
00050                01  PAYROLL-IN-AREA                  PIC X(100).
00051                FD  PAYROLL-MAST-ORD-FILE-OUT
00052                        LABEL RECORDS STANDARD
00053                        BLOCK CONTAINS 10 RECORDS.
00054                01  PAYROLL-MAST-ORD-AREA-OUT        PIC X(100).
00055                SD  SORT-WORK-FILE.
00056
00057                01  SORT-WORK-AREA.
00058                    02  FILLER                       PIC X(12).
00059                    02  PAY-WORK-EMP-NAME            PIC X(20).
00060                    02  FILLER                       PIC X(68).
00061           *
00062                WORKING-STORAGE SECTION.
00063                01  END-OF-FILE-SW                   PIC X.
00064                    88  NO-MORE-DATA   VALUE 'Y'.
00065                01  PAYROLL-MAST-IN-REC.
00066                    02  FILLER                       PIC X.
00067                    02  PAY-IN-DEPT-CODE             PIC S9(2).
00068                        88  DEPT-ON-VACATION     VALUE 1 7 10.
00069                    02  FILLER                       PIC X(97).
00070           *
00071                PROCEDURE DIVISION.
00072           *
00073                SORT-CONTROL SECTION.
00074           *
00075                SORT-PROCESS-CONTROL.
00076                    PERFORM SORT-PROCESS.
00077                    DISPLAY ' CREATION OF SORTED FILE COMPLETE'.
00078                    STOP RUN.
```

```
00079        *
00080            SORT-PROCESS.
00081                SORT SORT-WORK-FILE
00082                    ON ASCENDING KEY PAY-WORK-EMP-NAME
00083                    INPUT PROCEDURE READ-IN
00084                    GIVING PAYROLL-MAST-ORD-FILE-OUT.
00085        *
00086        READ-IN SECTION.
00087        *
00088        READ-IN-CONTROL.
00089            PERFORM START-PROCESS.
00090            PERFORM READ-INPUT-FILE.
00091            PERFORM PROCESS-INPUT-FILE UNTIL NO-MORE-DATA.
00092            CLOSE PAYROLL-MAST-FILE-IN
00093            GO TO READ-IN-SECTION-EXIT.
00094        *
00095        START-PROCESS.
00096            MOVE 'N' TO END-OF-FILE-SW.
00097            OPEN INPUT PAYROLL-MAST-FILE-IN.
00098        *
00099        PROCESS-INPUT-FILE.
00100            IF NOT DEPT-ON-VACATION
00101                PERFORM RELEASE-PAYROLL-MAST-IN-REC.
00102            PERFORM READ-INPUT-FILE.
00103        *
00104        READ-INPUT-FILE.
00105            READ PAYROLL-MAST-FILE-IN
00106                INTO PAYROLL-MAST-IN-REC
00107                AT END MOVE 'Y' TO END-OF-FILE-SW.
00108        *
00109        RELEASE-PAYROLL-MAST-IN-REC.
00110            RELEASE SORT-WORK-AREA FROM PAYROLL-MAST-IN-REC.
00111        *
00112        READ-IN-SECTION-EXIT.
00113            EXIT.
```

Figure 5.10
Sorting a file using the INPUT PROCEDURE/GIVING options for Example 5.2.

For an INPUT PROCEDURE, the following rules apply:

1. The INPUT PROCEDURE must consist of one or more sections that are written consecutively and do not form a part of any OUTPUT PROCEDURE.
2. The INPUT PROCEDURE must include at least one RELEASE statement in order to transfer records to the sort work file.
3. With the following exceptions, the INPUT PROCEDURE may contain any type of executable statement:
   a. The INPUT PROCEDURE must not contain any SORT statements.
   b. The INPUT PROCEDURE must not contain any transfers of control to points outside the INPUT PROCEDURE.[2]
   c. The remainder of the PROCEDURE DIVISION must not contain any transfers of control to points inside the INPUT PROCEDURE.[2]

OUTPUT PROCEDURE

An OUTPUT PROCEDURE contains statements to process records from the sort work file after the sorting has taken place. Like INPUT PROCEDURE(s), OUTPUT PROCEDURE(s) will in most cases consist of a single SECTION.

---

[2] Some compilers have extensions that allow these exceptions; however, their use is questionable programming practice.

As an example of an OUTPUT PROCEDURE, suppose that SORTER-FILE must be processed after sorting to create the file CENSUS-DATA-FILE-OUT (Figure 5.6); then we may write

```
SORT  SORTER-FILE
      ON ASCENDING KEY SORT-STATE-CODE,
                       SORT-CITY-NAME
      INPUT PROCEDURE PROCESS-DATA-FILE-IN
      OUTPUT PROCEDURE PROCESS-SORTER-FILE
```

PROCESS-SORTER-FILE is the name of a SECTION that will contain the statements to process SORTER-FILE after sorting is complete.

Within the SECTION(s) named in the OUTPUT PROCEDURE clause, the records are transferred from the sort work file to the program work area one at a time via the RETURN statement

---

FORMAT

RETURN sort-work-file-name [INTO identifier]

    AT END imperative-statement

The following rules apply:

1. A RETURN statement may only be used within the SECTION(s) named in the OUTPUT PROCEDURE clause.
2. An OUTPUT PROCEDURE must contain at least one RETURN statement to make records in the sort work file available.
3. Sort-work-file-name is the name given in the SD entry.
4. The record retrieved from sort-work-file-name will be located in the buffer area described in the 01-entry under the SD. If the INTO option is used, the record will also be located in the identifier named.
5. The identifier must be the name of a WORKING-STORAGE area or output record area. Use of the INTO option is equivalent to

```
RETURN sort-work-file-name
     AT END imperative-statement.
MOVE sort-record-name TO identifier.
```

   The rules for alphanumeric MOVE(s) apply. The RETURN/INTO is similar in effect to READ/INTO.
6. The imperative-statement in the AT END clause specifies the action to be taken when all records have been obtained from the sort work file.

To obtain the next record from SORTER-FILE and place it in SORT-WORK-OUT-REC, we may write

```
RETURN SORTER-FILE INTO SORT-WORK-OUT-REC
     AT END MOVE 'YES' TO EOF-SW.
```

The effect is the same as a READ/INTO for a file opened as INPUT.

Example 5.3

Each department head at Mega-Tronics needs a report of the total salary to date paid to employees in his or her department.

The following points concerning the program solution to Example 5.3, as shown in Figure 5.12 (structure charts in Figure 5.11), are important:

1. There are two keys specified for sorting, namely, PAY-WORK-DEPT-CODE and PAY-WORK-EMP-NAME. The sorting will cause the departments to be arranged in ascending order on department code and, within a department, the employees to be arranged in alphabetical order by name.
2. Only SALARY-REP-PRINT-FILE was explicitly opened and closed in the program. All other files were opened and closed automatically.
3. The choice of the OUTPUT PROCEDURE option causes one complete execution of the SECTION named GENERATE-REPORT *after* the sorting of SORT-WORK-FILE is complete. Control then returns to the statement following the SORT statement.
4. The RETURN obtains input from the file SORT-WORK-FILE and is similar to a READ.
5. The record formats of PAYROLL-MAST-IN-AREA, SORT-WORK-AREA, and SORT-RET-REC are identical and only the fields needed are explicitly named.
6. No permanent copy of SORT-WORK-FILE was output to tape or disk. This could easily have been done by adding the necessary WRITE statement in GENERATE-REPORT.

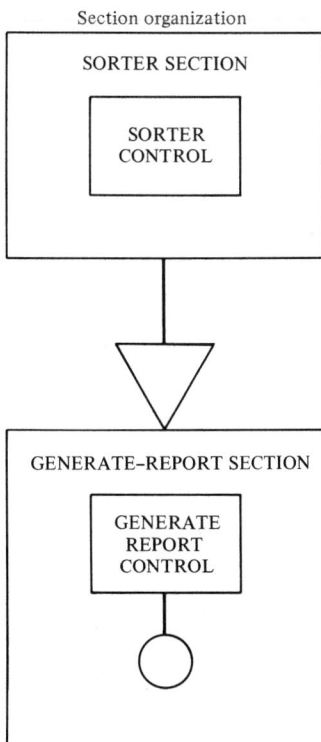

Figure 5.11a
Structure charts for the program in Figure 5.12.

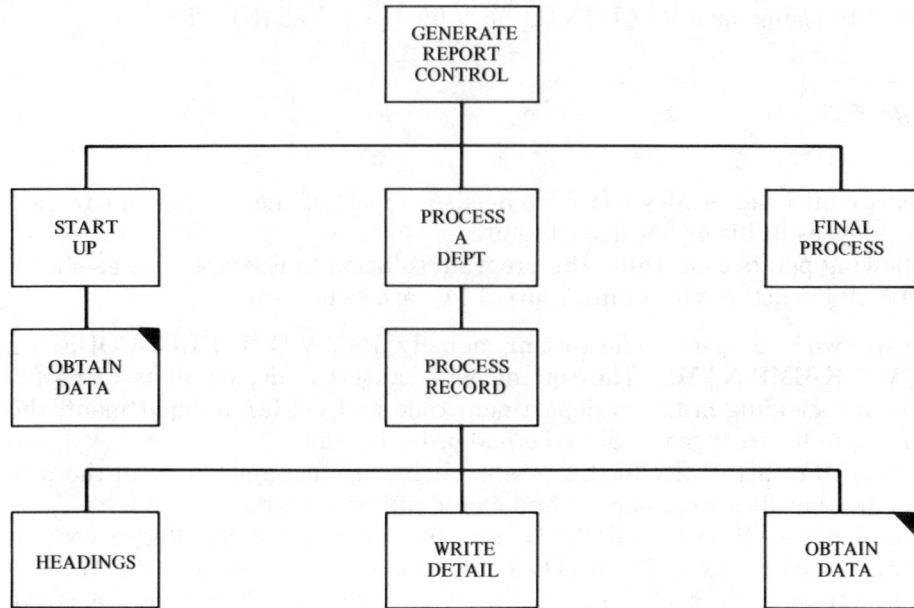

Figure 5.11b
Organization of GENERATE REPORT SECTION for the program in Figure 5.12.

```
00001          IDENTIFICATION DIVISION.
00002     *
00003      PROGRAM-ID.
00004         EX-5-3.
00005     ***********************************************************************
00006     *                                                                     *
00007     *    PROGRAMMER TEAM          SUMMERS/WALSTROM/LINDAHL               *
00008     *    PROGRAM COMPLETION DATE JANUARY 26, 1984.                       *
00009     *                                                                     *
00010     *                      PROGRAM SUMMARY                                *
00011     *    INPUT                                                            *
00012     *         THE INPUT FILE IS THE PAYROLL MASTER FILE. THE DATA         *
00013     *         NECESSARY FOR THIS APPLICATION                              *
00014     *              - DEPARTMENT CODE RECORD POSITIONS 2-3                 *
00015     *              - NAME RECORD POSITIONS 20-41                          *
00016     *              - YEAR-TO-DATE GROSS RECORD POSITIONS 81-87            *
00017     *                                                                     *
00018     *    PROCESSING                                                       *
00019     *         SORTING IS DONE USING THE TWO KEYS DEPARTMENT CODE          *
00020     *         AND EMPLOYEE NAME BY THE SORT VERB                          *
00021     *                                                                     *
00022     *    OUTPUT                                                           *
00023     *         A PRINTED REPORT IS PRODUCED. EACH DEAPRTMENTAL REPORT      *
00024     *         BEGINS ON A NEW PAGE. THE REPORT FOR A DEPARTMENT IS        *
00025     *         IN ALPHABETICAL ORDER BY EMPLOYEE NAME. REPORTED FOR        *
00026     *         EACH EMPLOYEE IS                                            *
00027     *              - EMPLOYEE NAME                                        *
00028     *              - YEAR-TO-DATE GROSS PAY                               *
00029     ***********************************************************************
00030     *
00031      ENVIRONMENT DIVISION.
```

Figure 5.12
Sorting a file using the USING/OUTPUT PROCEDURE options for Example 5.3.

Figure 5.12 (cont.)

```
00032                  *
00033                  CONFIGURATION SECTION.
00034                  SOURCE-COMPUTER.
00035                      IBM-370-155.
00036                  OBJECT-COMPUTER.
00037                      IBM-370-155.
00038                  SPECIAL-NAMES.
00039                      C01 IS TOP-OF-PAGE.
00040                  INPUT-OUTPUT SECTION.
00041                  FILE-CONTROL.
00042                      SELECT PAYROLL-MAST-FILE-IN
00043                          ASSIGN TO SYS023-DA-3330-S-PAYFILE.
00044                      SELECT SORT-WORK-FILE
00045                          ASSIGN TO SYS001-DA-3330-S-SORTWK1.
00046                      SELECT SALARY-REP-PRINT-FILE
00047                          ASSIGN TO SYS009-UR-1403-S.
00048                  *
00049                  DATA DIVISION.
00050                  *
00051                  FILE SECTION.
00052                  FD  PAYROLL-MAST-FILE-IN
00053                          LABEL RECORDS STANDARD
00054                          BLOCK CONTAINS 10 RECORDS.
00055                  01  PAYROLL-MAST-IN-AREA            PIC X(100).
00056                  SD  SORT-WORK-FILE.
00057
00058                  01  SORT-WORK-AREA.
00059                      02  FILLER                      PIC X.
00060                      02  PAY-WORK-DEPT-CODE          PIC S9(2).
00061                      02  FILLER                      PIC X(9).
00062                      02  PAY-WORK-EMP-NAME           PIC X(20).
00063                      02  FILLER                      PIC X(68).
00064                  FD  SALARY-REP-PRINT-FILE
00065                          LABEL RECORDS OMITTED.
00066                  01  SALARY-REP-PRINT-AREA           PIC X(133).
00067                  *
00068                  WORKING-STORAGE SECTION.
00069                  01  SWITCHES.
00070                      02  END-OF-FILE-SW              PIC X.
00071                          88  NO-MORE-DATA VALUE 'Y'.
00072                  01  COUNTERS.
00073                      02  LINE-COUNT                  PIC 9(2).
00074                  01  CONSTANTS.
00075                      02  PAGE-SIZE                   PIC 9(2) VALUE 55.
00076                  01  SAVE-AREAS.
00077                      02  SAVE-DEPT-CODE              PIC S9(2).
00078                  01  SORT-RET-REC.
00079                      02  FILLER                      PIC X.
00080                      02  SORT-RET-DEPT-CODE          PIC S9(2).
00081                      02  FILLER                      PIC X(9).
00082                      02  SORT-RET-EMP-NAME           PIC X(20).
00083                      02  FILLER                      PIC X(48).
00084                      02  SORT-RET-YTD-GROSS          PIC S9(5)V9(2).
00085                      02  FILLER                      PIC X(13).
00086                  01  HDG-LINE-1.
00087                      02  FILLER                      PIC X(24) VALUE SPACE.
00088                      02  FILLER                      PIC X(22)
00089                          VALUE 'REPORT FOR DEPARTMENT'.
00090                      02  HDG-DEPT-CODE               PIC Z9.
00091                      02  FILLER                      PIC X(84) VALUE SPACE.
00092                  01  HDG-LINE-2.
00093                      02  FILLER                      PIC X(15) VALUE SPACE.
00094                      02  FILLER                      PIC X(23) VALUE 'NAME'.
00095                      02  FILLER                      PIC X(95)
00096                          VALUE 'TOTAL SALARY TO DATE'.
00097                  01  EMP-REP-PRINT-REC.
00098                      02  FILLER                      PIC X(7) VALUE SPACE.
00099                      02  REP-EMP-NAME                PIC X(43).
00100                      02  REP-YTD-GROSS               PIC $Z(4)9.9(2).
00101                      02  FILLER                      PIC X(76) VALUE SPACE.
00102                  *
00103                  PROCEDURE DIVISION.
00104                  *
00105                  SORTER-SECTION.
```

Figure 5.12 (*cont.*)

```
00106               *
00107                   SORTER-CONTROL.
00108                       SORT SORT-WORK-FILE
00109                           ON ASCENDING KEY PAY-WORK-DEPT-CODE PAY-WORK-EMP-NAME
00110                           USING PAYROLL-MAST-FILE-IN
00111                           OUTPUT PROCEDURE GENERATE-REPORT.
00112                       STOP RUN.
00113               *
00114               GENERATE-REPORT SECTION.
00115               *
00116               GENERATE-REPORT-CONTROL.
00117                   PERFORM START-UP.
00118                   PERFORM PROCESS-A-DEPT UNTIL NO-MORE-DATA.
00119                   PERFORM FINAL-PROCESS.
00120                   GO TO GENERATE-REPORT-SECTION-EXIT.
00121               *
00122               START-UP.
00123                   MOVE 'N' TO END-OF-FILE-SW.
00124                   PERFORM OBTAIN-DATA.
00125                   OPEN OUTPUT SALARY-REP-PRINT-FILE.
00126               *
00127               PROCESS-A-DEPT.
00128                   COMPUTE LINE-COUNT = PAGE-SIZE + 1.
00129                   MOVE SORT-RET-DEPT-CODE TO SAVE-DEPT-CODE.
00130                   MOVE SAVE-DEPT-CODE TO HDG-DEPT-CODE.
00131                   PERFORM PROCESS-RECORD
00132                           UNTIL (NO-MORE-DATA
00133                                  OR
00134                                  SAVE-DEPT-CODE IS NOT EQUAL TO
00135                                  SORT-RET-DEPT-CODE).
00136               *
00137               FINAL-PROCESS.
00138                   CLOSE SALARY-REP-PRINT-FILE.
00139               *
00140               PROCESS-RECORD.
00141                   IF LINE-COUNT IS GREATER THAN PAGE-SIZE
00142                       PERFORM HEADINGS
00143                       MOVE 3 TO LINE-COUNT.
00144                   MOVE SORT-RET-EMP-NAME TO REP-EMP-NAME.
00145                   MOVE SORT-RET-YTD-GROSS TO REP-YTD-GROSS.
00146                   PERFORM WRITE-DETAIL.
00147                   ADD 1 TO LINE-COUNT.
00148                   PERFORM OBTAIN-DATA.
00149               *
00150               HEADINGS.
00151                   WRITE SALARY-REP-PRINT-AREA FROM HDG-LINE-1
00152                       AFTER ADVANCING TOP-OF-PAGE.
00153                   WRITE SALARY-REP-PRINT-AREA FROM HDG-LINE-2
00154                       AFTER ADVANCING 2 LINES.
00155               *
00156               WRITE-DETAIL.
00157                   WRITE SALARY-REP-PRINT-AREA FROM EMP-REP-PRINT-REC
00158                       AFTER ADVANCING 1 LINES.
00159               *
00160               OBTAIN-DATA.
00161                   RETURN SORT-WORK-FILE INTO SORT-RET-REC
00162                       AT END MOVE 'Y' TO END-OF-FILE-SW.
00163               *
00164               GENERATE-REPORT-SECTION-EXIT.
00165                   EXIT.
```

For OUTPUT PROCEDURE(s), the following rules apply:

1. The OUTPUT PROCEDURE must consist of one or more sections that are written consecutively and do not form a part of any INPUT PROCEDURE.
2. The OUTPUT PROCEDURE must include at least one RETURN statement in order to make sorted records available for processing.
3. With the following exceptions, the OUTPUT PROCEDURE may contain any type of executable statement:
   a. The OUTPUT PROCEDURE must not contain any SORT statements.

b. The OUTPUT PROCEDURE must not contain any transfers of control to points outside the OUTPUT PROCEDURE.[3]

c. The remainder of the PROCEDURE DIVISION must not contain any transfers of control to points inside the OUTPUT PROCEDURE.[3]

Example 5.4

The plant manager at Mega's plant site 1 has requested a list of employees and total salary-to-date for each employee. The listing is to be in alphabetical order by employee name within each department.

A solution to this problem is given in Figures 5.13 and 5.14.

The general organization of the program in Figure 5.14 is that statements related only to the input phase of the sort are in GET-PLANT-DATA, whereas statements related only to the output phase of the sort are in GENERATE-PLANT-REPORT. Other statements appear in SORTER. We feel that this is consistent with structured design techniques. Although it would be possible to delete employee information for plant site 2 in GENERATE-PLANT REPORT and choose the USING option, this would cause the entire input file to be transferred to SORT-WORK-FILE. This approach would unnecessarily increase the time required for sorting SORT-WORK-FILE.

---

[3] Some compilers have extensions that allow these exceptions; however, their use is questionable programming practice.

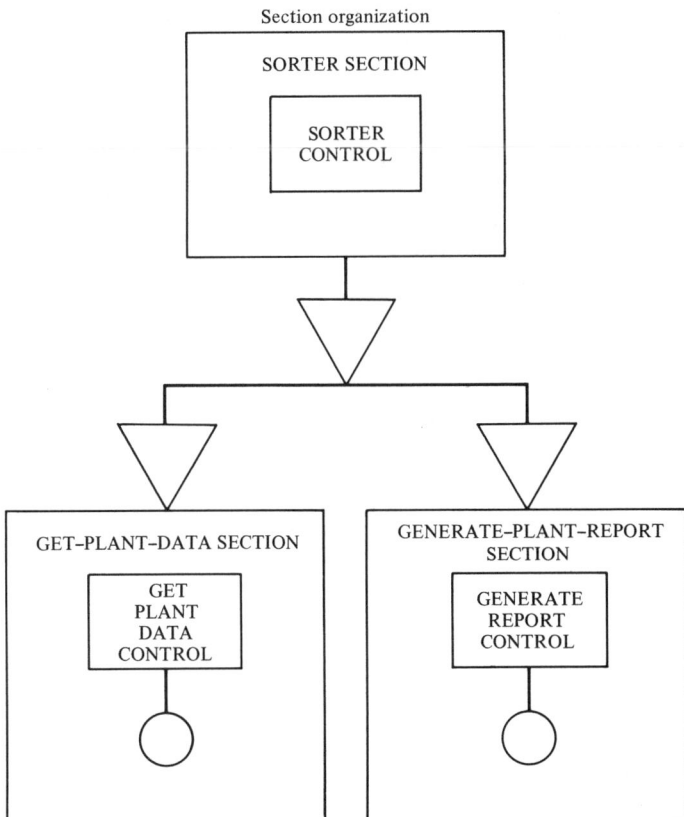

Figure 5.13a
Structure charts for the program in Figure 5.14.

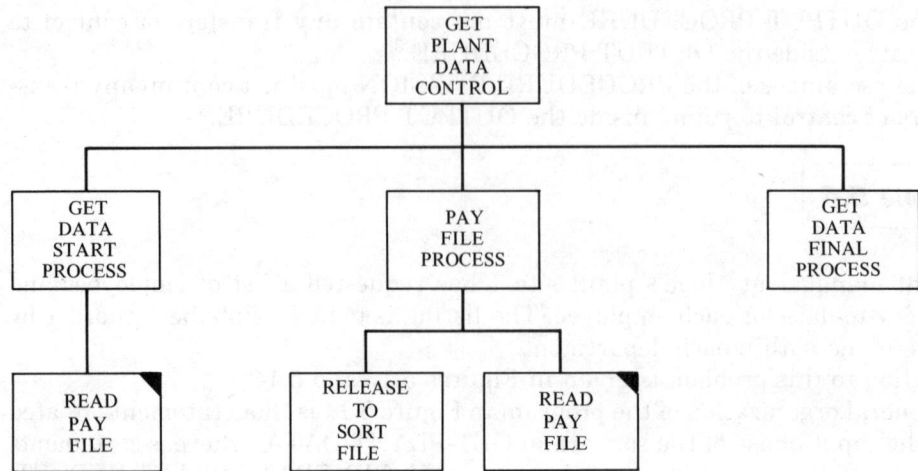

Figure 5.13b
Organization of GET-PLANT-DATA SECTION for the program in Figure 5.14.

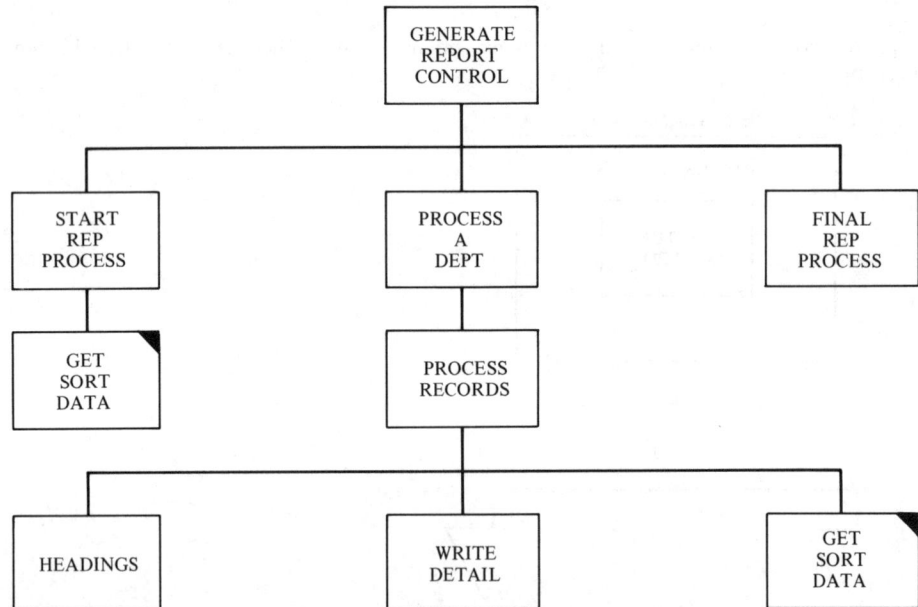

Figure 5.13c
Organization of GENERATE-PLANT-DATA SECTION for the program in Figure 5.14.

```
00001                 IDENTIFICATION DIVISION.
00002            *
00003                 PROGRAM-ID.
00004                     EX-5-4.
00005            ***********************************************************
00006            *                                                         *
00007            *   PROGRAMMER TEAM          SUMMERS/WALSTROM/LINDAHL      *
00008            *   PROGRAM COMPLETION DATE FEBRUARY 3, 1984               *
00009            *                                                         *
00010            *                    PROGRAM SUMMARY                       *
00011            *   INPUT                                                  *
00012            *       THE INPUT FILE IS THE PAYROLL MASTER FILE. THE DATA*
00013            *       NECESSARY FOR THIS APPLICATION:                    *
00014            *       DATA ITEM                     RECORD POSITIONS     *
00015            *          - PLANT SITE CODE             1                 *
00016            *          - DEPARTMENT CODE             2-3               *
00017            *          - NAME                        20-41             *
00018            *          - YEAR-TO-DATE GROSS          81-87             *
00019            *                                                         *
00020            *   PROCESSING                                             *
00021            *       SORTING IS DONE USING THE TWO KEYS DEPARTMENT CODE *
00022            *       AND EMPLOYEE NAME USING THE SORT VERB FOR ALL EMPLOYEE *
00023            *       RECORDS FOR THE SPECIFIED PLANT SITE.              *
00024            *                                                         *
00025            *   OUTPUT                                                 *
00026            *       A PRINTED REPORT IS PRODUCED. FOR THE SPECIFIED PLANT *
00027            *       EACH DEPARTMENTAL REPORT BEGINS ON A NEW PAGE. THE *
00028            *       REPORT FOR A DEPARTMENT IS IN ALPHABETICAL ORDER BY*
00029            *       EMPLOYEE NAME.   REPORTED FOR EACH EMPLOYEE IS     *
00030            *          - EMPLOYEE NAME                                 *
00031            *          - YEAR-TO-DATE GROSS PAY                        *
00032            ***********************************************************
00033            *
00034                 ENVIRONMENT DIVISION.
00035            *
00036                 CONFIGURATION SECTION.
00037                 SOURCE-COMPUTER.
00038                     IBM-370-155.
00039                 OBJECT-COMPUTER.
00040                     IBM-370-155.
00041                 SPECIAL-NAMES.
00042                     C01 IS TOP-OF-PAGE.
00043                 INPUT-OUTPUT SECTION.
00044                 FILE-CONTROL.
00045                     SELECT PAYROLL-MAST-FILE-IN
00046                         ASSIGN TO SYS023-DA-3330-S-PAYFILE.
00047                     SELECT SORT-WORK-FILE
00048                         ASSIGN TO SYS001-DA-3330-S-SORTWK1.
00049                     SELECT SALARY-REP-PRINT-FILE
00050                         ASSIGN TO SYS009-UR-1403-S.
00051            *
00052                 DATA DIVISION.
00053            *
00054                 FILE SECTION.
00055                 FD  PAYROLL-MAST-FILE-IN
00056                         LABEL RECORDS STANDARD
00057                         BLOCK CONTAINS 10 RECORDS.
00058                 01  PAYROLL-MAST-IN-AREA          PIC X(100).
00059                 SD  SORT-WORK-FILE.
00060
00061                 01  SORT-WORK-AREA.
00062                     02  FILLER                    PIC X.
00063                     02  PAY-WORK-DEPT-CODE        PIC S9(2).
00064                     02  FILLER                    PIC X(9).
00065                     02  PAY-WORK-EMP-NAME         PIC X(20).
00066                     02  FILLER                    PIC X(68).
00067                 FD  SALARY-REP-PRINT-FILE
00068                         LABEL RECORDS OMITTED.
00069                 01  SALARY-REP-PRINT-AREA         PIC X(133).
00070            *
00071                 WORKING-STORAGE SECTION.
00072                 01  SWITCHES.
00073                     02  END-OF-PAY-FILE-SW        PIC X.
00074                         88  NO-MORE-PAY-FILE      VALUE 'Y'.
00075                     02  END-OF-SORT-FILE-SW       PIC X.
00076                         88  NO-MORE-SORT-FILE     VALUE 'Y'.
```

Figure 5.14
Sorting a file using the INPUT PROCEDURE/OUTPUT PROCEDURE options for Example 5.4.

Figure 5.14 (*cont.*)

```
00077              01   COUNTERS.
00078                   02   LINE-COUNT                PIC 9(2).
00079              01   CONSTANTS.
00080                   02   PAGE-SIZE                 PIC 9(2) VALUE 55.
00081                   02   REPORT-PLANT-SITE         PIC S9    VALUE 1.
00082              01   SAVE-AREAS.
00083                   02   SAVE-DEPT-CODE            PIC S9(2).
00084              01   SORT-RET-REC.
00085                   02   FILLER                    PIC X.
00086                   02   SORT-RET-DEPT-CODE        PIC S9(2).
00087                   02   FILLER                    PIC X(9).
00088                   02   SORT-RET-EMP-NAME         PIC X(20).
00089                   02   FILLER                    PIC X(48).
00090                   02   SORT-RET-YTD-GROSS        PIC S9(5)V9(2).
00091                   02   FILLER                    PIC X(13).
00092              01   PAY-IN-REC.
00093                   02   PAY-IN-PLANT-SITE         PIC S9.
00094                   02   FILLER                    PIC X(99).
00095              01   HDG-LINE-1.
00096                   02   FILLER                    PIC X(24) VALUE SPACE.
00097                   02   FILLER                    PIC X(22)
00098                        VALUE 'REPORT FOR DEPARTMENT'.
00099                   02   HDG-DEPT-CODE             PIC Z9.
00100                   02   FILLER                    PIC X(85).
00101              01   HDG-LINE-2.
00102                   02   FILLER                    PIC X(15) VALUE SPACE.
00103                   02   FILLER                    PIC X(23) VALUE 'NAME'.
00104                   02   FILLER                    PIC X(95)
00105                        VALUE 'TOTAL SALARY TO DATE'.
00106              01   EMP-REP-PRINT-REC.
00107                   02   FILLER                    PIC X(7)  VALUE SPACE.
00108                   02   REP-EMP-NAME              PIC X(43).
00109                   02   REP-YTD-GROSS             PIC $Z(4)9.9(2).
00110                   02   FILLER                    PIC X(76) VALUE SPACE.
00111         *
00112         PROCEDURE DIVISION.
00113         *
00114         SORTER SECTION.
00115         *
00116         SORTER-CONTROL.
00117              SORT SORT-WORK-FILE
00118                   ON ASCENDING KEY PAY-WORK-DEPT-CODE PAY-WORK-EMP-NAME
00119                   INPUT PROCEDURE GET-PLANT-DATA
00120                   OUTPUT PROCEDURE GENERATE-PLANT-REPORT.
00121              STOP RUN.
00122         *
00123         GET-PLANT-DATA SECTION.
00124         *
00125         GET-PLANT-DATA-CONTROL.
00126              PERFORM GET-DATA-START-PROCESS.
00127              PERFORM PAY-FILE-PROCESS UNTIL NO-MORE-PAY-FILE.
00128              PERFORM GET-DATA-FINAL-PROCESS.
00129              GO TO GET-PLANT-DATA-SECTION-EXIT.
00130         *
00131         GET-DATA-START-PROCESS.
00132              OPEN INPUT PAYROLL-MAST-FILE-IN.
00133              MOVE 'N' TO END-OF-PAY-FILE-SW.
00134              PERFORM READ-PAY-FILE.
00135         *
00136       ' PAY-FILE-PROCESS.
00137              IF PAY-IN-PLANT-SITE = REPORT-PLANT-SITE
00138                   PERFORM RELEASE-TO-SORT-FILE.
00139              PERFORM READ-PAY-FILE.
00140         *
00141         GET-DATA-FINAL-PROCESS.
00142              CLOSE PAYROLL-MAST-FILE-IN.
00143         *
00144         READ-PAY-FILE.
00145              READ PAYROLL-MAST-FILE-IN INTO PAY-IN-REC
00146                   AT END MOVE 'Y' TO END-OF-PAY-FILE-SW.
00147         *
00148         RELEASE-TO-SORT-FILE.
00149              RELEASE SORT-WORK-AREA FROM PAY-IN-REC.
00150         *
00151         GET-PLANT-DATA-SECTION-EXIT.
00152              EXIT.
00153         GENERATE-PLANT-REPORT SECTION.
```

Figure 5.14 (*cont.*)

```
00154        *
00155          GENERATE-REPORT-CONTROL.
00156              PERFORM START-REP-PROCESS.
00157              PERFORM PROCESS-A-DEPT UNTIL NO-MORE-SORT-FILE.
00158              PERFORM FINAL-REP-PROCESS.
00159              GO TO GENERATE-PLANT-REPORT-EXIT.
00160        *
00161          START-REP-PROCESS.
00162              MOVE 'N' TO END-OF-SORT-FILE-SW.
00163              PERFORM GET-SORT-DATA.
00164              OPEN OUTPUT SALARY-REP-PRINT-FILE.
00165        *
00166          PROCESS-A-DEPT.
00167              COMPUTE LINE-COUNT = PAGE-SIZE + 1.
00168              MOVE SORT-RET-DEPT-CODE TO SAVE-DEPT-CODE.
00169              MOVE SAVE-DEPT-CODE TO HDG-DEPT-CODE.
00170              PERFORM PROCESS-RECORDS UNTIL  (NO-MORE-SORT-FILE
00171                                        OR
00172                             SAVE-DEPT-CODE IS NOT EQUAL
00173                             TO SORT-RET-DEPT-CODE).
00174        *
00175          FINAL-REP-PROCESS.
00176              CLOSE SALARY-REP-PRINT-FILE.
00177        *
00178          PROCESS-RECORDS.
00179              IF LINE-COUNT IS GREATER THAN PAGE-SIZE
00180                  PERFORM HEADINGS
00181                      MOVE 3 TO LINE-COUNT.
00182              MOVE SORT-RET-EMP-NAME TO REP-EMP-NAME.
00183              MOVE SORT-RET-YTD-GROSS TO REP-YTD-GROSS.
00184              PERFORM WRITE-DETAIL.
00185              ADD 1 TO LINE-COUNT.
00186              PERFORM GET-SORT-DATA.
00187        *
00188          GET-SORT-DATA.
00189              RETURN SORT-WORK-FILE INTO SORT-RET-REC
00190                  AT END MOVE 'Y' TO END-OF-SORT-FILE-SW.
00191        *
00192          HEADINGS.
00193              WRITE SALARY-REP-PRINT-AREA FROM HDG-LINE-1
00194                  AFTER ADVANCING TOP-OF-PAGE.
00195              WRITE SALARY-REP-PRINT-AREA FROM HDG-LINE-2
00196                  AFTER ADVANCING 2 LINES.
00197        *
00198          WRITE-DETAIL.
00199              WRITE SALARY-REP-PRINT-AREA FROM EMP-REP-PRINT-REC
00200                  AFTER ADVANCING 1 LINES.
00201        *
00202          GENERATE-PLANT-REPORT-EXIT.
00203              EXIT.
```

THE SEQUENTIAL FILE PROBLEM REVISITED

We would like to return to the problem that began our discussion of sorting. In Example 4.1 (Chapter 4), no mention was made of arranging the cards in order by social security number. This can be accomplished using a card sorter, and the program organization used for Example 4.1 assumed that this had been done. Sorting cards is a slow tedious procedure; using the SORT verb to create a sorted file from the information in the card file is a much faster and less error-prone approach.

As a final illustration of the use of the SORT verb, we outline in Figure 5.15 the changes necessary to the programming logic for Example 4.1, Chapter 4, to eliminate the need to physically sort the card file. Only the necessary changes are indicated; other changes might improve efficiency or readability.

```
                        .
                        .
                        .
        FILE-CONTROL.
            SELECT PAYROLL-FILE-IN
                ASSIGN TO SYS007-UR-2501-S.
            SELECT PAYROLL-MAST-FILE-OUT
                ASSIGN TO SYS023-DA-3330-S-PAYFILE.
            SELECT ERROR-REPORT-PRINT-FILE
            ASSIGN TO SYS009-UR-1403-S.
        SELECT PAYROLL-SORT-WORK-FILE
                ASSIGN TO SYS001-DA-3330-S-SORTWK1.
    *
    DATA DIVISION.
    *
    FILE SECTION.
    FD  PAYROLL-FILE-IN
            LABEL RECORDS ARE OMITTED.
    01  PAYROLL-IN-AREA                   PIC X(80).
    FD  PAYROLL-MAST-FILE-OUT
            LABEL RECORDS ARE STANDARD
            BLOCK CONTAINS 10 RECORDS.
    01  PAYROLL-MAST-OUT-AREA             PIC X(100).
    FD  ERROR-REPORT-PRINT-FILE
            LABEL RECORDS ARE OMITTED.
    01  ERROR-LINE-OUT-AREA               PIC X(132).
    SD  PAYROLL-SORT-WORK-FILE.
    01  PAYROLL-SORT-WORK-AREA.
        02  FILLER                        PIC X(3).
        02  PAY-SORT-SS-NUM               PIC X(9).
        02  FILLER                        PIC X(88).
    *
    WORKING-STORAGE SECTION.

                        .
                        .
                        .
    *
    PROCEDURE DIVISION.
    *
    SORT-CONTROL SECTION.
    *
    MAST-FILE-CREATE-CONTROL.
        SORT PAYROLL-SORT-WORK-FILE
            ON ASCENDING KEY PAY-SORT-SS-NUM
            INPUT PROCEDURE EDIT-INPUT-FILE
            GIVING PAYROLL-MAST-FILE-OUT.
        DISPLAY 'PROCESSING COMPLETE'.
        STOP RUN.
    *
    EDIT-INPUT-FILE SECTION.
    *
    EDIT-INPUT-FILE CONTROL.
        PERFORM START-UP.
        PERFORM CREATE-PAYROLL-MAST
            UNTIL END-OF-FILE.
        PERFORM FINISH-UP.
        GO TO EDIT-INPUT-FILE-EXIT.
    *
    START-UP.
        OPEN INPUT PAYROLL-FILE-IN.
            OUTPUT ERROR-REPORT-PRINT-FILE.
            MOVE 'N' TO END-OF-FILE-SW.
            PERFORM PRINT-HEADING.
            PERFORM READ-PAY-FILE.
    *
    CREATE-PAYROLL-MAST.

                        .
                        .
                        .
    *
    FINISH-UP.
        CLOSE PAYROLL-FILE-IN
            ERROR-REPORT-PRINT-FILE.
```

Figure 5.15

Illustration of changes to data validation and file creation program (Figure 4.5, Chapter 4) necessary to avoid physical card sorting.

Figure 5.15 (*cont.*)

```
*
 EDIT-PAYROLL-DATA.
              .
              .
              .
*
 PRINT-OUT-ERROR-TABLE.
              .
              .
              .
*
 PRINT-HEADING.
              .
              .
              .
*
 PRINT-TERMINATING-MESSAGE.
              .
              .
              .
*
 PRINT-BAD-RECORD.
              .
              .
              .
*
 WRITE-PAY-MAST-FILE.
       RELEASE PAYROLL-SORT-WORK-AREA
            FROM PAYROLL-MAST-OUT-REC.
*
 READ-PAY-FILE.
              .
              .
              .
*
 PRINT-ERROR-MESSAGE.
              .
              .
              .
*
 EDIT-INPUT-FILE-EXIT.
       EXIT.
```

COBOL SORT FEATURE VS. UTILITY SORTS

As we have seen in this chapter, the COBOL SORT verb has powerful options. However, its use generates the need for GO TO statements, SECTIONs, and so on, which increases coding complexity and may present problems in developing structured programs.

The operating system sort utility provides a procedure for *stand-alone sorts;* that is, the sorting process does not have to be done in the context of, or in conjunction with, a COBOL program. The sort utility program may be called, sort specifications supplied, and the file actually sorted through job-control statements. If records require no processing prior to sorting, the stand-alone sort frequently involves less effort on the part of the programmer than will use of the COBOL SORT verb. On the other hand, if input file processing is necessary before the sort, the INPUT PROCEDURE option of the SORT verb has clear advantages.

If there is no need to retain a copy of the sorted file after processing, using an OUTPUT PROCEDURE with the SORT verb can reduce the amount of I/O involved, because you can work with records as they are returned from the sort-work file. This eliminates the need to first copy the records to an output file (as the stand-alone sort must do) and then to use the output file as an input file requiring that records be read before processing.

Currently, opinion among authorities is divided concerning their preference for using the SORT feature embedded in a COBOL program as opposed to the stand-alone sort utility.

Programming Exercises for Chapter 5

The following exercises are designed to allow you to gain experience in writing programs that use the various options of the COBOL SORT feature.

EXERCISE 5.1

Create the output hours-worked file in Example 4.2, Chapter 4, by using the SORT feature to generate the file. Sort input time-card data in order by social security number.

EXERCISE 5.2

Complete coding and then test the data validation and file creation program presented in outline form in Figure 5.15 of this chapter.

EXERCISE 5.3

The objective of this exercise is to write a program involving the USING and OUTPUT PROCEDURE options of the SORT verb. Input to the program will be a batch of unsorted transaction records (blocking factor is 20). The format of the input record is as follows:

Record Positions	Contents	Format
1–2	Territory code	9(2)
3–6	Product number	9(4)
7–26	Product description	X(20)
27–32	Transaction amount	9(4)V9(2)

Output is to be a printed report consisting of totals by product within territory.

Remember that there may be multiple transactions involving each product within each territory (for example, 10 transactions involving product number 1496 in territory 25).

Output should be similar to the following:

TERRITORY	PRODUCT NO.	TOTAL BY PRODUCT	TOTAL BY TERRITORY
XX	XXXX		
.	.		
.	.		
.	XXXX	XX,XXX.XX	
.	.		
.	.		
XX	XXXX	XX,XXX.XX	XX,XXX.XX
.	.		
.	.		
.	XXXX	XX,XXX.XX	
.	.		
.	.		
XX	XXXX	XX,XXX.XX	XX,XXX.XX

EXERCISE 5.4

Redo Exercise 5.3 under the assumption that no transactions in territory 15 are to be included in the report, nor are any transactions involving product numbers 1947 or 2463 (regardless of territory). The INPUT PROCEDURE and OUTPUT PRO-CEDURE options of the SORT verb are to be used in this exercise.

EXERCISE 5.5

Redo Exercise 5.3 under the assumption that a sorted version of the input file is to be produced in addition to the printed report.

6 Creating and Processing Indexed Sequential Files

INTRODUCTION

Mega-Tronics is not completely satisfied with the performance of the payroll system as it is currently designed. One problem encountered is that hiring a single new employee involves re-creating the entire sequentially organized payroll master file. Another problem is that for pay periods in which only a few employees are to be paid, the payroll master file still must be read from the beginning until the necessary records are located. This is costly and time-consuming. Mega's president would like for the data processing department to consider alternative designs to eliminate these problems. After some consideration, Mega's EDP department agrees that the new file organization must meet the following requirements:

1. Additions to the file are to be possible *without* re-creating the file.
2. Access to an employee's record must be fast and simple, based on the social security number.
3. It must not be significantly more costly to process the entire payroll master file than it is under the current system.

The preceding requirements occur frequently and a file organization, called *indexed sequential*, has been developed to meet them. Such a file consists of two parts: (1) a data part, which will contain the records, and (2) two or more indexes. The indexes allow the operating system to locate a record based on a key field. They contain information similar to that found in the index to this book. The programmer will not normally need to be concerned with the indexes in any detail, since they are created and updated automatically by the operating system. Indexed sequential file organization is applicable only to direct-access storage devices.

There are two indexed sequential file organizations in use on IBM computers, an older one called ISAM (*I*ndexed *S*equential *A*ccess *M*ethod) and a newer one supported by VSAM (*V*irtual *S*torage *A*ccess *M*ethod). VSAM also supports additional file organizations, which allow it to replace all of the earlier IBM access methods.

ISAM ORGANIZATION

Records in an ISAM file may be blocked. Initially, records will be stored in ascending order on the record key. Each block will also have the key of the last record in the block associated with it. The key, stored separately, precedes the block (physical record) and is separated from it by an interrecord gap (IRG).

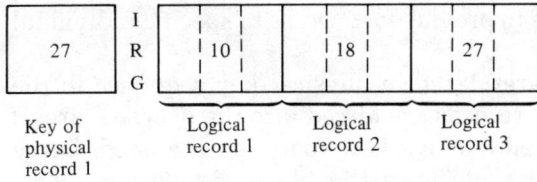

An ISAM file consists of several areas: two or more *index areas,* a *prime data area,* and *overflow areas.*

The records in the prime data area are always in physical key sequence. The overflow area contains records that cannot be placed in the proper key sequence in the prime data area. There are three possible levels of indexes:

1. A mandatory *track index,* which contains the highest key associated with a track of the prime data area.
2. A mandatory *cylinder index,* which contains the highest key on each cylinder.
3. An optional *master index,* which contains the highest key associated with each track of the cylinder index.

These relationships are illustrated in Figure 6.1. Typically, each cylinder that contains data will contain a prime data area and an overflow area. However, if many additions are expected, additional cylinders may be designated to contain only overflow records.

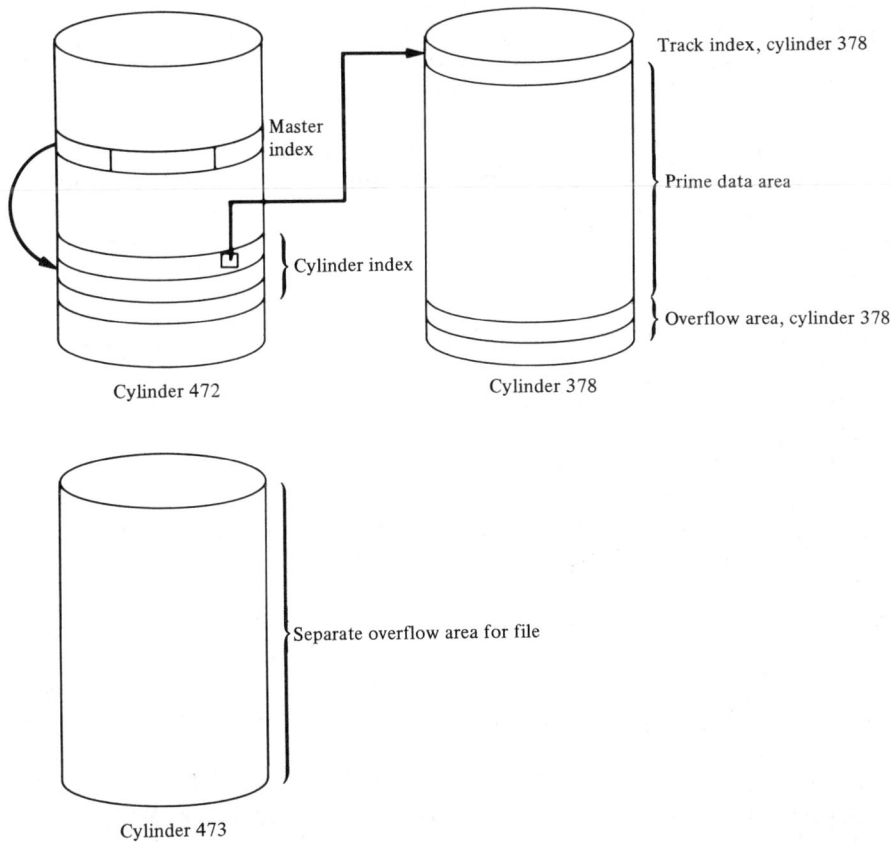

Figure 6.1
Sample cylinder allocation for an ISAM file.

The operating system uses the indexes to provide fast access to specific individual records.

When the file is created, all records are placed in physical key sequence in the prime data area. As additions are made, records are forced into the overflow areas. The file must be recreated when the available overflow space is exhausted. Large numbers of overflow records cause retrievals from the file to be slower; consequently, a reorganization of the file would normally be done as soon as the performance is unacceptably slow.

VSAM KEY SEQUENCED ORGANIZATION

Records in a KSDS (*Key Sequenced Data Set*) VSAM file (hereafter referred to as VSAM-indexed) are grouped into *control intervals*. Each control interval will initially contain free space to be used when additions are made.

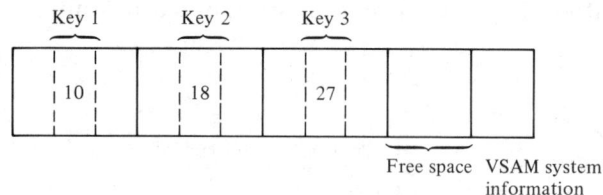

Key 1   Key 2   Key 3

| 10 | | 18 | | 27 |

Free space   VSAM system information

The VSAM system information will contain certain location and key information for the records and the location of free space in the control interval. Control intervals are grouped into *control areas*. Within a control interval, records are kept in physical key sequence.

There are three levels of indexes:

1. The *control interval index,* which contains the highest key in each of the control intervals for a given control area.
2. An index to the control interval index, called the *control area index,* which contains the highest key in a control area.
3. An index to the control area index.

These roughly approximate the track, cylinder, and master indexes under ISAM. The concepts are illustrated in Figure 6.2.

When additions are made, the record is inserted into the appropriate control interval, where records are shifted to maintain the ascending key sequence. If the control interval has no free space, the control interval is divided into two new control intervals, each containing free space. If the control area has no free space, the control area is divided. All these operations are done automatically by the VSAM facility.

Unlike ISAM, the space released by a deletion may be reused. Thus, there will seldom be any need to recreate the file. Since there is no separate overflow area, additions to the file will not reduce access speed to the same extent that they do under ISAM.

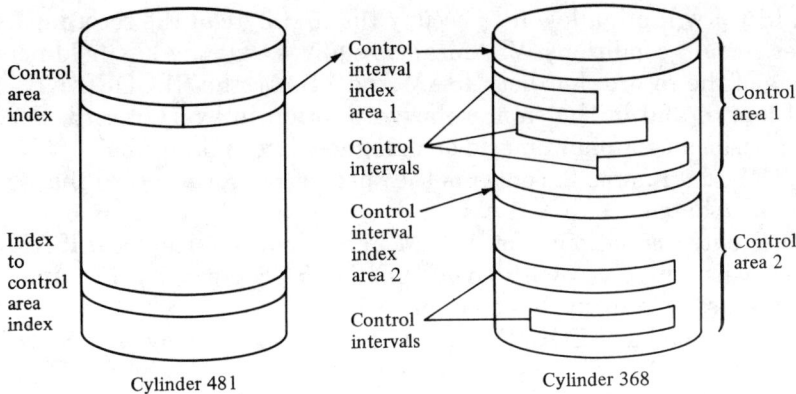

Figure 6.2
Sample cylinder allocation for KSDS VSAM file.

COBOL CONSIDERATIONS

Although there are major differences between the physical structure of ISAM and VSAM-Indexed files and the VSAM-Indexed file organization has more flexibility, the actual differences in the COBOL statements needed to manipulate the two file organizations are small.

ENVIRONMENT DIVISION ENTRIES

ISAM and VSAM-Indexed files must be named in a SELECT sentence in the FILE-CONTROL paragraph.

FORMAT	
ISAM	*VSAM Indexed*

SELECT file-name
 	
ASSIGN TO system-name
 	
ACCESS IS ⎰RANDOM ⎱
        ⎰SEQUENTIAL⎱
 	
RECORD KEY is data-name-1
 	
[NOMINAL KEY IS data-name-2]
	SELECT file-name
	
	ASSIGN TO system-name
	
	ORGANIZATION IS INDEXED
	
	ACCESS IS ⎧RANDOM ⎫
	        ⎨SEQUENTIAL⎬
	        ⎩DYNAMIC ⎭
	
	RECORD KEY IS data-name-1
	
	[FILE STATUS IS data-name-2]

The RECORD KEY, data-name-1, is the field on which the file is to be ordered. This name must appear in at least one 01-record entry description for the FD describing the file. ISAM will not allow it to occupy the first byte of the record. On some systems under certain conditions, VSAM also requires that the key field not include the first byte of the record. For both ISAM and VSAM, the RECORD KEY field must be fixed length and in the same relative position in every record. For VSAM it must be described as alphanumeric or unsigned external decimal.

The NOMINAL KEY, data-name-2, contains the specific key for a record that is to be read, written, or updated.

The FILE STATUS entry is optional for VSAM and is not applicable to ISAM files. We will not concern ourselves with the FILE STATUS entry at this time; however, it will be discussed later in this chapter.

Types of access are specified as SEQUENTIAL to process in order by key; RANDOM to process by designated key values; or DYNAMIC, which allows SEQUENTIAL and RANDOM in the same program.

Suppose we have a file that contains census data and uses the standard ZIP code as the record key.

SELECT statements that would allow the file to be read sequentially are

```
(ISAM)
        SELECT CENSUS-FILE-IN
            ASSIGN TO SYS023-DA-3330-I-CENFILE
            ACCESS IS SEQUENTIAL
            RECORD KEY IS CEN-ZIP-CODE.
(VSAM)
        SELECT CENSUS-FILE-IN
            ASSIGN TO SYS023-CENFILE
            ORGANIZATION IS INDEXED
            ACCESS IS SEQUENTIAL
            RECORD KEY IS CEN-ZIP-CODE.
```

The "I" following the entry "3330" in the ASSIGN statement specifies *indexed* file organization for ISAM files. For VSAM, the statement ORGANIZATION IS INDEXED is used.

If you wish to randomly read records by specific ZIP code, then the ACCESS would be specified as RANDOM for both ISAM and VSAM, and a NOMINAL KEY must be specified for ISAM.

FORMAT
ISAM
I-O-CONTROL.   <u>APPLY CORE-INDEX</u> TO data-name ON file-name

The APPLY CORE-INDEX entry is optional. If it is used, the highest-level index will be kept in main memory. This increases ISAM processing efficiency.

DATA DIVISION ENTRIES

There are no entries in the DATA DIVISION unique to indexed sequential organization. It should be noted that the RECORD KEY and, if needed, the NOMINAL KEY, which are *named* in the ENVIRONMENT DIVISION, must be *described* in the DATA DIVISION. The description of a NOMINAL KEY must be in the WORKING-STORAGE SECTION and must match that given for the RECORD KEY.

For VSAM, a NOMINAL KEY is not used, and the BLOCK CONTAINS clause is omitted from the FD statement.

FDs for the file given in the previous section would appear as follows:

```
(ISAM)

    FD   CENSUS-FILE-IN
             LABEL RECORDS STANDARD
             BLOCK CONTAINS 5 RECORDS.

    01   CEN-IN-AREA.
         02   CEN-STATUS-CODE            PIC X.
         02   CEN-ZIP-CODE               PIC X(5).
         02   FILLER                     PIC X(300).

(VSAM)

    FD   CENSUS-FILE-IN
             LABEL RECORDS STANDARD.

    01   CEN-IN-AREA.
         02   CEN-STATUS-CODE            PIC X.
         02   CEN-ZIP-CODE               PIC X(5).
         02   FILLER                     PIC X(300).
```

The LABEL RECORDS clause must be specified as STANDARD. The first byte of the record is reserved for a deletion code. If the information in the record is no longer needed, it is flagged for deletion by a programmer-written routine. There is a special verb to delete the record automatically under VSAM-indexed organization. Recall, however, that the record key field must exclude the first byte of the record on some systems under certain conditions.

PROCEDURE DIVISION ENTRIES

A record is retrieved from either an ISAM or VSAM indexed file by a READ statement.

FORMAT	
ISAM	*VSAM Indexed*

<u>READ</u> file-name
 	
[<u>INTO</u> data-name]
 	
$\begin{Bmatrix} \text{AT } \underline{\text{END}} \\ \underline{\text{INVALID}} \text{ KEY} \end{Bmatrix}$ imperative statement
	1. <u>READ</u> file-name [<u>NEXT</u>]
	
	    [<u>INTO</u> data-name]
	
	    [AT <u>END</u> imperative statement]
	2. <u>READ</u> file-name
	
	    [<u>INTO</u> data-name]
	    [<u>INVALID</u> KEY imperative statement]

If ACCESS IS SEQUENTIAL is specified for either ISAM or VSAM, the AT END clause should be specified. The optional reserved word NEXT is not needed for VSAM. Thus, both READ statements reduce to the same form and have the same effect as the READ did for files having sequential organization.

If ACCESS IS RANDOM is specified, the INVALID KEY clause should be chosen for both ISAM and VSAM; and the READ statement will have the same form for both. The processing difference, from the programmer's viewpoint, is that under ISAM the value of the key of the record to be retrieved is placed in the NOMINAL KEY field, whereas under VSAM it is placed in the RECORD KEY field.

Thus, for ISAM:

```
MOVE 61455 TO SEARCH-ZIP-CODE        (where SEARCH-
                                        ZIP-CODE is
                                        the NOMINAL-
                                        KEY)



              .
              .
              .

READ CENSUS-FILE-IN INTO CEN-IN-REC
     INVALID KEY MOVE 'Y' TO NOT-IN-FILE-SW.
```

and for VSAM:

```
MOVE 61455 TO CEN-ZIP-CODE           (where CEN-ZIP-
                                        CODE is the
                                        RECORD-KEY)



            .
            .
            .

READ CENSUS-FILE-IN INTO CEN-IN-REC
     INVALID KEY MOVE 'Y' TO NOT-IN-FILE-SW.
```

For VSAM, when ACCESS IS DYNAMIC, the NEXT clause must be coded for a sequential READ.

```
READ CEN-FILE-IN NEXT INTO CEN-IN-REC
    AT END MOVE 'Y' TO END-OF-FILE-SW.
```

The random retrieval of a record when ACCESS IS DYNAMIC is done exactly the same as it would be for ACCESS IS RANDOM.

To add records to an existing ISAM or VSAM-indexed file, the WRITE statement is used. Note that the format is the same for both file organizations.

FORMAT	
ISAM	*VSAM Indexed*

<u>WRITE</u> record-name
 	
  [<u>FROM</u> data-name]
  <u>INVALID</u> KEY imperative
           statement
	<u>WRITE</u> record-name
	
	  [<u>FROM</u> data-name]
	  [<u>INVALID</u> KEY imperative
	           statement]

In both cases, when the file is being created, it will be opened as OUTPUT. The INVALID KEY clause imperative statement will be executed if the records being written to the file contain either duplicate or out-of-sequence key fields or if an attempt is made to write outside the file limits. If an existing file is opened I-O, the INVALID KEY clause is executed if there is an existing record on the file with the same key.

To alter the contents of any non-key field in an existing record, the REWRITE statement is used. Its form is the same for both ISAM- and VSAM-indexed files.

FORMAT	
ISAM	*VSAM Indexed*

<u>REWRITE</u> record-name
 	
  [<u>FROM</u> data-name]
  <u>INVALID</u> KEY imperative
           statement
	<u>REWRITE</u> record-name
	
	  [<u>FROM</u> data-name]
	  [<u>INVALID</u> KEY imperative
	           statement]

To use REWRITE, the file must be opened for I-O. The technique to update a record is to READ the existing record, modify the data fields, and then use RE-WRITE to place the new version of the record back in the same location. The INVALID KEY clause will be executed if the original record location cannot be found when attempting to REWRITE the record. This would be an unusual situation, but it can easily be caused if the contents of NOMINAL KEY (RECORD KEY for VSAM files) are inadvertently changed *after* the record has been read but *prior* to the execution of the REWRITE statement.

```
REWRITE CEN-IO-AREA
    FROM NEW-CEN-DATA
    INVALID KEY MOVE 'Y' TO NOT-FOUND-SW.
```

We will now consider the processing involved to create (load) an indexed sequential file.

Example 6.1

The data processing department for Mega-Tronics has decided that the existing payroll system is to be converted to an ISAM-based system. This decision was prompted in part by the president's refusal to consider the purchase of new hardware to support VSAM. The first step in the conversion will be the conversion of the existing payroll master file to ISAM organization.

A program to create the new master file is given in Figure 6.4. Figure 6.3 illustrates the simple program structure involved.

Several important points concerning the program in Figure 6.4 should be discussed. The record key MAST-SS-NUM is specified, as is required, as an entry under the 01 record description for the FD that describes PAYROLL-MAST-FILE-OUT. Other fields may be described here if needed. The only field required that is not in the original sequential input file records is the deletion code field. By convention, it is located in the first byte of the record, and the figurative constant LOW-VALUES is typically used to indicate an active (nondeleted) record, whereas HIGH-VALUES indicates that a record has been deleted. PAY-OUT-DELETE-CODE (line 80) is used as the deletion code field in Figure 6.4.

Recall that the sequential master file (Example 4.1) is supposed to be in order by social security number. The INVALID KEY clause on line 117 signals program execution to stop if it is not in order.

All records from PAYROLL-MAST-FILE-IN are sequentially copied to the prime data area of the ISAM file. Approximately 20 percent of the available track space on each cylinder is automatically reserved for overflow. To reserve more (or less) overflow space, the APPLY statement can be used.[1] The statement on line 92 causes all switches to be set to 'N' initially.

If Mega's president should change his mind and implement VSAM, only minor changes would be needed. To convert the program in Figure 6.4 to VSAM-indexed, the following changes are needed:

1. Lines 51–53 would be replaced by

```
SELECT PAYROLL-MAST-FILE-OUT
    ASSIGN TO SYS023-PAYFIL
    ORGANIZATION IS INDEXED
    ACCESS IS SEQUENTIAL
    RECORD KEY IS MAST-SS-NUM.
```

2. Line 63 would need a period to end the sentence.
3. Line 64 would be deleted.

No changes would be required in the programming logic (that is, the PROCEDURE DIVISION).

---

[1] See the appropriate vendor manual for a discussion of this technique.

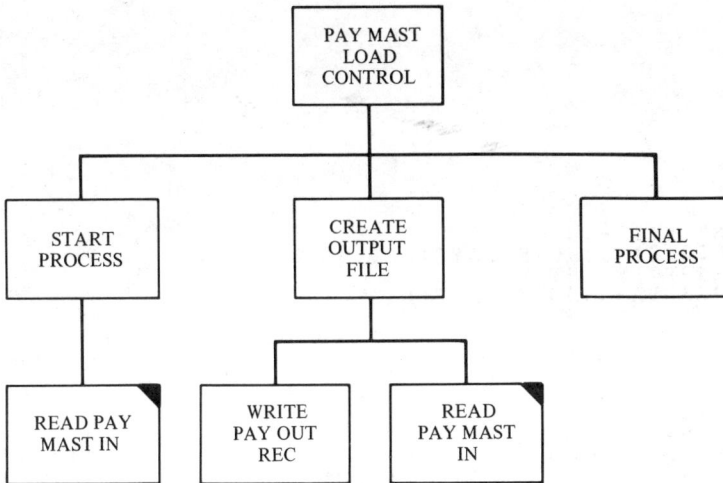

Figure 6.3
Structure chart for the program in Figure 6.4.

```
00001          IDENTIFICATION DIVISION.
00002        *
00003         PROGRAM-ID.
00004          EX-6-1.
00005        *****************************************************************
00006        *                                                               *
00007        *    PROGRAMMER TEAM          SUMMERS/WALSTROM/LINDAHL          *
00008        *    PROGRAM COMPLETION DATE NOVEMBER 20, 1984                  *
00009        *                                                               *
00010        *                   PROGRAM SUMMARY                             *
00011        *                                                               *
00012        *    INPUT                                                      *
00013        *        THE SEQUENTIAL PAYROLL MASTER FILE. IT IS IN ASCENDING *
00014        *        ORDER BY SOCIAL SECURITY NUMBER. EACH RECORD CONTAINS  *
00015        *            - CODE FOR PLANT LOCATION                          *
00016        *            - CODE FOR THE DEPARTMENT TO WHICH THE EMPLOYEE    *
00017        *              IS ASSIGNED                                      *
00018        *            - NAME                                             *
00019        *            - OTHER PERSONAL DATA                              *
00020        *            - TAX CLASSIFICATION                               *
00021        *            - PAY RATE                                         *
00022        *            - YEAR-TO-DATE TOTALS FOR GROSS PAY, TAX WITHHELD, *
00023        *              AND FICA WITHHELD                                *
00024        *                                                               *
00025        *    PROCESSING                                                 *
00026        *            - A DELETE CODE IS ADDED TO THE INPUT RECORD       *
00027        *            - THE DELETE CODE IS SET TO LOW-VALUES FOR ALL     *
00028        *              RECORDS                                          *
00029        *                                                               *
00030        *    OUTPUT                                                     *
00031        *        A NEW PAYROLL MASTER FILE IS CREATED. IT HAS INDEXED   *
00032        *        ORGANIZATION. THE INDEX IS BASED ON THE SOCIAL SECURITY*
00033        *        NUMBER. EACH RECORD CONTAINS                          *
00034        *            - DELETE CODE                                      *
00035        *            - DATA FROM RECORD OF THE INPUT FILE               *
00036        *        A MESSAGE IS WRITTEN TO INDICATE THE OUTCOME OF THE    *
00037        *        ATTEMPT TO LOAD THE FILE                               *
00038        *****************************************************************
00039        *
00040          ENVIRONMENT DIVISION.
```

Figure 6.4
Creation of an indexed file for Example 6.1.

Figure 6.4 (cont.)

```
00041                   *
00042                      CONFIGURATION SECTION.
00043                      SOURCE-COMPUTER.
00044                          IBM-370.
00045                      OBJECT-COMPUTER.
00046                          IBM-370
00047                      INPUT-OUTPUT SECTION.
00048                      FILE-CONTROL.
00049                          SELECT PAYROLL-MAST-FILE-IN
00050                              ASSIGN TO SYS023-DA-3330-S-PAYFILE.
00051                          SELECT PAYROLL-MAST-FILE-OUT
00052                              ASSIGN TO SYS023-DA-3330-I-PAYFIL
00053                              RECORD KEY IS MAST-SS-NUM.
00054                   *
00055                      DATA DIVISION.
00056
00057                      FILE SECTION.
00058                      FD  PAYROLL-MAST-FILE-IN
00059                              LABEL RECORDS ARE STANDARD
00060                              BLOCK CONTAINS 10 RECORDS.
00061                      01  PAYROLL-MAST-IN-AREA              PIC X(100).
00062                      FD  PAYROLL-MAST-FILE-OUT
00063                              LABEL RECORDS ARE STANDARD
00064                              BLOCK CONTAINS 5   RECORDS.
00065                      01  PAYROLL-MAST-OUT-AREA.
00066                          02  FILLER                        PIC X(4).
00067                          02  MAST-SS-NUM                   PIC X(9).
00068                          02  FILLER                        PIC X(88).
00069                   *
00070                      WORKING-STORAGE SECTION.
00071                      01  SWITCHES.
00072                          02   STOP-PROCESSING-SW           PIC X.
00073                              88   PROCESSING-SHOULD-STOP   VALUE 'Y'.
00074                          02   END-OF-FILE-SW               PIC X.
00075                              88   END-OF-FILE              VALUE 'Y'.
00076                          02   BAD-WRITE-SW                 PIC X.
00077                              88   BAD-WRITE                VALUE 'Y'.
00078                              88   GOOD-WRITE               VALUE 'N'.
00079                      01  PAY-OUT-REC.
00080                          02   PAY-OUT-DELETE-CODE          PIC X.
00081                          02   PAY-OUT-EMP-INFO             PIC X(100).
00082                   *
00083                      PROCEDURE DIVISION.
00084                   *
00085                      PAY-MAST-LOAD-CONTROL.
00086                          PERFORM START-PROCESS.
00087                          PERFORM CREATE-OUTPUT-FILE UNTIL PROCESSING-SHOULD-STOP.
00088                          PERFORM FINAL-PROCESS.
00089                          STOP RUN.
00090                   *
00091                      START-PROCESS.
00092                          MOVE ALL 'N' TO SWITCHES.
00093                          OPEN INPUT PAYROLL-MAST-FILE-IN
00094                              OUTPUT PAYROLL-MAST-FILE-OUT.
00095                          MOVE LOW-VALUE TO PAY-OUT-DELETE-CODE.
00096                          PERFORM READ-PAY-MAST-IN.
00097                   *
00098                      CREATE-OUTPUT-FILE.
00099                          PERFORM WRITE-PAY-OUT-REC.
00100                          PERFORM READ-PAY-MAST-IN.
00101                   *
00102                      FINAL-PROCESS.
00103                          IF BAD-WRITE
00104                              DISPLAY ' PROBABLE SEQUENCE ERROR'
00105                              DISPLAY ' RECORD KEY', MAST-SS-NUM
00106                          ELSE
00107                              DISPLAY ' INDEXED PAYROLL MASTER CREATED'.
00108                          CLOSE PAYROLL-MAST-FILE-IN, PAYROLL-MAST-FILE-OUT.
00109                   *
00110                      READ-PAY-MAST-IN.
00111                          READ PAYROLL-MAST-FILE-IN INTO PAY-OUT-EMP-INFO
00112                              AT END MOVE 'Y' TO STOP-PROCESSING-SW
00113                                              END-OF-FILE-SW.
00114                   *
00115                      WRITE-PAY-OUT-REC.
00116                          WRITE PAYROLL-MAST-OUT-AREA FROM PAY-OUT-REC
00117                              INVALID KEY  MOVE 'Y' TO STOP-PROCESSING-SW
00118                                                      BAD-WRITE-SW.
```

Example 6.2

A program to update the year-to-date totals will be needed in the new payroll system. The results of the new update program must be consistent with those of Example 4.3. (The only exception is that the payroll register report will not be printed, in order to shorten the programming and to allow a simpler illustration of record updating.) The update processing now will not require the file containing hours worked to be in order by social security number.

A program solution to this problem is given in Figure 6.6, with program organization shown in Figure 6.5.

The following are points concerned with the program shown in Figure 6.6:

1. Since HRS-WORKED-PAY-PERIOD-FILE-IN is not assumed to be in key sequence, ACCESS must be RANDOM and a NOMINAL KEY must be given.
2. The NOMINAL KEY, PAY-MAST-SEARCH-KEY, is named in the ENVIRONMENT DIVISION and is described in the WORKING-STORAGE SECTION. The length must be exactly the same as the RECORD KEY length.
3. Line 123 sets the NOMINAL KEY field to the social security number of the specific employee whose record is to be obtained from PAYROLL-MAST FILE-IO.
4. Line 170 contains the REWRITE statement to replace the record after updating.
5. PAYROLL-MAST-FILE-IO must be opened I-O.

Once again, only minimal changes would be necessary to convert the ISAM update program in Figure 6.6 to one that updates a VSAM-indexed file. Changes required are

1. Lines 53 through 57:

```
SELECT PAYROLL-MAST-FILE-IO
    ASSIGN TO SYS023-PAYFIL
    ORGANIZATION IS INDEXED
    RECORD KEY IS MAST-SS-NUM
    ACCESS IS RANDOM.
```

2. Delete lines 56, 68, 91, and 92.
3. Line 67 should have a period to end the sentence.
4. Line 123 should read

```
MOVE HRS-IN-SS-NUM TO MAST-SS-NUM.
```

This is because VSAM uses the contents of the RECORD KEY field to search for a record.

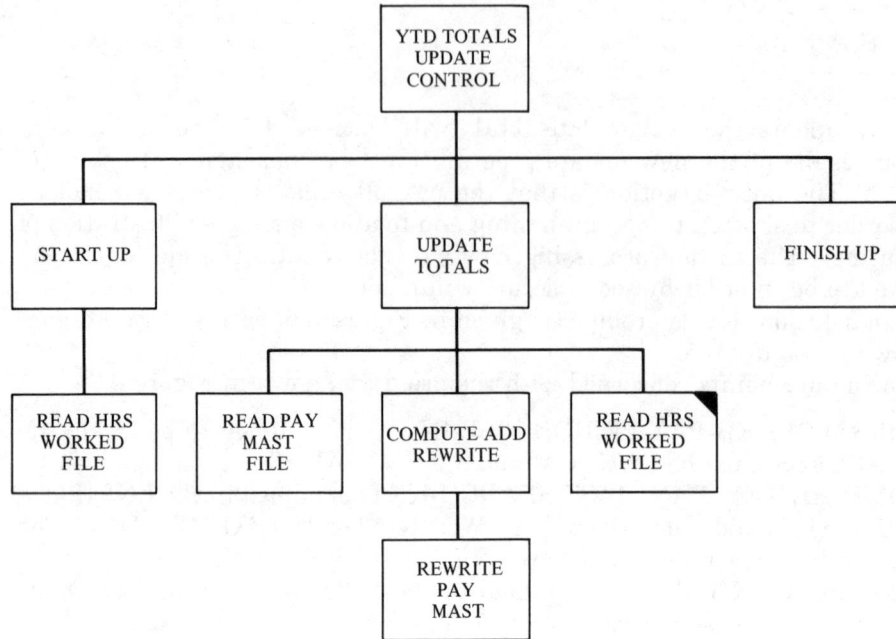

Figure 6.5
Structure chart for the program in Figure 6.6.

```
00001              IDENTIFICATION DIVISION.
00002         *
00003            PROGRAM-ID.
00004                EX-6-2.
00005            ****************************************************************
00006         *  *                                                              *
00007         *  *   PROGRAMMER TEAM            SUMMERS/WALSTROM/LINDAHL         *
00008         *  *   PROGRAM COMPLETION DATE DECEMBER 3, 1984.                  *
00009         *  *                                                              *
00010         *  *                    PROGRAM SUMMARY                           *
00011         *  *  INPUT                                                       *
00012         *  *      INPUT FILES USED ARE THE PAYROLL MASTER FILE AND THE    *
00013         *  *      HOURS WORKED. THE PAYROLL MASTER FILE IS INDEXED BY     *
00014         *  *      SOCIAL SECURITY NUMBER.                                 *
00015         *  *  DATA FROM THE PAYROLL MASTER FILE NECESSARY FOR THIS        *
00016         *  *  APPLICATION:                                               *
00017         *  *          - SOCIAL SECURITY NUMBER                            *
00018         *  *          - TAX CLASSIFICATION                                *
00019         *  *          - PAY RATE                                          *
00020         *  *          - YEAR-TO-DATE TOTALS FOR GROSS PAY, TAX AND FICA   *
00021         *  *  RECORDS ON THE HOURS WORKED FILE CONSIST OF                 *
00022         *  *          - SOCIAL SECURITY NUMBER                            *
00023         *  *          - TOTAL HOURS WORKED                                *
00024         *  *                                                              *
00025         *  *  PROCESSING                                                  *
00026         *  *      FOR EACH RECORD ON THE HOURS WORKED FILE THE            *
00027         *  *      CORRESPONDING RECORD IS LOOKED FOR ON THE MASTER FILE   *
00028         *  *      IF A MASTER RECORD IS FOUND                             *
00029         *  *          - GROSS PAY FOR THE PAY PERIOD IS COMPUTED          *
00030         *  *          - WITHOLDING TAX AND FICA FOR THE PAY PERIOD ARE    *
00031         *  *            COMPUTED                                          *
00032         *  *          - YEAR-TO-DATE GROSS PAY, TAX, AND FICA ARE UPDATED*
00033         *  *            ON THE MASTER FILE                                *
00034         *  *                                                              *
00035         *  *  OUTPUT                                                      *
00036         *  *          - THE UPDATED PAYROLL MASTER FILE                   *
00037         *  *          - A LIST OF HOURS WORKED RECORDS WITH NO MASTER     *
00038         *  *            RECORDS                                           *
00039         *  *          - A PROCESS STATUS MESSAGE                          *
00040            ****************************************************************
```

Figure 6.6
Random update of an indexed file for Example 6.2.

Figure 6.6 (cont.)

```
00041          *
00042           ENVIRONMENT DIVISION.
00043          *
00044           CONFIGURATION SECTION.
00045           SOURCE-COMPUTER.
00046               IBM-370.
00047           OBJECT-COMPUTER.
00048               IBM-370.
00049           INPUT-OUTPUT SECTION.
00050           FILE-CONTROL.
00051               SELECT  HRS-WORKED-PAY-PERIOD-FILE-IN
00052                   ASSIGN TO SYS023-DA-3330-S-HRSFILE.
00053               SELECT PAYROLL-MAST-FILE-IO
00054                   ASSIGN TO SYS023-DA-3330-I-PAYFIL
00055                   RECORD KEY IS MAST-SS-NUM
00056                   NOMINAL KEY IS PAY-MAST-SEARCH-KEY
00057                   ACCESS IS RANDOM.
00058          *
00059           DATA DIVISION.
00060          *
00061           FILE SECTION.
00062           FD  HRS-WORKED-PAY-PERIOD-FILE-IN
00063                   LABEL RECORDS ARE STANDARD
00064                   BLOCK CONTAINS 10 RECORDS.
00065           01  HRS-WORKED-IN-AREA              PIC X(13).
00066           FD  PAYROLL-MAST-FILE-IO
00067                   LABEL RECORDS ARE STANDARD
00068                   BLOCK CONTAINS 05 RECORDS.
00069           01  PAY-MAST-IO-AREA.
00070               02  FILLER                      PIC X(4).
00071               02  MAST-SS-NUM                 PIC X(9).
00072               02  FILLER                      PIC X(88).
00073          *
00074           WORKING-STORAGE SECTION.
00075           01  SWITCHES.
00076               02  END-OF-HRS-WORKED-FILE-SW   PIC X.
00077                   88  END-OF-HRS-WORKED-FILE  VALUE 'Y'.
00078               02  NOT-ON-MAST-FILE-SW         PIC X.
00079                   88  NOT-ON-MAST-FILE        VALUE 'Y'.
00080               02  UPDATE-SUCCESSFUL-SW        PIC X.
00081                   88  UPDATE-SUCCESSFUL       VALUE 'Y'.
00082               02  STOP-PROCESSING-SW          PIC X.
00083                   88  PROCESSING-SHOULD-STOP  VALUE 'Y'.
00084           01  CONSTANTS.
00085               02  MAX-REG-HRS                 PIC S9(2)   VALUE +40.
00086               02  OVERTIME-ADJUSTMENT         PIC SV9 VALUE +.5.
00087               02  MAX-SS-WITHHOLD             PIC S9(5)   VALUE +29700.
00088               02  SS-WITHHOLD-RATE            PIC SV9(3) VALUE +.067.
00089               02  TAXABLE-INCOME-ADJUSTMENT   PIC S9(2)   VALUE +13.
00090               02  EST-FED-TAX-RATE            PIC SV9(2)  VALUE +.18.
00091           01  THE-NOMINAL-KEY.
00092               02  PAY-MAST-SEARCH-KEY         PIC X(9).
00093           01  WORK-AREA.
00094               02  PAY-AMT                     PIC S9(4)V9(2).
00095           01  HRS-WORKED-IN-REC.
00096               02  HRS-IN-SS-NUM               PIC 9(9).
00097               02  HRS-IN-HRS-WORKED           PIC S9(2)V9(2).
00098           01  PAY-MAST-IO-REC.
00099               02  FILLER                      PIC X(4).
00100               02  PAY-IO-SS-NUM               PIC 9(9).
00101               02  FILLER                      PIC X(62).
00102               02  PAY-IO-TAX-CLASS            PIC S9(2).
00103               02  PAY-IO-PAY-RATE             PIC S9(2)V9(2).
00104               02  PAY-IO-YTD-GROSS            PIC S9(5)V9(2).
00105               02  PAY-IO-YTD-TAX              PIC S9(5)V9(2).
00106               02  PAY-IO-YTD-FICA             PIC S9(4)V9(2).
00107          *
00108           PROCEDURE DIVISION.
00109          *
00110           YTD-TOTALS-UPDATE-CONTROL.
00111               PERFORM START-UP.
00112               PERFORM UPDATE-TOTALS UNTIL PROCESSING-SHOULD-STOP.
00113               PERFORM FINISH-UP.
00114               STOP RUN.
```

Figure 6.6 (*cont.*)

```
00115                   *
00116                    START-UP.
00117                        MOVE ALL 'N' TO SWITCHES.
00118                        OPEN INPUT HRS-WORKED-PAY-PERIOD-FILE-IN
00119                              I-O PAYROLL-MAST-FILE-IO.
00120                        PERFORM READ-HRS-WORKED-FILE.
00121                   *
00122                    UPDATE-TOTALS.
00123                        MOVE HRS-IN-SS-NUM TO PAY-MAST-SEARCH-KEY.
00124                        PERFORM READ-PAY-MAST-FILE.
00125                        IF NOT-ON-MAST-FILE
00126                            DISPLAY ' INVALID SOCIAL SECURITY NUMBER',
00127                                  HRS-WORKED-IN-REC
00128                            MOVE 'N' TO NOT-ON-MAST-FILE-SW
00129                        ELSE
00130                            PERFORM COMPUTE-ADD-REWRITE.
00131                        PERFORM READ-HRS-WORKED-FILE.
00132                   *
00133                    FINISH-UP.
00134                        IF END-OF-HRS-WORKED-FILE
00135                            DISPLAY ' PROCESSING COMPLETE'
00136                        ELSE
00137                            DISPLAY ' INVALID REWRITE TO MASTER FILE',
00138                                  PAY-MAST-IO-REC.
00139                        CLOSE HRS-WORKED-PAY-PERIOD-FILE-IN,
00140                              PAYROLL-MAST-FILE-IO.
00141                   *
00142                    COMPUTE-ADD-REWRITE.
00143                        COMPUTE PAY-AMT = HRS-IN-HRS-WORKED * PAY-IO-PAY-RATE.
00144                        IF HRS-IN-HRS-WORKED IS GREATER THAN MAX-REG-HRS
00145                            COMPUTE PAY-AMT = PAY-AMT +
00146                                  OVERTIME-ADJUSTMENT * PAY-IO-PAY-RATE *
00147                                  (HRS-IN-HRS-WORKED - MAX-REG-HRS).
00148                        COMPUTE PAY-IO-YTD-TAX = PAY-IO-YTD-TAX + (PAY-AMT -
00149                              PAY-IO-TAX-CLASS * TAXABLE-INCOME-ADJUSTMENT)
00150                              * EST-FED-TAX-RATE.
00151                        IF PAY-IO-YTD-GROSS + PAY-AMT IS LESS THAN MAX-SS-WITHHOLD
00152                            COMPUTE PAY-IO-YTD-FICA = SS-WITHHOLD-RATE *
00153                                          (PAY-AMT + PAY-IO-YTD-GROSS)
00154                        ELSE
00155                            COMPUTE PAY-IO-YTD-FICA = SS-WITHHOLD-RATE *
00156                                          MAX-SS-WITHHOLD.
00157                        COMPUTE PAY-IO-YTD-GROSS = PAY-AMT + PAY-IO-YTD-GROSS.
00158                        PERFORM REWRITE-PAY-MAST.
00159                   *
00160                    READ-HRS-WORKED-FILE.
00161                        READ HRS-WORKED-PAY-PERIOD-FILE-IN INTO HRS-WORKED-IN-REC
00162                            AT END MOVE 'Y' TO END-OF-HRS-WORKED-FILE-SW,
00163                                          STOP-PROCESSING-SW.
00164                   *
00165                    READ-PAY-MAST-FILE.
00166                        READ PAYROLL-MAST-FILE-IO INTO PAY-MAST-IO-REC
00167                            INVALID KEY MOVE 'Y' TO NOT-ON-MAST-FILE-SW.
00168                   *
00169                    REWRITE-PAY-MAST.
00170                        REWRITE PAY-MAST-IO-AREA FROM PAY-MAST-IO-REC
00171                            INVALID KEY MOVE 'Y' TO STOP-PROCESSING-SW.
```

Example 6.3

Under the new system, new employee records will still be validated by the edit program of Example 4.1. However, since the file generated will contain only records of new employees, it will be used as an additions file to the ISAM master file. Under this system, the input to the edit program will no longer have to be in order by social security number. A structure chart and a program solution for the problem of Example 6.3 are given in Figures 6.7 and 6.8.

The programming logic required to add records to an ISAM file is much simpler than the logic for adding records to a sequential file.

We would like to emphasize several points about the program:

1. The NOMINAL KEY field must be specified.
2. ACCESS must be RANDOM.
3. Although updating of the indexes is automatic, it is the value in the NOMINAL KEY field that is used for the updating. Placing the new record key in the NOMINAL KEY field before attempting to WRITE a new record is necessary, and this is done on line 109.
4. Since the data items PAY-DELETE-CODE, PAY-YTD-TAX, and PAY-YTD-FICA are in WORKING-STORAGE, their values only have to be set once. (See lines 102 and 103.)
5. The WRITE statement on line 122 is used to transfer the new records to the file. The INVALID KEY clause will be executed if there is an existing record on the file with the same key.

Again, only minimal changes (shown subsequently) are required to the program in Figure 6.8 if PAYROLL-MAST-FILE-IO is a VSAM key-sequenced file:

1. Line 54 should be ASSIGN TO SYS023-PAYFIL.
2. Insert ORGANIZATION IS INDEXED after line 54 and delete line 56.
3. In the DATA DIVISION, line 63 should have a period following LABEL RECORDS ARE STANDARD; and lines 64, 80, and 81 should be deleted.
4. Only one change is necessary in the PROCEDURE DIVISION: Line 109 should read MOVE PAY-ADD-SS-NUM TO MAST-SS-NUM.

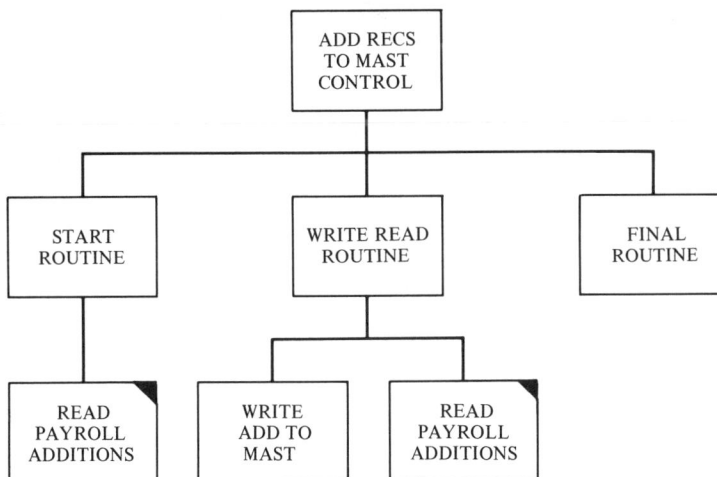

Figure 6.7
Structure chart for the program in Figure 6.8.

```
00001              IDENTIFICATION DIVISION.
00002         *
00003           PROGRAM-ID.
00004               EX-6-3.
00005         ******************************************************************
00006         *                                                                *
00007         *     PROGRAMMER TEAM            SUMMERS/WALSTROM/LINDAHL         *
00008         *     PROGRAM COMPLETION DATE DECEMBER 3, 1984.                  *
00009         *                                                                *
00010         *                    PROGRAM SUMMARY                             *
00011         *     INPUT                                                      *
00012         *         INPUT FILES ARE CURRENT PAYROLL MASTER FILE AND NEW    *
00013         *         EMPLOYEE FILE. THE PAYROLL MASTER FILE IS INDEXED      *
00014         *         BY SOCIAL SECURITY NUMBER. BOTH FILES CONTAIN THE      *
00015         *         FOLLOWING INFORMATION IN THE SAME FORMAT               *
00016         *                 - CODE FOR THE PLANT LOCATION                  *
00017         *                 - CODE FOR THE DEPARTMENT TO WHICH THE EMPLOYEE *
00018         *                   IS ASSIGNED                                  *
00019         *                 - SOCIAL SECURITY NUMBER                       *
00020         *                 - NAME                                         *
00021         *                 - OTHER PERSONAL INFORMATION                   *
00022         *                 - TAX CLASSIFICATION                           *
00023         *                 - PAY RATE                                     *
00024         *         IN ADDITION RECORDS ON THE CURRENT MASTER FILE CONTAIN *
00025         *                 - DELETE CODE                                  *
00026         *                 - YEAR-TO-DATE TOTALS FOR GROSS PAY, TAX WITHHELD *
00027         *                   AND FICA WITHHELD                            *
00028         *                                                                *
00029         *     PROCESSING                                                 *
00030         *         FOR A NEW EMPLOYEE RECORD                              *
00031         *                 - DELETE CODE IS SET TO LOW-VALUES             *
00032         *                 - ALL YEAR-TO-DATE TOATLS ARE SET TO ZERO      *
00033         *                 - THE RECORDS IS ADDED TO THE CURRENT MASTER FILE *
00034         *                                                                *
00035         *     OUTPUT                                                     *
00036         *         AN UPDATED MASTER FILE IS PROVIDED. IT CONTAINS        *
00037         *                 - EMPLOYEE RECORDS FROM BOTH INPUT FILES       *
00038         *         A PRINTED REPORT IS PRODUCED. IT CONTAINS              *
00039         *                 - A LIST OF EMPLOYEES ON BOTH INPUT FILES      *
00040         ******************************************************************
00041         *
00042           ENVIRONMENT DIVISION.
00043         *
00044           CONFIGURATION SECTION.
00045           SOURCE-COMPUTER.
00046               IBM-370.
00047           OBJECT-COMPUTER.
00048               IBM-370.
00049           INPUT-OUTPUT SECTION.
00050           FILE-CONTROL.
00051               SELECT PAYROLL-ADDITONS-FILE-IN
00052                   ASSIGN TO SYS023-DA-3330-S-ADDFILE.
00053               SELECT PAYROLL-MAST-FILE-IO
00054                   ASSIGN TO SYS023-DA-3330-I-PAYFIL
00055                   RECORD KEY IS MAST-SS-NUM
00056                   NOMINAL KEY IS PAY-MAST-SEARCH-KEY
00057                   ACCESS IS RANDOM.
00058         *
00059           DATA DIVISION.
00060         *
00061           FILE SECTION.
00062           FD  PAYROLL-MAST-FILE-IO
00063                   LABEL RECORDS ARE STANDARD
00064                   BLOCK CONTAINS 05 RECORDS.
00065           01  PAYROLL-MAST-OUT-AREA.
00066               02  FILLER                      PIC X(4).
00067               02  MAST-SS-NUM                 PIC X(9).
00068               02  FILLER                      PIC X(88).
00069           FD  PAYROLL-ADDITIONS-FILE-IN
00070                   LABEL RECORDS ARE STANDARD
00071                   BLOCK CONTAINS 10 RECORDS.
00072           01  PAY-ADDITIONS-IN-AREA           PIC X(80).
```

Figure 6.8

Addition of records to an indexed file for Example 6.3.

Figure 6.8 (cont.)

```
00073                *
00074                  WORKING-STORAGE SECTION.
00075                  01  SWITCHES.
00076                      02   END-OF-ADDITIONS-SW          PIC X.
00077                           88   END-OF-ADDITIONS        VALUE 'Y'.
00078                      02   DUPLICATE-KEY-SW             PIC X.
00079                           88   DUPLICATE-KEY           VALUE 'Y'.
00080                  01  THE-NOMINAL-KEY.
00081                      02   PAY-MAST-SEARCH-KEY          PIC X(9).
00082                  01  PAY-MAST-OUT-REC.
00083                      02   PAY-DELETE-CODE              PIC X.
00084                      02   PAY-ADD-EMP-INFO.
00085                           03   FILLER                 PIC X(3).
00086                           03   PAY-ADD-SS-NUM          PIC X(9).
00087                           03   FILLER                 PIC X(68).
00088                      02   PAY-YTD-GROSS               PIC S9(5)V9(2).
00089                      02   PAY-YTD-TAX                 PIC S9(5)V9(2).
00090                      02   PAY-YTD-FICA                PIC S9(4)V9(2).
00091                *
00092                  PROCEDURE DIVISION.
00093                *
00094                  ADD-RECS-TO-MAST-CONTROL.
00095                      PERFORM START-ROUTINE.
00096                      PERFORM WRITE-READ-ROUTINE UNTIL END-OF-ADDITIONS.
00097                      PERFORM FINAL-ROUTINE.
00098                      STOP RUN.
00099                *
00100                  START-ROUTINE.
00101                      MOVE ALL 'N' TO SWITCHES.
00102                      MOVE ZERO TO PAY-YTD-GROSS, PAY-YTD-TAX, PAY-YTD-FICA.
00103                      MOVE LOW-VALUE TO PAY-DELETE-CODE.
00104                      OPEN INPUT PAYROLL-ADDITIONS-FILE-IN
00105                           I-O PAYROLL-MAST-FILE-IO.
00106                      PERFORM READ-PAYROLL-ADDITIONS.
00107                *
00108                  WRITE-READ-ROUTINE.
00109                      MOVE PAY-ADD-SS-NUM TO PAY-MAST-SEARCH-KEY
00110                      PERFORM WRITE-ADD-TO-MAST.
00111                      IF DUPLICATE-KEY
00112                          DISPLAY 'DUPLICATE KEY', PAY-MAST-OUT-REC
00113                          MOVE 'N' TO DUPLICATE-KEY-SW.
00114                      PERFORM READ-PAYROLL-ADDITIONS.
00115                *
00116                  FINAL-ROUTINE.
00117                      DISPLAY 'PROCESSING OF ADDITIONS FILE COMPLETE'
00118                      CLOSE PAYROLL-ADDITIONS-FILE-IN,
00119                            PAYROLL-MAST-FILE-IO.
00120                *
00121                  WRITE-ADD-TO-MAST.
00122                      WRITE PAYROLL-MAST-OUT-AREA FROM PAY-MAST-OUT-REC
00123                          INVALID KEY MOVE 'Y' TO DUPLICATE-KEY-SW.
00124                *
00125                  READ-PAYROLL-ADDITIONS.
00126                      READ PAYROLL-ADDITIONS-FILE-IN INTO PAY-ADD-EMP-INFO
00127                          AT END MOVE 'Y' TO END-OF-ADDITIONS-SW.
```

START STATEMENT

Recall that processing of a sequential file must begin with the first record in the file. Sequential processing of an ISAM or VSAM-indexed file can begin with any record in the file. The START statement is used to select the appropriate record at which to begin processing.

FORMAT	
ISAM	*VSAM Indexed*
START file-name KEY IS $\left\{ {EQUAL\ TO \atop =} \right\}$ data-name INVALID KEY imperative statement	START file-name KEY IS $\left\{ {EQUAL\ TO \atop =} \atop {GREATER\ THAN \atop >} \atop {NOT\ LESS\ THAN \atop NOT\ <} \right\}$ data-name [INVALID KEY imperative statement]

If processing is to begin at other than the first record in the file, a START statement must be executed after the OPEN but before the first READ.

For ISAM files, the value of the key at which processing is to begin must be placed in data-name before the START is executed. The test for an equal value on the file is always a character comparison. The number of bytes compared is determined by the length of data-name, which can be any data item with length less than or equal to that of the record key.

Suppose the file contains records with keys 297641, 337681, 337682, 339440, 779611, 794811 . . . ; then a value of 337681 in data-name would begin processing with this record. If data-name has a length of 3 bytes and contains the value 779, processing would begin with the *first* occurrence of a record whose key has as its first three digits 779, in this case it is 779611. If data-name had a length of 3 and a value of 338, the INVALID KEY would be activated.

To illustrate the situation where processing would START with the first record containing a ZIP code index key beginning with the digits 614, we would write:

```
    MOVE 614 TO LOCAL-ZIP
            .

            .

            .

    START CEN-FILE-IN
        KEY IS LOCAL-ZIP
        INVALID KEY MOVE 'Y' TO DID-NOT-FIND-SW.
```

For VSAM, data-name must be the record key field or a subfield of the record key that begins in the first position of the record key. Suppose a VSAM file is indexed according to phone number:

```
    01  PHONE-IN-AREA.
        02    .
               .

               .

        02  WHOLE-PHONE-NUM.
            03  LOCATION-PART.
                04   AREA-CODE          PIC 9(3).
                04   EXCHANGE           PIC 9(3).
            03  REST-OF-PHONE-NUM       PIC 9(4).
```

Then the choices for data-name are WHOLE-PHONE-NUM, LOCATION-PART, and AREA-CODE.

To retrieve beginning with a specific phone number

```
MOVE 3092981452 TO WHOLE-PHONE-NUM.
```

To retrieve beginning with a specific exchange within an area code

```
MOVE 309298 TO LOCATION-PART.
```

To retrieve beginning with a specific area code

```
MOVE 309 TO AREA-CODE.
```

Example 6.4

Mega's data processing department has a request for a list of names and social security numbers for all employees whose numbers were issued in a certain region of the country.

Figure 6.10 contains a program solution for the problem of Example 6.4. The structure chart is given in Figure 6.9.

We note the following special points about the program:

1. The NOMINAL KEY is required for use in conjunction with the START statement.
2. The ACCEPT statement on line 122 allows for entering the smallest possible social security number for a given region and places it in REGION-INDICATOR.
3. The ACCEPT statement on line 123 allows for entering the largest possible social security number for a given region and places it in END-OF-REGION-INDICATOR.
4. The execution of the START statement (line 124) may alter the initial value of REGION-INDICATOR.
5. Termination of processing after all records for a given region have been listed is a programmer responsibility. This is done by setting STOP-PROCESSING-SW (lines 155–157).

Changes needed to convert the program in Figure 6.10 to a VSAM version are

1. Lines 48–51 should read

```
ASSIGN TO SYS023-PAYFIL
ORGANIZATION IS INDEXED
RECORD KEY IS MAST-SS-NUM
ACCESS IS SEQUENTIAL.
```

2. Lines 82–84 in the DATA DIVISION should be deleted.
3. In the PROCEDURE DIVISION, line 122 should be

```
ACCEPT MAST-SS-NUM.
```

and line 125 should be

```
KEY IS NOT LESS THAN MAST-SS-NUM.
```

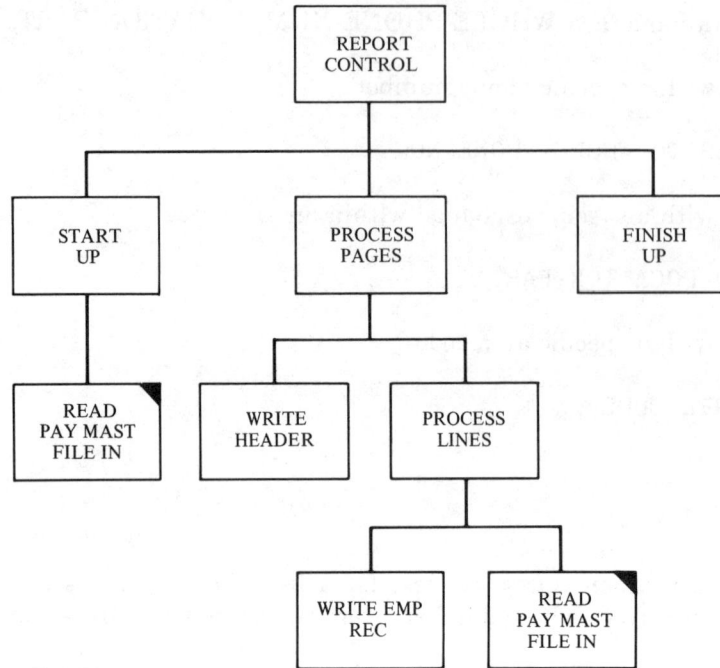

Figure 6.9
Structure chart for the program in Figure 6.10.

```
00001          IDENTIFICATION DIVISION.
00002      *
00003       PROGRAM-ID.
00004          EX-6-4.
00005      ****************************************************************
00006      *                                                              *
00007      *    PROGRAMMER TEAM              SUMMERS/WALSTROM/LINDAHL      *
00008      *    PROGRAM COMPLETION DATE DECEMBER 3, 1984                  *
00009      *                                                              *
00010      *                   PROGRAM SUMMARY                            *
00011      *    INPUT                                                     *
00012      *        THE PAYROLL MASTER FILE IS THE ONLY FILE NECESSARY.   *
00013      *        DATA ITEMS USED ARE                                   *
00014      *            - THE DELETION CODE                               *
00015      *            - EMPLOYEE SOCIAL SECURITY NUMBER                 *
00016      *            - EMPLOYEE NAME                                   *
00017      *        INPUT OF THE BEGINNING AND END OF THE REGION TO BE    *
00018      *        PROCESSED IS ALSO NECESSARY                           *
00019      *                                                              *
00020      *    PROCESSING                                                *
00021      *            - BEGINNING AND END OF REGION TO BE PROCESSED IS  *
00022      *              OBTAINED                                        *
00023      *            - FILE IS POSITIONED TO THE BEGINNING OF THE      *
00024      *              REGION                                          *
00025      *            - RECORDS ARE TESTED FOR DELETION AND FLAGGED     *
00026      *              ON OUTPUT IF THEY ARE DELETED                   *
00027      *                                                              *
00028      *    OUTPUT                                                    *
00029      *        A PRINTED REPORT IS PRODUCED. IT CONTAINS             *
00030      *            - EMPLOYEE SOCIAL SECURITY NUMBER                 *
00031      *            - EMPLOYEE NAME                                   *
00032      *            - MESSAGE TO INDICATE IF THE EMPLOYEE IS NO LONGER *
00033      *              EMPLOYED                                        *
00034      ****************************************************************
00035      *
00036       ENVIRONMENT DIVISION.
```

Figure 6.10
Sequential processing of an indexed file using the START statement for Example 6.4.

Figure 6.10 (*cont.*)

```
00037              *
00038              CONFIGURATION SECTION.
00039              SOURCE-COMPUTER.
00040                  IBM-370.
00041              OBJECT-COMPUTER.
00042                  IBM-370
00043              SPECIAL-NAMES.
00044                  C01 IS TO-TOP-OF-PAGE.
00045              INPUT-OUTPUT SECTION.
00046              FILE-CONTROL.
00047                  SELECT PAYROLL-MAST-FILE-IN
00048                      ASSIGN TO SYS023-DA-3330-I-PAYFIL
00049                      RECORD KEY IS MAST-SS-NUM
00050                      NOMINAL KEY IS REGION-INDICATOR
00051                      ACCESS IS SEQUENTIAL.
00052                  SELECT EMP-REPORT-PRINT-FILE
00053                      ASSIGN TO SYS009-UR-1403-S.
00054              *
00055              DATA DIVISION.
00056              *
00057              FILE SECTION.
00058              FD  PAYROLL-MAST-FILE-IN
00059                      LABEL RECORDS STANDARD
00060                      BLOCK CONTAINS 05 RECORDS.
00061                  01  PAY-MAST-IN-AREA.
00062                      02  FILLER                       PIC X(4).
00063                      02  MAST-SS-NUM                  PIC X(9).
00064                      02  FILLER                       PIC X(88).
00065              FD  EMP-REPORT-PRINT-FILE
00066                      LABEL RECORDS ARE OMITTED.
00067                  01  EMP-REPORT-AREA                  PIC X(133).
00068              *
00069              WORKING-STORAGE SECTION.
00070              01  SWITCHES.
00071                  02  END-OF-REGION-SW                 PIC X.
00072                      88  END-OF-REGION                VALUE 'Y'.
00073                  02  STOP-PROCESSING-SW               PIC X.
00074                      88  PROCESSING-SHOULD-STOP       VALUE 'Y'.
00075                  02  END-OF-PAGE-SW                   PIC X.
00076                      88  END-PAGE                     VALUE 'Y'.
00077              01  CONSTANTS.
00078                  02  PAGE-SIZE                        PIC 9(2) VALUE 55.
00079              01  COUNTERS.
00080                  02  PAGE-COUNT                       PIC 9(3).
00081                  02  LINE-COUNT                       PIC 9(2).
00082              01  REGION-INDICATOR.
00083                  02  REGION-NUM                       PIC X.
00084                  02  FILLER                           PIC X(8).
00085              01  END-OF-REGION-INDICATOR.
00086                  02  FILLER                           PIC X(9).
00087              01  PAYROLL-MAST-IN-REC.
00088                  02  PAY-IN-DELETE-CODE               PIC X.
00089                  02  FILLER                           PIC X(3).
00090                  02  PAY-IN-SS-NUM                    PIC 9(9).
00091                  02  PAY-IN-EMP-NAME                  PIC X(20).
00092                  02  FILLER                           PIC X(68).
00093              01  EMP-PRINT-LINE.
00094                  02  FILLER                           PIC X(10) VALUE SPACE.
00095                  02  EMP-PRINT-SS-NUM                 PIC 9(9).
00096                  02  FILLER                           PIC X(10)  VALUE SPACE.
00097                  02  EMP-PRINT-EMP-NAME               PIC X(25).
00098                  02  EMP-PRINT-STATUS                 PIC X(30).
00099              01  HEADER-LINE.
00100                  02  FILLER                           PIC X(24)
00101                          VALUE ' SOCIAL SECURITY NUMBER'.
00102                  02  FILLER                           PIC X(10) VALUE SPACE.
00103                  02  FILLER                           PIC X(25)
00104                          VALUE ' EMPLOYEE NAME'.
00105                  02  FILLER                           PIC X(4) VALUE 'PAGE'.
00106                  02  HEAD-PAGE-NUM                    PIC Z(2).
00107              *
00108              PROCEDURE DIVISION.
00109              *
00110              REPORT-CONTROL.
00111                  PERFORM START-UP.
00112                  PERFORM PROCESS-PAGES UNTIL PROCESSING-SHOULD-STOP.
00113                  PERFORM FINISH-UP.
00114                  STOP RUN.
```

Figure 6.10 (*cont.*)

```
00115        *
00116           START-UP.
00117              OPEN INPUT PAYROLL-MAST-FILE-IN
00118                   OUTPUT EMP-REPORT-PRINT-FILE.
00119              MOVE 'N' TO END-OF-REGION-SW, STOP-PROCESSING-SW.
00120              MOVE 1 TO PAGE-COUNT,
00121                        HEAD-PAGE-NUM.
00122              ACCEPT REGION-INDICATOR.
00123              ACCEPT END-OF-REGION-INDICATOR.
00124              START PAYROLL-MAST-FILE-IN
00125                   KEY IS = REGION-NUM
00126                   INVALID KEY MOVE ALL 'Y' TO SWITCHES.
00127              IF PROCESSING-SHOULD-STOP
00128                 DISPLAY ' INVALID STARTING POINT IN FILE'
00129              ELSE
00130                 PERFORM READ-PAY-MAST-FILE-IN.
00131        *
00132           PROCESS-PAGES.
00133              PERFORM WRITE-HEADER.
00134              MOVE 1 TO LINE-COUNT
00135              ADD 1 TO PAGE-COUNT.
00136              PERFORM  PROCESS-LINES UNTIL END-PAGE.
00137              MOVE PAGE-COUNT TO HEAD-PAGE-NUM.
00138              MOVE 'N' TO END-OF-PAGE-SW.
00139        *
00140           FINISH-UP.
00141              CLOSE PAYROLL-MAST-FILE-IN, EMP-REPORT-PRINT-FILE.
00142        *
00143           PROCESS-LINES.
00144              MOVE PAY-IN-SS-NUM TO EMP-PRINT-SS-NUM.
00145              MOVE PAY-IN-EMP-NAME TO EMP-PRINT-EMP-NAME.
00146              IF   PAY-IN-DELETE-CODE = LOW-VALUES
00147                   MOVE SPACE TO EMP-PRINT-STATUS
00148              ELSE
00149                   MOVE 'NO LONGER EMPLOYED' TO EMP-PRINT-STATUS.
00150              PERFORM WRITE-EMP-REC.
00151              ADD 1 TO LINE-COUNT.
00152              IF LINE-COUNT = PAGE-SIZE
00153                 MOVE 'Y' TO END-OF-PAGE-SW.
00154              PERFORM READ-PAY-MAST-FILE-IN.
00155              IF PAY-IN-SS-NUM IS GREATER THAN END-OF-REGION-INDICATOR
00156                 MOVE 'Y' TO STOP-PROCESSING-SW,
00157                            END-OF-PAGE-SW.
00158        *
00159           WRITE-HEADER.
00160              WRITE EMP-REPORT-AREA FROM HEADER-LINE
00161                  AFTER ADVANCING TO-TOP-OF-PAGE.
00162        *
00163           WRITE-EMP-REC.
00164              WRITE EMP-REPORT-AREA FROM EMP-PRINT-LINE
00165                  AFTER ADVANCING 1 LINES.
00166        *
00167           READ-PAY-MAST-FILE-IN.
00168              READ PAYROLL-MAST-FILE-IN INTO PAYROLL-MAST-IN-REC
00169                  AT END MOVE 'Y' TO STOP-PROCESSING-SW,
00170                            END-OF-PAGE-SW.
```

Example 6.5

Mega's data processing staff is now satisfied that they are well enough acquainted with ISAM to write a general maintenance program to keep the master file up to date. This program will add new records to the file, change employee personal information, update the YTD totals, and change the status of employees who no longer work for the company.

A program to perform these tasks is shown in Figure 6.12, along with a structure chart, shown in Figure 6.11.

This program incorporates many of the techniques used in previous examples. However, there are some new features worth special mention.

The file, PAYROLL-CHANGES-FILE-IN, has two record formats. However, all records are the same length, and all contain the social security number in the same location. All records have a code in the last byte to indicate the type of modification to PAYROLL-MAST-FILE-IO. If the code denotes a deletion, social security number is the only other field necessary. If the code denotes an addition, then all employee personal information must be given.

If personal data is to be updated, only the data to be changed need to be specified. For an update of year-to-date totals, social security number and hours worked need to be specified. The possible changes to an employee's personal data are described under CHGS-IN-REC, beginning at line 129, in Figure 6.12. CHGS-IN-YTD-REC, line 143, describes the data for a YTD totals update.

REDEFINES, used in line 143, allows us to have all record types from PAYROLL-CHANGES-FILE-IN read into the same physical location in internal storage. Having the same internal storage area defined to accommodate two different record descriptions eliminates the need for testing the code and then moving one record type to another location.

A table contains the error messages, and error messages are selected using the table subscript ERROR-SUB.

Deletions are indicated by placing HIGH-VALUES in PAY-IO-DELETE-CODE.

Note on lines 226–229 that the permanent file copy of a record will not be changed if an error is found. Also note that changes to a deleted record are not allowed (lines 224–225).

As before, only minimal changes are required to convert the program in Figure 6.12 to one that processes a VSAM-indexed file. As they are almost the same as those for Example 6.3, we will leave them as an exercise to the reader.

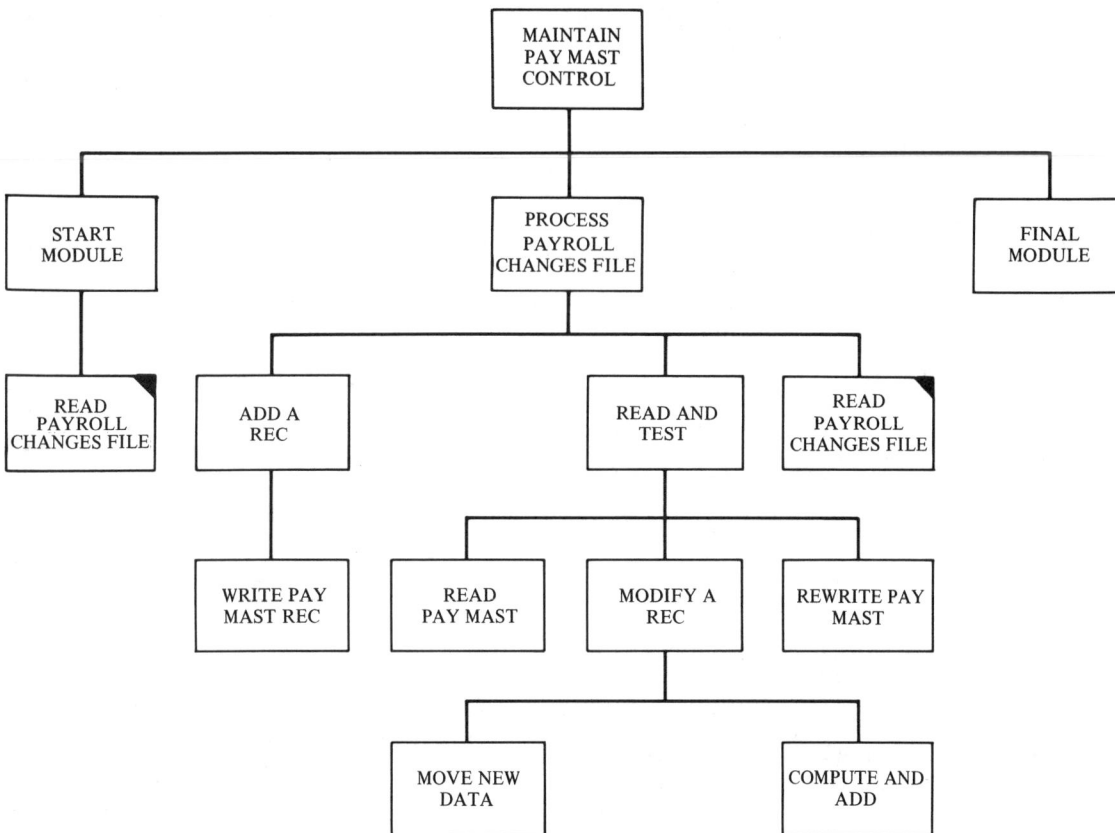

Figure 6.11
Structure chart for the program in Figure 6.12.

```
00001              IDENTIFICATION DIVISION.
00002            *
00003             PROGRAM-ID.
00004                EX-6-5.
00005            **********************************************************************
00006            *                                                                    *
00007            *     PROGRAMMER TEAM          SUMMERS/WALSTROM/LINDAHL               *
00008            *     PROGRAM COMPLETION DATE DECEMBER 10, 1984                       *
00009            *                                                                    *
00010            *                     PROGRAM SUMMARY                                 *
00011            *                                                                    *
00012            *     INPUT                                                           *
00013            *         INPUT FILES ARE THE PAYROLL MASTER FILE AND A               *
00014            *         TRANSACTIONS FILE CONTAINING INFORMATION FOR CHANGES        *
00015            *         TO THE MASTER FILE.                                         *
00016            *         PAYROLL MASTER RECORDS CONSIST OF                           *
00017            *             - DELETE CODE                                           *
00018            *             - CODE FOR PLANT LOCATION                               *
00019            *             - CODE FOR THE DEPARTMENT TO WHICH THE EMPLOYEE          *
00020            *               IS ASSIGNED                                           *
00021            *             - SOCIAL SECURITY NUMBER                                 *
00022            *             - NAME                                                  *
00023            *             - OTHER PERSONAL DATA                                   *
00024            *             - TAX CLASSIFICATION                                    *
00025            *             - PAY RATE                                              *
00026            *             - YEAR-TO-DATE TOTALS FOR GROSS PAY, TAX WITHHELD       *
00027            *               AND FICA WITHHELD                                     *
00028            *         THERE ARE TWO TYPES OF CHANGE RECORDS. ONE IS USED          *
00029            *         TO UPDATE YEAR-TO-DATE TOTALS AND ANOTHER FOR               *
00030            *         CHANGES TO OTHER FIELDS OF THE MASTER RECORDS OR            *
00031            *         ADDITIONS TO THE MASTER FILE                                *
00032            *         FOR YEAR-TO-DATE TOTALS CHANGES RECORD CONSIST OF           *
00033            *             - SOCIAL SECURITY NUMBER                                 *
00034            *             - TOTAL HOURS WORKED                                    *
00035            *             - TRANSACTION CODE                                      *
00036            *         FOR OTHER CHANGES THE RECORD CONTAINS THE NEW VALUES        *
00037            *         OF FIELDS TO BE CHANGED. POSSIBLE CHANGES ARE TO            *
00038            *             - CODE FOR PLANT LOCATION                               *
00039            *             - CODE FOR THE DEPARTMENT TO WHICH THE EMPLOYEE          *
00040            *               IS ASSIGNED                                           *
00041            *             - NAME                                                  *
00042            *             - OTHER PERSOANL DATA                                   *
00043            *             - TAX CLASSIFICATION                                    *
00044            *             - PAY RATE                                              *
00045            *         THE RECORD ALSO CONTAINS                                    *
00046            *             - SOCIAL SECURITY NUMBER                                 *
00047            *             - TRANSACTION CODE                                      *
00048            *                                                                    *
00049            *     PROCESSING                                                      *
00050            *         THE TYPE OF CHANGE TO THE MASTER FILE IS DETERMINED         *
00051            *         FOR A VALID UPDATE OF YEAR-TO-DATE TOTALS                   *
00052            *             - THE GROSS PAY FOR PAY PERIOD IS CALCULATED            *
00053            *             - THE TAX FOR THE PAY PERIOD IS COMPUTED                *
00054            *             - THE FICA FOR THE PAY PERIOD IS COMPUTED               *
00055            *             - THE YEAR-TO-DATE TOTALS ARE UPDATED                   *
00056            *         FOR A VALID UPDATE TO OTHER FIELDS OF A MASTER RECORD       *
00057            *             - NON-BLANK VALUES OF THE CHANGE RECORD ARE             *
00058            *               SUBSTITUED FOR THE CORRESPONDING FIELDS ON            *
00059            *               THE MASTER RECORD                                     *
00060            *         FOR A VALID ADDITION                                        *
00061            *             - DELETE CODE IS SET TO LOW-VALUES                      *
00062            *             - YEAR-TO-DATE TOTALS ARE SET TO ZERO                   *
00063            *             - CHANGE INFO PLACED IN MASTER RECORD                   *
00064            *         FOR A VALID DELETION                                        *
00065            *             - DELETE CODE IS SET TO HIGH-VALUES                     *
00066            *         FOR AN INVALID CHANGE A CODE IS SET TO INDICATE THE         *
00067            *         TYPE OF ERROR                                               *
00068            *                                                                    *
00069            *     OUTPUT                                                          *
00070            *         AN UPDATED PAYROLL MASTER FILE IS PRODUCED                  *
00071            *         A PRINTED REPORT OF RECORDS WITH ERRORS IN THE              *
00072            *         REQUESTED CHANGE IS PRODUCED. IT CONTAINS                   *
00073            *             - THE ERRONEOUS CHANGE RECORD                           *
00074            *             - A MESSAGE INDICATING THE TYPE OF ERROR                *
00075            **********************************************************************
```

Figure 6.12
Addition, modification, and deletion of records in an indexed file for Example 6.5.

Figure 6.12 (*cont.*)

```
00076          *
00077            ENVIRONMENT DIVISION.
00078          *
00079            CONFIGURATION SECTION.
00080            SOURCE-COMPUTER.
00081                IBM-370.
00082            OBJECT-COMPUTER.
00083                IBM-370.
00084            INPUT-OUTPUT SECTION.
00085            FILE-CONTROL.
00086                SELECT PAYROLL-MAST-FILE-IO
00087                    ASSIGN TO SYS023-DA-3330-I-PAYFYL
00088                    RECORD KEY IS PAY-REC-SS-NUM
00089                    NOMINAL KEY IS PAY-MAST-SEARCH-KEY
00090                    ACCESS IS RANDOM.
00091                SELECT PAYROLL-CHANGES-FILE-IN
00092                    ASSIGN TO SYS023-DA-3330-S-CHGSFYL.
00093          *
00094            DATA DIVISION.
00095          *
00096            FILE SECTION.
00097            FD  PAYROLL-MAST-FILE-IO
00098                    BLOCK CONTAINS  5 RECORDS
00099                    LABEL RECORDS ARE STANDARD.
00100            01  PAY-MAST-IO-AREA.
00101                02  FILLER                       PIC X(4).
00102                02  PAY-REC-SS-NUM               PIC X(9).
00103                02  FILLER                       PIC X(88).
00104            FD  PAYROLL-CHANGES-FILE-IN
00105                    LABEL RECORDS ARE STANDARD
00106                    BLOCK CONTAINS 20 RECORDS.
00107            01  PAY-CHANGES-IN-AREA              PIC X(81).
00108          *
00109            WORKING-STORAGE SECTION.
00110            01  SWITCHES.
00111                02  END-OF-FILE-SW               PIC X.
00112                    88  END-OF-CHANGES-FILE  VALUE 'Y'.
00113                02  STOP-PROCESSING-SW           PIC X.
00114                    88  PROCESSING-SHOULD-STOP   VALUE 'Y'.
00115            01  COUNTERS.
00116                02  ERROR-SUB                    PIC S9.
00117                    88  NO-ERROR VALUE ZERO.
00118            01  CONSTANTS.
00119                02  MAX-SS-WITHHOLD              PIC S9(5) VALUE +29700.
00120                02  SS-WITHHOLD-RATE             PIC SV9(3) VALUE +.067.
00121                02  OVERTIME-ADJUSTMENT          PIC SV9 VALUE +.5.
00122                02  MAX-REG-HRS                  PIC S9(2) VALUE 40.
00123                02  TAXABLE-INCOME-ADJUSTMENT    PIC S9(2) VALUE 13.
00124                02  EST-FED-TAX-RATE             PIC V9(2) VALUE +.18.
00125            01  WORK-AREAS.
00126                02  PAY-AMT                      PIC S9(4)V9(2).
00127            01  THE-NOMINAL-KEY.
00128                02  PAY-MAST-SEARCH-KEY          PIC X(9).
00129            01  CHGS-IN-REC.
00130                02  CHGS-IN-EMP-INFO.
00131                    03  CHGS-IN-PLANT-SITE       PIC S9.
00132                    03  CHGS-IN-DEPT-CODE        PIC S9(2).
00133                    03  CHGS-IN-SS-NUM           PIC X(9).
00134                    03  CHGS-IN-EMP-NAME         PIC X(20).
00135                    03  CHGS-IN-PERSONAL-DATA    PIC X(42).
00136                    03  CHGS-IN-TAX-CLASS        PIC S9(2).
00137                    03  CHGS-IN-PAY-RATE         PIC S9(2)V9(2).
00138                02  CHGS-IN-TRANS-CODE           PIC X.
00139                    88  ADD-TO-FILE    VALUE 'A'.
00140                    88  CHANGE-EMP-DATA VALUE 'E'.
00141                    88  CHANGE-TOTALS VALUE 'T'.
00142                    88  DELETE-EMP-REC  VALUE 'D'.
00143            01  CHGS-IN-YTD-REC REDEFINES CHGS-IN-REC.
00144                02  FILLER                       PIC X(3).
00145                02  CHGS-IN-YTD-SS-NUM           PIC X(9).
00146                02  FILLER                       PIC X(2).
00147                02  CHGS-IN-YTD-HRS-WRKED        PIC S9(2)V9(2).
00148                02  FILLER                       PIC X(63).
```

Figure 6.12 (*cont.*)

```
00149                 01   PAY-MAST-IO-REC.
00150                      02   PAY-IO-DELETE-CODE           PIC X.
00151                      02   PAY-IO-EMP-INFO.
00152                           03   PAY-IO-PLANT-SITE       PIC S9.
00153                           03   PAY-IO-DEPT-CODE        PIC S9(2).
00154                           03   PAY-IO-SS-NUM           PIC X(9).
00155                           03   PAY-IO-EMP-NAME         PIC X(20).
00156                           03   PAY-IO-PERSONAL-DATA    PIC X(42).
00157                           03   PAY-IO-TAX-CLASS        PIC S9(2).
00158                           03   PAY-IO-PAY-RATE         PIC S9(2)V9(2).
00159                      02   PAY-IO-YTD-GROSS             PIC S9(5)V9(2).
00160                      02   PAY-IO-YTD-TAX               PIC S9(5)V9(2).
00161                      02   PAY-IO-YTD-FICA              PIC S9(4)V9(2).
00162                 01   ERROR-MESSAGES.
00163                      02   FILLER                       PIC X(25)
00164                           VALUE ' DUPLICATE RECORD'.
00165                      02   FILLER                       PIC X(25)
00166                           VALUE ' NO RECORD ON FILE'.
00167                      02   FILLER                       PIC X(25)
00168                           VALUE ' RECORD ALREADY DELETED'.
00169                      02   FILLER                       PIC X(25)
00170                           VALUE ' INVALID TRANS CODE'.
00171                 01   ERROR-MESSAGE-TABLE REDEFINES ERROR-MESSAGES.
00172                      02   ERROR-MESSAGE OCCURS 4 TIMES
00173                                                        PIC X(25).
00174            *
00175            PROCEDURE DIVISION.
00176            *
00177            MAINTAIN-PAY-MAST-CONTROL.
00178                 PERFORM START-MODULE.
00179                 PERFORM PROCESS-PAYROLL-CHANGES-FILE
00180                      UNTIL PROCESSING-SHOULD-STOP.
00181                 PERFORM FINAL-MODULE.
00182                 STOP RUN.
00183            *
00184            START-MODULE.
00185                 OPEN INPUT PAYROLL-CHANGES-FILE-IN
00186                      I-O PAYROLL-MAST-FILE-IO.
00187                 DISPLAY ' LIST OF RECORDS WITH ERRORS'.
00188                 PERFORM READ-PAYROLL-CHANGES-FILE.
00189                 MOVE 'N' TO END-OF-FILE-SW
00190                           STOP-PROCESSING-SW.
00191            *
00192            PROCESS-PAYROLL-CHANGES-FILE.
00193                 MOVE 0 TO ERROR-SUB.
00194                 MOVE CHGS-IN-SS-NUM TO PAY-MAST-SEARCH-KEY.
00195                 IF ADD-TO-FILE
00196                      PERFORM ADD-A-REC
00197                 ELSE
00198                      PERFORM READ-AND-TEST.
00199                 IF ERROR-SUB IS POSITIVE
00200                      DISPLAY CHGS-IN-REC, SPACE,
00201                           ERROR-MESSAGE (ERROR-SUB).
00202                 PERFORM READ-PAYROLL-CHANGES-FILE.
00203            *
00204            FINAL-MODULE.
00205                 CLOSE PAYROLL-CHANGES-FILE-IN
00206                      PAYROLL-MAST-FILE-IO.
00207                 IF END-OF-CHANGES-FILE
00208                      DISPLAY ' PAYROLL MAST CHANGES PROCESSED '
00209                 ELSE
00210                      DISPLAY
00211                           ' INVALID REWRITE ATTEMPTED ',
00212                           ' PROCESSING STOPPED'
00213                      DISPLAY PAY-MAST-IO-REC.
00214            *
00215            ADD-A-REC.
00216                 MOVE LOW-VALUES TO PAY-IO-DELETE-CODE.
00217                 MOVE CHGS-IN-EMP-INFO TO PAY-IO-EMP-INFO.
00218                 MOVE ZERO TO PAY-IO-YTD-GROSS, PAY-IO-YTD-TAX,
00219                           PAY-IO-YTD-FICA.
00220                 PERFORM WRITE-PAY-MAST-REC.
```

Figure 6.12 (cont.)

```
00221          *
00222            READ-AND-TEST.
00223                PERFORM READ-PAY-MAST.
00224                IF NO-ERROR AND PAY-IO-DELETE-CODE = HIGH-VALUES
00225                    MOVE 3 TO ERROR-SUB.
00226                IF NO-ERROR
00227                    PERFORM MODIFY-A-REC.
00228                IF NO-ERROR
00229                    PERFORM REWRITE-PAY-MAST.
00230          *
00231            MODIFY-A-REC.
00232                IF CHANGE-EMP-DATA
00233                    PERFORM MOVE-NEW-DATA
00234                ELSE
00235                    IF CHANGE-TOTALS
00236                        PERFORM COMPUTE-AND-ADD
00237                    ELSE
00238                        IF DELETE-EMP-REC
00239                            MOVE HIGH-VALUES TO PAY-IO-DELETE-CODE
00240                        ELSE
00241                            MOVE 4 TO ERROR-SUB.
00242          *
00243            MOVE-NEW-DATA.
00244                IF CHGS-IN-PLANT-SITE IS NUMERIC
00245                    MOVE CHGS-IN-PLANT-SITE TO PAY-IO-PLANT-SITE.
00246                IF CHGS-IN-DEPT-CODE IS NUMERIC
00247                    MOVE CHGS-IN-DEPT-CODE TO PAY-IO-DEPT-CODE.
00248                IF CHGS-IN-EMP-NAME IS NOT EQUAL TO SPACE
00249                    MOVE CHGS-IN-EMP-NAME TO PAY-IO-EMP-NAME.
00250                IF CHGS-IN-PERSONAL-DATA IS NOT EQUAL TO SPACE
00251                    MOVE CHGS-IN-PERSONAL-DATA TO PAY-IO-PERSONAL-DATA.
00252                IF CHGS-IN-TAX-CLASS IS NUMERIC
00253                    MOVE CHGS-IN-TAX-CLASS TO PAY-IO-TAX-CLASS.
00254                IF CHGS-IN-PAY-RATE IS NUMERIC
00255                    MOVE CHGS-IN-PAY-RATE TO PAY-IO-PAY-RATE.
00256          *
00257            COMPUTE-AND-ADD.
00258                COMPUTE PAY-AMT = CHGS-IN-YTD-HRS-WRKED * PAY-IO-PAY-RATE.
00259                IF CHGS-IN-YTD-HRS-WRKED IS GREATER THAN MAX-REG-HRS
00260                    COMPUTE PAY-AMT = PAY-AMT +
00261                            OVERTIME-ADJUSTMENT * PAY-IO-PAY-RATE *
00262                            (CHGS-IN-YTD-HRS-WRKED - MAX-REG-HRS).
00263                COMPUTE PAY-IO-YTD-TAX = EST-FED-TAX-RATE *
00264                        (PAY-AMT - (PAY-IO-TAX-CLASS *
00265                            TAXABLE-INCOME-ADJUSTMENT)) +
00266                        PAY-IO-YTD-TAX.
00267                IF PAY-IO-YTD-GROSS + PAY-AMT IS LESS THAN MAX-SS-WITHHOLD
00268                    COMPUTE PAY-IO-YTD-FICA = SS-WITHHOLD-RATE * (PAY-AMT
00269                            + PAY-IO-YTD-GROSS)
00270                ELSE
00271                    COMPUTE PAY-IO-YTD-FICA = SS-WITHHOLD-RATE *
00272                            MAX-SS-WITHHOLD.
00273                COMPUTE PAY-IO-YTD-GROSS = PAY-AMT + PAY-IO-YTD-GROSS.
00274          *
00275            READ-PAYROLL-CHANGES-FILE.
00276                READ PAYROLL-CHANGES-FILE-IN INTO CHGS-IN-REC
00277                    AT END MOVE 'Y' TO END-OF-FILE-SW,
00278                                        STOP-PROCESSING-SW.
00279          *
00280            WRITE-PAY-MAST-REC.
00281                WRITE PAY-MAST-IO-AREA FROM PAY-MAST-IO-REC
00282                    INVALID KEY MOVE 1 TO ERROR-SUB.
00283          *
00284            READ-PAY-MAST.
00285                READ PAYROLL-MAST-FILE-IO INTO PAY-MAST-IO-REC
00286                    INVALID KEY MOVE 2 TO ERROR-SUB.
00287          *
00288            REWRITE-PAY-MAST.
00289                REWRITE PAY-MAST-IO-AREA FROM PAY-MAST-IO-REC
00290                    INVALID KEY MOVE 'Y' TO STOP-PROCESSING-SW.
```

ADDITIONAL VSAM FEATURES

Deletion of records in a VSAM-indexed file may be accomplished by using the DELETE verb. When the DELETE verb is used, the record is logically removed from the file and is no longer accessible to the programmer. Consequently, no program logic is needed to check for a deleted record, since they can no longer be read.

FORMAT
VSAM
<u>DELETE</u> file-name RECORD [<u>INVALID</u> KEY imperative-statement]

Using the DELETE verb, an employee record could be removed from the file by

```
DELETE PAY-MAST-FILE-IO RECORD
    INVALID KEY MOVE 2 TO ERROR-SUB.
```

Though the record is logically deleted initially, under VSAM, when the record space is needed, the system may physically delete the record so the space may be reused. Care should be exercised when deleting records. In most cases, the information contained in a deleted record should be saved in an inactive, but permanent, file, thus making the record available for later use should the need arise.

DYNAMIC ACCESS applies only to VSAM files and allows for both SEQUENTIAL and RANDOM processing in the same program.

FORMAT
VSAM
<u>ACCESS</u> IS <u>DYNAMIC</u>

DYNAMIC may be specified if, for example, you want to report changes made from a random update program in the same program. An outline of the technique is given in Figure 6.13.

In the program outline illustrated in Figure 6.13, your attention is directed to the following points:

1. The ACCESS IS DYNAMIC clause in the SELECT/ASSIGN sentence will allow for both sequential and random processing.
2. The statement PERFORM PROCESS-PAYROLL-CHANGES UNTIL PROCESSING-SHOULD-STOP provides the main loop control for processing the file randomly during the file update.

3. The statements MOVE ZERO TO PAY-REC-SS-NUM, START, and PER-FORM-SEQ-READ-IN will allow the first record in the file to be accessed in preparation for processing the file sequentially.
4. The statement PERFORM LIST-THE-FILE UNTIL PROCESSING-SHOULD-STOP provides the main loop control for processing the file sequentially to print out the records in the updated file.
5. In the paragraph named SEQ-READ-IN, the READ statement contains the reserved word NEXT, which specifies a sequential read when access is DYNAMIC.

```
FILE-CONTROL.
    SELECT PAYROLL-MAST-FILE-IO
        ASSIGN TO SYS023-PAYFIL
        ORGANIZATION IS INDEXED
        ACCESS IS DYNAMIC
        RECORD KEY IS MAST-SS-NUM.

        .
        .
        .

*
 PROCEDURE DIVISION.
*

    PERFORM START-MODULE.
    PERFORM PROCESS-PAYROLL-CHANGES
        UNTIL PROCESSING-SHOULD-STOP.
    MOVE 'N' TO STOP-PROCESSING-SW.
    MOVE ZERO TO PAY-REC-SS-NUM.
    START PAYROLL-MAST-FILE-IO
        KEY IS NOT LESS THAN PAY-REC-SS-NUM
        INVALID KEY MOVE 'Y' TO BAD-KEY-SW.
    PERFORM SEQ-READ-IN.
    PERFORM LIST-THE-FILE
        UNTIL PROCESSING-SHOULD-STOP.

        .
        .
        .

*
 SEQ-READ-IN.
    READ PAYROLL-MAST-FILE-IO NEXT INTO PAY-MAST-IO-REC
        AT END MOVE 'Y' TO STOP-PROCESSING-SW.

        .
        .
        .
```

Figure 6.13
Dynamic processing of a VSAM-indexed file.

FILE STATUS FOR INPUT—OUTPUT OPERATIONS

The *FILE STATUS* clause, introduced in the 74 ANSI COBOL standard, can be used with VSAM-indexed files but cannot be used with ISAM files. The clause is also applicable to sequential and to relative files as covered by the standard.

The FILE STATUS clause may be used to provide a programmer with specific information concerning the status of input–output operations during program execution. The system will automatically update a two-position programmer-defined *alphanumeric* data-field in WORKING-STORAGE after execution of each I/O operation for a specified file. This field must be named in a FILE STATUS clause in the SELECT entry for the file in the FILE-CONTROL paragraph. Values placed in the FILE STATUS data-field by the system can be tested to determine the outcome of an I/O operation.

Selected examples of FILE STATUS values for indexed files are as follows:

"00"   Successful completion of I/O operation

"10"   End-of-file

"21"   Sequence error

"22"   Duplicated key

"24"   Boundary violation

For additional information concerning FILE STATUS values and the file structures to which they pertain, see Figure 6.15 at the end of this chapter.

> ### Example 6.6

If the Mega-Tronics Corporation makes the decision to switch from ISAM to VSAM at some later date, and if its programmers wish to use the FILE STATUS clause, this will not be difficult. The program listing in Figure 6.14 is essentially the same as the ISAM file-creation program solution for Example 6.1 (shown in Figure 6.4), except that it now contains a FILE STATUS clause and has been modified into a VSAM program. Also, in this program, processing is allowed to continue if duplicate or out-of-sequence keys are encountered, thereby permitting file creation to continue. Records with problem keys can be corrected and then added to the file on a later file update run.

Several points concerning the program in Figure 6.14 should be called to your attention. Note the FILE STATUS entry on line 55 naming WRITE-STATUS as the data-field to be updated by the system. This field, and the specific FILE STATUS code values to be tested, are established on lines 77–83. After attempting to write a record, the statement on line 105 tests the FILE STATUS code value placed in WRITE-STATUS to determine if the write was successful. If it was not, the module ERROR-CHECK, beginning on line 119, is executed and WRITE-STATUS is tested to determine the specific cause of the unsuccessful write. An appropriate message indicating the problem is displayed, as well as the contents of the record. Program control then returns to line 107, where WRITE-STATUS is again tested to determine if program execution should continue. If the unsuccessful write was caused by any condition other than a duplicate key or a sequence error, processing will be terminated.

```
00051          SELECT PAYROLL-MAST-FILE-OUT
00052              ASSIGN TO SYS023-PAYFIL
00053              ORGANIZATION IS INDEXED
00054              RECORD KEY IS MAST-SS-NUM
00055              FILE STATUS IS WRITE-STATUS.
00056      *
00057      DATA DIVISION.
```

Figure 6.14
The use of FILE STATUS codes illustrated in a VSAM-indexed file creation program for Example 6.6.

Figure 6.14 (cont.)

```
00058              *
00059              FILE SECTION.
00060              FD  PAYROLL-MAST-FILE-IN
00061                       LABEL RECORDS ARE STANDARD
00062                       BLOCK CONTAINS 10 RECORDS.
00063              01  PAYROLL-MAST-IN-AREA              PIC X(100).
00064              FD  PAYROLL-MAST-FILE-OUT
00065                       LABEL RECORDS ARE STANDARD.
00066              01  PAYROLL-MAST-OUT-AREA.
00067                  02  FILLER                        PIC X(4).
00068                  02  MAST-SS-NUM                   PIC X(9).
00069                  02  FILLER                        PIC X(88).
00070              *
00071              WORKING-STORAGE SECTION.
00072              01  SWITCHES.
00073                  02  STOP-PROCESSING-SW            PIC X.
00074                      88  PROCESSING-SHOULD-STOP    VALUE 'Y'.
00075                  02  END-OF-FILE-SW                PIC X.
00076                      88  END-OF-FILE               VALUE 'Y'.
00077              01  MAST-STATUS-KEY.
00078                  02  WRITE-STATUS                  PIC X(2).
00079                      88  GOOD-WRITE VALUE '00'.
00080                      88  SEQUENCE-ERROR  VALUE '21'.
00081                      88  DUPLICATE-KEY VALUE '22'.
00082                      88  OUT-OF-FILE-LIMITS VALUE '24'.
00083                      88  PROCESSING-SHOULD-CONTINUE VALUE '00' '21' '22'.
00084              01  PAY-OUT-REC.
00085                  02  PAY-OUT-DELETE-CODE           PIC X.
00086                  02  PAY-OUT-EMP-INFO              PIC X(100).
00087              *
00088              PROCEDURE DIVISION.
00089              *
00090              PAY-MAST-LOAD-CONTROL.
00091                  PERFORM START-PROCESS.
00092                  PERFORM CREATE-OUTPUT-FILE UNTIL PROCESSING-SHOULD-STOP.
00093                  PERFORM FINAL-PROCESS.
00094                  STOP RUN.
00095              *
00096              START-PROCESS.
00097                  MOVE ALL 'N' TO SWITCHES.
00098                  OPEN INPUT PAYROLL-MAST-FILE-IN
00099                       OUTPUT PAYROLL-MAST-FILE-OUT.
00100                  MOVE LOW-VALUE TO PAY-OUT-DELETE-CODE.
00101                  PERFORM READ-PAY-MAST-IN.
00102              *
00103              CREATE-OUTPUT-FILE.
00104                  PERFORM WRITE-PAY-OUT-REC.
00105                  IF NOT GOOD-WRITE
00106                      PERFORM ERROR-CHECK.
00107                  IF PROCESSING-SHOULD-CONTINUE
00108                      PERFORM READ-PAY-MAST-IN
00109                  ELSE
00110                      MOVE 'Y' TO STOP-PROCESSING-SW.
00111              *
00112              FINAL-PROCESS.
00113                  IF END-OF-FILE
00114                      DISPLAY ' INDEXED PAYROLL MASTER CREATED '
00115                  ELSE
00116                      DISPLAY ' FILE CREATION NOT COMPLETE'
00117                  CLOSE PAYROLL-MAST-FILE-IN, PAYROLL-MAST-FILE-OUT.
00118              *
00119              ERROR-CHECK.
00120                  IF SEQUENCE-ERROR
00121                      DISPLAY ' OUT OF ORDER'
00122                  ELSE
00123                      IF DUPLICATE-KEY
00124                          DISPLAY ' DUPLICATE KEY'
00125                      ELSE
00126                          IF OUT-OF-FILE-LIMITS
00127                              DISPLAY ' BOUNDARY VIOLATION'
00128                          ELSE
00129                              DISPLAY ' UNDETERMINED ERROR ENCOUNTERED'.
00130                  DISPLAY PAY-OUT-REC.
00131              *
00132              READ-PAY-MAST-IN.
00133                  READ PAYROLL-MAST-FILE-IN INTO PAY-OUT-EMP-INFO
00134                      AT END MOVE 'Y' TO STOP-PROCESSING-SW
00135                                        END-OF-FILE-SW.
00136              *
00137              WRITE-PAY-OUT-REC.
00138                  WRITE PAYROLL-MAST-OUT-AREA FROM PAY-OUT-REC.
```

ADVANTAGES AND DISADVANTAGES OF INDEXED FILES

The following points are among the more important advantages of indexed files, and they apply to both ISAM and VSAM:

1. Records in an indexed file may be accessed either sequentially or randomly.
2. Processing of unsequenced transactions is possible. This eliminates the need to sort transactions.
3. Transactions may be processed immediately as they take place (real time), or they may be batched for later processing. If batched, the transactions may be sorted, thus making sequential processing of the indexed file possible.
4. When accessing the indexed file sequentially, processing may begin at any point in the file by using the START statement.
5. Adding records to an existing indexed file does not require recreation of the file.

COBOL File Status Chart	
File status Code Value	Meaning of Status Code Value
"00"	Successful completion of I/O operation. Any input–output operation: sequential, indexed, and relative files.
"02"	Successful completion of I/O operation with a duplicate alternate key, DUPLICATES specified; thus, duplicate keys allowed. WRITE, REWRITE: indexed files.
"10"	End of file, sequential access mode. READ: sequential, indexed, and relative files.
"20"	Invalid key, no further information supplied by system.
"21"	Invalid key, sequence error. 1. Key not greater than last record written. WRITE: indexed files. 2. Key not equal to last record read. REWRITE, DELETE: sequential, indexed, and relative files.
"22"	Invalid key, duplicate key, with duplicate keys not allowed. 1. WRITE: indexed and relative files. 2. REWRITE: indexed files.
"23"	Invalid key, no record found (that is, key not found). READ, REWRITE, DELETE, START: indexed and relative files.
"24"	Invalid key, boundary violation. WRITE: indexed and relative files.
"30"	Permanent I/O error, such as data check, parity error, or transmission error. Any Input/Output operation: sequential, indexed, and relative files.
"34"	Boundary violation. WRITE: sequential files.

Figure 6.15
COBOL file status chart for COBOL '74 under VSAM.

Disadvantages of indexed file organization include the following:

1. Since random access of an indexed file involves searching two or more indexes, with associated movements of the disk unit's access mechanism, random access is less efficient for an indexed file than for relative files or direct files. (Relative file and direct file organizations will be discussed in later chapters.)
2. Utilization of file space in an indexed file is usually less efficient than in a standard sequential file since (1) ISAM overflow areas, and the free space existing in VSAM control intervals, often contain unused space; and (2) records must be formatted with keys.

Additional disadvantages that apply to ISAM, but *not* to VSAM-indexed files, are

1. A file for which there are many record additions and/or deletions may have to be reorganized frequently.
2. Since ISAM overflow records are not in sequence, sequential processing of the file is not as efficient as it would be for a standard sequential file.

We would like to conclude this chapter by pointing out that, although the physical structure of indexed files is complex, as a programmer, you will find it relatively easy to work with indexed files.

Programming Exercises for Chapter 6

The following programming exercises are designed to allow you to gain experience in working with files that have indexed organization.

EXERCISE 6.1

The Boulder Subscription Service maintains subscription files for magazine publishers. A file is maintained for each magazine. These files all have indexed organization with the subscription identification code as the key. All subscription files have the following record format:

Record Positions	Contents	Format
1	Delete code	X
2–16	Subscription identification	X(15)
17–46	Name	X(30)
47–76	Street address	X(30)
77–91	City	X(15)
92–93	State	X(2)
94–98	ZIP code	X(5)
99–101	Amount paid per copy	9V9(2)
102–103	Number of issues remaining to be mailed	9(2)

Write a program to update and maintain the subscription files. Possible transaction codes and their meanings are

Transaction Code	Action
AS	Add a new subscriber
CS	Cancel subscription
RS	Renew subscription
CN	Change name
CA	Change address
CB	Change name and address

All transaction records contain a transaction code in record positions 1 and 2, followed by the subscription identification in positions 3 through 17. The remainder of the record is formatted as shown in the following illustration.

Transaction Code	Record Position	Contents	Format
AS	18–47	Name	X(30)
	48–77	Street address	X(30)
	78–92	City	X(15)
	93–94	State	X(2)
	95–99	ZIP code	X(5)
	100–104	Total paid	9(3)V9(2)
	105–106	Number of issues	9(2)
CS		No further information	
RS	18–22	Total renewal amount paid	9(3)V9(2)
	23–24	Number of renewal issues purchased	9(2)
CN	18–47	Name	X(30)
CA	18–47	Street address	X(30)
	48–64	City	X(15)
	65–66	State	X(2)
	67–71	ZIP code	X(5)
CB	18–47	Name	X(30)
	48–77	Street address	X(30)
	78–92	City	X(15)
	93–94	State	X(2)
	95–99	ZIP code	X(5)

Your output should consist of the updated subscription file and a printed report. For each transaction, print the action requested by the transaction and the action taken on the transaction. For each transaction you are unable to process, print an *informative* error message and the transaction record (for example, SUBSCRIPTION FILE RECORD NOT FOUND, and then print out contents of transaction record). For a subscription cancellation, print the amount of the customer refund.

Use the following formula to calculate the amount to be refunded to the customer from a subscription cancellation:

$$\text{(Amount paid per copy)} \times \text{(Number of issues remaining)}$$

Use the following formula to calculate the price paid per copy (in the subscription file record) for a current subscriber who renews a subscription before all of the previously purchased issues are mailed.

Amount paid per copy (for subscription file

record) = ((Amount paid per copy) ×

(Number of issues remaining to be mailed)

+ (Total renewal amount paid)) ÷

(Number of issues remaining to be mailed

+ Number of renewal issues purchased)

EXERCISE 6.2

The Boulder Subscription Service needs a program to print address labels for mailing magazines to subscribers. The form of the mailing labels is given in Chapter 4, Exercise 4.2. In addition, in the subscription file record, the program should subtract one from the number of issues remaining to be mailed. If this results in no issues remaining, then the delete code should be changed to indicate a deleted record.

The format of subscription file records is given in Exercise 6.1.

EXERCISE 6.3

The employees' credit union at Mega-Tronics has requested a program for daily updating of its accounts. The master file organization is indexed and contains records with the following format:

Record Position	Contents	Format
1	Account status code	X
2–6	Account number	X(5)
7–8	Department code	9(2)
9–17	Social security number	X(9)
18–37	Name	X(20)
38–67	Address	X(30)
68–74	Current balance	S9(5)V9(2)
75–81	Total deposits (month)	S9(5)V9(2)
82–88	Total withdrawals (month)	S9(5)V9(2)

Account number is the record key; the master file is in ascending order by account number.

The transaction file is not ordered on account number (it is in the physical order in which the transactions were made).

Records on the transaction file have a transaction code in position 1 followed by the account number in positions 2–6. The transaction code is as follows:

Code	Meaning
D	Deposit
W	Withdrawal
N	New account
C	Close account

If the transaction code is a D or W, the amount of the depositor withdrawal is in positions 7–13.

For a new account, the record also contains:

Record Position	Contents	Format
7–8	Department code	9(2)
9–17	Social security number	X(9)
18–37	Name	X(20)
38–67	Address	X(30)
68–74	Initial deposit	9(5)V9(2)

Output should consist of the updated master file and a printed report that contains all invalid transaction records and informative error messages.

EXERCISE 6.4

For purposes of printing monthly activity reports for accounts, Mega-Tronics maintains a file that contains a record of all deposits and withdrawals made during the month. It contains the account number, amount for each deposit or withdrawal, and the date of the deposit or withdrawal.

A program is needed that daily updates this file from the current day's transactions file.

A second program is required for activity report printing. This program must obtain the name and address from the master file (master file records described in Exercise 6.3).

The form of the monthly transaction file is

Record Positions	Contents	Format
1–5	Account number	X(5)
6–12	Transaction amount (positive if deposit, negative if withdrawal)	S9(5)V9(2)
13–27	Date of transaction (MM/DD/YY)	X(8)

If the operating system you are using permits duplicate keys, organize this file as an indexed file. Otherwise, it is to be a sequential file. It is to be ordered by account number and within an account number by date. (You may find the SORT verb useful if you are creating this file sequentially.)

Since this is an indexed file, records are only added to the file. You may wish to add a key to the record contents given. (On most systems that permit duplicates, this will not be necessary since the duplicates will be maintained on a "first in–first out" basis.)

First, write an update program that adds the daily withdrawals and deposits to the monthly deposits and withdrawals file.

Second, write a program that prints the monthly activity report.

Obtain the name and address from the master file. See the printer layout chart for the general output format. The heading should contain the name of the month and the year. Print as many transactions as possible on each line. The transaction amounts should be printed with DB for a deposit or CR for a withdrawal.

```
   MEGA-TRONICS ACCOUNT ACTIVITY REPORT FOR XXXXXXXXX 19XX      Page XX
                                     TRANSACTION
ACCOUNT            NAME              DATE      AMOUNT      DATE      AMOUNT
 XXXXX   XXXXXXXXXXXXXXXXXXXXXXXXXX XX/XX/XX $$$,$$$.99XX XX/XX/XX $$$,$$$.99XX
                      .                .          .          .          .
                      .                .          .          .          .
                      .                .          .          .          .
```

7 Creating and Processing Relative Files

INTRODUCTION

There are data processing applications in which the records to be processed will nearly always be randomly accessed by a key associated with the record. It will rarely be necessary to process all records in the entire file at any one time. Any type of reservation system (airline, hotel, dentist's office) is an example of this type of application. Another frequently encountered application of this type is inventory control.

Margo's Mail Order Boutique is a catalogue order firm that sells unusual clothing and accessories through a catalogue, which is published four times a year. As merchandise is shipped to customers and received from suppliers, a master inventory file is updated to reflect the number of units of a given catalogue item in stock. New items are added from time to time and items are sometimes discontinued. There is a significant amount of carry-forward of items from one catalogue to the next. Consequently, a complete recreation of the file should not have to be done very often. In addition to normal processing, a complete list of the file will be needed for tax purposes once a year. A description of the record structure is shown in Figure 7.1.

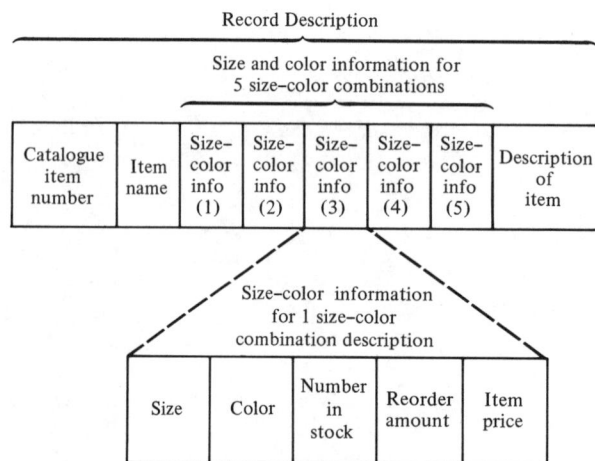

Figure 7.1
Logical Description of the data in a record in MARGO'S inventory file.

One file organization that is suitable for Margo's inventory processing is standard for 74 COBOL or later and is called *relative* (VSAM/RRDS). Relative files may be used only on direct-access storage facilities. It is a simple organization in which each record is retrieved by its record number, which indicates the relative position of the record in the file. Thus, each record must contain information that can be used to provide the relative record number of the record. We will examine this file organization in detail.

ENVIRONMENT DIVISION ENTRIES

Like all files, relative files must have a SELECT entry that names and describes the physical organization of the file.

```
                          FORMAT

   SELECT file-name
        ASSIGN TO system-name
        ORGANIZATION IS RELATIVE
                     ┌ SEQUENTIAL [RELATIVE KEY IS data-name-1] ┐
        [ACCESS IS ⎨ ⎰ RANDOM  ⎱                                ⎬
                     ⎩ ⎩ DYNAMIC ⎭ RELATIVE KEY IS data-name-2 ] ┘
```

When ACCESS IS SEQUENTIAL is specified, records will be read or written in ascending order of the relative record number. If ACCESS IS RANDOM, the relative record number placed in data-name-2 determines the record to be written or retrieved. When specifying that ACCESS IS DYNAMIC, records may be accessed either randomly or sequentially. If random access is desired, the relative record number for the record to be retrieved or written must be placed in data-name-2.

A sample SELECT statement for a hotel reservation file might have the following form:

```
SELECT HOTEL-RES-FILE-IN
    ASSIGN TO SYS023-RESFILE
    ORGANIZATION IS RELATIVE
    ACCESS IS DYNAMIC
    RELATIVE KEY IS REL-ROOM-NUM.
```

HOTEL-RES-FILE-IN may be read sequentially by REL-ROOM-NUM or randomly by a specific value placed in REL-ROOM-NUM.

DATA DIVISION ENTRIES

Since the DATA DIVISION entries are essentially the same as those with which we are already familiar, we will simply illustrate the DATA DIVISION entries for the file HOTEL-RES-FILE-IN of the previous section.

```
FD  HOTEL-RES-FILE-IN
    LABEL RECORDS STANDARD.
01  RES-IN-AREA                 PIC X(150).
                .
                .
                .

WORKING-STORAGE SECTION.
01  REL-ROOM-NUM                PIC 9(5).
                .
                .
                .
```

PROCEDURE DIVISION ENTRIES

Access to a record on a VSAM/RRDS file is done with a READ statement.

FORMAT
1. <u>READ</u> file-name [<u>NEXT</u>]
[<u>INTO</u> data-name]
[AT <u>END</u> imperative-statement.]
2. <u>READ</u> file-name
[<u>INTO</u> data-name]
[<u>INVALID</u> KEY imperative-statement.]

If ACCESS IS SEQUENTIAL is specified, the optional word NEXT is not needed. To sequentially process a file when ACCESS IS DYNAMIC has been specified, the NEXT option is required. In either case, if sequential processing is to be done, the AT END clause should be specified. For random processing, the INVALID KEY clause would be specified.

As an example of random processing:

```
MOVE HOTEL-ROOM-NUM-IN TO REL-ROOM-NUM.
READ HOTEL-RES-FILE-IN INTO RES-IN-REC
    INVALID KEY MOVE 'Y' TO BAD-DATA-SW.
```

To create a relative file, or to add records to an existing relative file, the WRITE statement is used.

```
                    ┌──────────────────────────────────────────┐
                    │                FORMAT                     │
                    ├──────────────────────────────────────────┤
                    │  WRITE record-name                        │
                    │      [FROM data-name]                     │
                    │      [INVALID KEY imperative-statement.]   │
                    └──────────────────────────────────────────┘
```

The imperative-statement following the INVALID KEY clause will be executed when writing: (1) if access is random or dynamic and the value of the relative key specifies a record position that is already filled (a duplicate key), or (2) when an attempt is made to write outside the limits of the file.

To alter the contents of a field in a record, the REWRITE statement is used.

```
                    ┌──────────────────────────────────────────┐
                    │                FORMAT                     │
                    ├──────────────────────────────────────────┤
                    │  REWRITE record-name                      │
                    │      [FROM data-name]                     │
                    │      [INVALID KEY imperative-statement]    │
                    └──────────────────────────────────────────┘
```

This statement replaces an existing record with the contents of record-name. In general, this statement will be preceded by a READ statement.

If the file is being processed sequentially, a REWRITE statement must be preceded by a READ statement.

```
        REWRITE RES-IO-AREA FROM RES-IO-REC
            INVALID KEY MOVE 'Y' TO BAD-UPDATE-SW.
```

Let's now consider several examples of relative file processing.

Example 7.1

As part of the initial design for Margo's Boutique, catalogue numbers were created to represent relative record numbers. A maximum of 5200 catalogue items is expected to exist at any one time. The items for the beginning catalogue were simply assigned catalog numbers of 1, 6, 11 . . . 5201, with 5201 representing a dummy record to allow for 5200 records on the file. New catalogue items will be assigned unused numbers. When all 5200 catalogue numbers are used, the file will be reorganized.

Program organization is illustrated in Figure 7.2, and the program listing is given in Figure 7.3.

The following important points concerning the program in Figure 7.3 should be noted.

1. The file is being created using ACCESS IS RANDOM (line 44). This allows the records to be presented in any order. If a file load is done under ACCESS IS SEQUENTIAL, the records must be in order by relative record number.
2. The relative key, RELATIVE-RECORD-NUMBER (line 65), is assigned a value in INV-IN-CAT-NUM (line 88) before the WRITE statement (line 106) is executed. Duplicate key values will cause the INVALID KEY clause (line 107) to be executed.

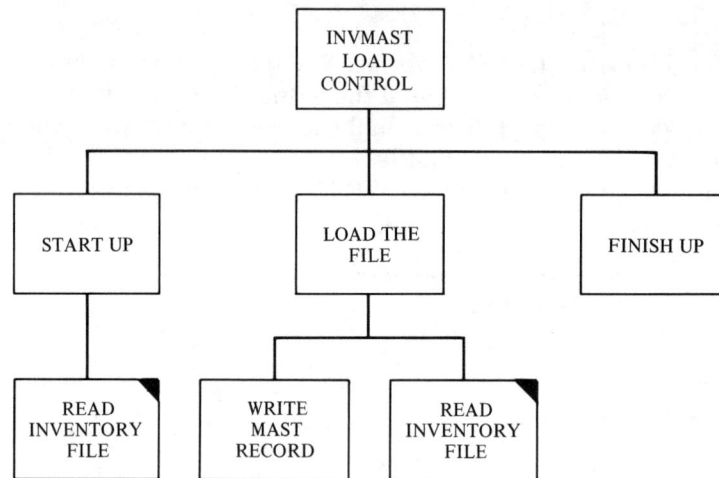

Figure 7.2
Structure chart for the program in Figure 7.3.

```
00001          IDENTIFICATION DIVISION.
00002       *
00003        PROGRAM-ID.
00004          EX-7-1.
00005       ***********************************************************************
00006       *                                                                     *
00007       *   PROGRAMMER TEAM            WALSTROM/SUMMERS/LINDAHL               *
00008       *   PROGRAM COMPLETION DATE AUGUST 2, 1984.                           *
00009       *                                                                     *
00010       *                  PROGRAM SUMMARY                                    *
00011       *    INPUT                                                            *
00012       *        EACH RECORD CONTAINS                                         *
00013       *               - CATALOGUE NUMBER                                    *
00014       *               - NAME OF THE ITEM                                    *
00015       *               - A TABLE CONTAINING IN EACH TABLE ENTRY:             *
00016       *                   SIZE, COLOR, NUMBER IN STOCK, REORDER AMOUNT,    *
00017       *                   PRICE                                             *
00018       *               - CATALOGUE DESCRIPTION                               *
00019       *                                                                     *
00020       *    PROCESSING                                                       *
00021       *               - EACH RECORD IS ASSIGNED ITS CATALOGUE NUMBER        *
00022       *                 AS ITS RELATIVE RECORD NUMBER                       *
00023       *                                                                     *
00024       *    OUTPUT                                                           *
00025       *               - A COPY OF THE INPUT FILE WITH RELATIVE              *
00026       *                 ORGANIZATION                                        *
00027       *               - A PROCESSING OUTCOME MESSAGE                        *
00028       ***********************************************************************
```

Figure 7.3
Creation of a relative file for Example 7.1.

Figure 7.3 (cont.)

```
00029              *
00030                ENVIRONMENT DIVISION.
00031              *
00032                CONFIGURATION SECTION.
00033                SOURCE-COMPUTER.
00034                    IBM.
00035                OBJECT-COMPUTER.
00036                    IBM.
00037                INPUT-OUTPUT SECTION.
00038                FILE-CONTROL.
00039                    SELECT INVENTORY-FILE-IN
00040                        ASSIGN TO SYS023-DA-3330-S-MAST701.
00041                    SELECT INVEN-MAST-FILE-OUT
00042                        ASSIGN TO SYS022-INVFLE
00043                            ORGANIZATION IS RELATIVE
00044                            ACCESS IS RANDOM
00045                            RELATIVE KEY IS RELATIVE-RECORD-NUMBER.
00046              *
00047                DATA DIVISION.
00048              *
00049                FILE SECTION.
00050                FD  INVENTORY-FILE-IN
00051                        LABEL RECORDS STANDARD.
00052                01  INVEN-IN-AREA                PIC X(304).
00053                FD  INVEN-MAST-FILE-OUT
00054                        LABEL RECORDS STANDARD.
00055                01  INVEN-OUT-AREA               PIC X(304).
00056              *
00057                WORKING-STORAGE SECTION.
00058                01  SWITCHES.
00059                    02  END-OF-INPUT-FILE-SW     PIC X.
00060                        88  END-OF-INPUT-FILE        VALUE 'Y'.
00061                    02  PROCESSING-SHOULD-STOP-SW  PIC X.
00062                        88  PROCESSING-SHOULD-STOP   VALUE 'Y'.
00063
00064                01  WORK-AREA.
00065                    02  RELATIVE-RECORD-NUMBER   PIC 9(4).
00066                01  INVENTORY-IN-REC.
00067                    02  INV-IN-CAT-NUM           PIC 9(4).
00068                    02  FILLER                   PIC X(300).
00069              *
00070                PROCEDURE DIVISION.
00071              *
00072                INV-MAST-LOAD-CONTROL.
00073                    PERFORM START-UP.
00074                    PERFORM LOAD-THE-FILE
00075                        UNTIL PROCESSING-SHOULD-STOP.
00076                    PERFORM FINISH-UP.
00077                    STOP RUN.
00078
00079              *
00080                START-UP.
00081                    OPEN INPUT INVENTORY-FILE-IN
00082                        OUTPUT INVEN-MAST-FILE-OUT.
00083                    MOVE 'N' TO END-OF-INPUT-FILE-SW
00084                             PROCESSING-SHOULD-STOP-SW.
00085                    PERFORM READ-INVENTORY-FILE.
00086              *
00087                LOAD-THE-FILE.
00088                    MOVE INV-IN-CAT-NUM TO RELATIVE-RECORD-NUMBER.
00089                    PERFORM WRITE-MAST-RECORD.
00090                    PERFORM READ-INVENTORY-FILE.
00091              *
00092                FINISH-UP.
00093                    IF END-OF-INPUT-FILE
00094                        DISPLAY 'MASTER INVENTORY RELATIVE FILE CREATED'
00095                    ELSE
00096                        DISPLAY 'PROBLEM IN CREATING RELATIVE FILE'
00097                        DISPLAY 'LAST RECORD READ WAS ' INVENTORY-IN-REC.
00098                    CLOSE INVENTORY-FILE-IN   INVEN-MAST-FILE-OUT.
00099              *
00100                READ-INVENTORY-FILE.
00101                    READ INVENTORY-FILE-IN INTO INVENTORY-IN-REC
00102                        AT END MOVE 'Y' TO END-OF-INPUT-FILE-SW
00103                                     PROCESSING-SHOULD-STOP-SW.
00104              *
00105                WRITE-MAST-RECORD.
00106                    WRITE INVEN-OUT-AREA FROM INVENTORY-IN-REC
00107                        INVALID KEY MOVE 'Y' TO PROCESSING-SHOULD-STOP-SW.
```

Example 7.2

From time to time, new sizes and colors are added to those already available for a catalogue item. A program to add new sizes or colors is desired.

A program solution to the problem of Example 7.2 is presented in Figure 7.5. A structure chart is shown in Figure 7.4.

To more easily follow the program solution given in Figure 7.5, it is important to note that the table INV-IO-NUM-STOCK-TAB (which is part of the inventory record INV-IO-REC) uses spaces to indicate that a specific element or location in the table within that record is empty.

The master file, of course, must be OPENed as I-O. The technique then involves setting a value for the relative key (line 121); retrieving the record specified by the relative key (line 161); locating a vacant entry in the size–color table by using the SEARCH statement (line 140); moving the new data into the table within the record (lines 151–157); and REWRITEing the record back to the file (line 170). (How much would this procedure differ if this same update problem solution was programmed using ISAM or VSAM/KSDS file organization?)

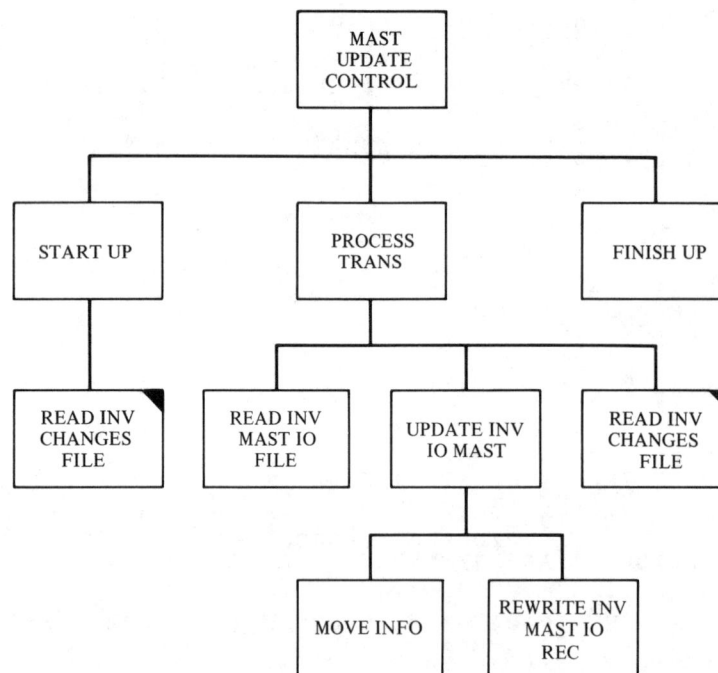

Figure 7.4
Structure chart for the program in Figure 7.5.

```
00001          IDENTIFICATION DIVISION.
00002      *
00003        PROGRAM-ID.
00004          EX-7-2.
00005      ****************************************************************
00006      *                                                              *
00007      *    PROGRAMMER TEAM          WALSTROM/SUMMERS/LINDAHL         *
00008      *    PROGRAM COMPLETION DATE AUGUST 13, 1984.                  *
00009      *                                                              *
00010      *                    PROGRAM SUMMARY                           *
00011      *                                                              *
00012      *    INPUT                                                     *
00013      *        THERE ARE TWO INPUT FILES, THE INVENTORY MASTER FILE  *
00014      *        AND THE FILE USED FOR UPDATING THE MASTER FILE. RECORDS *
00015      *        ON THE UPDATE FILE CONTAIN                            *
00016      *                - CATALOGUE NUMBER                            *
00017      *                - ITEM NAME                                   *
00018      *                - ITEM SIZE                                   *
00019      *                - ITEM COLOR                                  *
00020      *                - NUMBER OF ITEMS RECEIVED                    *
00021      *                - PRICE                                       *
00022      *                                                              *
00023      *    PROCESSING                                                *
00024      *        FOR EACH RECORD IN THE UPDATE FILE                    *
00025      *                - THE RECORD FROM THE MASTER FILE WITH THE SAME *
00026      *                  CATALOGUE NUMBER IS OBTAINED                *
00027      *                - AN UNUSED ENTRY IN THE SIZE-COLOR TABLE IS  *
00028      *                  LOCATED USING INDEXING                      *
00029      *                - THE NEW SIZE-COLOR INFORMATION IS PLACED IN *
00030      *                  THE SIZE-COLOR TABLE                        *
00031      *                                                              *
00032      *    OUTPUT                                                    *
00033      *                - THE UPDATED MASTER FILE                     *
00034      *                - A LIST OF RECORDS IN THE UPDATE FILE WITH   *
00035      *                  CATALOGUE NUMBERS NOT ON THE MASTER FILE OR *
00036      *                  WITH CATALOGUE NUMBERS OF RECORDS WHOSE SIZE- *
00037      *                  COLOR TABLE IS FULL                         *
00038      ****************************************************************
00039      *
00040        ENVIRONMENT DIVISION.
00041      *
00042        CONFIGURATION SECTION.
00043        SOURCE-COMPUTER.
00044          IBM.
00045        OBJECT-COMPUTER.
00046          IBM.
00047        INPUT-OUTPUT SECTION.
00048        FILE-CONTROL.
00049            SELECT INV-MAST-FILE-IO
00050                ASSIGN TO SYS033-INVFLE
00051                ORGANIZATION IS RELATIVE
00052                ACCESS MODE IS RANDOM
00053                RELATIVE KEY IS RELATIVE-RECORD-NUMBER.
00054            SELECT INV-CHANGES-FILE-IN
00055                ASSIGN TO SYS023-DA-3330-S-CHG702.
00056      *
00057        DATA DIVISION.
00058      *
00059        FILE SECTION.
00060        FD  INV-MAST-FILE-IO
00061                LABEL RECORDS STANDARD.
00062        01  INV-MAST-IO-AREA                    PIC X(304).
00063        FD  INV-CHANGES-FILE-IN
00064                LABEL RECORDS STANDARD.
00065        01  INV-CHANGES-IN-AREA                 PIC X(80).
00066      *
00067        WORKING-STORAGE SECTION.
00068        01  SWITCHES.
00069            02  END-OF-CHANGES-FILE-SW          PIC X.
00070                88  END-OF-CHANGES-FILE             VALUE 'Y'.
00071            02  PROCESSING-SHOULD-STOP-SW       PIC X.
00072                88  PROCESSING-SHOULD-STOP         VALUE 'Y'.
00073            02  CAT-NUM-ERROR-SW               PIC X.
00074                88  CAT-NUM-ERROR                  VALUE 'Y'.
00075                88  NO-CAT-NUM-ERROR               VALUE 'N'.
00076            02  ROOM-IN-TABLE-SW               PIC X.
00077                88  ROOM-IN-TABLE                  VALUE 'Y'.
```

Figure 7.5

Updating a relative file for Example 7.2.

Figure 7.5 (cont.)

```
00078              01   WORK-AREA.
00079                   02   RELATIVE-RECORD-NUMBER        PIC 9(4).
00080              01   INV-IN-CHANGES-REC.
00081                   02   INV-IN-CAT-NUM               PIC 9(4).
00082                   02   INV-IN-NAME                  PIC X(15).
00083                   02   INV-IN-SIZE                  PIC X(2).
00084                   02   INV-IN-COLOR                 PIC X(10).
00085                   02   INV-IN-NUM-OF-ITEMS          PIC 9(5).
00086                   02   INV-IN-REORDER-AMT           PIC 9(5).
00087                   02   INV-IN-ITEM-PRICE            PIC 9(3)V9(2).
00088                   02   FILLER                       PIC X(34).
00089              01   INV-IO-REC.
00090                   02   INV-IO-CAT-NUM               PIC 9(4).
00091                   02   INV-IO-NAME                  PIC X(15).
00092                   02   INV-IO-NUM-STOCK-TAB.
00093                        03   INV-IO-SIZE-COLOR-INFO
00094                                 OCCURS 5 TIMES
00095                                 INDEXED BY NUM-IN-STOCK-INDEX.
00096                             04   INV-IO-SIZE         PIC X(2).
00097                             04   INV-IO-COLOR        PIC X(10).
00098                             04   INV-IO-NUM-IN-STOCK PIC S9(5).
00099                             04   INV-IO-REORDER-AMT  PIC S9(5).
00100                             04   INV-IO-ITEM-PRICE   PIC S9(3)V9(2).
00101                   02   FILLER                       PIC X(150).
00102          *
00103          PROCEDURE DIVISION.
00104          *
00105          MAST-UPDATE-CONTROL.
00106              PERFORM START-UP.
00107              PERFORM PROCESS-TRANS
00108                   UNTIL PROCESSING-SHOULD-STOP.
00109              PERFORM FINISH-UP.
00110              STOP RUN.
00111          *
00112           START-UP.
00113              OPEN INPUT INV-CHANGES-FILE-IN
00114                   I-O INV-MAST-FILE-IO.
00115              MOVE 'N' TO END-OF-CHANGES-FILE-SW,
00116                          PROCESSING-SHOULD-STOP-SW.
00117              PERFORM READ-INV-CHANGES-FILE.
00118          *
00119          PROCESS-TRANS.
00120              MOVE 'N' TO CAT-NUM-ERROR-SW.
00121              MOVE INV-IN-CAT-NUM TO RELATIVE-RECORD-NUMBER.
00122              PERFORM READ-INV-MAST-IO-FILE.
00123              IF NO-CAT-NUM-ERROR
00124                   PERFORM UPDATE-INV-IO-MAST
00125              ELSE
00126                   DISPLAY ' CATALOGUE NUMBER NOT FOUND IN FILE ',
00127                           INV-IN-CHANGES-REC.
00128              PERFORM READ-INV-CHANGES-FILE.
00129          *
00130          FINISH-UP.
00131              IF END-OF-CHANGES-FILE
00132                   DISPLAY ' CHANGES TO INVENTORY MASTER FILE ARE COMPLETE '
00133              ELSE
00134                   DISPLAY ' PROBLEM IN PROCESSING CHANGES '
00135                   DISPLAY ' LAST CHANGES RECORD WAS ', INV-IN-CHANGES-REC.
00136              CLOSE INV-MAST-FILE-IO, INV-CHANGES-FILE-IN.
00137          *
00138          UPDATE-INV-IO-MAST.
00139              SET NUM-IN-STOCK-INDEX TO 1.
00140              SEARCH INV-IO-SIZE-COLOR-INFO
00141                   AT END MOVE 'N' TO ROOM-IN-TABLE-SW
00142                   WHEN INV-IO-SIZE-COLOR-INFO (NUM-IN-STOCK-INDEX) = SPACE
00143                        MOVE 'Y' TO ROOM-IN-TABLE-SW.
00144              IF ROOM-IN-TABLE
00145                   PERFORM MOVE-INFO
00146                   PERFORM REWRITE-INV-MAST-IO-REC
00147              ELSE
00148                   DISPLAY ' RECORD IS FULL ', INV-IN-CHANGES-REC.
```

Figure 7.5 (*cont.*)

```
00149              *
00150               MOVE-INFO.
00151                  MOVE INV-IN-SIZE TO INV-IO-SIZE (NUM-IN-STOCK-INDEX).
00152                  MOVE INV-IN-NUM-OF-ITEMS TO INV-IO-NUM-IN-STOCK
00153                                            (NUM-IN-STOCK-INDEX).
00154                  MOVE INV-IN-COLOR TO INV-IO-COLOR (NUM-IN-STOCK-INDEX).
00155                  MOVE INV-IN-REORDER-AMT TO INV-IO-REORDER-AMT
00156                                            (NUM-IN-STOCK-INDEX).
00157                  MOVE INV-IN-ITEM-PRICE TO INV-IO-ITEM-PRICE
00158                                            (NUM-IN-STOCK-INDEX).
00159              *
00160               READ-INV-CHANGES-FILE.
00161                  READ INV-CHANGES-FILE-IN INTO INV-IN-CHANGES-REC
00162                      AT END MOVE 'Y' TO END-OF-CHANGES-FILE-SW
00163                                         PROCESSING-SHOULD-STOP-SW.
00164              *
00165               READ-INV-MAST-IO-FILE.
00166                  READ INV-MAST-FILE-IO INTO INV-IO-REC
00167                      INVALID KEY MOVE 'Y' TO CAT-NUM-ERROR-SW.
00168              *
00169               REWRITE-INV-MAST-IO-REC.
00170                  REWRITE INV-MAST-IO-AREA FROM INV-IO-REC
00171                      INVALID KEY MOVE 'Y' TO PROCESSING-SHOULD-STOP-SW.
```

It is a rare situation in which key values can be assigned to fit the file organization. In general, the record keys are designed to encode other information, in which case the programmer will have to design a technique to convert the key value to a relative record number. A common technique used for this purpose is *division-remainder hashing. Hashing* is an addressing technique in which the value in a specified control field is converted into an appropriate address or, in this case, an appropriate relative record number. To illustrate, assume there will be 200 records in the file. Choose the largest prime number less than or equal to 200 (199 in this case). Divide the key value by 199 and use the remainder + 1 as the relative record number.

$$199 \overline{)00008 \text{ key value}} \quad 0 \text{ quotient}$$
$$8 \text{ remainder}$$

$$199 \overline{)00437 \text{ key value}} \quad 2 \text{ quotient}$$
$$39 \text{ remainder}$$

(relative record number = 8 + 1 = 9)   (relative record number = 39 + 1 = 40)

When this technique is used, multiple key values may generate the same relative record number. Values that hash to the same record location are called *synonyms.* If this occurs, the record will be written to the location generated only if that location is free. Once a record location is filled, additional synonym records, termed *overflow records,* will be written to the first free record location. This is only one of several methods for handling synonym or overflow records; however, it is frequently used.

The following table shows the relative record numbers actually written for a series of key values encountered in the specific sequence shown.

Key Value	Remainder + 1	Relative Record Number Written
00008	9	9
00001	2	2
00010	11	11
00207	9 (synonym)	10
00406	9 (synonym)	12

Example 7.3

Suppose the decision to use relative files is made after the assignment of catalogue numbers for Margo's Boutique has already been done. Consequently, the catalogue numbers *were not* assigned in the sequence 1, 6, 11, . . . 5200, as was true in Example 7.1. Instead, items are identified by a 6-digit catalogue number. There are still, at most, 5200 items. The largest prime number less than or equal to 5200 is 5197.

As you will recall, access to a disk file is rather time-consuming. Therefore, it has been arbitrarily decided to limit the number of file accesses to 10 when attempting to write any one record, the assumption being that records in the file are too dense and the file should be reorganized if more than 10 attempts are required to write a record.

Taking the factors just stated into account, a revised version of the program to create the master inventory file is shown in Figure 7.7. The program control structure is given in Figure 7.6. This program solution is very similar to the one for Example 7.1, except that a division-remainder hashing technique is used to generate, or derive, the relative record numbers.

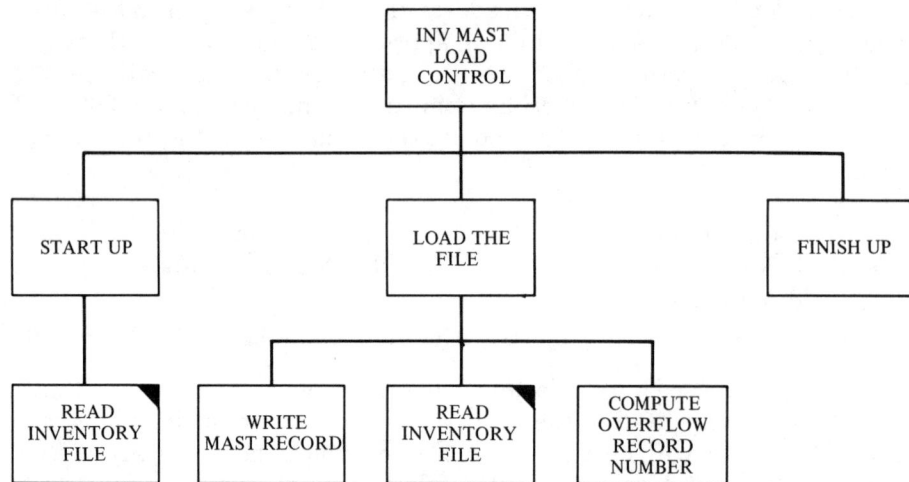

Figure 7.6
Structure chart for the program in Figure 7.7.

```
00001              IDENTIFICATION DIVISION.
00002          *
00003           PROGRAM-ID.
00004              EX-7-3.
00005          ****************************************************************
00006          *                                                              *
00007          *    PROGRAMMER TEAM           WALSTROM/SUMMERS/LINDAHL         *
00008          *    PROGRAM COMPLETION DATE SEPTEMBER 4, 1984                  *
00009          *                                                              *
00010          *                     PROGRAM SUMMARY                          *
00011          *    INPUT                                                     *
00012          *         EACH RECORD CONTAINS                                 *
00013          *              - CATALOGUE NUMBER                              *
00014          *              - NAME OF THE ITEM                             *
00015          *              - A TABLE CONTAINING IN EACH TABLE ENTRY:       *
00016          *                  SIZE, COLOR, NUMBER IN STOCK, REORDER AMOUNT, *
00017          *                  PRICE                                      *
00018          *              - CATALOGUE DESCRIPTION                         *
00019          *                                                              *
00020          *    PROCESSING                                                *
00021          *         EACH RECORD IS ASSIGNED A RELATIVE RECORD NUMBER USING *
00022          *              - DIVISION REMAINDER HASHING OF THE CATALOGUE    *
00023          *                NUMBER                                        *
00024          *              - NEXT AVAILABLE RECORD OVERFLOW TECHNIQUE       *
00025          *                                                              *
00026          *    OUTPUT                                                    *
00027          *              - A COPY OF THE INPUT FILE WITH RELATIVE         *
00028          *                ORGANIZATION                                  *
00029          *              - A PROCESSING OUTCOME MESSAGE                   *
00030          ****************************************************************
00031          *
00032           ENVIRONMENT DIVISION.
00033          *
00034           CONFIGURATION SECTION.
00035           SOURCE-COMPUTER.
00036              IBM.
00037           OBJECT-COMPUTER.
00038              IBM.
00039           INPUT-OUTPUT SECTION.
00040           FILE-CONTROL.
00041              SELECT INVENTORY-FILE-IN
00042                 ASSIGN TO SYS023-DA-3330-S-MAST703.
00043              SELECT INVEN-MAST-FILE-OUT
00044                 ASSIGN TO SYS030-INVTWO
00045                    ORGANIZATION IS RELATIVE
00046                    ACCESS MODE IS RANDOM
00047                    RELATIVE KEY IS RELATIVE-RECORD-NUMBER.
00048          *
00049           DATA DIVISION.
00050          *
00051           FILE SECTION.
00052           FD  INVENTORY-FILE-IN
00053               LABEL RECORDS STANDARD.
00054           01  INVEN-IN-AREA              PIC X(306).
00055           FD  INVEN-MAST-FILE-OUT
00056               LABEL RECORDS STANDARD.
00057           01  INVEN-OUT-AREA            PIC X(306).
00058          *
00059           WORKING-STORAGE SECTION.
00060           01  SWITCHES.
00061               02  PROCESSING-SHOULD-STOP-SW    PIC X.
00062                   88  PROCESSING-SHOULD-STOP     VALUE 'Y'.
00063               02  WRITE-STATUS-SW              PIC X.
00064                   88  RECORD-POSITION-ALREADY-FILLED VALUE 'F'.
00065                   88  GOOD-WRITE                    VALUE 'G'.
00066               02  NEW-INPUT-RECORD-SW         PIC X.
00067                   88  NEW-INPUT-RECORD           VALUE 'Y'.
00068               02  END-OF-INPUT-FILE-SW        PIC X.
00069                   88  END-OF-INPUT-FILE          VALUE 'Y'.
00070           01  CONSTANTS.
00071               02  PRIME-FOR-DIVISOR           PIC S9(4) VALUE +5197.
00072               02  MAX-NUM-OF-TRIES            PIC S9(2) VALUE +10.
00073               02  MAXIMUM-RECORD-NUMBER       PIC S9(4) VALUE +5200.
00074           01  COUNTERS.
00075               02  WRITE-TRY-COUNT             PIC S9(2).
```

Figure 7.7

Using a hashing technique to assign relative record numbers for Example 7.3.

Figure 7.7 (*cont.*)

```
00076                   01   CALCULATION-WORK-AREAS.
00077                        02   QUOTIENT                   PIC S9(6).
00078                        02   RELATIVE-RECORD-NUMBER      PIC 9(4).
00079                   01   INVENTORY-IN-REC.
00080                        02   INV-IN-CAT-NUM             PIC S9(6).
00081                        02   FILLER                    PIC X(300).
00082              *
00083              PROCEDURE DIVISION.
00084              *
00085              INV-MAST-LOAD-CONTROL.
00086                   PERFORM START-UP.
00087                   PERFORM LOAD-THE-FILE
00088                        UNTIL PROCESSING-SHOULD-STOP.
00089                   PERFORM FINISH-UP.
00090                   STOP RUN.
00091              *
00092              START-UP.
00093                   OPEN INPUT INVENTORY-FILE-IN
00094                        OUTPUT INVEN-MAST-FILE-OUT.
00095                   MOVE 'N' TO END-OF-INPUT-FILE-SW.
00096                   MOVE 'Y' TO NEW-INPUT-RECORD-SW.
00097                   PERFORM READ-INVENTORY-FILE.
00098              *
00099              LOAD-THE-FILE.
00100                   IF NEW-INPUT-RECORD
00101                        MOVE 0 TO WRITE-TRY-COUNT
00102                        DIVIDE INV-IN-CAT-NUM BY PRIME-FOR-DIVISOR
00103                             GIVING QUOTIENT
00104                                  REMAINDER RELATIVE-RECORD-NUMBER
00105                        ADD 1 TO RELATIVE-RECORD-NUMBER.
00106                   MOVE 'G' TO WRITE-STATUS-SW.
00107                   PERFORM WRITE-MAST-RECORD.
00108                   IF GOOD-WRITE
00109                        MOVE 'Y' TO NEW-INPUT-RECORD-SW
00110                        PERFORM READ-INVENTORY-FILE
00111                   ELSE
00112                        IF RECORD-POSITION-ALREADY-FILLED
00113                             PERFORM COMPUTE-OVERFLOW-RECORD-NUMBER
00114                        ELSE
00115                             DISPLAY 'SOME OTHER ERROR'.
00116              *
00117              FINISH-UP.
00118                   IF END-OF-INPUT-FILE
00119                        DISPLAY 'RELATIVE ORGANIZATION INVENTORY FILE CREATED'
00120                   ELSE
00121                        DISPLAY 'PROBLEM IN CREATING THE FILE'
00122                        DISPLAY 'LAST RECORD READ ' INVENTORY-IN-REC.
00123                   CLOSE INVENTORY-FILE-IN   INVEN-MAST-FILE-OUT.
00124              *
00125              COMPUTE-OVERFLOW-RECORD-NUMBER.
00126                   ADD 1 TO RELATIVE-RECORD-NUMBER.
00127                   ADD 1 TO WRITE-TRY-COUNT.
00128                   IF RELATIVE-RECORD-NUMBER = MAXIMUM-RECORD-NUMBER
00129                        MOVE 1 TO RELATIVE-RECORD-NUMBER.
00130                   IF WRITE-TRY-COUNT IS GREATER THAN MAX-NUM-OF-TRIES
00131                        DISPLAY 'TOO MANY TRIES, RECREATE FILE WITH MORE SPACE'
00132                        MOVE 'Y' TO PROCESSING-SHOULD-STOP-SW.
00133              *
00134              READ-INVENTORY-FILE.
00135                   READ INVENTORY-FILE-IN INTO INVENTORY-IN-REC
00136                        AT END MOVE 'Y' TO END-OF-INPUT-FILE-SW
00137                                          PROCESSING-SHOULD-STOP-SW.
00138              *
00139              WRITE-MAST-RECORD.
00140                   WRITE INVEN-OUT-AREA FROM INVENTORY-IN-REC
00141                        INVALID KEY MOVE 'N' TO NEW-INPUT-RECORD-SW
00142                                         MOVE 'F' TO WRITE-STATUS-SW.
```

Example 7.4

Margo's DP personnel have found that the performance of the relative file organization is not as good as was expected. Originally, it had been decided to limit to 10 the number of attempts to find an empty record location in which to write a record during the file load. It only took a short time, however, before it became clear that as the file began to fill, a much larger number of write attempts is actually necessary to allow new records to be added to the file. The DP personnel suspect that an excessive amount of external file searching is being done. The chief programmer has decided to experiment with a method of searching for the records internally to see if performance can be improved.

No longer will an access to the disk bring in only a single logical record. Instead, a group of 13 logical records will be accessed at one time. This new organization will be as shown in Figure 7.8. The relative record key is now used as the block number for a group of records. Each of the records, up to a maximum of 13, to be placed in the block will either hash to the block or overflow to it from another block. Alternate blocks are reserved for overflow. Once accessed, blocks will then be searched internally for available space in which to place records to be added.

The program organization is described in the structure chart of Figure 7.9. The program listing is given in Figure 7.10. It is fundamentally a two-part organization. Lines 111–120, 127–128, and 193–195 fill the file with dummy blocks containing 0 for all the catalogue numbers. The second part of the program uses the input file as an update to the dummy records, replacing them with input data. There is a strong similarity between this example and that of Example 7.2.

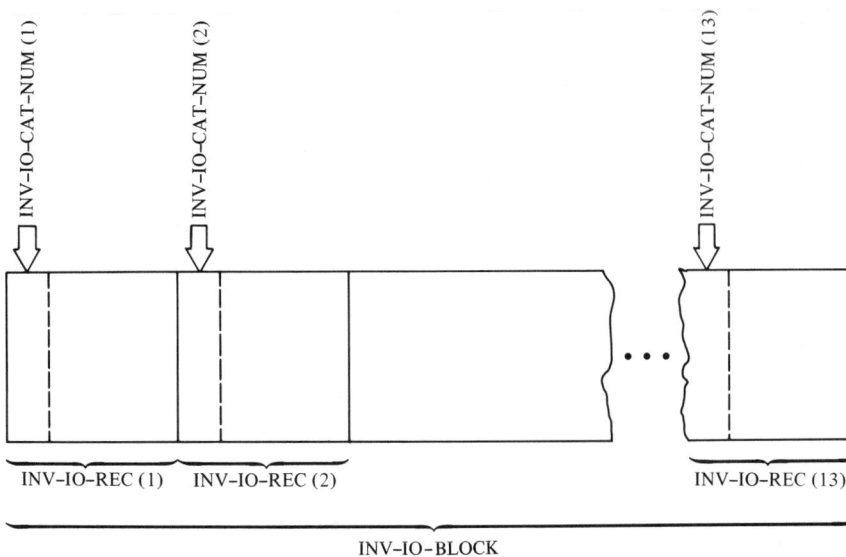

Figure 7.8
Description of a block (INV-IO-BLOCK) for Example 7.4.

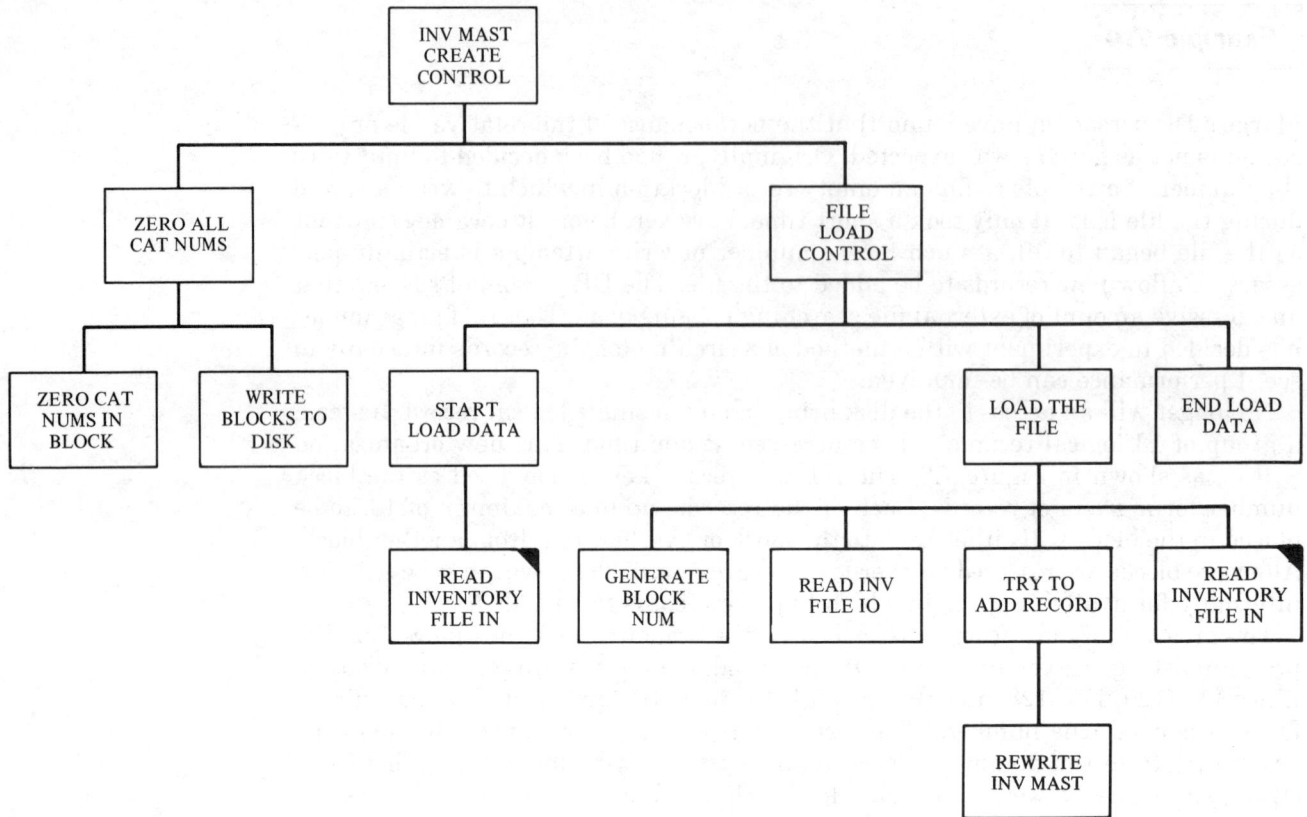

Figure 7.9
Structure charts for the program in Figure 7.10.

```
00001              IDENTIFICATION DIVISION.
00002              PROGRAM-ID.
00003                 EX-7-4.
00004    ************************************************************
00005    *                                                          *
00006    *     PROGRAMMER TEAM          WALSTROM/SUMMERS/LINDAHL     *
00007    *     PROGRAM COMPLETION DATE NOVEMBER 1, 1984              *
00008    *                                                          *
00009    *               PROGRAM SUMMARY                            *
00010    *                                                          *
00011    * INPUT                                                    *
00012    *     THE INVENTORY MASTER FILE                            *
00013    *                                                          *
00014    * PROCESSING                                               *
00015    *     EACH RECORD IN THE MASTER FILE IS ASSIGNED A RELATIVE *
00016    *     RECORD NUMBER BASED ON                               *
00017    *         - DIVISION REMAINDER HASHING OF THE CATALOGUE    *
00018    *           NUMBER                                         *
00019    *         - NEXT AVAILABLE RECORD OVERFLOW TECHNQIUE       *
00020    *     THE RECORD IS THEN PLACED IN THE FIRST FREE TABLE    *
00021    *     ENTRY OF THE OUTPUT RECORD                           *
00022    *                                                          *
00023    * OUTPUT                                                   *
00024    *     EACH RECORD OF THE OUTPUT FILE CONSISTS OF A TABLE   *
00025    *     WITH ENTRIES WHICH CONTAIN COPIES OF THE RECORDS     *
00026    *     FROM THE INVENTORY MASTER FILE.                      *
00027    *     THE FILE ORGANIZATION IS RELATIVE                    *
00028    *                                                          *
00029    *     A MESSAGE IS WRITTEN TO INDICATE THE OUTCOME OF THE  *
00030    *     ATTEMPT TO CREATE THE NEW MASTER FILE                *
00031    ************************************************************
```

Figure 7.10
Using user-defined blocking and unblocking routines with a relative file for Example 7.4.

Figure 7.10 (*cont.*)

```
00032        *
00033          ENVIRONMENT DIVISION.
00034        *
00035          CONFIGURATION SECTION.
00036          SOURCE-COMPUTER.
00037             IBM.
00038          OBJECT-COMPUTER.
00039             IBM.
00040          INPUT-OUTPUT SECTION.
00041          FILE-CONTROL.
00042             SELECT INVEN-MAST-FILE-IO
00043                 ASSIGN TO SYS025-INVFILE
00044                 ORGANIZATION IS RELATIVE
00045                 ACCESS IS RANDOM
00046                 RELATIVE KEY IS BLOCK-NUM.
00047             SELECT INVENTORY-FILE-IN
00048                 ASSIGN TO SYS025-INVTWO
00049                 ORGANIZATION IS RELATIVE
00050                 ACCESS IS SEQUENTIAL.
00051        *
00052          DATA DIVISION.
00053        *
00054          FILE SECTION.
00055          FD  INVEN-MAST-FILE-IO
00056                 LABEL RECORDS STANDARD.
00057          01   INVEN-IO-AREA                  PIC X(3978).
00058
00059          FD  INVENTORY-FILE-IN
00060                 LABEL RECORDS STANDARD.
00061          01   INVENTORY-IN-AREA              PIC X(80).
00062        *
00063          WORKING-STORAGE SECTION.
00064          01   SWITCHES.
00065               02   STOP-PROCESSING-SW        PIC X.
00066                    88   PROCESSING-SHOULD-STOP  VALUE 'Y'.
00067               02   WRITE-STATUS-SW           PIC X.
00068                    88   BAD-WRITE              VALUE 'W'.
00069               02   READ-STATUS-SW            PIC X.
00070                    88 KEY-NOT-FOUND            VALUE 'Y'.
00071               02   BLOCK-FULL-SW             PIC X.
00072                    88   BLOCK-FULL             VALUE 'Y'.
00073               02   END-OF-INPUT-SW           PIC X.
00074                    88   NO-MORE-INPUT          VALUE 'Y'.
00075               02   NEW-INPUT-RECORD-SW       PIC X.
00076                    88   NEW-INPUT-RECORD       VALUE 'Y'.
00077                    88   BAD-REWRITE            VALUE 'R'.
00078          01   COUNTERS.
00079               02   READ-TRY-COUNT            PIC S9.
00080          01   CONSTANTS.
00081               02   PRIME-FOR-DIVISOR         PIC S9(3)  VALUE +199.
00082               02   MAX-BLOCK-NUM             PIC S9(3)  VALUE +400.
00083               02   MAX-NUM-TRIES             PIC S9     VALUE +6.
00084               02   RECS-PER-BLOCK            PIC 9(2) VALUE 13.
00085          01   WORK-NUMBERS.
00086               02   TRACK-NUM                 PIC 9(3).
00087               02   SAVE-CAT-NUM              PIC 9(6).
00088               02   QUOTIENT                  PIC 9(6).
00089               02   BLOCK-NUM                 PIC 9(4).
00090          01   INVENTORY-IN-REC.
00091               02   INV-IN-CAT-NUM            PIC 9(6).
00092               02   FILLER                    PIC X(300).
00093          01   INV-IO-BLOCK.
00094               02   INV-IO-REC
00095                      OCCURS 13 TIMES
00096                      INDEXED BY RECS-PER-BLOCK-COUNT.
00097                 03   INV-IO-CAT-NUM          PIC 9(6).
00098                 03   FILLER                  PIC X(300).
00099        *
00100          PROCEDURE DIVISION.
00101        *
00102          INV-MAST-CREATE-CONTROL.
00103             PERFORM ZERO-ALL-CAT-NUMS.
00104             IF BAD-WRITE
00105                 DISPLAY 'NOT ENOUGH SPACE',
00106                         'ALL BLOCKS NOT ZEROED'
00107             ELSE
00108                 PERFORM FILE-LOAD-CONTROL.
00109             STOP RUN.
```

Figure 7.10 (*cont.*)

```
00110          *
00111              ZERO-ALL-CAT-NUMS.
00112                  MOVE 'G' TO WRITE-STATUS-SW.
00113                  OPEN OUTPUT INVEN-MAST-FILE-IO.
00114                  PERFORM ZERO-CAT-NUMS-IN-BLOCK
00115                      VARYING RECS-PER-BLOCK-COUNT FROM 1 BY 1 UNTIL
00116                      RECS-PER-BLOCK-COUNT IS GREATER THAN RECS-PER-BLOCK.
00117                  PERFORM WRITE-BLOCKS-TO-DISK VARYING BLOCK-NUM
00118                      FROM 1 BY 1 UNTIL BLOCK-NUM IS GREATER THAN
00119                      MAX-BLOCK-NUM OR BAD-WRITE.
00120                  CLOSE INVEN-MAST-FILE-IO.
00121          *
00122              FILE-LOAD-CONTROL.
00123                  PERFORM START-LOAD-DATA.
00124                  PERFORM LOAD-THE-FILE UNTIL PROCESSING-SHOULD-STOP.
00125                  PERFORM END-LOAD-DATA.
00126          *
00127              ZERO-CAT-NUMS-IN-BLOCK.
00128                  MOVE ZERO TO INV-IO-CAT-NUM (RECS-PER-BLOCK-COUNT).
00129          *
00130              START-LOAD-DATA.
00131                  OPEN INPUT INVENTORY-FILE-IN
00132                      I-O INVEN-MAST-FILE-IO.
00133                  MOVE 'Y' TO NEW-INPUT-RECORD-SW.
00134                  MOVE 'N' TO END-OF-INPUT-SW,
00135                      STOP-PROCESSING-SW.
00136                  PERFORM READ-INVENTORY-FILE-IN.
00137          *
00138              LOAD-THE-FILE.
00139                  IF NEW-INPUT-RECORD
00140                      MOVE ZERO TO READ-TRY-COUNT.
00141                  PERFORM GENERATE-BLOCK-NUM.
00142                  MOVE 'N' TO READ-STATUS-SW.
00143                  PERFORM READ-INV-FILE-IO.
00144                  IF KEY-NOT-FOUND
00145                      DISPLAY 'INVALID KEY', INVENTORY-IN-REC
00146                      MOVE 'Y' TO NEW-INPUT-RECORD-SW
00147                  ELSE
00148                      PERFORM TRY-TO-ADD-RECORD.
00149                  IF NEW-INPUT-RECORD
00150                      PERFORM READ-INVENTORY-FILE-IN.
00151          *
00152              END-LOAD-DATA.
00153                  CLOSE INVENTORY-FILE-IN, INVEN-MAST-FILE-IO.
00154                  IF NO-MORE-INPUT
00155                      DISPLAY 'ALL RECORDS PROCESSED'
00156                  ELSE
00157                      DISPLAY 'PROBLEM ENCOUNTERED'
00158                      DISPLAY 'LAST INPUT RECORD', INVENTORY-IN-REC.
00159          *
00160              GENERATE-BLOCK-NUM.
00161                  IF READ-TRY-COUNT = ZERO
00162                      MOVE INV-IN-CAT-NUM TO SAVE-CAT-NUM
00163                      DIVIDE SAVE-CAT-NUM BY PRIME-FOR-DIVISOR
00164                          GIVING QUOTIENT REMAINDER TRACK-NUM
00165                      COMPUTE BLOCK-NUM = 2 * TRACK-NUM + 1
00166                  ELSE
00167                      ADD 1 TO BLOCK-NUM.
00168                  ADD 1 TO READ-TRY-COUNT.
00169                  IF BLOCK-NUM IS GREATER THAN MAX-BLOCK-NUM
00170                      MOVE 1 TO BLOCK-NUM.
00171                  IF READ-TRY-COUNT IS GREATER THAN MAX-NUM-TRIES
00172                      MOVE 'Y' TO STOP-PROCESSING-SW
00173                      DISPLAY ' FILE TOO FULL'.
```

Figure 7.10 (cont.)

```
00174            *
00175                 TRY-TO-ADD-RECORD.
00176                     SET  RECS-PER-BLOCK-COUNT TO 1.
00177                     MOVE 'G' TO WRITE-STATUS-SW.
00178                     SEARCH INV-IO-REC
00179                         AT END MOVE 'Y' TO BLOCK-FULL-SW
00180                         WHEN INV-IO-CAT-NUM (RECS-PER-BLOCK-COUNT) = ZERO
00181                             MOVE 'N' TO BLOCK-FULL-SW.
00182                     MOVE 'Y' TO NEW-INPUT-RECORD-SW
00183                     IF BLOCK-FULL
00184                         MOVE 'N' TO NEW-INPUT-RECORD-SW
00185                     ELSE
00186                         MOVE INVENTORY-IN-REC TO
00187                             INV-IO-REC (RECS-PER-BLOCK-COUNT)
00188                         PERFORM REWRITE-INVENTORY-MAST.
00189                     IF BAD-REWRITE
00190                         MOVE 'Y' TO STOP-PROCESSING-SW
00191                         MOVE 'N' TO NEW-INPUT-RECORD-SW.
00192            *
00193                 WRITE-BLOCKS-TO-DISK.
00194                     WRITE INVEN-IO-AREA FROM INV-IO-BLOCK
00195                         INVALID KEY MOVE 'W' TO WRITE-STATUS-SW.
00196            *
00197                 READ-INVENTORY-FILE-IN.
00198                     READ INVENTORY-FILE-IN INTO INVENTORY-IN-REC
00199                         AT END MOVE 'Y' TO END-OF-INPUT-SW,
00200                                            STOP-PROCESSING-SW.
00201            *
00202                 READ-INV-FILE-IO.
00203                     READ INVEN-MAST-FILE-IO INTO INV-IO-BLOCK
00204                         INVALID KEY MOVE 'Y' TO READ-STATUS-SW.
00205            *
00206                 REWRITE-INVENTORY-MAST.
00207                     REWRITE INVEN-IO-AREA FROM INV-IO-BLOCK
00208                         INVALID KEY MOVE 'R' TO WRITE-STATUS-SW.
```

To logically remove a record from a relative file, the DELETE statement is used.

FORMAT
DELETE file-name [INVALID KEY imperative-statement]

To use the DELETE verb, the file must be opened for I-O. After execution of the DELETE statement, the record can no longer be accessed. For random access, the relative record number of the record to be deleted must be placed in the relative key. For sequential access, the last record read will be deleted. The location of a deleted record may be reused.

To begin sequential processing of a relative file at a point other than the beginning of the file, the START statement is used.

```
                    ┌─────────────────────────────────────────┐
                    │                 FORMAT                    │
                    ├─────────────────────────────────────────┤
                    │  START file-name                          │
                    │                ⎧ EQUAL TO     ⎫           │
                    │                ⎪     =        ⎪           │
                    │      [KEY IS  ⎨ GREATER THAN ⎬ data-name] │
                    │                ⎪     >        ⎪           │
                    │                ⎪ NOT LESS THAN⎪           │
                    │                ⎩   NOT <      ⎭           │
                    │                                           │
                    │  [INVALID KEY imperative-statement]       │
                    └─────────────────────────────────────────┘
```

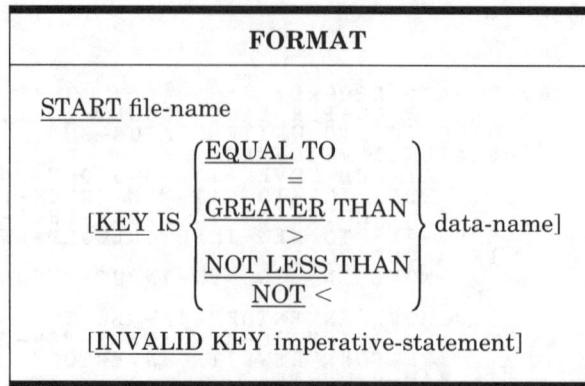

Access must be specified as either SEQUENTIAL or DYNAMIC. Processing will begin with the first record whose relative record number satisfies the condition specified in the START statement. If the KEY clause is omitted, processing begins with the record whose relative record number is in the relative key.

ADVANTAGES AND DISADVANTAGES OF RELATIVE FILES

The following are among the advantages of relative files:

1. Records in the file may be accessed either sequentially or randomly.
2. Processing of unsequenced transactions is possible, thus eliminating the need to sort transactions.
3. Transactions may be processed as they occur (real time) or batched for later processing. If batched, the transactions may be sorted, thus making sequential processing of the relative file possible.
4. Updating records does not require re-creation of the file.
5. Adding records does not require re-creation of the file.
6. Random access to records in a relative file is very efficient and fast; that is, there are no indexes to search, as is required with indexed files.

Disadvantages of relative files include the following:

1. If record keys, such as part number, social security number, and the like, do not contain values that will directly correspond to relative record numbers, then a programmer-written hashing routine is required for random access to records.
2. Processing overflow records involves extra computer time and increases program complexity.
3. If a hashing technique is used, a large number of synonyms, or an increase or decrease in the file size, will require reprogramming of the hashing routine.

Programming Exercises for Chapter 7

Dr. James' Neighborhood Emporium

Dr. James, owner of Dr. James' Neighborhood Emporium, wants to computerize the prescription records for the pharmacy department.

There must be direct access to records by prescription number. Prescription numbers are assigned in order as prescriptions are filled. When the numbers reach 50,000, they will be started over again at 1. There will not be more than 10,000 prescriptions filled in a given year.

The prescription file has relative organization, and each prescription record contains:

Record Positions	Contents	Format
1–5	Prescription number	9(5)
16–30	Physician	X(15)
31–50	Patient name	X(20)
51–80	Patient address	X(30)
81–95	Medicine name	X(15)
96–105	Amount prescribed	X(10)
106–108	Number of refills allowed	9(3)
109–114	Date first dispensed	9(6)
115–119	Charge	9(3)V9(2)
120–125	Date refilled	9(6)
126–130	Charge	9(3)V9(2)
.		
.		
.		
230–235	Date refilled	9(6)
236–240	Charge	9(3)V9(2)

The record contains space for a maximum of 12 dates and charges, which will allow for filling the prescription up to 12 times (fields are blank until refills occur).

The prescription file will be used with Exercises 7.1 and 7.2.

EXERCISE 7.1

You are to write a program that updates the prescription file just described. Your program should allow for

1. Adding a new prescription record.
2. Updating an existing prescription record for a refill; the update should be rejected if dispensing the drug will exceed the number of refills allowed.

A record to be added to the file contains the same information as columns 1–119 of the prescription file records. In addition, an 'A' appears in column 120. A record for a prescription refill contains the prescription number, date, charge, and code of 'R' in column 120.

EXERCISE 7.2

Write a program that lists and deletes all prescription records that were filled for the first time more than one year ago.

The Tired Traveler Hotel

The Tired Traveler Hotel maintains a room occupancy and status information file. This file has relative organization and uses the room number as the relative record number. Each record contains:

Record Position	Contents	Format
1	Room type	X
2	Number twin beds	9
3	Number double beds	9
4	Number queen beds	9
5	Number king beds	9
6	Room status	X
7–12	Check-in date	9(6)
13–14	Number of nights	9(2)
15	Number of people	9

Room status is

O	occupied
V	vacant
U	unusable

The occupancy file for the Tired Traveler Hotel will be used with Exercises 7.3 and 7.4.

EXERCISE 7.3

Write a COBOL program that will update the occupancy file when a customer checks into a specified room in the Tired Traveler Hotel. Your program should also allow for updating occupancy records when a customer checks out, or when room status for a specified room should be changed to unusable.

Your input transaction record format is

Record Position	Contents	Format
1–3	Room number	9(3)
4–5	Action requested code (IN is for check in, OT is for check out, UN means change room status to unusable)	X(2)
6–11	Check-in date	9(6)
12–13	Number of nights	9(2)
14	Number of people	9

(NOTE: Transaction record positions 6 through 14 will be blank for records containing either a checkout code or change room status to unusable code in positions 4–5.)

EXERCISE 7.4

A table contains the rates of rooms based on the room type and the number of persons in the room. Not all combinations are possible, and the table contains zero rates for impossible combinations. Room types are

S = Standard
D = Deluxe
L = Luxury

You are to write a COBOL program that will use the table in combination with the records in the occupancy file of the Tired Traveler Hotel. Your program should compute and print out the amount of room charge due when the room number is entered for a customer checking out. The occupancy file record should also be updated.

Use the following rate table in your program.

Number of Occupants	Standard	Deluxe	Luxury
1	48	50	55
2	51	56	61
3	57	59	67
4	0	62	0
5	0	68	0

Hospital Research Study

A researcher is studying patterns in the spread of communicable diseases beginning in 1978. Fifty hospitals throughout the United States were selected. Each hospital will supply data from which the number of cases admitted and the number of deaths attributed to the disease can be determined.

Each record will contain the information for a given year and hospital for all 10 diseases.

Year	Hospital	Cases Disease 1	Deaths Disease 1	. . .	Cases Disease 10	Deaths Disease 10

Table for 10 diseases for 1 year for 1 hospital

Each record has the following format:

Record Position	Contents	Format
1–2	Year	9(2)
3–4	Hospital	9(2)
5–7	Cases reported (disease 1)	9(3)
8–10	Deaths (disease 1)	9(3)
11–13	Cases reported (disease 2)	9(3)
14–16	Deaths (disease 2)	9(3)
	.	
	.	
	.	
59–61	Cases reported (disease 10)	9(3)
62–64	Deaths (disease 10)	9(3)

The relative record number is computed on the basis of year and hospital number. Use the formula

$$\text{relative record number} = (\text{year} - 78) * 50 + \text{hospital number}.$$

With this technique, all the records for a given year are together in the file.
The hospital file just described will be used with Exercises 7.5 and 7.6.

EXERCISE 7.5

Write a program that provides a report of total cases and total deaths for the years 1978–1980. The starting and ending years should be input so the program can be used for other time spans.

EXERCISE 7.6

Write a program that will produce a summary report for total cases and total deaths for a given hospital. Note that a given hospital's records occur every 50th record in the file.

Creating and Processing Files Having Direct File Organization

The nature of some data processing applications, as stated in the preceding chapter, is such that records to be processed will nearly always be accessed randomly by a key associated with the record. Typically, there is also a need to quickly access selected records in the file. Airline and hotel reservation systems and inventory control are frequently encountered examples of such applications.

For those of you who may not have read about Margo's Mail Order Boutique in the previous chapter, a few comments concerning that company should be repeated. These will provide us with an appropriate context for beginning the study of yet another type of file organization.

Margo's is a catalogue order firm that sells unusual clothing and accessories through a catalogue, which is published four times a year. As merchandise is shipped to customers and received from suppliers, a master inventory file is updated to reflect the number of units in stock for a given catalogue item. New items are added from time to time and items are sometimes discontinued. There is a significant amount of carry-forward of items from one catalogue to the next. Consequently, complete reloading of all records in the file should rarely be necessary. Figure 8.1 provides a description of the records contained in the firm's inventory file.

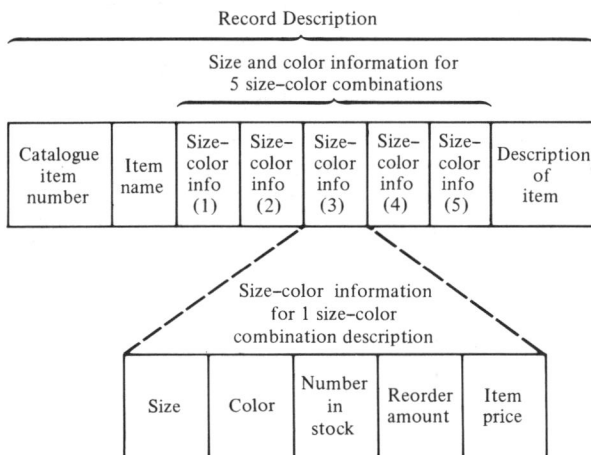

Figure 8.1
Logical description of the data in a record in MARGO'S inventory file.

There are currently at least two file organizations that are suitable for Margo's inventory processing system. One, called *relative* (VSAM/RRDS), was described in detail in the preceding chapter; therefore, it will not be given further consideration here. The other, an older organization called *direct* file organization, is not included in the standard for 74 COBOL. However, it does exist as an IBM extension to that standard. Direct files are compatible with the processing requirements of Margo's inventory system.

Direct file organization requires that the programmer specify a unique key for the record, as well as the cylinder and head designation for the track on which the record is to be located. More detailed information will be presented in the following sections.

DIRECT FILE CONCEPTS

When direct file organization is used, the file must be on a direct-access device and the position of the logical record in the file is controlled by programmer-written routines. The key that will be used by the operating system to place a record on the file or to retrieve a record from the file will consist of two parts: a *track identifier* and a *record identifier*. The track identifier specifies the physical location of the record—for example, cylinder 202, head 5. The record identifier contains a unique key for the logical record in the file—for example, a catalogue number, identification number, or social security number. Records in a direct file are normally unblocked and the key is stored separately from the record.

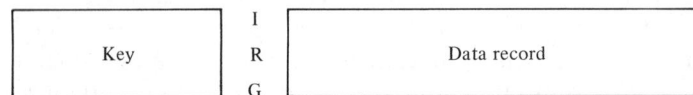

```
┌──────────────────┐ I ┌────────────────────────────────────┐
│                  │ R │                                      │
│       Key        │ G │             Data record              │
│                  │   │                                      │
└──────────────────┘   └────────────────────────────────────┘
```

Generally, the record identifier will be in both the key and the record. Since the record identifier will be known to the programmer, it is generally used to generate the value for the track identifier.

A common technique for this is *division/remainder hashing.* To illustrate, suppose a file requires 10 cylinders (which is 190 tracks on an IBM 3336 disk pack), and the record identifier is a 6-digit number. Choose the largest prime number less than or equal to 190, namely 181. Divide the record identifier by 181 and find the remainder. If the remainder is divided by 19 (the number of tracks per cylinder), the quotient and remainder obtained can be used to give the cylinder and head designation within the file.

Record Identifier	Remainder	Cylinder	Head
614427	113	5	18
814710	29	1	10

In general, many record identifiers will generate the same track identifier. Records that hash to the same track are called *synonyms.* Once a track is full, additional synonym records are termed *overflow records,* and the programmer must develop a separate processing routine for these overflow records. Since they are more complicated to process, it is desirable to minimize the number of overflow records. Both increasing the amount of space allocated for a file and changing the hashing routine can reduce the number of overflow records.

ENVIRONMENT DIVISION ENTRIES

In order to (1) describe the file organization as direct, (2) give a name to the file, and (3) describe how it is to be accessed, we must specify a SELECT sentence.

```
                    FORMAT

SELECT file-name

    ASSIGN TO system-name

    ACCESS IS  { SEQUENTIAL }
               { RANDOM     }

    [ACTUAL KEY IS data-name]
```

For ACCESS IS RANDOM, the ACTUAL KEY clause must be specified. Although sequential processing is possible, our discussion will primarily be concerned with random processing of the files. If ACCESS IS SEQUENTIAL, the file may be OPENed only for INPUT. The file will then be accessed in the physical order in which records are positioned on the tracks.

The data-name associated with the ACTUAL KEY must be described in the WORKING-STORAGE SECTION.

Assume a hotel reservation file is to be organized as a direct file. The SELECT sentence may have the following form:

```
SELECT HOTEL-RES-FILE-IN
    ASSIGN TO SYS023-DA-3330-W-RESFILE
    ACCESS IS RANDOM
    ACTUAL KEY IS ROOM-ACCESS-INFO.
```

The choice of W in system-name specifies the form of the ACTUAL KEY and how update processing is to be done. This will be described more fully a little later. Since ACCESS IS RANDOM is specified, the record identifier and track identifier parts of ROOM-ACCESS-INFO must both be set by the programmer before an attempt is made to access the file.

DATA DIVISION ENTRIES

There are no additional features for the FD entry for direct files. On some systems, the BLOCK CONTAINS clause must be omitted or be specified as 1. This is generally desirable, even if blocking factors greater than 1 are allowed. The structure of the ACTUAL KEY depends upon the type of disk addressing being done. The term *actual address* refers to a cylinder and head number, whereas a *relative address* is a track number relative to the beginning of file. Suppose a file is to occupy 5 cylinders beginning with cylinder 204.[1] Then cylinder 207, head 8, is an actual address for a track assigned to the file. The same track has relative address 65, which was derived by the calculation $((207 - 204) * 19 + 8)$. Relative addressing is much more commonly used than actual addressing, so we will restrict our discussion to relative addressing. The conversion of a relative track specification to an actual address is done automatically by the operating system.

For relative track addressing, the actual key has the form:

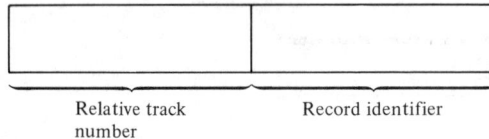

Relative track number	Record identifier

The data-item description for the relative track number must be 4 bytes long and in internal binary form. This data-item is described as PIC S9(8) COMP SYNC. However, it will occupy only 4 bytes internally because COMP specifies its form to be binary. The length of the record identifier portion of the ACTUAL KEY is determined by the number of bytes in the unique identifier used for the records, such as social security number, part number, and so on.

The entries for our hotel reservation file would be

```
              FILE SECTION.
              FD   HOTEL-RES-FILE-IN
                   LABEL RECORDS ARE STANDARD.
              01   RES-IN-AREA                PIC X(150).
                                 .
                                 .
                                 .


              WORKING-STORAGE SECTION.
                                 .
                                 .
                                 .

              01   ROOM-ACCESS-INFO.
relative track
address   ⟶ 02   ROOM-TRACK-NUM             PIC S9(8) COMP SYNC.
record
identifier ⟶ 02  ROOM-ACCESS-ROOM-NUM       PIC 9(5).
                                 .
                                 .
                                 .
```

---

[1] Throughout the rest of this chapter, we shall assume we are using disk devices having disk packs with 19 tracks per cylinder.

We will limit our discussion of PROCEDURE DIVISION entries to the READ, WRITE, and REWRITE verbs.

To access a record in an existing direct file, the READ statement is used.

FORMAT

READ file-name
 	
   [INTO data-name]
 	
   $\left\{ \begin{array}{l} \text{AT END} \\ \text{INVALID KEY} \end{array} \right\}$ imperative-statement

If the ACCESS IS SEQUENTIAL clause is specified, the READ for a direct file functions logically, just as it did for sequential files.

For a direct file to be accessed randomly, the ACTUAL KEY fields must be set to the desired values before the READ statement is executed. Only the track specified will be searched for the desired record.

The imperative-statement following the INVALID KEY clause will be executed if either of the following conditions exists:

1. The relative track number is outside the limits specified for the file.
2. There is no record on the track with the value specified in the record identifier.

The AT END clause applies only if the file is being read sequentially. To add a record to the file, the WRITE statement is used.

FORMAT

WRITE record-name
 	
   [FROM data-name]
 	
   INVALID KEY imperative-statement

The ACTUAL KEY fields must be set to the desired values prior to execution of the WRITE statement.

The imperative-statement following the INVALID KEY phase will be executed if

1. The track address is outside the limits specified for the file, or
2. The WRITE statement is being used to update a record and the record identifier specified is not found.

Although it is possible to use WRITE to update a record (if D, rather than W, is specified in the ASSIGN statement), we recommend use of the REWRITE statement, as it more clearly describes the type of I/O operation actually being done.

FORMAT

REWRITE record-name

[FROM data-name]

INVALID KEY imperative-statement

As you might expect, the use of REWRITE requires that the ACTUAL KEY fields be set. The REWRITE statement must be preceded by the execution of a READ statement.

The imperative-statement will be executed when

1. A relative track number is outside the file limits, or
2. The desired record identifier is not found on the track specified.

Example 8.1

Margo's Mail Order Boutique has decided to organize the inventory file as a direct file. Space is allocated for 5200 records, which is the maximum number expected to exist at any one time. The initial loading of records in the file is done for the items printed in the very first catalogue. No record overflow is expected to occur, since there are fewer than 1000 records to be loaded on the file.

Program organization is given in Figure 8.2, with the program listing for the file load presented in Figure 8.3.

Points of importance in the program are

1. 200 tracks are allocated for the file. Thus, the relative track numbers are 0 to 199.
2. The module CREATE-ACCESS-INFO (lines 119–123) is executed to determine a value for the two fields in RECORD-ACCESS INFO, the actual key, before the WRITE statement is executed.
3. Should there be overflow records, the program terminates abnormally (ABENDS). The INVALID KEY clause would not be executed in this case.

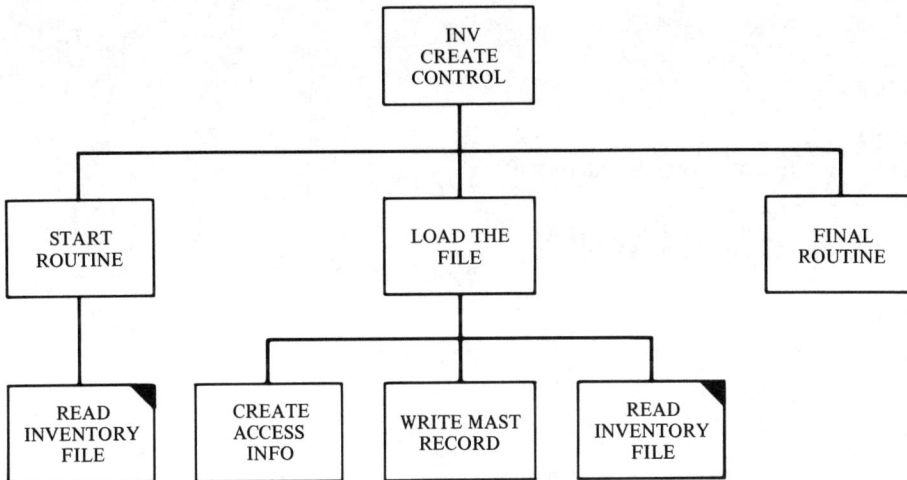

Figure 8.2
Structure chart for the program in Figure 8.3.

```
00001          IDENTIFICATION DIVISION.
00002      *
00003       PROGRAM-ID.
00004          EX-8-1.
00005      ****************************************************************
00006      *                                                              *
00007      *   PROGRAMMER TEAM          SUMMERS/WALSTROM/LINDAHL          *
00008      *   PROGRAM COMPLETION DATE AUGUST 2, 1984                     *
00009      *                                                              *
00010      *                    PROGRAM SUMMARY                           *
00011      *   INPUT                                                      *
00012      *       EACH RECORD CONTAINS                                   *
00013      *           - CATALOGUE NUMBER                                 *
00014      *           - NAME OF THE ITEM                                 *
00015      *           - A TABLE CONTAINING IN EACH TABLE ENTRY:          *
00016      *             SIZE, COLOR, NUMBER IN STOCK, REORDER AMOUNT,    *
00017      *             PRICE                                            *
00018      *           - CATALOGUE DESCRIPTION                            *
00019      *                                                              *
00020      *   PROCESSING                                                 *
00021      *       EACH RECORD IS ASSIGNED A RELATIVE TRACK NUMBER        *
00022      *           - DIVISION REMAINDER HASHING IS USED               *
00023      *           - NO OVERFLOW HANDLING IS DONE                     *
00024      *                                                              *
00025      *   OUTPUT                                                     *
00026      *       FOR NO TRACK OVERFLOW                                  *
00027      *           - A COPY OF THE INPUT FILE WITH DIRECT ORGANIZATION*
00028      *           - A PROGRAM COMPLETION MESSAGE                     *
00029      *       FOR TRACK OVERFLOW                                     *
00030      *           - ABNORMAL TERMINATION OCCURS                      *
00031      ****************************************************************
00032      *
00033       ENVIRONMENT DIVISION.
00034      *
00035       CONFIGURATION SECTION.
00036       SOURCE-COMPUTER.
00037          IBM-370.
00038       OBJECT-COMPUTER.
00039          IBM-370.
00040       INPUT-OUTPUT SECTION.
00041       FILE-CONTROL.
00042           SELECT INVEN-MAST-FILE-OUT
00043               ASSIGN TO SYS023-DA-3330-W-INVFILE
00044               ACCESS IS RANDOM
00045               ACTUAL KEY IS RECORD-ACCESS-INFO.
00046           SELECT INVENTORY-FILE-IN
00047               ASSIGN TO SYS023-DA-3330-S-DATFILE.
```

Figure 8.3
Creation of a direct file for Example 8.1.

Figure 8.3 (cont.)

```
00048              *
00049              DATA DIVISION.
00050              *
00051                 FILE SECTION.
00052                 FD   INVEN-MAST-FILE-OUT
00053                         LABEL RECORDS ARE STANDARD.
00054                 01   INVEN-OUT-AREA                    PIC  X(306).
00055                 FD   INVENTORY-FILE-IN
00056                         LABEL RECORDS ARE STANDARD
00057                         BLOCK CONTAINS 20 RECORDS.
00058                 01   INVEN-IN-AREA                     PIC  X(306).
00059              *
00060                 WORKING-STORAGE SECTION.
00061                 01   SWITCHES.
00062                      02   STOP-PROCESSING-SW           PIC X.
00063                           88  STOP-PROCESSING   VALUE 'Y'.
00064                      02   WRITE-STATUS-SW              PIC X.
00065                           88  GOOD-WRITE         VALUE 'G'.
00066                           88  BAD-KEY            VALUE 'I'.
00067                      02   END-OF-INPUT-SW              PIC X.
00068                           88  NO-MORE-INPUT     VALUE 'Y'.
00069                 01   CONSTANTS.
00070                      02   PRIME-FOR-DIVISOR            PIC S9(4) COMP SYNC
00071                                             VALUE 199.
00072                 01   WORK-NUMBERS.
00073                      02   SAVE-CAT-NUMBER              PIC S9(6) COMP SYNC.
00074                      02   QUOTIENT                     PIC S9(6) COMP SYNC.
00075                 01   RECORD-ACCESS-INFO.
00076                      02   REL-TRACK-NUMBER             PIC S9(8) COMP SYNC.
00077                      02   REC-KEY-CAT-NUM              PIC S9(6).
00078                 01   INVENTORY-IN-REC.
00079                      02   INV-IN-CAT-NUM               PIC S9(6).
00080                      02   FILLER                       PIC X(300).
00081              *
00082              PROCEDURE DIVISION.
00083              *
00084                 INV-CREATE-CONTROL.
00085                      PERFORM START-ROUTINE.
00086                      PERFORM LOAD-THE-FILE UNTIL STOP-PROCESSING.
00087                      PERFORM FINAL-ROUTINE.
00088                      STOP RUN.
00089              *
00090                 START-ROUTINE.
00091                      OPEN INPUT INVENTORY-FILE-IN
00092                           OUTPUT INVEN-MAST-FILE-OUT.
00093                      MOVE 'N' TO END-OF-INPUT-SW, STOP-PROCESSING-SW.
00094                      PERFORM READ-INVENTORY-FILE.
00095              *
00096                 LOAD-THE-FILE.
00097                      PERFORM CREATE-ACCESS-INFO.
00098                      MOVE 'G' TO WRITE-STATUS-SW.
00099                      PERFORM WRITE-MAST-RECORD.
00100                      IF GOOD-WRITE
00101                          PERFORM READ-INVENTORY-FILE
00102                      ELSE
00103                          IF BAD-KEY
00104                              DISPLAY ' INVALID KEY CONDITION'
00105                              DISPLAY ' CATALOG NUMBER ', REC-KEY-CAT-NUM
00106                              DISPLAY 'RELATIVE TRACK ', REL-TRACK-NUMBER
00107                          ELSE
00108                              MOVE 'Y' TO STOP-PROCESSING-SW
00109                              DISPLAY ' OTHER ERROR '.
00110              *
00111                 FINAL-ROUTINE.
00112                      IF NO-MORE-INPUT
00113                          DISPLAY 'DIRECT ACCESS FILE CREATED'
00114                      ELSE
00115                          DISPLAY ' PROBLEM IN CREATING THE FILE'
00116                          DISPLAY ' LAST RECORD READ', INVENTORY-IN-REC.
00117                      CLOSE INVENTORY-FILE-IN, INVEN-MAST-FILE-OUT.
00118              *
00119                 CREATE-ACCESS-INFO.
00120                      MOVE INV-IN-CAT-NUM TO SAVE-CAT-NUMBER.
00121                      DIVIDE SAVE-CAT-NUMBER BY PRIME-FOR-DIVISOR
00122                          GIVING QUOTIENT REMAINDER REL-TRACK-NUMBER.
00123                      MOVE INV-IN-CAT-NUM TO REC-KEY-CAT-NUM.
```

Figure 8.3 (cont.)

```
00124            *
00125                WRITE-MAST-RECORD.
00126                    WRITE INVEN-OUT-AREA FROM INVENTORY-IN-REC
00127                        INVALID KEY MOVE 'I' TO WRITE-STATUS-SW
00128                                    MOVE 'Y' TO STOP-PROCESSING-SW.
00129            *
00130                READ-INVENTORY-FILE.
00131                    READ INVENTORY-FILE-IN INTO INVENTORY-IN-REC
00132                        AT END MOVE 'Y' TO STOP-PROCESSING-SW,
00133                                           END-OF-INPUT-SW.
```

Although the approach taken in Example 8.1 would probably be sufficient for the initial startup of the inventory system, as time passes, it will be necessary to add new records to the file. Eventually, the problem of overflow records can be expected to occur.

Example 8.2

Margo's data processing manager has decided that the program in Figure 8.3 is to be revised to take into consideration the overflow problem.

Special routines must be written to handle overflow records, since no single COBOL statement provides this capability. Fundamental to the process of handling overflow records is the fact that attempting to WRITE a record to a track that is already full will cause an I-O error condition to exist. COBOL provides for error checking of this type by way of a DECLARATIVES subdivision within the PROCEDURE DIVISION. The general form of the DECLARATIVES subdivision is

---

FORMAT

PROCEDURE DIVISION.

DECLARATIVES.

section-name SECTION. USE sentence.

    [programmer routines]

END DECLARATIVES.

If a DECLARATIVE section is used in a program, it must appear as the first section in the PROCEDURE DIVISION, and the remainder of the PROCEDURE DIVISION must also be made up of one or more sections. (See Chapter 5 for additional information about sections, if desired.)

Although DECLARATIVES have several functions in COBOL, we will limit our discussion to their use in processing certain error conditions that can result from I-O operations. Examples of these errors are

1. Wrong length record.
2. Record contains invalid characters.
3. No room on track.

The USE sentence, within a DECLARATIVES section, will allow testing for these kinds of I-O errors. It has the following format.

FORMAT

USE AFTER STANDARD ERROR PROCEDURE

ON $\left\{ \begin{array}{l} \text{file-name-1} \\ \text{file-name-2 GIVING data-name-1} \\ \underline{\text{INPUT}} \\ \underline{\text{OUTPUT}} \\ \underline{\text{I-O}} \end{array} \right\}$

There are three additional forms of the USE sentence. One is associated with user-defined labels on files. They are rarely used and will not be discussed in this book. Another form will be discussed later in the chapter describing the REPORT WRITER feature of COBOL. The remaining form of the USE sentence will be covered in Chapter 11, when the COBOL source language debugging feature is presented.

The formal rules governing the USE sentence follow.

RULES AND CONSIDERATIONS PERTAINING TO THE USE SENTENCE

USE declaratives that specify error-handling procedures are activated when an input/output error occurs during execution of a READ or WRITE statement.

Within the section, the file associated with the USE sentence may not be referred to by an OPEN, START, SEEK, READ, WRITE, or REWRITE statement.

Within a USE procedure, there must be no reference to nondeclarative procedures except when an exit is taken with a GO TO statement. Conversely, in the nondeclarative portion, there must be no reference to procedure-names that appear in the declaratives portion, except that PERFORM statements may refer to a USE declarative or to procedures associated with such a declarative.

When either the file-name-1 or file-name-2 option is used, user error-handling procedures are executed for input/output errors occurring during execution of a READ or WRITE statement for that file only.

A file-name must not be referred to, implicitly or explicitly, in more than one USE sentence.

The user-error procedures are executed when the INPUT, OUTPUT, or I-O options are specified and an input/output error occurs, as follows:

When INPUT is specified, only for files opened as INPUT.

When OUTPUT is specified, only for files opened as OUTPUT.

When I-O is specified, only for files opened as I-O.

An exit from this type of declarative section can be effected by executing the last statement in the section (normal return), or by means of a GO TO statement. The normal return from an error declarative is to the statement following the input/output statement that caused the error.

The GIVING option allows the programmer to test the specific type of error that has occurred. Data-name-1 must be an 8-byte field defined in WORKING-STOR-AGE. The contents of this field will automatically be set to reflect the error condition that occurred. A "track full" condition will be indicated by a 1 in the third byte of the 8-byte error field.

A revised program is given in Figure 8.8, which loads the file, subject to the following conditions:

1. If a record can be placed on the track it hashes to, it will be placed there.
2. If a record is an overflow record, two additional attempts will be made to write the record. If the record can not be written in three attempts, the program terminates.

SECTION control organization of the program is given in Figure 8.4. A structure chart for the nonDECLARATIVES subdivision of the program is given in Figure 8.5.

Since the program logic is complex, module descriptions are given in Figures 8.6 and 8.7.

Note the following points about the program listed in Figure 8.8:

1. The only error that is tested for, and for which recovery is attempted, is "track full." Other errors causing entry into the DECLARATIVES will result in a switch being set to signal program termination (line 104).
2. The CREATE-NEW-ADDRESS module generates the next relative track address prior to each attempt to write an overflow record. If a record hashes originally to say, relative track 198 and there is not room on the track, there will still be two additional attempts, if needed, to write the record: first on track 199, and then on track 000.
3. The decision to try to write a record any given number of times is an arbitrary (but presumably reasonable) one made by the programmer.
4. Execution of the program begins on line 107.
5. If no error occurs when writing records to the file, lines 95–104 will never be executed.
6. An error that causes lines 168–169 to be executed as a result of an INVALID KEY condition *will not* cause the DECLARATIVES to be executed.

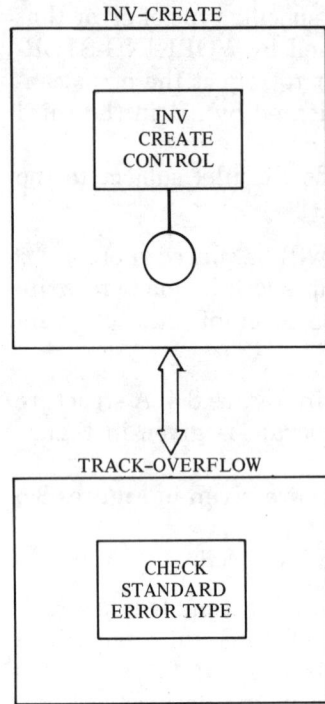

Figure 8.4
SECTION organization for the program in Figure 8.8.

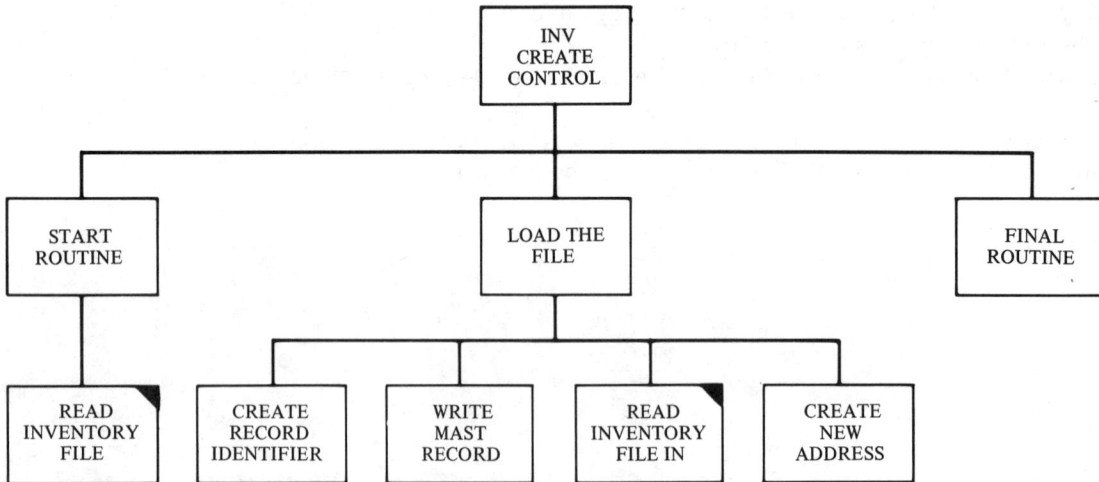

Figure 8.5
Structure chart for the INV-CREATE SECTION of the program in Figure 8.8.

INV-CREATE-CONTROL

This module controls execution of the routines START-ROUTINE, LOAD-THE-FILE, and FINAL-ROUTINE.   It also terminates execution of the program.

START-ROUTINE

This module opens all files, sets switches to indicate first processing of a record and that there is data to be processed, and causes the READ-INVENTORY-FILE module to be executed to obtain the first input record.

LOAD-THE-FILE

This module tests to see if an input record is being processed for the first time. If it is, then the DA record identifier is created. A switch is set to indicate that it is anticipated that the write to the DA file will be successful. The WRITE-MAST-RECORD module is called to try to write the record to the DA file. If the write is successful, the NEW-INPUT-RECORD switch is set to indicate that a new record is being obtained, and the READ-INVENTORY-FILE module is called to obtain a new record.

If the write is not successful because the track is full, the CREATE-NEW-ADDRESS module is executed to prepare for another attempt to write the record.

If the write is unsuccessful because an invalid key condition is encountered on the write, a switch is set to end creation of the file, and error information is displayed

If none of the previous write conditions are encountered, an appropriate message is displayed.

FINAL-ROUTINE

Tests are made to determine if all input data have been read. If so, a successful completion message is displayed; otherwise, an unsuccessful completion message is displayed. All files are closed.

CREATE-ACCESS-INFO

A relative track number is computed, using the division/remainder hashing technique. The input record key is copied to the actual key field.

CREATE-NEW-ADDRESS

A new relative track address is generated based on the next available track. Wrap-around from the last track in the file to the first track is done when appropriate.

If there have been too many tries to write a record, a switch is set to terminate creation of the file, and a descriptive message is displayed.

WRITE-MAST-RECORD

This module attempts to add the input record to the DA file. If the attempt is unsuccessful because of a track-full condition, the DECLARATIVES section is executed. If the attempt is unsuccessful because of an invalid key, two switches are set, one to terminate creation of the file and the other to indicate that an invalid key condition was encountered.

READ-INVENTORY-FILE

The next record is obtained from the input file. If the input file has been exhausted, switches are set to indicate that the input file has been completely read and processing should stop.

Figure 8.6
Module description for INV-CREATE SECTION of the program in Figure 8.8.

CHECK-STANDARD-ERROR-TYPE

When this DECLARATIVES module is entered, the system will automatically set the I-0 error bytes to reflect the error condition that occurred. This module then tests to see if the track is full.

If the track is not full, a switch is set that will result in no more attempts being made to write the record, and a second switch is set to indicate that processing should stop.

If the track is full, a switch is set to indicate that there is no more room on that track, and the new input record switch is set to indicate that a new input record should not be read.

Figure 8.7
Module description for DECLARATIVES for the program in Figure 8.8.

```
00001        IDENTIFICATION DIVISION.
00002       *
00003        PROGRAM-ID.
00004            EX-8-2.
00005       ****************************************************************
00006       *                                                              *
00007       *    PROGRAMMER TEAM          SUMMERS/WALSTROM/LINDAHL         *
00008       *    PROGRAM COMPLETION DATE AUGUST 9, 1984                    *
00009       *                                                              *
00010       *               PROGRAM SUMMARY                                *
00011       *    INPUT                                                     *
00012       *        EACH RECORD CONTAINS                                  *
00013       *            - CATALOGUE NUMBER                                *
00014       *            - NAME OF THE ITEM                                *
00015       *            - A TABLE CONTAINING IN EACH TABLE ENTRY:         *
00016       *              SIZE, COLOR, NUMBER IN STOCK, REORDER AMOUNT,   *
00017       *              PRICE                                           *
00018       *            - CATALOGUE DESCRIPTION                           *
00019       *                                                              *
00020       *    PROCESSING                                                *
00021       *        EACH RECORD IS ASSIGNED A RELATIVE TRACK NUMBER       *
00022       *            - DIVISION REMAINDER HASHING IS USED              *
00023       *            - NEXT AVAILABLE TRACK OVERFLOW HANDLING IS DONE  *
00024       *                                                              *
00025       *    OUTPUT                                                    *
00026       *            - A COPY OF THE INPUT FILE WITH DIRECT ORGANIZATION*
00027       *            - A PROGRAM OUTCOME MESSAGE                       *
00028       ****************************************************************
00029       *
00030        ENVIRONMENT DIVISION.
00031       *
00032        CONFIGURATION SECTION.
00033        SOURCE-COMPUTER.
00034            IBM-370.
00035        OBJECT-COMPUTER.
00036            IBM-370.
00037        INPUT-OUTPUT SECTION.
00038        FILE-CONTROL.
00039            SELECT INVEN-MAST-FILE-OUT
00040                ASSIGN TO SYS023-DA-3330-W-INVFILE
00041                ACCESS IS RANDOM
00042                ACTUAL KEY IS RECORD-ACCESS-INFO.
00043            SELECT INVENTORY-FILE-IN
00044                ASSIGN TO SYS023-DA-3330-S-DATFILE.
00045       *
00046        DATA DIVISION.
00047       *
00048        FILE SECTION.
00049        FD  INVEN-MAST-FILE-OUT
00050                LABEL RECORDS ARE STANDARD.
00051        01  INVEN-OUT-AREA                    PIC  X(306).
00052        FD  INVENTORY-FILE-IN
00053                LABEL RECORDS ARE STANDARD
00054                BLOCK CONTAINS 20 RECORDS.
```

Figure 8.8
Use of DECLARATIVES for handling overflow records for Example 8.2.

Figure 8.8 (cont.)

```
00055              01   INVEN-IN-AREA                    PIC X(306).
00056          *
00057          WORKING-STORAGE SECTION.
00058          01   SWITCHES.
00059              02   STOP-PROCESSING-SW               PIC X.
00060                  88   STOP-PROCESSING   VALUE 'Y'.
00061              02   WRITE-STATUS-SW                  PIC X.
00062                  88   NO-ROOM-FOUND     VALUE 'F'.
00063                  88   GOOD-WRITE        VALUE 'G'.
00064                  88   BAD-KEY           VALUE 'I'.
00065              02   END-OF-INPUT-SW                  PIC X.
00066                  88   NO-MORE-INPUT     VALUE 'Y'.
00067              02   NEW-INPUT-RECORD-SW              PIC X.
00068                  88   NEW-INPUT-RECORD  VALUE 'Y'.
00069          01   DECLARATIVES-ERROR-STATUS.
00070              02   FILLER                           PIC X(2).
00071              02   TRACK-FULL-ERROR                 PIC 9.
00072                  88   TRACK-IS-FULL     VALUE 1.
00073              02   FILLER                           PIC 9(5).
00074          01   COUNTERS.
00075              02   WRITE-TRY-COUNT                  PIC 9(2).
00076          01   CONSTANTS.
00077              02   MAX-TRACK-NUM                    PIC S9(4) COMP SYNC
00078                                        VALUE 199.
00079              02   PRIME-FOR-DIVISOR                PIC S9(4) COMP SYNC
00080                                        VALUE 199.
00081              02   MAX-NUM-OF-TRIES                 PIC S9(2) VALUE 3.
00082          01   WORK-NUMBERS.
00083              02   SAVE-CAT-NUMBER                  PIC S9(6) COMP SYNC.
00084              02   QUOTIENT                         PIC S9(6) COMP SYNC.
00085          01   RECORD-ACCESS-INFO.
00086              02   REL-TRACK-NUMBER                 PIC S9(8) COMP SYNC.
00087              02   REC-KEY-CAT-NUM                  PIC S9(6).
00088          01   INVENTORY-IN-REC.
00089              02   INV-IN-CAT-NUM                   PIC 9(6).
00090              02   FILLER                           PIC X(300).
00091          *
00092          PROCEDURE DIVISION.
00093          *
00094          DECLARATIVES.
00095          TRACK-OVERFLOW SECTION.
00096              USE AFTER STANDARD ERROR PROCEDURE ON INVEN-MAST-FILE-OUT
00097              GIVING DECLARATIVES-ERROR-STATUS.
00098          CHECK-STANDARD-ERROR-TYPE.
00099              IF TRACK-IS-FULL
00100                  MOVE 'F' TO WRITE-STATUS-SW
00101                  MOVE 'N' TO NEW-INPUT-RECORD-SW
00102              ELSE
00103                  MOVE 'O' TO WRITE-STATUS-SW
00104                  MOVE 'Y' TO STOP-PROCESSING-SW.
00105          END DECLARATIVES.
00106          *
00107          INV-CREATE SECTION.
00108          INV-CREATE-CONTROL.
00109              PERFORM START-ROUTINE.
00110              PERFORM LOAD-THE-FILE UNTIL STOP-PROCESSING.
00111              PERFORM FINAL-ROUTINE.
00112              STOP RUN.
00113          *
00114          START-ROUTINE.
00115              OPEN INPUT INVENTORY-FILE-IN
00116                   OUTPUT INVEN-MAST-FILE-OUT.
00117              MOVE 'Y' TO NEW-INPUT-RECORD-SW.
00118              MOVE 'N' TO END-OF-INPUT-SW, STOP-PROCESSING-SW.
00119              PERFORM READ-INVENTORY-FILE.
```

Figure 8.8 (cont.)

```
00120          *
00121              LOAD-THE-FILE.
00122              IF NEW-INPUT-RECORD
00123                  MOVE 0 TO WRITE-TRY-COUNT
00124                  PERFORM CREATE-ACCESS-INFO.
00125              MOVE 'G' TO WRITE-STATUS-SW.
00126              PERFORM WRITE-MAST-RECORD.
00127              IF GOOD-WRITE
00128                  MOVE 'Y' TO NEW-INPUT-RECORD-SW
00129                  PERFORM READ-INVENTORY-FILE
00130              ELSE
00131                  IF NO-ROOM-FOUND
00132                      PERFORM CREATE-NEW-ADDRESS
00133                  ELSE
00134                      IF BAD-KEY
00135                          DISPLAY ' INVALID KEY CONDITION '
00136                          DISPLAY ' CATALOG NUMBER',
00137                              REC-KEY-CAT-NUM
00138                          DISPLAY 'RELATIVE TRACK ', REL-TRACK-NUMBER
00139                      ELSE
00140                          DISPLAY ' OTHER STANDARD ERROR'
00141                          DISPLAY ' RELATIVE TRACK', REL-TRACK-NUMBER
00142                          DISPLAY ' CATALOGUE NUMBER ', REC-KEY-CAT-NUM.
00143          *
00144              FINAL-ROUTINE.
00145              IF NO-MORE-INPUT
00146                  DISPLAY 'DIRECT ACCESS FILE CREATED'
00147              ELSE
00148                  DISPLAY ' PROBLEM IN CREATING THE FILE'
00149                  DISPLAY ' LAST RECORD READ', INVENTORY-IN-REC.
00150              CLOSE INVENTORY-FILE-IN, INVEN-MAST-FILE-OUT.
00151          *
00152              CREATE-ACCESS-INFO.
00153              MOVE INV-IN-CAT-NUM TO SAVE-CAT-NUMBER.
00154              DIVIDE SAVE-CAT-NUMBER BY PRIME-FOR-DIVISOR
00155                  GIVING QUOTIENT REMAINDER REL-TRACK-NUMBER.
00156              MOVE INV-IN-CAT-NUM TO REC-KEY-CAT-NUM.
00157          *
00158              CREATE-NEW-ADDRESS.
00159              ADD 1 TO REL-TRACK-NUMBER, WRITE-TRY-COUNT.
00160              IF REL-TRACK-NUMBER IS GREATER THAN MAX-TRACK-NUM
00161                  MOVE 0 TO REL-TRACK-NUMBER.
00162              IF WRITE-TRY-COUNT IS GREATER THAN MAX-NUM-OF-TRIES
00163                  DISPLAY 'TOO MANY TRIES,RECREATE WITH MORE SPACE'
00164                  MOVE 'Y' TO STOP-PROCESSING-SW.
00165          *
00166              WRITE-MAST-RECORD.
00167              WRITE INVEN-OUT-AREA FROM INVENTORY-IN-REC
00168                  INVALID KEY MOVE 'I' TO WRITE-STATUS-SW
00169                          MOVE 'Y' TO STOP-PROCESSING-SW.
00170          *
00171              READ-INVENTORY-FILE.
00172              READ INVENTORY-FILE-IN INTO INVENTORY-IN-REC
00173                  AT END MOVE 'Y' TO STOP-PROCESSING-SW,
00174                          END-OF-INPUT-SW.
```

Example 8.3

A program is needed that will add a new size or color to an existing catalogue item in Margo's inventory file.

A structure chart for a program solution for Example 8.3 is given in Figure 8.9. The program listing is given in Figure 8.10.

The following observations should be made concerning the program:

1. The specification of W in the ASSIGN clause of line 49 allows the use of RE-WRITE to update records and indicates that relative track addressing will be used.
2. The maximum number of attempts to READ, and the tracks specified for READing, must be exactly the same as was specified when attempting to WRITE records when the file was created. If a record hashes to relative track 198, then tracks 198, 199, and 000 must be read before you can conclude that the desired record is not on the file.
3. The inventory master file, INV-MAST-FILE-IO, must be OPENed for I-O (Line 125).

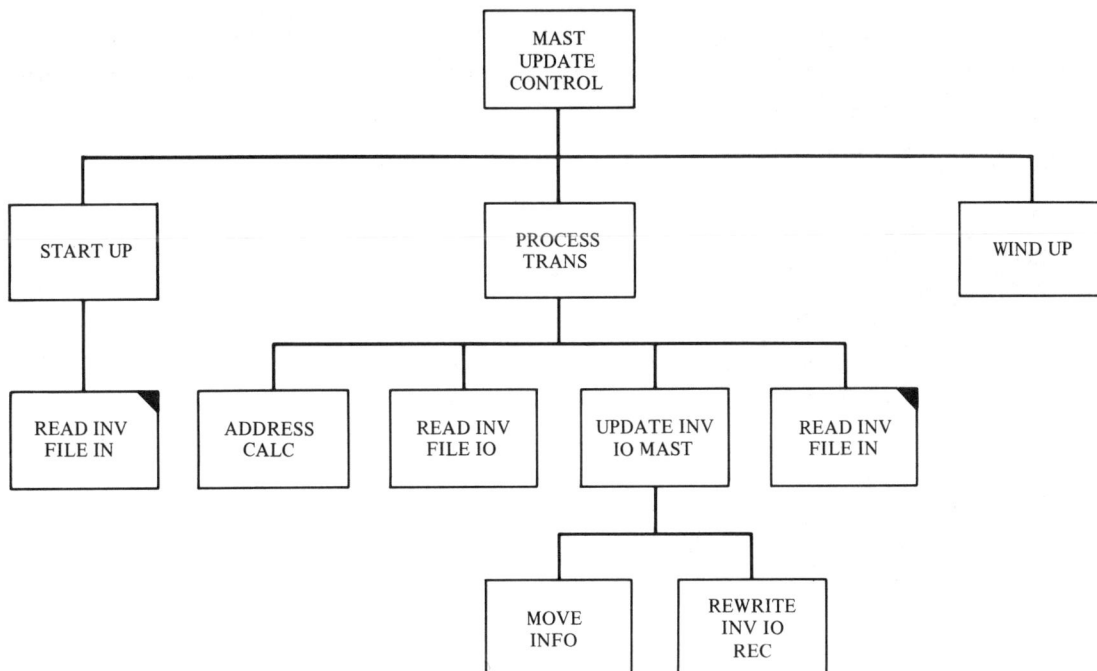

Figure 8.9
Structure chart for the program in Figure 8.10.

```
00001              IDENTIFICATION DIVISION.
00002         *
00003              PROGRAM-ID.
00004                  EX-8-3.
00005         ****************************************************************
00006         *                                                              *
00007         *    PROGRAMMER TEAM            SUMMERS/WALSTROM/LINDAHL        *
00008         *    PROGAM COMPLETION DATE AUGUST 20, 1984                     *
00009         *                                                              *
00010         *                    PROGRAM SUMMARY                           *
00011         *    INPUT                                                     *
00012         *        THERE ARE TWO INPUT FILES, THE INVENTORY MASTER FILE  *
00013         *        AND THE FILE TO BE USED FOR UPDATING THE MASTER FILE  *
00014         *        RECORDS ON THE UPDATE FILE CONTAIN                    *
00015         *                - CATALOGUE NUMBER                            *
00016         *                - ITEM NAME                                   *
00017         *                - ITEM SIZE                                   *
00018         *                - ITEM COLOR                                  *
00019         *                - NUMBER OF ITEMS RECEIVED                    *
00020         *                - PRICE                                       *
00021         *                                                              *
00022         *    PROCESSING                                                *
00023         *        FOR EACH RECORD IN THE UPDATE FILE                    *
00024         *                - THE RECORD FROM THE MASTER FILE WITH THE SAME *
00025         *                  CATALOGUE NUMBER IS OBTAINED                 *
00026         *                - AN UNUSED ENTRY IN THE SIZE-COLOR TABLE IS   *
00027         *                  LOCATED USING INDEXING                      *
00028         *                - THE NEW SIZE-COLOR INFORMATION IS PLACED IN  *
00029         *                  THE SIZE-COLOR TABLE                        *
00030         *                                                              *
00031         *    OUTPUT                                                    *
00032         *                - THE UPDATED MASTER FILE                     *
00033         *                - A LIST OF RECORDS IN THE UPDATE FILE WITH    *
00034         *                  CATALOGUE NUMBERS NOT ON THE MASTER FILE     *
00035         *                  OR CATALOGUE NUMBERS OR RECORDS WHOSE SIZE-COLOR *
00036         *                  TABLE IS FULL                               *
00037         ****************************************************************
00038         *
00039              ENVIRONMENT DIVISION.
00040         *
00041              CONFIGURATION SECTION.
00042              SOURCE-COMPUTER.
00043                  IBM-370.
00044              OBJECT-COMPUTER.
00045                  IBM-370.
00046              INPUT-OUTPUT SECTION.
00047              FILE-CONTROL.
00048                  SELECT INV-MAST-FILE-IO
00049                      ASSIGN TO SYS023-DA-3330-W-INVFILE
00050                      ACCESS IS RANDOM
00051                      ACTUAL KEY IS RECORD-ACCESS-INFO.
00052                  SELECT INV-CHANGES-FILE-IN
00053                      ASSIGN TO SYS007-UR-2501-S.
00054         *
00055              DATA DIVISION.
00056         *
00057              FILE SECTION.
00058              FD  INV-MAST-FILE-IO
00059                      LABEL RECORDS ARE STANDARD.
00060              01  INV-IO-AREA                     PIC X(306).
00061              FD  INV-CHANGES-FILE-IN
00062                      LABEL RECORDS ARE OMITTED.
00063              01  INV-IN-CHANGES-AREA             PIC X(80).
00064         *
00065              WORKING-STORAGE SECTION.
00066              01  SWITCHES.
00067                  02  END-OF-CHANGES-FILE-SW      PIC X.
00068                      88  END-OF-CHANGES-FILE VALUE 'Y'.
00069                  02  ROOM-IN-TABLE-SW            PIC X.
00070                      88  ROOM-IN-TABLE           VALUE 'Y'.
00071                  02  NEW-CHANGE-REC-SW           PIC X.
00072                      88  NEW-CHANGE-REC      VALUE 'Y'.
00073                  02  PROCESSING-SHOULD-STOP-SW   PIC X.
00074                      88  PROCESSING-SHOULD-STOP    VALUE 'Y'.
00075                  02  CAT-NUM-ERROR-SW            PIC X.
00076                      88  CAT-NUM-ERROR              VALUE 'Y'.
00077                      88  NO-CAT-NUM-ERROR           VALUE 'N'.
```

Figure 8.10
Updating a direct file for Example 8.3.

Figure 8.10 (cont.)

```
00078              01    COUNTERS.
00079                    02    READ-TRY-COUNT                   PIC 9(2).
00080              01    CONSTANTS.
00081                    02    PRIME-FOR-DIVISOR                PIC S9(4) COMP SYNC
00082                                       VALUE 199.
00083                    02    MAX-TRACK-NUM                    PIC S9(4) COMP SYNC
00084                                       VALUE 199.
00085                    02    MAX-NUM-OF-TRIES                 PIC S9(2) VALUE 3.
00086              01    RECORD-ACCESS-INFO.
00087                    02    REL-TRACK-NUM                    PIC S9(8) COMP SYNC.
00088                    02    REL-KEY-CAT-NUM                  PIC S9(6).
00089              01    WORK-NUMS.
00090                    02    SAVE-CAT-NUM                     PIC S9(6) COMP SYNC.
00091                    02    QUOTIENT                         PIC S9(6) COMP SYNC.
00092              01    INV-IN-CHANGES-REC.
00093                    02    INV-IN-CAT-NUM                   PIC 9(6).
00094                    02    INV-IN-NAME                      PIC X(15).
00095                    02    INV-IN-SIZE                      PIC X(2).
00096                    02    INV-IN-COLOR                     PIC X(10).
00097                    02    INV-IN-NUM-OF-ITEMS              PIC 9(5).
00098                    02    INV-IN-REORDER-AMT               PIC 9(5).
00099                    02    INV-IN-ITEM-PRICE                PIC 9(3)V9(2).
00100                    02    FILLER                           PIC X(58).
00101              01    INV-IO-REC.
00102                    02    INV-IO-CAT-NUM                   PIC 9(6).
00103                    02    INV-IO-NAME                      PIC X(15).
00104                    02    INV-IO-NUM-IN-STOCK-TAB.
00105                          03    INV-IO-SIZE-COLOR-INFO
00106                                     OCCURS 5 TIMES
00107                                     INDEXED BY NUM-IN-STOCK-INDEX.
00108                                04    INV-IO-SIZE        PIC X(2).
00109                                04    INV-IO-COLOR       PIC X(10).
00110                                04    INV-IO-NUM-IN-STOCK PIC S9(5).
00111                                04    INV-IO-REORDER-AMT PIC S9(5).
00112                                04    INV-IO-ITEM-PRICE  PIC S9(3)V99.
00113                    02    FILLER                           PIC X(150).
00114        *
00115          PROCEDURE DIVISION.
00116        *
00117          MAST-UPDATE-CONTROL.
00118              PERFORM START-UP.
00119              PERFORM PROCESS-TRANS UNTIL PROCESSING-SHOULD-STOP.
00120              PERFORM WIND-UP.
00121              STOP RUN.
00122        *
00123          START-UP.
00124              OPEN INPUT INV-CHANGES-FILE-IN
00125                   I-O INV-MAST-FILE-IO.
00126              DISPLAY ' LIST OF RECORDS WITH ERRORS'
00127              MOVE 'N' TO END-OF-CHANGES-FILE-SW,
00128                   PROCESSING-SHOULD-STOP-SW.
00129              MOVE 0 TO READ-TRY-COUNT.
00130              PERFORM READ-INV-FILE-IN.
00131        *
00132          PROCESS-TRANS.
00133              MOVE 'N' TO CAT-NUM-ERROR-SW.
00134              MOVE 'Y' TO NEW-CHANGE-REC-SW.
00135              PERFORM ADDRESS-CALC.
00136              PERFORM READ-INV-FILE-IO.
00137              ADD 1 TO READ-TRY-COUNT.
00138              IF NO-CAT-NUM-ERROR
00139                   PERFORM UPDATE-INV-IO-MAST
00140              ELSE
00141                   IF READ-TRY-COUNT IS LESS THAN MAX-NUM-OF-TRIES
00142                        MOVE 'N' TO NEW-CHANGE-REC-SW
00143                   ELSE
00144                        DISPLAY ' CAT NUMBER NOT FOUND ',
00145                             INV-IN-CHANGES-REC
00146                        MOVE 'Y' TO NEW-CHANGE-REC-SW.
00147              IF NEW-CHANGE-REC
00148                   MOVE 0 TO READ-TRY-COUNT
00149              PERFORM READ-INV-FILE-IN.
00150        *
00151          WIND-UP.
00152              CLOSE INV-MAST-FILE-IO, INV-CHANGES-FILE-IN.
00153              IF END-OF-CHANGES-FILE
00154                   DISPLAY ' CHANGES TO MAST FILE COMPLETE'
00155              ELSE
00156                   DISPLAY ' PROCESSING DIFFICULTY', INV-IO-REC.
```

Figure 8.10 (cont.)

```
00157         *
00158             ADDRESS-CALC.
00159                 IF READ-TRY-COUNT = 0
00160                     MOVE INV-IN-CAT-NUM TO REL-KEY-CAT-NUM,
00161                                             SAVE-CAT-NUM
00162                     DIVIDE SAVE-CAT-NUM BY PRIME-FOR-DIVISOR
00163                             GIVING QUOTIENT REMAINDER REL-TRACK-NUM
00164                 ELSE
00165                     ADD 1 TO REL-TRACK-NUM.
00166                 IF REL-TRACK-NUM IS GREATER THAN  MAX-TRACK-NUM
00167                     MOVE 0 TO REL-TRACK-NUM.
00168         *
00169             UPDATE-INV-IO-MAST.
00170                 SET NUM-IN-STOCK-INDEX TO 1.
00171                 SEARCH INV-IO-SIZE-COLOR-INFO
00172                     AT END MOVE 'N' TO ROOM-IN-TABLE-SW
00173                     WHEN INV-IO-SIZE-COLOR-INFO (NUM-IN-STOCK-INDEX)
00174                                             = SPACE
00175                         MOVE 'Y' TO ROOM-IN-TABLE-SW.
00176                 IF ROOM-IN-TABLE
00177                     PERFORM MOVE-INFO
00178                     PERFORM REWRITE-INV-IO-REC
00179                 ELSE
00180                         DISPLAY ' RECORD FULL', INV-IN-CHANGES-REC.
00181         *
00182             MOVE-INFO.
00183                 IF INV-IN-NAME IS NOT EQUAL TO SPACE
00184                     MOVE INV-IN-NAME TO INV-IO-NAME.
00185                 MOVE INV-IN-SIZE TO INV-IO-SIZE (NUM-IN-STOCK-INDEX).
00186                 MOVE INV-IN-NUM-OF-ITEMS TO INV-IO-NUM-IN-STOCK
00187                                         (NUM-IN-STOCK-INDEX).
00188                 MOVE INV-IN-COLOR TO INV-IO-COLOR (NUM-IN-STOCK-INDEX).
00189                 MOVE INV-IN-REORDER-AMT TO INV-IO-REORDER-AMT
00190                                         (NUM-IN-STOCK-INDEX).
00191                 MOVE INV-IN-ITEM-PRICE TO INV-IO-ITEM-PRICE
00192                                         (NUM-IN-STOCK-INDEX).
00193         *
00194             READ-INV-FILE-IO.
00195                 READ INV-MAST-FILE-IO INTO INV-IO-REC
00196                     INVALID KEY MOVE 'Y' TO CAT-NUM-ERROR-SW.
00197         *
00198             READ-INV-FILE-IN.
00199                 READ INV-CHANGES-FILE-IN INTO INV-IN-CHANGES-REC
00200                     AT END MOVE 'Y' TO END-OF-CHANGES-FILE-SW
00201                                         PROCESSING-SHOULD-STOP-SW.
00202         *
00203             REWRITE-INV-IO-REC.
00204                 REWRITE INV-IO-AREA FROM INV-IO-REC
00205                     INVALID KEY MOVE 'Y' TO PROCESSING-SHOULD-STOP-SW.
```

ADVANTAGES AND DISADVANTAGES OF DIRECT FILES

The following are among the advantages of direct files:

1. Processing of unsequenced transactions is possible. This eliminates the need to sort transactions.
2. Transactions may be processed immediately or batched for later processing.
3. Updating records does not require re-creation of the file.
4. Adding records does not require re-creation of the file.

Disadvantages of direct files include:

1. Processing overflow records involves extra computer time and increases program complexity.
2. There will nearly always be wasted space in a direct file. It is difficult to develop a method of deriving track identifier values that will result in records being

uniformly distributed throughout the entire file. Typically, some tracks will overflow while other tracks will not be filled.

3. A large number of synonyms, or an increase or decrease in the file size, will require reprogramming of the hashing technique.

4. Direct files are very device-oriented. Thus, changing from one type of disk device to another type with different characteristics (such as, different number of tracks per cylinder, different track capacities, different number of cylinders, and so on) will require reprogramming the hashing routine.

Programming Exercises for Chapter 8

Dr. James' Neighborhood Emporium

Dr. James, owner of Dr. James' Neighborhood Emporium, wants to computerize the prescription records for the pharmacy department.

There must be direct access to records by prescription number. Prescription numbers are assigned in the order that prescriptions are filled. When the prescription numbers reach 50,000, they will be started over again at 1. There will not be more than 10,000 prescriptions filled in one year.

The file is to have direct organization with .80 load factor and relative track addressing. Division-remainder hashing is to be used.

Each prescription record contains:

Record Position	Contents	Format
1–5	Prescription number	9(5)
16–30	Physician	X(15)
31–50	Patient name	X(20)
51–80	Patient address	X(30)
81–95	Medicine name	X(15)
96–105	Amount prescribed	X(10)
106–108	Number of refills allowed	9(3)
109–114	Date first dispensed	9(6)
115–119	Charge	9(3)V9(2)
120–125	Date refilled	9(6)
126–130	Charge	9(3)V9(2)
.		
.		
.		
230–235	Date refilled	9(6)
236–240	Charge	9(3)V9(2).

The record contains space for a maximum of 12 dates and charges, which will allow for filling the prescription up to 12 times (fields are blank until refills occur).

The prescription file will be used with Exercises 8.1 and 8.2.

EXERCISE 8.1

Write a program that updates the master prescription file just described. The program should allow for

1. Adding a new prescription record.
2. Updating an existing prescription record for a refill. The update should be rejected if dispensing the drug will exceed the number of refills allowed.

A record to be added to the file contains the same information as positions 1–119 in the master prescription file records. In addition, an 'A' appears in column 120. A record for a prescription refill contains the prescription number (1–5), date (6–11), the charge (11–15), and a code of 'R' in column 120.

EXERCISE 8.2

Write a program that lists all prescriptions in the prescription file that were filled for the first time more than one year ago.

Western State University

Western State University maintains a master file of directory information, which can be released to interested individuals.

Records have the following format:

Record Positions	Contents	Format
1–6	Student number	9(6)
7–26	Student name	X(20)
27–66	Address	X(40)
67–73	Phone number	X(7)

The file has direct organization with relative track addressing. The record identifier is the student number, and this field should also be used to determine the relative track number.

The master directory file for the university will be used with Exercises 8.3 and 8.4.

EXERCISE 8.3

You are to write a program that will change information in the master directory file. Input records have the same form as master records. The student number is always present; however, only fields that need to be changed in the master record are entered in the input record. All other fields are blank.

EXERCISE 8.4

At the beginning of each academic year, Western State University uses the directory master file to prepare a student directory. This directory is printed in alphabetical order by student name. Access the directory master file sequentially and use an INPUT PROCEDURE with the SORT verb to produce a file in the appropriate sequence for printing the directory.

The problems encountered in the daily operation of a data processing department will, in general, require programs that are much longer and more complex than any presented in this text. Large problems can often be subdivided into smaller problems, each requiring a relatively short and simple program for its solution. For these programs to be combined to generate an overall problem solution, some technique must be used to allow for communication between each of the separate programs. Control must be passed from one program to another as needed, and data items needed by several programs must be shared. Three advantages of this approach are (1) testing and debugging can be done on the smaller units; (2) common code used in multiple programs can be placed in a library, thus reducing the amount of duplicate code a programmer must write; and (3) a different programmer may work independently on each of these shorter programs, thereby reducing the length of time required to complete the total project.

Interprogram communication requires the specification of how control is to be transferred from one program to another and the designation of shared data items.

The various separately compiled programs will be combined by the operating system into a *run unit*. (A run unit consists of all machine code necessary to solve the problem.) Although the source programs may be in different languages, we will consider only the situation in which all the source programs are written in COBOL. The program in which execution of the run unit begins is generally referred to as the *main program*. The others are referred to as *subprograms*. A *calling program* transfers control to another program. The program to which control is transferred is a *called program*.

A program may be both a calling and a called program. That is, a called program may itself call another program.

In a called program, shared data items are described in the LINKAGE SECTION of the DATA DIVISION. No storage will be reserved in the called program for these items, as space has already been allocated in the calling program. The descriptions (such as PIC clause, USAGE clause, and so on) of the shared data items in the called program must be compatible, with respect to length and intended use, with the description given in the calling program. The PROCEDURE DIVISION statement in a called program contains a list of the shared data items.

DATA DIVISION ENTRIES

The general form of the DATA DIVISION for a called program is

```
DATA DIVISION.
[FILE SECTION.

        .

        .

        .          ]
[WORKING-STORAGE SECTION.

        .

        .

        .          ]
[LINKAGE SECTION.

        .

        .

        .          ]
```

Sections must be written in the order shown. Descriptions in the LINKAGE SECTION have the same form as entries in the WORKING-STORAGE SECTION. VALUE clauses are allowed only for 88-level items.

Items defined in the LINKAGE SECTION may be referenced in the PROCEDURE DIVISION only if they appear as

1. An operand of a USING clause.
2. A data item subordinate to an operand and the USING clause.
3. A data name associated with a USING operand such as a condition name.

PROCEDURE DIVISION ENTRIES

The PROCEDURE DIVISION statement in a called subprogram must contain a USING clause to specify the shared data items.

FORMAT
PROCEDURE DIVISION
[USING data-name-1, data-name-2, . . .]

The items in the USING clause must be defined in the LINKAGE SECTION at either the 01 or 77 level. These data names specify all shared data.

The CALL statement is used in the calling program to transfer control to a subprogram.

FORMAT

CALL 'subprogram name'

    [USING data-name-1, data-name-2, . . .]

The data items in the USING clause must be 01- or 77-level data items in the DATA DIVISION of the calling program. They may *not* be items in the REPORT SECTION (discussed in Chapter 10). Since the name of the subprogram must be known to the operating system, and because most operating systems will truncate or modify subprogram names, care must be taken in choosing the name so duplicates do not result from the operating system modifications.

The program containing the CALL statement is the calling program, whereas the program whose name appears in the CALL statement is the subprogram.

When a CALL is issued, subprogram execution begins with the first nondeclarative statement in the PROCEDURE DIVISION. Each time a called program is entered, all data items in the subprogram retain the values they had at the completion of the previous execution of the subprogram. If values initialized in the DATA DIVISION of a called program are altered during execution, they will *not be reinitialized* on later calls.

The EXIT PROGRAM statement is used in a subprogram to transfer control back to the calling program.

FORMAT

paragraph-name.

    EXIT PROGRAM.

Execution of this statement causes termination of the subprogram. The next statement following the CALL statement that transferred control to the subprogram will then be executed. The relationships between calling and called programs are illustrated in Figure 9.1.

There are two sets of data names that must be specified, one set in the calling program and the second set in the called program. Each program must use the names defined in its own DATA DIVISION. The names specified in the LINKAGE SECTION of COMPUTE-GPA in Figure 9.1 refer to exactly the same storage as the WORKING-STORAGE names given in CALLER-PROGRAM.

```
IDENTIFICATION DIVISION.
*
PROGRAM-ID.
    CALLER-PROGRAM.
    . . .
*
DATA DIVISION.
*
    . . .
*
WORKING-STORAGE SECTION.
01  SHARED-DATA-LIST.
    02  CREDIT-HOURS        PIC 9(4).
    02  HONOR-POINTS        PIC 9(5).
    02  GPA                 PIC 9V9(3).
    . . .
*
PROCEDURE DIVISION.
*
    . . .
    CALL 'COMPUTE-GPA'
        USING SHARED-DATA-LIST.
    . . .
    STOP RUN.
```

```
IDENTIFICATION DIVISION.
*
PROGRAM-ID.
    COMPUTE-GPA.
    . . .
*
DATA DIVISION.
*
    . . .
*
LINKAGE SECTION.
01  PROC-USING-LIST.
    02  LS-CREDIT-HOURS     PIC 9(4).
    02  LS-HONOR-POINTS     PIC 9(5).
    02  LS-GPA              PIC 9V9(3).
    . . .
*
PROCEDURE DIVISION
    USING PROC-USING-LIST.
*
    . . .
    COMPUTE LS-GPA = LS-HONOR-POINTS / LS-CREDIT-HOURS.
    . . .
*
GO-BACK-TO-CALLER.
    EXIT PROGRAM.
```

Figure 9.1
Relationship between calling program and called program.

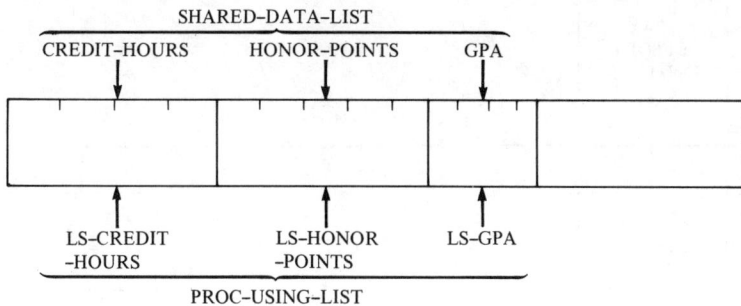

We will now consider several examples from previous chapters to explore subprogram concepts further.

Example 9.1

This example is based on an earlier one, Example 2.1, in Chapter 2. Recall that each employee's input data contained employee social security number, name, pay rate, and an hours-worked-per-day table.

We will modify the program solution given in Figure 2.3 so that the employee's gross pay is computed in a subprogram. You are urged to compare the two program organizations.

A hierarchy chart for the calling program is given in Figure 9.2. Since only sequential execution is used in the subprogram, its structure chart will be omitted. Note the new symbol for the execution of the subprogram COMPUTE-PAY. This is called a *predefined process symbol*.

The program listing of the calling program is given in Figure 9.3. Its structure is very similar to the program in Figure 2.2. On line 159, the CALL statement causes a transfer to the subprogram COMPUTE-PAY. The contents of all data items that appear in the description of EMP-TOTALS and PAY-WORK-RATE in the main program are available to be used by the subprogram COMPUTE-PAY. After execution of COMPUTE-PAY is complete, control will return to the calling program and execution will resume at line 160.

In Figure 9.4, the listing for the subprogram COMPUTE-PAY is given. The data items listed in WORKING-STORAGE are not shared with the main program. The items in the LINKAGE SECTION have descriptions that match those given for the corresponding items in the calling program. The order in which the shared items are listed on line 45 matches the order given in the CALL statement.

The EXIT PROGRAM statement on line 59 causes transfer of control back to the calling program.

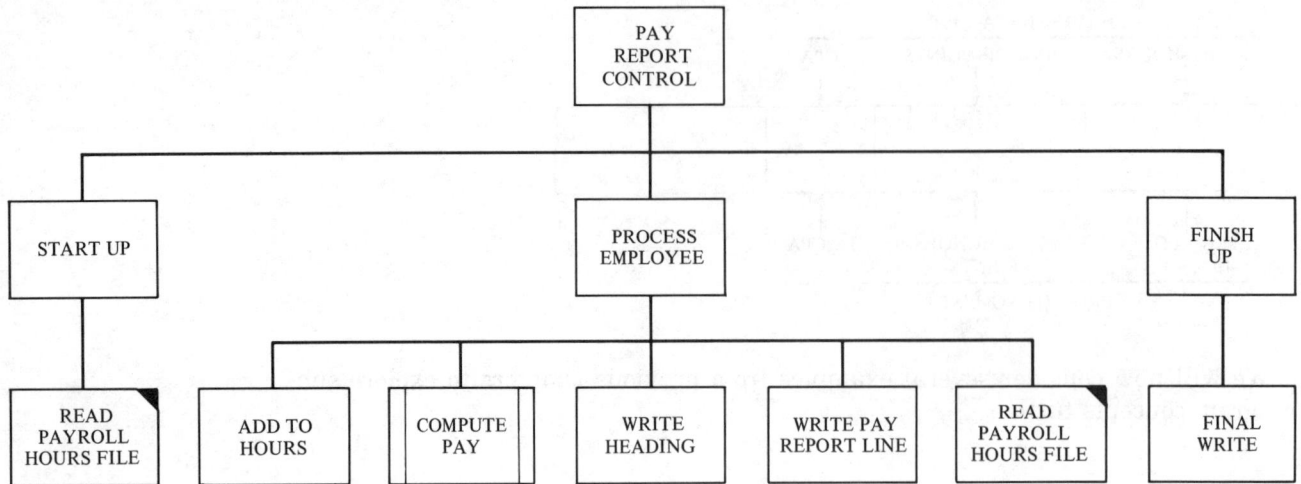

Figure 9.2
Structure chart for the calling program in Figure 9.3.

```
00001              IDENTIFICATION DIVISION.
00002          *
00003            PROGRAM-ID.
00004              EX-9-1.
00005          ***************************************************************
00006          *                                                             *
00007          *   PROGRAMMER TEAM            SUMMERS/WALSTROM/LINDAHL        *
00008          *   PROGRAM COMPLETION DATE OCTOBER 15, 1984                  *
00009          *                                                             *
00010          *                  PROGRAM SUMMARY                            *
00011          *   INPUT                                                     *
00012          *       EACH EMPLOYEE INPUT RECORD CONTAINS                   *
00013          *            - SOCIAL SECURITY NUMBER                         *
00014          *            - NAME                                           *
00015          *            - HOURLY PAY RATE                                *
00016          *            - NUMBER OF HOURS WORKED FOR EACH DAY OF THE WEEK *
00017          *                                                             *
00018          *   PROCESSING                                                *
00019          *            - THE TOTAL NUMBER OF HOURS WORKED FOR AN EMPLOYEE*
00020          *              IS COMPUTED USING A SUBSCRIPTED TABLE FOR       *
00021          *              THE DAILY HOURS WORKED                         *
00022          *            - THE GROSS PAY FOR AN EMPLOYEE IS COMPUTED       *
00023          *              USING THE EXTERNAL SUBPROGRAM COMPUTE-PAY       *
00024          *            - THE NUMBER OF REGULAR AND OVERTIME HOURS IS     *
00025          *              COMPUTED                                       *
00026          *            - TOTALS FOR REGULAR AND OVERTIME HOURS FOR ALL   *
00027          *              EMPLOYEES IS COMPUTED                          *
00028          *            - TOTAL GROSS PAY FOR ALL EMPLOYEES IS COMPUTED   *
00029          *                                                             *
00030          *   OUTPUT                                                    *
00031          *       A PRINTED REPORT IS PRODUCED. OUTPUT FOR AN EMPLOYEE   *
00032          *       CONSISTS OF                                           *
00033          *            - SOCIAL SECURITY NUMBER                         *
00034          *            - NAME                                           *
00035          *            - NUMBER OF HOURS WORKED AT REGULAR RATE         *
00036          *            - NUMBER OF HOURS WORKED AT OVERTIME RATE        *
00037          *            - PAY RATE                                       *
00038          *            - GROSS PAY                                      *
00039          *       OUTPUT FOR THE COMPANY CONSISTS OF                    *
00040          *            - TOTAL OF ALL EMPLOYEE HOURS WORKED             *
00041          *            - TOTAL OF ALL EMPLOYEE OVERTIME HOURS WORKED    *
00042          *            - TOTAL AMOUNT OF THE PAYROLL                    *
00043          ***************************************************************
```

Figure 9.3
Calling program to compute employee pay using a subprogram to calculate gross pay for Example 9.1.

Figure 9.3 (*cont.*)

```
00044              *
00045                ENVIRONMENT DIVISION.
00046              *
00047                CONFIGURATION SECTION.
00048                SOURCE-COMPUTER.
00049                    IBM-370.
00050                OBJECT-COMPUTER.
00051                    IBM-370.
00052                SPECIAL-NAMES.
00053                    C01 IS TO-TOP-OF-PAGE.
00054                INPUT-OUTPUT SECTION.
00055                FILE-CONTROL.
00056                    SELECT PAYROLL-HOURS-FILE-IN
00057                        ASSIGN TO SYS007-UR-2501-S.
00058                    SELECT PAYROLL-REPORT-PRINT-FILE
00059                        ASSIGN TO SYS009-UR-1403-S.
00060              *
00061                DATA DIVISION.
00062              *
00063                FILE SECTION.
00064                FD  PAYROLL-HOURS-FILE-IN
00065                        LABEL RECORDS ARE OMITTED.
00066                01  PAYROLL-HOURS-IN-AREA          PIC X(80).
00067                FD  PAYROLL-REPORT-PRINT-FILE
00068                        LABEL RECORDS ARE OMITTED.
00069                01  PAYROLL-REPORT-PRINT-AREA      PIC X(133).
00070              *
00071                WORKING-STORAGE SECTION.
00072                01  SWITCHES.
00073                    02  END-OF-PAY-DATA-SW         PIC X.
00074                        88  NO-MORE-PAY-DATA  VALUE 'Y'.
00075                01  COUNTERS.
00076                    02  HOURS-WORKED-COUNTER       PIC 9.
00077                    02  LINE-COUNT                 PIC 9(2).
00078                01  CONSTANTS.
00079                    02  NUM-DAYS-IN-WEEK           PIC 9 VALUE 7.
00080                    02  LINES-PER-PAGE             PIC 9(2) VALUE 55.
00081                01  PAY-WORK-RATE                  PIC 9(2)V9(3).
00082                01  EMP-TOTALS.
00083                    02  EMP-TOTAL-HOURS            PIC 9(2)V9(2).
00084                    02  EMP-TOTAL-OVERTIME         PIC 9(2)V9(2).
00085                    02  EMP-TOTAL-PAY              PIC 9(3)V9(2).
00086                01  COMPANY-TOTALS.
00087                    02  COM-TOTAL-HOURS            PIC 9(6)V9(2).
00088                    02  COM-TOTAL-OVERTIME         PIC 9(5)V9(2).
00089                    02  COM-TOTAL-PAY              PIC 9(8)V9(2).
00090                01  PAYROLL-HOURS-IN-REC.
00091                    02  PAY-IN-SS-NUM              PIC 9(9).
00092                    02  PAY-IN-NAME                PIC X(20).
00093                    02  PAY-IN-RATE                PIC 9(2)V9(3).
00094                    02  PAY-IN-HOURS-WORKED
00095                            OCCURS 7 TIMES         PIC 9(2)V9(2).
00096                    02  FILLER                     PIC X(18).
00097                01  PAY-REPORT-LINE.
00098                    02  FILLER                     PIC X(5) VALUE SPACE.
00099                    02  PAY-OUT-SS-NUM             PIC 9(9).
00100                    02  FILLER                     PIC X(5) VALUE SPACE.
00101                    02  PAY-OUT-NAME               PIC X(25).
00102                    02  PAY-OUT-REG-HOURS          PIC Z9.9(2).
00103                    02  FILLER                     PIC X(5) VALUE SPACE.
00104                    02  PAY-OUT-OVER-HOURS         PIC Z9.9(2).
00105                    02  FILLER                     PIC X(5) VALUE SPACE.
00106                    02  PAY-OUT-RATE               PIC Z9.9(3).
00107                    02  FILLER                     PIC X(5) VALUE SPACE.
00108                    02  PAY-OUT-TOTAL-PAY          PIC Z(2)9.9(2).
00109                01  HEADING-LINE.
00110                    02  FILLER                     PIC X(25)
00111                        VALUE '        SS NUM'.
00112                    02  FILLER                     PIC X(16)
00113                        VALUE 'NAME'.
00114                    02  FILLER                     PIC X(35)
00115                        VALUE 'REG HOURS   OVERTIME    RATE'.
00116                    02  FILLER                     PIC X(3) VALUE 'PAY'.
00117                01  STARLINE.
00118                    02  FILLER                     PIC X(133) VALUE ALL '*'.
```

Figure 9.3 *(cont.)*

```
00119              01   COMPANY-HOURS-LINE.
00120                   02   FILLER                          PIC X VALUE SPACE.
00121                   02   FILLER                          PIC X(30)
00122                        VALUE 'COMPANY TOTAL HOURS'.
00123                   02   COM-HOURS-OUT                    PIC Z(5)9.9(2).
00124              01   COMPANY-OVERTIME-LINE.
00125                   02   FILLER                          PIC X VALUE SPACE.
00126                   02   FILLER                          PIC X(30)
00127                        VALUE 'COMPANY TOTAL OVERTIME'.
00128                   02   COM-OVERTIME-OUT                 PIC Z(5)9.9(2).
00129              01   COMPANY-PAY-LINE.
00130                   02   FILLER                          PIC X VALUE SPACE.
00131                   02   FILLER                          PIC X(27)
00132                        VALUE 'COMPANY TOTAL PAYROLL'.
00133                   02   COM-PAY-OUT                      PIC $(8)9.9(2).
00134          *
00135          PROCEDURE DIVISION.
00136          *
00137          PAY-REPORT-CONTROL.
00138               PERFORM START-UP.
00139               PERFORM PROCESS-EMPLOYEE UNTIL NO-MORE-PAY-DATA.
00140               PERFORM FINISH-UP.
00141               STOP RUN.
00142          *
00143          START-UP.
00144               OPEN INPUT PAYROLL-HOURS-FILE-IN
00145                    OUTPUT PAYROLL-REPORT-PRINT-FILE.
00146               MOVE 'N' TO END-OF-PAY-DATA-SW.
00147               COMPUTE LINE-COUNT = LINES-PER-PAGE + 1.
00148               MOVE ZERO TO COM-TOTAL-HOURS,
00149                            COM-TOTAL-OVERTIME,
00150                            COM-TOTAL-PAY.
00151               PERFORM READ-PAYROLL-HOURS-FILE.
00152          *
00153          PROCESS-EMPLOYEE.
00154               MOVE ZERO TO EMP-TOTAL-HOURS.
00155               PERFORM ADD-TO-HOURS VARYING HOURS-WORKED-COUNTER
00156                    FROM 1 BY 1 UNTIL HOURS-WORKED-COUNTER IS
00157                    GREATER THAN NUM-DAYS-IN-WEEK.
00158               MOVE PAY-IN-RATE TO PAY-WORK-RATE.
00159               CALL 'COMPUTE-PAY' USING EMP-TOTALS, PAY-WORK-RATE.
00160               ADD EMP-TOTAL-HOURS TO COM-TOTAL-HOURS.
00161               ADD EMP-TOTAL-OVERTIME TO COM-TOTAL-OVERTIME.
00162               ADD EMP-TOTAL-PAY TO COM-TOTAL-PAY.
00163               COMPUTE PAY-OUT-REG-HOURS = EMP-TOTAL-HOURS -
00164                                            EMP-TOTAL-OVERTIME.
00165               MOVE PAY-IN-SS-NUM TO PAY-OUT-SS-NUM.
00166               MOVE PAY-IN-NAME TO PAY-OUT-NAME.
00167               MOVE EMP-TOTAL-OVERTIME TO PAY-OUT-OVER-HOURS.
00168               MOVE EMP-TOTAL-PAY TO PAY-OUT-TOTAL-PAY.
00169               MOVE PAY-IN-RATE TO PAY-OUT-RATE.
00170               IF LINE-COUNT IS GREATER THAN LINES-PER-PAGE
00171                    PERFORM WRITE-HEADING
00172                    MOVE ZERO TO LINE-COUNT.
00173               PERFORM WRITE-PAY-REPORT-LINE.
00174               ADD 1 TO LINE-COUNT.
00175               PERFORM READ-PAYROLL-HOURS-FILE.
00176          *
00177          FINISH-UP.
00178               MOVE COM-TOTAL-HOURS TO COM-HOURS-OUT.
00179               MOVE COM-TOTAL-OVERTIME TO COM-OVERTIME-OUT.
00180               MOVE COM-TOTAL-PAY TO COM-PAY-OUT.
00181               PERFORM FINAL-WRITE.
00182               CLOSE PAYROLL-HOURS-FILE-IN
00183                     PAYROLL-REPORT-PRINT-FILE.
00184          *
00185          ADD-TO-HOURS.
00186               ADD PAY-IN-HOURS-WORKED (HOURS-WORKED-COUNTER)
00187                   TO EMP-TOTAL-HOURS.
00188          *
00189          WRITE-HEADING.
00190               WRITE PAYROLL-REPORT-PRINT-AREA FROM HEADING-LINE
00191                   AFTER ADVANCING TO-TOP-OF-PAGE.
00192          *
00193          WRITE-PAY-REPORT-LINE.
00194               WRITE PAYROLL-REPORT-PRINT-AREA FROM PAY-REPORT-LINE
00195                   AFTER ADVANCING 1 LINES.
00196          *
00197          READ-PAYROLL-HOURS-FILE.
00198               READ PAYROLL-HOURS-FILE-IN INTO PAYROLL-HOURS-IN-REC
00199                   AT END MOVE 'Y' TO END-OF-PAY-DATA-SW.
```

Figure 9.3 (*cont.*)

```
00200        *
00201                FINAL-WRITE.
00202                    WRITE PAYROLL-REPORT-PRINT-AREA FROM STARLINE
00203                        AFTER ADVANCING 3 LINES.
00204                    WRITE PAYROLL-REPORT-PRINT-AREA FROM COMPANY-HOURS-LINE
00205                        AFTER ADVANCING 2 LINES.
00206                    WRITE PAYROLL-REPORT-PRINT-AREA FROM COMPANY-OVERTIME-LINE
00207                        AFTER ADVANCING 1 LINES.
00208                    WRITE PAYROLL-REPORT-PRINT-AREA FROM COMPANY-PAY-LINE
00209                        AFTER ADVANCING 1 LINES.
```

```
00001                IDENTIFICATION DIVISION.
00002        *
00003                PROGRAM-ID.
00004                    COMPUTE-PAY.
00005        ****************************************************************
00006        *                                                              *
00007        *     PROGRAMMER TEAM           SUMMERS/WALSTROM/LINDAHL        *
00008        *     PROGRAM COMPLETION DATE OCTOBER 10, 1984                  *
00009        *                                                              *
00010        *     DATA TO BE SUPPLIED BY CALLING PROGRAM                    *
00011        *             - TOTAL HOURS WORKED                              *
00012        *             - HOURLY PAY RATE                                 *
00013        *                                                              *
00014        *     DATA TO BE RETURNED TO CALLING PROGRAM                    *
00015        *             - OVERTIME HOURS                                  *
00016        *             - GROSS PAY                                       *
00017        *                                                              *
00018        *     PROCESSING                                                *
00019        *             - OVERTIME HOURS ARE COMPUTED                     *
00020        *             - GROSS PAY IS COMPUTED                           *
00021        ****************************************************************
00022        *
00023                ENVIRONMENT DIVISION.
00024        *
00025                CONFIGURATION SECTION.
00026                SOURCE-COMPUTER.
00027                    IBM-370.
00028                OBJECT-COMPUTER.
00029                    IBM-370.
00030        *
00031                DATA DIVISION.
00032        *
00033                WORKING-STORAGE SECTION.
00034                01   CONSTANTS.
00035                    02   REG-PAY-PERIOD              PIC 9(2) VALUE 40.
00036                    02   OVERTIME-RATE               PIC V9(2) VALUE .50.
00037        *
00038                LINKAGE SECTION.
00039                01   LS-EMP-TOTALS.
00040                    02   LS-EMP-TOTAL-HOURS          PIC 9(2)V9(2).
00041                    02   LS-EMP-TOTAL-OVERTIME       PIC 9(2)V9(2).
00042                    02   LS-EMP-TOTAL-PAY            PIC 9(3)V9(2).
00043                01   LS-PAY-RATE                     PIC 9(2)V9(3).
00044        *
00045                PROCEDURE DIVISION USING LS-EMP-TOTALS, LS-PAY-RATE.
00046        *
00047                COMPUTE-PAY-CONTROL.
00048                    COMPUTE LS-EMP-TOTAL-PAY = LS-EMP-TOTAL-HOURS * LS-PAY-RATE.
00049                    IF LS-EMP-TOTAL-HOURS IS GREATER THAN REG-PAY-PERIOD
00050                        COMPUTE LS-EMP-TOTAL-OVERTIME = LS-EMP-TOTAL-HOURS -
00051                                                        REG-PAY-PERIOD
00052                    ELSE
00053                        MOVE ZERO TO LS-EMP-TOTAL-OVERTIME.
00054                    COMPUTE LS-EMP-TOTAL-PAY = LS-EMP-TOTAL-PAY +
00055                                               LS-EMP-TOTAL-OVERTIME *
00056                                               OVERTIME-RATE * LS-PAY-RATE.
00057        *
00058                RETURN-TO-CALLER.
00059                    EXIT PROGRAM.
```

Figure 9.4
Called subprogram "COMPUTE-PAY" for Example 9.1.

As our next example, we will consider once again the payroll editing program presented in Chapter 4, Figure 4.5.

Example 9.2

Since the edit routine given in Figure 4.5 will be needed for other programs, we would like to have the program rewritten with the edit routine as a subprogram.

The structure chart for the calling program is given in Figure 9.5, with the listing of this program shown in Figure 9.6.

The CALL statement on line 165 transfers control to the subprogram EDIT-PAYROLL-DATA. Execution will resume in the main program with the statement on line 167. Note also that the data items on lines 90–100 and lines 128–145 are all available to the subprogram, should they be needed.

The listing for the subprogram EDIT-PAYROLL-DATA is given in Figure 9.7. Note there are no additional data defined in the subprogram—only shared data. The subprogram does not need all the data passed to it. Therefore, the description of the unneeded areas is specified as FILLER so that storage is matched properly.

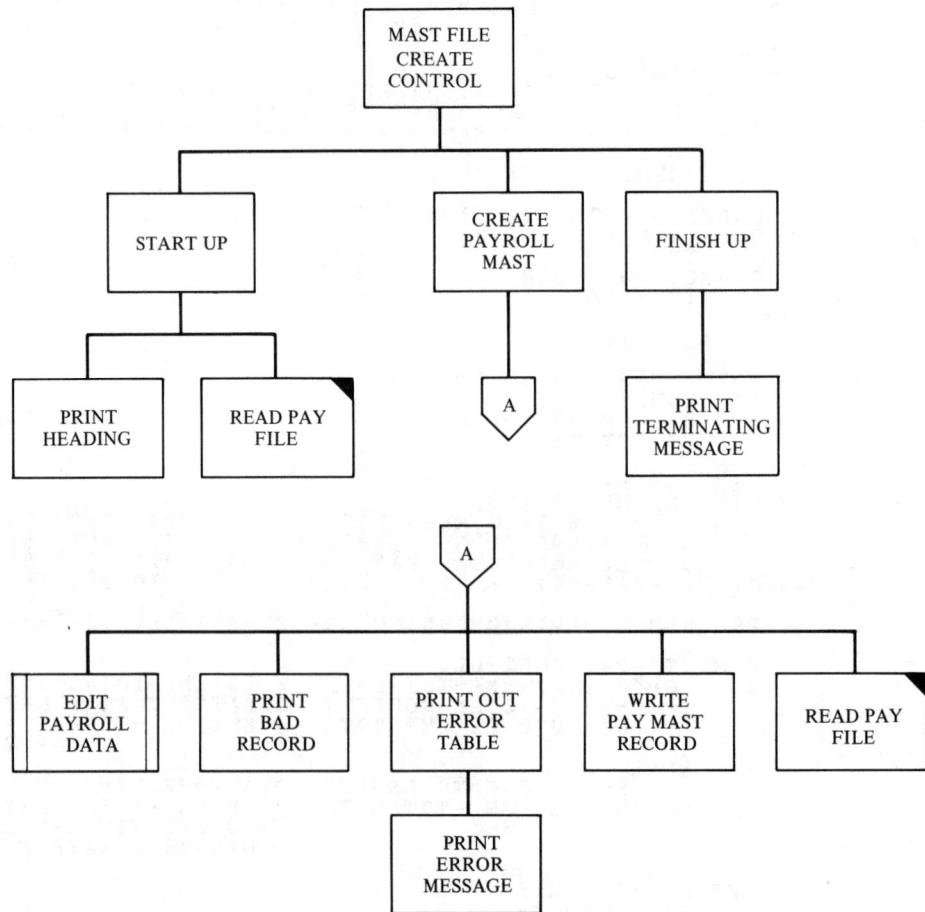

Figure 9.5
Structure chart for the calling program in Figure 9.6.

```
00001          IDENTIFICATION DIVISION.
00002      *
00003       PROGRAM-ID.
00004          EX-9-2.
00005      ***********************************************************************
00006      *                                                                     *
00007      *    PROGRAMMER TEAM          WALSTROM/SUMMERS/LINDAHL                 *
00008      *    PROGRAM COMPLETION DATE NOVEMBER 28,1983                          *
00009      *                                                                     *
00010      *                   PROGRAM SUMMARY                                    *
00011      *    INPUT                                                             *
00012      *        THE INPUT FILE IS IN ASCENDING ORDER                         *
00013      *        BY SOCIAL SECURITY NUMBER. EACH INPUT RECORD CONSISTS OF*
00014      *               - CODE FOR THE PLANT LOCATION                         *
00015      *               - CODE FOR THE DEPARTMENT TO WHICH THE EMPLOYEE       *
00016      *                 IS ASSIGNED                                         *
00017      *               - SOCIAL SECURITY NUMBER                              *
00018      *               - NAME                                                *
00019      *               - OTHER PERSONAL DATA                                 *
00020      *               - TAX CLASSIFICATION                                  *
00021      *               - PAY RATE                                            *
00022      *                                                                     *
00023      *    PROCESSING                                                        *
00024      *               - THE EMPLOYEE DATA IS CHECKED FOR ERRORS             *
00025      *                 USING THE SUBPROGRAM EDIT-PAYROLL-DATA              *
00026      *               - FOR A VALID INPUT RECORD, ZERO IS MOVED TO THE      *
00027      *                 YEAR-TO-DATE TOTALS FOR GROSS PAY, TAX WITHHELD     *
00028      *                 AND FICA WITHHELD                                   *
00029      *                                                                     *
00030      *    OUTPUT                                                            *
00031      *        FOR VALID EMPLOYEE INPUT DATA A RECORD IS OUTPUT TO          *
00032      *        A SEQUENTIAL DISK FILE. THIS FILE IS ORDERED BY             *
00033      *        SOCIAL SECURITY NUMBER. EACH RECORD CONSISTS OF            *
00034      *               - CODE FOR THE PLANT LOCATION                         *
00035      *               - CODE FOR THE DEPARTMENT TO WHICH THE EMPLOYEE       *
00036      *                 IS ASSIGNED                                         *
00037      *               - NAME                                                *
00038      *               - OTHER PERSONAL DATA                                 *
00039      *               - TAX CLASSIFICATION                                  *
00040      *               - PAY RATE                                            *
00041      *               - YEAR-TO-DATE TOTALS FOR GROSS PAY, TAX WITHHELD,    *
00042      *                 AND FICA WITHHELD                                   *
00043      *        FOR EMPLOYEE DATA WITH ERRORS A PRINTED REPORT IS           *
00044      *        PRODUCED. THE OUTPUT CONSISTS OF                             *
00045      *               - THE INPUT RECORD                                    *
00046      *               - A LIST OF ERROR MESSAGES DESCRIBING THE FIELDS      *
00047      *                 WHICH WERE ERRONEOUS                                *
00048      ***********************************************************************
00049      *
00050       ENVIRONMENT DIVISION.
00051      *
00052        CONFIGURATION SECTION.
00053        SOURCE-COMPUTER.
00054          IBM-370.
00055        OBJECT-COMPUTER.
00056          IBM-370.
00057        SPECIAL-NAMES.
00058          C01 IS TOP-OF-PAGE.
00059        INPUT-OUTPUT SECTION.
00060        FILE-CONTROL.
00061          SELECT PAYROLL-FILE-IN
00062             ASSIGN TO SYS007-UR-2501-S.
00063          SELECT PAYROLL-MAST-FILE-OUT
00064             ASSIGN TO SYS023-DA-3330-S-PAYFILE.
00065          SELECT ERROR-REPORT-PRINT-FILE
00066             ASSIGN TO SYS009-UR-1403-S.
00067      *
00068       DATA DIVISION.
00069      *
00070        FILE SECTION.
00071        FD  PAYROLL-FILE-IN
00072              LABEL RECORDS ARE OMITTED.
00073        01  PAYROLL-IN-AREA                    PIC X(80).
00074        FD  PAYROLL-MAST-FILE-OUT
00075              LABEL RECORDS ARE STANDARD
00076              BLOCK CONTAINS 10 RECORDS.
```

Figure 9.6

Calling program for data validation and sequential file creation using a subprogram to edit payroll data for Example 9.2.

Figure 9.6 (*cont.*)

```
00077            01    PAYROLL-MAST-OUT-AREA              PIC X(100).
00078            FD    ERROR-REPORT-PRINT-FILE
00079                     LABEL RECORDS ARE OMITTED.
00080            01    ERROR-LINE-OUT-AREA               PIC X(133).
00081         *
00082            WORKING-STORAGE SECTION.
00083            01    SWITCHES.
00084                  02    END-OF-FILE-SW              PIC X.
00085                        88    END-OF-FILE    VALUE 'Y'.
00086            01    COUNTERS.
00087                  02    ERR-SUB                     PIC 9.
00088            01    CONSTANTS.
00089                  02    NUMB-OF-ERROR-MESSAGES      PIC 9 VALUE 5.
00090            01    PAYROLL-IN-REC.
00091                  02    PAY-IN-PLANT-SITE           PIC 9.
00092                        88    POSSIBLE-PLANT-SITE    VALUES 1, 2.
00093                  02    PAY-IN-DEPT-CODE            PIC 9(2).
00094                        88    POSSIBLE-DEPT-CODE    VALUES 1 THRU 15.
00095                  02    PAY-IN-SS-NUM               PIC X(9).
00096                  02    PAY-IN-EMP-NAME             PIC X(20).
00097                  02    PAY-IN-PERSONAL-DATA        PIC X(42).
00098                  02    PAY-IN-TAX-CLASS            PIC 9(2).
00099                  02    PAY-IN-PAY-RATE             PIC 9(2)V9(2).
00100                        88    VALID-PAY-RATE    VALUES 3.35 THRU 18.75.
00101            01    PAYROLL-MAST-OUT-REC.
00102                  02    PAY-OUT-PLANT-SITE          PIC S9.
00103                  02    PAY-OUT-DEPT-CODE           PIC S9(2).
00104                  02    PAY-OUT-SS-NUM              PIC X(9).
00105                  02    PAY-OUT-EMP-NAME            PIC X(20).
00106                  02    PAY-OUT-PERSONAL-DATA       PIC X(42).
00107                  02    PAY-OUT-TAX-CLASS           PIC S9(2).
00108                  02    PAY-OUT-PAY-RATE            PIC S9(2)V9(2).
00109                  02    PAY-OUT-YTD-GROSS           PIC S9(5)V9(2).
00110                  02    PAY-OUT-YTD-TAX             PIC S9(5)V9(2).
00111                  02    PAY-OUT-YTD-FICA            PIC S9(4)V9(2).
00112            01    ERR-HDG-PRINT-LINE.
00113                  02    FILLER                      PIC X(47) VALUE SPACES.
00114                  02    FILLER                      PIC X(38)
00115                        VALUE 'LIST OF ERRORS IN PAYROLL DATA RECORDS'.
00116                  02    FILLER                      PIC X(47) VALUE SPACES.
00117            01    ERR-DETAIL-PRINT-LINE-1.
00118                  02    FILER                       PIC X(26) VALUE SPACES.
00119                  02    BAD-REC-OUT                 PIC X(80).
00120                  02    FILLER                      PIC X(26) VALUE SPACES.
00121            01    ERR-DETAIL-PRINT-LINE-2.
00122                  02    FILLER                      PIC X(58) VALUE SPACES.
00123                  02    ERR-MESSAGE-OUT             PIC X(17).
00124                  02    FILLER                      PIC X(57) VALUE SPACES.
00125            01    TERMINATING-MSG-PRINT-LINE.
00126                  02    FILLER                      PIC X(5) VALUE SPACE.
00127                  02    TERMINATING-MESSAGE         PIC X(127).
00128            01    ERROR-PROCESSING-TABLES.
00129                  02    ERROR-MESSAGE-SWITCH-TABLE.
00130                        03    ERROR-MESSAGE-SW
00131                              OCCURS 5 TIMES        PIC X.
00132                  02    ERROR-MESSAGE-CONTENT.
00133                        03    FILLER                PIC X(17)
00134                              VALUE 'PLANT SITE ERROR '.
00135                        03    FILLER                PIC X(17)
00136                              VALUE 'DEPT CODE ERROR  '.
00137                        03    FILLER                PIC X(17)
00138                              VALUE 'SOC SEC NUM ERROR'.
00139                        03    FILLER                PIC X(17)
00140                              VALUE 'TAX CLASS ERROR  '.
00141                        03    FILLER                PIC X(17)
00142                              VALUE 'PAY RATE ERROR   '.
00143                  02    ERROR-MESSAGE-TABLE REDEFINES ERROR-MESSAGE-CONTENT.
00144                        03    ERROR-MESSAGE
00145                              OCCURS 5 TIMES        PIC X(17).
00146         *
00147            PROCEDURE DIVISION.
00148         *
00149            MAST-FILE-CREATE-CONTROL.
00150                  PERFORM START-UP.
00151                  PERFORM CREATE-PAYROLL-MAST
00152                        UNTIL END-OF-FILE.
00153                  PERFORM FINISH-UP.
00154                  STOP RUN.
```

Figure 9.6 (*cont.*)

```
00155              *
00156                  START-UP.
00157                      OPEN INPUT PAYROLL-FILE-IN
00158                           OUTPUT PAYROLL-MAST-FILE-OUT
00159                                  ERROR-REPORT-PRINT-FILE.
00160                      MOVE 'N' TO END-OF-FILE-SW.
00161                      PERFORM PRINT-HEADING.
00162                      PERFORM READ-PAY-FILE.
00163              *
00164                  CREATE-PAYROLL-MAST.
00165                      CALL 'EDIT-PAYROLL-DATA'
00166                           USING PAYROLL-IN-REC, ERROR-PROCESSING-TABLES.
00167                      IF (ERROR-MESSAGE-SWITCH-TABLE IS NOT EQUAL TO ALL 'N')
00168                          MOVE PAYROLL-IN-REC TO BAD-REC-OUT
00169                          PERFORM PRINT-BAD-RECORD
00170                          PERFORM PRINT-OUT-ERROR-TABLE VARYING ERR-SUB FROM 1 BY 1
00171                              UNTIL ERR-SUB IS GREATER THAN NUMB-OF-ERROR-MESSAGES
00172                      ELSE
00173                          MOVE PAY-IN-PLANT-SITE TO PAY-OUT-PLANT-SITE
00174                          MOVE PAY-IN-DEPT-CODE TO PAY-OUT-DEPT-CODE
00175                          MOVE PAY-IN-SS-NUM TO PAY-OUT-SS-NUM
00176                          MOVE PAY-IN-EMP-NAME TO PAY-OUT-EMP-NAME
00177                          MOVE PAY-IN-PERSONAL-DATA TO PAY-OUT-PERSONAL-DATA
00178                          MOVE PAY-IN-TAX-CLASS TO PAY-OUT-TAX-CLASS
00179                          MOVE PAY-IN-PAY-RATE TO PAY-OUT-PAY-RATE
00180                          MOVE ZEROS TO PAY-OUT-YTD-GROSS
00181                                       PAY-OUT-YTD-TAX
00182                                       PAY-OUT-YTD-FICA
00183                          PERFORM WRITE-PAY-MAST-REC.
00184                      PERFORM READ-PAY-FILE.
00185              *
00186                  FINISH-UP.
00187                      IF END-OF-FILE
00188                          MOVE 'PAYROLL MASTER FILE CREATED'
00189                              TO TERMINATING-MESSAGE
00190                      ELSE
00191                          MOVE 'PROBLEM ENCOUNTERED CREATING PAYROLL MASTER FILE'
00192                              TO TERMINATING-MESSAGE.
00193                      PERFORM PRINT-TERMINATING-MESSAGE.
00194                      CLOSE PAYROLL-FILE-IN
00195                            PAYROLL-MAST-FILE-OUT
00196                            ERROR-REPORT-PRINT-FILE.
00197              *
00198                  PRINT-OUT-ERROR-TABLE.
00199                      IF (ERROR-MESSAGE-SW (ERR-SUB) IS EQUAL TO 'Y')
00200                          MOVE ERROR-MESSAGE (ERR-SUB) TO ERR-MESSAGE-OUT
00201                          PERFORM PRINT-ERROR-MESSAGE.
00202              *
00203                  PRINT-HEADING.
00204                      WRITE ERROR-LINE-OUT-AREA FROM ERR-HDG-PRINT-LINE
00205                          AFTER ADVANCING TOP-OF-PAGE.
00206              *
00207                  PRINT-TERMINATING-MESSAGE.
00208                      WRITE ERROR-LINE-OUT-AREA FROM TERMINATING-MSG-PRINT-LINE
00209                          AFTER ADVANCING TOP-OF-PAGE.
00210              *
00211                  PRINT-BAD-RECORD.
00212                      WRITE ERROR-LINE-OUT-AREA FROM ERR-DETAIL-PRINT-LINE-1
00213                          AFTER ADVANCING 3 LINES.
00214              *
00215                  WRITE-PAY-MAST-REC.
00216                      WRITE PAYROLL-MAST-OUT-AREA FROM PAYROLL-MAST-OUT-REC.
00217              *
00218                  READ-PAY-FILE.
00219                      READ PAYROLL-FILE-IN INTO PAYROLL-IN-REC
00220                          AT END MOVE 'Y' TO END-OF-FILE-SW.
00221              *
00222                  PRINT-ERROR-MESSAGE.
00223                      WRITE ERROR-LINE-OUT-AREA FROM ERR-DETAIL-PRINT-LINE-2
00224                          AFTER ADVANCING 1 LINES.
```

```
00001              IDENTIFICATION DIVISION.
00002          *
00003           PROGRAM-ID.
00004              EDIT-PAYROLL-DATA.
00005          ****************************************************************
00006          *                                                              *
00007          *    PROGRAMMER TEAM          WALSTROM/SUMMERS/LINDAHL          *
00008          *    PROGRAM COMPLETION DATE NOVEMBER 21, 1983                  *
00009          *                                                              *
00010          *    DATA TO BE SUPPLIED BY THE CALLING PROGRAM                 *
00011          *         - PLANT LOCATION CODE                                 *
00012          *         - DEPARTMENT CODE                                     *
00013          *         - SOCIAL SECURITY NUMBER                              *
00014          *         - TAX CLASSIFICATION                                  *
00015          *         - PAY RATE                                           *
00016          *                                                              *
00017          *    DATA TO BE RETURNED TO THE CALLING PROGRAM                 *
00018          *         - A SWITCH FOR EACH DATA ITEM SUPPLIED BY THE         *
00019          *           CALLING PROGRAM                                     *
00020          *                                                              *
00021          *    PROCESSING                                                 *
00022          *         - EACH DATA ITEM IS TESTED FOR PERMISSABLE VALUES     *
00023          *           AND A SWITCH IS SET TO INDICATE IF THE VALUE        *
00024          *           IS PERMISSABLE                                      *
00025          ****************************************************************
00026          *
00027           ENVIRONMENT DIVISION.
00028          *
00029           CONFIGURATION SECTION.
00030           SOURCE-COMPUTER.
00031              IBM-370.
00032           OBJECT-COMPUTER.
00033              IBM-370.
00034          *
00035           DATA DIVISION.
00036          *
00037           LINKAGE SECTION.
00038           01  LS-PAYROLL-REC.
00039               02  LS-PAY-PLANT-SITE            PIC 9.
00040                   88  POSSIBLE-PLANT-SITE VALUES 1 2.
00041               02  LS-PAY-DEPT-CODE            PIC 9(2).
00042                   88  POSSIBLE-DEPT-CODE VALUES 1 THRU 15.
00043               02  LS-PAY-SS-NUM              PIC 9(9).
00044               02  FILLER                     PIC X(62).
00045               02  LS-PAY-TAX-CLASS           PIC 9(2).
00046               02  LS-PAY-RATE                PIC 9(2)V9(2).
00047                   88  VALID-RATE VALUES 3.35 THRU 18.75.
00048           01  LS-ERROR-MESSAGE-SWITCH-TABLE.
00049               02  LS-ERROR-MESSAGE-SW
00050                   OCCURS 5 TIMES             PIC X.
00051               02  FILLER                     PIC X(85).
00052          *
00053           PROCEDURE DIVISION USING LS-PAYROLL-REC,
00054                                    LS-ERROR-MESSAGE-SWITCH-TABLE.
00055          *
00056           EDIT-PAYROLL-DATA-CONTROL.
00057               IF LS-PAY-PLANT-SITE IS NOT NUMERIC
00058                   MOVE 'Y' TO LS-ERROR-MESSAGE-SW (1)
00059               ELSE
00060                   IF NOT POSSIBLE-PLANT-SITE
00061                       MOVE 'Y' TO LS-ERROR-MESSAGE-SW (1)
00062                   ELSE
00063                       MOVE 'N' TO LS-ERROR-MESSAGE-SW (1).
00064
00065               IF LS-PAY-DEPT-CODE IS NOT NUMERIC
00066                   MOVE 'Y' TO LS-ERROR-MESSAGE-SW (2)
00067               ELSE
00068                   IF NOT POSSIBLE-DEPT-CODE
00069                       MOVE 'Y' TO LS-ERROR-MESSAGE-SW (2)
00070                   ELSE
00071                       MOVE 'N' TO LS-ERROR-MESSAGE-SW (2).
00072
00073               IF LS-PAY-SS-NUM IS NOT NUMERIC
00074                   MOVE 'Y' TO LS-ERROR-MESSAGE-SW (3)
00075               ELSE
```

Figure 9.7
Called subprogram "EDIT-PAYROLL-DATA" for Example 9.2.

Figure 9.7 (*cont.*)

```
00076                    MOVE 'N' TO LS-ERROR-MESSAGE-SW (3).
00077
00078              IF LS-PAY-TAX-CLASS IS NOT NUMERIC
00079                    MOVE 'Y' TO LS-ERROR-MESSAGE-SW (4)
00080              ELSE
00081                    MOVE 'N' TO LS-ERROR-MESSAGE-SW (4).
00082
00083
00084              IF LS-PAY-RATE IS NOT NUMERIC
00085                    MOVE 'Y' TO LS-ERROR-MESSAGE-SW (5)
00086              ELSE
00087                    IF NOT VALID-RATE
00088                          MOVE 'Y' TO LS-ERROR-MESSAGE-SW (5)
00089                    ELSE
00090                          MOVE 'N' TO LS-ERROR-MESSAGE-SW (5).
00091        *
00092           RETURN-TO-CALLER.
00093              EXIT PROGRAM.
```

As our next example, we will look again at the problem posed in Chapter 8, Example 8.2.

Example 9.3

All programs that access the master inventory file randomly will need to use the same hashing routine, the same limit on the number of attempts to access records, and the same overflow techniques used in the file load. The hashing and overflow routines will be coded as a subprogram.

The hierarchy chart for the nondeclaratives section of the calling program is given in Figure 9.8. The listing for the main program is given in Figure 9.9.

The CALL statement (line 119) in the main program that invokes the subprogram CREATE-ACCESS-INFO causes the track identifier to be computed and placed in REL-TRACK-NUM. This is done for an overflow record, as well as for a record that needs only hashing of the initial track identifier.

The listing for CREATE-ACCESS-INFO is given in Figure 9.10. It is important to note that the catalogue number must be moved to REC-KEY-CAT-NUM (line 118 in main program) before the transfer to the subprogram CREATE-ACCESS-INFO, since the subprogram has no access to INV-IN-CAT-NUM.

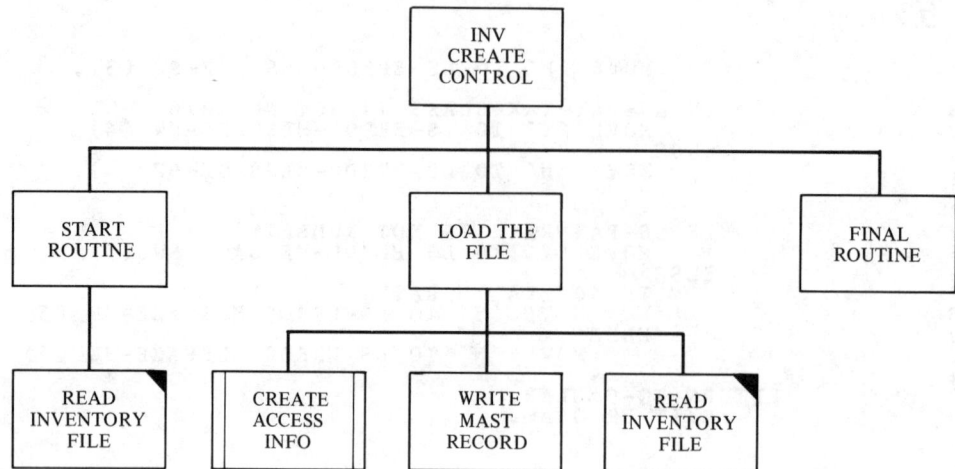

Figure 9.8
Structure chart for non-DECLARATIVES section of the calling program in Figure 9.9.

```
00001          IDENTIFICATION DIVISION.
00002        *
00003          PROGRAM-ID.
00004              EX-9-3.
00005        ************************************************************************
00006        *                                                                      *
00007        *    PROGRAMMER TEAM          SUMMERS/WALSTROM/LINDAHL                  *
00008        *    PROGRAM COMPLETION DATE AUGUST 9, 1984                            *
00009        *                                                                      *
00010        *                    PROGRAM SUMMARY                                   *
00011        *    INPUT                                                             *
00012        *        EACH RECORD CONTAINS                                          *
00013        *            - CATALOGUE NUMBER                                        *
00014        *            - NAME OF THE ITEM                                        *
00015        *            - A TABLE CONTAINING IN EACH TABLE ENTRY:                 *
00016        *              SIZE, COLOR, NUMBER IN STOCK, REORDER AMOUNT,           *
00017        *              PRICE                                                   *
00018        *            - CATALOGUE DESCRIPTION                                   *
00019        *                                                                      *
00020        *    PROCESSING                                                        *
00021        *        EACH RECORD IS ASSIGNED A RELATIVE TRACK NUMBER               *
00022        *    USING THE SUBPROGRAM CREATE-ACCESS-INFO                           *
00023        *            - DIVISION REMAINDER HASHING IS USED                      *
00024        *            - NEXT AVAILABLE TRACK OVERFLOW HANDLING IS DONE          *
00025        *                                                                      *
00026        *    OUTPUT                                                            *
00027        *            - A COPY OF THE INPUT FILE WITH DIRECT ORGANIZATION*
00028        *            - A PROGRAM OUTCOME MESSAGE                               *
00029        ************************************************************************
00030        *
00031          ENVIRONMENT DIVISION.
00032        *
00033          CONFIGURATION SECTION.
00034          SOURCE-COMPUTER.
00035              IBM-370.
00036          OBJECT-COMPUTER.
00037              IBM-370.
00038          INPUT-OUTPUT SECTION.
00039          FILE-CONTROL.
00040              SELECT INVEN-MAST-FILE-OUT
00041                  ASSIGN TO SYS023-DA-3330-W-INVFILE
00042                  ACCESS IS RANDOM
00043                  ACTUAL KEY IS RECORD-ACCESS-INFO.
00044              SELECT INVENTORY-FILE-IN
00045                  ASSIGN TO SYS023-DA-3330-S-DATFILE.
```

Figure 9.9
Calling program for creation of a direct file using a subprogram for the address hashing and record overflow routines for Example 9.3.

Figure 9.9 (*cont.*)

```
00046              *
00047                DATA DIVISION.
00048              *
00049                FILE SECTION.
00050                FD  INVEN-MAST-FILE-OUT
00051                        LABEL RECORDS ARE STANDARD.
00052                01  INVEN-OUT-AREA                 PIC X(306).
00053                FD  INVENTORY-FILE-IN
00054                        LABEL RECORDS ARE STANDARD
00055                        BLOCK CONTAINS 20 RECORDS.
00056                01  INVEN-IN-AREA                  PIC X(306).
00057              *
00058                WORKING-STORAGE SECTION.
00059                01  SWITCHES.
00060                    02  STOP-PROCESSING-SW             PIC X.
00061                        88  STOP-PROCESSING   VALUE 'Y'.
00062                    02  WRITE-STATUS-SW               PIC X.
00063                        88  NO-ROOM-FOUND     VALUE 'F'.
00064                        88  GOOD-WRITE        VALUE 'G'.
00065                        88  BAD-KEY           VALUE 'I'.
00066                    02  END-OF-INPUT-SW               PIC X.
00067                        88  NO-MORE-INPUT     VALUE 'Y'.
00068                    02  NEW-INPUT-RECORD-SW          PIC X.
00069                        88  NEW-INPUT-RECORD VALUE 'Y'.
00070                01  DECLARATIVES-ERROR-STATUS.
00071                    02  FILLER                        PIC X(2).
00072                    02  TRACK-FULL-ERROR             PIC 9.
00073                        88  TRACK-IS-FULL    VALUE 1.
00074                    02  FILLER                        PIC 9(5).
00075                01  COUNTERS.
00076                    02  WRITE-TRY-COUNT              PIC 9(2).
00077                01  CONSTANTS.
00078                    02  MAX-NUM-OF-TRIES             PIC S9(2) VALUE 3.
00079                01  RECORD-ACCESS-INFO.
00080                    02  REL-TRACK-NUMBER             PIC S9(8) COMP SYNC.
00081                    02  REC-KEY-CAT-NUM              PIC S9(6).
00082                01  INVENTORY-IN-REC.
00083                    02  INV-IN-CAT-NUM               PIC 9(6).
00084                    02  FILLER                        PIC X(300).
00085              *
00086                PROCEDURE DIVISION.
00087              *
00088                DECLARATIVES.
00089                TRACK-OVERFLOW SECTION.
00090                    USE AFTER STANDARD ERROR PROCEDURE ON INVEN-MAST-FILE-OUT
00091                        GIVING DECLARATIVES-ERROR-STATUS.
00092                CHECK-STANDARD-ERROR-TYPE.
00093                    IF TRACK-IS-FULL
00094                        MOVE 'F' TO WRITE-STATUS-SW
00095                        MOVE 'N' TO NEW-INPUT-RECORD-SW
00096                    ELSE
00097                        MOVE 'O' TO WRITE-STATUS-SW
00098                        MOVE 'Y' TO STOP-PROCESSING-SW.
00099                END DECLARATIVES.
00100              *
00101                INV-CREATE SECTION.
00102                INV-CREATE-CONTROL.
00103                    PERFORM START-ROUTINE.
00104                    PERFORM LOAD-THE-FILE UNTIL STOP-PROCESSING.
00105                    PERFORM FINAL-ROUTINE.
00106                    STOP RUN.
00107              *
00108                START-ROUTINE.
00109                    OPEN INPUT INVENTORY-FILE-IN
00110                        OUTPUT INVEN-MAST-FILE-OUT.
00111                    MOVE 'Y' TO NEW-INPUT-RECORD-SW.
00112                    MOVE 'N' TO END-OF-INPUT-SW, STOP-PROCESSING-SW.
00113                    PERFORM READ-INVENTORY-FILE.
```

Figure 9.9 (*cont.*)

```
00114               *
00115                   LOAD-THE-FILE.
00116                       IF NEW-INPUT-RECORD
00117                           MOVE ZERO TO WRITE-TRY-COUNT
00118                           MOVE INV-IN-CAT-NUM TO REC-KEY-CAT-NUM.
00119                       CALL 'CREATE-ACCESS-INFO' USING
00120                           RECORD-ACCESS-INFO, COUNTERS.
00121                       MOVE 'G' TO WRITE-STATUS-SW.
00122                       PERFORM WRITE-MAST-RECORD.
00123                       IF GOOD-WRITE
00124                           MOVE 'Y' TO NEW-INPUT-RECORD-SW
00125                           PERFORM READ-INVENTORY-FILE
00126                       ELSE
00127                           IF NO-ROOM-FOUND
00128                               ADD 1 TO WRITE-TRY-COUNT
00129                           ELSE
00130                               IF BAD-KEY
00131                                   DISPLAY 'BAD KEY', REC-KEY-CAT-NUM,
00132                                       ' TRACK NUM', REL-TRACK-NUMBER
00133                               ELSE
00134                                   DISPLAY 'OTHER STANDARD ERROR',
00135                                       ' CATALOGUE NUMBER', REC-KEY-CAT-NUM.
00136                       IF WRITE-TRY-COUNT IS EQUAL TO MAX-NUM-OF-TRIES
00137                           MOVE 'Y' TO STOP-PROCESSING-SW.
00138               *
00139                   FINAL-ROUTINE.
00140                       IF NO-MORE-INPUT
00141                           DISPLAY 'DIRECT ACCESS FILE CREATED'
00142                       ELSE
00143                           DISPLAY ' PROBLEM IN CREATING THE FILE'
00144                           DISPLAY ' LAST RECORD READ', INVENTORY-IN-REC.
00145                       CLOSE INVENTORY-FILE-IN, INVEN-MAST-FILE-OUT.
00146               *
00147                   WRITE-MAST-RECORD.
00148                       WRITE INVEN-OUT-AREA FROM INVENTORY-IN-REC
00149                           INVALID KEY MOVE 'I' TO WRITE-STATUS-SW
00150                                       MOVE 'Y' TO STOP-PROCESSING-SW.
00151               *
00152                   READ-INVENTORY-FILE.
00153                       READ INVENTORY-FILE-IN INTO INVENTORY-IN-REC
00154                           AT END MOVE 'Y' TO STOP-PROCESSING-SW,
00155                                               END-OF-INPUT-SW.
```

```
00001               IDENTIFICATION DIVISION.
00002               *
00003               PROGRAM-ID.
00004                   CREATE-ACCESS-INFO.
00005               ***************************************************************
00006               *                                                             *
00007               *    PROGRAMMER TEAM          SUMMERS/WALSTROM/LINDAHL         *
00008               *    PROGRAM COMPLETION DATE AUGUST 7, 1984                    *
00009               *                                                             *
00010               *    DATA TO BE SUPPLIED BY THE CALLING PROGRAM               *
00011               *       - THE CATALOGUE NUMBER                                 *
00012               *       - THE NUMBER OF ATTEMPTS WHICH HAVE BEEN              *
00013               *         MADE TO WRITE THE RECORD                            *
00014               *                                                             *
00015               *    DATA TO BE RETURNED TO THE CALLING PROGRAM               *
00016               *       - THE RELATIVE TRACK NUMBER                           *
00017               *                                                             *
00018               *    PROCESSING                                               *
00019               *       EACH CATALOGUE NUMBER GENERATES A RELATIVE TRACK      *
00020               *       NUMBER USING DIVISION REMAINDER HASHING WITH          *
00021               *       NEXT AVAILABLE TRACK OVERFLOW HANDLING                *
00022               ***************************************************************
00023               *
00024               ENVIRONMENT DIVISION.
```

Figure 9.10
Called subprogram "CREATE-ACCESS-INFO" for Example 9.3.

Figure 9.10 (*cont.*)

```
00025              *
00026               CONFIGURATION SECTION.
00027               SOURCE-COMPUTER.
00028                  IBM-370.
00029               OBJECT-COMPUTER.
00030                  IBM-370.
00031              *
00032              DATA DIVISION.
00033              *
00034              WORKING-STORAGE SECTION.
00035              01   WORK-NUMBERS.
00036                  02   SAVE-CAT-NUM              PIC S9(6) COMP SYNC.
00037                  02   QUOTIENT                  PIC S9(6) COMP SYNC.
00038
00039              01   CONSTANTS.
00040                  02   MAX-TRACK-NUM             PIC S9(4) COMP SYNC
00041                           VALUE 199.
00042                  02   PRIME-FOR-DIVISOR         PIC S9(4) COMP SYNC
00043                           VALUE 199.
00044
00045              LINKAGE SECTION.
00046              01   LS-RECORD-ACCESS-INFO.
00047                  02   LS-REL-TRACK-NUM          PIC S9(8) COMP SYNC.
00048                  02   LS-REC-KEY-CAT-NUM        PIC S9(6).
00049
00050              01   LS-COUNTERS.
00051                  02   LS-WRITE-TRY-COUNT        PIC 9(2).
00052              *
00053              PROCEDURE DIVISION USING
00054                  LS-RECORD-ACCESS-INFO, LS-COUNTERS.
00055              *
00056              CREATE-ACCESS-INFO-CONTROL.
00057                  IF LS-WRITE-TRY-COUNT = ZERO
00058                      MOVE LS-REC-KEY-CAT-NUM TO SAVE-CAT-NUM
00059                      DIVIDE SAVE-CAT-NUM BY PRIME-FOR-DIVISOR
00060                          GIVING QUOTIENT REMAINDER LS-REL-TRACK-NUM
00061                  ELSE
00062                      ADD 1 TO LS-REL-TRACK-NUM.
00063                  IF LS-REL-TRACK-NUM IS GREATER THAN MAX-TRACK-NUM
00064                      MOVE ZERO TO LS-REL-TRACK-NUM.
00065              *
00066              EXIT-PROGRAM.
00067                  EXIT PROGRAM.
```

As our final example, we will consider a subprogram with a somewhat more complex organization.

Example 9.4

A routine to sort a table can be written as a subprogram before the full details of the processing necessary in the main program to load the table are known. The information needed to sort a table is

1. The length of a table entry.
2. The number of elements in the table.
3. The location of the key field.
4. The description of the key field.

To illustrate this, we will modify Example 2.7 in Chapter 2, so that the sort routine is now a subprogram.

Structure charts for a program solution are given in Figures 9.11 and 9.12.

The listing for the calling program is given in Figure 9.13, with the sort subprogram listing shown in Figure 9.14.

The DATA DIVISION entries have been separated, since the indexes used for sorting in Example 2.7 are no longer needed in the calling program; rather, they are now needed in the subprogram. For this same reason, the sort-save-areas have been omitted in the calling program. The CALL statement on line 166 is all that is needed for the table to be sorted.

Note that the *index* RATE-TABLE-COUNTER, defined in the main program, is *not* the same as the *subscript* RATE-TABLE-COUNTER, defined in the subprogram SORT-CODE-RATE-TABLE. The only names that correspond are as follows:

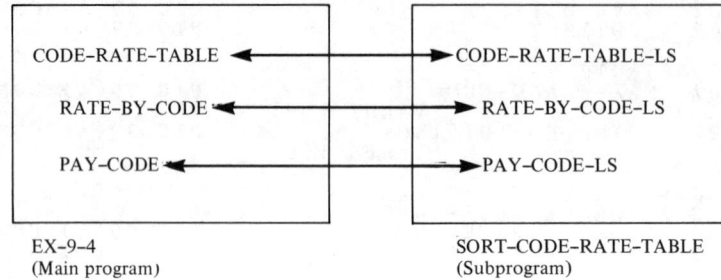

EX-9-4
(Main program)

SORT-CODE-RATE-TABLE
(Subprogram)

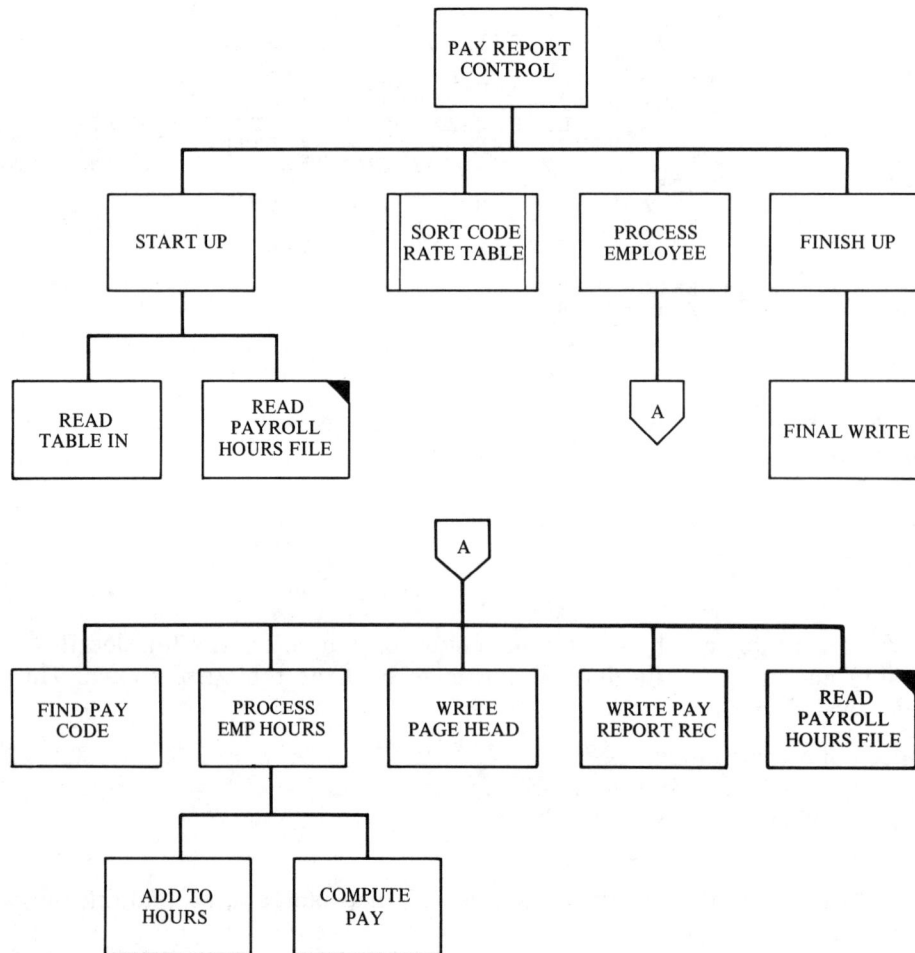

Figure 9.11
Structure chart for the calling program in Figure 9.13.

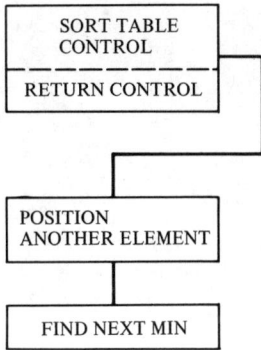

Figure 9.12
Structure chart for the called program in Figure 9.14.

```
00001          IDENTIFICATION DIVISION.
00002     *
00003        PROGRAM-ID.
00004           EX-9-4.
00005     ********************************************************************
00006     *                                                                  *
00007     *    PROGRAMMER TEAM              SUMMERS/WALSTROM/LINDAHL          *
00008     *    PROGRAM COMPLETION DATE  DECEMBER 5, 1984.                     *
00009     *                                                                  *
00010     *                    PROGRAM SUMMARY                                *
00011     *    INPUT                                                          *
00012     *         THE FIRST INPUT RECORD CONSISTS OF CODE RATE PAIRS        *
00013     *         FOR THE CODE RATE TABLE                                   *
00014     *              - PAY CODE                                           *
00015     *              - PAY RATE                                           *
00016     *         EACH EMPLOYEE INPUT RECORD CONTAINS                       *
00017     *              - SOCIAL SECURITY NUMBER                             *
00018     *              - NAME                                               *
00019     *              - PAY CODE                                          *
00020     *              - NUMBER OF HOURS WORKED FOR EACH DAY OF THE WEEK    *
00021     *                                                                  *
00022     *    PROCESSING                                                     *
00023     *              - THE SUBPROGRAM SORT-CODE-RATE-TABLE IS USED TO     *
00024     *                SORT THE CODE RATE TABLE IN ASCENDING ORDER        *
00025     *                BY PAY CODE                                        *
00026     *         FOR A VALID EMPLOYEE RECORD                               *
00027     *              - THE PAY RATE IS LOCATED IN THE CODE RATE TABLE     *
00028     *                USING A BINARY SEARCH TECHNIQUE                    *
00029     *              - THE TOAL NUMBER OF HOURS WORKED FOR AN EMPLOYEE    *
00030     *                IS COMPUTED                                        *
00031     *              - ALL TABLES ARE INDEXED                             *
00032     *              - THE GROSS PAY FOR AN EMPLOYEE IS COMPUTED          *
00033     *              - THE NUMBER OF REGULAR AND OVERTIME HOURS           *
00034     *                IS COMPUTED                                        *
00035     *              - TOTALS FOR REGULAR AND OVERTIME HOURS FOR ALL      *
00036     *                EMPLOYEES ARE ACCUMULATED                          *
00037     *              - TOTAL GROSS PAY FOR ALL EMPLOYEES IS COMPUTED      *
```

Figure 9.13
Calling program to compute employee pay using a subprogram to sort the code rate table for Example 9.4.

Figure 9.13 (cont.)

```
00038              *       OUTPUT                                            *
00039              *          A PRINTED REPORT IS PRODUCED                   *
00040              *          VALID EMPLOYEE OUTPUT CONSISTS OF              *
00041              *             - SOCIAL SECURITY NUMBER                    *
00042              *             - NAME                                      *
00043              *             - NUMBER OF HOURS WORKED AT OVERTIME RATE   *
00044              *             - PAY RATE                                  *
00045              *             - GROSS PAY                                 *
00046              *          INVALID EMPLOYEE OUTPUT CONSISTS OF            *
00047              *             - SOCIAL SECURITY NUMBER                    *
00048              *             - NAME                                      *
00049              *             - ZERO FOR HOURS AT REGULAR RATE, HOURS AT  *
00050              *               OVERTIME RATE, AND GROSS PAY              *
00051              *             - THE INVALID PAY CODE                      *
00052              *             - AN ERROR MESSAGE                          *
00053              *          COMPANY OUTPUT CONSISTS OF                     *
00054              *             - TOTAL OF ALL EMPLOYEE HOURS WORKED        *
00055              *             - TOTAL OF ALL EMPLOYEE OVERTIME HOURS WORKED *
00056              *             - TOTAL AMOUNT OF THE PAYROLL               *
00057              *                                                         *
00058              ***********************************************************************
00059              *
00060              ENVIRONMENT DIVISION.
00061              *
00062                CONFIGURATION SECTION.
00063                SOURCE-COMPUTER.
00064                  IBM-370.
00065                OBJECT-COMPUTER.
00066                  IBM-370.
00067                SPECIAL-NAMES.
00068                  C01 IS TO-TOP-OF-PAGE.
00069                INPUT-OUTPUT SECTION.
00070                FILE-CONTROL.
00071                    SELECT PAYROLL-HOURS-FILE-IN
00072                        ASSIGN TO SYS007-UR-2501-S.
00073                    SELECT PAYROLL-REPORT-PRINT-FILE
00074                        ASSIGN TO SYS009-UR-1403-S.
00075              *
00076              DATA DIVISION.
00077              *
00078                FILE SECTION.
00079                FD  PAYROLL-HOURS-FILE-IN
00080                    LABEL RECORDS ARE OMITTED.
00081                01  PAYROLL-HOURS-IN-AREA         PIC X(80).
00082                FD  PAYROLL-REPORT-PRINT-FILE
00083                    LABEL RECORDS ARE OMITTED.
00084                01  PAYROLL-REPORT-PRINT-AREA     PIC X(133).
00085              *
00086                WORKING-STORAGE SECTION.
00087                01  SWITCHES.
00088                    02  END-OF-PAY-DATA-SW        PIC X.
00089                        88  NO-MORE-PAY-DATA VALUE 'Y'.
00090                    02  PAY-CODE-FOUND-SW         PIC X.
00091                        88  PAY-CODE-FOUND    VALUE 'Y'.
00092                01  COUNTERS.
00093                    02  LINE-COUNT               PIC 9(2).
00094                01  CONSTANTS.
00095                    02  NUM-DAYS-IN-WEEK         PIC 9 VALUE 7.
00096                    02  NUM-OF-CODES             PIC 9(2) VALUE 10.
00097                    02  LINES-PER-PAGE           PIC 9(2) VALUE 55.
00098                    02  REG-PAY-PERIOD           PIC 9(2) VALUE 40.
00099                    02  OVERTIME-RATE            PIC V9(2) VALUE .50.
00100                01  EMPLOYEE-TOTALS.
00101                    02  EMP-TOTAL-HOURS          PIC 9(2)V9(2).
00102                    02  EMP-TOTAL-OVERTIME       PIC 9(2)V9(2).
00103                    02  EMP-TOTAL-PAY            PIC 9(3)V9(2).
00104                01  COMPANY-TOTALS.
00105                    02  COM-TOTAL-HOURS          PIC 9(6)V9(2).
00106                    02  COM-TOTAL-OVERTIME       PIC 9(5)V9(2).
00107                    02  COM-TOTAL-PAY            PIC 9(8)V9(2).
00108                01  PAYROLL-HOURS-IN-REC.
00109                    02  PAY-IN-SS-NUM            PIC 9(9).
00110                    02  PAY-IN-NAME             PIC X(20).
00111                    02  PAY-IN-CODE             PIC X.
00112                    02  PAY-IN-HOURS-WORKED
00113                            OCCURS 7 TIMES
00114                            INDEXED BY HOURS-WORKED-TABLE-COUNTER
00115                                          PIC 9(2)V9(2).
00116                    02  FILLER                  PIC X(22).
```

Figure 9.13 (*cont.*)

```
00117              01   PAY-REPORT-LINE.
00118                   02   FILLER                        PIC X(5) VALUE SPACE.
00119                   02   PAY-OUT-SS-NUM                PIC 9(9).
00120                   02   FILLER                        PIC X(5) VALUE SPACE.
00121                   02   PAY-OUT-NAME                  PIC X(25).
00122                   02   PAY-OUT-REG-HOURS             PIC Z9.9(2).
00123                   02   FILLER                        PIC X(5) VALUE SPACE.
00124                   02   PAY-OUT-OVER-HOURS            PIC Z9.9(2).
00125                   02   FILLER                        PIC X(5) VALUE SPACE.
00126                   02   PAY-OUT-RATE                  PIC Z9.9(3).
00127                   02   FILLER                        PIC X(5) VALUE SPACE.
00128                   02   PAY-OUT-TOTAL-PAY             PIC Z(2)9.9(2).
00129                   02   PAY-OUT-MESSAGE-INFO.
00130                        03   PAY-OUT-MESSAGE          PIC X(30).
00131                        03   PAY-OUT-CODE             PIC X.
00132              01   HEADING-LINE.
00133                   02   FILLER                        PIC X(44)
00134                        VALUE '        SS NUM      EMPLOYEE NAME'.
00135                   02   FILLER                        PIC X(35)
00136                        VALUE ' REG HOURS   OVERTIME   RATE     PAY'.
00137              01   STARLINE.
00138                   02   FILLER                        PIC X(133) VALUE ALL '*'.
00139              01   COMPANY-HOURS-LINE.
00140                   02   FILLER                        PIC X VALUE SPACE.
00141                   02   FILLER                        PIC X(30)
00142                        VALUE 'COMPANY TOTAL HOURS'.
00143                   02   COM-HOURS-OUT                 PIC Z(5)9.9(2).
00144              01   COMPANY-OVERTIME-LINE.
00145                   02   FILLER                        PIC X VALUE SPACE.
00146                   02   FILLER                        PIC X(30)
00147                        VALUE 'COMPANY TOTAL OVERTIME'.
00148                   02   COM-OVERTIME-OUT              PIC Z(5)9.9(2).
00149              01   COMPANY-PAY-LINE.
00150                   02   FILLER                        PIC X VALUE SPACE.
00151                   02   FILLER                        PIC X(27)
00152                        VALUE 'COMPANY TOTAL PAYROLL'.
00153                   02   COM-PAY-OUT                   PIC $(8)9.9(2).
00154              01   CODE-RATE-TABLE.
00155                   02   RATE-BY-CODE
00156                        OCCURS 10 TIMES
00157                        ASCENDING KEY IS PAY-CODE
00158                        INDEXED BY RATE-TABLE-COUNTER.
00159                        03   PAY-CODE                 PIC X.
00160                        03   PAY-RATE                 PIC 9(2)V9(3).
00161         *
00162              PROCEDURE DIVISION.
00163         *
00164              PAY-REPORT-CONTROL.
00165                   PERFORM START-UP.
00166                   CALL 'SORT-CODE-RATE-TABLE' USING CODE-RATE-TABLE.
00167                   PERFORM PROCESS-EMPLOYEE UNTIL NO-MORE-PAY-DATA.
00168                   PERFORM FINISH-UP.
00169                   STOP RUN.
00170         *
00171              START-UP.
00172                   OPEN INPUT PAYROLL-HOURS-FILE-IN
00173                        OUTPUT PAYROLL-REPORT-PRINT-FILE.
00174                   MOVE 'N' TO END-OF-PAY-DATA-SW.
00175                   COMPUTE LINE-COUNT = LINES-PER-PAGE + 1.
00176                   MOVE ZERO TO COM-TOTAL-HOURS,
00177                                COM-TOTAL-OVERTIME,
00178                                COM-TOTAL-PAY.
00179                   PERFORM READ-TABLE-IN.
00180                   PERFORM READ-PAYROLL-HOURS-FILE.
00181         *
00182              PROCESS-EMPLOYEE.
00183                   MOVE 'N' TO PAY-CODE-FOUND-SW.
00184                   .PERFORM FIND-PAY-CODE.
00185                   MOVE PAY-IN-NAME TO PAY-OUT-NAME.
00186                   MOVE PAY-IN-SS-NUM TO PAY-OUT-SS-NUM.
00187                   IF PAY-CODE-FOUND
00188                        MOVE SPACE TO PAY-OUT-MESSAGE-INFO
00189                        PERFORM PROCESS-EMP-HOURS
00190                   ELSE
00191                        MOVE 'INVALID PAY-CODE' TO PAY-OUT-MESSAGE
00192                        MOVE ZERO TO PAY-OUT-REG-HOURS, PAY-OUT-OVER-HOURS,
00193                                     PAY-OUT-RATE, PAY-OUT-TOTAL-PAY
00194                   MOVE PAY-IN-CODE TO PAY-OUT-CODE.
00195                   PERFORM WRITE-PAY-REPORT-REC.
00196                   ADD 1 TO LINE-COUNT.
00197                   PERFORM READ-PAYROLL-HOURS-FILE.
```

Figure 9.13 (cont.)

```
00198                    *
00199                        FINISH-UP.
00200                            MOVE COM-TOTAL-HOURS TO COM-HOURS-OUT.
00201                            MOVE COM-TOTAL-OVERTIME TO COM-OVERTIME-OUT.
00202                            MOVE COM-TOTAL-PAY TO COM-PAY-OUT.
00203                            PERFORM FINAL-WRITE.
00204                            CLOSE PAYROLL-HOURS-FILE-IN,
00205                                  PAYROLL-REPORT-PRINT-FILE.
00206                    *
00207                       FIND-PAY-CODE.
00208                            SEARCH ALL RATE-BY-CODE
00209                                WHEN PAY-CODE (RATE-TABLE-COUNTER) = PAY-IN-CODE
00210                                MOVE 'Y' TO PAY-CODE-FOUND-SW.
00211                    *
00212                       PROCESS-EMP-HOURS.
00213                            MOVE ZERO TO EMP-TOTAL-HOURS.
00214                            PERFORM ADD-TO-HOURS VARYING HOURS-WORKED-TABLE-COUNTER
00215                                FROM 1 BY 1 UNTIL HOURS-WORKED-TABLE-COUNTER
00216                                GREATER THAN NUM-DAYS-IN-WEEK.
00217                            PERFORM COMPUTE-PAY.
00218                            ADD EMP-TOTAL-HOURS TO COM-TOTAL-HOURS.
00219                            ADD EMP-TOTAL-OVERTIME TO COM-TOTAL-OVERTIME.
00220                            ADD EMP-TOTAL-PAY TO COM-TOTAL-PAY.
00221                            COMPUTE PAY-OUT-REG-HOURS = EMP-TOTAL-HOURS -
00222                                                        EMP-TOTAL-OVERTIME.
00223                            MOVE EMP-TOTAL-OVERTIME  TO PAY-OUT-OVER-HOURS.
00224                            MOVE PAY-RATE (RATE-TABLE-COUNTER) TO PAY-OUT-RATE.
00225                            MOVE EMP-TOTAL-PAY TO PAY-OUT-TOTAL-PAY.
00226                            IF LINE-COUNT   IS GREATER THAN LINES-PER-PAGE
00227                                PERFORM WRITE-PAGE-HEAD
00228                                MOVE ZERO TO LINE-COUNT.
00229                    *
00230                       ADD-TO-HOURS.
00231                            COMPUTE EMP-TOTAL-HOURS = EMP-TOTAL-HOURS +
00232                                    PAY-IN-HOURS-WORKED (HOURS-WORKED-TABLE-COUNTER).
00233                    *
00234                       COMPUTE-PAY.
00235                            COMPUTE EMP-TOTAL-PAY =   EMP-TOTAL-HOURS *
00236                                    PAY-RATE (RATE-TABLE-COUNTER).
00237                            IF EMP-TOTAL-HOURS IS GREATER THAN REG-PAY-PERIOD
00238                                COMPUTE EMP-TOTAL-OVERTIME = EMP-TOTAL-HOURS -
00239                                                            REG-PAY-PERIOD
00240                            ELSE
00241                                MOVE ZERO TO EMP-TOTAL-OVERTIME.
00242                            COMPUTE EMP-TOTAL-PAY =   EMP-TOTAL-PAY + EMP-TOTAL-OVERTIME
00243                                          * PAY-RATE (RATE-TABLE-COUNTER)
00244                                          * OVERTIME-RATE.
00245                    *
00246                       READ-TABLE-IN.
00247                            READ PAYROLL-HOURS-FILE-IN INTO CODE-RATE-TABLE
00248                                AT END MOVE 'Y' TO END-OF-PAY-DATA-SW.
00249                    *
00250                       WRITE-PAGE-HEAD.
00251                            WRITE PAYROLL-REPORT-PRINT-AREA FROM HEADING-LINE
00252                                AFTER ADVANCING TO-TOP-OF-PAGE.
00253                    *
00254                       WRITE-PAY-REPORT-REC.
00255                            WRITE PAYROLL-REPORT-PRINT-AREA FROM PAY-REPORT-LINE
00256                                AFTER ADVANCING 1 LINES.
00257                    *
00258                       READ-PAYROLL-HOURS-FILE.
00259                            READ PAYROLL-HOURS-FILE-IN INTO PAYROLL-HOURS-IN-REC
00260                                AT END MOVE 'Y' TO END-OF-PAY-DATA-SW.
00261                    *
00262                       FINAL-WRITE.
00263                            WRITE PAYROLL-REPORT-PRINT-AREA FROM STARLINE
00264                                AFTER ADVANCING 3 LINES.
00265                            WRITE PAYROLL-REPORT-PRINT-AREA FROM COMPANY-HOURS-LINE
00266                                AFTER ADVANCING 2 LINES.
00267                            WRITE PAYROLL-REPORT-PRINT-AREA FROM COMPANY-OVERTIME-LINE
00268                                AFTER ADVANCING 1 LINES.
00269                            WRITE PAYROLL-REPORT-PRINT-AREA FROM COMPANY-PAY-LINE
00270                                AFTER ADVANCING 1 LINES.
```

```
00001               IDENTIFICATION DIVISION.
00002               PROGRAM-ID.
00003                  SORT-CODE-RATE-TABLE.
00004               **********************************************************
00005               *                                                        *
00006               *    PROGRAMMER TEAM         SUMMERS/WALSTROM/LINDAHL     *
00007               *    PROGRAM COMPLETION DATE NOVEMBER 26, 1984            *
00008               *                                                        *
00009               *    DATA TO BE SUPPLIED BY THE CALLING PROGRAM           *
00010               *       - THE CODE RATE TABLE                             *
00011               *                                                        *
00012               *    DATA TO BE RETURNED TO THE CALLING PROGRAM           *
00013               *       - THE CODE RATE TABLE IN ASCENDING ORDER BY PAY CODE *
00014               *                                                        *
00015               *    PROCESSING                                          *
00016               *       - A DELAYED EXCHANGE SORT IS USED                 *
00017               *       - THE TABLE IS ACCESSED USING SUBSCRIPTS          *
00018               **********************************************************
00019               *
00020               ENVIRONMENT DIVISION.
00021               *
00022               CONFIGURATION SECTION.
00023               SOURCE-COMPUTER.
00024                  IBM.
00025               OBJECT-COMPUTER.
00026                  IBM.
00027               *
00028               DATA DIVISION.
00029               *
00030               WORKING-STORAGE SECTION.
00031               01   COUNTERS.
00032                    02   RATE-TABLE-COUNTER          PIC 9(2).
00033                    02   START-UNSORTED             PIC 9(2).
00034                    02   SAVE-MIN-LOCATION          PIC 9(2).
00035                    02   UNSORTED-COUNTER           PIC 9(2).
00036                    02   SORT-NUM-OF-CODES          PIC 9(2)   VALUE 10.
00037               01   SORT-SAVE-AREA.
00038                    02   SAVE-PAY-CODE              PIC X.
00039                    02   SAVE-PAY-RATE              PIC 9(2)V9(3).
00040               *
00041               LINKAGE SECTION.
00042               01   CODE-RATE-TABLE-LS.
00043                    02   RATE-BY-CODE-LS
00044                         OCCURS 10 TIMES.
00045                         03   PAY-CODE-LS           PIC X.
00046                         03   FILLER                PIC X(5).
00047               *
00048               PROCEDURE DIVISION
00049                    USING CODE-RATE-TABLE-LS.
00050               *
00051               SORT-TABLE-CONTROL.
00052                    PERFORM POSITION-ANOTHER-ELEMENT VARYING
00053                         RATE-TABLE-COUNTER FROM 1 BY 1
00054                         UNTIL RATE-TABLE-COUNTER = SORT-NUM-OF-CODES.
00055               *
00056               RETURN-CONTROL.
00057                    EXIT PROGRAM.
00058               *
00059               POSITION-ANOTHER-ELEMENT.
00060                    MOVE RATE-BY-CODE-LS (RATE-TABLE-COUNTER)
00061                         TO SORT-SAVE-AREA.
00062                    MOVE RATE-TABLE-COUNTER TO SAVE-MIN-LOCATION.
00063                    COMPUTE START-UNSORTED = RATE-TABLE-COUNTER + 1.
00064                    PERFORM FIND-NEXT-MIN VARYING UNSORTED-COUNTER
00065                         FROM START-UNSORTED BY 1 UNTIL UNSORTED-COUNTER
00066                         IS GREATER THAN SORT-NUM-OF-CODES.
00067                    MOVE RATE-BY-CODE-LS (RATE-TABLE-COUNTER) TO
00068                         RATE-BY-CODE-LS (SAVE-MIN-LOCATION).
00069                    MOVE SORT-SAVE-AREA TO
00070                         RATE-BY-CODE-LS (RATE-TABLE-COUNTER).
00071               *
00072               FIND-NEXT-MIN.
00073                    IF PAY-CODE-LS (UNSORTED-COUNTER) IS LESS THAN SAVE-PAY-CODE
00074                         MOVE RATE-BY-CODE-LS (UNSORTED-COUNTER) TO
00075                         SORT-SAVE-AREA
00076                         MOVE UNSORTED-COUNTER TO SAVE-MIN-LOCATION.
```

Figure 9.14
Called subprogram *"SORT-CODE-RATE-TABLE"* for Example 9.4.

CONCLUDING COMMENTS

Subprogram linkage is a complex topic with considerably more features than have been discussed in this chapter. The techniques for storage sharing and control transfer tend to be system-dependent. You should consult your vendor manual for more details.

The use of a subprogram is usually motivated by factors other than program efficiency. Extra code must be generated to establish the linkage between calling and called programs. Placing the code in the source program library and using the COPY statement (discussed in Chapter 11) will give more efficient execution.

In summary, we would emphasize the importance of a programmer having a clear understanding of subprograms. As previously stated, their effective use can significantly reduce the amount of duplicate code that programmers must write. Also subprograms allow us to work with smaller units; consequently, testing and debugging should be simplified. Further, since programmers can work independently on each of the subprograms, a shorter span of time should be required to complete the total programming project.

Programming Exercises for Chapter 9

EXERCISE 9.1

Most computer operating systems make the current date accessible to the COBOL programmer. The following statement may be used to obtain the date.

```
ACCEPT DATE-OF-TODAY FROM system-name.
```

Two date forms are common: (1) YYMMDD, where July 4, 1983, is 830704, and (2) YYDDD, where July 4, 1983, is 83185, which represents the 185th day of 1983. It is useful to be able to print the date in report headings to identify when the reports were printed.

Write a subprogram that converts the date in the specific form supplied by your system to its more common representation with the name of the month and complete specification of a year. A table of month names will be needed.

If the elapsed-day form (YYDDD) is used in your system, a table of elapsed days in the previous months will be useful. A year is a leap year if it is (1) not a century year (1700, 1800, and so on) and is evenly divisible by 4, or (2) it is a century year and is evenly divisible by 400.

EXERCISE 9.2

The file created in Exercise 7.5, Chapter 7, required that a relative record number be computed from the year and hospital number. Since all programs that access the file randomly will need this routine, write a subprogram to compute the relative record number for their use.

EXERCISE 9.3

Write a subprogram that computes the number of nights stayed at the Tired Traveler Hotel using the check-in and checkout dates. The record format for the Tired Traveler Hotel file is given in the exercises at the end of Chapter 7. You may assume that no dates will differ by more than one year. Assume that check-in and checkout dates placed on the file were obtained from the system. This subprogram should be usable by the billing program in Exercise 7.4, Chapter 7.

10 Report Writer Overview

Much of a programmer's time and effort will be directed toward producing printed reports for individuals within and outside the organization. Fairly complex logic is involved in maintaining line and page counters. Many of the reports will require control-break processing, which is also logically complex.[1] When these two techniques must be combined, much time may be spent debugging programming logic. The *Report Writer* feature of COBOL was designed to simplify the coding logic necessary to produce printed reports. The fundamental concept of Report Writer is that the form of the printed report will be described in the DATA DIVISION. All page counting, line counting, and producing of headings will be done automatically. Frequently, special processing is required when a control break occurs. If the special processing is related to the printed output, the Report Writer feature can also detect the control break and produce the appropriate output desired when the control break occurs.

Central to the Report Writer feature is the concept of a *report group*. A report group consists of one or more lines that typically will all be printed together (grouped). However, sometimes the report group contains no lines to be printed. Instead, it may be used for summing items or for control purposes. Let's look at these concepts in the context of a grade reporting problem. Assume we have a file (Figure 10.1) that contains the student's identification number, course names, grades earned, and the number of credit hours for each course the student has taken. All courses for a given student are grouped together in the file. Illustrated in Figure 10.2 is a sample page format for a grade report.

In the generation of a report, there are several kinds of report groups that we might be interested in using. We might want to print the individual course information; this is a *DETAIL* type of report group. We might want to print something special before or after a key group is processed; these are *CONTROL HEADING* and *CONTROL FOOTING* types of report groups, respectively. We might wish to print something special at the beginning or end of a page. These are *PAGE HEADING* and *PAGE FOOTING* types of report groups. Similarly, a *REPORT HEADING* is printed at the start of the report and a *REPORT FOOTING* at the end. To produce a report, the usual entries in the ENVIRONMENT DIVISION are needed. However,

---

[1] See Chapter 4 for a review of control-break processing. See also multiple sort keys discussed and used in Example 5.3 in Chapter 5, as *multiple control-break processing* is common on files containing records that are ordered on multiple sort keys.

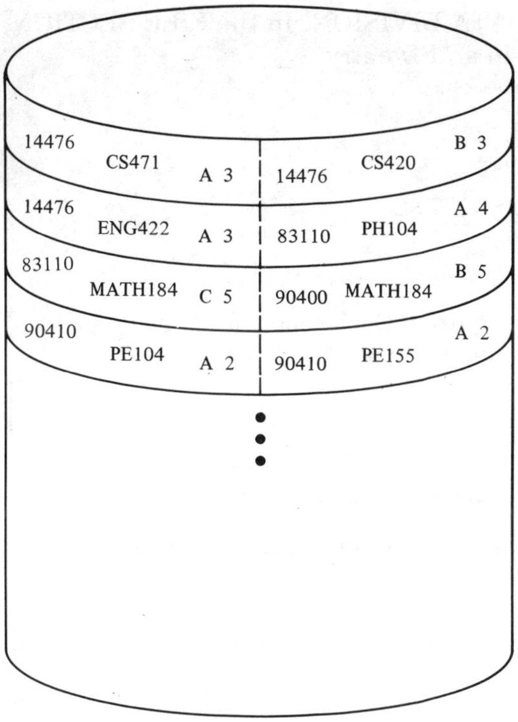

Figure 10.1
Sample grade report data file.

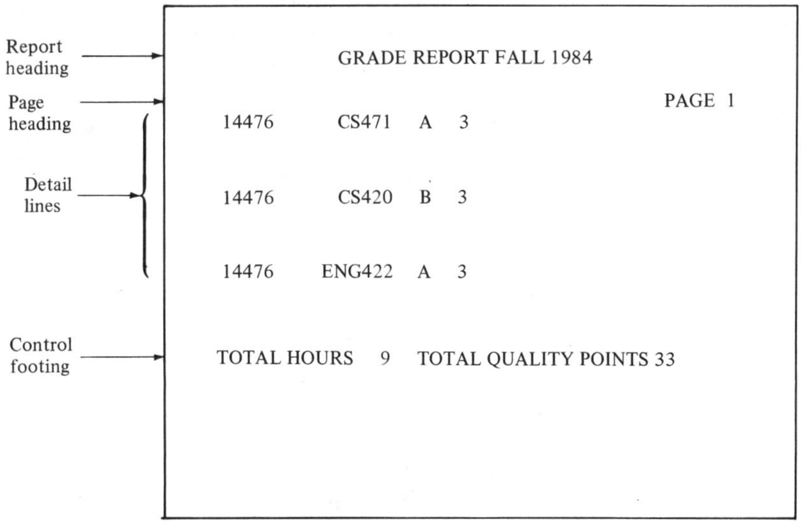

Figure 10.2
Sample page format for grade report.

many new entries are necessary in the DATA DIVISION. In the FILE SECTION, the name of the report must be specified in an FD entry:

```
FD  GRADE-REPORT-PRINT-FILE
    LABEL RECORDS ARE OMITTED
    RECORD CONTAINS 133 CHARACTERS
    REPORT IS GRADE-REPORT.
```

A new section, *REPORT SECTION,* is required. Each report must be named and described there. An *RD* (*report description*) entry is used for this purpose. The report description contains

1. A description of the format of a page.
2. A description of each report group.
3. A list of the data items to be used for control breaks.

For example, the grade report *page format* might be specified as follows:

```
RD  GRADE-REPORT
    CONTROLS ARE FINAL, STUDENT-ID
    PAGE LIMITS ARE 60 LINES
    HEADING 2
    FIRST DETAIL 4
    LAST DETAIL  55
    FOOTING      58.
```

The page format spacing specified by the preceding RD entry is given in Figure 10.3. Note that this page format leaves room for a three-line page or report footing to be printed on the last page of the report.

For each report group, we must specify spacing of the items to be printed (line and column), a description of the items to be printed, and how the values for these items are to be obtained. A report group will require a name if the report group will be referenced in other program statements. Report group descriptions have 01-level numbers.

To illustrate a report group, suppose a report title is to be centered on a cover sheet for the report.

```
01  TYPE IS REPORT HEADING
    LINE IS 28
    COLUMN IS 48
    PIC X(26)
    VALUE IS
    'GRADE REPORT EAST PODUNK U'.
```

The spacing of output for this example is shown in Figure 10.4.

Another example of report groups, this time a control footing, is described in the following entries.

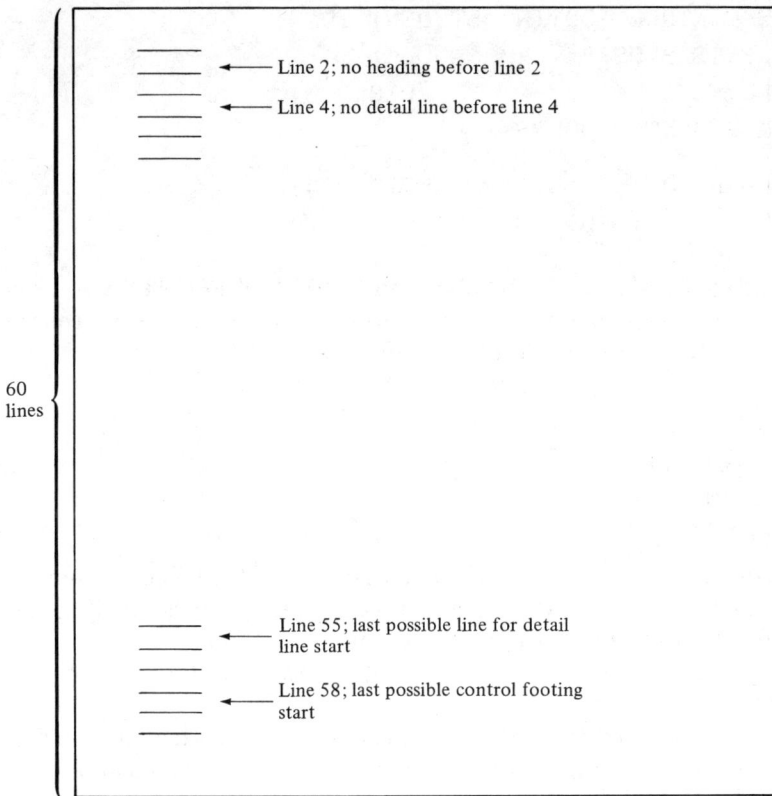

Figure 10.3
Sample page format spacing as specified by RD (record description) entry for GRADE-REPORT.

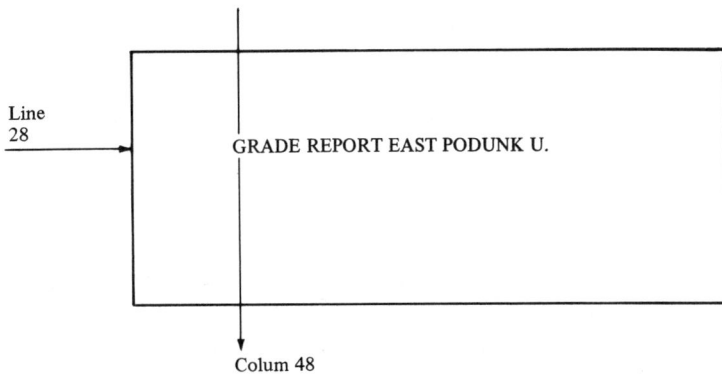

Figure 10.4
Sample report title spacing.

```
.01  TYPE IS CONTROL FOOTING STUDENT-ID.
     02  LINE IS PLUS 2
         COLUMN 35                    PIC 9(3)
         SUM SEMESTER-HOURS.

     02  COLUMN 50                    PIC 9(4)
         SUM QUALITY-POINTS.
```

When the line is printed, SEMESTER-HOURS and QUALITY-POINTS will have been *SUM*med for each student to generate the values to be printed when a control break occurs. Spacing will be as illustrated in Figure 10.5.

PROCEDURE DIVISION entries unique to the Report Writer feature are

1. *INITIATE* report-name.
2. *TERMINATE* report-name.
3. *GENERATE* $\begin{Bmatrix} \text{report-name} \\ \text{detail-line-name.} \end{Bmatrix}$

INITIATE initializes *LINE-COUNTER* and *PAGE-COUNTER* (special counters automatically generated by Report Writer) and produces the report heading and the first page heading if these report groups are defined.

TERMINATE produces the last control footing, page footing, and the report footing if these report groups are specified.

If a detail-line name is specified in the *GENERATE* statement, the detail report group is printed. However, if the report name is specified, only footings and headings will be printed when control breaks occur.

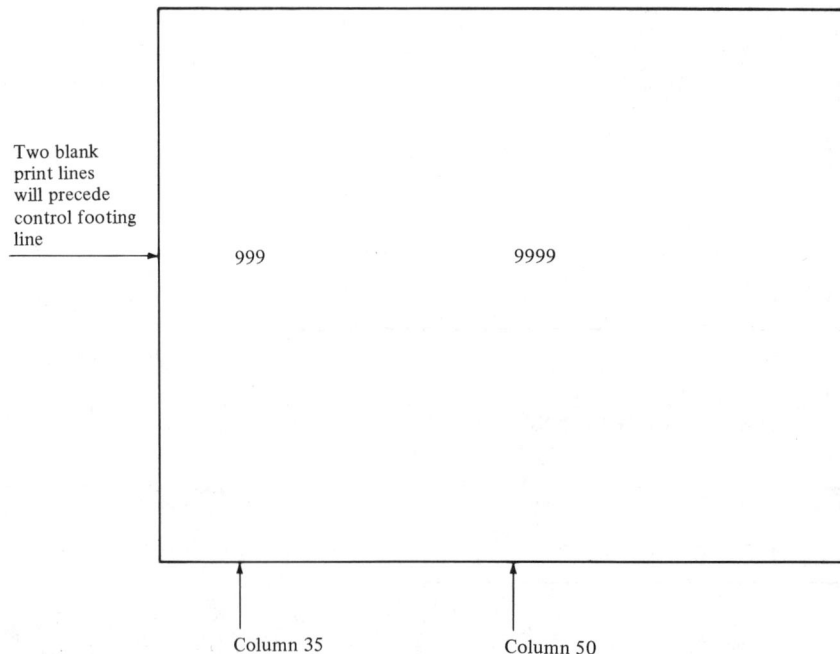

Two blank print lines will precede control footing line

          999   9999

          ↑   ↑
      Column 35   Column 50

Figure 10.5
Sample control footing spacing.

Both types of reports might be desired for GRADE-REPORT. *DETAIL* reporting could be used to print grade reports for mailing to students, whereas the registrar's office might wish only a summary report of students' performance.

BASIC REPORT WRITER EXAMPLES

We will now present several examples to illustrate different processing capabilities of Report Writer. Complete versions of the many forms of the DATA DIVISION entries are given in Appendix B.

Example 10.1

A report is to be generated from the project-hours-worked file in Example 4.2. You are encouraged to return to Chapter 4 and review Example 4.2, the module descriptions in Figure 4.7, and the program listing in Figure 4.8. By refreshing your memory concerning the original problem, you should be able to more easily follow what is taking place in this Report Writer example. The report to be generated should show the social security number and the total hours worked for each employee. (Recall that an employee may have multiple records in the hours-worked file; thus, control-break processing on social security number is required.) The printer layout chart for the output is illustrated in Figure 10.6. The program logic required in using Report Writer is much simpler than that originally required to create the total-hours report in Example 4.2. The structure chart is given in Figure 10.7. A program solution is shown in Figure 10.8.

The following points about the program in Figure 10.8 are called to your attention:

1. There are two control-break items (line 79)—a change in the social security number (HRS-IN-SS-NUM) and end of file (FINAL). It is important to be aware of the fact that the last social security key group read does not have a key value change when end of file occurs. Thus, a FINAL control break is needed to cause the last group to be properly processed.
2. The data item *PAGE-COUNTER* is numeric and is converted according to its edited description (line 95) only for printing.
3. The *LINE PLUS* phrase (lines 97, 102, 114) specifies how many lines to advance the printer before printing.
4. Since an item to be *SUM*med must appear in a *TYPE DETAIL* line, the entry on line 97, PROJ-HRS-LINE, is necessary so that the item in line 112 will be properly *SUM*med. PROJ-HRS-LINE will not be printed.
5. Creation of the summary report is accomplished by using the name of the report (TOTAL-HOURS-REPORT) in the *GENERATE* statement on line 145.

The output is shown in Figure 10.9.

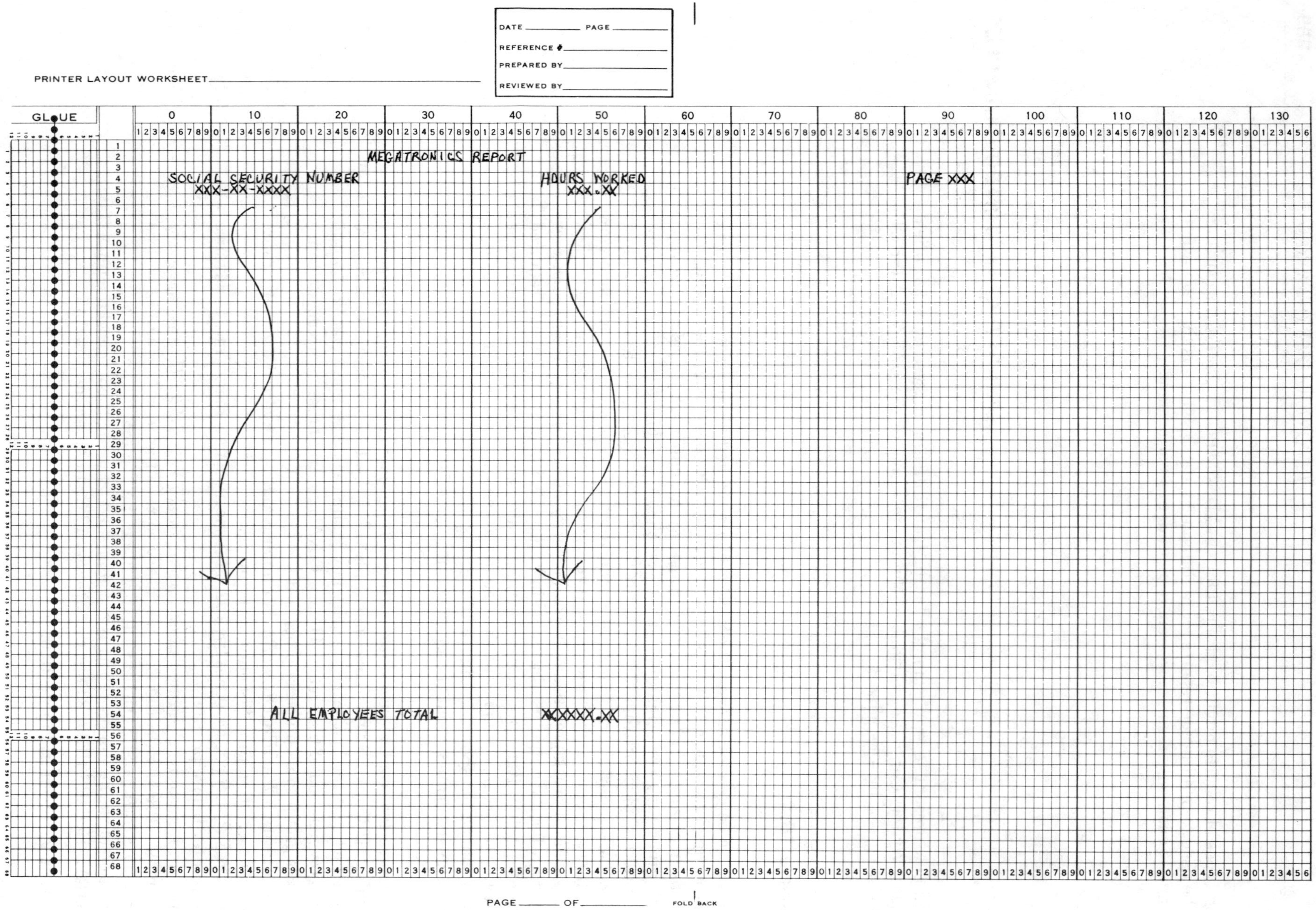

Figure 10.6
Printer layout for report to be generated for Example 10.1.

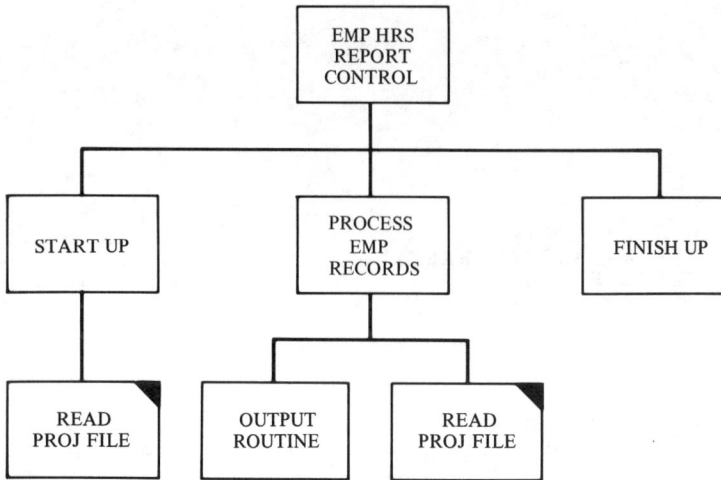

Figure 10.7
Structure chart for the program in Figure 10.8.

```
00001              IDENTIFICATION DIVISION.
00002         *
00003           PROGRAM-ID.
00004              EX-10-1.
00005         *********************************************************************
00006         *                                                                   *
00007         *     PROGRAMMER TEAM              WALSTROM/SUMMERS/LINDAHL          *
00008         *     PROGRAM COMPLETION DATE NOVEMBER 30, 1983                     *
00009         *                                                                   *
00010         *                    PROGRAM SUMMARY                                *
00011         *     INPUT                                                         *
00012         *          THE INPUT FILE IS A SEQUENTIAL FILE, ORDERED BY          *
00013         *          SOCIAL SECURITY NUMBER. THERE MAY BE MULTIPLE RECORDS    *
00014         *          FOR AN EMPLOYEE. EACH RECORDS CONSISTS OF                *
00015         *               - SOCIAL SECURITY NUMBER                           *
00016         *               - TASK PERFORMED BY EMPLOYEE                        *
00017         *               - PROJECT BUDGET NUMBER                             *
00018         *               - HOURS WORKED BY THE EMPLOYEE FOR THE TASK AND     *
00019         *                 PROJECT                                           *
00020         *                                                                   *
00021         *     PROCESSING                                                    *
00022         *          THE REPORT WRITER FEATURE CONTROLS PROCESSING OF         *
00023         *          THE INPUT DATA                                           *
00024         *               - THE TOTAL HOURS WORKED BY AN EMPLOYEE             *
00025         *                 IS CALCULATED                                     *
00026         *               - THE TOTAL NUMBER OF HOURS WORKED BY ALL           *
00027         *                 EMPLOYEES IS ACCUMULATED                          *
00028         *                                                                   *
00029         *     OUTPUT                                                        *
00030         *          A PRINTED REPORT IS PRODUCED USING THE REPORT WRITER     *
00031         *          FEATURE. FOR EACH EMPLOYEE THE OUTPUT CONSISTS OF        *
00032         *               - SOCIAL SECURITY NUMBER                           *
00033         *               - TOTAL HOURS WORKED                               *
00034         *          THE TOTAL NUMBER OF HOURS WORKED BY ALL EMPLOYEES        *
00035         *          IS ALSO PRINTED                                          *
00036         *********************************************************************
00037         *
00038           ENVIRONMENT DIVISION.
```

Figure 10.8
*Generation of a report requiring control-break processing on social security number and a FINAL control
break, using Report Writer for Example 10.1.*

Figure 10.8 (cont.)

```
00039          *
00040            CONFIGURATION SECTION.
00041            SOURCE-COMPUTER.
00042               IBM.
00043            OBJECT-COMPUTER.
00044               IBM.
00045            INPUT-OUTPUT SECTION.
00046            FILE-CONTROL.
00047               SELECT HRS-WORKED-PROJ-FILE-IN
00048                  ASSIGN TO SYS023-DA-3330-S-PHRSFIL.
00049               SELECT HRS-WORKED-PRINT-FILE
00050                  ASSIGN TO SYS009-UR-1403-S.
00051          *
00052           DATA DIVISION.
00053          *
00054            FILE SECTION.
00055            FD  HRS-WORKED-PROJ-FILE-IN
00056                  LABEL RECORDS ARE STANDARD
00057                  BLOCK CONTAINS 20 RECORDS.
00058            01  HRS-WORKED-PROJ-IN-AREA          PIC X(20).
00059            FD  HRS-WORKED-PRINT-FILE
00060                  REPORT IS TOTAL-HOURS-REPORT
00061                  RECORD CONTAINS 133 CHARACTERS
00062                  LABEL RECORDS ARE OMITTED.
00063          *
00064            WORKING-STORAGE SECTION.
00065            01  SWITCHES.
00066                02  END-OF-FILE-SW               PIC X.
00067                    88  NO-MORE-RECORDS   VALUE 'Y'.
00068            01  HRS-WORKED-IN-REC.
00069                02  HRS-IN-SS-NUM.
00070                    03  FIRST-3-DIGITS           PIC 9(3).
00071                    03  NEXT-2-DIGITS            PIC 9(2).
00072                    03  LAST-4-DIGITS            PIC 9(4).
00073                02  HRS-IN-DEPT-CODE             PIC S9(2).
00074                02  HRS-IN-PROJ-NUM              PIC 9(5).
00075                02  HRS-IN-HRS-WORKED            PIC S9(2)V9(2).
00076          *
00077           REPORT SECTION.
00078            RD  TOTAL-HOURS-REPORT
00079                  CONTROLS ARE FINAL HRS-IN-SS-NUM
00080                  PAGE LIMIT IS 55 LINES
00081                  HEADING   2
00082                  FIRST DETAIL 5
00083                  LAST DETAIL  50
00084                  FOOTING      54.
00085            01  TYPE REPORT HEADING.
00086                02  LINE 2  COLUMN 28             PIC X(18)
00087                    VALUE 'MEGATRONICS REPORT'.
00088            01  PAGE-HEADING TYPE PAGE HEADING LINE 4.
00089                02  COLUMN 5                     PIC X(22)
00090                    VALUE 'SOCIAL SECURITY NUMBER'.
00091                02  COLUMN 48                    PIC X(12)
00092                    VALUE 'HOURS WORKED'.
00093                02  COLUMN 90                    PIC X(4)
00094                    VALUE 'PAGE'.
00095                02  COLUMN 95                    PIC ZZ9
00096                    SOURCE  PAGE-COUNTER.
00097            01  PROJ-HRS-LINE TYPE DETAIL LINE PLUS 1.
00098                02  COLUMN 20                    PIC --9.9(2)
00099                    SOURCE HRS-IN-HRS-WORKED.
00100            01  EMP-HRS-TOTAL-LINE TYPE CONTROL FOOTING
00101                HRS-IN-SS-NUM
00102                LINE PLUS 1.
00103                02  COLUMN 8                     PIC 9(3)
00104                    SOURCE FIRST-3-DIGITS.
00105                02  COLUMN 11                    PIC X VALUE '-'.
00106                02  COLUMN 12                    PIC 9(2)
00107                    SOURCE NEXT-2-DIGITS.
00108                02  COLUMN 14                    PIC X VALUE '-'.
00109                02  COLUMN 15                    PIC 9(4)
00110                    SOURCE LAST-4-DIGITS.
00111                02  EMP-TOT COLUMN 51            PIC -9(2).9(2)
00112                    SUM HRS-IN-HRS-WORKED.
```

Figure 10.8 (*cont.*)

```
00113              01   TYPE CONTROL FOOTING FINAL
00114                   LINE PLUS 4.
00115                   02   COLUMN 27                    PIC X(21)
00116                        VALUE 'ALL EMPLOYEES TOTAL'.
00117                   02   COLUMN 48                    PIC -Z(5).99
00118                        SUM EMP-TOT.
00119          *
00120          PROCEDURE DIVISION.
00121          *
00122          EMP-HRS-REPORT-CONTROL.
00123              PERFORM START-UP.
00124              PERFORM PROCESS-EMP-RECORDS UNTIL NO-MORE-RECORDS.
00125              PERFORM FINISH-UP.
00126              STOP RUN.
00127          *
00128          START-UP.
00129              OPEN INPUT HRS-WORKED-PROJ-FILE-IN
00130                   OUTPUT HRS-WORKED-PRINT-FILE.
00131              MOVE 'N' TO END-OF-FILE-SW.
00132              INITIATE TOTAL-HOURS-REPORT
00133              PERFORM READ-PROJ-FILE.
00134          *
00135          PROCESS-EMP-RECORDS.
00136              PERFORM OUTPUT-ROUTINE.
00137              PERFORM READ-PROJ-FILE.
00138          *
00139          FINISH-UP.
00140              TERMINATE TOTAL-HOURS-REPORT
00141              CLOSE HRS-WORKED-PROJ-FILE-IN
00142                    HRS-WORKED-PRINT-FILE.
00143          *
00144          OUTPUT-ROUTINE.
00145              GENERATE TOTAL-HOURS-REPORT.
00146          *
00147          READ-PROJ-FILE.
00148              READ HRS-WORKED-PROJ-FILE-IN INTO HRS-WORKED-IN-REC
00149                   AT END MOVE 'Y' TO END-OF-FILE-SW.
```

```
                         MEGATRONICS REPORT

SOCIAL SECURITY NUMBER                          HOURS WORKED
      011-86-7322                                   39.00
      074-13-9821                                   50.00
      124-38-6752                                   42.00
      175-92-6415                                   40.00
      195-55-2633                                   40.00
      212-28-8534                                   40.00
      223-52-5542                                   51.25
      257-45-8211                                   40.00
      275-27-8640                                   46.00
      305-38-9742                                   46.00
      323-42-3765                                   50.00
      330-94-8326                                   40.00
      351-41-4122                                   40.00
      360-15-8021                                   40.00
      372-58-6742                                   41.50
      395-32-1760                                   40.00
      425-54-8624                                   40.00
      502-68-4265                                   40.00
      540-05-5298                                   46.00
      563-89-7521                                   42.00
      564-89-7521                                   51.00
      592-76-4831                                   40.00
      613-56-8442                                   40.00
      643-82-4694                                   40.00
      661-14-3880                                   45.00
      826-62-4853                                   40.00
      909-84-3920                                   40.00


         ALL EMPLOYEES TOTAL      1149.75
```

Figure 10.9
Sample output generated from program in Figure 10.8.

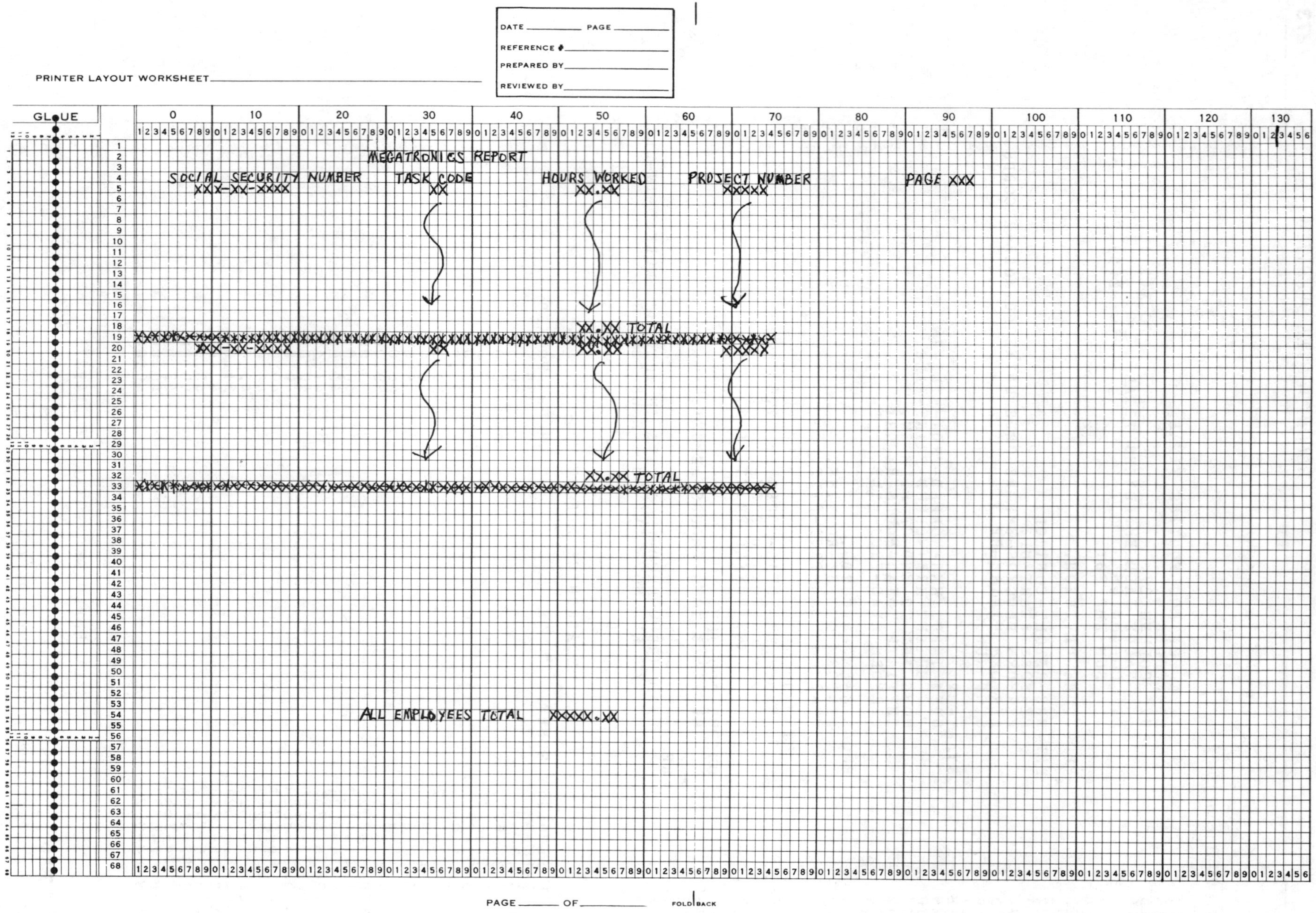

Figure 10.10
Printer layout for report to be generated for Example 10.2.

274

Example 10.2

Suppose the report shown in Figure 10.9 should also contain the hours an employee worked on each project, as well as the employee's total hours worked. Using Report Writer, the generation of the additional information will require little change to the solution presented for Example 10.1. The detail line must be described in the DATA DIVISION, and the *GENERATE* statement must specify the name of the detail line. A program solution is given in Figure 10.11 (see Figure 10.10 for printer layout form and Figure 10.12 for program output). The following points should be noted about the program:

1. The *GROUP INDICATE* phrase on lines 105, 107, 108, 110, and 111 causes these items to be printed only for the first entry of a key group.
2. The *CONTROL FOOTING* report group consists of two lines of output (lines 119–128).
3. The name of the detail line, PROJ-HRS-LINE, is specified in the *GENERATE* statement on line 161.
4. Control breaks, specified on line 82, are social security number (HRS-IN-SS-NUM) and FINAL.

```
00001          IDENTIFICATION DIVISION.
00002      *
00003       PROGRAM-ID.
00004         EX-10-2.
00005      *****************************************************************
00006      *                                                               *
00007      *    PROGRAMMER TEAM          WALSTROM/SUMMERS/LINDAHL           *
00008      *    PROGRAM COMPLETION DATE NOVEMBER 30, 1983                   *
00009      *                                                               *
00010      *                 PROGRAM SUMMARY                               *
00011      *    INPUT                                                      *
00012      *        THE INPUT FILE IS A SEQUENTIAL FILE, ORDERED BY        *
00013      *        SOCIAL SECURITY NUMBER. THERE MAY BE MULTIPLE RECORDS  *
00014      *        FOR AN EMPLOYEE. EACH RECORD CONSISTS OF               *
00015      *            - SOCIAL SECURITY NUMBER                           *
00016      *            - TASK PERFORMED BY EMPLOYEE                       *
00017      *            - PROJECT BUDGET NUMBER                            *
00018      *            - HOURS WORKED BY THE EMPLOYEE FOR THE TASK AND     *
00019      *              PROJECT                                          *
00020      *                                                               *
00021      *    PROCESSING                                                 *
00022      *        THE REPORT WRITER FEATURE CONTROLS PROCESSING OF       *
00023      *        THE INPUT DATA                                         *
00024      *            - THE TOTAL HOURS WORKED BY AN EMPLOYEE            *
00025      *              IS CALCULATED                                    *
00026      *            - THE TOTAL NUMBER OF HOURS WORKED BY ALL          *
00027      *              EMPLOYEES IS ACCUMULATED                         *
00028      *                                                               *
00029      *    OUTPUT                                                     *
00030      *        A PRINTED REPORT IS PRODUCED USING THE REPORT WRITER   *
00031      *        FEATURE. FOR EACH EMPLOYEE THE OUTPUT CONSISTS OF      *
00032      *            - SOCIAL SECURITY NUMBER                           *
00033      *            - PROJECT BUDGET NUMBER                            *
00034      *            - TASK CODE                                        *
00035      *            - HOURS WORKED                                     *
00036      *            - TOTAL HOURS WORKED                               *
00037      *        THE TOTAL NUMBER OF HOURS WORKED BY ALL EMPLOYEES      *
00038      *        IS ALSO PRINTED                                        *
00039      *****************************************************************
00040      *
00041       ENVIRONMENT DIVISION.
```

Figure 10.11
Control-break processing and generation of a report showing the hours an employee worked on each project, in addition to the employee's total hours worked, using Report Writer for Example 10.2.

Figure 10.11 (cont.)

```
00042          *
00043              CONFIGURATION SECTION.
00044              SOURCE-COMPUTER.
00045                  IBM.
00046              OBJECT-COMPUTER.
00047                  IBM.
00048              INPUT-OUTPUT SECTION.
00049              FILE-CONTROL.
00050                  SELECT HRS-WORKED-PROJ-FILE-IN
00051                      ASSIGN TO SYS023-DA-3330-S-PHRSFIL.
00052                  SELECT HRS-WORKED-PRINT-FILE
00053                      ASSIGN TO SYS009-UR-1403-S.
00054          *
00055          DATA DIVISION.
00056          *
00057              FILE SECTION.
00058              FD  HRS-WORKED-PROJ-FILE-IN
00059                      LABEL RECORDS ARE STANDARD
00060                      BLOCK CONTAINS 20 RECORDS.
00061              01  HRS-WORKED-PROJ-IN-AREA          PIC X(20).
00062              FD  HRS-WORKED-PRINT-FILE
00063                      REPORT IS TOTAL-HOURS-REPORT
00064                      RECORD CONTAINS 133 CHARACTERS
00065                      LABEL RECORDS ARE OMITTED.
00066          *
00067              WORKING-STORAGE SECTION.
00068              01  SWITCHES.
00069                  02  END-OF-FILE-SW               PIC X.
00070                      88  NO-MORE-RECORDS   VALUE 'Y'.
00071              01  HRS-WORKED-IN-REC.
00072                  02  HRS-IN-SS-NUM.
00073                      03  FIRST-3-DIGITS           PIC 9(3).
00074                      03  NEXT-2-DIGITS            PIC 9(2).
00075                      03  LAST-4-DIGITS            PIC 9(4).
00076                  02  HRS-IN-TASK-CODE             PIC S9(2).
00077                  02  HRS-IN-PROJ-NUM              PIC 9(5).
00078                  02  HRS-IN-HRS-WORKED            PIC S9(2)V9(2).
00079          *
00080              REPORT SECTION.
00081              RD  TOTAL-HOURS-REPORT
00082                      CONTROLS ARE FINAL HRS-IN-SS-NUM
00083                      PAGE LIMIT IS 55 LINES
00084                      HEADING    2
00085                      FIRST DETAIL 5
00086                      LAST DETAIL  50
00087                      FOOTING      54.
00088              01  TYPE REPORT HEADING.
00089                  02  LINE 2   COLUMN 28           PIC X(18)
00090                          VALUE 'MEGATRONICS REPORT'.
00091              01  PAGE-HEADING TYPE PAGE HEADING LINE 4.
00092                  02  COLUMN 5                     PIC X(22)
00093                          VALUE 'SOCIAL SECURITY NUMBER'.
00094                      02  COLUMN 31                PIC X(9)
00095                          VALUE 'TASK CODE'.
00096                  02  COLUMN 48                    PIC X(12)
00097                          VALUE 'HOURS WORKED'.
00098                  02  COLUMN 65                    PIC X(14)
00099                          VALUE 'PROJECT NUMBER'.
00100                  02  COLUMN 90                    PIC X(4)
00101                          VALUE 'PAGE'.
00102                  02  COLUMN 95                    PIC ZZ9
00103                          SOURCE   PAGE-COUNTER.
00104              01  PROJ-HRS-LINE TYPE DETAIL LINE PLUS 1.
00105                  02  COLUMN 8 GROUP INDICATE      PIC 9(3)
00106                          SOURCE FIRST-3-DIGITS.
00107                  02  COLUMN 11 GROUP INDICATE     PIC X VALUE '-'.
00108                  02  COLUMN 12 GROUP INDICATE     PIC 9(2)
00109                          SOURCE NEXT-2-DIGITS.
00110                  02  COLUMN 14 GROUP INDICATE     PIC X VALUE '-'.
00111                  02  COLUMN 15 GROUP INDICATE     PIC 9(4)
00112                          SOURCE LAST-4-DIGITS.
00113                  02  COLUMN 34                    PIC -9(2)
00114                          SOURCE HRS-IN-TASK-CODE.
00115                  02  COLUMN 51                    PIC -9(2).9(2)
00116                          SOURCE HRS-IN-HRS-WORKED.
00117                  02  COLUMN 69                    PIC 9(5)
00118                          SOURCE HRS-IN-PROJ-NUM.
```

Figure 10.11 (cont.)

```
00119              01  EMP-HRS-TOTAL-LINE TYPE CONTROL FOOTING
00120                  HRS-IN-SS-NUM.
00121                  02  EMP-TOT LINE PLUS 2 COLUMN 51
00122                                              PIC -9(2).9(2)
00123                      SUM HRS-IN-HRS-WORKED.
00124                  02  COLUMN 58               PIC X(5)
00125                      VALUE 'TOTAL'.
00126                  02  LINE PLUS 1             PIC X(74)
00127                      COLUMN 5
00128                      VALUE ALL '*'.
00129              01  TYPE CONTROL FOOTING FINAL
00130                  LINE PLUS 4.
00131                  02  COLUMN 27               PIC X(21)
00132                      VALUE 'ALL EMPLOYEES TOTAL'.
00133                  02  COLUMN 48               PIC -Z(5).99
00134                      SUM EMP-TOT.
00135          *
00136          PROCEDURE DIVISION.
00137          *
00138          EMP-HRS-REPORT-CONTROL.
00139              PERFORM START-UP.
00140              PERFORM PROCESS-EMP-RECORDS UNTIL NO-MORE-RECORDS.
00141              PERFORM FINISH-UP.
00142              STOP RUN.
00143          *
00144          START-UP.
00145              OPEN INPUT HRS-WORKED-PROJ-FILE-IN
00146                   OUTPUT HRS-WORKED-PRINT-FILE.
00147              MOVE 'N' TO END-OF-FILE-SW.
00148              INITIATE TOTAL-HOURS-REPORT
00149              PERFORM READ-PROJ-FILE.
00150          *
00151          PROCESS-EMP-RECORDS.
00152              PERFORM OUTPUT-ROUTINE.
00153              PERFORM READ-PROJ-FILE.
00154          *
00155          FINISH-UP.
00156              TERMINATE TOTAL-HOURS-REPORT
00157              CLOSE HRS-WORKED-PROJ-FILE-IN
00158                    HRS-WORKED-PRINT-FILE.
00159          *
00160          OUTPUT-ROUTINE.
00161              GENERATE PROJ-HRS-LINE.
00162          *
00163          READ-PROJ-FILE.
00164              READ HRS-WORKED-PROJ-FILE-IN INTO HRS-WORKED-IN-REC
00165                   AT END MOVE 'Y' TO END-OF-FILE-SW.
```

```
                        MEGATRONICS REPORT                                        PAGE    1
SOCIAL SECURITY NUMBER      TASK CODE           HOURS WORKED      PROJECT NUMBER
     011-86-7322                26                 25.00              00032
                                26                 14.00              00032

                                                   39.00 TOTAL
*******************************************************************************
     074-13-9821                22                 25.00              00032
                                26                 25.00              00032

                                                   50.00 TOTAL
*******************************************************************************
     124-38-6752                20                 20.00              00035
                                20                 02.00              00035
                                20                 10.00              00040
                                20                 10.00              00050

                                                   42.00 TOTAL
*******************************************************************************
     175-92-6415                21                 20.00              00050
                                21                 20.00              00050

                                                   40.00 TOTAL
*******************************************************************************
     195-55-2633                21                 20.00              00050
                                21                 20.00              00050

                                                   40.00 TOTAL
*******************************************************************************
     212-28-8534                21                 20.00              00050
                                21                 20.00              00050

                                                   40.00 TOTAL
*******************************************************************************
     223-52-5542                10                 15.00              10000
                                10                 15.00              20000
                                10                 05.50              55500
                                10                 15.75              32143

                                                   51.25 TOTAL
*******************************************************************************
     257-45-8211                21                 20.00              00050
                                21                 20.00              00050

                                                   40.00 TOTAL
*******************************************************************************
     275-27-8640                22                 23.00              11111
                                28                 23.00              11111

                                                   46.00 TOTAL
*******************************************************************************
```

Figure 10.12a
Sample output (first page) generated from the program in Figure 10.11.

```
                                                                                  PAGE    4
SOCIAL SECURITY NUMBER      TASK CODE           HOURS WORKED      PROJECT NUMBER
     826-62-4853                27                 05.00              00500

                                                   40.00 TOTAL
*******************************************************************************
     909-84-3920                22                 10.00              00125
                                22                 10.00              00125
                                25                 10.00              00125
                                25                 10.00              00125

                                                   40.00 TOTAL
*******************************************************************************


                    ALL EMPLOYEES TOTAL      1149.75
```

Figure 10.12b
Final page of output.

Example 10.3

Recall in Example 4.3 that the payroll master file was to be updated and a payroll register printed. We will redo that example using Report Writer to print the payroll register. The printer layout is shown in Figure 4.9 in the sequential files chapter.

The structure chart for the new version of the program is shown in Figure 10.13. Note that all modules needed for headings and page and line control have vanished and that the structure chart is a simpler one than required in Figure 4.10. Program output is shown in Figure 10.15.

The program solution is given in Figure 10.14. Since there are three different output line formats, there are three detail report groups specified. The only totals to be accumulated are company totals, so the only footing needed is a *CONTROL FOOTING FINAL*. Also, the DISPLAYs in lines 288–290 would be executed only if problems were encountered from which processing recovery is not possible.

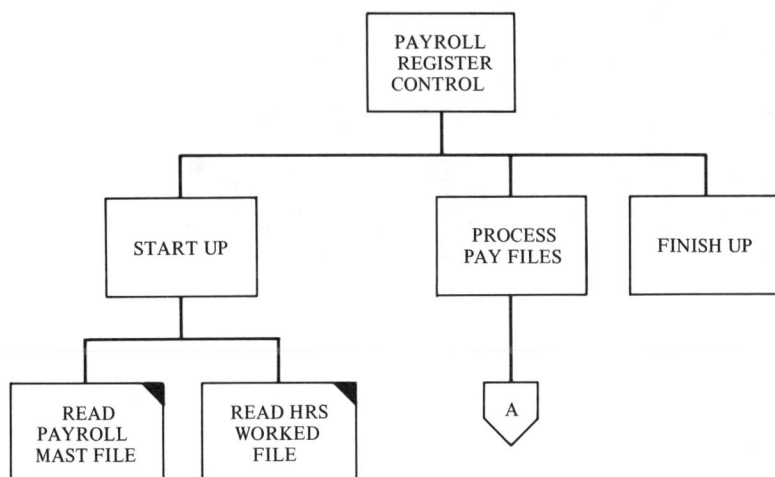

Figure 10.13
Structure chart for the program in Figure 10.14.

Figure 10.13 (*cont.*)

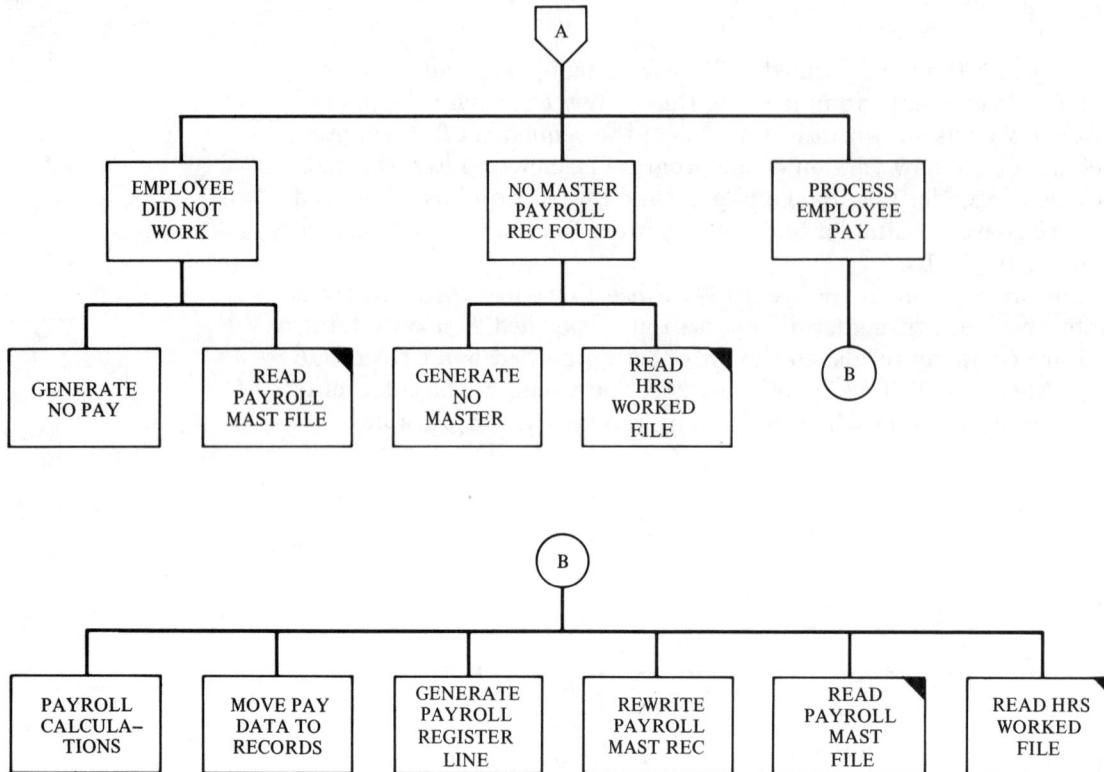

```
00001              IDENTIFICATION DIVISION.
00002         *
00003           PROGRAM-ID.
00004              EX-10-3.
00005         ****************************************************************
00006         *                                                              *
00007         *   PROGRAMMER TEAM          WALSTROM/SUMMERS/LINDAHL           *
00008         *   PROGRAM COMPLETION DATE DECEMBER 8, 1983.                   *
00009         *                                                              *
00010         *              PROGRAM SUMMARY                                  *
00011         *   INPUT                                                       *
00012         *       INPUT FILES USED ARE THE PAYROLL MASTER FILE AND        *
00013         *       THE HOURS WORKED FILE. BOTH ARE ORDERED ON THE          *
00014         *       SOCIAL SECURITY NUMBER.                                 *
00015         *   PAYROLL MASTER RECORDS CONSIST OF                           *
00016         *            - CODE FOR THE PLANT LOCATION                      *
00017         *            - CODE FOR THE DEPARTMENT TO WHICH THE EMPLOYEE     *
00018         *              IS ASSIGNED                                      *
00019         *            - SOCIAL SECURITY NUMBER                           *
00020         *            - NAME                                             *
00021         *            - OTHER PERSONAL DATA                              *
00022         *            - TAX CLASSIFICATION                               *
00023         *            - PAY RATE                                         *
00024         *            - YEAR-TO-DATE TOTALS FOR GROSS PAY,TAX WITHHELD,   *
00025         *              AND FICA WITHHELD                                 *
00026         *   HOURS WORKED RECORDS CONSIST OF                             *
00027         *            - SOCIAL SECURITY NUMBER                           *
00028         *            - TOTAL HOURS WORKED                               *
```

Figure 10.14
Updating a sequential master file and generating a payroll register using Report Writer for Example 10.3.

Figure 10.14 (cont.)

```
00029        *                                                                    *
00030        *      PROCESSING                                                     *
00031        *          THE STATUS OF EACH SOCIAL SECURITY NUMBER IS DETERMINED*
00032        *              - ONLY ON PAYROLL MASTER FILE                         *
00033        *              - ONLY ON HOURS WORKED FILE                           *
00034        *              - ON BOTH                                             *
00035        *          FOR EMPLOYEES APPEARING ON A SINGLE FILE A STATUS         *
00036        *          MESSAGE IS DETERMINED. FOR AN EMPLOYEE ON BOTH FILES      *
00037        *              - THE GROSS PAY FOR PAY PERIOD IS COMPUTED            *
00038        *              - THE TAX FOR PAY PERIOD IS COMPUTED                  *
00039        *              - THE FICA FOR PAY PERIOD IS COMPUTED                 *
00040        *              - THE NET PAY FOR PAY PERIOD IS COMPUTED              *
00041        *              - YEAR-TO-DATE TOTALS FOR GROSS PAY, TAX WITHHELD     *
00042        *                AND FICA WITHHELD ARE UPDATED                       *
00043        *          COMPANY TOTALS ARE ACCUMULATED USING REPORT WRITER FOR    *
00044        *              - YEAR-TO-DATE GROSS PAY, TAX WITHHELD,               *
00045        *                FICA WITHHELD                                       *
00046        *              - PAY PERIOD GROSS PAY, TAX WITHHELD,                 *
00047        *                FICA WITHHELD, NET PAY, REGULAR HOURS WORKED,       *
00048        *                OVERTIME HOURS WORKED                               *
00049        *                                                                    *
00050        *      OUTPUT                                                        *
00051        *          AN UPDATED PAYROLL MASTER FILE IS PRODUCED.               *
00052        *          A PRINTED REPORT IS PRODUCED USING REPORT WRITER. FOR     *
00053        *          AN EMPLOYEE ON BOTH FILES OUTPUT CONSISTS OF              *
00054        *              - SOCIAL SECURITY NUMBER                             *
00055        *              - YEAR-TO-DATE GROSS,TAX,FICA                         *
00056        *              - PLANT LOCATION CODE                                *
00057        *              - DEPARTMENT CODE                                    *
00058        *              - NAME                                               *
00059        *              - PAY RATE                                           *
00060        *              - REGULAR AND OVERTIME HOURS                         *
00061        *              - PAY PERIOD GROSS,TAX,FICA,NET                      *
00062        *          OTHER EMPLOYEE OUTPUT CONSISTS OF                         *
00063        *              - SOCIAL SECURITY NUMBER                             *
00064        *              - STATUS MESSAGE                                     *
00065        *          COMPANY OUTPUT CONSISTS OF                               *
00066        *              - YEAR-TO-DATE GROSS,TAX,FICA                         *
00067        *              - REGULAR AND OVERTIME HOURS                         *
00068        *              - PAY PERIOD GROSS,FICA,TAX,NET                       *
00069        ****************************************************************
00070        *
00071        ENVIRONMENT DIVISION.
00072        *
00073        CONFIGURATION SECTION.
00074        SOURCE-COMPUTER.
00075            IBM-370.
00076        OBJECT-COMPUTER.
00077            IBM-370.
00078        INPUT-OUTPUT SECTION.
00079        FILE-CONTROL.
00080            SELECT HRS-WORKED-PAY-PERIOD-FILE-IN
00081                ASSIGN TO SYS023-DA-3330-S-THRSFIL.
00082            SELECT PAYROLL-MAST-FILE-IO
00083                ASSIGN TO SYS023-DA-3330-S-PAYFILE.
00084            SELECT PAYROLL-REGISTER-REPORT-FILE
00085                ASSIGN TO SYS009-UR-1403-S.
00086        *
00087        DATA DIVISION.
00088        *
00089        FILE SECTION.
00090        FD  HRS-WORKED-PAY-PERIOD-FILE-IN
00091                LABEL RECORDS ARE STANDARD
00092                BLOCK CONTAINS 10 RECORDS.
00093        01  HRS-WORKED-IN-AREA                    PIC X(13).
00094        FD  PAYROLL-MAST-FILE-IO
00095                LABEL RECORDS ARE STANDARD
00096                BLOCK CONTAINS 10 RECORDS.
00097        01  PAY-MAST-IO-AREA                      PIC X(100).
00098        FD  PAYROLL-REGISTER-REPORT-FILE
00099                REPORT IS PAYROLL-REGISTER
00100                LABEL RECORDS ARE OMITTED.
```

Figure 10.14 (cont.)

```
00101          *
00102                    WORKING-STORAGE SECTION.
00103                    01    SWITCHES.
00104                          02    END-OF-HRS-WORKED-FILE-SW    PIC X.
00105                                88    END-OF-HRS-WORKED-FILE    VALUE 'Y'.
00106                          02    END-OF-PAYROLL-MAST-FILE-SW PIC X.
00107                                88    END-OF-PAYROLL-MAST-FILE    VALUE 'Y'.
00108                          02    STOP-PROCESSING-SW          PIC X.
00109                                88    PROCESSING-SHOULD-STOP    VALUE 'Y'.
00110                          02    INVALID-REWRITE-PAY-MAST-SW PIC X.
00111                                88    INVALID-REWRITE-PAY-MAST VALUE 'Y'.
00112                    01    CONSTANTS.
00113                          02    MAX-REG-HRS                 PIC S9(2)    VALUE +40.
00114                          02    OVERTIME-ADJUSTMENT         PIC S9V9     VALUE +1.5.
00115                          02    MAX-SS-WITHHOLD             PIC S9(5)    VALUE +29700.
00116                          02    SS-WITHHOLD-RATE            PIC SV9(3)   VALUE +.067.
00117                          02    TAXABLE-INCOME-ADJUSTMENT   PIC S9(2)    VALUE +13.
00118                          02    EST-FED-TAX-RATE            PIC SV9(2)   VALUE +.18.
00119                    01    ERROR-MESSAGE.
00120                          02    FILLER                      PIC X(20).
00121                    01    CALCULATION-WORK-AREAS.
00122                          02    EMPLOYEE-PAY-CALCULATION-AREA.
00123                                03    EMP-YTD-GROSS         PIC S9(5)V9(2).
00124                                03    EMP-YTD-TAX           PIC S9(4)V9(2).
00125                                03    EMP-YTD-FICA          PIC S9(4)V9(2).
00126                                03    EMP-REG-HR            PIC S9(2)V9(2).
00127                                03    EMP-OT-HR             PIC S9(2)V9(2).
00128                                03    EMP-GROSS             PIC S9(4)V9(2).
00129                                03    EMP-FICA              PIC S9(2)V9(2).
00130                                03    EMP-TAX               PIC S9(3)V9(2).
00131                                03    EMP-NET               PIC S9(4)V9(2).
00132                    01    HRS-WORKED-IN-REC.
00133                          02    HRS-IN-SS-NUM               PIC X(9).
00134                          02    HRS-IN-HRS-WORKED           PIC S9(2)V9(2).
00135                    01    PAY-MAST-IO-REC.
00136                          02    PAY-IO-PLANT-SITE           PIC S9.
00137                          02    PAY-IO-DEPT-CODE            PIC S9(2).
00138                          02    PAY-IO-SS-NUM               PIC X(9).
00139                          02    PAY-IO-EMP-NAME             PIC X(20).
00140                          02    PAY-IO-PERSONAL-DATA        PIC X(42).
00141                          02    PAY-IO-TAX-CLASS            PIC S9(2).
00142                          02    PAY-IO-PAY-RATE             PIC S9(2)V9(2).
00143                          02    PAY-IO-YTD-GROSS            PIC S9(5)V9(2).
00144                          02    PAY-IO-YTD-TAX              PIC S9(5)V9(2).
00145                          02    PAY-IO-YTD-FICA             PIC S9(4)V9(2).
00146          *
00147                    REPORT SECTION.
00148                    RD    PAYROLL-REGISTER CONTROL IS FINAL
00149                          PAGE LIMIT IS 55 LINES
00150                          HEADING   1
00151                          FIRST DETAIL 5
00152                          LAST DETAIL   53
00153                          FOOTING    55.
00154                    01    TYPE REPORT HEADING LINE 1.
00155                          02    COLUMN 48                   PIC X(18)
00156                                VALUE  'MEGA-TRONICS, INC.'.
00157                          02    COLUMN 70                   PIC X(16)
00158                                VALUE 'PAYROLL REGISTER'.
00159                    01    TYPE PAGE HEADING.
00160                          02    LINE 2 COLUMN 122           PIC X(4) VALUE 'PAGE'.
00161                          02    COLUMN 127                  PIC 9(2)
00162                                SOURCE PAGE-COUNTER.
00163                          02    LINE 3 COLUMN 1             PIC X(10) VALUE 'SOC-SEC-NO'.
00164                          02    COLUMN 13                   PIC X(9) VALUE 'YTD-GROSS'.
00165                          02    COLUMN 25                   PIC X(7) VALUE 'YTD-TAX'.
00166                          02    COLUMN 34                   PIC X(8) VALUE 'YTD-FICA'.
00167                          02    COLUMN 43                   PIC X(5) VALUE 'PLANT'.
00168                          02    COLUMN 49                   PIC X(4)
00169                                VALUE 'DEPT'.
00170                          02    COLUMN 57                   PIC X(13)
00171                                VALUE 'EMPLOYEE-NAME'.
00172                          02    COLUMN 76                   PIC X(4) VALUE 'RATE'.
00173                          02    COLUMN 83                   PIC X(6) VALUE 'REG-HR'.
00174                          02    COLUMN 90                   PIC X(5) VALUE 'OT-HR'.
00175                          02    COLUMN 99                   PIC X(5) VALUE 'GROSS'.
00176                          02    COLUMN 108                  PIC X(4) VALUE 'FICA'.
00177                          02    COLUMN 117                  PIC X(3) VALUE 'TAX'.
00178                          02    COLUMN 127                  PIC X(3) VALUE 'NET'.
00179                          02    LINE PLUS 1 COLUMN 1        PIC X(132) VALUE ALL '-'.
```

Figure 10.14 (*cont.*)

```
00180          01   PAY-REG-EMP-PRINT-LINE TYPE DETAIL LINE PLUS 1.
00181               02   COLUMN 1                        PIC 9(9)
00182                    SOURCE PAY-IO-SS-NUM.
00183               02   COLUMN 14                       PIC Z(5).9(2)
00184                    SOURCE EMP-YTD-GROSS.
00185               02   COLUMN 25                       PIC Z(4).9(2)
00186                    SOURCE EMP-YTD-TAX.
00187               02   COLUMN 35                       PIC Z(4).9(2)
00188                    SOURCE EMP-YTD-FICA.
00189               02   COLUMN 45                       PIC 9
00190                    SOURCE PAY-IO-PLANT-SITE.
00191               02   COLUMN 50                       PIC 9(2)
00192                    SOURCE PAY-IO-DEPT-CODE.
00193               02   COLUMN 54                       PIC X(20)
00194                    SOURCE PAY-IO-EMP-NAME.
00195               02   COLUMN 76                       PIC Z9.9(2)
00196                    SOURCE PAY-IO-PAY-RATE.
00197               02   COLUMN 83                       PIC Z9.9(2)
00198                    SOURCE EMP-REG-HR.
00199               02   COLUMN 90                       PIC Z9.9(2)
00200                    SOURCE EMP-OT-HR.
00201               02   COLUMN 98                       PIC Z(4).9(2)
00202                    SOURCE EMP-GROSS.
00203               02   COLUMN 108                      PIC Z9.9(2)
00204                    SOURCE EMP-FICA.
00205               02   COLUMN 116                      PIC Z(3).9(2)
00206                    SOURCE EMP-TAX.
00207               02   COLUMN 125                      PIC Z(4).9(2)
00208                    SOURCE EMP-NET.
00209          01   PAY-REG-ERROR-LINE TYPE DETAIL LINE PLUS 1.
00210               02   COLUMN 1                        PIC 9(9)
00211                    SOURCE PAY-IO-SS-NUM.
00212               02   COLUMN 14                       PIC Z(5).9(2)
00213                    SOURCE EMP-YTD-GROSS.
00214               02   COLUMN 25                       PIC Z(4).9(2)
00215                    SOURCE EMP-YTD-TAX.
00216               02   COLUMN 35                       PIC Z(4).9(2)
00217                    SOURCE EMP-YTD-FICA.
00218               02   COLUMN 45                       PIC 9
00219                    SOURCE PAY-IO-PLANT-SITE.
00220               02   COLUMN 50                       PIC 9(2)
00221                    SOURCE PAY-IO-DEPT-CODE.
00222               02   COLUMN 54                       PIC X(20)
00223                    SOURCE PAY-IO-EMP-NAME.
00224               02   COLUMN 76                       PIC Z9.9(2)
00225                    SOURCE PAY-IO-PAY-RATE.
00226               02   COLUMN 83                       PIC X(20)
00227                    SOURCE ERROR-MESSAGE.
00228          01   HR-IN-ERROR-LINE TYPE DETAIL LINE PLUS 1.
00229               02   COLUMN 1                        PIC 9(9)
00230                    SOURCE HRS-IN-SS-NUM.
00231               02   COLUMN 83                       PIC X(20)
00232                    SOURCE ERROR-MESSAGE.
00233          01   TYPE CONTROL FOOTING FINAL LINE PLUS 2.
00234               02   COLUMN 2                        PIC X(6) VALUE 'TOTALS'.
00235               02   COLUMN 13                       PIC Z(6).9(2)
00236                    SUM EMP-YTD-GROSS.
00237               02   COLUMN 24                       PIC Z(5).9(2)
00238                    SUM EMP-YTD-TAX.
00239               02   COLUMN 34                       PIC Z(5).9(2)
00240                    SUM EMP-YTD-FICA.
00241               02   COLUMN 81                       PIC Z(4).9(2)
00242                    SUM EMP-REG-HR.
00243               02   COLUMN 89                       PIC Z(3).9(2)
00244                    SUM EMP-OT-HR.
00245               02   COLUMN 96                       PIC Z(6).9(2)
00246                    SUM EMP-GROSS.
00247               02   COLUMN 106                      PIC Z(4).9(2)
00248                    SUM EMP-FICA.
00249               02   COLUMN 114                      PIC Z(5).9(2)
00250                    SUM EMP-TAX.
00251               02   COLUMN 123                      PIC Z(6).9(2)
00252                    SUM EMP-NET.
00253      *
00254          PROCEDURE DIVISION.
```

Figure 10.14 (*cont.*)

```
00255                *
00256                  PAYROLL-REGISTER-CONTROL.
00257                     PERFORM START-UP.
00258                     PERFORM PROCESS-PAY-FILES
00259                         UNTIL PROCESSING-SHOULD-STOP.
00260                     PERFORM FINISH-UP.
00261                     STOP RUN.
00262                *
00263                  START-UP.
00264                     OPEN INPUT   HRS-WORKED-PAY-PERIOD-FILE-IN
00265                          I-O     PAYROLL-MAST-FILE-IO
00266                          OUTPUT  PAYROLL-REGISTER-REPORT-FILE.
00267                     MOVE ALL 'N' TO SWITCHES.
00268                     INITIATE PAYROLL-REGISTER.
00269                     PERFORM READ-PAYROLL-MAST-FILE.
00270                     PERFORM READ-HRS-WORKED-FILE.
00271                *
00272                  PROCESS-PAY-FILES.
00273                     IF (PAY-IO-SS-NUM IS LESS THAN HRS-IN-SS-NUM)
00274                         PERFORM EMPLOYEE-DID-NOT-WORK
00275                     ELSE
00276                         IF (PAY-IO-SS-NUM IS GREATER THAN HRS-IN-SS-NUM)
00277                             PERFORM  NO-MASTER-PAYROLL-REC-FOUND
00278                         ELSE
00279                             PERFORM PROCESS-EMPLOYEE-PAY.
00280                     IF END-OF-HRS-WORKED-FILE
00281                             AND
00282                         END-OF-PAYROLL-MAST-FILE
00283                         MOVE 'Y' TO STOP-PROCESSING-SW.
00284                *
00285                  FINISH-UP.
00286                     TERMINATE PAYROLL-REGISTER.
00287                     IF INVALID-REWRITE-PAY-MAST
00288                         DISPLAY 'BAD REWRITE TO PAYROLL MASTER FILE '
00289                             PAY-MAST-IO-REC
00290                         DISPLAY 'PROGRAM IS BEING TERMINATED'.
00291                     CLOSE HRS-WORKED-PAY-PERIOD-FILE-IN    PAYROLL-MAST-FILE-IO
00292                         PAYROLL-REGISTER-REPORT-FILE.
00293                *
00294                  EMPLOYEE-DID-NOT-WORK.
00295                     MOVE PAY-IO-YTD-GROSS TO EMP-YTD-GROSS.
00296                     MOVE PAY-IO-YTD-TAX TO EMP-YTD-TAX.
00297                     MOVE PAY-IO-YTD-FICA TO EMP-YTD-FICA.
00298                     MOVE 'NOT IN PAY STATUS' TO ERROR-MESSAGE.
00299                     PERFORM GENERATE-NO-PAY.
00300                     PERFORM READ-PAYROLL-MAST-FILE.
00301                *
00302                  NO-MASTER-PAYROLL-REC-FOUND.
00303                     MOVE 'NO PAYROLL MASTER' TO ERROR-MESSAGE.
00304                     PERFORM GENERATE-NO-MASTER.
00305                     PERFORM READ-HRS-WORKED-FILE.
00306                *
00307                  PROCESS-EMPLOYEE-PAY.
00308                     PERFORM PAYROLL-CALCULATIONS.
00309                     PERFORM MOVE-PAY-DATA-TO-RECORDS.
00310                     PERFORM GENERATE-PAYROLL-REGISTER-LINE.
00311                     PERFORM REWRITE-PAYROLL-MAST-REC.
00312                     PERFORM READ-PAYROLL-MAST-FILE.
00313                     PERFORM READ-HRS-WORKED-FILE.
```

Figure 10.14 (*cont.*)

```
00314            *
00315                    PAYROLL-CALCULATIONS.
00316                        IF (HRS-IN-HRS-WORKED IS GREATER THAN MAX-REG-HRS)
00317                            MOVE MAX-REG-HRS TO EMP-REG-HR
00318                            COMPUTE EMP-OT-HR = (HRS-IN-HRS-WORKED) - (MAX-REG-HRS)
00319                            COMPUTE EMP-GROSS = (EMP-REG-HR * PAY-IO-PAY-RATE) +
00320                                (EMP-OT-HR * (OVERTIME-ADJUSTMENT * PAY-IO-PAY-RATE))
00321                        ELSE
00322                            MOVE HRS-IN-HRS-WORKED TO EMP-REG-HR
00323                            MOVE ZEROES TO EMP-OT-HR
00324                            COMPUTE EMP-GROSS = (EMP-REG-HR * PAY-IO-PAY-RATE).
00325                        COMPUTE EMP-TAX = ((EMP-GROSS) - (PAY-IO-TAX-CLASS) *
00326                            (TAXABLE-INCOME-ADJUSTMENT)) * (EST-FED-TAX-RATE).
00327                        IF (PAY-IO-YTD-GROSS IS GREATER THAN MAX-SS-WITHHOLD)
00328                            MOVE ZEROS TO EMP-FICA
00329                        ELSE
00330                            IF ((PAY-IO-YTD-GROSS + EMP-GROSS)
00331                                    IS LESS THAN MAX-SS-WITHHOLD)
00332                                COMPUTE EMP-FICA = EMP-GROSS * SS-WITHHOLD-RATE
00333                            ELSE
00334                                COMPUTE EMP-FICA = ((MAX-SS-WITHHOLD) -
00335                                    (PAY-IO-YTD-GROSS)) * SS-WITHHOLD-RATE.
00336                        COMPUTE EMP-NET = EMP-GROSS - (EMP-FICA + EMP-TAX).
00337                        COMPUTE EMP-YTD-GROSS = PAY-IO-YTD-GROSS + EMP-GROSS.
00338                        COMPUTE EMP-YTD-TAX = PAY-IO-YTD-TAX + EMP-TAX.
00339                        COMPUTE EMP-YTD-FICA = PAY-IO-YTD-FICA + EMP-FICA.
00340            *
00341                    MOVE-PAY-DATA-TO-RECORDS.
00342                        MOVE EMP-YTD-GROSS TO PAY-IO-YTD-GROSS.
00343                        MOVE EMP-YTD-TAX TO PAY-IO-YTD-TAX.
00344                        MOVE EMP-YTD-FICA TO PAY-IO-YTD-FICA.
00345            *
00346                    GENERATE-NO-PAY.
00347                        GENERATE PAY-REG-ERROR-LINE.
00348            *
00349                    GENERATE-NO-MASTER.
00350                        GENERATE HR-IN-ERROR-LINE.
00351            *
00352                    GENERATE-PAYROLL-REGISTER-LINE.
00353                        GENERATE PAY-REG-EMP-PRINT-LINE.
00354            *
00355                    REWRITE-PAYROLL-MAST-REC.
00356                        REWRITE PAY-MAST-IO-AREA FROM PAY-MAST-IO-REC
00357                            INVALID KEY MOVE 'Y' TO INVALID-REWRITE-PAY-MAST-SW
00358                                            STOP-PROCESSING-SW.
00359            *
00360                    READ-PAYROLL-MAST-FILE.
00361                        READ PAYROLL-MAST-FILE-IO INTO PAY-MAST-IO-REC
00362                            AT END MOVE HIGH-VALUES TO PAY-IO-SS-NUM
00363                                MOVE 'Y' TO END-OF-PAYROLL-MAST-FILE-SW.
00364            *
00365                    READ-HRS-WORKED-FILE.
00366                        READ HRS-WORKED-PAY-PERIOD-FILE-IN INTO HRS-WORKED-IN-REC
00367                            AT END MOVE HIGH-VALUES TO HRS-IN-SS-NUM
00368                                MOVE 'Y' TO END-OF-HRS-WORKED-FILE-SW.
```

MEGA-TRONICS, INC.   PAYROLL REGISTER   PAGE 01

SOC-SEC-NO	YTD-GROSS	YTD-TAX	YTD-FICA	PLANT	DEPT	EMPLOYEE-NAME	RATE	REG-HR	OT-HR	GROSS	FICA	TAX	NET
011867322	154.05	20.70	10.32	2	12	WILLIAMSON SHIRLEY A	3.95	39.00	0.00	154.05	10.32	20.70	123.03
024765852	.00	.000	.000	1	01	CARLSON LEONARD O	3.55	NOT IN PAY STATUS					
035102698	.00	.000	.000	1	02	JACKSON PAMELA S	3.85	NOT IN PAY STATUS					
046345658	.00	.000	.000	1	06	ADAMS WAYNE P	7.30	NOT IN PAY STATUS					
061597324	.00	.000	.000	2	07	MADISON JERRY L	5.65	NOT IN PAY STATUS					
074139821	269.50	39.15	18.05	2	01	KENNEDY COLLEEN E	4.90	40.00	10.00	269.50	18.05	39.15	212.30
085464975	169.85	25.89	11.37	1	15	ZIMMERMAN WALTER B	3.95	40.00	2.00	169.85	11.37	25.89	132.59
124386752	.00	.000	.000	2	10	LAMBERT STEVEN J	4.50	NOT IN PAY STATUS					
149871046	.00	.000	.000	2	01	GALLOWAY DENISE J	6.80	NOT IN PAY STATUS					
158652450	208.00	28.08	13.93	2	01	DENNING SUSAN B	5.20	40.00	0.00	208.00	13.93	28.08	165.99
175926415	290.00	45.18	19.43	1	07	HAGGERTY RAYMOND M	7.25	40.00	0.00	290.00	19.43	45.18	225.39
186527540	156.00	18.72	10.45	2	01	SWANSON KATHLEEN A	3.90	40.00	0.00	156.00	10.45	18.72	126.83
195526330	241.71	38.82	16.19	2	02	OLDFIELD MERRILEE S	4.25	40.00	11.25	241.71	16.19	38.82	186.70
212288534	.00	.000	.000	1	15	YOUNG RICHARD E	4.25	NOT IN PAY STATUS					
224876452	.00	.000	.000	1	01	REED GLORIA S	8.35	NOT IN PAY STATUS					
235255424	420.00	73.26	28.14	2	10	MARTIN JAMES A	10.50	40.00	0.00	420.00	28.14	73.26	318.60
245745883	352.80	51.80	23.63	1	01	UNDERWOOD MARY L	7.20	40.00	6.00	352.80	23.63	51.80	277.37
257278640	267.05	45.72	17.89	1	05	COLLINS RUTH	5.45	40.00	6.00	267.05	17.89	45.72	203.44
305243885	577.50	87.57	38.69	1	06	JANSEN JEFFREY J	10.50	40.00	10.00	577.50	38.69	87.57	451.24
313345458	.00	.000	.000	2	10	NELSON CHARLES P	6.40	NOT IN PAY STATUS					
316271468	.00	.000	.000	2	07	ERICKSON MARTIN D	4.90	NOT IN PAY STATUS					
324243765	336.00	53.46	22.51	2	10	HOLBROOK VICTORIA L	8.40	40.00	0.00	336.00	22.51	53.46	260.03
330948326	238.00	40.50	15.94	1	15	EVANS ARTHUR J	5.95	40.00	0.00	238.00	15.94	40.50	181.56
354159820	190.00	24.84	12.73	2	07	STEVENS PHYLLIS K	4.75	40.00	0.00	190.00	12.73	24.84	152.43
352239764	200.68	33.78	13.44	1	05	KRAMER CHARLES J	4.75	40.00	1.50	200.68	13.44	33.78	153.46
360158021	.00	.000	.000	2	10	TOWNSEND JAMES J	3.65	NOT IN PAY STATUS					
372589742	.00	.000	.000	1	15	PATTON RICHARD H	3.80	NOT IN PAY STATUS					
386114880	254.00	41.04	17.01	1	15	FAIRBANKS MARGARET A	6.35	40.00	0.00	254.00	17.01	41.04	195.95
388452260	.00	.000	.000	1	15	LARSON GORDON R	5.10	NOT IN PAY STATUS					
395321760	.00	.000	.000	1	01	SULLIVAN KENNETH A	4.75	NOT IN PAY STATUS					
403842266	.00	.000	.000	2	07	PETERSON KERMIT T	5.10	NOT IN PAY STATUS					
425486624	150.00	24.66	10.05	2	05	WOODS ROBERT L	3.75	40.00	0.00	150.00	10.05	24.66	115.29
483565421	.00	.000	.000	2	02	BAKER CHRISTY J	6.35	NOT IN PAY STATUS					
502684265	382.00	64.08	25.59	2	06	COOPER ANDREW J	9.55	40.00	0.00	382.00	25.59	64.08	292.33
513179986	.00	.000	.000	1	08	HUNTER JOHANNA M	3.75	NOT IN PAY STATUS					
517256574	.00	.000	.000	1	06	ANDREWS WENDY A	8.45	NOT IN PAY STATUS					
520289972	.00	.000	.000	2	06	HILL WAYNE T	9.55	NOT IN PAY STATUS					
524728445	.00	.000	.000	1	15	KIMBALL JOHN T	7.25	NOT IN PAY STATUS					
528297644	.00	.000	.000	2	15	LITTLE FREDRICK R	4.35	NOT IN PAY STATUS					
532843760	.00	.000	.000	2	06	GREENFIELD REBECCA A	4.90	NOT IN PAY STATUS					
540055298	.00	.000	.000	1	02	JOHNSON ELMER L	5.60	NOT IN PAY STATUS					
556046543	.00	.000	.000	1	15	ELLIOTT RANDALL L	6.45	NOT IN PAY STATUS					
564897521	.00	.000	.000	1	07	IRWIN WALTER A	7.30	NOT IN PAY STATUS					
	318.50	50.31	21.33	2	08	THOMPSON LORRAINE M	6.50	40.00	6.00	318.50	21.33	50.31	246.86
	169.85	25.89	11.37	1	02	MONROE ROBERT J	3.95	40.00	2.00	169.85	11.37	25.89	132.59
				2	02	ZINKMAN MAYNARD V	5.25	NOT IN PAY STATUS					
				1	05	OLSON LINDA L	3.95	NO PAYROLL MASTER					

Figure 10.15a

Sample output (first page) generated from the program in Figure 10.14.

SOC-SEC-NO	YTD-GROSS	YTD-TAX	YTD-FICA	PLANT	DEPT	EMPLOYEE-NAME	RATE	REG-HR	OT-HR	GROSS	FICA	TAX	NET
571569876	.00	.00	.00	1	01	ASPEGREN FLORENCE T	4.80	NOT IN PAY STATUS					
584311524	.00	.00	.00	2	06	LEE HERMAN E	5.25	NOT IN PAY STATUS					
592764831	150.00	22.32	10.05	2	02	REDFIELD SANDRA L	3.75	40.00	0.00	150.00	10.05	22.32	117.63
608912953	338.00	58.50	22.64	1	06	LIVINGSTON WOODROW J	9.25	40.00	0.00	338.00	22.64	58.50	256.86
613568442	.00	.00	.00	2	05	NORRIS LAVONNE C	8.45	NOT IN PAY STATUS					
629372263	202.00	29.34	13.53	2	07	HAWKINS RALPH N	6.65	40.00	0.00	202.00	13.53	29.34	159.13
643824694	593.75	97.51	39.78	1	08	TEMPLE MERCEDES E	12.50	40.00	5.00	593.75	39.78	97.51	456.46
661143880	.00	.00	.00	2	07	WILLIAMSON ANNETTE L	14.80	NOT IN PAY STATUS					
680298634	.00	.00	.00	1	08	MURPHY RICHARD H	9.40	NOT IN PAY STATUS					
715278105	.00	.00	.00	1	10	DRAKE T DONALD D	11.25	NOT IN PAY STATUS					
725384426	.00	.00	.00	2	15	ROBERTS THOMAS H	10.50	NOT IN PAY STATUS					
745493208	.00	.00	.00	2	08	WEBER JACK B	8.95	NOT IN PAY STATUS					
752792654	.00	.00	.00	2	07	KING STEPHEN S	5.65	NOT IN PAY STATUS					
763846215	.00	.00	.00	1	15	BLACKBURN PAULETTE M	4.80	NOT IN PAY STATUS					
784769258	.00	.00	.00	2	07	WALTON MARTHA K	3.95	NOT IN PAY STATUS					
801692643	.00	.00	.00	1	15	SHAW STANLEY G	9.40	NOT IN PAY STATUS					
815279180	314.00	51.84	21.03	2	07	HORTON RICHARD N	7.85	40.00	0.00	314.00	21.03	51.84	241.13
826624853	.00	.00	.00	2	15	OWENS KELLY L	5.55	NOT IN PAY STATUS					
835586480	.00	.00	.00	1	02	LEWIS DAVID J	3.90	NOT IN PAY STATUS					
855697299	.00	.00	.00	1	08	GRABOWSKI KATHERINE	3.85	NOT IN PAY STATUS					
864215845	.00	.00	.00	2	02	WHITE JOHN R	3.40	NOT IN PAY STATUS					
875384264	410.00	71.46	27.47	1	08	SMITH FRANCES T	16.75	40.00	0.00	410.00	27.47	71.46	311.07
882584264	.00	.00	.00	1	10	JONES RICHARD G	10.25	NOT IN PAY STATUS					
909843920	.00	.00	.00	2	06	VINSON DURWOOD A	4.75	NOT IN PAY STATUS					
918847261	.00	.00	.00	1	10	EDWARDS WILLIAM C	3.95	NOT IN PAY STATUS					
949258301	.00	.00	.00	1	08	CUNNINGHAM BARBARA J	4.50	NOT IN PAY STATUS					
952658422	.00	.00	.00	2		ROPER CARL A		NOT IN PAY STATUS					
TOTALS	7353.24	1164.42	492.56					1039.00	59.75	7353.24	492.56	1164.42	5696.26

Figure 10.15b
Final page of output.

THE USE OF DECLARATIVES WITH REPORT WRITER

Sometimes additional processing will be needed before a control group should be generated. Suppose that in our grade report example we want to print the grade point average, as well as the total hours and quality points. Report Writer allows this type of special processing to be done using DECLARATIVES. To do this, the PROCEDURE DIVISION is coded in SECTIONS. The DECLARATIVES must be placed at the beginning of the PROCEDURE DIVISION and must contain a USE statement that specifies that the section is to be executed before a specified report group is printed.[2] The report group may not be a detail report group.

To illustrate, suppose the control is the STUDENT-ID. Then the following statements might be coded.

```
DECLARATIVES.
    USE BEFORE REPORTING STUDENT-SUMMARY-COMPUTE-GPA.
    COMPUTE GPA = TOTAL-QUALITY-POINTS / TOTAL-HOURS.
END DECLARATIVES.
```

These DECLARATIVES could then be used in conjunction with a control footing report group similar to the following entries.

```
01  STUDENT-SUMMARY
    TYPE IS CONTROL FOOTING STUDENT-ID.
    02  TOTAL-HOURS
        LINE IS PLUS 2
        COLUMN 35                           PIC 9(3)
        SUM SEMESTER-HOURS.

    02  TOTAL-QUALITY-POINTS
        COLUMN 50                           PIC 9(4)
        SUM QUALITY-POINTS.

    02  COLUMN 75                           PIC 9.99
        SOURCE GPA.
```

Example 10.4

Suppose the report generated for Example 10.2 should contain a message that flags the employees who have worked more than 40 hours in a week.

As will be illustrated shortly, only a slight modification in the control footing report group will be necessary to accommodate printing the message. In Figure 10.16, the SECTION organization is given. The structure chart for REPORT-GENERATION SECTION is identical to that of Figure 10.7. Figure 10.18 contains program output. The program listing is given in Figure 10.17. Note that

---

[2] This is not the first time we have used DECLARATIVES for special processing. DECLARATIVES, the USE statement, and SECTIONS were discussed in Chapter 8 in connection with processing overflow records. SECTIONS were also described in some detail in Chapter 5.

1. The control footing line that starts on line 128 now contains a message area (lines 133, 134).
2. The *USE BEFORE REPORTING* entry on line 146 specifies that statements in the DECLARATIVES section are to be executed prior to printing the report group EMP-HRS-TOTAL-LINE.
3. Execution of the program begins on line 157, which follows the DECLARATIVES SECTION.
4. On each execution of line 180, a test is made for a new social security number. If a new social security number is encountered, all DECLARATIVES statements will be executed, and then the footing will be printed.

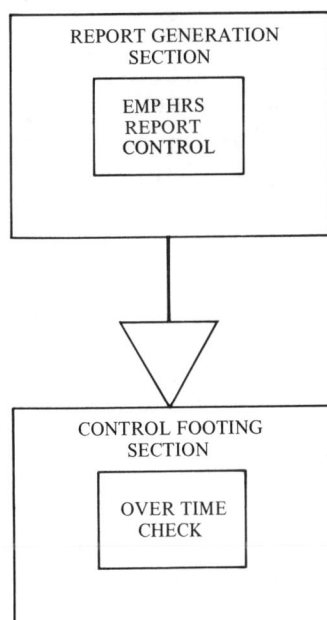

Figure 10.16
Section organization for the program in Figure 10.17.

```
00001                IDENTIFICATION DIVISION.
00002          *
00003           PROGRAM-ID.
00004             EX-10-4.
00005          *****************************************************************
00006          *                                                               *
00007          *    PROGRAMMER TEAM         WALSTROM/SUMMERS/LINDAHL            *
00008          *    PROGRAM COMPLETION DATE DECEMBER 5, 1983                    *
00009          *                                                               *
00010          *                    PROGRAM SUMMARY                            *
00011          *    INPUT                                                      *
00012          *        THE INPUT FILE IS A SEQUENTIAL FILE, ORDERED BY        *
00013          *        SOCIAL SECURITY NUMBER. THERE MAY BE MULTIPLE RECORDS  *
00014          *    FOR AN EMPLOYEE. EACH RECORD CONSISTS OF                   *
00015          *            - SOCIAL SECURITY NUMBER                           *
00016          *            - TASK PERFORMED BY AN EMPLOYEE                     *
00017          *            - PROJECT BUDGET NUMBER                            *
00018          *            - HOURS WORKED BY EMPLOYEE FOR THE TASK AND         *
00019          *              PROJECT                                         *
```

Figure 10.17
Control-break processing and report generation using a DECLARATIVES section in Report Writer for Example 10.4.

Figure 10.17 *(cont.)*

```
00020     *
00021     *      PROCESSING                                               *
00022     *         THE REPORT WRITER FEATURE CONTROLS THE ACCUMULATION   *
00023     *         OF TOTALS.                                            *
00024     *            -  THE TOTAL HOURS WORKED BY AN EMPLOYEE           *
00025     *               IS CALCULATED                                   *
00026     *            -  THE TOTAL HOURS WORKED BY ALL                   *
00027     *               EMPLOYEES IS ACCUMULATED                        *
00028     *            -  THE TOTAL HOURS WORKED BY AN EMPLOYEE           *
00029     *               IS CHECKED TO DETERMINE IF THE EMPLOYEE WORKED  *
00030     *               OVERTIME                                        *
00031     *                                                               *
00032     *      OUTPUT                                                   *
00033     *         A PRINTED REPORT IS PRODUCED USING THE REPORT WRITER  *
00034     *         FEATURE. FOR EACH EMPLOYEE THE OUTPUT CONSISTS OF     *
00035     *            -  SOCIAL SECURITY NUMBER                          *
00036     *            -  PROJECT BUDGET NUMBER                           *
00037     *            -  TASK CODE                                       *
00038     *            -  HOURS WORKED                                    *
00039     *            -  TOTAL HOURS WORKED                              *
00040     *            -  A MESSAGE TO INDICATE AN EMPLOYEE WHO WORKED    *
00041     *               OVERTIME                                        *
00042     *         THE TOTAL NUMBER OF HOURS WORKED BY ALL EMPLOYEES     *
00043     *         IS ALSO PRINTED                                       *
00044     **************************************************************
00045     *
00046      ENVIRONMENT DIVISION.
00047     *
00048      CONFIGURATION SECTION.
00049      SOURCE-COMPUTER.
00050          IBM.
00051      OBJECT-COMPUTER.
00052          IBM.
00053      INPUT-OUTPUT SECTION.
00054      FILE-CONTROL.
00055          SELECT HRS-WORKED-PROJ-FILE-IN
00056              ASSIGN TO SYS023-DA-3330-S-PHRSFIL.
00057          SELECT  HRS-WORKED-PRINT-FILE
00058              ASSIGN TO SYS009-UR-1403-S.
00059     *
00060      DATA DIVISION.
00061     *
00062      FILE SECTION.
00063      FD  HRS-WORKED-PROJ-FILE-IN
00064              LABEL RECORDS ARE STANDARD
00065              BLOCK CONTAINS 20 RECORDS.
00066      01  HRS-WORKED-PROJ-IN-AREA           PIC X(20).
00067      FD  HRS-WORKED-PRINT-FILE
00068              LABEL RECORDS ARE OMITTED
00069              RECORD CONTAINS 133 CHARACTERS
00070              REPORT IS TOTAL-HOURS-REPORT.
00071     *
00072      WORKING-STORAGE SECTION.
00073      01  SWITCHES.
00074          02  END-OF-FILE-SW                PIC X.
00075              88  NO-MORE-RECORDS VALUE 'Y'.
00076      01  CONSTANTS.
00077          02  MAX-REG-HRS                   PIC S9(2) VALUE +40.
00078      01  OVERTIME-MESSAGE.
00079          02  FILLER                        PIC X(21).
00080      01  HRS-WORKED-IN-REC.
00081          02  HRS-IN-SS-NUM.
00082              03  FIRST-3-DIGITS            PIC 9(3).
00083              03  NEXT-2-DIGITS             PIC 9(2).
00084              03  LAST-4-DIGITS             PIC 9(4).
00085          02  HRS-IN-TASK-CODE              PIC S9(2).
00086          02  HRS-IN-PROJ-NUM               PIC 9(5).
00087          02  HRS-IN-HRS-WORKED             PIC S9(2)V9(2).
00088     *
00089      REPORT SECTION.
00090      RD  TOTAL-HOURS-REPORT
00091              CONTROLS ARE FINAL HRS-IN-SS-NUM
00092              PAGE LIMIT IS 55 LINES
00093              HEADING 2
00094              FIRST DETAIL 5
00095              LAST DETAIL  50
00096              FOOTING      54.
00097      01  TYPE REPORT HEADING.
00098          02  LINE 2 COLUMN 28              PIC X(18)
00099                  VALUE 'MEGATRONICS REPORT'.
```

Figure 10.17 (*cont.*)

```
00100         01   PAGE-HEADING TYPE PAGE HEADING LINE 4.
00101              02   COLUMN 5                    PIC X(22)
00102                   VALUE 'SOCIAL SECURITY NUMBER'.
00103              02   COLUMN 31                   PIC X(9)
00104                   VALUE 'TASK CODE'.
00105              02   COLUMN 48                   PIC X(12)
00106                   VALUE 'HOURS WORKED'.
00107              02   COLUMN 65                   PIC X(14)
00108                   VALUE 'PROJECT NUMBER'.
00109              02   COLUMN 90                   PIC X(4)
00110                   VALUE 'PAGE'.
00111              02   COLUMN 95                   PIC ZZ9
00112                   SOURCE PAGE-COUNTER.
00113         01   PROJ-HRS-LINE TYPE DETAIL LINE PLUS 1.
00114              02   COLUMN 8 GROUP INDICATE     PIC 9(3)
00115                   SOURCE FIRST-3-DIGITS.
00116              02   COLUMN 11 GROUP INDICATE    PIC X VALUE '-'.
00117              02   COLUMN 12 GROUP INDICATE    PIC 9(2)
00118                   SOURCE NEXT-2-DIGITS.
00119              02   COLUMN 14 GROUP INDICATE    PIC X VALUE '-'.
00120              02   COLUMN 15 GROUP INDICATE    PIC 9(4)
00121                   SOURCE LAST-4-DIGITS.
00122              02   COLUMN 34                   PIC -9(2)
00123                   SOURCE HRS-IN-TASK-CODE.
00124              02   COLUMN 51                   PIC -9(2).9(2)
00125                   SOURCE HRS-IN-HRS-WORKED.
00126              02   COLUMN 69                   PIC 9(5)
00127                   SOURCE HRS-IN-PROJ-NUM.
00128         01   EMP-HRS-TOTAL-LINE TYPE CONTROL FOOTING HRS-IN-SS-NUM.
00129              02   EMP-TOT LINE PLUS 2 COLUMN 51
00130                                               PIC -Z(2).9(2)
00131                   SUM HRS-IN-HRS-WORKED.
00132              02   COLUMN 58                   PIC X(5) VALUE 'TOTAL'.
00133              02   COLUMN 65                   PIC X(21)
00134                   SOURCE OVERTIME-MESSAGE.
00135              02   LINE PLUS 1 COLUMN 5        PIC X(98) VALUE ALL '*'.
00136         01   TYPE CONTROL FOOTING FINAL LINE PLUS 4.
00137              02   COLUMN 27                   PIC X(21)
00138                   VALUE 'ALL EMPLOYEES TOTAL'.
00139              02   COLUMN 48                   PIC -Z(5).9(2)
00140                   SUM EMP-TOT.
00141    *
00142         PROCEDURE DIVISION.
00143    *
00144         DECLARATIVES.
00145         CONTROL-FOOTING SECTION.
00146              USE BEFORE REPORTING EMP-HRS-TOTAL-LINE.
00147    *
00148         OVERTIME-CHECK.
00149              IF EMP-TOT IS GREATER THAN MAX-REG-HRS
00150                   MOVE 'OVERTIME RATE APPLIES' TO OVERTIME-MESSAGE
00151              ELSE
00152                   MOVE SPACE TO OVERTIME-MESSAGE.
00153         END DECLARATIVES.
00154    *
00155         REPORT-GENERATION SECTION.
00156    *
00157         EMP-HRS-REPORT-CONTROL.
00158              PERFORM START-UP.
00159              PERFORM PROCESS-EMP-RECORDS UNTIL NO-MORE-RECORDS.
00160              PERFORM FINISH-UP.
00161              STOP RUN.
00162    *
00163         START-UP.
00164              OPEN INPUT HRS-WORKED-PROJ-FILE-IN
00165                   OUTPUT HRS-WORKED-PRINT-FILE.
00166              MOVE 'N' TO END-OF-FILE-SW.
00167              INITIATE TOTAL-HOURS-REPORT.
00168              PERFORM READ-PROJ-FILE.
00169    *
00170         PROCESS-EMP-RECORDS.
00171              PERFORM OUTPUT-ROUTINE.
00172              PERFORM READ-PROJ-FILE.
00173    *
00174         FINISH-UP.
00175              TERMINATE TOTAL-HOURS-REPORT.
00176              CLOSE HRS-WORKED-PROJ-FILE-IN
00177                   HRS-WORKED-PRINT-FILE.
00178    *
00179         OUTPUT-ROUTINE.
00180              GENERATE PROJ-HRS-LINE.
00181    *
00182         READ-PROJ-FILE.
00183              READ HRS-WORKED-PROJ-FILE-IN INTO HRS-WORKED-IN-REC
00184                   AT END MOVE 'Y' TO END-OF-FILE-SW.
```

MEGATRONICS REPORT

SOCIAL SECURITY NUMBER	TASK CODE	HOURS WORKED	PROJECT NUMBER	PAGE 1
011-86-7322	26	25.00	00032	
	26	14.00	00032	
		39.00 TOTAL		
074-13-9821	22	25.00	00032	
	26	25.00	00032	
		50.00 TOTAL OVERTIME RATE APPLIES		
124-38-6752	20	20.00	00035	
	20	02.000	00035	
	20	10.00	00040	
	20	10.00	00050	
		42.00 TOTAL OVERTIME RATE APPLIES		
175-92-6415	21	20.00	00050	
	21	20.00	00050	
		40.00 TOTAL		
195-55-2633	21	20.00	00050	
	21	20.00	00050	
		40.00 TOTAL		
212-28-8534	21	20.00	00050	
	21	20.00	00050	
		40.00 TOTAL		
223-52-5542	10	15.00	100000	
	10	15.00	200000	
	10	05.50	55500	
	10	15.75	32143	
		51.25 TOTAL OVERTIME RATE APPLIES		
257-45-8211	21	20.00	00050	
	21	20.00	00050	
		40.00 TOTAL OVERTIME RATE APPLIES		
275-27-8640	22	23.00	11111	
	28	23.00	11111	
		46.00 TOTAL OVERTIME RATE APPLIES		

Figure 10.18a
Sample output (first page) generated from the program in Figure 10.17.

```
SOCIAL SECURITY NUMBER     TASK CODE          HOURS WORKED      PROJECT NUMBER              PAGE    4
   826-62-4853                27                 05.00             00500

                                                 40.00 TOTAL
****************************************************************************************************
   909-84-3920                22                 10.00             00125
                              22                 10.00             00125
                              25                 10.00             00125
                              25                 10.00             00125

                                                 40.00 TOTAL
****************************************************************************************************


                      ALL EMPLOYEES TOTAL     1149.75
```

Figure 10.18b
Final page of output.

CONCLUDING COMMENTS ABOUT REPORT WRITER

Report Writer is a powerful feature in the COBOL language and, where applicable, should reduce programming time. The feature allows you to generate a report by specifying the physical appearance of the report, rather than having to specify and code all of the detailed procedures otherwise required to generate the report if Report Writer is not used.

As implied in the chapter title, our intention has been to present only an overview of the Report Writer feature. The statements that are unique to Report Writer have many formats, with phrases and options available that require extensive discussion if comprehensive treatment is to be given to them.

Programming Exercises for Chapter 10

EXERCISE 10.1

Assume that a copy of the payroll master file is in order by department code. Within a department, the employee records are in alphabetical order. For a description of the record, see Example 4.1 in Chapter 4.

Write a program using the Report Writer feature to produce a report showing gross pay by department. Each department's report should begin on a new page. The page format is given in the following printer layout.

```
              REPORT FOR DEPARTMENT XX

        EMPLOYEE NAME          SALARY TO DATE

     XXXXXXXXXXXXXXXXXXXX          XXXXX.XX
              .                        .
              .                        .
              .                        .



        DEPARTMENTAL TOTAL         XXXXXXX.XX
```

EXERCISE 10.2

A file is available that contains all the deposit and withdrawal records for customers of Mega-Tronics' credit union. This file is in order by account number. Write a program that produces a report for each account.

Input records are in the following format:

Record Position	Contents	Format
1–5	Account number	X(5)
6–12	Transaction amount (positive if deposit, negative if withdrawal)	S9(5)V9(2)
13–20	Date of transaction (MM/DD/YY)	X(8)

The report description is given in the following printer layout. The BLANK WHEN ZERO and GROUP INDICATE clauses should be used. A transaction amount should be printed in the appropriate column.

```
          MEGA-TRONICS CREDIT UNION TRANSACTION REPORT
                                          PAGE XX

      ACCOUNT      DEPOSIT      WITHDRAWAL
      NUMBER       AMOUNT         AMOUNT

      XXXXXXX      XXXXX.XX      XXXXX.XX
                      .             .
                      .             .
                      .             .


            XXXXXXX.XX      XXXXXXX.XX     ACCOUNT TOTALS
```

EXERCISE 10.3

A file is available that contains sales information for a company's products by territory. The file is ordered by territory code and within a territory by product number.

Input records have the following format:

Record Position	Contents	Format
1–2	Territory code	9(2)
3–6	Product number	9(4)
7–26	Product description	X(20)
27–32	Transaction amount	9(4)V9(2)

Write a program using the Report Writer feature that produces a report of total sales for each product within a territory and the total sales of all products within each territory. The output format is given in the following printer layout.

```
                    SALES REPORT
                                              PAGE XX

   TERRITORY    PRODUCT    TOTAL BY PRODUCT    TOTAL BY TERRITORY

      XX         XXXX         XXXXXX.XX
                   .             .
                   .             .
                   .             .




                                              XXXXXXXX.XX

   TERRITORY    PRODUCT    TOTAL BY PRODUCT    TOTAL BY TERRITORY

      XX         XXXX         XXXXXX.XX
                   .             .
                   .             .
                   .             .




                                              XXXXXXXX.XX
```

11 Miscellaneous Topics

INTRODUCTION

In this chapter, we will provide a brief introduction to several additional COBOL features. They are the COPY statement, with the associated source program library; the string manipulation verbs; and the USE FOR DEBUGGING declarative. We will also describe the debugging language extension supplied with IBM compilers.

SOURCE PROGRAM LIBRARIES AND THE COPY STATEMENT

As you have probably noticed, there is a lot of code repeated in a sequence of COBOL programs that processes the same files. In many organizations, the names of data items that refer to fields, records, and files are established and then made an organization standard. Thus, much of the DATA DIVISION in several programs would consist of exactly the same COBOL entries. The *COPY* feature allows segments of COBOL programs to be placed in a library on disk and then later to be inserted into programs as needed.

$$
\begin{array}{|c|}
\hline
\textbf{FORMAT} \\
\\
\underline{\text{COPY}} \text{ text-name} \left[\left\{ \begin{array}{l} \underline{\text{OF}} \\ \underline{\text{IN}} \end{array} \right\} \text{library-name} \right] \\
\\
[\underline{\text{REPLACING}} \left\{ \begin{array}{l} ==\text{pseudo-text-1}== \\ \text{identifier-1} \\ \text{literal-1} \\ \text{word-1} \end{array} \right\} \\
\\
\underline{\text{BY}} \left\{ \begin{array}{l} ==\text{pseudo-text-2}== \\ \text{identifier-2} \\ \text{literal-2} \\ \text{word-2} \end{array} \right\}] \ldots \\
\hline
\end{array}
$$

The COPY statement may appear anywhere in a program that a delimiter or a character string may appear. The text from the library is substituted for the entire COPY statement. The procedure for creating the source program library is installation-dependent; your local user consultant (or instructor) can provide you with necessary information.

Let's consider several examples related to the inventory master file for Margo's Boutique. The description of the inventory master relative file is given in Chapter 7.

Suppose the library contains the following entry with the text name MASTDSC.

```
SELECT INV-MAST-FILE
     ASSIGN TO SYS023-INVFILE
     ORGANIZATION IS RELATIVE
     ACCESS IS RANDOM
     RELATIVE KEY IS BLOCK-NUM.
```

Then any program working with INV-MAST-FILE can use the description in the library simply by invoking the name MASTDSC with a COPY statement:

```
COPY MASTDSC.
```

The *REPLACING* option of the COPY verb allows us to modify statements being copied from the library, changing them as they are inserted in the program containing the COPY verb.[1]

Suppose a program requires dynamic access rather than random access as specified in the previous library entry. Then the statement

```
COPY MASTDSC
     REPLACING RANDOM BY DYNAMIC.
```

would cause the library entry to be inserted into the program, with the word "RANDOM" replaced by the word "DYNAMIC".

Since the relative key is not part of the file, it might not be included as one of the items with standard data names. If so, we could make the entry

```
COPY MASTDSC
     REPLACING BLOCK-NUM BY REL-KEY
     REPLACING RANDOM BY DYNAMIC.
```

The preceding COPY statement results in the program containing

```
SELECT INV-MAST-FILE
     ASSIGN TO SYS023-INVFILE
     ORGANIZATION IS RELATIVE
     ACCESS IS DYNAMIC
     RELATIVE KEY IS REL-KEY.
```

---

[1] We encourage the use of standard names for items to be used in multiple programs. Use of the REPLACING option tends to generate nonstandard names; consequently, its extensive use is a questionable practice. Also, some systems may not support this option.

Any items that are related to the description of the file could reasonably be copied. Hashing routines and editing routines are also reasonable items to place in a COPY library.

> ### Example 11.1

Recall the payroll master file that was described in Chapter 4, Example 4.1. Suppose the DP manager had decided to enforce naming conventions so that the master file record fields will have standard names. The record description and the edit routine are to be placed in a library for use by all programs that access this file.

The original structure chart in Figure 4.3 has been modified and is shown in Figure 11.1. Note that execution of the module EDIT-PAYROLL-DATA is now indicated with a predefined process symbol. Figure 11.2 contains the modifications made to the original program solution for Example 4.1, which are necessary to use the entries in the COPY library. We call your attention to the COPY statements on lines 93 and 173. All entries with the character "C" preceding them are generated by the compiler as a result of the COPY statements.

Figure 11.3 shows the contents of the source library.

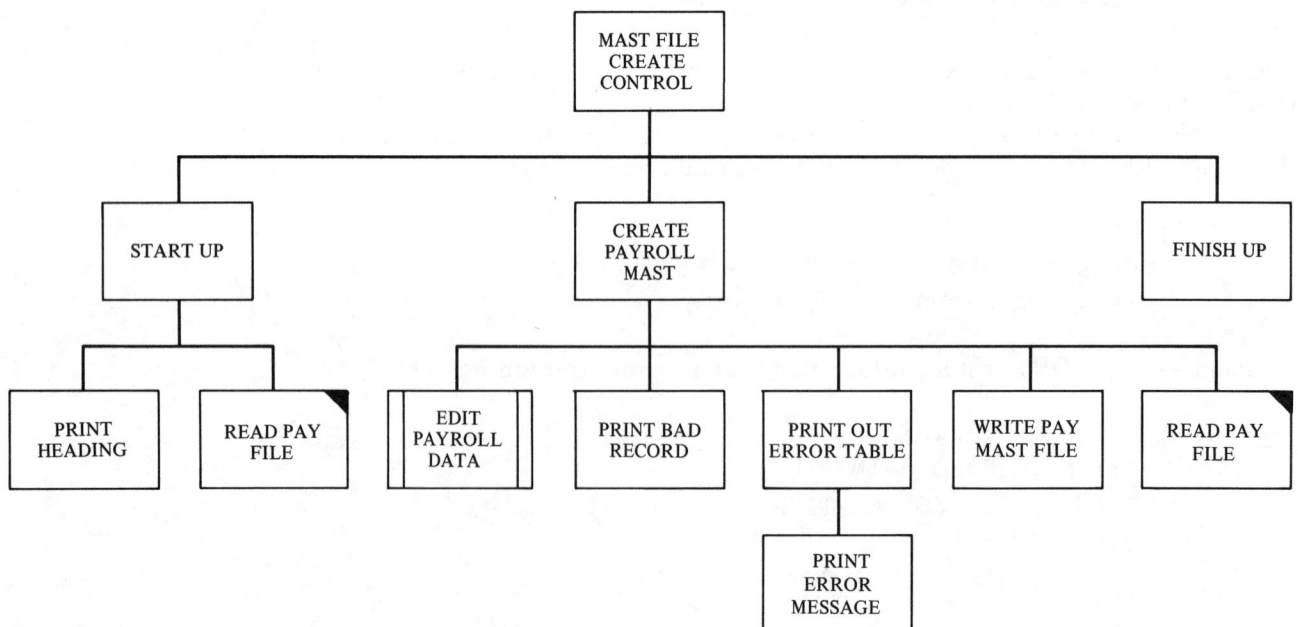

Figure 11.1
Structure chart for the program in Figure 11.2.

```
00001          IDENTIFICATION DIVISION.
00002        *
00003         PROGRAM-ID.
00004            EX-11-1.
00005         ***********************************************************************
00006         *                                                                     *
00007         *    PROGRAMMER TEAM              WALSTROM/SUMMERS/LINDAHL             *
00008         *    PROGRAM COMPLETION DATE NOVEMBER 28,1983                         *
00009         *                                                                     *
00010         *                    PROGRAM SUMMARY                                  *
00011         *    INPUT                                                            *
00012         *        THE INPUT FILE IS IN ASCENDING ORDER                         *
00013         *        BY SOCIAL SECURITY NUMBER. EACH INPUT RECORD CONSISTS OF*
00014         *            - CODE FOR THE PLANT LOCATION                            *
00015         *            - CODE FOR THE DEPARTMENT TO WHICH THE EMPLOYEE          *
00016         *              IS ASSIGNED                                            *
00017         *            - SOCIAL SECURITY NUMBER                                 *
00018         *            - NAME                                                   *
00019         *            - OTHER PERSONAL DATA                                    *
00020         *            - TAX CLASSIFICATION                                     *
00021         *            - PAY RATE                                              *
00022         *                                                                     *
00023         *    PROCESSING                                                       *
00024         *            - THE EMPLOYEE DATA IS CHECKED FOR ERRORS IN             *
00025         *              THE PLANT LOCATION CODE, DEPARTMENT CODE,              *
00026         *              SOCIAL SECURITY NUMBER, TAX CLASSIFICATION, AND        *
00027         *              PAY RATE                                              *
00028         *            - FOR A VALID INPUT RECORD, ZERO IS MOVED TO THE         *
00029         *              YEAR-TO-DATE TOTALS FOR GROSS PAY, TAX WITHHELD        *
00030         *              AND FICA WITHHELD                                      *
00031         *                                                                     *
00032         *    OUTPUT                                                           *
00033         *        FOR VALID EMPLOYEE INPUT DATA A RECORD IS OUTPUT TO          *
00034         *        A SEQUENTIAL DISK FILE. THIS FILE IS ORDERED BY              *
00035         *        SOCIAL SECURITY NUMBER. EACH RECORD CONSISTS OF              *
00036         *            - CODE FOR THE PLANT LOCATION                            *
00037         *            - CODE FOR THE DEPARTMENT TO WHICH THE EMPLOYEE          *
00038         *              IS ASSIGNED                                            *
00039         *            - NAME                                                   *
00040         *            - OTHER PERSONAL DATA                                    *
00041         *            - TAX CLASSIFICATION                                     *
00042         *            - PAY RATE                                              *
00043         *            - YEAR-TO-DATE TOTALS FOR GROSS PAY, TAX WITHHELD,       *
00044         *              AND FICA WITHHELD                                      *
00045         *        FOR EMPLOYEE DATA WITH ERRORS A PRINTED REPORT IS            *
00046         *        PRODUCED. THE OUTPUT CONSISTS OF                             *
00047         *            - THE INPUT RECORD                                       *
00048         *            - A LIST OF ERROR MESSAGES DESCRIBING THE FIELDS         *
00049         *              WHICH WERE ERRONEOUS                                   *
00050         ***********************************************************************
00051         *
00052          ENVIRONMENT DIVISION.
00053        *
00054          CONFIGURATION SECTION.
00055          SOURCE-COMPUTER.
00056             IBM.
00057          OBJECT-COMPUTER.
00058             IBM.
00059          SPECIAL-NAMES.
00060             C01 IS TOP-OF-PAGE.
00061          INPUT-OUTPUT SECTION.
00062          FILE-CONTROL.
00063             SELECT PAYROLL-MAST-FILE
00064                ASSIGN TO SYS023-DA-3330-S-PAYFILE.
00065             SELECT PAYROLL-FILE-IN
00066                ASSIGN TO SYS007-UR-2501-S.
00067             SELECT ERROR-REPORT-PRINT-FILE
00068                ASSIGN TO SYS009-UR-1403-S.
00069        *
00070          DATA DIVISION.
00071        *
00072          FILE SECTION.
00073          FD  PAYROLL-FILE-IN
00074                LABEL RECORDS ARE OMITTED.
```

Figure 11.2
Use of the COPY statement to retrieve a record description and a data editing module stored in a source statement library.

Figure 11.2 (*cont.*)

```
00075                01   PAYROLL-IN-AREA                     PIC X(80).
00076                FD   PAYROLL-MAST-FILE
00077                        LABEL RECORDS ARE STANDARD
00078                        BLOCK CONTAINS 10 RECORDS.
00079                01   PAYROLL-MAST-AREA                   PIC X(100).
00080                FD   ERROR-REPORT-PRINT-FILE
00081                        LABEL RECORDS ARE OMITTED.
00082                01   ERROR-LINE-OUT-AREA                 PIC X(133).
00083            *
00084            WORKING-STORAGE SECTION.
00085                01   SWITCHES.
00086                     02   STOP-PROCESSING-SW             PIC X.
00087                        88  PROCESSING-SHOULD-STOP VALUE 'Y'.
00088                     02   END-OF-FILE-SW                 PIC X.
00089                        88  END-OF-FILE VALUE 'Y'.
00090                01   COUNTERS.
00091                     02   ERR-SUB                        PIC 9.
00092                01   PAYROLL-MAST-REC.
00093                                     COPY PAYREC.
00094   C            02   PAY-EMP-MAST-DATA.
00095   C                 03   PAY-MAST-PLANT-SITE       PIC 9.
00096   C                    88 POSSIBLE-PLANT-SITE     VALUES 1, 2.
00097   C                 03   PAY-MAST-DEPT-CODE        PIC 9(2).
00098   C                    88 POSSIBLE-DEPT-CODE VALUES 1 THRU 15.
00099   C                 03   PAY-MAST-SS-NUM           PIC 9(9).
00100   C                 03   PAY-MAST-EMP-NAME         PIC X(20).
00101   C                 03   PAY-MAST-PERSONAL-DATA    PIC X(42).
00102   C                 03   PAY-MAST-TAX-CLASS        PIC 9(2).
00103   C                 03   PAY-MAST-RATE             PIC 9(2)V9(2).
00104   C                    88 POSSIBLE-PAY-RATE VALUE 3.35 THRU 18.75.
00105   C            02   PAY-MAST-YTD-TOTALS.
00106   C                 03   PAY-MAST-YTD-GROSS        PIC S9(5)V9(2).
00107   C                 03   PAY-MAST-YTD-TAX          PIC S9(5)V9(2).
00108   C                 03   PAY-MAST-YTD-FICA         PIC S9(4)V9(2).
00109                01   ERROR-HDG-PRINT-LINE.
00110                     02   FILLER                        PIC X(47) VALUE SPACE.
00111                     02   FILLER                        PIC X(38)
00112                        VALUE 'LIST OF ERRORS IN PAYROLL DATA RECORDS'.
00113                01   ERROR-DETAIL-PRINT-LINE-1.
00114                     02   FILLER                        PIC X(26) VALUE SPACE.
00115                     02   BAD-REC-OUT                   PIC X(80).
00116                01   ERROR-DETAIL-PRINT-LINE-2.
00117                     02   FILLER                        PIC X(58) VALUE SPACE.
00118                     02   ERROR-MESSAGE-OUT             PIC X(17).
00119                01   ERROR-PROCESSING-TABLES.
00120                     02   ERROR-MESSAGE-SWITCH-TABLE.
00121                          03   ERROR-MESSAGE-SW
00122                             OCCURS 5 TIMES             PIC X.
00123                     02   ERROR-MESSAGE-CONTENT.
00124                          03   FILLER                   PIC X(17)
00125                             VALUE 'PLANT SITE ERROR'.
00126                          03   FILLER                   PIC X(17)
00127                             VALUE 'DEPT CODE ERROR'.
00128                          03   FILLER                   PIC X(17)
00129                             VALUE 'SOC SEC NUM ERROR'.
00130                          03   FILLER                   PIC X(17)
00131                             VALUE 'TAX CLASS ERROR'.
00132                          03   FILLER                   PIC X(17)
00133                             VALUE 'PAY RATE ERROR'.
00134                     02   ERROR-MESSAGE-TABLE REDEFINES ERROR-MESSAGE-CONTENT.
00135                          03   ERROR-MESSAGE
00136                             OCCURS 5 TIMES             PIC X(17).
00137            *
00138            PROCEDURE DIVISION.
00139            *
00140            MAST-FILE-CREATE-CONTROL.
00141                     PERFORM START-UP.
00142                     PERFORM CREATE-PAYROLL-MAST UNTIL END-OF-FILE.
00143                     PERFORM FINISH-UP.
00144                     STOP RUN.
00145            *
00146            START-UP.
00147                     OPEN INPUT PAYROLL-FILE-IN
00148                          OUTPUT PAYROLL-MAST-FILE, ERROR-REPORT-PRINT-FILE.
00149                     MOVE 'N' TO END-OF-FILE-SW.
00150                     PERFORM PRINT-HEADING.
00151                     MOVE ZERO TO PAY-MAST-YTD-GROSS,
00152                                  PAY-MAST-YTD-TAX,
00153                                  PAY-MAST-YTD-FICA.
00154                     PERFORM READ-PAY-FILE.
```

Figure 11.2 (*cont.*)

```
00155              *
00156                  CREATE-PAYROLL-MAST.
00157                      PERFORM EDIT-PAYROLL-DATA.
00158                      IF (ERROR-MESSAGE-SWITCH-TABLE IS NOT EQUAL TO ALL 'N')
00159                          MOVE PAY-EMP-MAST-DATA TO BAD-REC-OUT
00160                          PERFORM PRINT-BAD-RECORD
00161                          PERFORM PRINT-OUT-ERROR-TABLE VARYING ERR-SUB
00162                              FROM 1 BY 1 UNTIL ERR-SUB IS GREATER THAN 5
00163                      ELSE
00164                          PERFORM WRITE-PAY-MAST-FILE.
00165                      PERFORM READ-PAY-FILE.
00166              *
00167                  FINISH-UP.
00168                      CLOSE PAYROLL-FILE-IN
00169                          PAYROLL-MAST-FILE
00170                          ERROR-REPORT-PRINT-FILE.
00171              *
00172                  EDIT-PAYROLL-DATA.
00173                      COPY PAYEDIT.
00174   C                  IF PAY-MAST-PLANT-SITE IS NOT NUMERIC
00175   C                      MOVE 'Y' TO ERROR-MESSAGE-SW (1)
00176   C                  ELSE
00177   C                      IF NOT POSSIBLE-PLANT-SITE
00178   C                          MOVE 'Y' TO ERROR-MESSAGE-SW (1)
00179   C                      ELSE
00180   C                          MOVE 'N' TO ERROR-MESSAGE-SW (1).
00181   C                  IF PAY-MAST-DEPT-CODE IS NOT NUMERIC
00182   C                      MOVE 'Y' TO ERROR-MESSAGE-SW (2)
00183   C                  ELSE
00184   C                      IF NOT POSSIBLE-DEPT-CODE
00185   C                          MOVE 'Y' TO ERROR-MESSAGE-SW (2)
00186   C                      ELSE
00187   C                          MOVE 'N' TO ERROR-MESSAGE-SW (2).
00188   C                  IF PAY-MAST-SS-NUM IS NOT NUMERIC
00189   C                      MOVE 'Y' TO ERROR-MESSAGE-SW (3)
00190   C                  ELSE
00191   C                          MOVE 'N' TO ERROR-MESSAGE-SW (3).
00192   C                  IF PAY-MAST-TAX-CLASS IS NOT NUMERIC
00193   C                      MOVE 'Y' TO ERROR-MESSAGE-SW (4)
00194   C                  ELSE
00195   C                          MOVE 'N' TO ERROR-MESSAGE-SW (4).
00196   C                  IF PAY-MAST-RATE IS NOT NUMERIC
00197   C                      MOVE 'Y' TO ERROR-MESSAGE-SW (5)
00198   C                  ELSE
00199   C                      IF NOT POSSIBLE-PAY-RATE
00200   C                          MOVE 'Y' TO ERROR-MESSAGE-SW (5)
00201   C                      ELSE
00202   C                          MOVE 'N' TO ERROR-MESSAGE-SW (5).
00203              *
00204                  PRINT-HEADING.
00205                      WRITE ERROR-LINE-OUT-AREA FROM ERROR-HDG-PRINT-LINE
00206                          AFTER ADVANCING TOP-OF-PAGE.
00207              *
00208                  PRINT-BAD-RECORD.
00209                      WRITE ERROR-LINE-OUT-AREA FROM ERROR-DETAIL-PRINT-LINE-1
00210                          AFTER ADVANCING 3 LINES.
00211              *
00212                  PRINT-OUT-ERROR-TABLE.
00213                      IF (ERROR-MESSAGE-SW (ERR-SUB) = 'Y')
00214                          MOVE ERROR-MESSAGE (ERR-SUB) TO ERROR-MESSAGE-OUT
00215                          PERFORM PRINT-ERROR-MESSAGE.
00216              *
00217                  READ-PAY-FILE.
00218                      READ PAYROLL-FILE-IN INTO PAY-EMP-MAST-DATA
00219                          AT END MOVE 'Y' TO END-OF-FILE-SW.
00220              *
00221                  WRITE-PAY-MAST-FILE.
00222                      WRITE PAYROLL-MAST-AREA FROM PAYROLL-MAST-REC.
00223              *
00224                  PRINT-ERROR-MESSAGE.
00225                      WRITE ERROR-LINE-OUT-AREA FROM ERROR-DETAIL-PRINT-LINE-2
00226                          AFTER ADVANCING 1 LINES.
```

Contents of entry named PAYREC:

```
02   PAY-EMP-MAST-DATA.
     03   PAY-MAST-PLANT-SITE       PIC 9.
          88 POSSIBLE-PLANT-SITE    VALUES 1, 2.
     03   PAY-MAST-DEPT-CODE        PIC 9(2).
          88  POSSIBLE-DEPT-CODE VALUES 1 THRU 15.
     03   PAY-MAST-SS-NUM           PIC 9(9).
     03   PAY-MAST-EMP-NAME         PIC X(20).
     03   PAY-MAST-PERSONAL-DATA    PIC X(42).
     03   PAY-MAST-TAX-CLASS        PIC 9(2).
     03   PAY-MAST-RATE             PIC 9(2)V9(2).
          88  POSSIBLE-PAY-RATE VALUE 3.35 THRU 18.75.
02   PAY-MAST-YTD-TOTALS.
     03   PAY-MAST-YTD-GROSS        PIC S9(5)V9(2).
     03   PAY-MAST-YTD-TAX          PIC S9(5)V9(2).
     03   PAY-MAST-YTD-FICA         PIC S9(4)V9(2).
```

Contents of entry named PAYEDIT:

```
IF PAY-MAST-PLANT-SITE IS NOT NUMERIC
   MOVE 'Y' TO ERROR-MESSAGE-SW (1)
ELSE
   IF NOT POSSIBLE-PLANT-SITE
      MOVE 'Y' TO ERROR-MESSAGE-SW (1)
   ELSE
      MOVE 'N' TO ERROR-MESSAGE-SW (1).
IF PAY-MAST-DEPT-CODE IS NOT NUMERIC
   MOVE 'Y' TO ERROR-MESSAGE-SW (2)
ELSE
   IF NOT POSSIBLE-DEPT-CODE
      MOVE 'Y' TO ERROR-MESSAGE-SW (2)
   ELSE
      MOVE 'N' TO ERROR-MESSAGE-SW (2).
IF PAY-MAST-SS-NUM IS NOT NUMERIC
   MOVE 'Y' TO ERROR-MESSAGE-SW (3)
ELSE
   MOVE 'N' TO ERROR-MESSAGE-SW (3).
IF PAY-MAST-TAX-CLASS IS NOT NUMERIC
   MOVE 'Y' TO ERROR-MESSAGE-SW (4)
ELSE
   MOVE 'N' TO ERROR-MESSAGE-SW (4).
IF PAY-MAST-RATE IS NOT NUMERIC
   MOVE 'Y' TO ERROR-MESSAGE-SW (5)
ELSE
   IF NOT POSSIBLE-PAY-RATE
      MOVE 'Y' TO ERROR-MESSAGE-SW (5)
   ELSE
      MOVE 'N' TO ERROR-MESSAGE-SW (5).
```

Figure 11.3
Contents of the source statement library.

STRING MANIPULATION STATEMENTS

Several statements are available in COBOL for processing data items as character strings. These verbs are most useful for processing items whose contents vary in length or items in which the position of the contents is not known. Another use is to insert editing symbols that are not part of COBOL standard editing symbols into a data item. We will consider examples of each of these different uses.

Use of the INSPECT Statement

Suppose a check identification number consists of three parts: a 9-digit identifier for the bank, a 10-digit customer identifier, and 5 digits for the check number. Assume the following entries.

```
01          .
            .
            .
   02  IN-CHECK-ID         PIC X(24).
            .
            .
            .
01          .
            .
            .
   02  OUT-CHECK-ID        PIC X(9)BX(10)BX(5).
```

If one of the usual COBOL insertion symbols (such as a blank) is desired, then

```
MOVE IN-CHECK-ID TO OUT-CHECK-ID
```

will insert the symbol.

However, if some nonstandard editing symbol is desired, the *INSPECT* statement with the *REPLACING* option can be used to insert the appropriate symbol.

FORMAT
INSPECT identifier-1
REPLACING $\left\{\begin{array}{l}\underline{\text{ALL}}\\\underline{\text{LEADING}}\\\underline{\text{FIRST}}\end{array}\right\}\left\{\begin{array}{l}\text{identifier-2}\\\text{literal-1}\end{array}\right\}$
BY $\left\{\begin{array}{l}\text{identifier-3}\\\text{literal-2}\end{array}\right\}$
$\left[\left\{\begin{array}{l}\underline{\text{BEFORE}}\\\underline{\text{AFTER}}\end{array}\right\}\text{INITIAL}\left\{\begin{array}{l}\text{identifier-4}\\\text{literal-3}\end{array}\right\}\right]\cdots$

Insertion of the character ':' in the check identifier can be accomplished with the statement

```
INSPECT OUT-CHECK-ID
    REPLACING ALL SPACE
    BY ':'.
```

If there is *any* possibility that later a different separator character will be used, then for easy program modification, place the separator character in a data item:

```
02  SEPARATOR              PIC X VALUE ':'.
```

Then write the INSPECT statement as

```
INSPECT OUT-CHECK-ID
    REPLACING ALL SPACE
    BY SEPARATOR.
```

Use of the *UNSTRING* Statement

Unfortunately, data are not always presented to a programmer in the most convenient fashion. Suppose a name field is 50 characters long and the name consists of three parts at most: first name (or initial), middle name (or initial), and last name. For example, Mary Squires, Mary Floyd Squires, or M. F. Squires.

A directory is to be prepared with the names listed in alphabetical order. However, the manner in which names are currently arranged in the name field (that is, last name last) will cause a problem when sorting. The *UNSTRING* statement can be used to separate, or break apart, the contents of a field. This will be useful in rearranging the contents of our name field. The format of the UNSTRING statement is

```
                        FORMAT

UNSTRING identifier-1

    [DELIMITED BY [ALL] { identifier-2 }
                        { literal-1    }

    [ OR ALL { identifier-3 } ] ...
             { literal-2    }

    INTO identifier-4 [identifier-5] ...

    [TALLYING IN identifier-6]
```

The *DELIMITED BY* clause defines delimiters that serve as indicators, or markers, specifying the place(s) where character strings are to be separated (or joined together, as we will see later when we discuss the *STRING* statement). Consecutive occurrences of a DELIMITER are considered as only a single occurrence when the *ALL* option is used.

It is decided that the specific order for directory names will be (1) by last name, (2) by first name or initial, and (3) by middle name or initial. Periods after initials are to be removed.

The following segment of code will UNSTRING the contents of the complete name field, as DELIMITED BY a space between each part of the name, into three separate fields.

```
MOVE ZERO TO NAME-FIELDS-COUNT.
MOVE SPACE TO NAME-FIELDS.
UNSTRING WHOLE-NAME
    DELIMITED BY ALL SPACE
    INTO NAME-FIELD-1
        NAME-FIELD-2
        NAME-FIELD-3
    TALLYING IN NAME-FIELDS-COUNT.
```

The following actions take place when the code is executed, if we assume the name involved is "MARY FLOYD SQUIRES".

WHOLE–NAME

MARY	FLOYD	SQUIRES

NAME–FIELDS

MARY	FLOYD	SQUIRES

NAME–FIELD–1|NAME–FIELD–2 NAME–FIELD–3

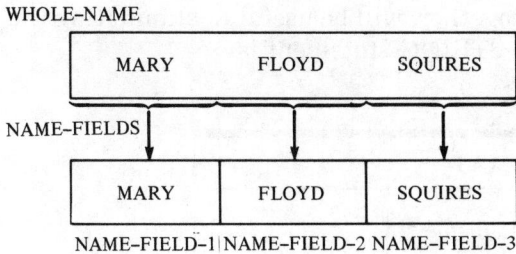

The *TALLYING IN* option will count the number of receiving fields to which data is moved (three in this case) and place the count in NAME-FIELDS-COUNT. If NAME-FIELDS-COUNT is 3, then the name is separated, and the last name is in NAME-FIELD-3. Assuming the name involved is "MARY SQUIRES", then

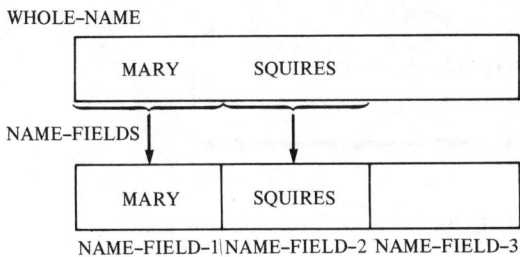

WHOLE–NAME

MARY	SQUIRES	

NAME–FIELDS

MARY	SQUIRES	

NAME–FIELD–1|NAME–FIELD–2 NAME–FIELD–3

NAME-FIELD-COUNT now contains a 2, and the last name is in NAME-FIELD-2.

The following statements should be added to our program segment in order to align fields for correct sorting, to move spaces to that portion of NAME-FIELDS not containing part of a name, and to remove periods after initials.

```
IF NAME-FIELDS-COUNT is equal to 2
    MOVE FIELD-2 TO FIELD-3
    MOVE SPACE TO FIELD-2.
INSPECT NAME-FIELDS
    REPLACING ALL '.' BY SPACE.
```

Using the name as it will appear in NAME-FIELDS with the SORT verb keys specified as NAME-FIELD-3, NAME-FIELD-1, NAME-FIELD-2 will generate the appropriate order for our directory file.

Use of the STRING Statement

Have you noticed lately that computer-generated junk mail is looking better? The large blank spaces frequently left in sentences for the variable parts of the letter seem to be disappearing. Consider the following paragraph:

```
line 1        WELCOME TO ''name-of-town''. WE ARE GLAD
line 2    THAT YOU HAVE CHOSEN OUR COMMUNITY AS
line 3    YOUR NEW HOME.
```

This paragraph has a much nicer appearance if there is not a lot of blank space left after the town name has been inserted in the space provided. The *STRING* statement, used to join character strings together, will be useful in eliminating the unwanted blank space. The format of the STRING statement is

```
                          FORMAT

    STRING  ⎰identifier-1⎱  ⎡identifier-2⎤ . . .
            ⎱literal-1   ⎰  ⎣literal-2  ⎦

              DELIMITED BY ⎰identifier-3⎱
                          ⎱literal-3   ⎰
                          ⎱SIZE        ⎰

            ⎡⎰identifier-4⎱ ⎡identifier-5⎤ DELIMITED BY
            ⎢⎱literal-4   ⎰ ⎣literal-5  ⎦
            ⎰identifier-6⎱⎤
            ⎱literal-6   ⎰⎥ . . . INTO identifier-7
            ⎱SIZE        ⎰⎦
```

To generate the variable line in the paragraph

```
    STRING '      WELCOME TO ',TOWN,'. WE ARE GLAD'
        INTO LETTER-OUT-LINE.
```

This will create the line with no extra spaces, and towns such as CINCINNATI and HOPE will both be spaced correctly.

For our final example of string manipulation, let's assume a date is to be entered through a terminal. The terminal operator might enter the date as 5/7/84, 05/07/84, 5/07/84, or 05/7/84 if the date is entered in the form month/day/year. Suppose the date entered is to be written out in its usual English form as May 7, 1984. Further assume that there is a table MONTH-NAME-TAB that contains the names of all months.

Consider the following DATA DIVISION entries:

```
    01  DATE-IN-REC.
        02  DATE-IN              PIC X(8).
    01  DATE-SEPARATED.
        02  MONTH-NUM            PIC 9(2).
        02  DAY-NUM              PIC X(2).
        02  YEAR-NUM             PIC 9(2).
    01  DATE-OUT-REC.
        02  DATE-OUT             PIC X(18).
```

Then we may split the date into month, day, and year by

```
    UNSTRING DATE-IN DELIMITED BY '/'
        INTO MONTH-NUM DAY-NUM YEAR-NUM.
```

If DATE-IN contains 5/7/84, then DATE-SEPARATED would contain 057ᵇ84 after execution of the UNSTRING statement. The following statements will complete generating the date in the desired output form.

```
MOVE SPACE TO DATE-OUT.
STRING MONTH-NAME-TAB  (MONTH-NUM)  DELIMITED BY
    SPACE
    ' ' DELIMITED BY SIZE
    DAY-NUM DELIMITED BY SPACE
    ', 19' YEAR-NUM DELIMITED BY SIZE
    INTO DATE-OUT.
```

In our date example, the STRING verb will cause the name "MAY" to be copied from the table MONTH-NAME-TAB, followed by a space, followed by the day of the month (note that DAY-NUM was declared as alphanumeric with PIC X(2); thus, single-digit days were left-justified when the previous UNSTRING statement was executed) followed by, ", 19", followed by the contents of YEAR-NUM (in this case, "84"). All of these characters will be strung into DATE-OUT.

The STRING statement does not cause unfilled positions in the receiving field to be padded with blanks. Consequently, in our example, it is necessary to MOVE SPACE TO DATE-OUT prior to execution of the STRING statement. The DELIMITED BY *SIZE* option means that the entire contents of the sending field are to be copied. The SIZE option specifies that field length (size) is to be used as the delimiter.

COBOL SOURCE LANGUAGE DEBUGGING

The COBOL source language *debugging feature* allows the programmer to access information that will be useful for finding errors in programming logic. It provides for tracing the execution flow of a program, for showing changes in the values of identifiers during program execution, and for tracing references to files. Use of the debugging feature involves a compile time switch, an execution time switch, a *USE FOR DEBUGGING* declarative section, debugging lines, and a special register, *DEBUG-ITEM*.

The compile time switch is set in the SOURCE-COMPUTER paragraph by specifying WITH DEBUGGING MODE.

FORMAT

SOURCE-COMPUTER.   Computer-name
                   WITH DEBUGGING MODE.

To illustrate, the following statement might be written:

```
SOURCE-COMPUTER.
    IBM-370 WITH DEBUGGING MODE.
```

Specification of *WITH DEBUGGING MODE* causes the debugging section and debugging lines to be compiled as part of the object program. If the WITH DEBUGGING MODE is omitted, the debugging section and all debugging lines are treated as comments. If the compile-time switch is set, debugging lines, those lines with a "D" in column 7 (to be discussed a bit later), will be executed regardless of whether or not the object-time debugging switch is set. The procedure for setting the object-time debugging switch may vary among systems; your local user consultant, or your instructor, can provide you with the necessary information.

Both the compile-time debugging switch and the object-time debugging switch must be set if USE FOR DEBUGGING sections are to be executed.

FORMAT

PROCEDURE DIVISION.

DECLARATIVES.

section-name SECTION.

USE FOR DEBUGGING

ON $\left\{ \begin{array}{l} \text{[ALL REFERENCES OF] identifier-1} \\ \text{file-name-1} \\ \text{procedure-name-1} \\ \text{ALL PROCEDURES} \end{array} \right\}$

$\left[\begin{array}{l} \text{[ALL REFERENCES OF] identifier-2} \\ \text{file-name-2} \\ \text{procedure-name-2} \\ \text{ALL PROCEDURES} \end{array} \right]$ . . .

The USE statement specifies when sections are to be executed. The formal rules for debugging sections follow:

FORMAL RULES THAT APPLY TO USE FOR DEBUGGING SECTIONS

1. All USE FOR DEBUGGING sections must be together immediately following the DECLARATIVES statement.
2. Except for the USE statement, there must be no reference to a nondeclarative procedure.
3. No statement in a debugging section may cause automatic execution of a debugging section.
4. A debugging section is executed only once as a result of execution of a single statement, no matter how many times the operand is specified. For example,
    COMPUTE YTD-PAY = YTD-PAY + PAY.
   would cause one execution of a section with
    USE ON YTD-PAY.
5. Statements outside the debugging section must not refer to produce names in the debugging section.
6. Except for the USE FOR DEBUGGING sentence, statements within a declarative section may refer only through a PERFORM to procedure names in a different USE procedure.
7. Procedure names within debugging sections must not appear in a USE FOR DEBUGGING statement.
8. A given operand may appear only once in a USE FOR DEBUGGING statement.
9. If the identifier is subscripted or indexed, it is specified without the subscript or index.
10. The identifier must not be a special register.
11. When ALL PROCEDURES is specified, no USE sentence may specify a procedure-name. The ALL PROCEDURES option may be specified only once.
12. References to DEBUG-ITEM may be made only in debugging sections.

In Table 11.1, the conditions for execution of debugging sections are summarized.

TABLE 11.1 Summary of Conditions that May Cause the USE FOR DEBUGGING Declaratives to be Executed

USE FOR DEBUGGING Operand Type	*Execution of the Following Statement Causes the USE FOR DEBUGGING Procedure Execution*
Identifier-n	Before REWRITE/WRITE/RELEASE identifier-n and after the MOVE for a FROM option.
	After each initialization, modification, or evaluation of identifier-n in a PERFORM statement that references identifier-n.
	After execution of any statement that explicitly references and alters identifier-n.
ALL REFERENCES of identifier-n	Before GO TO DEPENDING ON identifier-n control is transferred.
	Before REWRITE/WRITE/RELEASE identifier-n and after the MOVE for a FROM option.
	After each initialization, modification of evaluation of identifier-n in a PERFORM statement that references identifier-n.
	After any other COBOL statement that explicitly references to identifier-n.
File-name-n	After OPEN/CLOSE/START/DELETE file-name-n.
	After READ file-name-n if the AT END or INVALID key clause is not executed.
Procedure-name-n	Before execution of procedure-name-n.
	After execution of an ALTER statement that references procedure name-n.
ALL PROCEDURES	Before execution of all nondebugging procedures.
	After execution of ALTER statements in nondeclarative procedures.

When a USE FOR DEBUGGING declarative is executed, the DEBUG-ITEM special register will contain information about the program status. DEBUG-ITEM has the following format:

```
                              FORMAT

     01  DEBUG-ITEM.
         02  DEBUG-LINE                     PIC X(6).
         02  FILLER                         PIC X VALUE SPACE.
         02  DEBUG-NAME                     PIC X(30).
         02  FILLER                         PIC X VALUE SPACE.
         02  DEBUG-SUB-1                    PIC S9 (4)
             SIGN IS LEADING SEPARATE CHARACTER.
         02  FILLER                         PIC X VALUE SPACE.
         02  DEBUG-SUB-2                    PIC S9(4)
             SIGN IS LEADING SEPARATE CHARACTER.
         02  FILLER                         PIC X VALUE SPACE.
         02  DEBUG-SUB-3                    PIC S9(4)
             SIGN IS LEADING SEPARATE CHARACTER.
         02  FILLER                         PIC X VALUE SPACE.
         02  DEBUG-CONTENTS                 PIC X (n).
```

On entry to the debugging declarative, the DEBUG-ITEM subfields will be updated as follows:

DEBUG-LINE will contain the line number or the sequence number of the statement causing entry to the debugging section.

DEBUG-NAME will contain the name of the item that caused the debugging section to be executed.

DEBUG-SUB-1, DEBUG-SUB-2, DEBUG-SUB-3 will contain the occurrence numbers for each level of subscripting or indexing specified for the DEBUG-NAME.

DEBUG-CONTENTS will contain a message about the type of control transfer if DEBUG-NAME is a procedure-name. If DEBUG-NAME is an identifier, it will contain the contents of the identifier. If DEBUG-NAME is a file name and a READ is executed, it will contain the record contents, provided a record is retrieved. The size of the DEBUG-CONTENTS depends on the type of operand specified in the USE FOR DEBUGGING statement.

A *debugging line* must contain a D in column 7. If the compile-time switch is set, these lines are compiled as object code. If the compile-time switch is not set, they are treated as comments. Either way, care must be exercised to insure that statement syntax is correct. Consider the following paragraph:

```
        READ-INV-FILE-IN.
            READ INV-FILE-IN INTO INV-IN-REC
                INVALID KEY
    D           DISPLAY 'BAD KEY', TRANS-REL-KEY
                MOVE 'Y' TO BAD-TRANS-KEY-SW.
```

This code is correct either way. However, the following paragraph is not, because the period following the DISPLAY statement will be treated as part of the comment if the compile-time switch is not set.

```
        READ-INV-FILE-IN.
            READ INV-FILE-IN INTO INV-IN-REC
                INVALID KEY MOVE 'Y' TO BAD-TRANS-KEY-SW
    D           DISPLAY 'BAD KEY', TRANS-REL-KEY.
```

Example 11.2

In Figure 11.4, we give an illustration of the use of debugging lines and debugging declaratives in the relative files update program from Chapter 7, Example 7.2. Note the debugging section beginning on line 106 and the debugging line on line 130.

```
00001            IDENTIFICATION DIVISION.
00002        *
00003            PROGRAM-ID.
00004                EX-11-2.
00005        ***************************************************************
00006        *                                                             *
00007        *    PROGRAMMER TEAM            WALSTROM/SUMMERS/LINDAHL       *
00008        *    PROGRAM COMPLETION DATE AUGUST 13, 1984.                 *
00009        *                                                             *
00010        *                    PROGRAM SUMMARY                          *
00011        *                                                             *
00012        *    INPUT                                                    *
00013        *        THERE ARE TWO INPUT FILES, THE INVENTORY MASTER FILE *
00014        *        AND THE FILE USED FOR UPDATING THE MASTER FILE. RECORDS*
00015        *        ON THE UPDATE FILE CONTAIN                           *
00016        *            - CATALOGUE NUMBER                               *
00017        *            - ITEM NAME                                      *
00018        *            - ITEM SIZE                                      *
00019        *            - ITEM COLOR                                     *
00020        *            - NUMBER OF ITEMS RECEIVED                       *
00021        *            - PRICE                                          *
00022        *                                                             *
00023        *    PROCESSING                                               *
00024        *        FOR EACH RECORD IN THE UPDATE FILE                   *
00025        *            - THE RECORD FROM THE MASTER FILE WITH THE SAME   *
00026        *              CATALOGUE NUMBER IS OBTAINED                   *
00027        *            - AN UNUSED ENTRY IN THE SIZE-COLOR TABLE IS      *
00028        *              LOCATED USING INDEXING                         *
00029        *            - THE NEW SIZE-COLOR INFORMATION IS PLACED IN     *
00030        *              THE SIZE-COLOR TABLE                           *
00031        *                                                             *
00032        *    OUTPUT                                                   *
00033        *            - THE UPDATED MASTER FILE                        *
00034        *            - A LIST OF RECORDS IN THE UPDATE FILE WITH       *
00035        *              CATALOGUE NUMBERS NOT ON THE MASTER FILE OR     *
00036        *              WITH CATALOGUE NUMBERS OF RECORDS WHOSE SIZE-   *
00037        *              COLOR TABLE IS FULL                            *
00038        ***************************************************************
00039        *
00040            ENVIRONMENT DIVISION.
00041        *
00042            CONFIGURATION SECTION.
00043            SOURCE-COMPUTER.
00044                IBM-370 WITH DEBUGGING MODE.
00045            OBJECT-COMPUTER.
00046                IBM-370.
00047            INPUT-OUTPUT SECTION.
00048            FILE-CONTROL.
00049                SELECT INV-MAST-FILE-IO
00050                    ASSIGN TO SYS033-INVFLE
00051                    ORGANIZATION IS RELATIVE
00052                    ACCESS MODE IS RANDOM
00053                    RELATIVE KEY IS RELATIVE-RECORD-NUMBER.
00054                SELECT INV-CHANGES-FILE-IN
00055                    ASSIGN TO SYS023-DA-3330-S-CHG702.
00056        *
00057            DATA DIVISION.
00058        *
00059            FILE SECTION.
00060            FD  INV-MAST-FILE-IO
00061                    LABEL RECORDS STANDARD.
00062            01  INV-MAST-IO-AREA              PIC X(304).
00063            FD  INV-CHANGES-FILE-IN
00064                    LABEL RECORDS STANDARD.
```

Figure 11.4
Sample program containing DEBUG DECLARATIVES and a debug line.

Figure 11.4 (*cont.*)

```
00065                01   INV-CHANGES-IN-AREA              PIC X(80).
00066           *
00067                WORKING-STORAGE SECTION.
00068                01   SWITCHES.
00069                     02   END-OF-CHANGES-FILE-SW       PIC X.
00070                          88   END-OF-CHANGES-FILE          VALUE 'Y'.
00071                     02   PROCESSING-SHOULD-STOP-SW    PIC X.
00072                          88   PROCESSING-SHOULD-STOP       VALUE 'Y'.
00073                     02   CAT-NUM-ERROR-SW             PIC X.
00074                          88   CAT-NUM-ERROR                VALUE 'Y'.
00075                          88   NO-CAT-NUM-ERROR             VALUE 'N'.
00076                     02   ROOM-IN-TABLE-SW             PIC X.
00077                          88   ROOM-IN-TABLE                VALUE 'Y'.
00078                01   WORK-AREA.
00079                     02   RELATIVE-RECORD-NUMBER       PIC 9(4).
00080                01   INV-IN-CHANGES-REC.
00081                     02   INV-IN-CAT-NUM               PIC 9(4).
00082                     02   INV-IN-NAME                  PIC X(15).
00083                     02   INV-IN-SIZE                  PIC X(2).
00084                     02   INV-IN-COLOR                 PIC X(10).
00085                     02   INV-IN-NUM-OF-ITEMS          PIC 9(5).
00086                     02   INV-IN-REORDER-AMT           PIC 9(5).
00087                     02   INV-IN-ITEM-PRICE            PIC 9(3)V9(2).
00088                     02   FILLER                       PIC X(34).
00089                01   INV-IO-REC.
00090                     02   INV-IO-CAT-NUM               PIC 9(4).
00091                     02   INV-IO-NAME                  PIC X(15).
00092                     02   INV-IO-NUM-STOCK-TAB.
00093                          03   INV-IO-SIZE-COLOR-INFO
00094                               OCCURS 5 TIMES
00095                               INDEXED BY NUM-IN-STOCK-INDEX.
00096                               04   INV-IO-SIZE        PIC X(2).
00097                               04   INV-IO-COLOR       PIC X(10).
00098                               04   INV-IO-NUM-IN-STOCK PIC S9(5).
00099                               04   INV-IO-REORDER-AMT PIC S9(5).
00100                               04   INV-IO-ITEM-PRICE  PIC S9(3)V9(2).
00101                     02   FILLER                       PIC X(150).
00102           *
00103                PROCEDURE DIVISION.
00104           *
00105                DECLARATIVES.
00106                DEBUG-SECTION SECTION.
00107                     USE FOR DEBUGGING ON ALL PROCEDURES.
00108                DEBUG-ROUTINE.
00109                     DISPLAY 'DEBUG LINE ', DEBUG-LINE,
00110                             'DEBUG NAME ', DEBUG-NAME.
00111                END DECLARATIVES.
00112                FILE-LOAD-SECTION SECTION.
00113                MAST-UPDATE-CONTROL.
00114                     PERFORM START-UP.
00115                     PERFORM PROCESS-TRANS
00116                          UNTIL PROCESSING-SHOULD-STOP.
00117                     PERFORM FINISH-UP.
00118                     STOP RUN.
00119           *
00120                START-UP.
00121                     OPEN INPUT INV-CHANGES-FILE-IN
00122                          I-O INV-MAST-FILE-IO.
00123                     MOVE 'N' TO END-OF-CHANGES-FILE-SW,
00124                               PROCESSING-SHOULD-STOP-SW.
00125                     PERFORM READ-INV-CHANGES-FILE.
00126           *
00127                PROCESS-TRANS.
00128                     MOVE 'N' TO CAT-NUM-ERROR-SW.
00129                     MOVE INV-IN-CAT-NUM TO RELATIVE-RECORD-NUMBER.
00130           D         DISPLAY INV-IN-CHANGES-REC.
00131                     PERFORM READ-INV-MAST-IO-FILE.
00132                     IF NO-CAT-NUM-ERROR
00133                          PERFORM UPDATE-INV-IO-MAST
00134                     ELSE
00135                          DISPLAY ' CATALOGUE NUMBER NOT FOUND IN FILE ',
00136                                  INV-IN-CHANGES-REC.
00137                     PERFORM READ-INV-CHANGES-FILE.
```

Figure 11.4 (*cont.*)

```
00138          *
00139              FINISH-UP.
00140                  IF END-OF-CHANGES-FILE
00141                      DISPLAY ' CHANGES TO INVENTORY MASTER FILE ARE COMPLETE '
00142                  ELSE
00143                      DISPLAY ' PROBLEM IN PROCESSING CHANGES '
00144                      DISPLAY ' LAST CHANGES RECORD WAS ', INV-IN-CHANGES-REC.
00145                  CLOSE INV-MAST-FILE-IO, INV-CHANGES-FILE-IN.
00146          *
00147              UPDATE-INV-IO-MAST.
00148                  SET NUM-IN-STOCK-INDEX TO 1.
00149                  SEARCH INV-IO-SIZE-COLOR-INFO
00150                      AT END MOVE 'N' TO ROOM-IN-TABLE-SW
00151                      WHEN INV-IO-SIZE-COLOR-INFO (NUM-IN-STOCK-INDEX) = SPACE
00152                          MOVE 'Y' TO ROOM-IN-TABLE-SW.
00153                  IF ROOM-IN-TABLE
00154                      PERFORM MOVE-INFO
00155                      PERFORM REWRITE-INV-MAST-IO-REC
00156                  ELSE
00157                      DISPLAY ' RECORD IS FULL ', INV-IN-CHANGES-REC.
00158          *
00159              MOVE-INFO.
00160                  MOVE INV-IN-SIZE TO INV-IO-SIZE (NUM-IN-STOCK-INDEX).
00161                  MOVE INV-IN-NUM-OF-ITEMS TO INV-IO-NUM-IN-STOCK
00162                          (NUM-IN-STOCK-INDEX).
00163                  MOVE INV-IN-COLOR TO INV-IO-COLOR (NUM-IN-STOCK-INDEX).
00164                  MOVE INV-IN-REORDER-AMT TO INV-IO-REORDER-AMT
00165                          (NUM-IN-STOCK-INDEX).
00166                  MOVE INV-IN-ITEM-PRICE TO INV-IO-ITEM-PRICE
00167                          (NUM-IN-STOCK-INDEX).
00168          *
00169              READ-INV-CHANGES-FILE.
00170                  READ INV-CHANGES-FILE-IN INTO INV-IN-CHANGES-REC
00171                      AT END MOVE 'Y' TO END-OF-CHANGES-FILE-SW
00172                              PROCESSING-SHOULD-STOP-SW.
00173          *
00174              READ-INV-MAST-IO-FILE.
00175                  READ INV-MAST-FILE-IO INTO INV-IO-REC
00176                      INVALID KEY MOVE 'Y' TO CAT-NUM-ERROR-SW.
00177          *
00178              REWRITE-INV-MAST-IO-REC.
00179                  REWRITE INV-MAST-IO-AREA FROM INV-IO-REC
00180                      INVALID KEY MOVE 'Y' TO PROCESSING-SHOULD-STOP-SW.
```

THE IBM DEBUGGING LANGUAGE

As *extensions* to both the 68 and 74 COBOL standards, IBM supplied special statements to assist in debugging. These statements may be inserted within the source program, or they may be collected and placed at the end of the source code for easy removal once the program has been tested in a compile-time debugging packet.

To follow the flow of execution, the *TRACE* statement is used.

```
┌─────────────────────────┐
│         FORMAT          │
├─────────────────────────┤
│  ⎰ READY ⎱              │
│  ⎱ RESET ⎰ TRACE        │
└─────────────────────────┘
```

READY TRACE causes the line number of a procedure name to be listed when execution of each procedure begins. *RESET TRACE* stops the listing of procedure name line numbers.

To follow the values in identifiers, the *EXHIBIT* statement is used.

FORMAT
EXHIBIT $\left\{\begin{array}{l}\underline{\text{NAMED}} \\ \underline{\text{CHANGED NAMED}} \\ \underline{\text{CHANGED}}\end{array}\right\}$ identifier-1 . . .

The EXHIBIT statement provides for the display of the values in data items. For example, it can be used for verifying the accuracy of items being written to a file. If *NAMED* is specified, the name as well as the value is displayed. If *CHANGED* is specified, the display is done only if the value has been altered since the last execution of the EXHIBIT statement.

To reduce the amount of output being generated by EXHIBIT and TRACE, the *ON* statement can be used.

FORMAT
$\underline{\text{ON}} \left\{\begin{array}{l}\text{integer-1} \\ \text{identifier-1}\end{array}\right\} \left[\underline{\text{AND EVERY}} \left\{\begin{array}{l}\text{integer-2} \\ \text{identifier-2}\end{array}\right\}\right]$ $\left[\underline{\text{UNTIL}} \left\{\begin{array}{l}\text{integer-3} \\ \text{identifier-3}\end{array}\right\}\right]$ imperative-statement $\left\{\begin{array}{l}\underline{\text{ELSE}} \\ \underline{\text{OTHERWISE}}\end{array}\right\}$ statement . . .

The ON statement sets up a counter that is initialized to ZERO and incremented by the value of integer-2 (identifier-2). The statements are executed when the counter value is between the limits specified by integer-1 (identifier-1) and integer-3 (identifier-3). Consider the following entry:

```
ON 50 AND EVERY 2
    UNTIL 70
    EXHIBIT YTD-TOTAL.
```

The EXHIBIT statement will be executed for the counter values of 50, 52, 54, . . . , 68, 70.

The TRACE, EXHIBIT, and ON statements may appear anywhere in a program.

The *DEBUG* statement signals the beginning of a group of statements to be used for debugging purposes, called debugging packets, which must be placed at the end of the source code. Each packet is preceded by a DEBUG statement.

FORMAT
$\underline{\text{DEBUG}}$ procedure-name

The word DEBUG followed by the procedure-name may appear anywhere in positions 1–72. No other text may appear on the line. A sequence number may appear in positions 1–6. The procedure-name is the paragraph or section name indicating where the statements in the packet are to be executed.

Example 11.3

To illustrate use of IBM's debugging language, a TRACE statement and a DEBUG packet have been inserted into the program originally shown in Chapter 4, Figure 4.8. This program, with the debugging statements inserted and the output generated from the execution trace, is shown in Figure 11.5. The following points should be noted:

1. The TRACE is activated on line 92.
2. The path of program execution will be followed (traced), listing line numbers of procedures as they are executed, until paragraph PROCESS-SAME SS-NUM has been executed five times. The trace is then terminated by the ON 5 RESET TRACE statement on line 116.
3. The DEBUG packet (lines 129–132) will continue to EXHIBIT the item-name and value of HRS-IN-SS-NUM, HRS-IN-HRS-WORKED, and HRS-OUT-HRS-WORKED whenever there is a change in the values they contain until program termination. Note the absence of a period on line 129.
4. No editing of values takes place for the output generated by the EXHIBIT statement.

```
00001          IDENTIFICATION DIVISION.
00002       *
00003        PROGRAM-ID.
00004          EX-11-3.
00005       ******************************************************************
00006       *                                                                *
00007       *   PROGRAMMER TEAM          WALSTROM/SUMMERS/LINDAHL            *
00008       *   PROGRAM COMPLETION DATE NOVEMBER 28,1983                     *
00009       *                                                                *
00010       *              PROGRAM SUMMARY                                   *
00011       *   INPUT                                                        *
00012       *       THE INPUT FILE IS A SEQUENTIAL FILE, ORDERED BY          *
00013       *       SOCIAL SECURITY NUMBER. THERE MAY BE MULTIPLE RECORDS    *
00014       *       FOR AN EMPLOYEE. EACH RECORD CONSISTS OF                 *
00015       *           - SOCIAL SECURITY NUMBER                             *
00016       *           - TASK PERFORMED BY EMPLOYEE                         *
00017       *           - PROJECT BUDGET NUMBER                              *
00018       *           - HOURS WORKED BY EMPLOYEE FOR THE TASK              *
00019       *             AND PROJECT                                        *
00020       *                                                                *
00021       *   PROCESSING                                                   *
00022       *           - FOR EACH EMPLOYEE THE TOTAL NUMBER OF HOURS        *
00023       *             WORKED IS ACCUMULATED                              *
00024       *           - THE TOTAL NUMBER OF HOURS WORKED BY ALL            *
00025       *             EMPLOYEES IS ACCUMULATED                           *
00026       *                                                                *
00027       *   OUTPUT                                                       *
00028       *       THE OUTPUT FILE IS A SEQUENTIAL FILE ORDERED BY          *
00029       *       SOCIAL SECURITY NUMBER. EACH RECORD CONSISTS OF          *
00030       *           - SOCIAL SECURITY NUMBER                             *
00031       *           - TOTAL HOURS WORKED                                 *
00032       *       A PRINTED REPORT IS GENERATED. IT CONTAINS              *
00033       *           - THE TOTAL NUMBER OF HOURS WORKED BY ALL            *
00034       *             EMPLOYEES                                          *
00035       ******************************************************************
```

Figure 11.5
Sample program (with output generated) using a compile-time DEBUG packet and an execution trace.

Figure 11.5 (cont.)

```
00036            *
00037             ENVIRONMENT DIVISION.
00038            *
00039             CONFIGURATION SECTION.
00040             SOURCE-COMPUTER.
00041                 IBM-370.
00042             OBJECT-COMPUTER.
00043                 IBM-370.
00044             INPUT-OUTPUT SECTION.
00045             FILE-CONTROL.
00046                 SELECT HRS-WORKED-PAY-PERIOD-FILE-OUT
00047                     ASSIGN TO SYS023-DA-3330-S-THRSFIL.
00048                 SELECT HRS-WORKED-PROJ-FILE-IN
00049                     ASSIGN TO SYS023-DA-3330-S-PHRSFIL.
00050            *
00051             DATA DIVISION.
00052            *
00053             FILE SECTION.
00054             FD  HRS-WORKED-PAY-PERIOD-FILE-OUT
00055                     LABEL RECORDS ARE STANDARD
00056                     BLOCK CONTAINS 10 RECORDS.
00057             01  HRS-WORKED-OUT-AREA            PIC X(13).
00058             FD  HRS-WORKED-PROJ-FILE-IN
00059                     LABEL RECORDS ARE STANDARD
00060                     BLOCK CONTAINS 20 RECORDS.
00061             01  HRS-WORKED-PROJ-IN-AREA        PIC X(20).
00062            *
00063             WORKING-STORAGE SECTION.
00064             01  SWITCHES.
00065                 02  END-OF-FILE-SW             PIC X.
00066                     88  NO-MORE-RECORDS VALUE 'Y'.
00067                 02  END-OF-SS-NUM-GROUP-SW     PIC X.
00068                     88  NEW-SS-NUM      VALUE 'Y'.
00069             01  COMPANY-TOTALS.
00070                 02  COMPANY-HRS-WORKED-TOTAL   PIC S9(6)V9(2).
00071                 02  COMPANY-HRS-DISPLAY-TOTAL  PIC -Z(6).9(2).
00072             01  HRS-WORKED-IN-REC.
00073                 02  HRS-IN-SS-NUM              PIC X(9).
00074                 02  HRS-IN-TASK-CODE           PIC S9(2).
00075                 02  HRS-IN-PROJ-NUM            PIC 9(5).
00076                 02  HRS-IN-HRS-WORKED          PIC 9(2)V9(2).
00077             01  HRS-WORKED-OUT-REC.
00078                 02  HRS-OUT-SS-NUM             PIC X(9).
00079                 02  HRS-OUT-HRS-WORKED         PIC 9(2)V9(2).
00080            *
00081             PROCEDURE DIVISION.
00082            *
00083             EMP-HRS-FILE-CREATE-CONTROL.
00084                 PERFORM START-UP.
00085                 PERFORM PROCESS-SS-NUM-GROUP UNTIL NO-MORE-RECORDS.
00086                 PERFORM FINAL-ROUTINE.
00087                 STOP RUN.
00088            *
00089             START-UP.
00090                 OPEN INPUT HRS-WORKED-PROJ-FILE-IN
00091                      OUTPUT HRS-WORKED-PAY-PERIOD-FILE-OUT.
00092                 READY TRACE.
00093                 MOVE 'N' TO END-OF-FILE-SW.
00094                 PERFORM READ-PROJ-FILE.
00095                 MOVE 0 TO COMPANY-HRS-WORKED-TOTAL.
00096            *
00097             PROCESS-SS-NUM-GROUP.
00098                 MOVE HRS-IN-SS-NUM TO HRS-OUT-SS-NUM.
00099                 MOVE 0 TO HRS-OUT-HRS-WORKED.
00100                 MOVE 'N' TO END-OF-SS-NUM-GROUP-SW.
00101                 PERFORM PROCESS-SAME-SS-NUM UNTIL NEW-SS-NUM.
00102                 PERFORM WRITE-HRS-REC-OUT.
00103                 ADD HRS-OUT-HRS-WORKED TO COMPANY-HRS-WORKED-TOTAL.
00104            *
00105             FINAL-ROUTINE.
00106                 IF NO-MORE-RECORDS
00107                     MOVE COMPANY-HRS-WORKED-TOTAL TO
00108                          COMPANY-HRS-DISPLAY-TOTAL
00109                     DISPLAY 'HOURS FOR ALL WORKERS '
00110                          COMPANY-HRS-DISPLAY-TOTAL
00111                     DISPLAY 'HOURS WORKED FILE PROCESSING COMPLETE'.
00112                 CLOSE HRS-WORKED-PROJ-FILE-IN
00113                       HRS-WORKED-PAY-PERIOD-FILE-OUT.
```

Figure 11.5 (cont.)

```
00114            *
00115                PROCESS-SAME-SS-NUM.
00116                    ON 5 RESET TRACE.
00117                    ADD HRS-IN-HRS-WORKED TO HRS-OUT-HRS-WORKED.
00118                    PERFORM READ-PROJ-FILE.
00119                    IF HRS-IN-SS-NUM IS NOT EQUAL TO HRS-OUT-SS-NUM
00120                        MOVE 'Y' TO END-OF-SS-NUM-GROUP-SW.
00121            *
00122                WRITE-HRS-REC-OUT.
00123                    WRITE HRS-WORKED-OUT-AREA FROM HRS-WORKED-OUT-REC.
00124            *
00125                READ-PROJ-FILE.
00126                    READ HRS-WORKED-PROJ-FILE-IN INTO HRS-WORKED-IN-REC
00127                        AT END MOVE 'Y' TO END-OF-FILE-SW,
00128                                            END-OF-SS-NUM-GROUP-SW.
00129     DEBUG  PROCESS-SAME-SS-NUM
00130                SUM-CHECK.
00131                    EXHIBIT CHANGED NAMED
00132                        HRS-IN-SS-NUM, HRS-IN-HRS-WORKED, HRS-OUT-HRS-WORKED.
```

```
125
97
115
130
HRS-IN-SS-NUM = 011867322 HRS-IN-HRS-WORKED = 2500 HRS-OUT-HRS-WORKED = 0000
125
115
130
HRS-IN-HRS-WORKED = 1400 HRS-OUT-HRS-WORKED = 2500
125
122
97
115
130
HRS-IN-SS-NUM = 074139821 HRS-IN-HRS-WORKED = 2500 HRS-OUT-HRS-WORKED = 0000
125
115
130
HRS-OUT-HRS-WORKED = 2500
125
122
97
115
130
HRS-IN-SS-NUM = 124386752 HRS-IN-HRS-WORKED = 2000 HRS-OUT-HRS-WORKED = 0000
HRS-IN-HRS-WORKED = 0200 HRS-OUT-HRS-WORKED = 2000
HRS-IN-HRS-WORKED = 1000 HRS-OUT-HRS-WORKED = 2200
HRS-OUT-HRS-WORKED = 3200
HRS-IN-SS-NUM = 175926415 HRS-IN-HRS-WORKED = 2000 HRS-OUT-HRS-WORKED = 0000
HRS-OUT-HRS-WORKED = 2000
HRS-IN-SS-NUM = 195552633 HRS-OUT-HRS-WORKED = 0000
HRS-OUT-HRS-WORKED = 2000
HRS-IN-SS-NUM = 212288534 HRS-OUT-HRS-WORKED = 0000
HRS-OUT-HRS-WORKED = 2000
HRS-IN-SS-NUM = 223525542 HRS-IN-HRS-WORKED = 1500 HRS-OUT-HRS-WORKED = 0000
HRS-OUT-HRS-WORKED = 1500
HRS-IN-HRS-WORKED = 0550 HRS-OUT-HRS-WORKED = 3000
HRS-IN-HRS-WORKED = 1575 HRS-OUT-HRS-WORKED = 3550
HRS-IN-SS-NUM = 257458211 HRS-IN-HRS-WORKED = 2000 HRS-OUT-HRS-WORKED = 0000
HRS-OUT-HRS-WORKED = 2000
HRS-IN-SS-NUM = 275278640 HRS-IN-HRS-WORKED = 2300 HRS-OUT-HRS-WORKED = 0000
HRS-OUT-HRS-WORKED = 2300
HRS-IN-SS-NUM = 305389742 HRS-OUT-HRS-WORKED = 0000
HRS-OUT-HRS-WORKED = 2300
HRS-IN-SS-NUM = 323423765 HRS-IN-HRS-WORKED = 2500 HRS-OUT-HRS-WORKED = 0000
HRS-OUT-HRS-WORKED = 2500
HRS-IN-SS-NUM = 330948326 HRS-IN-HRS-WORKED = 2000 HRS-OUT-HRS-WORKED = 0000
HRS-OUT-HRS-WORKED = 2000
HRS-IN-SS-NUM = 351414122 HRS-IN-HRS-WORKED = 4000 HRS-OUT-HRS-WORKED = 0000
HRS-IN-SS-NUM = 360158021 HRS-IN-HRS-WORKED = 1000
HRS-OUT-HRS-WORKED = 1000
HRS-OUT-HRS-WORKED = 2000
HRS-OUT-HRS-WORKED = 3000
```

Figure 11.5 (cont.)

```
HRS-IN-SS-NUM = 372586742 HRS-IN-HRS-WORKED = 0750 HRS-OUT-HRS-WORKED = 0000
HRS-IN-HRS-WORKED = 1250 HRS-OUT-HRS-WORKED = 0750
HRS-IN-HRS-WORKED = 1000 HRS-OUT-HRS-WORKED = 2000
HRS-IN-HRS-WORKED = 1150 HRS-OUT-HRS-WORKED = 3000
HRS-IN-SS-NUM = 395321760 HRS-IN-HRS-WORKED = 2000 HRS-OUT-HRS-WORKED = 0000
HRS-OUT-HRS-WORKED = 2000
HRS-IN-SS-NUM = 425548624 HRS-IN-HRS-WORKED = 1000 HRS-OUT-HRS-WORKED = 0000
HRS-OUT-HRS-WORKED = 1000
HRS-OUT-HRS-WORKED = 2000
HRS-OUT-HRS-WORKED = 3000
HRS-IN-SS-NUM = 502684265 HRS-IN-HRS-WORKED = 2000 HRS-OUT-HRS-WORKED = 0000
HRS-OUT-HRS-WORKED = 2000
HRS-IN-SS-NUM = 540055298 HRS-IN-HRS-WORKED = 0700 HRS-OUT-HRS-WORKED = 0000
HRS-IN-HRS-WORKED = 0900 HRS-OUT-HRS-WORKED = 0700
HRS-IN-HRS-WORKED = 3000 HRS-OUT-HRS-WORKED = 1600
HRS-IN-SS-NUM = 563897521 HRS-IN-HRS-WORKED = 1400 HRS-OUT-HRS-WORKED = 0000
HRS-OUT-HRS-WORKED = 1400
HRS-OUT-HRS-WORKED = 2800
HRS-IN-SS-NUM = 564897521 HRS-IN-HRS-WORKED = 1700 HRS-OUT-HRS-WORKED = 0000
HRS-OUT-HRS-WORKED = 1700
HRS-OUT-HRS-WORKED = 3400
HRS-IN-SS-NUM = 592764831 HRS-IN-HRS-WORKED = 2000 HRS-OUT-HRS-WORKED = 0000
HRS-OUT-HRS-WORKED = 2000
HRS-IN-SS-NUM = 613568442 HRS-IN-HRS-WORKED = 4000 HRS-OUT-HRS-WORKED = 0000
HRS-IN-SS-NUM = 643824694 HRS-IN-HRS-WORKED = 1000
HRS-OUT-HRS-WORKED = 1000
HRS-OUT-HRS-WORKED = 2000
HRS-OUT-HRS-WORKED = 3000
HRS-IN-SS-NUM = 661143880 HRS-IN-HRS-WORKED = 2500 HRS-OUT-HRS-WORKED = 0000
HRS-IN-HRS-WORKED = 2000 HRS-OUT-HRS-WORKED = 2500
HRS-IN-SS-NUM = 826624853 HRS-IN-HRS-WORKED = 1500 HRS-OUT-HRS-WORKED = 0000
HRS-OUT-HRS-WORKED = 1500
HRS-IN-HRS-WORKED = 0500 HRS-OUT-HRS-WORKED = 3000
HRS-OUT-HRS-WORKED = 3500
HRS-IN-SS-NUM = 909843920 HRS-IN-HRS-WORKED = 1000 HRS-OUT-HRS-WORKED = 0000
HRS-OUT-HRS-WORKED = 1000
HRS-OUT-HRS-WORKED = 2000
HRS-OUT-HRS-WORKED = 3000
HOURS FOR ALL WORKERS    1149.75
HOURS WORKED FILE PROCESSING COMPLETE
```

Before ending our discussion of the IBM debugging language, we should again point out that, although their use is common on IBM systems, the TRACE, EXHIBIT, ON, and DEBUG location statements are not part of 74 ANSI standard COBOL. These statements are IBM extensions to the standard debugging feature (USE FOR DEBUGGING, debugging lines specified with a "D" in column 7, and so on) previously described.

CONCLUDING COMMENTS ABOUT MISCELLANEOUS TOPICS

Several COBOL features have been briefly discussed under this chapter heading, "Miscellaneous Topics." However, even as miscellaneous topics, these features should not be considered unimportant.

The COPY feature makes the use of standard data names within an organization very attractive and provides us with a procedure that will frequently reduce, by a significant amount, the number of lines of code a programmer is required to write.

The string manipulation verbs are useful when the need arises to process items whose contents vary in length or items in which the contents are not known, as well as items that need special editing.

Effective use of debugging statements can be of tremendous value to you in locating errors in program logic. We strongly recommend their use when appropriate, as they will often considerably shorten program debugging time.

A COBOL Reserved Words

Reserved Word	ANS COBOL-74	CODASYL COBOL-80 Only	IBM OS/VS COBOL
ACCEPT	X	—	X
ACCESS	X	—	X
ACTUAL	—	—	X
ADD	X	—	X
ADVANCING	X	—	X
AFTER	X	—	X
ALL	X	—	X
ALPHABET	—	X	—
ALPHABETIC	X	—	X
ALPHANUMERIC	—	X	—
ALPHANUMERIC-EDITED	—	X	—
ALSO	X	—	X
ALTER	X	—	X
ALTERNATE	X	—	X
AND	X	—	X
ANY	—	X	—
APPLY	—	—	X
ARE	X	—	X
AREA	X	—	X
AREAS	X	—	X
ASCENDING	X	—	X
ASSIGN	X	—	X
AT	X	—	X
AUTHOR	X	—	X
BASIS	—	X	—
BEFORE	X	—	X
BEGINNING	—	—	X
BINARY	—	X	—
BIT	—	X	—
BITS	—	X	—
BLANK	X	—	X
BLOCK	X	—	X
BOOLEAN	—	X	—

Reprinted by permission of IBM from *IBM VS COBOL for OS/VS*.

Reserved Word	ANS COBOL-74	CODASYL COBOL-80 Only	IBM OS/VS COBOL
BOTTOM	X	—	X
BY	X	—	X
CALL	X	—	X
CANCEL	X	—	X
CBL	—	—	X
CD	X	—	X
CF	X	—	X
CH	X	—	X
CHANGED	—	—	X
CHARACTER	X	—	X
CHARACTERS	X	—	X
CLOCK-UNITS	X	—	—
CLOSE	X	—	X
COBOL	X	—	—
CODE	X	—	X
CODE-SET	X	—	X
COLLATING	X	—	X
COLUMN	X	—	X
COMMA	X	—	X
COMMIT	—	X	—
COMMON	—	X	—
COMMUNICATION	X	—	X
COMP	X	—	X
COMP-1	—	—	X
COMP-2	—	—	X
COMP-3	—	—	X
COMP-4	—	—	X
COMPUTATIONAL	X	—	X
COMPUTATIONAL-1	—	—	X
COMPUTATIONAL-2	—	—	X
COMPUTATIONAL-3	—	—	X
COMPUTATIONAL-4	—	—	X
COMPUTE	X	—	X
CONFIGURATION	X	—	X
CONNECT	—	X	—
CONSOLE	—	—	X
CONTAINS	X	—	X
CONTENT	—	X	—
CONTINUE	—	X	—
CONTROL	X	—	X
CONTROLS	X	—	X
CONVERTING	—	X	—
COPY	X	—	X
CORE-INDEX	—	—	X
CORR	X	—	X
CORRESPONDING	X	—	X
COUNT	X	—	X
CSP	—	—	X
CURRENCY	X	—	X

Reserved Word	ANS COBOL-74	CODASYL COBOL-80 Only	IBM OS/VS COBOL
CURRENT	—	X	—
CURRENT-DATE	—	—	X
CO1	—	—	X
CO2	—	—	X
CO3	—	—	X
CO4	—	—	X
CO5	—	—	X
CO6	—	—	X
CO7	—	—	X
CO8	—	—	X
CO9	—	—	X
C10	—	—	X
C11	—	—	X
C12	—	—	X
DATA	X	—	X
DATE	X	—	X
DATE-COMPILED	X	—	X
DATE-WRITTEN	X	—	X
DAY	X	—	X
DAY-OF-WEEK	—	X	—
DB	—	X	—
DB-ACCESS-CONTROL-KEY	—	X	—
DB-DATA-NAME	—	X	—
DB-EXCEPTION	—	X	—
DB-RECORD-NAME	—	X	—
DB-SET-NAME	—	X	—
DB-STATUS	—	X	—
DE	X	—	X
DEBUG	—	—	X
DEBUG-CONTENTS	X	—	X
DEBUT-ITEM	X	—	X
DEBUT-LINE	X	—	X
DEBUG-NAME	X	—	X
DEBUG-SUB-1	X	—	X
DEBUG-SUB-2	X	—	X
DEBUG-SUB-3	X	—	X
DEBUGGING	X	—	X
DECIMAL-POINT	X	—	X
DECLARATIVES	X	—	X
DELETE	X	—	X
DELIMITED	X	—	X
DELIMITER	X	—	X
DEPENDING	X	—	X
DESCENDING	X	—	X
DESTINATION	X	—	X
DETAIL	X	—	X
DISABLE	X	—	X
DISCONNECT	—	X	—

Reserved Word	ANS COBOL-74	CODASYL COBOL-80 Only	IBM OS/VS COBOL
DIS	—	—	X
DISPLAY	X	—	X
DISPLAY-n	—	X	—
DISPLAY-ST	—	—	X
DIVIDE	X	—	X
DIVISION	X	—	X
DOWN	X	—	X
DUPLICATE	—	X	—
DUPLICATES	X	—	X
DYNAMIC	X	—	X
EGI	X	—	X
EJECT	—	—	X
ELSE	X	—	X
EMI	X	—	X
EMPTY	—	X	—
ENABLE	X	—	X
END	X	—	X
END-ADD	—	X	—
END-CALL	—	X	—
END-COMPUTE	—	X	—
END-DELETE	—	X	—
END-DIVIDE	—	X	—
END-EVALUATE	—	X	—
END-IF	—	X	—
END-MULTIPLY	—	X	—
END-OF-PAGE	X	—	X
END-PERFORM	—	X	—
END-READ	—	X	—
END-RECEIVE	—	X	—
END-RETURN	—	X	—
END-REWRITE	—	X	—
END-SEARCH	—	X	—
END-START	—	X	—
END-STRING	—	X	—
END-SUBTRACT	—	X	—
END-UNSTRING	—	X	—
END-WRITE	—	X	—
ENDING	—	—	X
ENTER	X	—	X
ENTRY	—	—	X
ENVIRONMENT	X	—	X
EOP	X	—	X
EQUAL	X	—	X
EQUALS	—	X	—
ERASE	—	X	—
ERROR	X	—	X
ESI	X	—	X
EVALUATE	—	X	—

Reserved Word	ANS COBOL-74	CODASYL COBOL-80 Only	IBM OS/VS COBOL
EVERY	X	—	X
EXAMINE	—	—	X
EXCEEDS	—	X	—
EXCEPTION	X	—	X
EXCLUSIVE	—	X	—
EXHIBIT	—	—	X
EXIT	X	—	X
EXOR	—	X	—
EXTEND	X	—	X
EXTERNAL	—	X	—
FALSE	—	X	—
FD	X	—	X
FILE	X	—	X
FILE-CONTROL	X	—	X
FILE-LIMIT	—	—	X
FILE-LIMITS	—	—	X
FILLER	X	—	X
FINAL	X	—	X
FIND	—	X	—
FINISH	—	X	—
FIRST	X	—	X
FOOTING	X	—	X
FOR	X	—	X
FREE	—	X	—
FROM	X	—	X
FUNCTION	—	X	—
GENERATE	X	—	X
GET	—	X	—
GIVING	X	—	X
GLOBAL	—	X	—
GO	X	—	X
GREATER	X	—	X
GROUP	X	—	X
HEADING	X	—	X
HIGH-VALUE	X	—	X
HIGH-VALUES	X	—	X
I-O	X	—	X
I-O-CONTROL	X	—	X
ID	—	—	X
IDENTIFICATION	X	—	X
IF	X	—	X
IN	X	—	X
INDEX	X	—	X
INDEX-n	—	X	—
INDEXED	X	—	X
INDICATE	X	—	X
INITIAL	X	—	X
INITIALIZE	—	X	X
INITIATE	X	—	X

Reserved Word	ANS COBOL-74	CODASYL COBOL-80 Only	IBM OS/VS COBOL
INPUT	X	—	X
INPUT-OUTPUT	X	—	X
INSERT	—	—	X
INSPECT	X	—	X
INSTALLATION	X	—	X
INTO	X	—	X
INVALID	X	—	X
IS	X	—	X
JUST	X	—	X
JUSTIFIED	X	—	X
KEEP	—	X	—
KEY	X	—	X
LABEL	X	—	X
LAST	X	—	X
LD	—	X	—
LEADING	X	—	X
LEAVE	—	—	X
LEFT	X	—	X
LENGTH	X	—	X
LESS	X	—	X
LIMIT	X	—	X
LIMITS	X	—	X
LINAGE	X	—	X
LINAGE-COUNTER	X	—	X
LINE	X	—	X
LINE-COUNTER	X	—	X
LINES	X	—	X
LINKAGE	X	—	X
LOCALLY	—	X	—
LOCK	X	—	X
LOW-VALUE	X	—	X
LOW-VALUES	X	—	X
MEMBER	—	X	—
MEMORY	X	—	X
MERGE	X	—	X
MESSAGE	X	—	X
MODE	X	—	X
MODIFY	—	X	—
MODULES	X	—	X
MORE-LABELS	—	—	X
MOVE	X	—	X
MULTIPLE	X	—	X
MULTIPLY	X	—	X
NAMED	—	—	X
NATIVE	X	—	X
NEGATIVE	X	—	X
NEXT	X	—	X
NO	X	—	X

Reserved Word	ANS COBOL-74	CODASYL COBOL-80 Only	IBM OS/VS COBOL
NOMINAL	—	X	X
NOT	X	—	X
NOTE	—	—	X
NULL	—	X	—
NUMBER	X	—	X
NUMERIC	X	—	X
NUMERIC-EDITED	—	X	—
OBJECT-COMPUTER	X	—	X
OCCURS	X	—	X
OF	X	—	X
OFF	X	—	X
OMITTED	X	—	X
ON	X	—	X
OPEN	X	—	X
OPTIONAL	X	—	X
OR	X	—	X
ORDER	—	X	—
ORGANIZATION	X	—	X
OTHER	—	X	—
OTHERWISE	—	—	X
OUTPUT	X	—	X
OVERFLOW	X	—	X
OWNER	—	X	—
PACKED-DECIMAL	—	X	—
PADDING	—	X	—
PAGE	X	—	X
PAGE-COUNTER	X	—	X
PASSWORD	—	—	X
PERFORM	X	—	X
PF	X	—	X
PH	X	—	X
PIC	X	—	X
PICTURE	X	—	X
PLUS	X	—	X
POINTER	X	—	X
POSITION	X	—	X
POSITIONING	—	—	X
POSITIVE	X	—	X
PRINTING	X	—	—
PRIOR	—	X	—
PROCEDURE	X	—	X
PROCEDURES	X	—	X
PROCEED	X	—	X
PROCESSING	—	—	X
PROGRAM	X	—	X
PROGRAM-ID	X	—	X
PROTECTED	—	X	—
PURGE	—	X	—

Reserved Word	ANS COBOL-74	CODASYL COBOL-80 Only	IBM OS/VS COBOL
QUEUE	X	—	X
QUOTE	X	—	X
QUOTES	X	—	X
RANDOM	X	—	X
RD	X	—	X
READ	X	—	X
READY	—	—	X
REALM	—	X	—
REALMS	—	X	—
RECEIVE	X	—	X
RECONNECT	—	X	—
RECORD	X	—	X
RECORD-NAME	—	X	—
RECORD-OVERFLOW	—	—	X
RECORDS	X	—	X
REDEFINES	X	—	X
REEL	X	—	X
REFERENCE	—	X	—
REFERENCES	X	—	X
RELATIVE	X	—	X
RELEASE	X	—	X
RELOAD	—	—	X
REMAINDER	X	—	X
REMARKS	—	—	X
REMOVAL	X	—	X
RENAMES	X	—	X
REORG-CRITERIA	—	—	X
REPEATED	—	X	—
REPLACE	—	X	—
REPLACING	X	—	X
REPORT	X	—	X
REPORTING	X	—	X
REPORTS	X	—	X
REREAD	—	—	X
RERUN	X	—	X
RESERVE	X	—	X
RESET	X	—	X
RETAINING	—	X	—
RETRIEVAL	—	X	—
RETURN	X	—	X
RETURN-CODE	—	—	X
REVERSED	X	—	X
REWIND	X	—	X
REWRITE	X	—	X
RF	X	—	X
RH	X	—	X
RIGHT	X	—	X

Reserved Word	ANS COBOL-74	CODASYL COBOL-80 Only	IBM OS/VS COBOL
ROLLBACK	—	X	—
ROUNDED	—	—	X
RUN	X	—	X
SAME	X	—	X
SD	X	—	X
SEARCH	X	—	X
SECTION	X	—	X
SECURITY	X	—	X
SEEK	—	—	X
SEGMENT	X	—	X
SEGMENT-LIMIT	X	—	X
SELECT	X	—	X
SELECTIVE	—	—	X
SEND	X	—	X
SENTENCE	X	—	X
SEPARATE	X	—	X
SEQUENCE	X	—	X
SEQUENTIAL	X	—	X
SET	X	—	X
SETS	—	X	—
SIGN	X	—	X
SIZE	X	—	X
SKIP-1	—	—	X
SKIP-2	—	—	X
SKIP-3	—	—	X
SORT	X	—	X
SORT-CORE-SIZE	—	—	X
SORT-FILE-SIZE	—	—	X
SORT-MERGE	X	—	X
SORT-MESSAGE	—	—	X
SORT-MODE-SIZE	—	—	X
SORT-RETURN	—	—	X
SOURCE	X	—	X
SOURCE-COMPUTER	X	—	X
SPACE	X	—	X
SPACES	X	—	X
SPECIAL-NAMES	X	—	X
STANDARD	X	—	X
STANDARD-1	X	—	X
STANDARD-2	—	X	—
START	X	—	X
STATUS	X	—	X
STOP	X	—	X
STORE	—	—	X
STRING	X	—	X
SUB-QUEUE-1	X	—	X
SUB-QUEUE-2	X	—	X

Reserved Word	ANS COBOL-74	CODASYL COBOL-80 Only	IBM OS/VS COBOL
SUB-QUEUE-3	X	—	X
SUB-SCHEMA	—	X	—
SUBTRACT	X	—	X
SUM	X	—	X
SUPPRESS	X	—	X
SYMBOLIC	X	—	X
SYNC	X	—	X
SYNCHRONIZED	X	—	X
SYSIN	—	—	X
SYSOUT	—	—	X
SYSPUNCH	—	—	X
S01	—	—	X
S02	—	—	X
TABLE	X	—	X
TALLY	—	—	X
TALLYING	X	—	X
TAPE	X	—	X
TENANT	—	X	—
TERMINAL	X	—	X
TERMINATE	X	—	X
TEST	—	X	—
TEXT	X	—	X
THAN	X	—	X
THEN	—	—	X
THROUGH	X	—	X
THRU	X	—	X
TIME	X	—	X
TIME-OF-DAY	—	—	X
TIMES	X	—	X
TO	X	—	X
TOP	X	—	X
TOTALED	—	—	X
TOTALING	—	—	X
TRACE	—	—	X
TRACK-AREA	—	—	X
TRACK-LIMIT	—	—	X
TRACKS	—	—	X
TRAILING	X	—	X
TRANSFORM	—	—	X
TRUE	—	X	—
TYPE	X	—	X
UNEQUAL	—	X	—
UNIT	X	—	X
UNSTRING	X	—	X
UNTIL	X	—	X
UP	X	—	X
UPDATE	—	X	—
UPON	X	—	X

Reserved Word	ANS COBOL-74	CODASYL COBOL-80 Only	IBM OS/VS COBOL
UPSI-0	—	—	X
UPSI-1	—	—	X
UPSI-2	—	—	X
UPSI-3	—	—	X
UPSI-4	—	—	X
UPSI-5	—	—	X
UPSI-6	—	—	X
UPSI-7	—	—	X
USAGE	X	—	X
USAGE-MODE	—	X	—
USE	X	—	X
USING	X	—	X
VALUE	X	—	X
VALUES	X	—	X
VARYING	X	—	X
WHEN	X	—	X
WHEN-COMPILED	—	—	X
WITH	X	—	X
WITHIN	—	X	—
WORDS	X	—	X
WORKING-STORAGE	X	—	X
WRITE	X	—	X
WRITE-ONLY	—	—	X
ZERO	X	—	X
ZEROES	X	—	X
ZEROS	X	—	X
+	X	—	X
−	X	—	X
*	X	—	X
/	X	—	X
**	X	—	X
<	X	—	X
>	X	—	X
=	X	—	X

COBOL Language Formats

COBOL Program Structure

```
{ IDENTIFICATION DIVISION.
{ ID DIVISION.

PROGRAM-ID. program-name.

[AUTHOR. [comment-entry] ... ]
[INSTALLATION. [comment-entry] ... ]
[DATE-WRITTEN. [comment-entry] ... ]
[DATE-COMPILED. [comment-entry] ... ]
[SECURITY. [comment-entry] ... ]

ENVIRONMENT DIVISION.

{ CONFIGURATION SECTION.
{ [CONFIGURATION SECTION.]

SOURCE-COMPUTER. entry
OBJECT-COMPUTER. entry
{ [SPECIAL-NAMES. entry]
{ [SPECIAL-NAMES. entry] ]

[INPUT-OUTPUT SECTION.
FILE-CONTROL. entry
[I-O-CONTROL. entry] ]

DATA DIVISION.
[FILE SECTION.
[file-description entry
[record-description entry] ... ] ... ]

[WORKING-STORAGE SECTION.

[data item description entry]
[record-description entry  ] ... ]

[LINKAGE SECTION.

[data item description entry]
[record-description entry  ] ... ]
```

```
[REPORT SECTION.
[report description entry
{report-group description entry } ... ] ... ]
```

Procedure Division – Format 1

```
PROCEDURE DIVISION [USING identifier-1 [identifier-2]...].

[DECLARATIVES.

{ section-name SECTION [priority-number]. USE Sentence.

[paragraph-name. [sentence] ... ] ... } ...
END DECLARATIVES.]
{ section-name SECTION [priority-number].
[paragraph-name. [sentence] ... ] ... } ...
```

Procedure Division – Format 2

```
PROCEDURE DIVISION [USING identifier-1 [identifier-2]...].

{ paragraph-name. [sentence] ... } ...
```

Identification Division Formats

```
{ IDENTIFICATION DIVISION.
{ ID DIVISION.

PROGRAM-ID. program-name.

[AUTHOR. [comment-entry] ... ]
[INSTALLATION. [comment-entry] ... ]
[DATE-WRITTEN. [comment-entry] ... ]
[DATE-COMPILED. [comment-entry] ... ]
[SECURITY. [comment-entry] ... ]
```

Reprinted by permission of IBM from "IBM VS COBOL for DOS/VSE Reference Summary—Format and Reserved Words," © Copyright International Business Machines Corporation, 1981.
IBM extensions to American National Standard COBOL X3.23-1974 are shown within boxes.

Environment Division Formats

Configuration Section

ENVIRONMENT DIVISION.

$$\begin{Bmatrix} [\underline{\text{CONFIGURATION SECTION}}. \\ [\underline{\text{CONFIGURATION SECTION}}.] \end{Bmatrix}$$

<u>SOURCE-COMPUTER</u>. computer-name [WITH <u>DEBUGGING</u> <u>MODE</u>].

<u>OBJECT-COMPUTER</u>. computer-name

    [<u>MEMORY</u> SIZE integer $\begin{Bmatrix} \underline{\text{WORDS}} \\ \underline{\text{CHARACTERS}} \\ \underline{\text{MODULES}} \end{Bmatrix}$]

    [PROGRAM COLLATING <u>SEQUENCE</u> IS alphabet-name]

    [<u>SEGMENT-LIMIT</u> <u>IS</u> priority-number].

[<u>SPECIAL-NAMES</u>.

    [function-name-1 <u>IS</u> mnemonic-name] ...

    [function-name-2 [<u>IS</u> mnemonic-name]

$$\begin{Bmatrix} \underline{\text{ON}}\ \text{STATUS}\ \underline{\text{IS}}\ \text{condition-name-1]} \\ \quad [\underline{\text{OFF}}\ \text{STATUS}\ \underline{\text{IS}}\ \text{condition-name-2]} \\ \underline{\text{OFF}}\ \text{STATUS}\ \underline{\text{IS}}\ \text{condition-name-2} \\ \quad [\underline{\text{ON}}\ \text{STATUS}\ \underline{\text{IS}}\ \text{condition-name-1]} \end{Bmatrix} \text{]} \ ...$$

    [alphabet-name IS

$$\begin{Bmatrix} \underline{\text{STANDARD-1}} \\ \underline{\text{NATIVE}} \\ \text{literal-1} \begin{bmatrix} \begin{Bmatrix} \underline{\text{THROUGH}} \\ \underline{\text{THRU}} \end{Bmatrix} \text{literal-2} \\ \underline{\text{ALSO}}\ \text{literal-3} \\ \quad [\underline{\text{ALSO}}\ \text{literal-4}] \ ... \end{bmatrix} \\ [\text{literal-5} \begin{bmatrix} \begin{Bmatrix} \underline{\text{THROUGH}} \\ \underline{\text{THRU}} \end{Bmatrix} \text{literal-6} \\ \underline{\text{ALSO}}\ \text{literal-7} \\ \quad [\underline{\text{ALSO}}\ \text{literal-8}] \ ... \end{bmatrix}] ... \end{Bmatrix}] ...$$

    [<u>CURRENCY</u> SIGN <u>IS</u> literal-9]

$$\begin{Bmatrix} [\underline{\text{DECIMAL-POINT}}\ \text{IS}\ \underline{\text{COMMA}}].] \\ [\underline{\text{DECIMAL-POINT}}\ \text{IS}\ \underline{\text{COMMA}}].]] \end{Bmatrix}$$

Input-Output Section

<u>Note</u>: The key word FILE-CONTROL appears only once, at the beginning of the paragraph before the first File-Control entry.

FILE-CONTROL Paragraph   Sequential Files

FILE-CONTROL.

    <u>SELECT</u> [<u>OPTIONAL</u>] file-name

    <u>ASSIGN</u> TO assignment-name-1 [assignment-name-2] ...

    [<u>RESERVE</u> integer $\begin{bmatrix} \text{AREA} \\ \text{AREAS} \end{bmatrix}$]

    [<u>ORGANIZATION</u> IS <u>SEQUENTIAL</u>]

    [<u>ACCESS</u> MODE IS <u>SEQUENTIAL</u>]

    [<u>PASSWORD</u> IS data-name-1]

    [FILE <u>STATUS</u> IS data-name-2].

<u>Note</u>:   PASSWORD is only for VSAM sequential files.

FILE-CONTROL Entry   Indexed Files

FILE-CONTROL.

    <u>SELECT</u> file-name

    <u>ASSIGN</u> TO assignment-name-1 [assignment-name-2] ...

    [<u>RESERVE</u> integer $\begin{bmatrix} \text{AREA} \\ \text{AREAS} \end{bmatrix}$]

    <u>ORGANIZATION</u> IS <u>INDEXED</u>

    [<u>ACCESS</u> MODE IS $\begin{Bmatrix} \underline{\text{SEQUENTIAL}} \\ \underline{\text{RANDOM}} \\ \underline{\text{DYNAMIC}} \end{Bmatrix}$]

    <u>RECORD</u> KEY IS data-name-3

        [<u>PASSWORD</u> IS data-name-1]

    [<u>ALTERNATE</u> <u>RECORD</u> KEY IS data-name-4

        [<u>PASSWORD</u> IS data-name-5]

        [WITH <u>DUPLICATES</u>]] ...

    [FILE <u>STATUS</u> IS data-name-2].

FILE-CONTROL Entry – Relative Files

FILE-CONTROL.

    <u>SELECT</u> file-name

    <u>ASSIGN</u> TO assignment-name-1 [assignment-name-2] ...

    [<u>RESERVE</u> integer $\begin{bmatrix} \text{AREA} \\ \text{AREAS} \end{bmatrix}$]

    <u>ORGANIZATION</u> IS <u>RELATIVE</u>

    [<u>ACCESS</u> MODE IS

        $\begin{Bmatrix} \underline{\text{SEQUENTIAL}} \ [\underline{\text{RELATIVE}} \ \text{KEY IS data-name-6}] \\ \underline{\text{RANDOM}} \\ \underline{\text{DYNAMIC}} \end{Bmatrix}$ <u>RELATIVE</u> KEY IS data-name-7 $\Big\}$]

    [<u>PASSWORD</u> IS data-name-1]

    [FILE <u>STATUS</u> IS data-name-2].

<u>Note</u>: The key word I-O-CONTROL appears only once, at the beginning of the paragraph before the first I-O-Control entry.

I-O-CONTROL Paragraph – Physical Sequential Files

I-O-CONTROL.

    [<u>RERUN</u> <u>ON</u> assignment-name

        EVERY   integer-1 <u>RECORDS</u> OF file-name-1] ...

    [<u>SAME</u> $\begin{bmatrix} \text{RECORD} \\ \underline{\text{SORT}} \\ \underline{\text{SORT-MERGE}} \end{bmatrix}$ AREA

    FOR file-name-2 $\big\{$file-name-3$\big\}$ ...] ...

    [<u>MULTIPLE</u> <u>FILE</u> TAPE CONTAINS

     file-name-4 [<u>POSITION</u> integer-2]

     [file-name-5 [<u>POSITION</u> integer-3]] ...] ... .

Data Division Formats

File Section Formats

Format 1 – Physical Sequential Files

FILE SECTION.

FD file-name

    [<u>BLOCK</u> CONTAINS [integer-1 <u>TO</u>] integer-2 $\begin{Bmatrix} \text{CHARACTERS} \\ \underline{\text{RECORDS}} \end{Bmatrix}$]

    [<u>RECORD</u> CONTAINS [integer-3 <u>TO</u>] integer-4 CHARACTERS]

    <u>LABEL</u> $\begin{Bmatrix} \underline{\text{RECORD}} \ \text{IS} \\ \underline{\text{RECORDS}} \ \text{ARE} \end{Bmatrix}$ $\begin{Bmatrix} \text{STANDARD} \\ \text{OMITTED} \end{Bmatrix}$

    [<u>VALUE</u> <u>OF</u> system-name-1 IS $\begin{Bmatrix} \text{data-name-1} \\ \text{literal-1} \end{Bmatrix}$

       [system-name-2 IS $\begin{Bmatrix} \text{data-name-2} \\ \text{literal-2} \end{Bmatrix}$] ...]

    [<u>DATA</u> $\begin{Bmatrix} \underline{\text{RECORD}} \ \text{IS} \\ \underline{\text{RECORDS}} \ \text{ARE} \end{Bmatrix}$ data-name-3 [data-name-4] ...]

    [<u>LINAGE</u> IS $\begin{Bmatrix} \text{data-name-5} \\ \text{integer-5} \end{Bmatrix}$ LINES

      [WITH <u>FOOTING</u> AT $\begin{Bmatrix} \text{data-name-6} \\ \text{integer-6} \end{Bmatrix}$]

        [LINES AT <u>TOP</u> $\begin{Bmatrix} \text{data-name-7} \\ \text{integer-7} \end{Bmatrix}$]

          [LINES AT <u>BOTTOM</u> $\begin{Bmatrix} \text{data-name-8} \\ \text{integer-8} \end{Bmatrix}$]]

    [$\begin{Bmatrix} \text{REPORT IS} \\ \underline{\text{REPORTS}} \ \text{ARE} \end{Bmatrix}$ report-name-1 [report-name-2] ...]

    [<u>CODE-SET</u> IS alphabet-name].

Format 2 – VSAM Files (Sequential, Indexed, Relative)

<u>FILE</u> SECTION.

FD file-name

    [<u>BLOCK</u> CONTAINS [integer-1 <u>TO</u>] integer-2 $\left\{ \begin{array}{l} \text{CHARACTERS} \\ \text{RECORDS} \end{array} \right\}$

    [<u>RECORD</u> CONTAINS [integer-3 <u>TO</u>] integer-4 CHARACTERS]

    <u>LABEL</u> $\left\{ \begin{array}{l} \text{RECORD IS} \\ \text{RECORDS ARE} \end{array} \right\}$ $\left\{ \begin{array}{l} \text{STANDARD} \\ \text{OMITTED} \end{array} \right\}$

    [<u>VALUE</u> OF system name-1 IS $\left\{ \begin{array}{l} \text{data-name-1} \\ \text{literal-1} \end{array} \right\}$

          [system-name-2 IS $\left\{ \begin{array}{l} \text{data-name-2} \\ \text{literal-2} \end{array} \right\}$] ...]

    [<u>DATA</u> $\left\{ \begin{array}{l} \text{RECORD IS} \\ \text{RECORDS ARE} \end{array} \right\}$ data-name-3 [data-name-4] ...].

1-49 $\left\{ \begin{array}{l} \text{data-name} \\ \text{FILLER Clause} \end{array} \right\}$

    [REDEFINES Clause]
    [BLANK WHEN ZERO Clause]
    [JUSTIFIED Clause]
    [OCCURS Clause]
    [PICTURE Clause]
    [SIGN Clause]
    [SYNCHRONIZED Clause]
    [USAGE Clause].

[88   condition-name VALUE Clause.]

[66   RENAMES Clause.]

<u>Note</u>: Details of the above data description clauses are
given in the following WORKING-STORAGE SECTION formats.

Working-Storage Section Formats

<u>WORKING-STORAGE</u> SECTION.

$\left\{ \begin{array}{l} \text{77} \\ \text{01-49} \end{array} \right\}$ $\left\{ \begin{array}{l} \text{data-name-1} \\ \text{FILLER} \end{array} \right\}$

    [<u>REDEFINES</u> data-name-2]

    [<u>BLANK</u> WHEN <u>ZERO</u>]

    [$\left\{ \begin{array}{l} \text{<u>JUSTIFIED</u>} \\ \text{<u>JUST</u>} \end{array} \right\}$ RIGHT]

    [OCCURS Clause -- See Table Handling formats]

    [$\left\{ \begin{array}{l} \text{<u>PICTURE</u>} \\ \text{<u>PIC</u>} \end{array} \right\}$ IS character-string]

    [[<u>SIGN</u> IS] $\left\{ \begin{array}{l} \text{<u>LEADING</u>} \\ \text{<u>TRAILING</u>} \end{array} \right\}$ [<u>SEPARATE</u> CHARACTER]]

    [$\left\{ \begin{array}{l} \text{<u>SYNCHRONIZED</u>} \\ \text{<u>SYNC</u>} \end{array} \right\}$ $\left[\begin{array}{l} \text{<u>LEFT</u>} \\ \text{<u>RIGHT</u>} \end{array} \right]$]

    [[<u>USAGE</u> IS] $\left\{ \begin{array}{l} \text{DISPLAY} \\ \text{INDEX} \\ \text{<u>COMPUTATIONAL</u>} \\ \text{<u>COMP</u>} \\ \text{<u>COMPUTATIONAL-3</u>} \\ \text{<u>COMP-3</u>} \\ \text{<u>COMPUTATIONAL-4</u>} \\ \text{<u>COMP-4</u>} \end{array} \right\}$]

    [<u>VALUE</u> IS literal].

[88 condition-name $\left\{ \begin{array}{l} \text{<u>VALUE</u> IS} \\ \text{<u>VALUES</u> ARE} \end{array} \right\}$

    literal-1 [$\left\{ \begin{array}{l} \text{<u>THROUGH</u>} \\ \text{<u>THRU</u>} \end{array} \right\}$ literal-2]

        [literal-3 [$\left\{ \begin{array}{l} \text{<u>THROUGH</u>} \\ \text{<u>THRU</u>} \end{array} \right\}$ literal-4]] ... .

[66 data-name-1 <u>RENAMES</u> data-name-2

    [$\left\{ \begin{array}{l} \text{<u>THROUGH</u>} \\ \text{<u>THRU</u>} \end{array} \right\}$ data-name-3].]

Note: Valid clauses in the LINKAGE SECTION are given with
the formats for the Subprogram Linkage feature.

Valid formats for the REPORT SECTION are given with the
formats for the Report Writer Feature.

Procedure Division Formats

Conditional Expressions

Class Condition

identifier is [NOT] { NUMERIC / ALPHABETIC }

Condition – Name Condition

condition-name

Relation Condition

operand-1 IS [NOT] { GREATER THAN / > / LESS THAN / < / EQUAL TO / = } operand-2

Note: Operand-1 and operand-2 may each be an identifier,
a literal, or an arithmetic expression. There must be at
least one reference to an identifier.

Sign Condition

operand IS [NOT] { POSITIVE / NEGATIVE / ZERO }

Note: Operand must be a numeric identifier or
an arithmetic expression.

Switch – Status Condition

condition-name

Negated Simple Condition

NOT simple-condition

Combined Condition

condition { AND / OR } condition ...

Abbreviated Combined Relation Condition

relation-condition { { AND / OR } [NOT]
[relational-operator] object } ...

Procedure Division Header

PROCEDURE DIVISION [USING identifier-1 [identifier-2] ...].

ACCEPT Statement (for Data Transfer)

ACCEPT identifier [FROM { mnemonic-name / [function-name] }]

ACCEPT Statement (for System Information Transfer)

ACCEPT identifier FROM { DATE / DAY / TIME }

ADD Statement – Format 1

ADD { identifier-1 / literal-1 } [identifier-2 / literal-2] ...

TO identifier-m [ROUNDED]
[identifier-n [ROUNDED]]...

[ON SIZE ERROR imperative-statement]

ADD Statement – Format 2

ADD { identifier-1 / literal-1 } { identifier-2 / literal-2 } [identifier-3 / literal-3] ...

GIVING identifier-m [ROUNDED]
[identifier-n [ROUNDED]] ...

[ON SIZE ERROR imperative-statement]

ADD Statement – Format 3

```
        ( CORRESPONDING )
ADD     {               }
        ( CORR          )

        identifier-1 TO identifier-2 [ROUNDED]
        [ON SIZE ERROR imperative-statement]
```

ALTER Statement

```
ALTER procedure-name-1
          TO [PROCEED TO] procedure-name-2
      [procedure-name-3
          TO [PROCEED TO] procedure-name-4] ...
```

CLOSE Statement – Physical Sequential Files

```
                       ⎡ (REEL) [WITH NO REWIND]      ⎤
                       ⎢ {UNIT} [FOR REMOVAL  ]       ⎥
CLOSE file-name-1      ⎢                              ⎥
                       ⎢         (NO REWIND)          ⎥
                       ⎣ WITH   {LOCK     }           ⎦

                       ⎡ (REEL) [WITH NO REWIND]      ⎤
                       ⎢ {UNIT} [FOR REMOVAL  ]       ⎥
      [file-name-2     ⎢                              ⎥ ] ...
                       ⎢         (NO REWIND)          ⎥
                       ⎣ WITH   {LOCK     }           ⎦
```

CLOSE Statement – VSAM Files

```
CLOSE file-name-1    [WITH LOCK]
     [file-name-2    [WITH LOCK]] ...
```

COMPUTE Statement

```
COMPUTE identifier-1 [ROUNDED]

        [identifier-2 [ROUNDED] ] ...

        = arithmetic-expression

        [ON SIZE ERROR imperative-statement]
```

DECLARATIVES Procedures

```
PROCEDURE DIVISION [USING identifier-1 [identifier-2] ...].
DECLARATIVES.
{section-name SECTION [priority-number]. USE sentence.

[paragraph-name. [sentence.] ...] ...] ... }
END DECLARATIVES.
```

DELETE Statement

```
DELETE file-name RECORD
        [INVALID KEY imperative-statement]
```

DISPLAY Statement

```
          (identifier-1) [identifier-2]
DISPLAY   {            } [          ] ...
          (literal-1   ) [literal-2 ]

          ( mnemonic-name  )
    [UPON {               }]
          ( function-name  )
```

DIVIDE Statement – Format 1

```
        (identifier-1)
DIVIDE  {            }
        (literal-1   )

    INTO   identifier-2 [ROUNDED]
          [identifier-3 [ROUNDED] ] ...
    [ON SIZE ERROR imperative-statement]
```

DIVIDE Statement – Format 2

```
        (identifier-1) (INTO) (identifier-2)
DIVIDE  {            } {    } {            }
        (literal-1   ) (BY  ) (literal-2   )

    GIVING   identifier-3 [ROUNDED]
            [identifier-4 [ROUNDED] ] ...
    [ON SIZE ERROR imperative-statement]
```

DIVIDE Statement – Format 3

$$\underline{\text{DIVIDE}}\begin{Bmatrix}\text{identifier-1}\\\text{literal-1}\end{Bmatrix}\begin{Bmatrix}\underline{\text{INTO}}\\\underline{\text{BY}}\end{Bmatrix}\begin{Bmatrix}\text{identifier-2}\\\text{literal-2}\end{Bmatrix}$$

        GIVING identifier-3 [ROUNDED]
        [REMAINDER identifier-4]
        [ON SIZE ERROR imperative-statement]

ENTER Statement

    ENTER language-name [routine-name].

EXIT Statement

paragraph-name. EXIT [PROGRAM].

Note: The paragraph-name is not part of the EXIT
statement format; however, it is always required
preceding an EXIT statement.

GO TO Statement – Unconditional

    GO TO procedure-name-1

GO TO Statement – Conditional

    GO TO procedure-name-1 [procedure-name-2] ...
        procedure-name-n DEPENDING ON identifier

GO TO Statement – Altered

    GO TO.

IF Statement

    IF condition $\begin{Bmatrix}\text{statement-1}\\\underline{\text{NEXT}}\;\underline{\text{SENTENCE}}\end{Bmatrix}\begin{Bmatrix}\underline{\text{ELSE}}\;\text{statement-2}\\\underline{\text{ELSE}}\;\underline{\text{NEXT}}\;\underline{\text{SENTENCE}}\end{Bmatrix}$

Note: ELSE NEXT SENTENCE may be omitted if it immediate
precedes the period for the conditional statement.

INSPECT Statement

    INSPECT identifier-1
      [TALLYING {identifier-2

$$\underline{\text{FOR}}\begin{Bmatrix}\begin{Bmatrix}\underline{\text{ALL}}\\\underline{\text{LEADING}}\\\underline{\text{CHARACTERS}}\end{Bmatrix}\begin{Bmatrix}\text{identifier-3}\\\text{literal-1}\end{Bmatrix}\end{Bmatrix}$$

$$\left[\begin{Bmatrix}\underline{\text{BEFORE}}\\\underline{\text{AFTER}}\end{Bmatrix}\text{INITIAL}\begin{Bmatrix}\text{identifier-4}\\\text{literal-2}\end{Bmatrix}\right]\}...\}\;...\;]$$

[REPLACING

$$\left\{\begin{array}{l}\underline{\text{CHARACTERS}}\;\underline{\text{BY}}\begin{Bmatrix}\text{identifier-6}\\\text{literal-4}\end{Bmatrix}\\\left[\begin{Bmatrix}\underline{\text{BEFORE}}\\\underline{\text{AFTER}}\end{Bmatrix}\text{INITIAL}\begin{Bmatrix}\text{identifier-7}\\\text{literal-5}\end{Bmatrix}\right]\\\begin{Bmatrix}\underline{\text{ALL}}\\\underline{\text{LEADING}}\\\underline{\text{FIRST}}\end{Bmatrix}\begin{Bmatrix}\begin{Bmatrix}\text{identifier-5}\\\text{literal-3}\end{Bmatrix}\underline{\text{BY}}\begin{Bmatrix}\text{identifier-6}\\\text{literal-4}\end{Bmatrix}\\\left[\begin{Bmatrix}\underline{\text{BEFORE}}\\\underline{\text{AFTER}}\end{Bmatrix}\text{INITIAL}\begin{Bmatrix}\text{identifier-7}\\\text{literal-5}\end{Bmatrix}\right]\end{Bmatrix}...\}\;...\end{array}\right\}\;]$$

Note: Either the TALLYING option or the REPLACING option
must be specified; both may be specified.

MOVE Statement – Format 1

$$\underline{\text{MOVE}}\begin{Bmatrix}\text{identifier-1}\\\text{literal}\end{Bmatrix}\underline{\text{TO}}\;\text{identifier-2 [identifier-3] ...}$$

MULTIPLY Statement – Format 1

$$\underline{\text{MOVE}}\begin{Bmatrix}\underline{\text{CORRESPONDING}}\\\underline{\text{CORR}}\end{Bmatrix}\text{identifier-1}\;\underline{\text{TO}}\;\text{identifier-2}$$

MULTIPLY Statement – Format 1

$$\underline{MULTIPLY} \quad \begin{Bmatrix} identifier\text{-}1 \\ literal\text{-}1 \end{Bmatrix} \quad \underline{BY} \; identifier\text{-}2$$

$$[\underline{ROUNDED}]$$

$$[identifier\text{-}3 \; [\underline{ROUNDED}] \;] \; ...$$
$$[ON \; \underline{SIZE} \; \underline{ERROR} \; imperative\text{-}statement]$$

MULTIPLY Statement – Format 2

$$\underline{MULTIPLY} \quad \begin{Bmatrix} identifier\text{-}1 \\ literal\text{-}1 \end{Bmatrix} \quad \underline{BY} \quad \begin{Bmatrix} identifier\text{-}2 \\ literal\text{-}2 \end{Bmatrix}$$

$$\underline{GIVING} \; identifier\text{-}3 \; [\underline{ROUNDED}]$$
$$[identifier\text{-}4 \; [\underline{ROUNDED}] \;] \; ...$$
$$[ON \; \underline{SIZE} \; \underline{ERROR} \; imperative\text{-}statement]$$

OPEN Statement – Sequential Files

$$\underline{OPEN} \begin{Bmatrix} \underline{INPUT} \; file\text{-}name\text{-}1 \begin{bmatrix} \underline{REVERSED} \\ WITH \; \underline{NO} \; REWIND \end{bmatrix} \\ [file\text{-}name\text{-}2 \begin{bmatrix} \underline{REVERSED} \\ WITH \; \underline{NO} \; REWIND \end{bmatrix}] \; ... \\ \underline{OUTPUT} \; file\text{-}name\text{-}3 \; [WITH \; \underline{NO} \; \underline{REWIND}] \\ [file\text{-}name\text{-}4 \; [WITH \; \underline{NO} \; \underline{REWIND}]] \; ... \\ \underline{I\text{-}O} \; file\text{-}name\text{-}5 \; [file\text{-}name\text{-}6] \; ... \\ \underline{EXTEND} \; file\text{-}name\text{-}7 \; [file\text{-}name\text{-}8] \; ... \end{Bmatrix} \; ...$$

<u>Note</u>: **EXTEND is only for VSAM Sequential Files.**

OPEN Statement – Indexed Files

$$\underline{OPEN} \begin{Bmatrix} \underline{INPUT} \; file\text{-}name\text{-}1 \; [file\text{-}name\text{-}2] \; ... \\ \underline{OUTPUT} \; file\text{-}name\text{-}3 \; [file\text{-}name\text{-}4] \; ... \\ \underline{I\text{-}O} \; file\text{-}name\text{-}5 \; [file\text{-}name\text{-}6] \; ... \\ \boxed{\underline{EXTEND} \; file\text{-}name\text{-}7 \; [file\text{-}name\text{-}8] \; ...} \end{Bmatrix}$$

OPEN Statement – Relative Files

$$\underline{OPEN} \begin{Bmatrix} \underline{INPUT} \; file\text{-}name\text{-}1 \; [file\text{-}name\text{-}2] \; ... \\ \underline{OUTPUT} \; file\text{-}name\text{-}3 \; [file\text{-}name\text{-}4] \; ... \\ \underline{I\text{-}O} \; file\text{-}name\text{-}5 \; [file\text{-}name\text{-}6] \; ... \end{Bmatrix} \; ...$$

PERFORM Statement – Basic PERFORM

$$\underline{PERFORM} \; procedure\text{-}name\text{-}1 \; [\begin{Bmatrix} \underline{THROUGH} \\ \underline{THRU} \end{Bmatrix} \; procedure\text{-}name\text{-}2]$$

PERFORM Statement   TIMES Option

$$\underline{PERFORM} \; procedure\text{-}name\text{-}1 \; [\begin{Bmatrix} \underline{THROUGH} \\ \underline{THRU} \end{Bmatrix} \; procedure\text{-}name\text{-}2]$$

$$\begin{Bmatrix} identifier\text{-}1 \\ integer\text{-}1 \end{Bmatrix} \underline{TIMES}$$

PERFORM Statement   Conditional PERFORM

$$\underline{PERFORM} \; procedure\text{-}name\text{-}1 \; [\begin{Bmatrix} \underline{THROUGH} \\ \underline{THRU} \end{Bmatrix} \; procedure\text{-}name\text{-}2]$$

$$\underline{UNTIL} \; condition\text{-}1$$

PERFORM Statement – VARYING Option

```
PERFORM procedure-name-1 [ {THROUGH}  procedure-name-2]
                          {THRU   }

    VARYING {index-name-1}  FROM {index-name-2}
            {identifier-1}       {literal-2   }
                                 {identifier-2}

        BY {literal-3   }  UNTIL condition-1
           {identifier-3}

    [AFTER {index-name-4}  FROM {index-name-5}
           {identifier-4}       {literal-5   }
                                {identifier-5}

        BY {literal-6   }  UNTIL condition-2
           {identifier-6}

    [AFTER {index-name-7}  FROM {index-name-8}
           {identifier-7}       {literal-8   }
                                {identifier-8}

        BY {literal-9   }  UNTIL condition-3] ]
           {identifier-9}
```

READ Statement – Sequential Retrieval

```
READ file-name [NEXT] RECORD [INTO identifier]
    [AT END imperative-statment]
```

READ Statement – Random Retrieval

```
READ file-name RECORD [INTO identifier]
    [KEY IS data-name]
    [INVALID KEY imperative-statemnt]
```

REWRITE Statement

```
REWRITE record-name [FROM identifier]
    [INVALID KEY imperative-statement]
```

START Statement

```
                          {EQUAL TO      }
                          {=             }
START file-name [KEY IS   {GREATER THAN  }  data-name]
                          {>             }
                          {NOT LESS THAN }
                          {NOT <         }

    [INVALID KEY imperative-statement]
```

STOP Statement

```
STOP {RUN    }
     {literal}
```

STRING Statement

```
STRING {identifier-1}  [identifier-2] ...
       {literal-1   }  [literal-2   ]

    DELIMITED BY {identifier-3}
                 {literal-3   }
                 {SIZE        }

    [ {identifier-4}  [identifier-5] ...
      {literal-4   }  [literal-5   ]

    DELIMITED BY {identifier-6}  ] ...
                 {literal-6   }
                 {SIZE        }

    INTO identifier-7
    [WITH POINTER identifier-8]
    [ON OVERFLOW imperative-statment]
```

SUBTRACT Statement – Format 1

```
SUBTRACT {identifier-1}  [identifier-2] ...
         {literal-1   }  [literal-2   ]

    FROM identifier-m [ROUNDED]
        [identifier-n [ROUNDED] ] ...
    [ON SIZE ERROR imperative-statement]
```

SUBTRACT Statement – Format 2

```
SUBTRACT {identifier-1}  [identifier-2] ...
         {literal-1   }  [literal-2   ]

    FROM {identifier-m}
         {literal-m   }

    GIVING identifier-n [ROUNDED]
        [identifier-o [ROUNDED] ] ...
    [ON SIZE ERROR imperative-statement]
```

SUBTRACT Statement – Format 3

```
SUBTRACT {CORRESPONDING}
         {CORR         }

    identifier-1 FROM identifier-2 [ROUNDED]
    [ON SIZE ERROR imperative-statement]
```

TRANSFORM Statement

```
┌─────────────────────────────────────────────┐
│ TRANSFORM identifier-3 CHARACTERS            │
│         ⎧ figurative-constant-1 ⎫            │
│  FROM   ⎨ nonnumeric-literal-1  ⎬            │
│         ⎩ identifier-1          ⎭            │
│         ⎧ figurative-constant-2 ⎫            │
│  TO     ⎨ nonnumeric-literal-2  ⎬            │
│         ⎩ identifier-2          ⎭            │
└─────────────────────────────────────────────┘
```

UNSTRING Statement

```
UNSTRING identifier-1

    [DELIMITED BY [ALL] ⎧ identifier-2 ⎫
                        ⎩ literal-1    ⎭

        [OR [ALL] ⎧ identifier-3 ⎫ ] ... ]
                  ⎩ literal-2    ⎭

    INTO identifier-4
            [DELIMITER IN identifier-5]
            [COUNT IN identifier-6]
         [identifier-7
            [DELIMITER IN identifier-8]
            [COUNT IN identifier-9] ] ...
    [WITH POINTER identifier-10]
    [TALLYING IN identifier-11]
    [ON OVERFLOW imperative-statement]
```

USE Sentence – EXCEPTION/ERROR Procedures

```
section-name SECTION [priority-number].

    USE AFTER STANDARD ⎧ EXCEPTION ⎫ PROCEDURE
                       ⎩ ERROR     ⎭

        ⎧ file-name-1 [file-name-2] ... ⎫
    ON  ⎨ INPUT                         ⎬
        ⎪ OUTPUT                        ⎪
        ⎪ I-O                           ⎪
        ⎩ EXTEND                        ⎭
```

WRITE Statement – Physical Sequential Files

```
WRITE record-name [FROM identifier]

    ⎡ ⎧ BEFORE ⎫           ⎧ identifier-2 ⎫ ⎡ LINE  ⎤ ⎤
    ⎢ ⎨        ⎬ ADVANCING ⎨ integer      ⎬ ⎣ LINES ⎦ ⎥
    ⎣ ⎩ AFTER  ⎭           ⎩ mnemonic-name ⎭          ⎦
                           ⎩ PAGE         ⎭

        [AT ⎧ END-OF-PAGE ⎫ imperative-statement]
            ⎩ EOP         ⎭
```

WRITE Statement   VSAM Sequential Files

```
WRITE record-name [FROM identifier]
```

WRITE Statement   VSAM Indexed and Relative Files

```
WRITE record-name [FROM identifier]
    [INVALID KEY imperative-statement]
```

Data Reference Formats

Qualification

Data Item References

```
⎧ data-name-1    ⎫ ⎡ ⎧ OF ⎫             ⎤
⎨               ⎬ ⎢ ⎨    ⎬ data-name-2 ⎥ ...
⎩ condition-name ⎭ ⎣ ⎩ IN ⎭             ⎦
```

Procedure Name References

```
paragraph-name [ ⎧ OF ⎫ section-name]
                 ⎩ IN ⎭
```

COPY Library References

```
text-name [ ⎧ OF ⎫ library-name]
            ⎩ IN ⎭
```

Subscripting

```
⎧ data-name-1    ⎫ ⎡ ⎧ OF ⎫             ⎤
⎨               ⎬ ⎢ ⎨    ⎬ data-name-2] ⎥ ...
⎩ condition-name ⎭ ⎣ ⎩ IN ⎭             ⎦
    (subscript [subscript [subscript]])
```

Indexing

$$\left\{\begin{array}{l}\text{data-name-1}\\\text{condition-name}\end{array}\right\}\quad[\ \left\{\begin{array}{l}\underline{OF}\\\underline{IN}\end{array}\right\}\ \text{data-name-2}]\ \ldots$$

$$\left(\left\{\begin{array}{l}\text{index-name-1}\ [\left\{\pm\right\}\ \text{literal-2}]\\\text{literal-1}\end{array}\right.\right.$$

$$\left[\ \left\{\begin{array}{l}\text{index-name-2}\ [\left\{\pm\right\}\ \text{literal-4}]\\\text{literal-3}\end{array}\right.\right.$$

$$\left[\ \left\{\begin{array}{l}\text{index-name-3}\ [\left\{\pm\right\}\ \text{literal-6}]\\\text{literal-5}\end{array}\right\}\ ]\ ])$$

Table Handling Formats

Table Handling Data Division

OCCURS Clause – Fixed Length Tables

```
OCCURS integer-2 TIMES

   [  { ASCENDING  }  KEY IS data-name-2 [data-name-3]...]...
      { DESCENDING }

   [INDEXED BY index-name-1 [index-name-2]...]
```

OCCURS Clause – Variable Length Tables

```
OCCURS integer-1 TO integer-2 TIMES

   DEPENDING ON data-name-1

   [  { ASCENDING  }  KEY IS data-name-2 [data-name-3]...]...
      { DESCENDING }

   [INDEXED BY index-name-1 [index-name-2]... ]
```

USAGE IS INDEX Clause

```
[USAGE IS] INDEX
```

Table Handling Procedure Division

Format 1 – Serial Search

```
SEARCH identifier-1 [VARYING  { identifier-2 }  ]
                               { index-name-1 }

   [AT END imperative-statement-1]

   WHEN condition-1  { imperative-statement-2 }
                     { NEXT SENTENCE          }

   [WHEN condition-2  { imperative-statement-3 }  ] ...
                      { NEXT SENTENCE          }
```

Format 2   Binary Search

```
SEARCH ALL identifier-1
   [AT END imperative-statement-1]

   WHEN  { relation-condition-1 }
         { condition-name-1     }

   [AND  { relation-condition-2 }  ] ...
         { condition-name-2     }

   [ imperative-statement-2 ]
   [ NEXT SENTENCE          ]
```

Note: In Format 2, each relation-condition must be an
EQUAL TO (=) condition with an ASCENDING/DESCENDING KEY
data item for this table element as the subject.

SET Statement – Direct Indexing

$$\underline{SET}\ \left\{\begin{array}{l}\text{index-name-1 [index-name-2] }\ldots\\\text{identifier-1 [identifier-2] }\ldots\end{array}\right\}\ \underline{TO}\ \left\{\begin{array}{l}\text{index-name-3}\\\text{identifier-3}\\\text{literal-1}\end{array}\right\}$$

SET Statement – Relative Indexing

$$\underline{SET}\ \text{index-name-4 [index-name-5] }\ldots$$

$$\left\{\begin{array}{l}\underline{UP}\ \underline{BY}\\\underline{DOWN}\ \underline{BY}\end{array}\right\}\ \left\{\begin{array}{l}\text{identifier-4}\\\text{literal-2}\end{array}\right\}$$

Sort Merge Formats

Sort/Merge Environment Division

FILE-CONTROL Entry

```
    SELECT file-name
    ASSIGN TO assignment-name-1 [assignment-name-2] ...
```

I-O-CONTROL Entry

```
    [RERUN ON assignment-name]

           ⎧ RECORD     ⎫
    [SAME  ⎨ SORT       ⎬ AREA
           ⎩ SORT-MERGE ⎭
           FOR file-name-1 [file-name-2] ... ].
```

Sort/Merge Data Division

SD Entry

```
SD  file-name
    [RECORD CONTAINS [integer-1 TO] integer-2 CHARACTERS]

           ⎧ RECORD IS   ⎫
    [DATA  ⎨ RECORDS ARE ⎬ data-name-1 [data-name-2] ... ].
           ⎩             ⎭
```

Sort/Merge Procedure Division Formats

MERGE Statement

```
    MERGE file-name-1

              ⎧ ASCENDING  ⎫
       ON     ⎨ DESCENDING ⎬ KEY data-name-1 [data-name-2]...
              ⎩            ⎭

              ⎧ ASCENDING  ⎫
       [ON    ⎨ DESCENDING ⎬ KEY data-name-3 [data-name-4]...]...
              ⎩            ⎭

       [COLLATING SEQUENCE IS alphabet-name]
       USING file-name-2 file-name-3 [file-name-4]...

       ⎧ GIVING file-name-5                                        ⎫
       ⎨ OUTPUT PROCEDURE                                          ⎬
       ⎩    IS section-name-1 [ ⎧THROUGH⎫ section-name-2]          ⎭
                               ⎩THRU   ⎭
```

RELEASE Statement (SORT Feature only)

```
    RELEASE record-name [FROM identifier]
```

RETURN Statement

```
    RETURN file-name RECORD [INTO identifier]
           AT END imperative-statement
```

SORT Statement

```
    SORT file-name-1

              ⎧ ASCENDING  ⎫
       ON     ⎨ DESCENDING ⎬ KEY data-name-1 [data-name-2]...
              ⎩            ⎭

              ⎧ ASCENDING  ⎫
       [ON    ⎨ DESCENDING ⎬ KEY data-name-3 [data-name-4]...]...
              ⎩            ⎭
```

[COLLATING SEQUENCE IS alphabet-name]

```
⎧ USING file-name-2 [file-name-3]...                              ⎫
⎪ INPUT PROCEDURE                                                 ⎪
⎪                      ⎧ THROUGH ⎫                                ⎪
⎪     IS section-name-1 [         ⎬ section-name-2]               ⎬
⎪                      ⎩ THRU    ⎭                                ⎪
⎪ GIVING file-name-4                                              ⎪
⎪ OUTPUT PROCEDURE                                                ⎪
⎪                      ⎧ THROUGH ⎫                                ⎪
⎩     IS section-name-3 [         ⎬ section-name-4]               ⎭
                       ⎩ THRU    ⎭
```

Report Writer Formats

Report Writer Environment Division

SPECIAL-NAMES.

   [function-name-1 IS mnemonic-name] ...

Report Writer Data Division

File Section – FD Entry

FD   file-name

   ⎧ REPORT IS ⎫
   ⎨   ⎬ report-name-1 [report-name-2] ...
   ⎩ REPORTS ARE ⎭

   [RECORD CONTAINS [integer-1 TO] integer-2 CHARACTERS]

   [BLOCK CONTAINS Clause]

   LABEL RECORDS Clause

   [DATA RECORDS Clause]

   [VALUE OF Clause].

Report Section – RD Entry

RD   report-name

   [WITH CODE mnemonic-name]

   ⎡⎧ CONTROL IS   ⎫⎧ FINAL   ⎫   ⎤
   ⎢⎨   ⎬⎨   ⎬ identifier-1 [identifier-2]...⎬⎥
   ⎣⎩ CONTROLS ARE ⎭⎩ [FINAL] ⎭   ⎦

   ⎡PAGE ⎡LIMIT IS ⎤ integer-1 ⎧ LINE ⎫
   ⎣   ⎣LIMITS ARE⎦   ⎩ LINES ⎭

      [HEADING   integer-2]
      [FIRST DETAIL integer-3]
      [LAST DETAIL integer-4]
      [FOOTING   integer-5]].

Report Group Description Entry – Format 1

01 [data-name]

        ⎧ REPORT HEADING ⎫
        ⎪ RH   ⎪
        ⎪ PAGE HEADING   ⎪
        ⎪ PH   ⎪
        ⎪ CONTROL HEADING ⎧ FINAL   ⎫
        ⎪ CH   ⎩ identifier-n ⎭
TYPE IS ⎨ DETAIL
        ⎪ DE
        ⎪ CONTROL FOOTING ⎧ identifier-n ⎫
        ⎪ CF   ⎩ FINAL   ⎭
        ⎪ PAGE FOOTING
        ⎪ PF
        ⎪ REPORT FOOTING
        ⎩ RF

   ⎧   ⎧ integer-1   ⎫
   [LINE NUMBER IS ⎨ PLUS integer-2 ⎬]
            ⎩ NEXT PAGE   ⎭

   ⎧   ⎧ integer-1   ⎫
   [NEXT GROUP IS ⎨ PLUS integer-2 ⎬]
          ⎩ NEXT PAGE   ⎭

   [USAGE Clause].

Report Group Description Entry – Format 2

   level-number [data-name]

      [LINE Clause]

      [USAGE Clause].

Report Group Description Entry – Format 3

```
level-number [data-name]

  [COLUMN NUMBER IS integer]
  [GROUP INDICATE]
  [LINE Clause]
  ⎧  SOURCE IS identifier                            ⎫
  ⎪  SUM identifier-1 [identifier-2] ... [UPON data-name-2] ⎪
  ⎨           ⎧ FINAL       ⎫              ⎬
  ⎪  [RESET ON ⎨ identifier-3 ⎬ ]          ⎪
  ⎩  VALUE IS literal                      ⎭

   PICTURE Clause
  [USAGE Clause]
  [BLANK WHEN ZERO Clause]
  [JUSTIFIED Clause].
```

Report Group Description Entry – Format 4

```
01 [data-name]
   TYPE Clause
   [LINE Clause]
   [NEXT GROUP Clause]
   [COLUMN Clause]
   [GROUP INDICATE Clause]
   ⎧ SOURCE Clause ⎫
   ⎨ SUM Clause    ⎬
   ⎩ VALUE Clause  ⎭
   PICTURE Clause
   [USAGE Clause]
   [BLANK WHEN ZERO Clause]
   [JUSTIFIED Clause].
```

Report Writer Procedure Division

GENERATE Statement

```
GENERATE ⎧ data-name   ⎫
         ⎨ report-name ⎬
```

INITIATE Statement

```
INITIATE report-name-1 [report-name-2] ...
```

PRINT-SWITCH Statement

```
MOVE 1 TO PRINT-SWITCH
```

TERMINATE Statement

```
TERMINATE report-name-1 [report-name-2] ...
```

USE BEFORE REPORTING Sentence

```
USE BEFORE REPORTING data-name .
```

Segmentation Formats

SEGMENT-LIMIT Clause – Environment Division

```
SEGMENT-LIMIT IS priority-number
```

Priority-numbers – Procedure Division

```
section-name SECTION [priority-number].
```

Source Program Library Formats

COPY Statement

COPY text-name [{ OF / IN } library-name]

[SUPPRESS]

[REPLACING { ==pseudo-text-1== / identifier-1 / literal-1 / word-1 }

BY { ==pseudo-text-2== / identifier-2 / literal-2 / word-2 } ...].

Extended Source Program Library Formats (IBM Extension)

BASIS Statement

[sequence-number] BASIS basis-name

INSERT/DELETE Statements

[sequence-number] { INSERT / DELETE } sequence-number-field

Subprogram Linkage Formats

LINKAGE SECTION – Data Division

LINKAGE SECTION.

{ 77 / 01-49 } { data-name / FILLER Clause }

   [REDEFINES Clause]
   [BLANK WHEN ZERO Clause]
   [JUSTIFIED Clause]
   [OCCURS Clause]
   [PICTURE Clause]
   [SIGN Clause]
   [SYNCHRONIZED Clause]
   [USAGE Clause].
[88 condition-name VALUE Clause.]
[66 RENAMES Clause.]] ...

Subprogram Linkage – Procedure Division

CALL Statement

CALL literal-1 [USING identifier-1 [identifier-2] ...]

ENTRY Statement

ENTRY literal [USING identifier-1 [identifier-2]...]

EXIT PROGRAM Statement

paragraph-name. EXIT PROGRAM.

Note: The paragraph-name is not part of the EXIT statement format; however, it is always required preceding an EXIT statement.

GOBACK Statement

GOBACK.

Procedure Division Header – Called Program

PROCEDURE DIVISION [USING identifier-1 [identifier-2]...].

STOP RUN Statement

STOP RUN.

Debugging Feature Formats

Debugging Feature Environment Division

SOURCE-COMPUTER Paragraph

SOURCE-COMPUTER. computer-name
                [WITH DEBUGGING MODE].

Debugging Feature Procedure Division

USE FOR DEBUGGING Sentence

section-name SECTION [priority-number].
   USE FOR DEBUGGING

ON { procedure-name-1 [procedure-name 2]... / ALL PROCEDURES } .

C COBOL Coding Conventions Used in Textbook Examples[1]

- Name all programmers who have written or modified program code.
- Give the date of each program modification.
- Provide a brief program summary.

- Use descriptive data names and relate them in a meaningful way to the logical use of the data in the program (for example, TOTAL-YTD-GROSS, not TOTAL-1; PAYROLL-MAST-FILE, not MAST-DISK-FILE).
- Use consecutive level numbers (01, 02, 03, 04, rather than 01, 05, 10, 15, and so on). This method allows level numbers to correspond to the logical subdivisions of data.
- Use a common prefix where data items constitute a logical record. This identifies data items with specific records and simplifies the process of developing unique names.
- Do not use qualification of data names (each data name should be unique).
- Do not use 77-level numbers. Group related data items under 01 level entries.
- Except for character strings used for editing, consecutively repeating the same character in a string should not be used in a PICTURE clause (for example, 9(4)V9(3), not 9999V999). This saves counting, improves scannability of entries, and reduces the probability of field-length errors.
- Programming constants (values that will not change during program execution, such as tax rates) should be described as data items and initialized with a VALUE clause.
- The value of data items initialized with a VALUE clause should not be altered or changed during program execution.

---

[1] Many, but not all, of the coding conventions that we follow and the rationale for their use can be found in H. F. Ledgard and W. C. Cane's article entitled "COBOL Under Control," published in the *Communications of the ACM*, Vol. 19, No. 11, November 1976, pp. 601–608. We have followed these coding conventions in programs throughout the textbook. In our opinion, they represent fundamentally sound programming practices. However, we are aware that not all authorities agree; consequently, your instructor may prefer to have you follow somewhat different practices.

- Each named programming constant should be used for one, and only one, function in a program. Using a named constant for more than one purpose detracts from program clarity.
- Condition names (88-level entries) should be used for testing the values of data items that have only a small number of possible values or that have a range of values (such as switches, codes, range limits on variables).

PROCEDURE DIVISION

- Paragraphs and sections must have only one entry point and one exit point.
- GO TO statements are not used except where *required* by COBOL syntax restrictions (such as INPUT PROCEDURE with SORT verb). When its use is *required,* the GO TO transfer of control should always be to an EXIT paragraph.
- Paragraphs should contain no more than 50 lines of code.
- Each paragraph is to be designed to contain code for a logical function in the program.
- SECTIONs are used only where required by COBOL syntax restrictions (such as SORT, DECLARATIVES).
- Only one STOP RUN or EXIT PROGRAM statement should be used in a program. It is used only to exit the main control routine.
- Simple IF statements are permitted; otherwise, every IF is paired with a corresponding ELSE and indented to indicate how the pairs are associated.
- The INTO option should be used for READ/RETURN input operations, and the FROM option should be used for WRITE/REWRITE/RELEASE output operations.
- The I/O operations READ/RETURN/WRITE/REWRITE/RELEASE/DELETE are to be written in separate paragraphs with only one I/O statement contained in a paragraph.
  EXCEPTION: Multiple WRITE statements for a printer file are permissible in a single paragraph (such as multiple-line report page headings).
- In general, all I/O modules should be placed at the end of program source statements. This isolates the I/O statements, making them easy to locate should the need arise and, as they contain no logic, it removes them from the main body of program logic flow.
- The AT END or INVALID KEY clauses should be used to set switches. They should never be used to execute other routines.
- Except for I/O modules, when possible, avoid short paragraphs containing only one or two statements. Short, choppy paragraphs reduce program readability, making program logic more difficult to follow as they often force the reader to jump needlessly from paragraph to paragraph.
- Switches should be tested in paragraphs that control execution, either directly or indirectly, of the paragraph in which the switch is set.
- Except for simple ADD, SUBTRACT, and DIVIDE with a REMAINDER clause, use the COMPUTE verb for calculations.
- Explicitly specify the order of evaluations of complex arithmetic or logical expressions using parentheses. For example, use

COMPUTE A = (B / C) + (D * E)
not
COMPUTE A = B / C + D * E

- Use condition names for testing the value of switches, codes, and for data validation of codes and range limits on variables.
- Many commercial print chains do not contain > or < symbols. Therefore, we recommend they not be used; instead, use the reserved words GREATER THAN or LESS THAN.
- Write only one verb per line. This improves program readability.
- Except for such system-dependent features as debugging tools, subprogram linkage conventions, and I/O, only standard ANS COBOL statements and conventions are to be used.

D Disk Capacity Tables

IBM 3330 RECORD CAPACITY TABLE

Some examples of how the IBM 3330 capacity table may be used follow. In the table, *records* refers to physical records.

Assume 140-byte logical records to be recorded unblocked (data length = 140) and without keys. The table indicates that 47 records can be placed on each track (893 on each cylinder, 360772 on each 3336 Model 1 pack, and 721544 on each 3336 Model 11 pack). Reducing the record length by 1 byte permits 48 records per track, an increase of 7676 records per pack. Alternatively, the record length can be increased by 5 bytes without decreasing the number of records per pack.

To see the effect of blocked records, assume the same 140-byte logical records are to be recorded without keys. Also assume a blocking factor of 20 (data length = 2800). The table indicates that 4 physical records can be written on each track for a total of 80 logical records per track (compared with 48 logical records if unblocked).

Assume 100-byte logical records, unblocked, and formatted with keys (data length = 100, key length = 8). The number to look up in the "with keys" part of the table is 108 (key length + data length). There will be 44 records per track.

IBM 3330 Record Capacity Table

Bytes per Record				Records Per				Bytes per Record				Records Per			
Without Keys		With Keys				3336 Model 1	3336 Model 11	Without Keys		With Keys				3336 Model 1	3336 Model 11
Min	Max	Min	Max	Trk	Cyl	Pack	Pack	Min	Max	Min	Max	Trk	Cyl	Pack	Pack
6448	13030	6392	12974	1	19	7676	15352	119	123	63	67	51	969	391476	782952
4254	6447	4198	6391	2	38	15352	30704	114	118	58	62	52	988	399152	798304
3157	4253	3101	4197	3	57	23028	46056	109	113	53	57	53	1007	406828	813656
2499	3156	2443	3100	4	76	30704	61408	105	108	49	52	54	1026	414504	829008
2060	2498	2004	2442	5	95	38380	76760	101	104	45	48	55	1045	422180	844360
1746	2059	1690	2003	6	114	46056	92112	96	100	40	44	56	1064	429856	859712
1511	1745	1455	1689	7	133	53732	107464	92	95	36	39	57	1083	437532	875064
1328	1510	1272	1454	8	152	61408	122816	89	91	33	35	58	1102	445208	890416
1182	1327	1126	1271	9	171	69084	138168	85	88	29	32	59	1121	452884	905768
1062	1181	1006	1125	10	190	76760	153520	81	84	25	28	60	1140	460560	921120
963	1061	907	1005	11	209	84436	168872	78	80	22	24	61	1159	468236	936472
878	962	822	906	12	228	92112	184224	74	77	18	21	62	1178	475912	951824
806	877	750	821	13	247	99788	199576	71	73	15	17	63	1197	483588	967176
743	805	687	749	14	266	107464	214928	68	70	12	14	64	1216	491264	982528
688	742	632	686	15	285	115140	230280	65	67	9	11	65	1235	498940	997880
640	687	584	631	16	304	122816	245632	62	64	6	8	66	1254	506616	1013232
597	639	541	583	17	323	130492	260984	59	61	3	5	67	1273	514292	1028584
558	596	502	540	18	342	138168	276336	56	58	2	2	68	1292	521968	1043936
524	557	468	501	19	361	145844	291688	54	55			69	1311	529644	1059288
492	523	436	467	20	380	153520	307040	51	53			70	1330	537320	1074640

| Bytes per Record | | | | | | Records Per | | Bytes per Record | | | | | | Records Per | |
| Without Keys | | With Keys | | | | 3336 Model 1 | 3336 Model 11 | Without Keys | | With Keys | | | | 3336 Model 1 | 3336 Model 11 |
Min	Max	Min	Max	Trk	Cyl	Pack	Pack	Min	Max	Min	Max	Trk	Cyl	Pack	Pack
464	491	408	435	21	399	161196	322392	48	50			71	1349	544996	1089992
438	463	382	407	22	418	168872	337744	46	47			72	1368	552672	1105344
414	437	358	381	23	437	176548	353096	43	45			73	1387	560348	1120696
392	413	336	357	24	456	184224	368448	41	42			74	1406	568024	1136048
372	391	316	335	25	475	191900	383800	39	40			75	1425	575700	1151400
353	371	297	315	26	494	199576	399152	36	38			76	1444	583376	1166752
336	352	280	296	27	513	207252	414504	34	35			77	1463	591052	1182104
319	335	263	279	28	532	214928	429856	32	33			78	1482	598728	1197456
304	318	248	262	29	551	222604	445208	30	31			79	1501	606404	1212808
290	303	234	247	30	570	230280	460560	28	29			80	1520	614080	1228160
277	289	221	233	31	589	237956	475912	26	27			81	1539	621756	1243512
264	276	208	220	32	608	245632	491264	24	25			82	1558	629432	1258864
253	263	197	207	33	627	253308	506616	22	23			83	1577	637108	1274216
242	252	186	196	34	646	260984	521968	20	21			84	1596	644784	1289568
231	241	175	185	35	665	268660	537320	19	19			85	1615	652460	1304920
221	230	165	174	36	684	276336	552672	17	18			86	1634	660136	1320272
212	220	156	164	37	703	284012	568024	15	16			87	1653	667812	1335624
203	211	147	155	38	722	291688	583376	13	14			88	1672	675488	1350976
195	202	139	146	39	741	299364	598728	12	12			89	1691	683164	1366328
187	194	131	138	40	760	307040	614080	10	11			90	1710	690840	1381680
179	186	123	130	41	779	314716	629432	9	9			91	1729	698516	1397032
172	178	116	122	42	798	322392	644784	7	8			92	1748	706192	1412384
165	171	109	115	43	817	330068	660136	6	6			93	1767	713868	1427736
158	164	102	108	44	836	337744	675488	4	5			94	1786	721544	1443088
152	157	96	101	45	855	345420	690840	3	3			95	1805	729220	1458440
146	151	90	95	46	874	353096	706192	1	2			96	1824	736896	1473792
140	145	84	89	47	893	360772	721544								
134	139	78	83	48	912	368448	736896								
129	133	73	77	49	931	376124	752248								
124	128	68	72	50	950	383800	767600								

Reprinted by permission of IBM from "3330 Series Disk Storage Reference Summary" (GX20-1920), track capacity tables.

IBM 3375 TRACK, CYLINDER, AND ACCESS MECHANISM CAPACITY TABLES

The following tables give the number of equal-length records that can be placed on a track and cylinder. The first table gives the number of records if there are no keys (KL = 0); the second table gives the number of records if there are keys: Part 1 is used for key lengths 1 through 32 bytes; part 2 is used for key lengths greater than 32 bytes up to a maximum of 255 bytes.

The number of 32-byte segments that can be placed on a track depends on the data length (DL). A range of data lengths results in a given number of segments. For example, for records without keys, data lengths from

5,601 to 6,816 bytes allow 5 records per track, 60 records per cylinder.

6,817 to 8,608 bytes allow 4 records per track, 48 records per cylinder.

8,609 to 11,616 bytes allow 3 records per track, 36 records per cylinder.

The tables show the maximum data lengths that can be used for the given number of records. Key and data areas are assumed to occupy the full 32-byte segments. These two tables include the total number of bytes used for the given number of records on a track and cylinder.

IBM 3375 Record (Without Keys) Capacity Table

Record Length (*Total Bytes)	Track Capacity		Cylinder Capacity		Access Mechanism Capacity	
	Records	Bytes	Records	Bytes	Records	Bytes
35,616	1	35,616	12	427,392	11,508	409,868,928
17,600	2	35,200	24	422,400	23,016	405,081,600
11,616	3	34,848	36	418,176	34,524	401,030,784
8,608	4	34,432	48	413,184	46,032	396,243,456
6,816	5	34,080	60	408,960	57,540	392,192,640
5,600	6	33,600	72	403,200	69,048	386,668,800
4,736	7	33,152	84	397,824	80,556	381,513,216
4,096	8	32,768	96	393,216	92,064	377,094,144
3,616	9	32,544	108	390,528	103,572	374,516,352
3,200	10	32,000	120	384,000	115,080	368,256,000
2,880	11	31,680	132	380,160	126,588	364,573,440
2,592	12	31,104	144	373,248	138,096	357,944,832
2,368	13	30,784	156	369,408	149,604	354,262,272
2,176	14	30,464	168	365,568	161,112	350,579,712
2,016	15	30,240	180	362,230	172,620	348,001,920
1,856	16	29,696	192	356,352	184,128	341,741,568
1,728	17	29,376	204	352,512	195,636	338,059,008
1,600	18	28,800	216	345,600	207,144	331,430,400
1,504	19	28,576	228	342,912	218,652	328,852,608
1,408	20	28,160	240	337,920	230,160	324,065,280
1,312	21	27,552	252	330,624	241,668	317,068,416
1,248	22	27,456	264	329,472	253,176	315,963,648
1,152	23	26,496	276	317,952	264,684	304,915,968
1,088	24	26,112	288	313,344	276,192	300,496,896
1,056	25	26,400	300	316,800	287,700	303,811,200
992	26	25,792	312	309,504	299,208	296,814,336
928	27	25,056	324	300,672	310,716	288,344,448
896	28	25,088	336	301,056	322,224	288,712,704
832	29	24,128	348	289,536	333,732	277,665,024
800	30	24,000	360	288,000	345,240	276,192,000
768	31	23,808	372	285,696	356,748	273,982,464
736	32	23,552	384	282,624	368,256	271,036,416
704	33	23,232	396	278,784	379,764	267,353,856
672	34	22,848	408	274,176	391,272	262,934,784
640	35	22,400	420	268,800	402,780	257,779,200
608	36	21,888	432	262,656	414,288	251,887,104
576	37	21,312	444	255,744	425,796	245,258,496
544	38	20,672	456	248,064	437,304	237,893,376
512	40	20,480	480	245,760	460,320	235,683,840
480	41	19,680	492	236,160	471,828	226,477,440
448	43	19,264	516	231,168	494,844	221,690,112
416	45	18,720	540	224,640	517,860	215,429,760
384	46	17,664	552	211,968	529,368	203,277,312
352	48	16,896	576	202,752	552,384	194,439,168
320	51	16,320	612	195,840	586,908	187,810,560
288	53	15,264	636	183,168	609,924	175,658,112
256	56	14,336	672	172,032	644,448	164,978,688
224	59	13,216	708	158,592	678,972	152,089,728
192	62	11,904	744	142,848	713,496	136,991,232
160	66	10,560	792	126,720	759,528	121,524,480
128	70	8,960	840	107,520	805,560	103,111,680
96	75	7,200	900	86,400	863,100	82,857,600
64	80	5,120	960	61,440	920,640	58,920,960
32	86	2,752	1,032	33,024	989,688	31,670,016

*Includes DL and unused bytes when rounding up to 32-byte segments.

Reprinted by permission of IBM from "IBM 3375 Direct Access Storage: Description and Users Guide" (GX26-1662), track capacity tables.

IBM 3375 Record (with Keys) Capacity Tables (Part 1 of 2)

Data Length (*Total Bytes)	Track Capacity		Cylinder Capacity		Access Mechanism Capacity	
	Records	Bytes	Records	Bytes	Records	Bytes
35,424	1	35,424	12	425,088	11,508	407,659,392
17,408	2	34,816	24	417,792	23,016	400,662,528
11,424	3	34,272	36	411,264	34,524	394,402,176
8,416	4	33,664	48	403,968	46,032	387,405,312
6,624	5	33,120	60	397,440	57,540	381,144,960
5,408	6	32,448	72	389,376	69,048	373,411,584
4,544	7	31,808	84	381,696	80,556	366,046,464
3,904	8	31,232	96	374,784	92,064	359,417,856
3,424	9	30,816	108	369,792	103,572	354,630,528
3,008	10	30,080	120	360,960	115,080	346,160,640
2,688	11	29,568	132	354,816	126,588	340,268,544
2,400	12	28,800	144	345,600	138,096	331,430,400
2,176	13	28,288	156	339,456	149,604	325,538,304
1,984	14	27,776	168	333,312	161,112	319,646,208
1,824	15	27,360	180	328,320	172,620	314,858,880
1,664	16	26,624	192	319,488	184,128	306,388,992
1,536	17	26,112	204	313,344	195,636	300,496,896
1,408	18	25,344	216	304,128	207,144	291,658,752
1,312	19	24,928	228	299,136	218,652	286,871,424
1,216	20	24,320	240	291,840	230,160	279,874,560
1,120	21	23,520	252	282,240	241,668	270,668,160
1,056	22	23,232	264	278,784	253,176	267,353,856
960	23	22,080	276	264,960	264,684	254,096,640
896	24	21,504	288	258,048	276,192	247,468,032
864	25	21,600	300	259,200	287,700	248,572,800
800	26	20,800	312	249,600	299,208	239,366,400
736	27	19,872	324	238,464	310,716	228,686,976
704	28	19,712	336	236,544	322,224	226,845,696
640	29	18,560	348	222,720	333,732	213,588,480
608	30	18,240	360	218,880	345,240	209,905,920
576	31	17,856	372	214,272	356,748	205,486,848
544	32	17,408	384	208,896	368,256	200,331,264
512	33	16,896	396	202,752	379,764	194,439,168
480	34	16,320	408	195,840	391,272	187,810,560
448	35	15,680	420	188,160	402,780	180,445,440
416	36	14,976	432	179,712	414,288	172,343,808
384	37	14,208	444	170,496	425,796	163,505,664
352	38	13,376	456	160,512	437,304	153,931,008
320	40	12,800	480	153,600	460,320	147,302,400
288	41	11,808	492	141,696	471,828	135,886,464
256	43	11,008	516	132,096	494,844	126,680,064
224	45	10,080	540	120,960	517,860	116,000,640
192	46	8,832	552	105,984	529,368	101,638,656
160	48	7,680	576	92,160	552,384	88,381,440
128	51	6,528	612	78,336	586,908	75,124,224
96	53	5,088	636	61,056	609,924	58,552,704
64	56	3,584	672	43,008	644,448	41,244,672
32	59	1,888	708	22,656	678,972	21,727,104

*Data length rounded up to 32-byte segments. This table also adjusted for key lengths of 1 through 32 bytes. See Figure 6 (Part 2 of 2) for key lengths of 32 through 255 bytes.

IBM 3375 Record (with Keys) Capacity Table (Part 2 of 2)

Record Length (*Total Bytes)	Track Capacity		Cylinder Capacity		Access Mechanism Capacity	
	Records	Bytes	Records	Bytes	Records	Bytes
35,456	1	35,456	12	425,472	11,508	408,027,648
17,440	2	34,880	24	418,560	23,016	401,399,040
11,456	3	34,368	36	412,416	34,524	395,506,944
8,448	4	33,792	48	405,504	46,032	388,878,336
6,656	5	33,280	60	399,360	57,540	382,986,240
5,440	6	32,640	72	391,680	69,048	375,621,120
4,576	7	32,032	84	384,384	80,556	368,624,256
3,936	8	31,488	96	374,856	92,064	362,363,904
3,456	9	31,104	108	373,248	103,572	357,944,832
3,040	10	30,400	120	364,800	115,080	349,843,200
2,720	11	29,920	132	359,040	126,588	344,319,360
2,432	12	29,184	144	350,208	138,096	335,849,472
2,208	13	28,704	156	344,448	149,604	330,325,632
2,016	14	28,224	168	338,688	161,112	324,801,792
1,856	15	27,840	180	334,080	172,620	320,382,720
1,696	16	27,136	192	325,632	184,128	312,281,088
1,568	17	26,656	204	319,872	195,636	306,757,248
1,440	18	25,920	216	311,040	207,144	298,287,360
1,344	19	25,536	228	306,342	218,652	293,868,288
1,248	20	24,960	240	299,520	230,160	287,239,680
1,152	21	24,192	252	290,304	241,668	278,401,536
1,088	22	23,936	264	287,232	253,176	275,455,488
992	23	22,816	276	273,792	264,684	262,566,528
928	24	22,272	288	267,264	276,192	256,306,176
896	25	22,400	300	268,800	287,700	257,779,200
832	26	21,632	312	259,584	299,208	248,941,056
768	27	20,736	324	248,832	310,716	238,629,888
736	28	20,608	336	247,296	322,224	237,156,864
672	29	19,488	348	233,856	333,732	224,267,904
640	30	19,200	360	230,400	345,240	220,953,600
608	31	18,848	372	226,176	356,748	216,902,784
576	32	18,432	384	221,184	368,256	212,115,456
544	33	17,952	396	215,424	379,764	206,591,616
512	34	17,408	408	208,896	391,272	200,331,264
480	35	16,800	420	201,600	402,780	193,334,400
448	36	16,128	432	193,536	414,288	185,601,024
416	37	15,392	444	184,704	425,796	177,131,136
384	38	14,592	456	175,104	437,304	167,924,736
352	40	14,080	480	168,960	460,320	162,032,640
320	41	13,120	492	157,440	471,828	150,984,960
288	43	12,384	516	148,608	494,844	142,515,072
256	45	11,520	540	138,240	517,860	132,572,160
224	46	10,304	552	123,648	529,368	118,578,432
192	48	9,216	576	110,592	552,384	106,057,728
160	51	8,160	612	97,920	586,908	93,905,280
128	53	6,784	636	81,408	609,924	78,070,272
96	56	5,376	672	64,512	644,448	61,867,008
64	59	3,776	708	45,312	678,972	43,454,208

*Includes KL, DL, and unused bytes when rounding up to 32-byte segments.

How To Use This Table

Assume DL=820, KL=48, then:

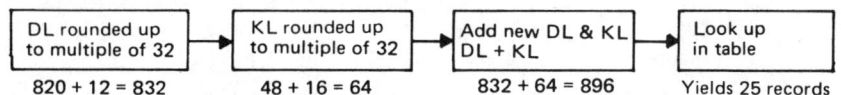

DL rounded up to multiple of 32	→	KL rounded up to multiple of 32	→	Add new DL & KL DL + KL	→	Look up in table
820 + 12 = 832		48 + 16 = 64		832 + 64 = 896		Yields 25 records

E List of Prime Numbers Between 2 and 10,000

2	3	5	7	11	13	17	19	23	29
31	37	41	43	47	53	59	61	67	71
73	79	83	89	97	101	103	107	109	113
127	131	137	139	149	151	157	163	167	173
179	181	191	193	197	199	211	223	227	229
233	239	241	251	257	263	269	271	277	281
283	293	307	311	313	317	331	337	347	349
353	359	367	373	379	383	389	397	401	409
419	421	431	433	439	443	449	457	461	463
467	479	487	491	499	503	509	521	523	541
547	557	563	569	571	577	587	593	599	601
607	613	617	619	631	641	643	647	653	659
661	673	677	683	691	701	709	719	727	733
739	743	751	757	761	769	773	787	797	809
811	821	823	827	829	839	853	857	859	863
877	881	883	887	907	911	919	929	937	941
947	953	967	971	977	983	991	997	1009	1013
1019	1021	1031	1033	1039	1049	1051	1061	1063	1069
1087	1091	1093	1097	1103	1109	1117	1123	1129	1151
1153	1163	1171	1181	1187	1193	1201	1213	1217	1223
1229	1231	1237	1249	1259	1277	1279	1283	1289	1291
1297	1301	1303	1307	1319	1321	1327	1361	1367	1373
1381	1399	1409	1423	1427	1429	1433	1439	1447	1451
1453	1459	1471	1481	1483	1487	1489	1493	1499	1511
1523	1531	1543	1549	1553	1559	1567	1571	1579	1583
1597	1601	1607	1609	1613	1619	1621	1627	1637	1657
1663	1667	1669	1693	1697	1699	1709	1721	1723	1733
1741	1747	1753	1759	1777	1783	1787	1789	1801	1811
1823	1831	1847	1861	1867	1871	1873	1877	1879	1889
1901	1907	1913	1931	1933	1949	1951	1973	1979	1987
1993	1997	1999	2003	2011	2017	2027	2029	2039	2053
2063	2069	2081	2083	2087	2089	2099	2111	2113	2129
2131	2137	2141	2143	2153	2161	2179	2203	2207	2213
2221	2237	2239	2243	2251	2267	2269	2273	2281	2287
2293	2297	2309	2311	2333	2339	2341	2347	2351	2357
2371	2377	2381	2383	2389	2393	2399	2411	2417	2423
2437	2441	2447	2459	2467	2473	2477	2503	2521	2531
2539	2543	2549	2551	2557	2579	2591	2593	2609	2617
2621	2633	2647	2657	2659	2663	2671	2677	2683	2687
2689	2693	2699	2707	2711	2713	2719	2729	2731	2741
2749	2753	2767	2777	2789	2791	2797	2801	2803	2819
2833	2837	2843	2851	2857	2861	2879	2887	2897	2903
2909	2917	2927	2939	2953	2957	2963	2969	2971	2999
3001	3011	3019	3023	3037	3041	3049	3061	3067	3079
3083	3089	3109	3119	3121	3137	3163	3167	3169	3181
3187	3191	3203	3209	3217	3221	3229	3251	3253	3257
3259	3271	3299	3301	3307	3313	3319	3323	3329	3331
3343	3347	3359	3361	3371	3373	3389	3391	3407	3413
3433	3449	3457	3461	3463	3467	3469	3491	3499	3511

3517	3527	3529	3533	3539	3541	3547	3557	3559	3571
3581	3583	3593	3607	3613	3617	3623	3631	3637	3643
3659	3671	3673	3677	3691	3697	3701	3709	3719	3727
3733	3739	3761	3767	3769	3779	3793	3797	3803	3821
3823	3833	3847	3851	3853	3863	3877	3881	3889	3907
3911	3917	3919	3923	3929	3931	3943	3947	3967	3989
4001	4003	4007	4013	4019	4021	4027	4049	4051	4057
4073	4079	4091	4093	4099	4111	4127	4129	4133	4139
4153	4157	4159	4177	4201	4211	4217	4219	4229	4231
4241	4243	4253	4259	4261	4271	4273	4283	4289	4297
4327	4337	4339	4349	4357	4363	4373	4391	4397	4409
4421	4423	4441	4447	4451	4457	4463	4481	4483	4493
4507	4513	4517	4519	4523	4547	4549	4561	4567	4583
4591	4597	4603	4621	4637	4639	4643	4649	4651	4657
4663	4673	4679	4691	4703	4721	4723	4729	4733	4751
4759	4783	4787	4789	4793	4799	4801	4813	4817	4831
4861	4871	4877	4889	4903	4909	4919	4931	4933	4937
4943	4951	4957	4967	4969	4973	4987	4993	4999	5003
5009	5011	5021	5023	5039	5051	5059	5077	5081	5087
5099	5101	5107	5113	5119	5147	5153	5167	5171	5179
5189	5197	5209	5227	5231	5233	5237	5261	5273	5279
5281	5297	5303	5309	5323	5333	5347	5351	5381	5387
5393	5399	5407	5413	5417	5419	5431	5437	5441	5443
5449	5471	5477	5479	5483	5501	5503	5507	5519	5521
5527	5531	5557	5563	5569	5573	5581	5591	5623	5639
5641	5647	5651	5653	5657	5659	5669	5683	5689	5693
5701	5711	5717	5737	5741	5743	5749	5779	5783	5791
5801	5807	5813	5821	5827	5839	5843	5849	5851	5857
5861	5867	5869	5879	5881	5897	5903	5923	5927	5939
5953	5981	5987	6007	6011	6029	6037	6043	6047	6053
6067	6073	6079	6089	6091	6101	6113	6121	6131	6133
6143	6151	6163	6173	6197	6199	6203	6211	6217	6221
6229	6247	6257	6263	6269	6271	6277	6287	6299	6301
6311	6317	6323	6329	6337	6343	6353	6359	6361	6367
6373	6379	6389	6397	6421	6427	6449	6451	6469	6473
6481	6491	6521	6529	6547	6551	6553	6563	6569	6571
6577	6581	6599	6607	6619	6637	6653	6659	6661	6673
6679	6689	6691	6701	6703	6709	6719	6733	6737	6761
6763	6779	6781	6791	6793	6803	6823	6827	6829	6833
6841	6857	6863	6869	6871	6883	6899	6907	6911	6917
6947	6949	6959	6961	6967	6971	6977	6983	6991	6997
7001	7013	7019	7027	7039	7043	7057	7069	7079	7103
7109	7121	7127	7129	7151	7159	7177	7187	7193	7207
7211	7213	7219	7229	7237	7243	7247	7253	7283	7297
7307	7309	7321	7331	7333	7349	7351	7369	7393	7411
7417	7433	7451	7457	7459	7477	7481	7487	7489	7499
7507	7517	7523	7529	7537	7541	7547	7549	7559	7561
7573	7577	7583	7589	7591	7603	7607	7621	7639	7643
7649	7669	7673	7681	7687	7691	7699	7703	7717	7723
7727	7741	7753	7757	7759	7789	7793	7817	7823	7829
7841	7853	7867	7873	7877	7879	7883	7901	7907	7919
7927	7933	7937	7949	7951	7963	7993	8009	8011	8017
8039	8053	8059	8069	8081	8087	8089	8093	8101	8111
8117	8123	8147	8161	8167	8171	8179	8191	8209	8219
8221	8231	8233	8237	8243	8263	8269	8273	8287	8291
8293	8297	8311	8317	8329	8353	8363	8369	8377	8387
8389	8419	8423	8429	8431	8443	8447	8461	8467	8501

8513	8521	8527	8537	8539	8543	8563	8573	8581	8597
8599	8609	8623	8627	8629	8641	8647	8663	8669	8677
8681	8689	8693	8699	8707	8713	8719	8731	8737	8741
8747	8753	8761	8779	8783	8803	8807	8819	8821	8831
8837	8839	8849	8861	8863	8867	8887	8893	8923	8929
8933	8941	8951	8963	8969	8971	8999	9001	9007	9011
9013	9029	9041	9043	9049	9059	9067	9091	9103	9109
9127	9133	9137	9151	9157	9161	9173	9181	9187	9199
9203	9209	9221	9227	9239	9241	9257	9277	9281	9283
9293	9311	9319	9323	9337	9341	9343	9349	9371	9377
9391	9397	9403	9413	9419	9421	9431	9433	9437	9439
9461	9463	9467	9473	9479	9491	9497	9511	9521	9533
9539	9547	9551	9587	9601	9613	9619	9623	9629	9631
9643	9649	9661	9677	9679	9689	9697	9719	9721	9733
9739	9743	9749	9767	9769	9781	9787	9791	9803	9811
9817	9829	9833	9839	9851	9857	9859	9871	9883	9887
9901	9907	9923	9929	9931	9941	9949	9967	9973	

Index